Printed by MAXWELL PRESS
Chicago, Illinois

Bound by BROCK & RANKIN, INC.
Chicago, Illinois

A

COMPLETE HISTORY

OF THE

MEXICAN WAR:

ITS CAUSES, CONDUCT, AND CONSEQUENCES

A

COMPLETE HISTORY

OF THE

MEXICAN WAR:

ITS CAUSES, CONDUCT, AND CONSEQUENCES:

COMPRISING AN ACCOUNT OF THE

VARIOUS MILITARY AND NAVAL OPERATIONS.

FROM ITS COMMENCEMENT TO THE

TREATY OF PEACE.

ILLUSTRATED AND EXPLAINED BY

MAPS, PLANS OF BATTLES, VIEWS, AND PORTRAITS.

BY N. C. BROOKS, A.M.

The Rio Grande Press Inc.,

1734 East 71st Place, Chicago 49, Illinois

HAROLD R. YEARY LIBRARY

E
404
.B88
1965

First edition from which
this printing was reproduced
was supplied by
GILBERTO ESPINOSA
Albuquerque, N. M.

973.62
B773

A RIO GRANDE CLASSIC
First published in 1849

LIBRARY OF CONGRESS CARD CATALOG
65-20151

1965

The ❦ Rio Grande Press Inc.,
1734 East 71st Place, Chicago 49, Illinois

OCT 1 6 2012

A NOTE FROM THE PUBLISHER

In selecting this book for publication as one of our beautiful Rio Grande Classics, we found very little substantial source material on the Mexican War in print. A great deal was written about the conflict in the decade following 1848, but very little on the subjcet has been published since. In our research, we have come to consider this particular title the best of several accounts contemporary to the time. It was originally published, in 1849, as a subscription edition. We have found few scholars who know the book, and we find it rarely listed in the standard bibliographies. It is, nevertheless, authentic source material of American history.

In our research, we discovered, also, an anonymously-written paperbound ephemera volume entitled *A Complete History of the Late Mexican War*. It is not related to the Brooks work, but it is too small to be reprinted as a separate volume. We consider it both germane and significant to our edition of the Brooks work. We have, accordingly, included it as part of this title. We have sought scholarly opinion as to the authorship of this appended ephemera, without success. Don Gilberto Espinosa, of Albuquerque, who wrote the introduction on the following pages, refers to the author of this material as 'The Unknown,' and for lack of further information we leave it at that.

More than anything else, it was the 'Unknown's' collected casualty lists and military rosters which caused us to include this anonymous work in this volume. So far as we have been able to determine, these are the only casualty lists of the Mexican War extant, outside of War Department files.

Robert B. McCoy
THE RIO GRANDE PRESS, INC.

Chicago, Illinois
October 1965

A COMPLETE HISTORY OF THE WAR WITH MEXICO

The Rio Grande Press is to be commended for making available to students, scholars and just plain readers of American history these two splendid source volumes combined into one magnificent book. Together, they present a first hand story of the war between the United States and Mexico.

The first of these books is *A Complete History of the Mexican War, its causes, conduct and consequences, comprising an account of the various military and naval operations from its commencement to the Treaty of Peace.* It was written by Nathan Covington Brooks, a distinguished scholar and writer of his time and a member of the Maryland Historical Society. The book was completed on June 4th, 1849, scarcely a year after the conflict ended; it is dedicated to Major General Zachary Taylor.

Despite the fact that the Brooks work is a most complete and correct story of the Mexican War, this precious volume seems to have been entirely ignored almost from the day it was published. Certainly it is the least known, while yet the most authentic, of the books published about the Mexican War.

Almost the same observation applies to the second work published in this volume, which I shall refer to as *The Chronicle of the Unknown.* There may be some historic excuse for this latter volume being overlooked. In its first and only edition, it was a paperbound booklet, not registered, and of limited circulation. It is fortunate that a few copies survived, and that one found its way into the offices of The Rio Grande Press. The author is not indicated; the account was published anonymously.

It seems to me that this booklet was written by several

authors, rather than one, for its literary style varies and varies again. Still, it is a very correct record. A comparison of the sequence of events recorded, of the campaigns, of the battles fought and other incidents agrees completely with the Brooks work of a year earlier. So far as official records corroborating the anonymous work, there are many — and they do.

A distinctive feature of this anonymous work is the Appendix listing all the men killed, wounded and missing. In some 18 pages of small print, the book records the name, rank and organization of each casualty of each division, regiment, battalion and platoon. The author(s?) lists the most important battles, and events surrounding each.

To point up the Unknown's accuracy: he gives an account of the casualties in the three day battle at Monterey. He accounts for 492 soldiers either killed, wounded or missing. These were men from the division of General Twiggs; from the Ohio, Tennessee, Mississippi and Kentucky regiments of General Butler's division; of the division of General Worth and of Hay's regiment and Colonel Wood's Texas Rangers. The account also lists a full inventory of the ordnance, small arms and munitions captured at Monterey.

I do not vouch for the completeness of this list, but who else has caused to be published such a splendid tabulation of statistical source material about the Mexican War? In my own study of the subject, I have seen this nowhere else, although complete records are perhaps available from the archives of the United States. Nevertheless, here they are, convenient and very germane to any complete history of the Mexican War.

The story of the war between Mexico and the United States has been told and retold, but a long time ago. As in every war, the first news of its progress must have come from reports of officers to their superiors or to the War Department. Many returning veterans set forth their personal version from recollections, or from notes. Versions of events and incidents without number appeared in pamphlet form and newspaper articles of the time.

In evaluating any history, it is logical to regard written accounts in two categories.

A 'source book' is an account written from first hand

information, such as diaries, journals, documents, official records or personal interviews. Such works are usually contemporaneous and set forth soon after the event. But, not always.

Non-source material is a book written long after the event (usually) and is most generally based on research *from* source materials. When a historian or a writer researching the past discovers a new *source* of information about his subject, his non-source book *can* contain source material.

The two books published in this volume are 'source material' *of the time.* Neither of the authors had available to them some of the records that are available today. For example, the Magoffin papers were not available when these two books were published, nor were details of the Gadsden purchase. While these historic facts in themselves have no bearing on the history of the war, they explain the WHY of the Mexican War — and thus give us a historic perspective we would not otherwise have on the subject.

The Brooks work covers not only the war in Mexico but relates many war activities in Texas, in New Mexico (and what is now Arizona) and in California. The author first presents a complete resume of the Texan revolution. A check of these first four chapters and of the numerous references to, and copies of, correspondence exchanged by American, Mexican and Texan officials with the account given by Dr. Carlos Castañeda *(The Mexican Side of the Texas Revolution,* Dallas, 1928). Castañeda sets forth in full the official reports of General Antonio Lopez de Santa Ana, General Vicente Filosola, General José Urrea and General José Maria Tornel (Mexican Secretary of War). These reports show little variance between each other, and are quite close to the Brooks figures.

I cite the following point to show the general accuracy of the Brooks work. On page 48, Brooks states that at the battle of San Jacinto, when Texas won its independence from Mexico, the Mexican loss was 630 men killed, 280 wounded and 730 taken prisoners. He states also there were two Texans killed and only 22 wounded.

It appeared to me that considering the bloody conflict and

the considerable number of soldiers involved (even considering that Houston had caught Santa Ana napping), the Texan casualties seemed unduly small. However, Castañeda quotes (page 262) from the dairy of General José Urrea:

" . . . *From all the information obtained, and it is confirmed by General Santa Ana as well as by the official reports of Señor Filosola, it seems certain that Houston had 720 men. Of these, two were killed and 22 were wounded.*"

Accuracy like this is the keynote of the Brooks work.

Brooks describes an interesting episode not too generally noted by historians — the San Patricio defection. This was an artillery battalion composed entirely of recent Irish immigrants. Almost *en mass*, for reasons of their own, they defected to the Mexican army. At the battles of Contreras and Churubusco, the Irishmen offered formidable resistance. General Winfield Scott captured and executed some 72 of them; their leader, one Captain Riley, was branded and punished as a traitor but was not executed because his defection occurred before war was declared.

The Unknown, in his description of the battle of Matamoros, mentioned that he observed Captain Riley of the San Patricio battalion fighting with the Mexicans, as well as some English and German soldiers — recent immigrants, no doubt, who had likewise defected to the Mexican side.

Destiny and the March of Empire decreed that this great America of ours should extend from the Atlantic to the Pacific. Morally, the war that accomplished this expansion cannot be justified any more than can the conquest of the Aztec empire by the Spaniards, or the stealing of this country from the American Indian. "Show me," President James Buchanan replied to a critic of the Mexican War, "one square foot of this earth that is not held by conquest."

President Ulysses S. Grant didn't like the Mexican War. In his memoirs he wrote (pp. 61, 62, Vol. I):

"*. . . Ostensibly we were intended to prevent filibustering into Texas, but really as a menace to Mexico in case she appeared to contemplate war. Generally, the officers of the army were indifferent as to whether annexation was* *contemplated or not, but not all of them . . .*

"For myself, I was bitterly opposed to the measure, and to this day regard the war which resulted as one of the most unjust ever waged by a strong against a weaker nation. It was the instance of a republic following the bad example of European monarchies in not considering justice in their desire to acquire additional territory."

There has been little question and no argument in the last century but that the annexation of Texas, and the dispute as to whether the Nueces River or the Rio Grande were the southern and western boundaries of Texas, were the events that triggered the actual hostilities.

But were these events alone the *causes* of the war? Definitely not. This was not a war to vindicate wrongs and to defend Texas boundary claims. The war with Mexico was essentially a war of conquest which had been dreamed of by American expansionists more than half a century before war actually came.

Some 16 years before the war began, the Mexican scholar José Tornel (later Mexican Secretary of War) wrote these words as translated by Castañeda in his book (previously cited):

". . . For more than 50 years, that is, from the very beginning of their political infancy, the prevailing thought of the United States of America has been the acquisition of the greater part of the territory once belonging to Spain — particularly, that part which today (1830) belongs to Mexico."

Even earlier, in 1810, New Mexico's first and only delegate to the Spanish Cortes, Don Pedro Bautista Pino, warned King Ferdinand VII thus:

" . . . I expect, Sir, that your Majesty will take note of this truth, that resulting from the purchase of Louisiana, by the United States, the door is left open to enable them to arm and incite the savage tribes, as well as for themselves to invade our province; once lost, its recovery is improbable."

Antonio de Barriero, a Mexican lawyer who lived in New Mexico for many years and was an adviser to the governors, wrote these prophetic words in 1830:

" . . . *The Supreme Government should not ignore that the savage tribes which surround New Mexico afford a most favorable weapon to the cabinet in Washington, to take a hand in a cruel and bloody war against the Republic, since with these lands devastated and ravaged, they could well cast those ulterior glances attributed to the United States with respect to the usurpation of these lands.*"

On March 2nd, 1836, former President John Quincy Adams (then representing his state in the Congress) spoke these words which were entered into the Congressional Record:

" . . . *Your war, sirs, is to be a war of races — the Anglo-Saxon against the Moorish-Mexican American . . . What will be the causes of such a war? . . . Sirs, the banners of freedom will be the banners of Mexico . . . and your banners, I blush to speak the word, will be the banners of slavery . . . You are talking about acknowledging the independence of Texas, and yet you are thirsting to annex Texas, Coahuila and Tamaulipas and Santa Fé, from the source to the mouth of the Bravo, to your already extended dominions. Five hundred thousand square miles of the territory of Mexico would not even now quench your burning thirst for aggrandizement.*

" . . . *And again I ask, what will be the cause for such a war? Aggression, conquest and the establishment of slavery where it has been abolished!*"

Some years ago, while traveling in the Far East, the then Attorney General Robert Kennedy was heckled by a student who threw at him the example of American imperialism in connection with the Mexican War. Kennedy answered him:

" . . . *We take little pride in that episode.*"

Nathan Covington Brooks was born in Cecil County, Maryland, in the year 1808. He was the son of parents who came to America from England and Wales in pre-Revolutionary times. He died in 1898 at the age of 89 years. During his lifetime he was prominent in the cultural, political and literary life of his community. He was the author of numerous works on historical subjects.

At the outbreak of the Mexican War, Brooks was 38 years of age. His evident literary and historical tendencies interested him in writing this book which he must have begun prior to the commence of actual hostilities. Otherwise, it would not have been possible for him to have it ready for publication on July 4, 1849, scarcely a year after the American flag was replaced by the Mexican banner over the national palace in Mexico City.

In his preface, Brooks remarks:

" . . . *The subscribers to this History of the Mexican War, who have patiently waited for some time for the reception of their copies, will pardon the delay which has insured the authenticity of the work and enhanced its value.*"

Subscription books were just that, in the middle of the 19th Century. Orders were taken before a book was published, and only enough books were manufactured to fill the orders. As a consequence, Brooks in effect published a limited edition, whether or not he planned to do so. I believe it to be historically important, probably more so than any other volume published about the war.

The War with Mexico is a matter of history, now, but it should not continue to be "The War That Nobody Knows;" every American should know at least *something* about it. It should, in my opinion, be required reading for every college student in every state of the Union. In publishing these two books together as one, The Rio Grande Press has performed a distinct and very real service to students, scholars, teachers, librarians and the general public at large. I consider it a privilege, as well as a pleasure, to have had the opportunity to set forth these words on behalf of the book. While the motivations for the war may be debatable, the results are not.

GILBERTO ESPINOSA

Albuquerque, New Mexico
October, 1965

A

COMPLETE HISTORY

OF THE

MEXICAN WAR:

ITS CAUSES, CONDUCT, AND CONSEQUENCES:

COMPRISING AN ACCOUNT OF THE

VARIOUS MILITARY AND NAVAL OPERATIONS,

FROM ITS COMMENCEMENT TO THE

TREATY OF PEACE.

ILLUSTRATED AND EXPLAINED BY

MAPS, PLANS OF BATTLES, VIEWS, AND PORTRAITS.

BY N. C. BROOKS, A. M.,

MEMBER OF THE MARYLAND HISTORICAL SOCIETY;

AUTHOR OF "SKETCHES OF THE BATTLES OF THE REVOLUTION," ETC. ETC.

PHILADELPHIA:

GRIGG, ELLIOT & CO., 14 NORTH FOURTH STREET.

BALTIMORE:

HUTCHINSON & SEEBOLD.

1849.

Entered according to Act of Congress, in the year 1849, by

HUTCHINSON & SEEBOLD,

in the Clerk's Office of the District Court of Maryland.

Printed by T. K. & P. G. Collins.

GEN. Z. TAYLOR.

Z. Taylor

TO

MAJOR-GENERAL ZACHARY TAYLOR,

THIS HISTORY OF

THE MEXICAN WAR

IS INSCRIBED,

WITH THE RESPECTFUL SALUTATIONS

OF THE AUTHOR.

PREFACE.

In relation to the origin of the Mexican War, which now forms an important part of the history of our country, public opinion has been divided, and much affected by the political bias of the two leading parties; so that it is impossible for an impartial chronicler to please both, and difficult even to avoid giving offence to·either.

I have therefore reviewed the causes which led to the war between the sister republics, unaffected by any party preferences or prejudices whatever; and after a careful examination of all the points at issue, and the diplomatic action of the two governments, have endeavoured at least to arrive at just and candid conclusions.

In the record of the events of the war—which may challenge comparison with the military achievements of any age or nation—I have endeavoured to award to each arm of the service—cavalry, artillery, and infantry, and to our navy—the meed of praise it has so nobly won ; and if, in any case, the claims of particular persons may have been overlooked, it is to be hoped that the circumstance will not be attributed to a disposition to do injustice to any.

For the details of the history, I am indebted mainly to the perusal of the diplomatic correspondence and public records—the letters and official reports of the general and subordinate officers, and interviews and correspondence with those who were active participators in the scenes described.

The subscribers to THE HISTORY OF THE MEXICAN WAR, who have patiently waited some time for the reception of their copies, will pardon a delay which has insured the authenticity of the work and enhanced its value.

BALTIMORE, *July 4th*, 1849.

CONTENTS.

CHAPTER I.

CHAPTER II.

CHAPTER III.

CHAPTER IV.

CHAPTER V.

CHAPTER VI.

CHAPTER VII.

CHAPTER VIII.

CHAPTER IX.

CHAPTER X.

CHAPTER XI.

CHAPTER XII.

CHAPTER XIII.

CHAPTER XIV.

CHAPTER XV.

CHAPTER XX.

CHAPTER XXI.

CHAPTER XXII.

CHAPTER XXIII.

CHAPTER XXIV.

CHAPTER XXV.

ILLUSTRATIONS.

---

3   (15)

HISTORY OF THE MEXICAN WAR.

CHAPTER I.

CAUSES OF THE MEXICAN WAR—Revolution of the Hispano-American Provinces —Consequent irregularities—Neutrality of the United States—Violations of it by Mexico—Forbearance of the United States—Treaty of Amity, Commerce, and Navigation—Revolt of Texas—Neutrality of the United States—Troops under General Gaines—Conduct of M. Gorostiza, the Mexican Minister.

WHILE in every war the civil authority of the country in which it is carried on, will be, to some extent, subordinate to the military power, it is an aggravation of the unnatural character of a civil war, that the disregard of law is general, and that the rights of persons and property, being without any adequate security, are liable to continual molestation. The overthrow of the existing government of a country, or resistance to its authority, with the excitement and confusion incident to the struggles of antagonistic factions for ascendancy, all tend directly to produce a lawless and aggressive spirit, which is hostile to personal liberty, while the wasting of the public resources of the country by the double exactions of intestine war, give rise to those pressing necessities which are often supplied by the forcible impressment and appropriation of private property.

This was exemplified in the struggles of the different Hispano-American countries for independence. The people were continually subjected to seizure of their property either by the republicans or monarchists, just as one party or the other happened to prevail, and was in want of necessary funds.

Nor in their efforts to raise means to support the contest in which they were engaged, did they evince much more respect for the law of nations than they did for the laws of their own country ; the property belonging to citizens of a neutral power, was appropriated to their own use, without scruple or reserve, whenever it was necessary to their purpose. Although, during the protracted struggle between Spain and her revolted colonies, the most perfect neutrality was observed by the government of the United States, this impartial course did not shield her from the depredations of both the belligerents. An extract from the first annual message of President Monroe, in 1817, will exhibit the aggressive conduct of the contending parties, and the just and liberal policy of the United States towards both .

" It was anticipated, at an early stage, that the contest between Spain and the colonies would become highly interesting to the United States. It was natural that our citizens should sympathize in events which affected their neighbours. It seemed probable, also, that the prosecution of the conflict, along our coasts and in contiguous countries, would occasionally interrupt our commerce, and otherwise affect the persons and property of our citizens. These anticipations have been realized. Such injuries have been received from persons acting under the authority of both the parties; and, for which, redress has in most instances been withheld. Through every stage of the conflict, the United States have maintained an impartial neutrality, giving aid to neither of the parties in men, money, ships, or munitions of war. They have regarded the contest not in the light of an ordinary insurrection or rebellion, but as a civil war between parties nearly equal, having, as to neutral powers, equal rights. Our ports have been open to both, and every article, the fruit of our soil or of the industry of our citizens, which either was permitted to take, has been equally free to the other. Should the colonies establish their independence, it is proper now to state, that this government neither seeks nor would accept from them any advantage in commerce or otherwise, which will not be equally open to all other nations. The colonies will, in that event, become independent states, free from any obligation to, or connexion with us, which it may not then be their interest to form on the basis of a fair reciprocity."

The property of American citizens, resident in the Spanish colonies, was often impressed, and merchandise protected by the American flag was confiscated under a pretended violation of blockades of extensive coasts ; which, considering the small force employed to sustain them, were merely declaratory, and had not the slightest foundation in any acknowledged principle of international law on which to rest their pretensions. So outrageous were some of these spoliations in their character, that the same President in a subsequent message designated them as "piratical practices," and asserted it was "incumbent on the United States to claim of each, with equal rigour, the faithful observance of the well-known law of nations."

In the case of all these injuries, much allowance was generously made by the United States government, in consideration of the distracted condition of the several countries during a period of civil war, and the difficulties attending an enforcement of any laws, either civil or international. Mexico, our immediate neighbour, like the other Spanish-American countries, had applied the appropriating code to the property of American resident citizens, and had been guilty of sundry violations of the American flag. Redress of grievances was not immediately demanded for these repeated violations of our neutrality, in the hope that, after Mexico had established her independence, a more just policy would prevail, at least towards the United States, which had been the first power to recognise her nationality.

And when, contrary to all reasonable expectation, the impressment of the property of our citizens, and spoliations on our commerce, were continued, the United States, evincing more than the courtesy which is due to nations, still exhibited a magnanimous forbearance towards a sister republic, just coming into existence, and was unwilling to demand redress with that promptitude which the magnitude of the injuries would have justified.

This magnanimous forbearance was mistaken for weakness, and Mexico therefore continued her unjust and aggressive policy. In 1828 a treaty of commerce and boundaries was negotiated between the two republics, but the ratification of that instrument was delayed by the government of Mexico upon the most trifling pretexts. In 1829, President Jackson, in his annual message, complained that the Mexican government still failed to ratify this "treaty negotiated and concluded in its own capital and under its own eye." This delay was the more vexatious, on account of the uncertainty of the boundary line, and the consequent acts of certain claimants under Mexican grants of territory, which had been under the jurisdiction of the United States. The same year, Mexico assumed an overbearing tone towards the United States, and requested the recall of our resident minister, Mr. Poinsett.

On the 5th of April, 1831, a treaty of amity, commerce, and navigation was concluded between the two republics, and ratified some time after. A convention was also agreed upon between the two powers, for the appointment of commissioners to make a demarcation of boundaries between the two countries, but Mexico did not observe the stipulations. She even permitted the time fixed, by the treaty of limits with the United States, for the meeting of the commissioners to define the boundaries, to expire without appointing any commissioners whatever, — all the derangements incidental to an undefined boundary, in the mean time, jeoparding the protection and quiet of citizens resident upon the border.

After the conclusion of the treaty of amity, commerce, and navigation, in 1831, it was hoped that Mexico would observe a just and friendly policy towards the United States; but, instead of redressing, or even acknowledging the former injuries which she had committed, in violation of the solemn obligations of the late treaty, she was guilty of new outrages, not only upon individual citizens of the United States, but upon her flag, and upon the persons of her consuls and other agents and officers of the government, as we will more particularly show hereafter.

❦ In the mean time new causes arose, which widened the breach between the two governments. Texas, a department of Mexico, settled to a considerable extent by emigrants from the United States, being absolved from its allegiance to Mexico by the entire overthrow of the constitution, and the tyranny of the Central government, refused to acknowledge any longer the Mexican rule, and raised the standard of revolt. In her heroic struggle for independence, she continually received subsidies of men, money, and munitions of war, from the people of the United States, which gave great offence to the Mexican government.

It was perfectly natural that the citizens of the United States would feel a strong sympathy with a people struggling for liberty, and endeared to them by kindred ties; and that they would give them such aid as was in their power. The Mexican people, however, failed to discriminate, as they should have done, between the people and the government of the United States, the latter of which determined to preserve that exact neutrality which was due to the two contending powers. If individual citizens did violate the neutrality of the United States, by supplying Texas with arms, ammunition, and troops, it is no reflection upon the government, which took all due means to prevent it, as will appear from the following circular from the Department of State, addressed to the United States District Attorneys, resident in the principal cities of the Union :—

" WASHINGTON, Nov. 4, 1835.

" SIR : It has become necessary for me to call your attention to the probable event of a contest between the different portions of the Mexican empire in the vicinity of the United States. Some of our citizens may, from their connexion with the settlers there, and from their enterprise and love of change, be induced to forget their duty to their own government, and its obligations to foreign powers; but it is the fixed determination of the Executive faithfully to discharge, so far as its power extends, all the obligations of the government, and more especially that which requires that we shall abstain, under every temptation, from intermeddling with the domestic disputes of other nations.

"You are, therefore, earnestly enjoined, should the contest begin, to be attentive to all movements of a hostile character which may be contemplated or attempted within your district, and to prosecute, without discrimination, all violations of those laws of the United States, which have been enacted for the purpose of preserving peace, and of fulfilling the obligations of treaties with foreign powers.

"I am, sir, your obedient servant,
                JOHN FORSYTH."

Notwithstanding the efforts of the government of the United States, to prevent her citizens from taking part in the contest between Mexico and Texas, many joined the standard of the latter, and furnished supplies of arms and ammunition. In addition to this, a portion of the United States troops. under General Gaines, advanced into the territory of Texas as far as Nacogdoches, which gave great offence to the other contending power. The President of the United States had stationed these troops upon the frontier, deeming it proper, while observing a strict neutrality himself, to require both the contending parties to respect his neutrality; and to prevent the employment of the Indians in the contest, which might cause incursions into the territories of the United States. The following extract from a letter of General Gaines, presents the reasons which, in his opinion, justified his advance into the Texan territory:—

"The 33d article of the treaty with Mexico requires both the contracting parties to prevent 'by force, all hostilities and incur-

sions on the part of the Indian nations living within their respective boundaries, so that the United States of America will not
suffer Indians to attack the citizens of the Mexican States,' &c.

" The provisions of this article, I am particularly instructed to
cause to be enforced ; and I have, pursuant to instructions, taken
measures to make known to the various Indian tribes inhabiting
that portion of the United States bordering upon the Mexican territory, on the waters of the Red and Arkansas rivers, the determination of the government to prevent any hostile incursions into
Texas, and have directed that the chiefs be called upon to incul-
cate upon their people the necessity of carefully abstaining from
any violation of the above-mentioned engagements.

" I have learned, from several of our citizens entitled to credit,
that one Manuel Flores, a Mexican Spaniard, but for several
years past a citizen of Spanish Town in this state, near the Sabine
Ridge, has been lately commissioned by persons professing to act
by the authority of the Mexican government, for the purpose of
enticing the Indians in the western prairies on our side of the
boundary line to join them in the war of extermination now waging
in Texas ; and that with this view, the agent, Manuel Flores,
accompanied by a stranger, has lately passed up the valley of the
Red river, and has already produced considerable excitement
among the Caddo Indians.   And I have very recently learned,
from several intelligent persons in Texas, and others who have
lately been there, that many of our Indians have gone over to the
Texas side of the line.

" These facts and circumstances present to me this most important question, whether I am to sit still and suffer these movements to be so far matured as to place the white settlements on
both sides of the line wholly within the power of the savages, or
whether I ought not instantly to prepare the means for protecting
the frontier settlements ; and if necessary, compelling the Indians
to return to their own homes and hunting-grounds ?

4

"I cannot but decide in favour of the last alternative which this question presents; for nothing can be more evident than that an Indian war, commencing on either side of the line, will as surely extend to both sides, as that a lighted quick match thrust into one side of a powder magazine would extend the explosion to both sides."

Mr. Gorostiza, the Mexican Minister, protested against the advance of the troops under General Gaines, as a positive violation of the Mexican territory; a long and somewhat angry correspondence ensued, in which Mr. Gorostiza at length demanded peremptorily the recall of the troops under General Gaines, and failing to effect his desire in that particular, on the 15th of October, 1836, abruptly terminated his mission to the United States, and returned home.

Before doing so, however, he adopted a course unexampled in the history of diplomacy, and highly indecorous to the government of the United States. On his own responsibility he issued a pamphlet containing portions of his correspondence with the American Secretary of State, and extracts from his letters to his own government—with an introduction to the whole, containing statements and comments defamatory of the people and government of the United States. This pamphlet was sent to editors of newspapers known generally to be unfavourable to the administration, and to the diplomatic agents accredited to the United States government.

The President felt himself greatly aggrieved by this extraordinary and disrespectful conduct, especially after the long forbearance that had been exercised towards the Mexican government, which still refused not only to redress, but even to acknowledge the many injuries and insults which had been offered to the persons and property of our citizens, to the American flag, and to the dignity of our consuls and other officers.

CHAPTER II.

Injuries and Insults offered by Mexico—Outrages on the Persons and Property of American Citizens—Insults to the American Flag—Application of Texas for the recognition of her Nationality—Just and candid Policy of General Jackson—Recognition of Texas—Refusal of Mexico to redress or even admit the Injuries committed against the United States—Jackson's special Message—Action of Congress—Special Messenger despatched—Promises of redress—Neglect of Mexico to perform her Promises—Renewal of Negotiations—Convention for the Settlement of Claims—Procrastination and Evasion of Mexico—Failure of Mexico to comply with the Stipulations.

AFTER the treaty of amity, commerce, and navigation, concluded in 1831, it was hoped that Mexico would observe a just and friendly policy towards our country; but, in violation of the most solemn articles, she committed outrages not only upon individual citizens of the United States, but upon her flag, and the persons of her consuls and other officers. The following list of grievances, as enumerated in a letter of July 20th, 1836, from the Department of State to Powhattan Ellis, our Charge d'Affaires in Mexico, will exhibit the outrages of Mexico, and the unexampled forbearance of the United States.

On the 31st of December, 1831, an alcalde of Menotillan, in the colony of Guazcualco, instituted what is said to have been an illegal, arbitrary, and oppressive proceeding against Doctor Baldwin, a citizen of the United States, under colour of a suit at law, preferred and carried on by a creature of the alcalde himself. Baldwin appeared before the alcalde to answer the charge; an altercation ensued, and the alcalde ordered him to the stocks,

13

which Baldwin refusing to submit to, attempted to escape, and was pursued by a party of soldiers who attended the court. In the race Baldwin fell, receiving an injury in one of his legs; was captured, carried back into the presence of the alcalde, placed in the stocks, and afterwards imprisoned.

In February 1832, the schooner Topaz, of Bangor, Maine, was employed by the Mexican government to carry troops from Matamoros to Galveston Bay. The master and mate were murdered by the soldiers on the passage, the crew imprisoned, and the vessel seized and converted to the Mexican service.

On the 21st of June, 1832, the American schooner Brazoria was seized in the port of Brazoria, by John Austin, the Mexican military commandant in that quarter, and employed to make an attack upon Anahuac, then in possession of insurgents. During the attack she was injured so as to be made unseaworthy, and was abandoned as a total loss, for which the underwriters have received no compensation.

In the summer of 1832, the steamboat Hidalgo, and schooner Consolation, belonging to Aaron Leggett, of New York, were forcibly taken possession of by Mexican officers at Tobasco, and used by them. The brig John, belonging to Leggett, was also detained, and money was extorted from him. The consequences resulting from these acts are represented to have been ruinous to the sufferer, and the Mexican government was clearly bound by the treaty to indemnify him for them.

In March 1834, Captain McCeige, of the schooner Industry, of Mobile, was imprisoned at Tobasco, and an exorbitant fine demanded of him without cause. The payment of the fine being made, the only condition upon which he could be allowed to depart, he abandoned his vessel and her cargo to the authorities, who afterwards sold them.

In the summer of 1834, the brig Paragon, of New York, was causelessly fired into on her way to Vera Cruz, by the Mexican

public-armed schooner Tampico.   In answer to an official representation on the subject by Mr. Butler, that government promised
that the affair should be inquired into ; but the promise was not
fulfilled.

In the beginning of May 1835, the answer of officers supposed
to belong to the custom-house, who boarded the brig Ophir, of
New York, on her arrival at Campeachy, to an inquiry of the
captain as to which of the ship's papers it would be necessary to
present at the custom-house, was accidentally, or intentionally,
misrepresented.   In consequence of this, notwithstanding all the
papers were shown to the boarding officers, the invoices only
being exhibited at the custom-house, the vessel was seized and
condemned.

In May 1835, also, the schooner Martha, from New Orleans,
was seized at Galveston Bay, by the Mexican armed schooner
Montezuma, for an alleged non-compliance with some of the formalities of their revenue laws.   Four of the passengers of the
Martha were put in irons, under the hatches of the Montezuma,
and otherwise treated with great barbarity, merely for an imputed
intention to use their firearms against a guard that had been
placed on board the Martha.

In November 1835, the schooner Hannah and Elizabeth, of
New Orleans, was stranded in attempting to enter Matagorda
Bay.   While in this condition, she was fired into by the Mexican
armed schooner Bravo, boarded by twenty armed soldiers, under
the command of two officers, who forcibly took the master, crew,
and passengers from the wreck, pillaged them of most of their
clothes, and chained them in the hold of the Bravo until their
arrival at Matamoros, where they were continued in confinement;
but through the urgent representations of our consul there, all but
the captain were eventually released, who was kept a long time
in confinement.

On the 17th of February, 1836, William Hallett and Zalmon

Hull, citizens of the United States, were arrested in the streets of Matamoros by a party of armed soldiers, who struck Hull in the face with a sword, and forcibly took both to the principal barrack in that city, where they were confined upon suspicion of being about to proceed to Texas. Shortly afterwards, sentinels were placed at the doors of the consul's residence, under false pretences, and all communication with the house prohibited. Armed soldiers broke open his gate during his absence, forcibly took a mare and two mules belonging to him, entered his house with drawn swords, and searched every room in it, for the avowed object of finding the consul.

In February 1836, an attempt was made at the city of Mexico to take from Mr. W. A. Slocum, protected by a courier's passport from the United States Department of State, public despatches of the United States government, addressed to Mr. Butler. The attempt failed, but Mr. Slocum was fined and detained, for carrying official letters on his person, authenticated by the endorsement of the American Department of State, and directed to the Chargé d'Affaires of the United States in Mexico.

In March 1836, the schooner Eclipse was detained at Tobasco, and her master and crew maltreated by the authorities.

In April 1836, the brig Jane, schooner Compeer, and other merchant vessels of the United States, were forcibly detained at Matamoros.

The same year, the military commandant of Tampico made the embargo a pretext for interrupting or obstructing the correspondence between the commander of the United States revenue cutter Jefferson and our consul there. When the Jefferson anchored off the port of Tampico, direct from Pensacola, being sent out by order of Commodore Dallas—Lieutenant Osborn and his boats' crew upon going on shore were seized and imprisoned, and the vessel prohibited from entering the river. A demand for satisfaction was made by the American Consul, but was indignantly refused. Some time after, the commandant was displaced on representation of our government, but he was speedily restored to a higher office on the same coast.

In the mean time, Texas, which, since the battle of San Jacinto, had not been molested by Mexico, pressed upon the American government its recognition as an independent nation; but President Jackson, although wounded by the conduct of the Mexican government, with that strong sense of justice and honour for which he was distinguished, in his special message to Congress of December 21st, 1836, advised that the United States should delay to recognise its nationality until the independence of Texas was indisputably established, that the policy of his country might be above all suspicion.

(" The title of Texas to the territory she claims is identified with her independence ; she asks us to acknowledge that title to the territory, with an avowed design to treat immediately of its transfer to the United States. It becomes us to beware of a too early movement, as it might subject us, however unjustly, to the imputation of seeking to establish the claim of our neighbours to a territory, with a view to its subsequent acquisition by ourselves.

" Prudence, therefore, seems to dictate that we should still stand aloof, and maintain our present attitude, if not until Mexico itself, or one of the great foreign powers, shall recognise the independence of the new government, at least until the lapse of time, or the course of events shall have proved, beyond cavil or dispute, the ability of the people of that country to maintain their separate sovereignty, and to uphold the government constituted by them.

" Neither of the contending parties can justly complain of this course. By pursuing it, we are but carrying out the long-established policy of our government—a policy which has secured to us respect and influence abroad, and inspired confidence at home."

Some time before this, to prevent any hasty action in the case of Texas, the President had sent a confidential agent to ascertain the civil, political, and military condition of the country.

On the acknowledgment of the independence of Texas, some time after, by the United States, the Mexican Minister of Foreign Affairs protested against the matter in the most solemn manner, and in a way calculated to do violence to the feelings of the government and people of the United States. In the interim, the representations of our Chargé d'Affaires in Mexico, in relation to the grave complaints which the United States made against the government of that country, had been entirely disregarded. Wherefore, the President, in carrying out his candid policy "to ask for nothing which was not clearly right, and to submit to nothing that was wrong," finding he could effect nothing with the Mexican government, called the attention of Congress to the difficulty in a special message of February 6th, 1837, from which we make the following extracts :—

" The length of time since some of the injuries have been committed, the repeated and unavailing applications for redress, the wanton character of some of the outrages upon the persons and property of our citizens, upon the officers and flag of the United States, independent of recent insults to this government and people, by the late Extraordinary Mexican Minister, would justify, in the eyes of all nations, immediate war.

" That remedy, however, should not be used by just and generous nations, confiding in their strength for injuries committed, if it can be honourably avoided ; and it has occurred to me that, considering the present embarrassed condition of that country, we should act with both wisdom and moderation, by giving to Mexico one more opportunity of atoning for the past, before we take redress into our own hands. To avoid all misconception on the part of Mexico, as well as to protect our national character from reproach, this opportunity should be given with the avowed design and full preparation to take immediate satisfaction, if it should not be obtained on a repetition of the demand for it. To this end, I recommend that an act be passed authorizing reprisals, and the use of the naval force of the United States, by the Executive, against Mexico, to force them, in the event of a refusal by the Mexican government, to come to an amicable adjustment of the matters in controversy between us, upon another demand thereof made from on board of one of our vessels of war on the coast of Mexico."

The President was entirely sustained by both houses of Congress in his views of the flagrant outrages committed by Mexico, as well as in the plan of redress; but it was recommended that she should have another opportunity to atone for her past misconduct.   In this, strict adherence was had to the 34th article of the treaty with Mexico, which provided that—" If any of the articles contained in the present treaty shall be violated or infracted in any manner whatever, it is stipulated that neither of the contracting parties will order or authorize any acts of reprisal, nor declare war against the other, on complaint of injuries or damages, until the said party considering itself offended shall first have presented to the other a statement of such injuries or damages, verified by competent proofs, and demanded justice and satisfaction, and the same shall have been either refused or unreasonably delayed."

In the House of Representatives, the report of the Committee on Foreign Affairs contained the following paragraph :—

" The committee fully concur with the President that ample cause exists for taking redress into our own hands, and believe that we should be justified, in the opinion of other nations, for taking such a step.   But they are willing to try the experiment of another demand, made in the most solemn form, upon the justice of the Mexican government, before any further proceedings are adopted."

5

The report of the similar committee in the Senate contained the following :—

" After such a demand, should prompt justice be refused by the Mexican government, we may appeal to all nations not only for the equity and moderation with which we shall have acted towards a sister republic, but for the necessity which will then compel us to seek redress for our wrongs, either by actual war or by reprisals. The subject will then be presented before Congress, at the commencement of the next session, in a clear and distinct form ; and the committee cannot doubt but that such measures will be immediately adopted as may be necessary to vindicate the honour of our country, and insure ample reparation to our injured citizens."

Pursuant to these recommendations, the President despatched a special messenger to Mexico to demand satisfaction and redress, who made the demand accordingly on the 20th of July, 1837. The government of Mexico replied on the 29th, and gave assurances that " nothing should be left undone which may contribute to the most speedy and equitable determination of the subjects which have so seriously engaged the attention of the American government." It further promised to " adopt, as the only guides of its conduct, the plainest principles of public right, the sacred obligations imposed by international law, and the religious faith of treaties ; and that whatever justice and reason may dictate respecting each case will be done."

How well Mexico adhered to the above pledges, will appear from the following extract from the annual message of President Van Buren, of December 5th, 1837 :—

" Although the large number, and many of them aggravated cases of personal wrongs, have been now for years before the Mexican government, and some of the causes of national complaint, and those of the most offensive character, admitted of immediate, simple, and satisfactory replies, it is only within a few days past that any specific communication in answer to your last demand, made five months ago, has been received from the Mexican Minister. By the report of the Secretary of State, herewith presented, and the accompanying documents, it will be seen that for not one of our public complaints has satisfaction been given or offered; that but one of the cases of personal wrong has been favourably considered, and that but four cases of both descriptions, out of all those formally presented and earnestly pressed, have as yet been decided upon by the Mexican government. * * * In accordance with the clearly-understood wishes of the legislature, another and formal demand for satisfaction has been made upon the Mexican government, with what success the documents now communicated will show. On a careful and deliberative examination of the contents, and considering the spirit manifested by the Mexican government, it has become my painful duty to return the subject, as it now stands, to Congress, to whom it belongs to decide upon the time, the mode, and the measures of redress."

Instead, now, of war or reprisals, Congress generously forbore to redress her wrongs in the case of a sister republic ; and negotiations were renewed between the countries. After a year's delay, the convention of April 11th, 1839, was agreed upon "for the adjustment of claims of citizens of the United States of America upon the government of the Mexican republic." The joint board of commissioners to examine and decide upon these claims met in August 1840, and the four first months were spent in frivolous points raised by the Mexican commissioners. The examination of claims, in consequence, did not commence till December 1840, though the time of session of the convention was limited to but eighteen months. When the time expired, in 1842, the claims allowed amounted to two million twenty-six thousand one hundred and thirty-nine dollars and sixty-eight cents. Before the umpire between the commissioners of the two countries, and

undecided for want of time, were claims amounting to nine hundred and twenty-eight thousand six hundred and twenty-seven
dollars and eighty-five cents; while still other claims submitted
to the board, amounting to three million three hundred and thirty-
six thousand eight hundred and thirty-seven dollars and five
cents, were not examined at all for want of time. The two million twenty-six thousand one hundred and thirty-nine dollars
and sixty-eight cents, were not paid by Mexico, according to
stipulation, and a postponement of the time of payment was
granted to Mexico at her request, in the spirit of forbearance that
had always actuated the American government.

A second convention was concluded on the 30th of January,
1843, which was declared to be " entered into for the accommodation of Mexico." This stipulated that Mexico should pay on the
30th of April, 1843, the interest then due on the awards of the
convention of the 11th of April, 1839; and that she should pay in
five years, in equal instalments every three months, the principal
of the awards, and the interest accruing thereon. Of the sum
thus acknowledged for acts of outrage and wrong committed
upon the citizens of the United States, and secured by the solemn
obligations of a treaty, Mexico paid only the interest due on the
30th of April, 1843, and three of the twenty instalments of the
principal. Nor was this all. To provide for a liquidation of the
claims not decided upon by the convention of April 1839, it was
stipulated by the sixth article of the convention of the 30th of
January, 1843, that a new convention should be entered into for
the settlement of these claims. A third convention was accordingly concluded on the 20th of November, 1843, and ratified by
the United States Senate in January 1844, with two amendments,
manifestly reasonable. On referring these amendments to the
government of Mexico, she was guilty of delays and evasions, in
violation of the faith of treaties; and, though the subject was
earnestly pressed upon her, she would not give an answer whether

she would or would not accede to the amendments, but preserved a gloomy and sullen silence.

It is but just, however, to state that an effort was made to pay our admitted claims, which fell through, partly in consequence of the anticipated annexation of Texas. This will appear from an extract from the letter of Mr. Voss to Mr. Slidell :—

" For the avowed purpose of liquidating the recognised American claims, General Santa Anna, the head of the Mexican government, in May 1843, decreed the collection of a forced loan, to be distributed in certain proportions through the departments of this Republic, and paid at periods corresponding to those stipulated in the convention to that effect with the government of the United States. This measure, essentially unpopular, could only have emanated from a government as absolute as that of Santa Anna then was, and, even with the aid of his unlimited powers, was very imperfectly enforced, while the temptation to a misapplication of the funds collected amidst the difficulties by which Santa Anna was surrounded is sufficiently obvious. From these concurring circumstances, the Mexican government was absolutely unable to pay the instalment which became due in April 1844 ; and in July of the same year, when another instalment should have been paid, the incapacity of the government to fulfil its engagements had become still greater.

" About this time public attention was directed to the Texan question with renewed force ; and amidst the angry excitement which it occasioned, the press found a popular theme for complaint in the payment of the American claims, and freely advocated its discontinuance."

To show that Mexico had no just right to complain of the conduct either of Texas or of the government of the United States, we will consider the circumstances attending the revolt of the former, and its annexation to the United States.

CHAPTER III.

BEFORE 1821, if we except the tribes of savages that wandered
over its wastes, Texas contained few inhabitants. These generally were Americans, settled, for the most part, in and around
the towns of San Antonio and Nacogdoches—adventurous and
hardy pioneers, who, with restless enterprise, had pushed their
fortunes beyond the confines of civilization.

Bearing with them the innate spirit of freedom, they diffused
abroad the love of liberty among the Spaniards, and contributed
in no small degree to induce them to throw off their foreign yoke,
and establish independence.

On the 17th of January, 1821, Moses Austin, of Connecticut,
obtained from the Spanish authorities permission to establish a
colony in Texas, with many important privileges. He was empowered to introduce into Texas three hundred families, upon a

24

specified territory, one hundred miles in breadth on the coast, and extending one hundred and fifty miles into the interior. The grant allotted to him crossed the rivers Brazos and Colorado, and included large tracts east and west of these rivers. By the conditions agreed upon between Austin and the Spanish authorities, each family of the settlers was to receive a grant in fee of a section of land of the extent of one Spanish league square. The colonists were permitted to bring with them all necessary implements, and other goods not exceeding the value of two thousand dollars, free from any duty, and, for a period of five or six years, they were to be exempt from taxes of every kind.

Before the colony was established the grantee deceased, and Stephen F. Austin, his son, who received the grant by bequest, led thither a colony of settlers in December 1821. At the outset of their career, the colonists endured many hardships, and suffered many privations, while they were continually harassed by the incursions and depredations of the Indians.

Notwithstanding, they bore up amid their discouragements, and, favoured by a mild climate, and cheered by the hope of future wealth from the richness and fertility of the soil, continued both to labour and to suffer, while they redeemed a home from the wilderness and the savage.

After a period of toil and dangers, during which the colony had steadily progressed in importance, the Mexican Revolution produced a change of government, and in consequence cast a degree of doubt upon the validity of the compact made with the elder Austin by the Spanish authorities. To superintend the interests of his colony, Austin went to Mexico, and after spending a year there, he obtained a confirmation of his grant from the National Congress of Mexico in August 1823. This revived the drooping spirits of the colonists, and reconciled them to their new homes, of which they had begun to grow weary. Emigration to the country, which had been checked, was now resumed

Laredo Junior College Library
Laredo, Texas

again, with alacrity and confidenc , under the naturalization laws of 1823, '24, and '25.

In 1824, when the Mexican territory was organized into states under the constitution which was then adopted, and which provided for a political system similar to our own, consisting of a general or national government, and local or state governments, Texas, on account of the smallness of its population, was united with Coahuila, under the name of the state of Coahuila and Texas. This union, which was with her own consent, was provisional, and to continue until she was in a condition to become a state herself, and assume the necessary powers of government; in the words of the organic act of the constituent congress of Mexico, of the 7th of May, 1824, "until Texas possessed the necessary elements to form a separate state of herself." Thus was guarantied to Texas a specific political existence, with all the rights of self-government, as an independent state of the Mexican confederation, as soon as she "possessed the necessary elements."

During the presidency of Guadaloupe Victoria, the constitution and the federal system adopted under it, were considered firmly established. The internal government of Texas was similar to that of our territories. It was divided into five municipalities, each of which chose its own judges, sheriffs, and other officers. The selection thus by the people, from their own citizens, of those who were to administer law and justice among them, was a security against violence and oppression. Their officers were identified with them in views, feelings, and interests. With these guaranties for the protection of person and property for the present, and the provision for the future state sovereignty of Texas, that country afforded strong inducements for agricultural enterprise to the citizens of the United States, who accordingly emigrated thither, in expectation of the permanent enjoyment of civil institutions like those of their own country.

At the close of Victoria's term of office, in 1828, when Gomez Pedraza had been elected president of the republic, Santa Anna, with his troops, pronounced in favour of General Guerrero, the rejected presidential candidate, and defeated the government troops, and thus gave to Mexico the example of prostrating the civil by the military power. Guerrero was, in consequence, installed president. Bustamente, who had received the suffrages of the friends of Pedraza, was vice-president. Santa Anna, in reward of his services, was appointed secretary of war.

In 1831 Bustamente organized a conspiracy, deposed Guerrero, and, under the formalities of a military tribunal, sentenced him to be shot, on the 10th of February, 1831. Though Bustamente pretended that this zeal was evinced in favour of " Constitutional order," he did not recall Pedraza, the rightful president, but, sustained by the aristocracy and clergy, who were alarmed at the influence of republican institutions on their privileges, he proceeded, under the humble title of Vice-President, to establish throughout the country a perfect military despotism, in utter disregard of all constitutional and loyal restraints. The tyrant and his military satraps exercised the most absolute sway over the life, liberty, and property of his subjects. All freedom of the press was destroyed. As an instance, in Guadalaxara, the publisher of a paper which had given offence to Inclon, the military commandant, was seized, his press and types destroyed, and he himself, in presence of the governor and state authorities, ordered to be shot in three hours.

Among the early acts of this iniquitous administration, was the repeal of the colonization laws in relation to Texas and the United States. Emigrants from that republic were forbidden to hold land in Mexico; and by a new construction of law, many of the settlers in Texas were to be deprived of their lands, endeared to them by their labours and their sufferings. Troops soon after were sent to Texas to harass the people, under the pre-

6

text of aiding the revenue officers. Forts erected for their accommodation at Nacogdoches, Anahuac, and Velasco, soon became the seats of military tribunals, for mock trials of popular and influential citizens, under the vague charges of disaffection to the government; and were made prisons for their incarceration, after they were condemned.

Determined to resist this military despotism, the planters united, and with such forces as they could raise, in one week took the forts at Velasco, Nacogdoches, and Anahuac, and drove the enemy from the country. About this time, but without any concert of action, the garrison of Vera Cruz declared against Bustamente, and invited Santa Anna to assume the command of that post. He accepted the offer, and addressed a remonstrance to Bustamente, after which he seduced over to his interest large bodies of the government troops, and marched upon the capital, when Bustamente resigned his power and fled from the country. With a seeming regard for " constitutional order," which he had violated in 1828, when he deposed Pedraza, Santa Anna now recalled to the executive chair that chieftain, whose term of office was about to expire. Aware of his popularity, and assured that he would be the next president, he hazarded nothing, but gained much by this show of disinterested action.

In the beginning of 1833 Santa Anna was elected to the presidential chair without opposition; and, from the popularity which he now enjoyed, as the restorer of the constitution of his country, the most sanguine expectations were entertained of a liberal execution of the powers of government. The members of the Congress were regarded as sincere friends of liberty, and the inhabitants of Texas thought the time favourable to petition the government for admission into the Mexican confederacy as a free state.

Their petition set forth, that " Coahuila and Texas were totally dissimilar in soil, climate, and productions: that the representa-

GEN. ANTONIO LOPEZ DE SANTA ANNA.

tives of the former were so much more numerous than the latter, that all legislation for the benefit of Texas could be only the effect of a generous courtesy: that laws happily adapted to the one, would on account of the great dissimilarity of their interests be ruinous to the other: that Texas was in continual danger from the aggression of the Indian tribes, without any efficient government to protect her in such cases: that the present legislation is calculated to exasperate the Indian tribes by withholding their rights; whereas, by doing them justice, valuable auxiliaries might be gained, instead of deadly enemies, which should be the policy of Texas: that Texas 'possessed the necessary elements for a state government, and that for her attachment to the federal constitution, and to the republic, the petitioners pledged their lives and honour.' "

For the above reasons and others, they prayed that Texas might be erected into a separate state of the Mexican confederacy, agreeably to the decree of the 7th of May, 1824, which annexed it provisionally to Coahuila.

Austin as Commissioner proceeded to Mexico with this petition, which he presented to Congress and had referred to a committee. He urged its importance upon Congress and the executive, but after waiting several months, during which he was unable to get the committee to report, to obtain a hearing from Congress, or the encouragement of the president, he despaired of success in the existing state of affairs. He wrote therefore to the municipal authorities of San Antonio, advising the call of a convention to organize a state government in Texas, with the view of rendering the action of Congress necessary in their behalf. In consequence of this letter, while on his return to Texas, he was arrested in Coahuila, and imprisoned on a charge of treason.

The circumstances of the election of Santa Anna, probably led him to aspire to the supreme power. Movements of the soldiery in which he was implicated soon after his inauguration, evince this disposition on his part.   But he was restrained in his designs by the Congress, which was liberal in its views and actions, and could not be induced to favour his ambitious inclinations.

During its session the Congress had turned its attention to ecclesiastical affairs, and made innovations that alarmed the clergy.   It was in favour of granting toleration to the different religious creeds; and appropriated to the national treasury some of the resources of the church, which it was conceived to hold without law or right.   This dissatisfaction of the clergy favoured the sinister designs of Santa Anna, and he soon resolved to render himself independent of Congress through their instrumentality. The clergy, wherever they had influence to dictate their views, now procured *pronunciamentos* which denounced Congress and its reforms, but expressed unbounded confidence in the president. Backed thus by the priesthood and those whose action they controlled, Santa Anna, in 1834, dissolved by force the Congress and the general council of the nation, and took measures to secure the return of a majority of members to the next Congress favourable to his designs.   For this purpose the power of the clergy was employed, and large bodies of troops were posted to overawe the suffrages of the people.

When this Congress assembled in January 1835, Santa Anna in his message plainly intimated that the people were not fitted for a free government.   He who, in 1823, on the fall of Iturbide, in order to forward his selfish views, had proclaimed himself " protector of the federal republic," now contrived its destruction.

Pronunciamentos in favour of a central government were effected among the people by the agency of the president and priesthood, when Congress, upon the 3d of October, passed a decree abolishing the constitution of 1824, and with it the state constitutions and state authorities.   The very name of State was annihilated.   To check the opposition that might arise, large forces were quartered in each state under the new governors or military prefects who were appointed by the usurper. The central government was in fact a military despotism; and the Congress was in the power of the creatures of the usurper, and served but to register his decrees.

If this change of government had been effected by a convention of the people, it would have been legal and binding. But it was not even the act of a constitutional congress; for, the usurper had dissolved by a military order the legitimate Congress while one-half of its term remained unexpired, and by a military order, under means that prevented the free action of public opinion, had procured the election of members in a revolutionary and unconstitutional manner.

Opposition to this revolutionary subversion of the government, was made by the people in the states of Mexico, Oaxaca, Puebla, and Jalisco. The inhabitants of the state of Zacatecas took up arms against the government in support of the federal constitution, but by a powerful army led by Santa Anna, and the treachery of that usurper, their efforts were crushed, and the horrid butchery of the citizens which followed, cast such a terror over the Mexican people, that they submitted to the military government which had been imposed, without further opposition.

The people of Texas, still attached to the Mexican federal system, and hoping that the Mexican people would rise and restore it, determined to call a general congress of consultation for Texas, and delegates elected for that purpose were directed to meet on the 15th of October.

Before that period, however, the war had commenced. General Cos, the governor, or military prefect of Texas, arrived with large bodies of troops, and attempted to disarm the inhabitants, which disclosed to the Texans the intended re-enactment of the bloody drama of Zacatecas, and animated them to a brave resistance. The repulse of the Mexicans at Gonzales, on the last day of September, the capture of Goliad, the victory at Conception, and the capture of Fort Lepanticlan, on the west bank of the Nueces, followed in quick succession, and gave confidence to the people; while the storming and capture of San Antonio, the last military post held by Mexico, by which General Cos and his army capitulated to the commander of the Texan troops, diffused the liveliest joy through the state. We copy the first article of the capitulation, as it proves even at this time, the sincere desire of Texas still to be a member of the Mexican confederation, agreeably to the constitution of 1824. It will also prove the faithlessness of Cos, in returning again to the war after being paroled :—

"Article 1st. That General Cos and his officers retire with their arms and private property, into the interior of the republic, under parole of honour, *that they will not in any way oppose the re-establishment of the federal constitution of* 1824."

This capitulation took place on the 11th of December, 1835, and closed the campaign of that year.

When the 15th of October came, the time appointed for the delegates to assemble in consultation, many were in the ranks of the army; but there was still a quorum, which published a declaration, in which they expressed their firm adherence to the federal constitution of 1824, and the lawful government of the country, and proffering their aid to restore them. It was made on the 11th of November, and was as follows:—

"Whereas, General Antonio Lopez de Santa Anna, and other military chieftains, have by force of arms overthrown the federal institutions of Mexico, and dissolved the social compact which existed between Texas and the other members of the Mexican confederacy, now the good people of Texas, availing themselves of their natural rights, SOLEMNLY DECLARE :

"1st. That they have taken up arms in defence of their rights and liberties, which were threatened by encroachments of military despots, and in defence of the republican principles of the federal constitution of Mexico in 1824.

" 2d. That Texas is no longer morally or civilly bound by the compact of union; yet, stimulated by the generosity and sympathy common to a free people, they offer their support and assistance to such of the members of the Mexican confederacy as will take up arms against military despotism.

" 3d. That they do not acknowledge that the present authorities of the nominal Mexican republic have the right to govern within the limits of Texas.

" 4th. That they will not cease to carry on war against the said authorities, whilst their troops are within the limits of Texas.

" 5th. That they hold it to be their right, during the disorganization of the federal system, and the reign of despotism, to withdraw from the union, to establish an independent government, or to adopt such measures as they may deem best calculated to protect their rights and liberties; but that they will continue faithful to the Mexican government so long as that nation is governed by the constitution and laws, that were framed for the government of the political association.

" 6th. That Texas is responsible for the expenses of her armies now in the field.

" 7th. That the public faith of Texas is pledged for the payment of any debts contracted by her agents.

" 8th. That she will reward, by donations in hand, all who volunteer their services in her present struggle, and receive them as citizens.

" These declarations we solemnly avow to the world, and call God to witness their truth and sincerity, and invoke defeat and disgrace upon our heads, should we prove guilty of duplicity."

It is certainly evident from the above that not Texas, but Mexico herself, was the revolutionary party. This will be further apparent from the views set forth in a report by Stephen F. Aus-

tin to the provisional government, on the 30th of November, of
of which we submit an extract:—

" That every people have the right to change their government,
is unquestionable; but it is equally certain and true, that this
change, to be morally or politically obligatory, must be effected
by the free expression of the community, and by legal and constitutional means; for otherwise, the stability of governments and
the rights of the people would be at the mercy of fortunate revolutionists, of violence, or faction.

"Admitting, therefore, that a central and despotic, or strong
government, is best adapted to the education and habits of a portion of the Mexican people, and that they wish it; this does not,
and cannot, give to them the right to dictate, by unconstitutional
means and force, to the other portion who have equal rights, and
differ in opinion.

" Had the change been effected by constitutional means, or had
a national convention been convened, and every member of the
confederacy been fairly represented, and a majority agreed to the
change, it would have placed the matter on different ground;
but, even then, it would be monstrous to admit the principle, that
a majority have the right to destroy the minority, for the reason,
that self-preservation is superior to political obligations.   That
such a government as is contemplated by the before-mentioned
decree of the 3d of October, would destroy the people of Texas,
must be evident to all, when they consider its geographical situation, so remote from the contemplated centre of legislation and
power; populated as it is, by a people who are so different in
education, habits, customs, language, and local wants, from all
the rest of the nation; and especially when a portion of the central party have manifested violent religious and other prejudices
and jealousies against them.   But no national convention was
convened, and the constitution has been, and now is, violated and
disregarded.   The constitutional authorities of the state of Coahuila

and Texas solemnly protested against the change of government, for which act they were driven by military force from office, and imprisoned. The people of Texas protested against it, as they had a right to do, for which they have been declared rebels by the government of Mexico.

"However necessary, then, the basis established by the decree of the 3d of October, may be to prevent civil wars and anarchy in other parts of Mexico, it is attempted to be effected by force and unconstitutional means. However beneficial it may be to some parts of Mexico, it would be ruinous to Texas. This view presents the whole subject to the people. If they submit to a forcible and unconstitutional destruction of the social compact, which they have sworn to support, they violate their oaths. If they submit to be tamely destroyed, they disregard their duty to themselves, and violate the first law which God stamped upon the heart of man, civilized or savage ; which is the law of the right of self-preservation.

" The decree of the 3d of October, therefore, if carried into effect, evidently leaves no remedy for Texas but resistance, secession from Mexico, and a direct resort to natural rights."

The members of the Consultation, after sundry acts calculated to meet the exigencies of the times, organized a provisional government, which consisted of a governor, lieutenant-governor, and general council. The council was composed of one member from each district represented in the Consultation. The provisional government went into operation on the 14th of November, and was to continue in force till the following March. It was made thus temporary, in order to await the action and co-operation of the other states, should they make an effort to restore the constitution of the country, and its legitimate political system.

In organization of the provisional government, Henry Smith was chosen governor, James W. Robinson, lieutenant-governor, and General Samuel Houston, commander-in-chief.

7

CHAPTER IV.

Rumours of Invasion—Want of Preparation by the Texans—Convention of the People—Intelligence of the Advance of the Mexican Army—Declaration of Independence—Constitution in conformity to it—General Houston's Orders—Lorenzo de Zavala, the Refugee—Advance of the Mexican Army—Urea marches on Goliad—Santa Anna marches on San Antonio—Colonel Travis in the Alamo—Besieged by General Siesma—Arrival of Santa Anna and Fall of the Alamo—Surrender of Colonel Fannin at Goliad—Massacre of the Prisoners after Capitulation—Policy of General Houston—Battle of San Jacinto—Complete Victory—Capture of Santa Anna—Texan Independence established.

DURING the winter, owing to the remoteness of the capital, and the variance of the two countries, the Texans had but little information respecting the intentions of Mexico. Frequent rumours, however, came, that Santa Anna contemplated an invasion. It was even said, that he was on his march, and alarm and preparation to meet him followed the annunciation. But, as the accounts proved unfounded, a sense of security and indifference lulled them to sleep, and in consequence, nearly all their forces were disbanded, when the Texans were startled by the intelligence that Santa Anna, at the head of ten thousand men, the choicest of his troops, had already entered the country, with the declared intention, if he found resistance, to spare neither age nor sex, but to make the country an utter desolation.

This intelligence, with that of the siege of San Antonio de Bexar, reached Washington on the 2d of March. A convention of the people was in session at that place, to provide for the exigencies of the time, as the period of the provisional government was about to expire, and decree the independence of the country

36

if it were deemed expedient. Convinced now, that nothing was to be expected from a change in the political system of Mexico, and preferring death to a state of slavery, the delegates, in full view of the terrible struggle that was before them, resolved to dissolve all connexion with Mexico whatever, and published to the world the following charter of freedom, upon the same day on which they learned the advance of the Mexican chief, and the siege of San Antonio de Bexar.

"*Unanimous Declaration of Independence, by the delegates of the people of Texas, in general convention, at the town of Washington, on the 2d day of March*, 1836.

" WHEN a government has ceased to protect the lives, liberty, and property of the people, from whom its legitimate powers are derived, and for the advancement of whose happiness it was instituted; and, so far from being a guaranty for their inestimable and inalienable rights, becomes an instrument in the hands of evil rulers for their oppression: When the federal republican constitution of their country, which they have sworn to support, no longer has a substantial existence, and the whole nature of their government has been forcibly changed, without their consent, from a restrictive federative republic, composed of sovereign states, to a consolidated central military despotism, in which every interest is disregarded but that of the army and the priesthood—both the eternal enemies of civil liberty, the ever-ready minions of power, and the usual instruments of tyrants: When, long after the spirit of the constitution has departed, moderation is at length so far lost by those in power, that even the semblance of freedom is removed, and the forms themselves of the constitution discontinued; and so far from their petitions and remonstrances being regarded, the agents who bear them are thrown into dungeons, and mercenary armies sent forth to force a new government upon them at the point of the bayonet:

" When, in consequence of such acts of malfeasance and abduction on the part of the government, anarchy prevails, and civil society is dissolved into its original elements; in such a crisis, the first law of nature—the right of self-preservation—the inherent and inalienable right of the people to appeal to first principles, and take their political affairs in their own hands in extreme cases, enjoins it as a right towards themselves, and a sacred obligation to their posterity, to abolish such government, and create another in its stead, calculated to rescue them from impending dangers, and to secure their welfare and happiness.

" Nations, as well as individuals, are amenable for their acts to the public opinion of mankind. A statement of a part of our grievances is therefore submitted to an impartial world, in justifi- cation of the hazardous but unavoidable step now taken of sever- ing our political connexion with the Mexican people, and assuming an independent attitude among the nations of the earth.

" The Mexican government, by its colonization laws, invited and induced the Anglo-American population of Texas to colonize its wilderness, under the pledged faith of a written constitution, that they should continue to enjoy that constitutional liberty and republican government to which they had been habituated in the land of their birth, the United States of America.

" In this expectation they have been cruelly disappointed, inas- much as the Mexican nation has acquiesced in the late changes made in the government by General Antonio Lopez de Santa Anna, who, having overturned the constitution of his country, now offers us the cruel alternative, either to abandon our homes, acquired by so many privations, or submit to that most intolerable of all tyranny, the combined despotism of the sword and the priesthood.

" It hath sacrificed our welfare to the state of Coahuila, by which our interests have been continually depressed, through a jealous and partial course of legislation, carried on at a far distant seat of government, by a hostile majority, in an unknown tongue; and this, too, notwithstanding we have petitioned in the humblest terms for the establishment of a separate state government; and have, in accordance with the provisions of the national constitution, presented to the General Congress a republican constitution, which was, without a just cause, contemptuously rejected.

" It incarcerated in a dungeon, for a long time, one of our citizens, for no other cause but a zealous endeavour to procure the acceptance of our constitution, and the establishment of a state government.

" It has failed and refused to secure, on a firm basis, the right of trial by jury—that palladium of civil liberty, and only safe guaranty for the life, liberty, and property of the citizen.

" It has failed to establish any public system of education, although possessed of almost boundless resources, (the public domain;) and although it is an axiom in political science, that unless a people are educated and enlightened, it is idle to expect the continuance of civil liberty, or the capacity for self-government.

" It has suffered the military commandants stationed among us to exercise arbitrary acts of oppression and tyranny, thus trampling upon the most sacred rights of the citizen, and rendering the military superior to the civil power.

" It has dissolved, by force of arms, the state Congress of Coahuila and Texas, and obliged our representatives to fly for their lives from the seat of government, thus depriving us of the fundamental political right of representation.

" It has demanded the surrender of a number of our citizens, and ordered military detachments to seize and carry them into the interior for trial, in contempt of the civil authorities, and in defiance of the laws and the constitution.

" It has made piratical attacks upon our commerce by commissioning foreign desperadoes, and authorizing them to seize our vessels and convey the property of our citizens to far distant parts for confiscation.

" It denies us the right of worshipping the Almighty according to the dictates of our own conscience, by the support of a national religion, calculated to promote the temporal interest of its human functionaries, rather than the glory of the true and living God.

" It has demanded us to deliver up our arms, which are essential to our defence—the rightful property of freemen—and formidable only to tyrannical governments.

" It has invaded our country both by sea and by land, with the intent to lay waste our territory, and drive us from our homes; and has now a large mercenary army advancing, to carry on against us a war of extermination.

" It has, through its emissaries, incited the merciless savage, with the tomahawk and scalping knife, to massacre the inhabitants of our defenceless frontiers.

" It has been, during the whole time of our connexion with it, the contemptible sport and victim of successive military revolutions, and hath continually exhibited every characteristic of a weak, corrupt, and tyrannical government.

" These and other grievances, were patiently borne by the people of Texas, until they reached that point at which forbearance ceases to be a virtue. We then took up arms in defence of the national constitution. We appealed to our Mexican brethren for assistance; our appeal has been made in vain; though months have elapsed, no sympathetic response has yet been heard from the interior. We are, therefore, forced to the melancholy conclusion, that the Mexican people have acquiesced in the destruction of their liberty, and the substitution therefore of a military government; that they are unfit to be free, and incapable of self-government.

" The necessity of self-preservation, therefore, now decrees our eternal political separation.

" We, therefore, the delegates with plenary powers of the people of Texas, in solemn convention assembled, appealing to a candid world for the necessities of our condition, do hereby resolve and declare, that our political connexion with the Mexican nation has for ever ended, and that the people of Texas do now constitute a Free, Sovereign, and Independent Republic, and are fully invested with all the rights and attributes which properly belong to independent nations; and, conscious of the rectitude of our intentions, we fearlessly and confidently commit the issue to the decision of the Supreme Arbiter of the destinies of nations."

Signed by RICHARD ELLIS, President,

and forty-nine delegates.

On the 17th the convention agreed upon a constitution, which was to be submitted to the people, and, if approved, the officers of the government were to be elected under it. Whatever was done, was in accordance with strict democratic principles, and the sovereignty of the people.

While the convention thus acted with decision in declaring the nationality of Texas, prompt measures were taken in its defence. General Houston, the Commander-in-chief, by the following brief but stirring appeal, announced independence and summoned the country to arms:—

"ARMY ORDERS.

"CONVENTION HALL, WASHINGTON, March 2d, 1836.

" War is raging on the frontiers. Bejar is besieged by two thousand of the enemy, under the command of General Siesma. Reinforcements are on their march to unite with the besieging army. By the last report our force in Bejar was only one hundred and fifty men strong. The citizens of Texas must rally to the aid of our army, or it will perish. Let the citizens of the East march to the combat. The enemy must be driven from our soil, or desolation will accompany their march upon us. IN-

DEPENDENCE IS DECLARED; it must be maintained. Immediate action united with valour alone can achieve the great work. 'The services of all are forthwith required in the field.'

SAM. HOUSTON,

Commander-in-chief of the Army."

The events of the former campaign were in the last degree wounding to the pride of the Mexican chief. The Texans, opposed to the central power, not only had refused to receive his military governor and had organized a government of their own; but, after taking the several forts, had forced the governor and his troops to capitulate and abandon the country.

While wounded executive and military pride thus urged him to subjugate the country, religious fanaticism stimulated him to vengeance against the Texans, because they refused to deliver up Lorenzo de Zavala, one of the purest men in Mexico, who had become a refugee in consequence of moving a law in the Mexican Congress, against certain church property. To render their action unpardonable, the Texans had elected Zavala vice-president of the provisional government.

The invading army entered Texas in two divisions. General Urea led the right and advanced upon Goliad, while Santa Anna, with the left, marched upon San Antonio de Bexar, which was reached by the van, consisting of a thousand men under General Siesma, on the 23d of February. The Texan garrison, under Colonel W. B. Travis, consisted of but one hundred and fifty men. Expecting no mercy from the infuriated chief, they determined to make a desperate resistance, and retired into the Alamo with what provisions they could collect. The intrepid commander then issued the following proclamation, which he observed to the letter:—

"COMMANDANCY OF THE ALAMO, BEJAR, Feb. 24th, 1836.

"Fellow-Citizens and Compatriots!

"I am besieged by a thousand or more of the Mexicans under Santa Anna. I have sustained a continual bombardment and cannonade for twenty-four hours, and have not lost a man. The enemy have demanded a surrender at discretion; otherwise the garrison is to be put to the sword, if the fort is taken. I have answered the summons with a cannon-shot, and our flag still waves proudly from the walls. I shall never surrender or retreat. Then I call on you in the name of liberty, patriotism, and every-thing dear to the American character, to come to our aid with all despatch. The enemy are receiving reinforcements daily, and will no doubt increase to three or four thousand in four or five days. Though this call may be neglected, I am determined to sustain myself as long as possible, and die like a soldier who never forgets what is due to his own honour and that of his country. Victory or death!

W. BARRETT TRAVIS,

Lieut. Col. Com't."

From the 23d of February to the 3d of March, the Mexicans, increased by the successive arrivals of troops, assailed the little garrison with an incessant cannonade. Various attempts too were made to carry the fortress by storm; but the Texans, anima-ted to a terrible resistance by the ominous blood-red flag which floated from the enemy's camp, repelled their efforts with heavy slaughter. In the mean time, the enemy encircled them with entrenched encampments, while the Texans increased their de-fences by entrenching on the inside.

On the 3d of March a deafening shout of acclamation announ-ced the arrival of Santa Anna, attended by additional troops. Closely invested now by an army of four thousand men, the brave Travis and his band withstood the furious onset that con-

8

tinued night and day. Human nature, however, could not bear up against this incessant labour and watching. On the morning of the 6th, a few hours before day, oppressed they sunk down to rest. Shortly after, Santa Anna, who was maddened at the resistance he had met, made a more furious assault than usual. Having drawn up his infantry, with his cavalry posted in the rear to shoot down any who would turn back, he forced them on to the attack. An hour before day the Mexicans advanced, slew the exhausted sentinels at their posts, and gained the walls. The noise roused the garrison to a desperate struggle, and on all sides round were strewed the bodies of the assailants, till the Texans, overcome with the fatigue of slaughter, and exhausted by wounds, sunk overpowered by the numbers of the enemy. When the Mexicans obtained full possession of the fort, they found but a single man alive; Santa Anna, infuriated at the resistance of the garrison, which had caused him the loss of a thousand of his best troops, immediately ordered him to be shot; and, with a savage ferocity, ordered the mangled bodies of the slain to be piled up together and reduced to ashes.

That the lamented Travis acted properly in refusing to surrender to the sanguinary tyrant, is proved by what took place at Goliad. Colonel Fannin, who commanded at this place, unable to resist the right division of the Mexican forces under General Urea, surrendered to that officer under the assurances of a treaty solemnly ratified as follows:—

"Seeing the Texan army entirely overpowered by a far superior force, and to avoid the effusion of blood, we surrender ourselves prisoners of war, under the following terms:

"Art. 1st. That we should be received and treated as prisoners of war, according to the usages of civilized nations.

"Art. 2d. That the officers should be paroled immediately upon their arrival at La Bahia; and the other prisoners should be sent to Copano, within eight days, there to await shipping to convey them to the United States, so soon as it was practicable to procure it: no more to take up arms against Mexico, until exchanged.

"Art. 3d. That all private property should be respected, and officers' swords should be returned on parole or release.

"Art. 4th. That our men should receive every comfort, and be fed as well as their own men. Signed,

Gen. UREA,

Col. MORATEAS,

Col. HOBZINGER,

on the part of the enemy, and our part. Signed by

Col. FANNIN, and

Maj. WALLACE."

Notwithstanding the pledges given above, the unfortunate Fannin and his men were treated with great brutality, and at length by order of Santa Anna were marched out between files of soldiers under circumstances of great treachery, and inhumanly butchered, and their bodies afterwards burned to ashes. And as if alike in disregard of God and humanity, this act of savage ferocity was committed upon the day of the Prince of Peace: the roar of musketry—the petitions and cries of the wounded—and the smoke of the burning bodies desecrating and polluting the still Sabbath air. The awful scene is depicted in the following extract from the letter of a Mexican officer:—

"This day, Palm Sunday, March 27, has been to me a day of heartfelt sorrow. At six in the morning, the execution of four hundred and twelve American prisoners was commenced, and continued till eight, when the last of the number was shot. At eleven, commenced the operation of burning their bodies. But what an awful scene did the field present, when the prisoners were executed, and fell dead in heaps! And what spectator could view it without horror! They were all young, the oldest not more than thirty, and of fine florid complexions.   When the unfortunate youths were brought to the place of death, their lamentations and the appeals which they uttered to heaven in their own language, with extended arms, kneeling or prostrate on the earth, were such as might have caused the very stones to cry out in compassion."

The slaughter of Fannin and his troops, and the fall of the Alamo, carried dismay into the hearts of the people.   The government panic-struck fled, and most of the citizens, giving up all for lost, imitated the example.   In this trying emergency, Houston, the commander-in-chief, having drawn to his standard about eight hundred men, with dauntless intrepidity resolved to attack the enemy before he would concentrate his forces, and thus cut up his army in detail.

By a providential circumstance, Houston, when near the division of the centre, which was commanded by Santa Anna, obtained every desirable information.   A courier was captured with a despatch detailing Santa Anna's movements, his force, route, and destination.   By a forced march, Houston reached on the 20th of April the place, near the confluence of Buffalo Bayou and San Jacinto, where Santa Anna intended to cross the San Jacinto river, on his way to Anahuac; and, before his army had prepared their refreshments, the troops of Santa Anna appeared.   A cannonade soon commenced on both sides, with skirmishes between the cavalry and detached bodies of infantry, shortly after which Santa Anna retired to a position three-fourths of a mile from the Texan camp, where he rested the right flank of his infantry on a wood that skirted the San Jacinto, and secured his left by a fortification of packs and baggage, with an opening in the centre for his artillery.

Thus, almost in presence of each other, the hostile armies slept till the bright sun of spring arose which was to light the young republic to independence, and usher in the day of doom to its enemies.

On the morning of the 21st, Santa Anna was reinforced by five hundred and forty men under General Cos, making his force nearly sixteen hundred men. These were choice troops, formed under his own eye, acquainted with the manœuvres and strifes of war, and equipped with all needful appointments. To oppose these, the Texan commander had under him less than eight hundred men. These were planters and men of every profession and trade, the most of whom had never seen service, who with scarcely any military exercise had taken upon them the duties and fatigues of a soldier. They had, however, every stimulant to excite them. If vanquished, they knew that they would be butchered in cold blood, and that the fire and sword of desolation would sweep over the settlements, till it reached the Sabine. Patriotism thus summoned them to every manly exertion for the defenceless living, while a voice from Goliad and the Alamo, called to vengeance for the butchered dead.

Under the cover of a wood, having completed his arrangements for battle, without exposing his designs to the enemy, General Houston led on his little army to the attack. The evolutions were made with alacrity and precision. Debouching from an island of timber, the army advanced rapidly in line across the prairie ; when the artillery took position within two hundred yards of the enemy's breastwork, and poured in a destructive fire of grape and canister. Colonel Sherman's regiment having commenced the action on the left, the centre and right advanced in double quick time, with the terrible war-cry, " Remember the Alamo !" which rose above the roar of battle, and carried dismay into the hearts of the Mexicans. Receiving the fire of the enemy, which mostly went over their heads and did little execution, they advanced within point-blank shot, and then with deadly aim delivered their fire with murderous effect. Not taking time to reload the pieces, they rushed on and used their pistols, and then, raising their rifles as war-clubs, sent them crashing through skull and bone.   Many of these were broken at the breech, when, still pressing on like furious lions, and shouting that deathful cry, " Remember the Alamo!" with their bowie-knives they hewed down those of the enemy that resisted, or stabbed them in retreat. The breastwork and artillery were soon in possession of the Texans, while the wings in the mean time had been put to slaughter or the rout.

The enemy's cavalry had been repulsed with great loss by that of the Texans under the brave Lamar, and it was now in full retreat.   Hotly pursued by the Texans, it sought retreat by a bridge which General Houston had taken the precaution to cut down.   On arriving here, a cry of horror announced the bridge was gone.   Some urged their coursers down the steep bank, and horse and rider went down together.   Others dismounted, and were struggling to swim over the stream.   Horses and men were jammed and crushed together, upon the banks and in the waters, while a heavy fire from their pursuers assailed them, till the waters were red with blood, and the channel choked up with the dead and the dying.   The victory was complete.   The Mexican loss was six hundred and thirty killed, two hundred and eighty wounded, and seven hundred and thirty prisoners.   Among the latter were General Santa Anna, and General Cos, who had treacherously broken his parole.   Of the army scarcely a man escaped. The Texans lost but two in killed, and twenty-three wounded. The battle of San Jacinto sealed the independence of the country, and the new star of Texas rose in beauty among the constellations of republics.   Santa Anna, who by his inhumanity to his prisoners had forfeited his life, was generously spared by the Texan commander.   As President of Mexico he made a treaty with General Houston, in which he recognised the full independence of Texas, and engaged to order the withdrawal of the remaining troops, upwards of four thousand in number. His generals immediately evacuated the country and returned to Mexico with their troops; but the Mexican Congress refused to acknowledge the treaty which he had made, and ordered a new invasion. This however was not attempted, and all warfare between the two countries was hereafter confined to desultory attacks and skirmishes.

Texas, which had been granted to the settlers as a part of Mexico, according to laws of naturalization—which had further become theirs by labours that redeemed it from the wilderness—which had been pledged to them with state sovereignty by the federal compact of 1824—all rightful control of which reverted from Mexico to them upon the forcible dissolution of that compact by military despotism—had lastly become theirs by right of conquest, and the inhabitants of Texas had an unquestionable right to organize a government of their own, or form any alliance or union with any government whatever.

Able to maintain the independence she had declared, she was admitted into the family of nations. President Jackson, after sending a confidential agent to examine her condition, people, and resources, first recognised her political existence; and the last time he put his hand officially to paper, it was on this interesting occasion. The act of recognition by the United States was soon followed by that of England, France, and Belgium.

We have thus at some length shown the rise of Texas as a nation, with the view of relieving her from the obloquy too often thrown upon her, and of demonstrating the fact, that instead of plundering the Mexican nation of a part of her territory, as her people have been accused of doing, they acknowledged and upheld the great principles of the Mexican constitution with truth and fidelity, until there was no hope of constitutional freedom, and a war of extermination denounced against them as rebels, drove them into independence.

CHAPTER V.

Having achieved the independence of their country, the people of Texas now turned their attention to the future, and considered whether they would best promote their security and happiness by a separate existence under the protection of some foreign state, or by merging their sovereignty in the great Northern Confederacy. The expenses of maintaining a government, and the distrust of foreign alliances, indisposed them to the former, while the circumstance of the majority of the inhabitants being emigrants from the United States, rendered a union with that country desirable. With this preference, and in the exercise of a legitimate act of sovereignty, the Executive of Texas, on the 4th of August, 1837, proposed to annex that country to the United States. An expression of opinion relative to this subject had been made in September 1836, at the first election held for choosing officers

50

under the constitution, and the desire for the union was found to be nearly unanimous.

The proposition of annexation was made during the presidency of Mr. Van Buren; but, as the United States and Mexico were bound by a treaty of amity and commerce, he conceived that annexation would be a breach of the comity existing between them; and, foreseeing that it involved the probability of a war with Mexico, he was unwilling to entertain the proposition with favour.

Having failed to secure incorporation with the republican family of the North, Texas opened negotiations with European powers, with the view of obtaining the acknowledgment of her independence by Mexico, through the intervention of France and England. England, especially, treated the young republic with great consideration, and exerted her influence to induce the recognition of her nationality on the part of Mexico. This was for no disinterested love of a republican state, but with the view of securing to herself by treaty the commercial advantages to be derived from the increasing importance of Texas. France, too, committed now to the intrigues of the Montpensier marriage, laboured to prevent the annexation of Texas to the United States, probably with the view of placing over Mexico and Texas, at no distant day, a French prince, through the Spanish union. Mexico herself, fearing that the annexation of Texas to the United States might lead to a further dismemberment of territory, would have consented to the recognition of Texas, on condition that she would preserve a distinct nationality; and accordingly an armistice had been concluded between them, through the intervention of France and England. While annexation was becoming thus less necessary and desirable to Texas, the importance of the measure claimed the attention of the politicians of the United States.

Accordingly, during Mr. Tyler's administration, negotiations

9

with a view to annexation were opened on the 6th of October, 1843, by Abel P. Upshur, Esq., Secretary of State. A treaty of annexation was signed by the Texan Ministers Plenipotentiary and by President Tyler, and on the 22d of April, 1844, submitted to the United States Senate, but was rejected by that body. While the subject of annexation was agitated, Mexico had steadily notified the government of the United States that it would consider the act a ground of war. The Mexican Minister of Foreign Relations, Mr. Bocanegra, on the 23d of August, 1843, in a letter to Waddy Thompson, our Minister in Mexico, had used the following explicit language :—

" His Excellency, the Provisional President, resting on this deep conviction, is obliged to prevent an aggression unprecedented in the annals of the world from being consummated ; and if it be indispensable for the Mexican nation to seek security for its rights at the expense of the disasters of war, it will call upon God, and rely on its own efforts for the defence of its just cause."

In November of the same year, General Almonte, the Mexican Minister at Washington, protested against the act of annexation in the following solemn manner :—

" But if, contrary to the hopes and wishes entertained by the government of the undersigned for the preservation of the good understanding and harmony which should reign between the two neighbouring and friendly republics, the United States should, in defiance of good faith and the principles of justice which they have constantly proclaimed, commit the unheard-of act of violence of appropriating to themselves an integrant part of the Mexican territory, the undersigned, in the name of his nation, and now for them, protests in the most solemn manner against such an aggression ; and he moreover declares, by express order of his government, that on sanction being given by the Executive of the Union to the incorporation of Texas into the United States, he will consider his mission ended, seeing that, as the Secretary of State will have learned, the Mexican government is resolved to declare war as soon as it receives intimation of such an act."

Though the treaty of annexation was defeated, the subject was favourably entertained by the people, who feared that the fertile province offered to them would, by a union with England, become in some measure a rival. The following extract from a letter of General Jackson of the date of January 1st, 1845, shows the importance of the subject:—

"I have just received from Major Donelson, a letter dated at Washington, in Texas, from which I would infer, that if Congress expect to annex Texas to the United States, they must act speedily, or it will be found to be beyond our grasp. The rejection of the advances of Texas has given offence to some, and a handle to others to press the liberal propositions of England upon the Texans, together with the splendid view of Texas independent, growing into a vast republic, in time to embrace not only the limits of Texas, but all the domain once Montezuma's. This view, to ambitious aspirants, added to the guaranties of England of her independence, and the loan of large sums for ten years, based upon a treaty that English manufactures shall be free of duty, is gaining a party in Texas. General Houston is still the leading star; and his influence alone can be counted upon to resist the present influence of England and its increasing power. How long this influence of England can be successfully withstood in Texas, is becoming a very questionable matter. I have taken a view of the whole ground, giving to all information its due weight, and I say to you that, unless Congress acts upon this subject promptly, Texas will be beyond our grasp, and lost to the United States for ever, unless regained by the sword. What will be the situation of our country, with British manufactures introduced duty free into Texas? Comment is unnecessary.

"I hazard nothing in saying, that, if the present Congress do not act promptly upon this subject, the next will not have the power. The consent of Texas cannot then be obtained. Great Britain will have laid the lion's paw upon her, and bound her by treaty."

During the session of 1844–45, the subject engaged the attention of Congress, and on the 1st of March, 1845, a joint resolution passed the two houses of Congress annexing Texas to the United States. We extract the principal part of the resolution, as we shall have occasion to refer to it hereafter :—

" *Resolved by the Senate and House of Representatives of the United States of America in Congress assembled :* That Congress doth consent that the territory properly included within and rightfully belonging to the Republic of Texas, may be erected into a new state, to be called the State of Texas, with a republican form of government to be adopted by the people of said republic by deputies in convention assembled, with the consent of the existing government, in order that the same may be admitted as one of the states of this Union.

" *Section 1st. And be it further resolved,* That the foregoing consent of Congress is given upon the following conditions, to wit :—

" *First.* Said state to be formed subject to the adjustment by this government of all questions of boundary that may arise with other governments ; and the constitution thereof, with the proper evidence of its adoption by the people of the said Republic of Texas, shall be transmitted to the President of the United States, to be laid before Congress for its final action, on or before the 1st of January, 1846."

Immediately after learning that this resolution was signed by the President of the United States, General Almonte, the Mexican Minister, protested against it in the name of his government, demanded his passports, and left the country.

As soon as the annexation of Texas became known in Mexico, Señor Cuevas, the Minister of Foreign Affairs, on the 23d of

COMMODORE DAVID CONNER

March addressed a long memorial to the Chambers upon the subject, in which he stated his reliance upon the interference of foreign powers; at the same time he notified the American Minister, Mr. Shannon, that all diplomatic intercourse between Mexico and the United States was at an end. He addressed also a circular to the ministers resident of all the foreign powers, in which he protested against the injustice of the United States, and announced the intention of Mexico to resist it; and on the 22d of March sent despatches to the governors of the different departments throughout the republic, asking their assistance to sustain the government and maintain the rights of the nation. On the 7th of April, the joint committee of the Mexican Congress to whom the memorial on the affairs of Texas had been referred, made a report, in which they asserted their right to Texas, and the duty to take up arms for its recovery; and made the most urgent appeals to the patriotism of the people to prevent its usurpation.

Meanwhile the American government, satisfied that Texas would accept the terms of annexation, had taken precautionary measures for the protection of the country. An efficient military force was concentrated on the frontier of Texas, under the command of Brigadier-General Zachary Taylor, who had distinguished himself in the Florida war; and a strong squadron under Captain Stockton was ordered to the Gulf of Mexico, with instructions to co-operate with the army.

By a despatch of the 21st of March, 1845, General Taylor, then at Fort Jesup, in Louisiana, was ordered to hold his troops in readiness to march into Texas upon notification by the Department of War. Subsequent to this, on the 28th of May, the Secretary of War reiterated the above instructions as follows:—

"Sir: I am directed by the President to cause the forces now under your command, and those which may be assigned to it, to be put into a position where they may most promptly and efficiently act in defence of Texas, in the event it shall become necessary or proper to employ them for that purpose. The information received by the Executive of the United States warrants the belief that Texas will shortly accede to the terms of annexation. As soon as the Texan Congress shall have given its consent to annexation, and a convention shall assemble and accept the terms offered in the resolutions of Congress, Texas will then be regarded by the executive government here so far a part of the United States as to be entitled from this government to defence and protection from foreign invasion and Indian incursions. The troops under your command will be placed and kept in readiness to perform this duty."

On the 15th of June, in accordance with a requisition of Mr. Donelson, the American *Charge d'Affaires* in Texas, Mr. Bancroft, the acting Secretary of War, addressed to Taylor the following confidential letter of instructions, which we give entire on account of its importance :—

"WAR DEPARTMENT, *June* 15, 1845.

" SIR: On the 4th day of July next, or very soon thereafter, the convention of the people of Texas will probably accept the proposition of annexation, under the joint resolutions of the late Congress of the United States. That acceptance will constitute Texas an integral portion of our country.

" In anticipation of that event, you will forthwith make a forward movement with the troops under your command, and advance to the mouth of the Sabine, or to such other point on the Gulf of Mexico, or its navigable waters, as in your judgment may be most convenient for an embarkation at the proper time for the western frontier of Texas.

" In leaving to your judgment to decide the route, it is intended that you choose the most expeditious, having due regard to the health and efficiency of the troops, on reaching the point of destination.

" The force under your immediate command, at and near Fort Jesup, to be put in motion on the receipt of these instructions, will be the 3d and 4th regiments of infantry, and seven companies of the 2d regiment of dragoons. The two absent companies of the 4th infantry have been ordered to join their regiments. Artillery will be ordered from New Orleans.

" It is understood that suitable forage for cavalry cannot be obtained in the region which the troops are to occupy; if this be so, the dragoons must leave their horses and serve as riflemen. But it is possible that horses of the country, accustomed to subsist on meagre forage, may be procured, if it be found necessary. You will therefore take the precaution to order a portion of the cavalry equipments to accompany the regiment, with a view to mounted service.

" The point of your ultimate destination is the western frontier of Texas, where you will select and occupy, on or near the Rio Grande del Norte, such a site as will consist with the health of the troops, and will be best adapted to repel invasion, and to protect what, in the event of annexation, will be our western border. You will limit yourself to the defence of the territory of Texas, unless Mexico should declare war against the United States.

" Your movement to the Gulf of Mexico, and your preparations to embark for the western frontier of Texas, are to be made without any delay; but you will not effect a landing on that frontier until you have yourself ascertained the due acceptance of Texas of the proffered terms of annexation, or until you receive directions from Mr. Donelson.

" I am, sir, very respectfully, your obedient servant,
                                        GEORGE BANCROFT.

To Brigadier-General Z. TAYLOR,
    U. S. Army, commanding 1st dep't. Fort Jesup, La."

This letter was forwarded to General Taylor by an express, and immediately upon its receipt, the army was put in motion. On the 2d of July, the 4th Infantry embarked on steamers, and arrived at New Orleans on the 4th. The 3d Infantry left Fort Jesup on the 7th, and reached New Orleans on the 10th. General Taylor and staff remained at Fort Jesup to arrange affairs for the departure of the Dragoons, and did not join the troops until the 15th. On the 19th, Lieutenant Bragg, with the 3d Artillery, arrived from Charleston, and joined the Army of Occupation. Here the general received the following despatch, which modified his former instructions:—

"WAR DEPARTMENT, July 8, 1845.

"SIR: This department is informed that Mexico has some military establishments on the east side of the Rio Grande, which are, and for some time have been, in the actual occupancy of her troops. In carrying out the instructions heretofore received, you will be careful to avoid any acts of aggression, unless an actual state of war should exist. The Mexican forces at the posts in their possession, and which have been so, will not be disturbed as long as the relations of peace between the United States and Mexico continue.

WM. L. MARCY.

Brigadier-General Z. TAYLOR."

The line of policy herein enjoined was much in accordance with the views of General Taylor, as appears in the following reply:—

"HEAD-QUARTERS FIRST MILITARY DEPARTMENT,
New Orleans, La., July 20, 1845.

"SIR: I respectfully acknowledge your communication of July 8, covering the instructions of the Secretary of War of the same date, relative to the Mexican settlements on this side of the Rio Grande. Those instructions will be closely obeyed;

and the department may rest assured that I will take no step to interrupt the friendly relations between the United States and Mexico. I am gratified at receiving these instructions, as they confirm my views, previously communicated, in regard to the proper line to be occupied at present by our troops.

" I am, sir, very respectfully, your obedient servant,

Z. TAYLOR,

Brevet Brig. Gen. U. S. A., commanding.

The Adjutant-General of the Army, Washington, D. C."

A despatch from Major Donelson, dated at Austin, July 7th, reached New Orleans on the 21st, and informed General Taylor that the Convention of Texas had unanimously accepted the terms of annexation, and the following day the troops embarked for Texas. On the morning of the 26th of July they reached St. Joseph's Island, in Aransas Bay, where they were temporarily established; and on the 31st the Army of Occupation took position at Corpus Christi. This location was at once healthy, easily supplied, and well situated to hold in observation the course of the Rio Grande from Matamoros to Laredo. While here the troops were regularly practised in the different evolutions and manœuvres of war, and reconnoissances were made with reference to an advance of the army towards the Rio Grande. Meanwhile Mexico made no declaration of war, and adopted no measures that looked like a determination to invade Texas. This induced the United States Executive to suppose that Mexico would be willing to settle the existing difficulties by diplomacy; and accordingly, Mr. Buchanan, the Secretary of State, by means of an indirect correspondence with Mr. Black, the American Consul of Mexico, attempted to renew negotiations with the Mexican cabinet. The government was evidently in favour of adjusting all difficulties with the United States, and agreed to receive an envoy for that purpose; but, fearing the prejudices of

10

the Mexican people, who were in favour of war, stipulated that, to avoid all appearance of coercion, the person deputed should be of a conciliatory disposition, and that before his arrival, the naval force of the United States should be withdrawn from Vera Cruz, where it lay in sight. Commodore Conner, who was now in command of the squadron, promptly withdrew the naval force, as requested. No doubt whatever can be entertained that President Herrera and his cabinet were desirous of peace; but before the minds of the Mexican people had been prepared for the renewal of friendly relations, the American envoy, Mr. Slidell, appeared and pressed his reception with earnestness, which greatly embarrassed the action of the administration. The council of government was to a great extent in open opposition to the Executive and his cabinet, and, instead of forwarding the movement in favour of negotiation, made it the subject of intrigue against the administration, with the view of overthrowing it. In consequence of this the Mexican government refused to receive Mr. Slidell, upon a point of etiquette, that having recalled her resident Minister, and dissolved the relations between the two countries, Mexico could not receive again a *resident* Minister from the United States, until a special envoy had by negotiations arranged the difficulties in relation to Texas. This will appear from the following extract of a letter from Mr. Black to Mr. Slidell, detailing the substance of a conversation between him and Pena y Pena, the Mexican Minister of Foreign Affairs:—

"On Saturday evening, the 13th instant, at the request of Mr. Slidell, I called on the Mexican Minister, Señor Pena, at his house, to inquire when an answer would be given to his (Mr. Slidell's) aforesaid note. He replied, that the affair had been submitted to the government council, in a special session of this day, and that it had been referred to a committee, and that as soon as the committee made a report, and the council should decide, he would then advise me, through Mr. Monasterio, when he was ready for the conference to present to me the answer for Mr. Slidell; as he said when he came to examine the credentials of Mr. Slidell, he found them to be the same as those presented by Mr. Shannon, and other former Ministers— as a Minister to reside near the government of Mexico, just as if there had been no suspension of the diplomatic and friendly relations between the two governments; that the Mexican government understood the present mission to be a special mission, and confined to the differences in relation to the Texas question, and not as a mission to reside near the Mexican government, as in ordinary cases; that of course would follow when the first question was decided.

" I replied, that as I understood it, the Mexican government had not only agreed to receive an envoy intrusted with full powers to settle the question in dispute in relation to the affairs of Texas, but *all* the questions in dispute between the two governments, as proposed by the government of the United States. He replied that the credentials of Mr. Slidell had not reference to any questions in dispute, but merely as a Minister to reside near the Mexican government, without reference to any questions in dispute, just as if the diplomatic and friendly relations between the two governments had not been and were not interrupted; that I knew the critical situation of the Mexican government, and that it had to proceed with great caution and circumspection in this affair; that the government itself was well disposed to arrange all differences."

The principal reason, however, that influenced the Executive in coming to this decision, was the fear of an anticipated revolution, which took place but nine days after, and caused the overthrow of Herrera's administration in favour of General Paredes, who was a military despot, and hostile to the United States.

Mr. Slidell now retired to Jalapa, and again made overtures to the Mexican government to renew their friendly relations by re-

ceiving him as "Envoy Extraordinary and Minister Plenipotentiary to reside near the government of Mexico;" but the administration of Paredes, adhering to the resolve of the former
administration, which had been accused of treason on account
of being favourably disposed to the United States, refused to
receive Mr. Slidell in any other character than that of a *special*
envoy to treat upon the subject of Texas alone. This will
appear more fully from an extract of a letter of Señor Castillo
y Luñas, dated March 12th, 1846 :—

"From these extracts it is manifest that it was the firm
intention of the Mexican government to admit only a plenipotentiary from the United States clothed with powers *ad hoc*—that
is to say, special powers to treat upon the question of Texas, and
upon this alone as preliminary to the renewal of friendly relations
between the two countries, if the result should be such as to
admit of their restoration; and then, but not before, of the
reception of an Envoy Extraordinary and Minister Plenipotentiary
near the same government.

"Nor could the government of the republic on that occasion
extend its engagement beyond this; for to admit any person sent
by the United States in the character simply of the ordinary
agents between friendly nations, whilst the grave question of
Texas was still pending, directly and immediately affecting, as
it does, the integrity of the Mexican territory, and the very
nationality itself, would be equivalent to an acknowledgment
that this question was at an end, thus prejudging it without even
touching it, and to a recognition that the relations of friendship
and harmony between the two nations were from that moment in
fact re-established."

Immediately on the receipt of this note, Mr. Slidell demanded
his passports, and returned to the United States.

Notwithstanding the hostile attitude of Mexico, war might
have been avoided if time had been allowed for the prejudices

and animosity of the people against the United States to subside. It is true Mexico had signified an intention to declare war and invade Texas, but would never have done so if she had not been provoked by the advance of the army of the United States. To substantiate this opinion, we should call to mind, that immediately after the battle of San Jacinto, the Mexican government had ordered an invasion of Texas, but never carried her order into execution. General Almonte had solemnly stated, in the event of the annexation of Texas, "the Mexican government is resolved to declare war as soon as it receives intimation of such an act," yet Mexico made no declaration of war.

And such would have been the issue of all the threats about the subjugation of Texas after its annexation to the United States. Even Paredes, who was known to be hostile to the United States, had declared in his manifesto to the people that "until the National Congress had considered the question, no act of aggression would be committed against the United States by the Mexican government, but that it would repel any that might be offered by them."

It is evident alike from the letters of General Taylor and of the War Department, that while the army remained at Corpus Christi, war was not expected by either. The following letters will show this to be the case :—

"HEAD-QUARTERS, ARMY OF OCCUPATION,
Corpus Christi, Texas, Sept. 6, 1845.

" SIR : I have the honour to report that a confidential agent, despatched some days since to Matamoras, has returned, and reports that no extraordinary preparations are going forword there; that the garrison does not seem to have been increased, and that our consul is of opinion there will be no declaration of war. A decree had been issued prohibiting, under penalty of death, any communication, by writing, across the frontier—a precaution which has been adopted on former occasions, and caused, no doubt, by our presence here. Nothing definite can be learned in relation to the march of troops from the interior. A body of 3,000 men was reported in march to Matamoros, but the information is too vague to merit much confidence. The agent, who is intelligent, and upon whose statements a good deal of reliance may, I think, be safely placed, says that the mass of the people, with whom he mingled, is opposed to a war with us, and that if war be declared, the frontier departments of Tamaulipas, Coahuila, and Nuevo Leon, will probably declare themselves independent of the central government and establish pacific relations with us.

" This is the substance of the information brought from Matamoros. Notwithstanding its character, I shall not relax my exertions to *prepare* for active operations and a state of war with Mexico. I must express the hope that no militia force will be ordered to join me without my requisition for it. I am entirely confident that none will be required.

" I am, sir, very respectfully, your obedient servant,

Z. TAYLOR,

Brevet Brig. Gen. U. S. A. commanding.

The Adjutant-General of the Army, Washington, D. C."

Subsequent to the reception of the above, and while admitting there was no probability of war, the Executive, through his secretary, directed an advance to the Rio Grande, into territory which was in dispute, and which had never been held by Texas at all :—

" WAR DEPARTMENT,
Washington, Oct. 16, 1845.

" SIR : The information which we have here, renders it probable that no serious attempts will, at present, be made by Mexico to invade Texas, although she continues to threaten incursions. Previous instructions will have put you in possession of the views of the government of the United States, not only as to the extent of its territorial claims, but of its determination to assert them. In carrying out these instructions, you will be left very much to your own judgment, by reason of your superior knowledge of localities, and the earlier notice you may receive of the probable views of Mexico, and the movements of her troops.

" On the supposition that no active operations on your part will be required during the approaching winter, an important question to be decided is the position or positions to be occupied by your forces. This must be determined mainly with reference to the objects for which the army under your command was sent into Texas. You will approach as near the western boundary of Texas (the Rio Grande) as circumstances will permit; having reference to reasonable security; to accommodations for putting your troops into winter huts, if deemed necessary; to the facility and certainty of procuring or receiving supplies; and to checking any attempted incursions by the Mexican forces or the Indian tribes.

* * * * * * *

" You are requested to avail yourself of all proper occasions, and employ the means you possess to collect information in regard to all these matters, and forward it to this department.

" Very respectfully, your obedient servant,

WM. L. MARCY,

Secretary of War.

Brigadier-General Z. TAYLOR,
    Commanding Army of Occupation in Texas."

While efforts were making to restore diplomatic relations between the two countries, and long before the Mexican government had finally refused to receive the United States' envoy, the President had ordered the advance of the army to the left bank of the Rio Grande, and a strong fleet into the Gulf of Mexico, and thus precluded all hopes of accommodation :

"WAR DEPARTMENT,
Washington, January 13, 1846.

"SIR: I am directed by the President to instruct you to advance and occupy, with the troops under your command, positions on or near the east bank of the Rio del Norte, as soon as it can be conveniently done with reference to the season and the routes by which your movements must be made. From the views heretofore presented to this department, it is presumed Point Isabel will be considered by you an eligible position. This point, or some one near it, and points opposite Matamoros and Mier, and in the vicinity of Laredo, are suggested for your consideration; but you are left to your better knowledge to determine the post or posts which you are to occupy, as well as the question of dividing your forces with a view to occupying two or more positions.

"In the positions you may take in carrying out these instructions and other movements that may be made, the use of the Rio del Norte may be very convenient, if not necessary. Should you attempt to exercise the right which the United States have in common with Mexico to the free navigation of this river, it is probable that Mexico would interpose resistance. You will not attempt to enforce this right without further instructions.

"You are requested to report to this department, without delay, what means you may require, if any, beyond those you now possess, to enforce and maintain our common right to navigate this river, as well as your views of the importance of this right in the defence and protection of the State of Texas.

"It is not designed, in our present relations with Mexico, that you should treat her as an enemy; but, should she assume that character by a declaration of war, or any open act of hostility towards us, you will not act merely on the defensive, if your relative means enable you to do otherwise.

"Since instructions were given you to draw aid from Texas, in case you should deem it necessary, the relations between that

State and the United States have undergone some modification. Texas is now fully incorporated into our Union of States, and you are hereby authorized by the President to make a requisition upon the Executive of that state for such of its militia force as may be needed to repel invasion or to secure the country against apprehended invasion.

"I have the honour to be, with great respect, your obedient servant,

WM. L. MARCY,
Secretary of War.

Brigadier General Z. Taylor."

The President, in his annual message to Congress, assigned the following reasons for ordering the advance of the American troops:—

"Instructions have been issued to the general in command, to occupy the left bank of the Del Norte. This river, which is the south-western boundary of the state of Texas, is an exposed frontier; from this quarter invasion was threatened; upon it and in its immediate vicinity, in the judgment of high military experience, are the proper stations for the protecting forces of the government. In addition to this important consideration, several others have occurred to induce this movement. Among these are the facilities afforded by the ports at Brazos Santiago and the mouth of the Del Norte, for the reception of supplies by sea; the stronger and more healthful military positions; the convenience for obtaining a ready and a more abundant supply of provisions, water, fuel, and forage; and the advantages which are afforded by the Del Norte, in forwarding supplies to such ports as may be established in the interior and upon the Indian frontier."

Now, were it true that the Rio Grande del Norte was the south-western boundary of the republic of Texas, the advance of the American army to that river for the defence of Texas, would have been justifiable. But let us consider this subject, and see

11

if it really was the boundary of the Texas annexed to the United States. That the Rio Grande was the *ancient* boundary of Texas, all must admit. While Texas belonged severally to France, to the United States, and to Spain, it was the acknowledged boundary. So Mexico received it upon the downfall of the Spanish power in that country. Holding now the entire country by right of revolution and by subjugation, it must be admitted that Mexico could make any partitions of her own territory, and establish any domestic boundaries which she deemed expedient. In doing this, she was at perfect liberty to abridge the extent of Texas, or amplify it by any additions from the territory of Mexico proper. In her internal divisions, Mexico saw fit to assign a portion of the territory east of the Rio Grande that had been included in the *ancient* Texas, to the states of Tamaulipas, Coahuila, and Chihuahua, and established the original line between Texas, Tamaulipas, and Coahuila, on the river Aransas, thirty miles east of the Nueces. This, then, was the boundary of Texas, when jointly with Coahuila it was admitted as a state into the Mexican Confederation.

This was its boundary when the unconstitutional establishment of a central government and military despotism resolved the Mexican Confederacy into its original elements, and thus left to each integrant portion the right to organize a government of its own. By right of revolution the people of Texas declared their independence, and established a government. This simple act, however, did not extend her boundaries. The independent republic of Texas would, of necessity, now be within the same metes and bounds that the state or department of Texas had been while a part of the Mexican confederacy, unless additions were made to it by annexation, or by conquest. To a certain extent, its boundaries *were* enlarged; for the people of Tamaulipas, living between the Aransas and the Nueces, and those in the valley of the Nueces to the west of that river as far as the great desert, united with the Texans in their revolt, and after the independence of Texas was declared, associated themselves with them in forming their government. They were thus *annexed* to Texas or *subjuga-- ted* by it, and became a part of Texas. The boundary of Texas, then, by revolutionary right or by subjugation, now became the great desert west of the valley of the Nueces. Up to this boundary the people had united in the Texan revolution, acknowledged the laws of Texas after the government was formed, and paid taxes for its support.

From the great desert west to the valley of the Rio Grande were Mexican settlements, composed of those born under Mexican laws—citizens of the states of Tamaulipas, Coahuila, and Chihuahua, who had not revolted with the Texans, but had always acknowledged the Mexican authority, and given it a ready support. Over these Texas had no control. She had not subjugated them; she exercised no jurisdiction over them; she attempted none, either to serve process, collect taxes, or enforce laws. True, the Congress of Texas, by act of December 19th, 1836, declared the Rio Grande, from its mouth to its source, to be their boundary; but with what propriety, or on what grounds? They might have gone further, and with equal justness declared the San Fernando to be the boundary. It is one thing to declare right to territory, *on paper*, and another to take it by conquest, and maintain it by arms. To the country lying between the desert and the Rio Grande, Texas had the same right that she had to the state of Zacatecas or New Leon, and no more. It was a claim simply asserted on *paper*, but founded upon no right, maintained by no force. The declaration of the Rio Grande as boundary by the Congress of Texas, according to a statement of Judge Ellis, who was President of the convention that formed the constitution, was an act of policy with the sole view of *giving sufficient margin in the negotiation with Mexico,* and with no expectation of so retaining it.

The above historical facts and inferences show that Texas had no just claim to the country up to the Rio Grande ; and consequently we could have none.   What follows will make the truth more apparent.   In the first place, President Tyler, who concluded the treaty of annexation which was rejected by the Senate, did not consider the Rio Grande as the certain boundary of Texas. Hence Mr. Calhoun, the Secretary of State, in his letter to Mr. Green, our Chargé at Mexico, says :—" You are enjoined also, by the President, to assure the Mexican government, that it is his desire to settle all questions between the two countries which may grow out of this treaty, or any other cause, on the most liberal and satisfactory terms, *including that of boundary.*"   And again, speaking of the government of the United States, says :—" It had left the boundary of Texas without specification, so that what the line of boundary should be, might be an open question to be fairly and fully discussed and settled according to the rights of each— the mutual interests and security of the two countries."

The Executive that ordered the advance to the Rio Grande, indirectly admits that our claim was not just ; for the American Minister, Mr. Shannon, acting under his instructions, when about to leave Mexico, in his letter to the Minister of Foreign Affairs, states :—" The undersigned can assure his excellency Señor Cuevas that his (Mr. Shannon's) government entertains the liveliest desire to cultivate amicable relations with that of Mexico ; and here he will improve this opportunity to repeat that which he has before communicated to the government of Mexico, to wit, that the United States has not adopted the measure of annexation in any spirit of hostility towards Mexico, and that the United States are anxious to settle all questions which may grow out of this measure, including that of boundaries, in terms the most just and liberal."

The *liberal terms* referred to, in connexion with boundaries, could have reference only to the purchase of territory.   The same is apparent from the letters of Mr. Slidell, who was sent to arrange all matters in dispute between the two governments.

It is evident that the Congress of the United States did not believe the claim of Texas to the Rio Grande tenable, for in the joint resolution of annexation, the language is: — "The territory properly included within and rightfully belonging to Texas." Indeed, the very phraseology employed was in consequence of a common conviction in the Senate, that Texas' claim to territory up to the Rio Grande was not just. In accordance with this belief, it was further resolved, that the United States should adjust all questions of boundary, the only one in dispute being the boundary between Texas and Mexico. The language employed was as follows:—

"Section 1st. *And be it further resolved*, That the foregoing consent of Congress is given upon the following conditions, to wit:—

" First, said state to be formed subject to the adjustment by this government of all questions of boundary that may arise with other governments."

The following resolution offered in the United States Senate by Senator Benton, will place the matter in a stronger light:—

" *Resolved*, That the incorporation of the left bank of the Rio del Norte into the American Union, by virtue of a treaty with Texas, comprehending, as the said incorporation would do, a part of the Mexican departments of New Mexico, Chihuahua, Coahuila, and Tamaulipas, would be an act of direct aggression on Mexico, for all the consequences of which the United States would stand responsible."

I shall now show that our agent sent to Texas, Mr. Donelson, did not regard the claim of Texas as just, to the country lying on the Rio Grande. This is apparent in his letter to the Secretary of State, under date of June 23d, 1845, in which he says:—" The territory between the Nueces and the Rio Grande, you are aware, has been in possession of both parties. Texas has held in peace

Corpus Christi. Mexico has held Santiago. Both parties have had occasional possession of Laredo and other higher points. Mexico, however, has threatened a renewal of war for the whole of Texas, if she accepts the proposals for the annexation to the Union. If she undertakes such an expedition, she of course puts upon the hazard of war the whole claim, and *gives us the right of going not only to the Rio Grande, but wherever else we may please.*" In a note to the Secretary, under date of July 2d, 1845, Mr. Donelson reiterates the same:—

"My position is, that we can hold Corpus Christi and all other points up the Nueces. *If attacked, the right of defence will authorize us to expel the Mexicans to the Rio Grande.*"

In a letter to General Taylor, of June 28th, Mr. Donelson uses language of the same import :-

"The occupation of the country between the Nueces and the Rio Grande, you are aware, is a disputed question. Texas holds Corpus Christi; Mexico holds Santiago, near the mouth of the Rio Grande.

*   *   *   *   *   *   *

"You can safely hold possession of Corpus Christi and all other points up the Nueces, *and if Mexico attempts to dislodge you,* drive her beyond the Rio Grande.'

The views which Mr. Donelson entertained respecting the real claim of Texas, were perfectly just. She was entitled to Corpus Christi and the settlements on the Nueces, east of the great desert, but to no territory beyond the desert.

More than this, in the preliminary treaty between Texas and Mexico, signed by the Texan Secretary of State, and approved by the President of Texas, the Texans themselves admitted the boundary between them and Mexico to be an unsettled question, as will appear from the 3d and 4th articles:—

"3. Limits and other conditions to be matter of arrangement in the final treaty.

" 4. Texas will be willing to *remit disputed points respecting territory* and other matters to the arbitration of umpires."

In a letter to Mr. Buchanan, of July 11th, 1845, Mr. Donelson shows the impropriety of vindicating by arms a claim to the territory on the Rio Grande, which Texas herself had agreed to settle by arbitration :—

" The proclamation of a truce between the two nations (Mexico and Texas), founded on propositions mutually acceptable to them, leaving the question of boundary not only an open one, but *Mexico in possession of the east bank of the Rio Grande*, seemed to me inconsistent with the expectation that in defence of the claim of Texas, our troops should march immediately to that river. What the Executive of Texas had determined not to fight for, but to settle by negotiation, to say the least of it, could be as well left to the United States on the same conditions."

The above views of Mr. Donelson on the question of the boundary of Texas, were consonant both with justice and prudence, and in direct opposition to the course pursued by the Executive of the United States.

But further, while the President claimed the territory as far as the Rio Grande, we were accustomed to pay duties to Mexico at the custom-house at Brazos Santiago or Point Isabel. We paid duties also at Santa Fe, far east of the Rio Grande, and we interceded with Mexico for the American citizens taken prisoners in the expedition against that place.

In March 3d, 1845, Congress passed an act relative to drawbacks on goods sent to " Santa Fe in Mexico." The Secretary of the Treasury, on referring to it in his report in the following December, recognises Santa Fe as a part of Mexico. The President of the United States, himself, in the same message in which he claims as the boundary of Texas, " the Rio Grande from its mouth to its source," in speaking of the victories of our troops, admits the futility of the claim in the following sentence :—" By rapid movements *the province of New Mexico, with Santa Fe, its capital,* has been captured without bloodshed." Moreover, after taking possession of this portion of the Mexican territory, the President provided for the establishment of a military government, such as would temporarily follow an acquisition of territory by conquest. If he had considered it really a portion of Texas, it would, as a matter of course, have come under the control of the state authorities of Texas, for even the President of the United States could not interfere with the internal government of a sovereign state.

The foregoing, in connexion with the letter of the Secretary of War, under date of July 8th, 1845, which we have given, and with the official despatch of General Taylor to the Department of War, of the date of February 26th, 1846, conclusively prove that the Rio Grande was not considered the real boundary of Texas, either by Texas herself, by the Congress of the United States, or its Executive, by the agent sent to Texas, by the Secretary of War, or by the commander of the forces sent to occupy Texas. As a military officer, however, General Taylor had no election in the matter, but was bound to obey the directions of the President as Commander-in-chief of the Army and Navy of the United States.

The following letters from General Taylor to the War Department, after he was ordered to advance to the Rio Grande, are necessary to an understanding of the causes which led directly to the commencement of hostilities between Mexico and the United States.

"HEAD-QUARTERS, ARMY OF OCCUPATION,
Corpus Christi, Texas, February 4, 1846.

" SIR : I respectfully acknowledge the communication of the Secretary of War, dated January 13th, and containing the instructions of the President to move forward with my force to the

Rio Grande. I shall lose no time in making the necessary pre-parations for carrying out those instructions.

" The occupation of Point Isabel or Brazos Santiago as a depot will be indispensable. That point, and a position on or near the river opposite Matamoros, will, I think, answer all present purposes. At any rate, I shall not separate my force further until the position of affairs shall render it entirely safe to do so.

" I propose to abandon this position entirely, as soon after our march as the stores, hospital, &c., can be transferred to St. Jo-seph's Island. It will be necessary to keep up an establishment at that point for the present, although our supplies will come to Point Isabel direct from New Orleans.

" In reply to the call of the Secretary for information as to what means, if any, will be required ' to enforce and maintain our common right to navigate' the Rio Grande, I would respectfully state that, until I reach the river and ascertain the condition of things in the frontier states of Mexico, temper of the people, &c., I cannot give any satisfactory answer to the question. I have every reason to believe that the people residing on the river are well disposed towards our government. Our advance to the Rio Grande will itself produce a powerful effect, and it may be that the common navigation of the river will not be disputed. It is very important to us, and will be indispensable when posts are established higher up, as must ultimately be the case.

" I shall not call for any militia force in addition to what I already have, unless unforeseen circumstances shall render its em-ployment necessary.

" I beg leave again to call the attention of the Department to the necessity of having our movement and position at Brazos Santiago covered by a small armed vessel. I deem this vitally important, and hope it will meet with favourable consideration.

" We have no news from the interior of Mexico more recent

12

than that derived from the New Orleans papers of the 26th of January.

" I am, sir, very respectfully, your obedient servant,

Z. TAYLOR,

Brevet Brig. Gen. U. S. A. commanding.

The Adjutant-General of the Army, Washington, D. C."

"Head-Quarters, Army of Occupation,
Corpus Christi, Texas, February 26, 1846.

" Sir : I have to report that the preparations for a forward movement of this command are now nearly completed. The examinations spoken of in my report of the 16th instant have shown the practicability of both routes—by the main land and by Padre Island. The reconnoissance of Padre Island extended to its southern extremity, and included the harbour of Brazos Santiago and Point Isabel; that of the main route reached to a point near the Little Colorado. A depot, with four days' forage, and subsistence for the army, will be thrown forward some forty miles, to the Santa Gertrudes. A detachment of two companies, to establish and cover this depot, will march, on the 28th, under Brevet Major Graham. In about a week thereafter, say the 7th of March, the cavalry will march, to be followed, at intervals of one day, by the brigades of infantry. By the 25th of March, at latest, I hope to be in position on the Rio Grande.

" I have taken occasion to represent to some citizens of Matamoros, who were here with a large number of mules for sale, and who are represented to have considerable influence at home, that the United States government, in occupying the Rio Grande, has no motive of hostility towards Mexico, and that the army will, in no case, go beyond the river, unless hostilities should be commenced by the Mexicans themselves; that the Mexicans living on this side will not be disturbed in any way by the troops; that they will be protected in all their usages; and that everything which the army may need will be purchased from them at fair prices. I also stated that, until the matter should be finally adjusted between the two governments, the harbour of Brazos Santiago would be open to the free use of the Mexicans as heretofore. The same views were impressed upon the Mexican custom-house officer at Brazos Santiago by Captain Hardee, who commanded the escort which covered the reconnoissance of Padre Island.

" We are entirely without news of interest from the frontier, or the interior of Mexico, our latest date from the capital being the 21st of January, and the same from Vera Cruz.

" I am, sir, very respectfully, your obedient servant,

Z. TAYLOR,

Brevet Brig. Gen. U. S. A. commanding.

The Adjutant-General of the Army, Washington, D. C."

Now, it has been contended by some, that the advance to the Rio Grande was not the cause of the war,—that Mexico would have declared war anyhow,—and that, as Paredes published his manifesto on the 23d of April, 1846, it is impossible that the arrival of General Taylor upon the Rio Grande, which took place on the 28th of March, could have been reported in Mexico, deliberated upon, and orders for the commencement of hostilities forwarded to General Arista, by the 24th of April. But, it will be recollected, that *direction* to march to the Rio Grande was given to General Taylor, October 16th, 1845, three months before the peremptory *order* of the 13th of January; and that General Taylor, while at Corpus Christi, made no secret of the intended advance to the Rio Grande, but openly conversed with influential citizens of Mexico respecting it, with the view of conciliating them. Hence we perceive that, long before he reached the Rio Grande, and possibly before he left Corpus Christi, his intended march was known to the Mexican government. The language of General Taylor, in his letter of February 26th, makes this clear:—" I have taken occasion to represent to some citizens of

Matamoros, who were here with a large number of mules for sale, and who are represented to have considerable influence at home, that the United States government, in occupying the Rio Grande, has no motive of hostility towards Mexico, and that the army will in no case go beyond the river, unless hostilities should be commenced by the Mexicans themselves."

In the final note of Señor Lanzas to Mr. Slidell, dated March 12th, from the following passage, it would seem that the Mexican government was already aware of the intended advance of the American army, in which he impugns the sincerity of the United States, which, he says, were " *proposing peace at the very moment when they are causing their squadrons and their troops to advance upon the ports and frontiers of Mexico*, exacting a humiliation impossible to be submitted to, in order to find a pretext, if no reason can be found, which may occasion the breaking out of hostilities."

But the manifesto of Paredes, which we shall give in the due course of narrative, will itself set the matter at rest, for he expressly states—that he does not declare war, but merely defends the Mexican territory which has been invaded. His language is :—" I solemnly announce that I do not declare war against the United States of America, because it pertains to the august Congress of the nation, and not to the Executive, to settle definitely the reparation which so many aggressions demand. But the defence of the Mexican territory, which the United States troops invade, is an urgent necessity, and my responsibility would be immense before the nation, if I did not give commands to repel those forces who act like enemies, and I have so commanded. From this day commences a defensive war, and those points of our territory which are invaded or attacked, will be energetically defended."

And, that Paredes knew of the advance of the American army, is beyond dispute ; for in his manifesto he enumerates among the acts of aggression, the occupation of Padre Island, Point Isabel,

MAJ. GEN. WILLIAM J. WORTH.

and the right bank of the Rio Bravo: "Meanwhile the army of the United States encamped at Corpus Christi, and occupied the *Isla del Padre;* following this, they then moved to the Point *Santa Isabel,* and their standard of the stars and stripes waved on the right bank of the Rio Bravo del Norte, opposite the city of Matamoros, blockading that river with their vessels of war."

Now, as the Army of Occupation remained seven months and eleven days at Corpus Christi without interruption, but was immediately opposed on passing the bounds over which Texas possessed jurisdiction, it is, I think, sufficiently evident that war would not have ensued, had it not been for the advance of our troops to the Rio Grande, into territory which never belonged to Texas, and which, therefore, she could not annex to us.

The reconnoissances which General Taylor had ordered being completed, he determined on the route by the main land. Accordingly, on the morning of the 8th of March, the advance of the Army of Occupation, under Colonel Twiggs, marched in a southerly direction for the Rio Grande. It consisted of the 2d regiment of dragoons, and Major Ringgold's light artillery, and numbered twenty-three officers and three hundred and seventy-eight men. On the 9th it was followed by the First Brigade, under General Worth, with Duncan's battery; and on the 10th by the Second Brigade, under Lieutenant-Colonel McIntosh. The Third Brigade, under Colonel Whistler, with Bragg's battery, struck their tents on the 11th, and were followed on the same day by General Taylor and his staff.

Major Monroe embarked for Brazos Santiago, accompanied by Captain Sanders, of the Engineers, and the officers of the ordnance and the pay departments. He had with him a siege-train and a field-battery, which, for want of horses, was of necessity shipped. The movement to Brazos Santiago was covered by the revenue cutter Woodbury.

Arrangements having been made by the staff departments for

supplying the army on their march, as well as for establishing a
depot at Point Isabel, the commanding general issued an order
to the troops, by which he intended to relieve the apprehensions
that might be felt by the Mexicans on account of his march into
their country.   Copies of the order were sent in advance to Matamoros, Camargo, and Mier.   It was as follows:—

" ORDER No. 30.

" HEAD-QUARTERS, ARMY OF OCCUPATION, }
Corpus Christi, March 8, 1846.   }

" The Army of Occupation of Texas being now about to take
a position upon the left bank of the Rio Grande, under the orders
of the Executive of the United States, the General-in-chief desires
to express the hope that the movement will be advantageous to
all concerned ; and with the object of attaining this laudable end,
he has ordered all under his command to observe, with the most
scrupulous respect, the rights of all the inhabitants who may be
found in peaceful prosecution of their respective occupations, as
well on the left as on the right side of the Rio Grande.   Under
no pretext, nor in any way, will any interference be allowed with
the civil rights or religious privileges of the inhabitants ; but the
utmost respect for them will be maintained.

" Whatsoever may be needed for the use of the army will be
bought by the proper surveyor, and paid for at the highest prices.
The General-in-chief has the satisfaction to say that he confides
in the patriotism and discipline of the army under his command,
and that he feels sure that his orders will be obeyed with the
utmost exactness.

Z. TAYLOR,
Brevet Brig. Gen. U. S. A. commanding."

The march of the army was of the most toilsome and exhaust-
ing nature.   The country over which they moved was sterile, and
destitute of vegetation, except the wiry grass of the prairie ; and

its surface was varied only by slight elevations, never rising to the dignity of hills, and by occasional skirtings of stunted wood, in which the musquete and prickly pear were predominant.

As they proceeded further south, the country became more desolate, till they entered the solitudes of a vast desert, where vegetation was suspended, and the weary soldier, encumbered with his burden, was ready to sink with exhaustion from the heat of a tropic sun and his toilsome progress over loose and burning sands like heated ashes, into which, at every step, the foot descended. At times, when faint with marching and fevered with thirst, the failing energies of nature were exhilarated by the appearance of blue mountains in the distance, beautiful lakes skirted with trees, and fields clothed with verdure—and the soldier forgot his suffering and toil in expectation of hospitable shade and refreshing streams; but as he advanced he either discovered that the *mirage* had spread a false verdure and beauty over barren sands, that mocked his sight, and then faded utterly away, or found the groves he had descried impenetrable thickets of thorn and cactus, that refused him shelter, and the glassy lakes pools of brine, which maddened the thirst they mocked.

Beyond this, and approaching the Arroya Colorado, the country was much improved in appearance—the wood was increased in quantity and of better growth, and the soil changed from sand to a dark-coloured clay, and covered with vegetation and flowers. The supply of fresh water, too, was abundant, and the troops in a measure forgot the hardships they had passed.

As General Taylor advanced, he formed a junction of the Dragoons and First and Second Brigades, and on the 20th he came to the Arroya Colorado, a narrow inlet of the sea, where the enemy made some demonstrations of an intention to resist his march. After ordering a reconnoissance, he made dispositions to cross the river, and effected the passage without opposition from the enemy.   The following letter to the War Department gives a detailed account of the affair:—

"Head-Quarters, Army of Occupation,
Camp Three Miles south of the Arroya Colorado, March 21, 1846.

"Sir:—I respectfully report that my forces are now concentrated at this point, the Third Brigade having joined me to-day. We are nearly north of Matamoros, and about thirty miles distant.

"The Arroya Colorado is a salt river, or rather lagoon, nearly one hundred yards broad, and so deep as barely to be fordable. It would have formed a serious obstruction to our march had the enemy chosen to occupy its right bank, even with a small force. On the 19th, the advanced corps encamped within three miles of the ford, and a reconnoissance was pushed forward to the river. A party of irregular cavalry (rancheros) was discovered on the opposite bank, but threw no obstacle in the way of examining the ford. They, however, signified to the officer charged with the reconnoissance that it would be considered an act of hostility if we attempted to pass the river, and that we should, in that case, be treated as enemies. Under these circumstances, not knowing the amount of force that might be on the other bank, I deemed it prudent to make dispositions to pass the river under fire, for which please see my 'Orders,' No. 33.   At an early hour on the 20th, the Cavalry and First Brigade of Infantry were in position at the ford, the batteries of field artillery being so placed as to sweep the opposite bank.   While these dispositions were in progress, the party that had shown themselves the day before again made their appearance.   I sent Captain Mansfield to communicate with the officer in command, who said that he had positive orders to fire upon us if we attempted to cross the river.   Another party then made its appearance, and passed the river to communicate with me.   One of them (who was represented as the adjutant-general of the Mexican troops) repeated substantially what had been sent before, viz.: that they had peremptory orders to fire upon us, and that it would be considered a declaration of war if we passed the river. He placed in my hands, at the same time, a proclamation of General Mejia, issued at Matamoros, a day or two previous, which I enclose. I informed the officer that I should immediately cross the river, and if any of his party showed themselves on the other bank after the passage commenced, they would receive the fire of our artillery. In the mean time, the Second Brigade (which had encamped some miles in my rear) came up and formed on the extreme right. The crossing was then commenced and executed in the order prescribed. Not a shot was fired ; and a reconnoissance of cavalry, sent immediately forward, discovered the party which had occupied the bank retreating in the direction of Matamoros. Agreeably to my orders, they were not molested. The Cavalry and First and Second Brigades of Infantry, with a train of two hundred wagons, crossed over and encamped at this point, three miles distant, at an early hour in the afternoon.

" I have thought proper to make a detailed report of this operation, as being the first occasion on which the Mexicans have shown themselves in an attitude decidedly hostile. It has also furnished an excellent opportunity for the instruction of the troops, and for displaying their discipline and spirit, which, I am gratified to be able to say, were everything that could be desired.

" I am compelled to remain at this point until joined by the supply train of the Third Brigade, which is unavoidably in the rear. On the 23d, at latest, I expect to resume the march, but am not fully decided as to the direction. While Matamoros is the point to be ultimately attained, it is necessary, at the same time, to cover our supplies, which will soon arrive at Point Isabel.

" From the best information I am able to obtain, the enemy is not in force on this side of the Rio Grande. A few rancheros are still on the route hence to Matamoros. It is believed that there may be nearly two thousand troops in that place, but what

13

proportion of regular troops I cannot state with confidence. The arrival of General Ampudia is expected from the interior; but the accounts I receive of his movements are quite contradictory.

"I am, sir, very respectfully, your obedient servant,

Z. TAYLOR,

Brevet Brig. Gen. U. S. A. commanding.

The Adjutant-General of the Army, Washington, D. C."

Of the proclamation to which General Taylor alludes in the foregoing letter, we give as much as is necessary to show that the Mexicans considered the advance of the Americans into their territory as equivalent to a declaration of war.

" *The general-in-chief of the forces assembled against the enemy, to the inhabitants of this department and the troops under his command.*

" FELLOW-CITIZENS :—The annexation of the department of Texas to the United States, projected and consummated by the tortuous policy of the cabinet of the Union, does not yet satisfy the ambitious desires of the degenerate sons of Washington. The civilized world has already recognised in that act all the marks of injustice, iniquity, and the most scandalous violation of the rights of nations. Indelible is the stain which will for ever darken the character for virtue falsely attributed to the people of the United States ; and posterity will regard with horror their perfidious conduct, and the immorality of the means employed by them to carry into effect that most degrading depredation. The right of conquest has always been a crime against humanity ; but nations jealous of their dignity and reputation have endeavoured at least to cover it by the splendour of arms and the prestige of victory. To the United States it has been reserved to put in practice dissimulation, fraud, and the basest treachery, in order to obtain possession, in the midst of peace, of the territory of a friendly nation, which generously relied upon the faith of promises and the solemnity of treaties.

" The cabinet of the United States does not, however, stop in its career of usurpation. Not only does it aspire to the possession of the department of Texas, but it covets also the regions on the left bank of the Rio Bravo. Its army, hitherto for some time stationed at Corpus Christi, is now advancing to take possession of a large part of Tamaulipas; and its vanguard has arrived at the Arroya Colorado, distant eighteen leagues from this place. What expectations, therefore, can the Mexican government have of treating with an enemy, who, whilst endeavouring to lull us into security, by opening diplomatic negotiations, proceeds to occupy a territory which never could have been the object of the pending discussion? The limits of Texas are certain and recognised; never have they extended beyond the river Neuces; notwithstanding which, the American army has crossed the line separating Tamaulipas from that department. Even though Mexico could forget that the United States urged and aided the rebellion of the former colonists, and that the principle, giving to an independent people the right to annex itself to another nation, is not applicable to the case, in which the latter has been the protector of the independence of the former, with the object of admitting it into its own bosom; even though it could be accepted as an axiom of international law, that the violation of every rule of morality and justice might serve as a legitimate title for acquisition; nevertheless, the territory of Tamaulipas would still remain beyond the law of annexation, sanctioned by the American Congress; because that law comprises independent Texas, the ground occupied by the rebellious colony, and in no wise includes other departments, in which the Mexican government has uninterruptedly exercised its legitimate authority.

" *Fellow-countrymen:* With an enemy which respects not its own laws, which shamelessly derides the very principles invoked by it previously, in order to excuse its ambitious views, we have no other resource than arms. We are fortunately always prepared to take them up with glory, in defence of our country; little do we regard the blood in our veins, when we are called on to shed it in vindication of our honour, to assure our nationality and independence. If to the torrent of devastation which threatens us it be necessary to oppose a dike of steel, our swords will form it; and on their sharp points will the enemy receive the fruits of his anticipated conquest. If the banks of the Panuco have been immortalized by the defeat of an enemy, respectable and worthy of the valour of Mexico, those of the Bravo shall witness the ignominy of the proud sons of the north, and its deep waters shall serve as the sepulchre of those who dare to approach it. The flame of patriotism which burns in our hearts will receive new fuel from the odious presence of the conquerors; and the cry of Dolores and Iguala shall be re-echoed with harmony to our ears, when we take up our march to oppose our naked breasts to the rifles of the hunters of the Mississippi.

     *   *   *   *   *   *   *

FRANCISCO MEJIA.

MATAMOROS, March 18, 1846.''

On the evening of the 21st, the Third Brigade crossed the Colorado and encamped near the other brigades, and the whole rested on the 22d, to enable the ox-teams to come up, which had been left behind in order to accelerate the movements of the troops.

General Taylor had intended to march direct to Matamoros, but hearing that the Mexicans in force occupied Point Isabel, the contemplated depot for his military stores, and unwilling to leave an enemy in his rear, so as to endanger his subsistence, he changed his intention and marched upon Point Isabel. That he might be ready in case of emergency to form the troops in line of battle with great readiness, the order of march was in four columns, the Dragoons being on the right, the Third Brigade on the left, and the First and Second Brigades in the centre.

On the 24th, upon reaching a point on the route from Matamoros to Point Isabel, eighteen miles from the former, and ten from the latter place, he learned that Point Isabel was not occupied by troops, and directed General Worth to move towards Matamoros, while he himself proceeded with the dragoons and the empty wagons of the train to Point Isabel. On approaching the place, General Taylor was met by a deputation of citizens of the state of Tamaulipas, who came to present a protest of the Prefect against his advance into their country. He promised to give them an audience when he halted the troops, but when near Point Isabel, the rising smoke indicated that the Mexicans had fired the place; when he dismissed the deputation, informing them that he would answer their protest when opposite to Matamoros. Having detached Colonel Twiggs with the advance of the dragoons to arrest the flames, General Taylor found on his arrival that the conflagration had done but little damage; and had the further good fortune to find that, agreeably to his well concerted arrangements, the steamboats from Corpus Christi with the supplies, had just entered the port.

The protest to which we have referred was as follows:—

"Office of the Prefect of the Northern District of the Department of Tamaulipas.

"*God and Liberty!*

"SANTA RITA, March 23, 1846.

" SIR : Although the pending question respecting the annexation of the department of Texas to the United States is subject to the decision of the supreme government of Mexico, the fact of the advance of the army, under your excellency's orders, over the line occupied by you at Corpus Christi, places me under the necessity, as the chief political authority of the northern district of

Tamaulipas, to address you, as I have now the honour to do, through the commissioners, who will place this in your hands, and to inform you that the people under this prefecture, being justly alarmed at the invasion of an army, which, without any previous declaration of war, and without announcing explicitly the object proposed by it, comes to occupy a territory which never belonged to the insurgent province, cannot regard with indifference a proceeding so contrary to the conduct observed towards each other by civilized nations, and to the clearest principles of the law of nations; that, directed by honour and patriotism, and certain that nothing has been said officially by the cabinet of the Union to the Mexican government, respecting the extension of the limits of Texas to the left bank of the Rio Bravo, trusting in the well-known justice of their cause, and using their natural right of defence, they (the citizens of this district) protest, in the most solemn manner, that neither now nor at any time do they, or will they consent to separate themselves from the Mexican republic, and to unite themselves with the United States, and that they are resolved to carry this firm determination into effect, resisting, so far as their strength will enable them, at all times and places, until the army under your excellency's orders shall recede and occupy its former positions; because, so long as it remains within the territory of Tamaulipas, the inhabitants must consider that whatsoever protestations of peace may be made, hostilities have been openly commenced by your excellency, the lamentable consequences of which will rest before the world exclusively on the heads of the invaders.

"I have the honour to say this to your excellency, with the object indicated, and to assure you of my consideration and esteem.

JENES CARDENAS.

JUAN JOSE PINEDA.

To General Z. TAYLOR, &c."

As Point Isabel was to be the depot of all military stores for the Army of Occupation, it was accordingly surveyed with a view to its defence, and Captain Sanders of the Engineers ordered to construct the necessary works. In addition to the troops originally intended for the defence of the post, Captain Porter's company was ordered to the place as a reinforcement; and the whole placed under the command of Major Monroe.

Having thrown forward a sufficient amount of supplies towards Matamoros, General Taylor proceeded with the dragoons and staff to join General Worth, who had advanced with the brigades on the 24th six miles towards Matamoros, and again three miles on the 25th, encamping at Palo Alto, near the place where the battle afterwards occurred, and which General Taylor then indicated as the place which the enemy would probably select, should he desire to meet them in an open field. The junction of the troops was effected on the 27th, and orders issued to march on the 28th for the town of Matamoros. At eight o'clock, on the morning of the 28th, the troops were put in motion; and after a march through a beautiful and picturesque country, reached the Rio Grande opposite Matamoros at eleven o'clock A. M., and planted upon its banks the standard of the " Stripes and Stars." The point of destination had been gained. At their feet rolled the waters of the far-famed river, and beyond rose the city of Matamoros in its beauty, with the Mexican colours gaily flying from the Place d'Artillerie, the quarters of the military commandant, and the prominent places of the city. When the American flag was spread to the breeze, its presence was greeted by the cross of St. George, and the French and Spanish colours run up from the different consulates.

As the American troops advanced towards the Rio Grande, large parties of irregular Mexican troops retreated before them, by whom two of our dragoons, far in advance of the rest, were captured, which created some excitement among our soldiers.

CHAPTER VI.

DIRECTLY after the planting of the American colours on the Rio
Grande, General Worth and staff were directed to cross the river
with an open communication for General Mejia, the commander
of the Mexican forces in Matamoros, and a sealed one for the civil
authorities. General Mejia, on a point of etiquette, refused to receive General Worth in person; but, after some delay, General
Vega, representing the military authorities of Matamoros, and the
Licenciado Casares the civil authorities, were deputed to meet
General Worth and receive any communication which he had to
make from his commanding-general.

In the interview which took place, General Vega complained
of the march of the American troops into the department of Tamaulipas as an act of aggression; to which General Worth replied
that the question of the right of territory was a matter to be settled
by the two governments. Finding that General Mejia refused to
receive from him the despatch with which he was charged, General Worth withdrew it, but delivered to the Licenciado Casares
the sealed document for the civil authorities.

During the interview, General Worth repeatedly requested permission to see the American Consul, and, when finally refused,

(90)

stated that the refusal was considered a belligerent act; and, after announcing that the commanding-general would regard the passage of any armed party of Mexicans across the Rio Grande as an act of war, promptly terminated the conference.

Both parties now prepared for the contest which was inevitable. General Taylor ordered Major Mansfield of the Engineers to make the necessary surveys and throw up suitable works, while the Mexicans were active in strengthening their former defences and establishing new ones. On the 29th the Mexicans mounted a heavy gun in a battery of sand-bags, and contemplated a night attack. The reported crossing of a large body of cavalry led General Taylor to believe their object was to attack Point Isabel, while at the same time they opened their batteries on the troops opposite Matamoros. Accordingly he gave out the watchword and ordered the men to sleep upon their arms, while he despatched Captain May with a squadron of dragoons to reach Point Isabel, twenty-seven miles distant, in the space of four hours, to put Major Monroe on his guard and reinforce the garrison. The morning of the 30th dawned, however, without an attack, and the Mexicans lost the golden opportunity of assailing their enemy while encamped in open field.

The defences under Major Mansfield, an active and accomplished officer, were prosecuted with energy. By the 6th of April a battery was completed for four 18-pounders, and the guns placed in battery bearing "directly upon the public square of Matamoros, and within good range for demolishing the town." In rear of the battery they broke ground on the 8th for the principal intrenchment, a strong field-fort with six bastions, capable of holding two thousand men. It was afterwards named Fort Brown, in honour of the brave Major Brown who was killed in its defence. Along the Rio Grande on either side, fronting each other for the space of two miles, thus lay the hostile armies within musket-range—their batteries shotted—the guns pointed at each

14

other—and the officers and men impatient for the order to light the matches, and commence the work of destruction.

On the 10th, Colonel Trueman Cross, Deputy Quartermaster-General of the army, rode out as usual for air and exercise, but the day passed away without his return, and fearful apprehensions began to be felt for his safety, as the country was known to be full of rancheros, or irregular cavalry, who were prowling about for plunder, and spared neither age nor rank. Towards evening cannon were fired to direct him, if lost, and parties were subse-sequently out to search for him. Letters were also sent to the commandant at Matamoros to inquire for him, but no intelligence could be obtained.

On the 11th, the firing of a salute, the ringing of the church-bells, the music of the bands, and a parade of all the troops in Matamoros, announced the arrival of General Ampudia; and all expected the immediate commencement of hostilities.

His advent had been preceded by the following ingenious appeal to the naturalized citizens of the United States in the army of General Taylor, and had probably been suggested by the frequent desertions that had taken place from that class of soldiers:—

"The Commander-in-chief of the Mexican Army, to the English and Irish under the orders of the American General Taylor:

" Know ye: That the government of the United States is com-mitting repeated acts of barbarous aggression against the mag-nanimous Mexican Nation; that the government which exists under 'the flag of the stars,' is unworthy of the designation of Christian. Recollect that you were born in Great Britain; that the American government looks with coldness upon the powerful flag of St. George, and is provoking to a rupture the warlike people to whom it belongs; President Polk boldly manifesting a desire to take possession of Oregon, as he has already done of Texas. Now, then, come with all confidence to the Mexican ranks; and I guaranty to you, upon my honour, good treatment, and that all your expenses shall be defrayed until your arrival in the beautiful capital of Mexico.

"Germans, French, Poles, and individuals of other nations! Separate yourselves from the Yankees, and do not contribute to defend a robbery and usurpation, which, be assured, the civilized nations of Europe look upon with the utmost indignation. Come, therefore, and array yourselves under the tri-coloured flag, in the confidence that the God of armies protects it, and that it will protect you equally with the English.

Head-quarters, upon the road to Matamoros, April 2d, 1846.

PEDRO DE AMPUDIA.

FRANCISCO R. MORENO, *Adj't of the Commander-in-chief.*"

The day after the arrival of General Ampudia in Matamoros, he addressed a letter to General Taylor, in which he required him to withdraw from his position before Matamoros to the other side of the Nueces. It is plainly to be inferred from this letter that the Mexican government would have settled by diplomacy the question of the annexation of Texas, if the American troops had not invaded the department of Tamaulipas. The contents of Ampudia's letter were as follows:—

"HEAD-QUARTERS AT MATAMOROS, 2 o'clock P. M.
Fourth Military Division, General-in-Chief.
April 12, 1846.

"*God and Liberty!*

"To explain to you the many grounds for the just grievances felt by the Mexican nation, caused by the United States government, would be a loss of time, and an insult to your good sense; I, therefore, pass at once to such explanation as I consider of absolute necessity.

"Your government, in an incredible manner—you will even permit me to say an extravagant one, if the usages, or general rules established and received among all civilized nations are regarded—has not only insulted, but has exasperated the Mexi-

can nation, bearing its conquering banner to the left bank of the
Rio Bravo del Norte; and in this case, by explicit and definitive
orders of my government, which neither can, will, nor should receive new outrages, I require you in all form, and at latest in the
peremptory term of twenty-four hours, to break up your camp and
retire to the other bank of the Nueces river, while our governments
are regulating the pending question in relation to Texas. If you
insist on remaining upon the soil of the department of Tamaulipas,
it will clearly result that arms, and arms alone, must decide the
question; and, in that case, I advise you that we accept the war
to which, with so much injustice on your part, you provoke us,
and that, on our part, this war shall be conducted conformably to
the principles established by the most civilized nations; that is to
say, that the law of nations and of war shall be the guide of my
operations; trusting that on your part the same will be observed.

  With this view, I tender you the considerations due to your
person and respectable office.

PEDRO DE AMPUDIA.

Senor General-in-chief of the U. S. Army,
    Don Z. TAYLOR."

  General Taylor sent word to Ampudia that he did not require
twenty-four hours for deliberation, but would reply at ten o'clock
the following day.   Shortly after, he removed the First Brigade of
his army to the right, out of the range of shot; and early on the
morning of the 13th moved the Second Brigade to the left, out
of range, while General Twiggs, with the dragoons and Ringgold's
battery, occupied the centre, and the Third Brigade, with Bragg's
and Duncan's batteries, took position within the interior of the
field-work.   Having made this prudent disposition of his troops
in expectation of an immediate attack, General Taylor despatched
the following manly reply to the peremptory requisition of General
Ampudia:—

"Head-Quarters Army of Occupation.
Camp near Matamoros, Texas, April 12, 1846.

"Senor: I have had the honour to receive your note of this date, in which you summon me to withdraw the forces under my command from their present position, and beyond the river Nueces, until the pending question between our governments, relative to the limits of Texas, shall be settled.

"I need hardly advise you that, charged as I am, in only a military capacity, with the performance of specific duties, I cannot enter into a discussion of the international question involved in the advance of the American army. You will, however, permit me to say, that the government of the United States has constantly sought a settlement, by negotiation, of the question of boundary; that an envoy was despatched to Mexico for that purpose, and that up to the most recent dates said envoy had not been received by the actual Mexican government, if indeed he has not received his passports and left the republic. In the mean time, I have been ordered to occupy the country up to the left bank of the Rio Grande, until the boundary shall be definitely settled. In carrying out these instructions I have carefully abstained from all acts of hostility, obeying, in this regard, not only the letter of my instructions, but the plain dictates of justice and humanity.

"The instructions under which I am acting will not permit me to retrograde from the position I now occupy. In view of the relations between our respective governments, and the individual suffering which may result, I regret the alternative which you offer; but, at the same time, wish it understood that I shall by no means avoid such alternative, leaving the responsibility with those who rashly commence hostilities. In conclusion, you will permit me to give the assurance that on my part the laws and customs of war among civilized nations shall be carefully observed.

"I have the honour to be, very respectfully, your obedient servant,   Z. TAYLOR.

Senor General Don Pedro de Ampudia."

Expecting an attack, and hearing that the enemy were crossing in great numbers, General Taylor despatched the 1st company of dragoons, 4th infantry, and Ringgold's battery to meet the train coming from Point Isabel, which arrived in safety on the 14th. The following day he blockaded the mouth of the river Bravo with the United States brig Lawrence, and a revenue cutter, and, on the 17th, ordered to the Brazos Santiago two vessels laden with stores for Ampudia's army.   This elicited another menacing letter from Ampudia, to which General Taylor replied in a calm and dignified manner, showing that the act was the result of the belligerent attitude which General Ampudia had assumed.

On the 19th, the first conflict took place between the Mexican and American troops.   Two days before, Lieutenant Dobbins of the 3d infantry, and Lieutenant Porter of the 4th, each with a detachment of two non-commissioned officers and ten privates, left camp for the purpose of finding the body of Colonel Cross, and punishing his murderers.   About noon on the 19th, Lieutenant Porter advanced upon a party of Mexicans, one of whom snapped his piece at him, whereupon he discharged both barrels of his gun, and his men rushing on, captured the camp of the Mexicans, with ten horses and their equipments, and twenty blankets.   Late in the evening he met a second larger party, which had probably been joined by those he encountered in the morning, and they immediately fired upon his command.   The lieutenant and one of his party fell, when the rest, unable to use their fire-arms on account of the rain, separated and fled.   Lieutenant Porter was the son of the late Commodore Porter, and was a gallant young officer, and much esteemed in his regiment.

On the 21st, a Mexican straggler came into camp, and stated that he knew where the body of an American officer was lying, and on sending out a party, the remains of Colonel Cross were found in a thicket, a short distance from the road leading to the river.   He was stripped of his clothing, and the flesh was torn

away from his body by the vultures.   On the 23d, a board of officers assembled to report upon his death, and came to the conclusion that he was attacked and stripped by the banditti of Romano
Falcon, and afterwards slain by that desperado by a blow upon
the head from the butt of his pistol.

Late in the evening of the 24th, the remains of the unfortunate
colonel were committed to the grave, under an escort composed
of a squadron of dragoons and eight companies of infantry, the
whole commanded by Colonel Twiggs.   The infantry occupied
the front of the procession, the dragoons came next, and the body
followed, drawn by six horses on the wheels of a caisson, and
enveloped in the flag of his country.   Next came a solitary
mourner, the son of the deceased; then a war-horse in black led
by dragoons, followed by all the officers who were not upon duty.

From the opposite bank of the river, and from the enemy's
works, groups of officers and soldiers looked upon the procession,
as the body was borne and laid in its resting-place at the foot of
the flag-staff, upon which the flag was at half-mast.   Colonel Childs
in an impressive manner read the burial-service for the dead,—
three volleys were fired over his grave—the flag was run up to its
former position, and the dead was left to his repose in silence.

Like his predecessor, Arista, when about to assume the command in Matamoros, insidiously endeavoured to corrupt the American soldiery, by disseminating the following artful address, the
original draft of which was subsequently found among his baggage
when his camp was captured on the 9th of May:—

"General Arista's advice to the Soldiers of the United States Army.
HEAD-QUARTERS AT MATAMOROS, April 20, 1846.

"Soldiers!—You have enlisted in time of peace to serve in that
army for a specific term; but your obligation never implied that
you were bound to violate the laws of God, and the most sacred
rights of friends!   The United States government, contrary to the

wishes of a majority of all honest and honourable Americans, has ordered you to take *forcible* possession of the territory of a *friendly* neighbour, who has never given her consent to such occupation. In other words, while the treaty of peace and commerce between Mexico and the United States is in full force, the United States, presuming on her strength and prosperity, and on our supposed imbecility and cowardice, attempts to make you the blind instruments of her unholy and mad ambition, and *force* you to appear as the hateful robbers of our dear homes, and the unprovoked violators of our dearest feelings as men and patriots. Such villany and outrage, I know, is perfectly repugnant to the noble sentiments of any gentleman, and it is base and foul to rush you on to certain death, in order to aggrandize a few lawless individuals, in defiance of the laws of God and man!

" It is to no purpose if they tell you, that the law for the annexation of Texas justifies your occupation of the Rio Bravo del Norte ; for by this act they rob us of a great part of *Tamaulipas, Coahuila, Chihuahua, and New Mexico ;* and it is barbarous to send a handful of men on such an errand against a powerful and warlike nation. Besides, the most of you are Europeans, and we are the *declared friends* of a majority of the nations of *Europe.* The North Americans are ambitious, overbearing, and insolent as a nation, and they will only make use of you as vile tools to carry out their abominable plans of pillage and rapine.

" I warn you in the name of justice, honour, and your own interests and self-respect, to abandon their desperate and unholy cause, and become *peaceful Mexican citizens.* I guarantee you, in such case, a half section of land, or three hundred and twenty acres, to settle upon, gratis. Be wise, then, and just, and honourable, and take no part in murdering us who have no unkind feelings for you. Lands shall be given to officers, sergeants, and corporals, according to rank, privates receiving three hundred and twenty acres, as stated.

" If, in time of action, you wish to espouse our cause, throw away your arms and run to us, and we will embrace you as true friends and Christians. It is not decent nor prudent to say more. But should any of you render important service to Mexico, you shall be accordingly considered and preferred.

M. ARISTA,

Commander-in-chief of the Mexican Army."

On the 23d of April, General Paredes issued a proclamation of defensive war to the people of Mexico, from which we make the following extracts:—

" At the time Mr. Slidell presented himself, the troops of the United States occupied our territory, their squadrons threatened our ports, and they prepared to occupy the peninsula of the Californias, of which the question of the Oregon with England is only a preliminary. Mr. Slidell was not received, because the dignity of the nation repelled this new insult. Meanwhile the army of the United States encamped at Corpus Christi, and occupied the *Isla del Padre;* following this, they then moved to the point *Santo Isabel,* and their standard of the stars and stripes waved on the right bank of the Rio Bravo del Norte, opposite the city of Matamoros, blockading that river with their vessels of war. The village of Laredo was surprised by a party of their troops, and a small party of our men, reconnoitring there, were disarmed. Hostilities, then, have been commenced, by the United States of North America, beginning new conquests upon the frontier territories of the departments of Tamaulipas and New Leon, and progressing at such a rate, that troops of the same United States threaten Monterey in Upper California. No one can doubt which of the two republics is responsible for this war: a war which any sense of equity and justice, and respect for the rights and laws of civilized nations, might have avoided.

" I have commanded the General-in-chief of our forces on the

15

Northern frontier, to repel all hostilities offered to us, which is actual war against any power making war on us, and calling upon the God of battles, He will preserve the valour of our troops, the unquestionable right to our territory, and the honour of those arms which are used only in defence of justice. Our general will govern himself by the established usages of civilized warfare. With orders from me to prevent, if possible, the effusion of blood, he will intimate to the General-in-chief of the American troops that he shall return to the other side of the Rio de las Nueces, the ancient limits of Texas. Those nations interested in preserving the peace of so many years, and who may be injured in their commercial relations with the Mexican republic, will perceive the hard alternative to which they are reduced, by the *politic* invasion of the United States, and they (the nations) must succumb or defend their existence thus compromised. I solemnly announce that I do not declare war against the United States of America, because it pertains to the august Congress of that nation, and not to the Executive, to settle definitely the reparation which so many aggressions demand.

" But the defence of the Mexican territory, which the United States troops invade, is an urgent necessity, and my responsibility would be immense before the nation, if I did not give commands to repel those forces who act like enemies, and I have so commanded. From this day commences a defensive war, and those points of our territory which are invaded or attacked will be energetically defended."

On the 24th, a grand review and great military rejoicing, announced the arrival of Arista in Matamoros. In the evening a parley was sounded on the Mexican side of the river, and a messenger brought to General Taylor the following letter directed to " the General-in-chief of the forces of the United States encamped opposite Matamoros."

" MEXICAN ARMY.

" The course of events since the annexation of Texas to the United States was declared, has been so clearly hostile to Mexico, and so foreign to the dignity and principles which the Americans have proclaimed to the world, that we come to the conclusion that their policy has changed, and their moderation is turned into a desire of aggrandizement, enriching themselves by humiliating their neighbours.

" The respect and consideration that friendly nations show to each other have been trampled upon, by which reason the justice and excessive moderation of Mexico shine forth still more. Pressed and forced into war, we enter into a struggle, that cannot be avoided without failing in what is most sacred in man.

" Political discussions do not appertain to military men, but to diplomatic agents; to us belongs the part to act, without it occasioning any surprise that the troops under my command should not wait for anything else to give battle.

" We Mexicans have been calumniated as barbarous, in the most caustic and unjust terms; the occasion has arrived to show what we are, and I do not believe that in the troops under my command there will be any cause to confirm such suppositions, as they will cause to shine the feelings of humanity and generosity that distinguish them.

" For the first time, I have the honour to offer your Excellency my great consideration. God and liberty!

MARIANO ARISTA.

HEAD-QUARTERS, MATAMOROS, April 24, 1846."

This official communication was accompanied by a polite private note, in which General Arista announced his intention to conduct the war in which they were about to engage according to the laws which courtesy and humanity impose on modern civilization.

We have now traced the progress of events from the first mis-

understanding between the two countries to the commencement
of actual hostilities; and, notwithstanding the belligerent attitude
which Mexico assumed by recalling her minister immediately
after the annexation of Texas to the United States, it is evident,
from the subsequent actions and correspondence of the Mexican
authorities, that war would not have occurred, had it not been for
the advance of the American army into territory which Mexico
believed to be, and which was, a part, not of Texas but of Mexico.
But we not only invaded the territory of the Mexican republic;
we first commenced hostilities, when on the 18th of April " Lieutenant Porter, at the head of his own detachment, surprised a
Mexican camp, drove away the men, and took possession of their
horses."* Though we are obliged, in candour, to make these
admissions, we would not be understood as holding the opinion
that there were not just grounds for war against a country which
had outraged the American flag, imprisoned our citizens and confiscated their property, and violated the solemn faith of treaties.
But, while there existed so many causes, all or any of which would
have justified a declaration of war on our part, it is a matter of
supreme regret, that, after the magnanimous forbearance which we
had exhibited towards Mexico, and unwillingness to appeal to the
last resort of nations, war was at length brought on by an act,
and in a manner, totally unjustifiable.

When the Mexican minister Almonte, after the annexation of
Texas, demanded his passports and menaced war, all usage, both
ancient and modern, of civilized nations, would have justified the
American Congress in declaring immediate war, and ordering the
armies of the republic into Mexico, without waiting for her to
strike the first blow. But, while the Congress of the United States
is disposed to continue the exercise of that magnanimous forbearance which had characterized her intercourse with a sister republic, the Executive, by an assumption of power not warranted in

---

* General Taylor's Letter to the Secretary of War, April 23.

the Constitution, and without the knowledge and consent of Congress, orders the American army into the territory of Mexico and precipitates the country into war. Had it not been for this, no conflict in arms between the republics would have arisen, and the outpouring of blood and treasure expended upon this contest would have been avoided; for it is evident, that, although Mexico felt herself aggrieved by the annexation of Texas to the United States, neither the people nor the government would have seriously contemplated war on that account, had not the invasion of the Mexican territory been superadded.

It is true, Mexico had no just cause of offence in the case of Texas, for that republic, free and independent, had a right to dispose of her own territory as she pleased; but some degree of allowance and forbearance was due even to the prejudices of a country which had seen a portion of its territory dismembered by those who had formerly been citizens of the United States, and afterwards annexed to that country. If a little time had been allowed for the wounded pride of Mexico to heal, and we had abstained from aggression upon her territory, better feelings and better counsels would have prevailed with her, and a treaty alike honourable to both would have arranged all difficulties between us. If the Rio Grande was desirable as a boundary, instead of the great desert, which was the true boundary, a very small part of the money that has been expended in the war, would have secured it to the nation by purchase.

I love my country much—I honour her brave sons—I admire the gallant chiefs and their soldiery, who throughout this war have wreathed their brows with the laurels of victory—I venerate the mighty dead, who ' with garments dyed in blood,' have made their beds of glory upon the battle-field, and have bequeathed names of immortality to the republic; but the love of truth with a historian should be paramount to the love of country. The eye of justice should not be blinded by the blaze of glory; and, whatever splendour has crowned the achievements of our troops in this war—however widely the power and majesty of our arms by means of it have been spread abroad among the nations, I can but feel that the manner in which it was brought on, was unjust, and reprehend as dangerous to the republic the precedent that has been set by the Executive, of involving the nation in war without the privity and consent of Congress.

Of what avail are the guaranties of the constitution that Congress alone shall declare war, when the American Executive can, at any time, bring on a war, by ordering the troops of the republic into foreign territory, or even into territory which we claim that lies in dispute? In the case of this weaker neighbour, though great have been the sacrifices of life and treasure, the consequences have not been serious; but who can imagine what the end would have been, if, in the dispute about Oregon, the President, without consulting Congress, had ordered the American army to the boundary as claimed in 54° 40′?

Another serious evil is, that a war thus brought on without preparation has for a time to be sustained with the inadequate men and means of a peace establishment; and thus, at the onset, the prestige of victory may be in favour of the enemy, and to some extent influence the future contest.

In 1845, with that prudent forecast for which he is remarkable, General Scott had recommended an increase of the army by filling up the skeleton regiments, but his prudent suggestions were neglected both by Congress and the President. In everything there was a want of due preparation. The meagre force comprising the Army of Occupation, was collected by withdrawing the troops from the forts and military posts, which in many cases upon the seaboard and the frontier were thus left without a garrison, while even for this small force, thrown forward into an enemy's territory, like a forlorn hope, to provoke and bring on a war, the provision for munitions, subsistence, and transportation, was totally insufficient.

CHAPTER VII.

REPORTS having reached the American camp, that the Mexicans
were crossing the river above and below, in great force, Captain
Ker was despatched to the lower ford with a body of dragoons to
ascertain the truth of the report, and on the evening of the 25th
Captain Thornton was despatched to the upper ford, for the like
purpose, accompanied by Captain Hardee, Lieutenants Kane and
Mason, and sixty-one non-commissioned officers and privates.
Captain Ker returned with his party without discovering any of
the enemy. Thornton proceeded with his command up the river
about twenty-four miles, and as he supposed within about three
miles of the camp of the enemy, when his Mexican guide refused
to proceed further, from a belief that the whole country was
occupied by Mexican soldiers. Thornton with his command
pressed on about two miles further, when he reached a farm-house
enclosed by a thicket of chaparral, except on the side lying next
to the river. The ground in this direction was boggy and
impassable. Entering the enclosure through a pair of bars,
Thornton with his command approached the house, when by a
sudden firing from the surrounding chaparral, the Americans perceived that they were encompassed by the enemy, who were

(105)

afterwards found to be about twenty-five hundred in number.
Promptly wheeling his command, Thornton ordered a charge,
and attempted to escape by the way he had entered, but the
dense files of the enemy prevented.   Captain Hardee now rode
up to offer some suggestion, when a shot struck Captain Thornton's horse, and the beast, maddened by the wound, ran with him
towards the chaparral, cleared it at a bound, and plunging down
a precipice with his rider, fell to the earth.   The captain lay
insensible for some hours, after which his consciousness returned,
when, mounting his charger, which like himself was badly
wounded, he endeavoured to make his way to the American camp.
Before he reached it, however, he was taken by a party of the
enemy, and carried to Matamoros.   As soon as the misfortune
occurred to Thornton, Captain Hardee assumed command, and
dashing towards the river bank, with the view of swimming the
river, he found that the marshy ground prevented escape.
Determined then on a vigorous resistance, he dismounted his
men, and examined their pieces; but while thus engaged, a
Mexican officer came up and demanded a surrender.   Hardee
agreed to surrender, provided he and his men would be treated
agreeably to the usages of civilized warfare.   The message was
borne by the officer to his commanding-general, who gave assurance that the prisoners should be treated with humanity.   Captain
Hardee then surrendered, and he and his men were carried
to Matamoros, where they were kindly treated by the Mexicans.
General Torrejon commanded the enemy's forces in this engagement.   Their success was owing to their numbers and the complete concealment afforded to their ambuscade by the chaparral.
The American loss was one lieutenant, two sergeants, and eight
privates killed, and fifty-three prisoners.   The loss, inconsiderable
as it was in numbers, was notwithstanding important, depriving
the American commander of nearly one-third of the mounted
force on the Rio Grande.   General Arista, on receiving the news

of this skirmish, affected to consider it a great victory, and addressed the following letter of congratulation to the commander, General Torrejon :—

"MATAMOROS, April 26.

"This has been a day of rejoicing to all the division of the North, it having this day been known of the triumph achieved by the brigade which your Excellency so worthily commands. The rejoiced country will doubtless celebrate this preliminary of glorious deeds that her happy sons will in future present to her. Your Excellency will communicate to your brave soldiers that I have seen with the greatest pleasure their valiant behaviour, and that I await for the detailed despatch to elevate it to the knowledge of the supreme government, so that the nation may learn the triumph of your arms.

MARIANO ARISTA.

To Gen. Don ANASTASIO TORREJON."

On the evening of the 27th, after the news of Thornton's defeat reached the American encampment, General Taylor called a council-of-war of a few confidential officers, to take into consideration the propriety of crossing the Rio Grande and attacking Arista at Matamoros. The primary arrangements were all made, and corps selected for the purpose, when the important question presented itself, How could the troops pass the river? All kinds of schemes and expedients were concerted, but none appeared feasible, and the general reluctantly abandoned it.

Could the troops have been transported suddenly over, Arista's forces would have been demolished without fighting at Palo Alto or Resaca de la Palma.

Here, as after the battle of the 9th of May, the improvidence of the War Department was apparent in not furnishing the Army of Occupation with a pontoon train, as had been requested by General Taylor; while, at the same time, he was under instruc-

16

tions, if attacked, not to limit himself to defensive operations, but carry the war into the enemy's country beyond the Rio Grande.*

About this time, Captain Walker, who had been identified with the border struggles of Texas, and one of the Mier prisoners, arrived at Point Isabel with a company of Texan Rangers, and prepared to participate in the contest, in which he subsequently acted so prominent a part.

The Mexicans, after the capture of Captain Thornton, had boldly crossed the Rio Grande in large detachments, and spread themselves between General Taylor and the depot at Point Isabel under Major Munroe, with the view of threatening both stations of the American army, and cutting off General Taylor from his supplies. Captain Walker with his command was directed, therefore, by Major Munroe to occupy a position west of the Point, for the purpose of gaining intelligence of the movements of the enemy, and of opening a communication with General Taylor. At this time some teams despatched from Point Isabel to Fort Brown were compelled to return; and Captain Walker, who went out with his company on the 28th to reconnoitre, encountered an overwhelming Mexican force, and after a short contest, in which his raw recruits were scattered in confusion, was obliged to retreat, and was pursued to within cannon-range of Point Isabel.

Major Munroe had put the Point in the best possible state of defence by strengthening the works, and adding to the regular force the masters and crews of the vessels in port. Still, as he was in expectation of an immediate attack, he desired to inform the commanding-general of his situation; and Captain Walker, notwithstanding his late discomfiture, volunteered his services to carry any message to General Taylor.

Late on the evening of the 29th, accompanied by six companions, Captain Walker set out on his perilous expedition, and

* Letter to the Secretary of War, August 30, 1845.

CAPT. SAMUEL WALKER.

after encountering the most imminent risks of capture, he succeeded in delivering his message to General Taylor.

The situation of the American commander had now reached a crisis. He must either fall back upon Point Isabel; or, leaving the garrison there to defend itself, remain at Fort Brown and brave the enemy; or, lastly, attempt with a portion of his forces to open a communication with Point Isabel. To bear back the flag that had been planted on the Rio Grande was out of the question; to remain stationary at Fort Brown, would soon reduce the troops to starvation. Nothing remained, then, but to leave a part of his force at Fort Brown, and with the residue open a communication with Point Isabel, and thus procure for the troops necessary supplies. In doing this he had to encounter the risk of an attack from the enemy upon either of the three portions into which his army would be divided; but the pressing necessities of his situation rendered the measure imperative, and General Taylor accordingly made arrangements for marching.

At four o'clock P. M. on the 1st May, he marched from Fort Brown with the main body of his army, and passed through the chaparral without meeting the enemy. At midnight the troops halted, fatigued and exhausted, and lay upon their arms in the open prairie, without fires to take off the chillness of the cold and damp night air. On the morning of the 2d the army resumed its march, and after suffering much from thirst and the heat of the weather, reached Point Isabel about noon.

On the evening of General Taylor's departure for Point Isabel, Arista had ordered his troops to cross the Rio Grande, for the purpose of attacking the Americans. After transporting his forces, he found that the American commander had departed for Point Isabel; and, with the vanity peculiar to the Mexican character, he supposed that General Taylor had been aware of his intention, and was desirous of avoiding a meeting, and he construed the march of the American army into a timorous flight from the valiant legions of Mexico. Conceiving the design of cutting off the Americans on their march, the Mexican general despatched his cavalry for that purpose, which accordingly made a forced march by night; but General Taylor with his troops had already passed beyond the place where the enemy had intended to intercept him. The disappointment which this occasioned the over-confident enemy, was in some measure alleviated by the fact, that General Taylor had left a small garrison in Fort Brown, which would of necessity soon be compelled to surrender to Mexican valour. The following document, from El Monitor Republicano of Matamoros, a semi-official paper, is a specimen of the arrogant and vainglorious feelings of the Mexicans on the above occasion.

"On the first of this month, at eleven o'clock in the morning, the general-in-chief left this place to join the army, who, several hours before, had left with the intention of crossing the river at a short distance from the camp of the enemy. In consequence of the orders given, so that this dangerous operation might be performed with due security, and according to the rules of military art, when our troops arrived at the spot designated for the crossing of the river, the left bank was already occupied by General D. Anastasio Torrejon, with all the force under his command. The enthusiasm of our soldiers to conquer the obstacles which separated them from the enemy was so great, that they showed themselves impatient of the delay occasioned by the bad condition of some of the flat-boats, which had been very much injured in the transportation by land, and could not be used, as they would fill up with water as soon as they were launched. In spite of that obstacle, the work went on with such activity, and so great was the ardour of the most excellent general-in-chief, whose orders were obeyed with the greatest promptness and precision, that a few hours were sufficient to transport, to the opposite bank of the Bravo, a strong division, with all its artillery and train.

"This rapid and well-combined movement ought to have

proved to the invaders not only that the Mexicans possess instruction and aptness for war, but that those qualities are now brought
forth by the purest patriotism.   The Northern Division, fearless
of fatigue, and levelling all difficulties, ran to seek an enemy
who, well sheltered under parapets, and defended with guns of a
large calibre, could wait for the attack with indisputable advantage.
With deep trenches, with a multitude of fortifications, the defence
was easy against those who presented themselves with their naked
breasts.

"But General Taylor dared not resist the valour and enthusiasm of the sons of Mexico.   Well did he foresee the intrepidity
with which our soldiers would rush against the usurpers of the
national territory.   Well did he know the many injuries which
were to be avenged by those who had taken up arms, not to
aggrandize themselves with the spoils of the property of others,
but to maintain the independence of their country.   Well did he
know, we repeat it, that the Mexicans would be stopped neither
by trenches, or fortresses, or large artillery.   Thus it was that
the chief of the American forces, frightened as soon as he.
perceived from the situation and proximity of his camp, that our
army were preparing to cross the river, left with precipitation for
Point Isabel, with almost all his troops, eight pieces of artillery,
and a few wagons.   Their march was observed from our position,
and the most excellent General D. Francisco Mejia immediately
sent an express extraordinary to communicate the news to the
most excellent general-in-chief.   Here let me pay to our brave
men the tribute which they deserve.   The express verbally
informed some of the troops, which had not yet arrived at the ford,
of the escape of the Americans; in one instant, all the soldiers
spontaneously crossed the river, almost racing one with another.
Such was the ardour with which they crossed the river to attack
the enemy.

"The terror and haste with which the latter fled to the fort, to shut themselves up in it and avoid a conflict, frustrated the active measures of the most excellent Señor General Arista, which were to order the cavalry to advance in the plain and cut off the flight of the fugitives. But it was not possible to do so, notwithstanding their forced march during the night. General Taylor left his camp at two o'clock in the afternoon, and, as fear has wings, he succeeded in shutting himself up in the fort. When our cavalry reached the point where they were to detain him, he had already passed, and was several leagues ahead. Great was the sorrow of our brave men, not to have been able to meet the enemy face to face; their defeat was certain, and the main body of that invading army, who thought that they inspired the Mexicans with so much respect, would have disappeared in the first important battle. But there was some fighting to be done; and the Americans do not know how to use other arms but those of duplicity and treachery. Why did they not remain with firmness under their colours? Why did they abandon the ground which they pretend to usurp with such iniquity? Thus has an honourable general kept his word. Had not General Taylor said, in all his communications, that he was prepared to repel all hostilities? Why, then, does he fly in so cowardly a manner to shut himself up at the Point? The commander-in-chief of the American army has covered himself with opprobrium and ignominy in sacrificing a part of his forces, whom he left in the fortifications, to save himself; for it is certain that he will not return to their assistance—not that he is ignorant of their peril, but he calculates that this would be greater if he had the temerity of attempting to resist the Mexican lances and bayonets in the open plain."

The garrison left in Fort Brown consisted of the 7th infantry, Captain Loud's company of 2d artillery, in charge of four 18-pounders, and Lieutenant Bragg with his light battery of four pieces; all under the command of Major Jacob Brown, a veteran

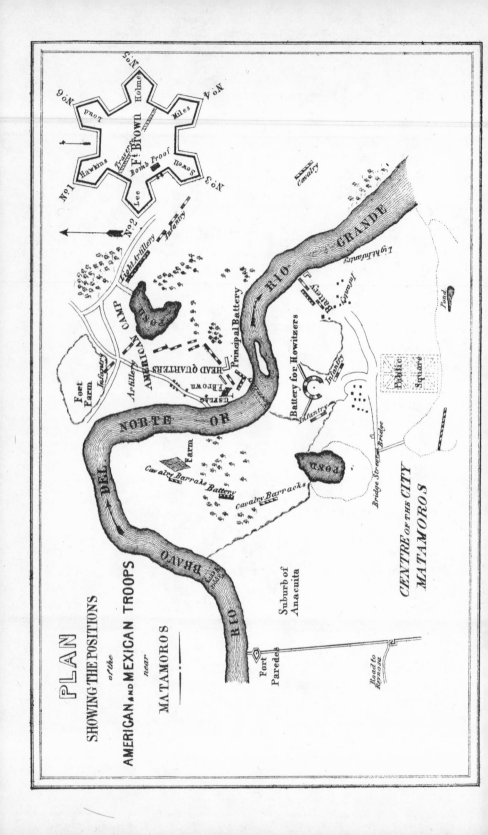

officer of great bravery. He was instructed to expend as little ammunition as possible, not to attempt offensive operations, and to defend the post to the last. Certain signals were arranged to be given by means of the 18-pounders, which were to be fired at half past six o'clock A. M., in case of the investment of the fort, or any particular accident.

On the afternoon of May 1st, Major Brown had his tents pitched, divided his forces to the several bastions, six in number, and apportioned the six senior officers to the command of them, viz: No. 1, Captain Hawkins; No. 2, Captain Lee; No. 3, Captain Miles; No. 4, Captain Loud; No. 5, Brevet Major Sewall, and No. 6, Captain Holmes.

On the morning of the 2d of May, all hands were turned out at the earliest dawn to work on the east bastion, by the gate; it had not yet been touched. By dint of hard labour, the ditch was dug and the parapet raised to some extent; when, just before sunset, officers' and men's attention was called to what was going on at Matamoros. There seemed to be a grand parade and festival; the bells rung continually, soldiers marched and countermarched; and at last was perceived a train of priests, monks, and friars, going round from battery to battery, consecrating and blessing the guns, shot, and shell. This pious ceremony continued until the night had set in, and convinced all who reflected, that it was a prelude to an attack.

Accordingly the guards were doubled, and orders given for *reveillé* at an earlier hour than usual.

On the morning of the 3d, reveillé beat and finished, when the Mexicans commenced theirs. The shrill bugles poured forth their discordant music amid the continued peal of their bells, for a longer period than usual, until the streaks of dawn made everything visible to the east, when the report of a gun was heard, and turning the eye quickly towards Matamoros, the first shell was seen as it was passing the bright and beautiful star **Venus**, whose tardiness in retiring to rest, seemed only to await this signal of the bloody strife, in this first gun of the war.

In quick succession followed many discharges from a battery of seven guns, upon the American works; the garrison was soon in a condition of resistance, and Loud opened with the 18-pounders upon the fort and town with tremendous effect, the consulate flags being respected. In twenty minutes after the American fire opened, an 18-pound ball struck one of the Mexican twelve-pounders directly in the muzzle, and dismounted it, wounding and maiming the officers and men that manned it. This incident, and the hotness of the American fire, so disconcerted the enemy, that the whole battery was silenced immediately after. The enemy then commenced firing shot and shell from the lower fort and mortar battery, but without doing any damage, though the cannonade continued with little interruption until night.

As soon as the cannonade commenced, one-third of the garrison were left to man the bastions, and the rest were directed to repair to the east bastion gate and drawbridge and finish it. To complete the curtain connecting the flanks of the north and east bastions, the troops worked under a continued shower of shot and shell for twenty-four hours without intermission, till it was completed. The men became more exposed as the parapet rose, and the enemy taking advantage of it, directed their guns upon the labourers, but without effect. The only man killed was Sergeant Weigart.

As the garrison found that their fire did but little execution except to the houses of the town, it was deemed prudent to suspend the cannonade, with the view of saving ammunition. The firing accordingly ceased at ten o'clock. From this circumstance, however, the enemy inferred our loss was severe, and that their fire had silenced our guns.

On the 4th of May, the firing from the enemy's batteries was continued during the day.

The men in the garrison having completed the defences at and around the east bastion, were now busily employed in making bomb-proofs for security against the iron tempest that relentlessly assailed them. They were built at points convenient for the soldiers when in their stations, and were formed by layers of barrels of pork, with poles laid across, and the whole covered with embankments of earth.

At nine o'clock in the evening, an irregular firing of musketry was heard in the rear of the fort, at a distance of three or four hundred yards, and extending up the river about a mile. Major Brown, supposing that the storming of the fort would take place immediately, put the entire garrison under arms, and ordered all the batteries and defences to be manned; but the assault was not attempted. During the night the enemy erected a battery in the field, which was intended to assail the American works by a cross-fire.

On the morning of the 5th, large parties of horse and foot were discovered in the rear of the fort, supported by the above-mentioned battery, which, simultaneously with those in Matamoros, opened upon the fort with a galling fire of round-shot and shells. This fire was answered from the 18-pounders, and the howitzer battery placed in embrazure on the south-east bastion, for the space of an hour, when the firing on both sides ceased. About nine o'clock some Mexican officers, under an escort of cavalry, with large bodies of mounted men and infantry within supporting distance, commenced a reconnoissance at the distance of half a mile, with the view of establishing a new battery. Lieutenant Hanson with a party of dragoons, by permission of Major Brown, with great gallantry sallied out to watch their movements, when they precipitately retreated behind their works.

On Wednesday, the 6th, the cannonade began with the dawn

17

of day, and round-shot and shells from the lower fort and mortar battery were thrown into the fort, tearing the tents to pieces and killing and wounding many of the artillery horses.   Large parties of mounted men and infantry were now seen hovering near; and Major Brown, finding himself surrounded by the enemy, gave to General Taylor the preconcerted signal, by firing at half-past six o'clock the 18-pounders.   The enemy's fire was now redoubled, as if in consequence of this; and the shot and shells from the several forts and batteries in front and rear, fell in an iron shower throughout the fort.   At about ten o'clock, while the brave Major Brown, attended by his adjutant, was performing his usual round, to see that the men were at their posts, he stopped to give some directions respecting a bomb-proof upon which they were engaged, when a descending shell struck him ; and amid the cloud of dust that arose he was seen to fall mortally wounded.   His right leg was torn off, leaving the muscles and the bare and jagged bones exposed to the view of his companions, who gathered in sympathy around him.   Calm in the endurance of suffering, as he had before been in danger, he reminded them of their duties, as he was borne to the hospital : " Men, go to your duties, stand by your posts ; I am but one among you."

He was carried to a bomb-proof; where, owing to the confined air, the violence of the wound, and the heat of the weather, he had but little chance of recovery.   He lingered until the evening of the 9th ; and while the roar of the artillery, as it became more distinct and nearer, proclaimed the retreat of the Mexicans before his victorious general at Resaca de la Palma, yielded up his life to his country, in whose honourable service he had been so long employed.

In his notice of the defence of Fort Brown, General Taylor pays the following handsome tribute to his memory :—

" The field-work opposite Matamoros has sustained itself handsomely, during a cannonade and bombardment of one hundred and sixty hours. But the pleasure is alloyed with profound regret at the loss of its heroic and indomitable commander, Major Brown, who died to-day from the effects of a shell. His loss would be a severe one to the service at any time, but to the army under my orders, it is indeed irreparable."

On the fall of Major Brown, the command of the fort devolved on Captain Hawkins, and his bastion on Brevet Major Rains. Soon after this, large parties of infantry and cavalry were seen advancing upon the fort in the rear, but they soon dispersed on receiving a few rounds of canister from Lieutenant Bragg's battery. From ten o'clock till half-past twelve P. M., the shot and shells fell in one continual shower. After this, a dull and sullen fire was kept up till between four and five o'clock, when a white flag was displayed in the rear, and the Mexican bugles sounded a parley. Soon after, two officers approached the fort with a flag, when they were met, at the distance of three hundred yards, by Major Sewall and Lieutenant Britton, who bore the following communication from General Arista to Captain Hawkins, written in Spanish:—

> " MEXICAN ARMY, DIVISION OF THE NORTH, }
> General-in-Chief. }

" You are besieged by forces sufficient to take you; and there is, moreover, a numerous division encamped near you, which, free from all other cares, will keep off any succours which you may expect to receive.

" The respect for humanity, acknowledged at the present age by all civilized nations, doubtless imposes upon me the duty of mitigating the disasters of war.

" This principle, which Mexicans observe above all other nations, obliges me to summon you, as all your efforts will be useless, to surrender, in order to avoid, by a capitulation, the entire destruction of all the soldiers under your command.

" You will thus afford me the pleasure of complying with the mild and benevolent wishes above expressed, which distinguish the character of my countrymen, whilst I at the same time fulfil the most imperious of the duties which my country requires for the offences committed against it.

"God and liberty!

Head-Quarters, at the Fanques del Raminero, May 6, 1846.

                                    M. ARISTA."

Captain Hawkins, though resolved to defend the fort to the last, thought it proper to submit the message which he had received to his officers. He accordingly assembled the commanders of bastions, with Captain Mansfield, principal engineer, and Lieutenant Bragg. The vote was taken, beginning with the youngest officer, and was unanimous, *to defend the fort to the death.*

The following reply was returned within the allotted hour :—

                    " HEAD QUARTERS U. S. FORCES, ⎫
                      Near Matamoros, May 6, 1846, 5 P. M. ⎭

"SIR : Your humane communication has just been received, and, after the consideration due to its importance, I must respectfully decline to surrender my forces to you.

"The exact purport of your despatch I cannot feel confident that I understood, as my interpreter is not skilled in your language; but if I have understood you correctly, you have my reply above.

          I am, sir, respectfully, your obedient servant,

                              E. S. HAWKINS,
                    Commanding U. S. Forces opposite Matamoros.

Gen. M. ARISTA,
    Commanding Division of the North."

On the receipt of this reply followed the most harassing fire of shot and shells that had yet been experienced; but the American troops could not answer it, as their ammunition was nearly expended, and that on hand had to be kept for close quarters, as the storming of the fort was momentarily expected.

At the dawn of the 7th the enemy's batteries opened as usual with great vigour, and parties seemed advancing on the fort, but several rounds of canister and grape fired into their picket-guards, at the houses in the rear, and at the old guard-house, caused them to fall back out of cannon-range. A random fire was kept up during the forenoon with musketry; but at half-past two commenced a regular bombardment with shot and shells, from howitzers and mortars, which was continued without intermission till after sunset.

The Mexicans had advanced the former night, and occupied a traverse left by the garrison to the north of the work near the river, which was only one hundred yards from it, and as high as our breast-work. At this place was a cover from which they fired their escopets into the fort, and which might serve them as a rallying-point, whence to rush upon it in the expected storm. It was determined to level it, at whatever cost.

Accordingly, on the night of the 7th, Captain Miles, with three subalterns, Lieutenants Potter, Van Dorn and Clitz, and one hundred men, under direction of Captain Mansfield the chief engineer, were sent, with spades only, on this dangerous enterprise. The traverse lay longitudinally perpendicular to the face of one of the enemy's strongest batteries, and not over five hundred yards from it: had a discovery been made, a single discharge of grape might have cut off the whole party. Happily, by eleven o'clock, the traverse was levelled and some clumps of chaparral adjacent cut away, much to the chagrin and mortification of the enemy, who returned about midnight to resume their firing of the previous night, but found their breast-work level with the ground.

At this time a random fire of musketry commenced, accompanied by the notes of bugles sounding the charge; and the defenders of the fort expected every moment the deadly assault. Arrangements had already been made for it in Matamoros, to take place this very night by a picked corps of five thousand men; but

Arista had ascertained that General Taylor was advancing, and the order was countermanded. The storming of the fort having been abandoned, the firing was now irregular until three o'clock A. M. At this time it became more severe, and was continued until daylight.

At sunrise on the 8th the enemy's batteries commenced their fire, and for several hours poured an incessant storm of shot and shells into the fort. At noon the bombardment was resumed, and an additional mortar, established in the chaparral across the river, opened upon the garrison. Worn down with watching, exhausted by labour, and harassed by a continual fire, the weary soldiers were becoming listless, and indifferent to the shot and shells that fell in dangerous proximity to their persons, when, about half-past two o'clock P. M. on the 8th, they were roused from their lethargy by a cannon-shot in the direction of Point Isabel. Another and another followed in quick succession, and then ensued a heavy cannonade like a continued volley of artillery. The countenances of the soldiers brightened, as they sprang to their feet and listened with intense interest to the roar of the distant battle, which was then raging on the plains of Palo Alto. The sounds grew nearer and more distinct, from which they inferred their general was driving the enemy before him ; and, mounting upon the parapets, regardless of the missiles that fell thick around them, they raised a shout that rose far above the thunder of the enemy's forts, and carried dismay to the hearts of the inhabitants of Matamoros. Soon after this the enemy redoubled his fire, and from mortars established in the north, south and west—four in number— round-shot and shells in a storm of iron hail strewed the earth in every direction. While the sounds of the distant battle were now heard, bodies of infantry and cavalry were seen crossing the river, and hurrying onward to reinforce their companions. About sunset, a Mexican came running to the fort with a flag, and announced to the garrison the pleasing intelligence, that General

Taylor had met the forces of Arista on his march, and after a severe fight, had driven him back towards Matamoros.

During the night there was no more firing, and the garrison, though on the alert should an assault be attempted, was enabled to obtain better rest than usual to their weary, exhausted frames.

The firing was resumed on the morning of the 9th, but the garrison was greatly encouraged on finding that the enemy's battery to the east of the fort was withdrawn and removed to Matamoros. The belief that General Taylor had been victorious on the preceding day, was confirmed by seeing troops hurrying in the direction of Arista's head-quarters. During the fire this morning, an act of great daring was performed by Lieutenant Van Dorn and Quartermaster-Sergeant Henry. The halyards of the flag had become unrigged the preceding evening; they ascended to adjust these, when the enemy turned upon them the fire of all their batteries; yet, amid the storm of grape, canister, and shells, they dauntlessly stood to their work until they had accomplished it, and descended amid the acclamations of their companions.

About midday the firing ceased for some time, and amid the silence of the pause, the gallant Major Brown breathed his last.

It was now after two o'clock; no message or tidings had been received from General Taylor, and anxiety was painfully depicted on the faces of many, when the booming of cannon in quick succession, told that their companions were again in deadly conflict with the enemy. Nearer and clearer came the sound, till amid the diapason of artillery was heard the sharp rattle of musketry, and the garrison knew that the brave army coming to their relief, were driving before them the proud legions of Mexico.

At length the sound of battle ceased, and the defenders of the fort were now anxious to gain intelligence of a result in which their own safety was so deeply concerned; when, towards set of sun, the Mexican troops emerged from the chaparral in the utmost confusion, and rushed in full retreat to the river, pursued by May's dragoons and Duncan's artillery. Transported at the sight, the garrison manned the parapets, and, lifting up the voice of exultation, silenced with their cheers the batteries of the enemy, for not another shot was fired afterwards. As the tide of Mexican cavalry and infantry rolled by, discharges of grape from a 6-pounder and one of the 18's of the fort, carried increasing confusion into their masses; but as it was difficult to distinguish friend from foe, the fire of the garrison was checked, lest the deadly missiles might be directed against the pursuers as well as the fugitives.

After a siege of one hundred and sixty hours, in which several thousand shot and shells were received, and every ten feet of its area ploughed up by a bomb, thus ended the defence of Fort Brown. It was undoubtedly one of the most brilliant achievements of the war. Throughout its continuance, the courage, patience, and perseverance of the American soldiery were severely tested, under the most disadvantageous and harassing circumstances; and well did they abide the fiery ordeal.

Besides its gallant defender Major Brown, Sergeant Weigart of the 7th infantry was the only one killed; the wounded were thirteen in number, and were all privates. The case of Sergeant Weigart was a remarkable one. The second bomb thrown by the Mexicans exploded near his company, and carried away a part of his head, killing him instantly. While laid out on a board in the hospital tent preparatory to burial, a shell entered the tent, burst, and blew off his head. After his burial, a bomb entered his grave, and exploding therein, partially exhumed him.

CHAPTER VIII.

Bombardment of Fort Brown heard at Point Isabel—Captain Walker sent with a Communication to Major Brown—May charges the Enemy's Lancers—Return of Captain Walker—March of General Taylor for Fort Brown—Published Order —Enemy discovered—Arista's Order of Battle—Taylor's Order of Battle— Daring Service of Lieutenant Blake—Enemy's Fire opened—Duncan's Battery— Ringgold's Artillery—Churchhill's 18-pounders—Charge of Cavalry—Lieutenant Ridgely—Fall of Ringgold—Artillery Battalion—Lieutenant-Colonel Childs— The Prairie fired—Duncan's Movement—Forces of the two Armies—The Loss on each side—Taylor's Despatch—Arista's Despatch.

THE cannonade that opened upon Fort Brown, on the 3d of May, was heard by General Taylor at Point Isabel. Anxious to relieve the garrison, he determined to return immediately to Fort Brown, and the troops were under order to march at one, P. M. Subsequently, he deemed it proper first to communicate with the fort; and Captain Walker was selected for that duty. About two o'clock, on the evening of the 3d, the captain set out with ten Texan Rangers, accompanied by Captain May, with a command of one hundred dragoons; and after proceeding a few miles, halted until dark.

About nine o'clock they came in sight of the enemy's camp-fires; and, by proceeding cautiously, succeeded in getting between their encampment and the fort. About seven miles from the latter, protected from observation by the edge of the chaparral, Captain May remained with his command; while Captain Walker, and six of the rangers, advanced to the fort. It was arranged between them, that Captain Walker should return as early as possible, so that they could pass the enemy's lines before daylight.

18   (123)

Captain May awaited the return of Captain Walker until near dawn; when, finding that he and his party were discovered by the enemy's scouts, and believing that some accident had happened to the captain, he returned to Point Isabel. When within twelve miles of the Point, he found his way obstructed by about one hundred and fifty lancers. These he charged, and drove before him towards their camp for two or three miles; when, fearing an ambuscade, he wheeled about and proceeded on to Point Isabel, which he reached at nine o'clock.

It was near three o'clock in the morning of the 4th, before Captain Walker succeeded in reaching the fort, and delivering his message to the commander. After some time, he received Major Brown's communications for General Taylor, and being furnished with fresh horses, hastened to join Captain May. On arriving at the spot where he had left the captain and his party, he found them gone—and the enemy prepared to cut off his return. He then rode back to Fort Brown, where he remained till night, and then set out again for Point Isabel. The enemy were everywhere in his pathway, but he managed to evade them, and bore to General Taylor the cheering intelligence that the fort had nobly sustained itself; and was able, for the present, to repel any force that could be brought against it. After the receipt of this news, General Taylor resolved to remain a while longer at Point Isabel, that he might place it in a better state of defence, and prepare for his return to Fort Brown.

During the week which he spent at Point Isabel, General Taylor had completed the defences of that post, and made arrangements for the transportation of the supplies and munitions of war intended for Fort Brown. Summoned thither by the booming of the deep-mouthed cannon that assailed the fort, he left Point Isabel on the evening of the 7th of May, and with the main body of his army, and a train of three hundred wagons, his light artillery, and two 18-pounders on siege-carriages, drawn by ten yoke of oxen, moved towards the Rio Grande.

In expectation of the enemy's disputing his return, and confident of his ability to repel their efforts, General Taylor issued the following order :—

"HEAD-QUARTERS, ARMY OF OCCUPATION,
May 7, 1846.

ORDER No. 58.

"The army will march to-day at three o'clock, in the direction of Matamoros. It is known the enemy has recently occupied the route in force. If still in possession, the general will give him battle. The commanding-general has every confidence in his officers and men. If his orders and instructions are carried out, he has no doubt of the result, let the enemy meet him in what numbers they may. He wishes to enjoin upon the battalions of infantry, that their main dependence must be in the bayonet.

W. W. S. BLISS,
Assistant Adjutant-General."

The weather was warm, and their march slow and toilsome, encumbered as it was with the train and the heavy artillery intended for Fort Brown ; so that, after making seven miles of their way, they halted and bivouacked on their arms for the night.

Early on the following morning it was reported by the scouts under Captain Walker, that the enemy had deserted their camp, from which it was inferred, that the enemy did not contemplate giving battle. The march was resumed about sunrise, and continued till noon. At this time, the advance of cavalry which had reached the water-hole of Palo Alto, brought intelligence to the general that the Mexicans were in front ; and it was soon discovered that they occupied the road in great force.

On reaching the water, the army was halted, with the view of resting and refreshing the men, and enabling the general to make a proper and deliberate disposition of his forces. The enemy in battle-array was now plainly visible at a distance of three-quarters of a mile, his banners gaily floating in the breeze, and his tall lances flashing in the sunlight. Compact lines of infantry extended from a thicket of chaparral on their right, about a mile over an open prairie of three miles in extent; while a heavy force of cavalry on their left, stretched across the road and rested upon a salt-marsh of difficult passage. At intervals along their line, batteries were planted to sweep the advancing column of the Americans.

Though he saw before him an army greatly superior in numbers, inured to arms in many a fight, and enjoying the advantages of a well-selected position, General Taylor, firm in his resolution to advance, and confident of the bravery of his troops, calmly disposed his forces in order of battle.

The line of battle was formed in two wings. The right wing was commanded by the veteran Colonel David E. Twiggs, and was composed of the following troops, commencing on the extreme right:—5th infantry, Lieutenant-Colonel McIntosh; Ringgold's light artillery; 3d infantry, Captain L. M. Morris; two 18-pounders, under Lieutenant Churchhill, 3d artillery; 4th infantry, Major G. W. Allen; and two squadrons of dragoons, under Captains Ker and May. The left wing, under the command of Lieutenant-Colonel Belknap, consisted of a battalion of artillery, serving as infantry, under Lieutenant-Colonel Childs; Captain Duncan's light artillery; and the 8th infantry, under Captain Montgomery. For security the wagon train was parked near the water, under the directions of Captains Crossman and Myers of the Quartermaster's department, and protected by the squadron of dragoons under Captain Ker.

Having refreshed themselves and filled their canteens, the troops were put in motion and ordered to advance by heads of columns. After the line of battle had been formed, General

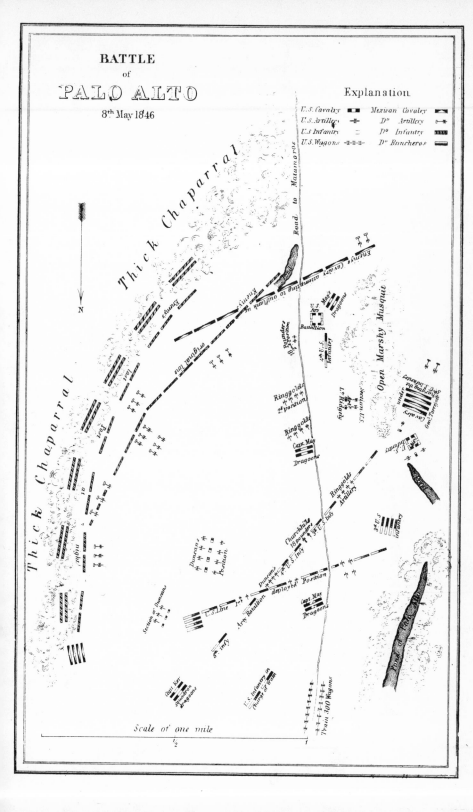

BATTLE
of
PALO ALTO
8th May 1846

Explanation

U.S. Cavalry		Mexican Cavalry	
U.S. Artillery		Do Artillery	
U.S Infantry		Do Infantry	
U.S Wagons		Do Rancheros	

Thick Chaparral

Thick Chaparral

Road to Matamoros

Open Marshy Musquit

N

Scale of one mile

Taylor rode along the line and encouraged the men, who seemed eager for the contest.   As yet he did not know whether the enemy had artillery or not; and anxious to learn that particular, he detached Captain May with his dragoons, to reconnoitre his lines, and, if possible, draw the fire of his artillery; but it was completely masked by the long prairie-grass and the men in front of the pieces, and the captain returned again, after an ineffectual effort.

Lieutenant Blake now volunteered a daring service.   He proposed to go forward alone, and make a reconnoissance of the enemy's position and forces.   With great gallantry he dashed forwards to within eighty yards of the enemy's line, while both armies looked on with admiration; and dismounting, took his glass, and deliberately surveyed the whole of their forces.   After this, he mounted his horse and galloped down the line to the other end, and, after a second examination with his glass, returned and reported to the general the presence and position of at least two batteries of artillery in the enemy's line.   Scarcely had he finished his report to General Taylor, when the enemy's battery on the right, with ball and grape, opened upon the American forces, and the work of destruction began.

As soon as the cannonade commenced, General Taylor halted his columns, and ordered them to deploy into line, which was performed with steadiness and precision.   The light artillery on the wings and the 18-pounders in the centre, were advanced about one hundred yards, and the order passed to answer the enemy's fire.   Duncan's battery on the left got into position a little in advance of the others, and first returned the challenge of the enemy.   Ringgold's artillery was soon engaged in the conflict; and the terrible 18-pounders from the centre, under the direction of the general, were brought to bear upon the enemy's left.

The battle now raged with fury from right to left, and the cannon on both sides dealt destruction.   The fire of the enemy was incessant, but inaccurate; Ringgold's artillery on the contrary mowed down whole platoons of cavalry on the Mexican left; the discharges of the 18-pounders in the same direction were murderous, while the Mexican right suffered terribly from the artillery of Duncan, which was served with deadly effect. Captain May, who had been ordered to support this battery, while contemplating a charge, received a severe fire from the Mexican artillery, by which he lost four horses killed and two wounded.

At this time the Mexican cavalry, which, unable to withstand the rapid discharges and precision of Ringgold's artillery, and the fire of the heavy pieces under Churchhill, had faltered and given way, advanced through the chaparral with two pieces of artillery, for the purpose of attacking the right flank of the Americans, or of making a demonstration upon the train which had been parked in the rear. To check this flank movement, troops were promptly detached. The 5th infantry was advanced to meet the enemy in that quarter, supported by a section of Major Ringgold's battery under Lieutenant Randolph Ridgely, Captain Walker's company of volunteers, and, shortly after, the 3d infantry. Thrown into cavalry square, the 5th sustained with great bravery the charge of the lancers under General Torrejon, and galled them with a severe fire, while Lieutenant Ridgely served his pieces with rapidity, and poured shot and shells upon their ranks with decisive effect. The lieutenant had his horse shot under him, at which time the horses at one of his caissons, affrighted, sprang madly forward in range of the gun. Regardless of danger, the lieutenant threw himself between the contending fires, and seizing the leader by the head, brought the horses to their places, and saved both them and the ammunition of his battery. Though severely wasted, a portion of the enemy's cavalry on the flank continued to press on, until they perceived the 3d infantry advancing in column by division to receive them, when they turned and retired with precipitation, lessened by the iron hail that pursued them.

In the mean time Churchhill's 18-pounders and the artillery under Ringgold, supported by the 4th infantry from the left, continued to assail the enemy with a steady fire, and with murderous effect. To check this fire, the enemy poured from his batteries a storm of grape and canister, which killed and wounded many of the 4th, and among them Captain Page, who was shockingly disfigured by a shot which tore away his lower jaw. Soon after, the gallant Ringgold, while directing the fire of his pieces, was mortally wounded by a 6-pound shot, which at the same time mangled and dashed to the earth the charger on which he was mounted. Colonel Payne, inspector-general of the army and one of General Taylor's aids, chanced to be near him at the time. By permission, he had just directed with effect one of the guns, and, summoned by the call of one of the men, ran with others to the wounded major, to afford such aid as was in their power; but with the true gallantry of a soldier, more concerned for the cause of his country than his own life, he wished to decline their services, and said: " Don't stay with me; you have work to do. Go ahead!"

After Major Ringgold was carried to the rear, Lieutenant Shover assumed the command of his pieces, and continued to serve them with precision and good effect until the close of the action.

While this flank movement was attempted by the enemy, the artillery battalion, under Lieutenant-Colonel Childs, had been brought up, for the purpose of supporting the batteries of Churchhill and Ringgold. As the enemy's cavalry came dashing on, a deadly fire from the 18-pounders gave them a severe check, while the artillery battalion, thrown into cavalry-square, were prepared to receive them. Again pressing on, the enemy opened a fire of small arms upon the square, by which Lieutenant Luther, of the

2d artillery, and others were wounded ; but a volley from the front
of the square, delivered with good effect, stopped their advance,
and closed the action upon the American right.   Evening was
now setting in ; and the enemy, foiled in all his attempts against
the American line, fell back from his position, and retired through
the chaparral out of sight.

While these things took place, Captain May had been ordered
to drive in the cavalry of the enemy on the Mexican left, but
while advancing for that purpose, received a heavy fire from their
artillery, which disabled a considerable portion of his command.
Having gained a position with the view of charging, he was
restrained by the consideration of the great disparity of forces,
which were as one to ten, and returned to his former position.

During the engagement, the prairie-grass on the left, parched
by the continued blaze of the cannon, had been fired by the discharge of Duncan's battery ; and dense wreaths of smoke rolling
up, entirely enveloped the two armies from each other, and hung
like the pall of death over the battle-field.   In consequence of
this, the fight was suspended ; but during its pause, while Duncan was advancing to gain a position somewhat to the right of the
one which he had occupied, the Mexicans were marching across
the prairie with the view of attacking the train ; which, during the
engagement, in consequence of the advance of our line, had also
been advanced and parked in the rear.

The temporary clearing away of the smoke, which the sea-
breeze lifted up like a curtain, and let fall again, disclosed to
each army the manœuvre of the other.   Penetrating the enemy's
intention, Colonel Belknap ordered Duncan to alter his direction,
and wheel his horses to the left, which was promptly obeyed.
Rushing in the direction of the enemy's advancing troops, Duncan
halted within musket-range of the lancers ; and, as the clearing
of the air revealed his position to the astonished enemy, poured
a volley of shot and shells upon the lancers from one section,

BATTLE OF PALO ALTO AND DEATH OF MAJOR RINGGOLD.

while he directed the fire of another against some regiments of infantry, that, supported by horse, were emerging from the chaparral. Bravely did the enemy sustain the fire for a time. They re-formed the broken ranks, and attempted to press on, but the shells and shrapnell shot soon carried confusion into their ranks; their own fire slackened, while the iron storm that assailed them was resistless. Their infantry fell back, and retired within the chaparral, in the rear of the position it had occupied; in which movement it was soon followed by the cavalry, while night coming on put an end to the contest.

During these movements, Ker's dragoons and the 8th infantry stood firm as veterans, ready to support the batteries; but were not called into action. The 8th was kept in column, instead of being deployed into line, and sustained a galling fire under circumstances demanding the coolest endurance.

The fire from both armies ceased with the setting sun, whose last rays gave a light tinge of gold to the heavy clouds of smoke that draped the battle-field, like the transient fame that gilds the gloom of war. Many an eye that brightened with his morning radiance was dim, and would now behold his beams no more for ever.

The regular force of the Mexicans in this battle was six thousand men, with twelve pieces of artillery, besides bodies of irregular troops. The Americans had in all but twenty-two hundred and eighty-eight men; yet, with this inferior force, the American general defeated a veteran army, with all the advantages of a select position. It was the first open action between the armies of the belligerents; and its complete success was a happy omen of the victories that were to follow.

The Mexicans lost two hundred killed, and four hundred wounded; the Americans lost nine killed, forty-four wounded, and two missing. Artillery was the main arm employed, and the rapidity and precision with which the American guns were served, caused the great disparity in the loss of the two armies.

19

Another cause of the disparity was, that the Mexicans directed their fire with the view of silencing the batteries; while the Americans directed their shot against the masses of men. But the chief cause was the difference in the abilities of the two commanders, and the bravery of their subordinate officers. Their men, with veteran firmness, withstood the volleys of our artillery, and, had they been led by superiors of dauntless bravery, though they might not have been victorious, would have rendered the fortunes of the day far different. Finding the great superiority of our artillery, Arista should have charged, with recklessness of the partial sacrifice, and by the very force of his numbers have overpowered his enemy. That General Taylor expected him to do this, is evident from his order: "He wishes to enjoin upon the battalions of infantry, that their chief dependence must be in the bayonet."

By the light of the burning prairie, and the soft rays of the moon, the Americans collected their wounded and buried the dead; and after the excitement was over, sank to repose on the bare earth, in expectation of resuming the battle on the morrow. The place of the battle, Palo Alto (tall timber), is so called on account of the timber which skirted the further end of the prairie, and which, though of stunted growth, is *tall* in comparison with the chaparral of that region. When first passing over this ground, General Taylor had predicted, that the enemy would select it for their place to give battle.

At the dawn of day, on the 9th, the enemy were seen retiring along the chaparral towards the road, as if to dispute the further progress of our army. Determined to advance and attack the enemy, General Taylor resolved to park the train, and mount some of the 12-pounders, which it carried for its defence. The wounded were left behind, to be sent to Point Isabel. The gallant Major Ringgold, who, while standing up in his stirrups watching the effect of his fire, had received a shot that passed

MAJOR SAMUEL RINGGOLD.

through both legs, carrying away the flesh and integuments, lingered until the 11th; when, with great composure, he closed a life which had been faithfully devoted to his country.

About sunrise General Taylor formed his troops in line of battle, and marched forward to meet the enemy; but the dragoons and Captain Walker's men, who were in advance, reported the chaparral free, and the enemy rapidly retiring along the road, upon which the general halted his army.

The commanding-general now rode back to the train, for the purpose of despatching his first bulletin, which had been prepared the preceding night. While here, an unfortunate occurrence took place. Lieutenant Blake, of the Topographical Engineers, whom we have mentioned as making the bold reconnoissance of the enemy's line, accidentally shot himself. On entering the tent in which General Taylor was sitting, he threw down his holsters, when the cap of one of his pistols exploded, discharging the contents into his body.

The despatch of General Taylor was brief and unpretending. In a subsequent communication he dwelt upon the details of the fight.

> "HEAD-QUARTERS, ARMY OF OCCUPATION,
> Camp at Palo Alto, Texas, May 9, 1846.

"SIR: I have the honour to report that I was met near this place yesterday, on my march from Point Isabel, by the Mexican forces, and after an action of about five hours, dislodged them from their position and encamped upon the field. Our artillery, consisting of two 18-pounders and two light batteries, was the arm chiefly engaged, and to the excellent manner in which it was manœuvred and served is our success mainly due.

"The strength of the enemy is believed to have been about 6000 men, with seven pieces of artillery, and 800 cavalry. His loss is probably at least one hundred killed. Our strength did not exceed, all told, twenty-three hundred, while our loss was comparatively trifling—four men killed, three officers and thirty-seven men wounded, several of the latter mortally. I regret to say that Major Ringgold, 2d artillery, and Captain Page, 4th infantry, are severely wounded. Lieutenant Luther, 2d artillery, slightly so.

" The enemy has fallen back, and it is believed, has repassed the river. I have advanced parties now thrown forward in his direction, and shall move the main body immediately.

" In the haste of this report, I can only say that the officers and men behaved in the most admirable manner throughout the action. I shall have the pleasure of making a more detailed report when those of the different commanders shall be received.

" I am, sir, very respectfully, your obedient servant,

Z. TAYLOR,

Brevet Brig. Gen. U. S. A., commanding.

The Adjutant-General of the Army, Washington, D. C."

In striking contrast with this plain statement is the account of the vanquished Arista, addressed to the Mexican Minister of War and Marine, and dated, " In sight of the enemy, May 8." Though in sight of the enemy, the Mexican commander was at the time in *retreat.* This omission, however, is of little moment, when we consider the many misstatements of his despatch.

" Constant in my purpose of preventing General Taylor from uniting the forces which he brought from the Fronton of Santa Isabel, with those which he left opposite Matamoros, I moved this day from the Fanques del Raminero, whence I despatched my last extraordinary courier, and took the direction of Palo Alto, as soon as my spies informed me that the enemy had left Fronton, with the determination of introducing into his fort wagons loaded with provisions and heavy artillery.

" I arrived opposite Palo Alto about one o'clock, and observed that the enemy was entering that position.

" With all my forces, I established the line of battle in a great plain, my right resting upon an elevation, and my left on a slough of difficult passage.

" Scarcely was the first cannon fired, when there arrived General D. Pedro de Ampudia, second in command, whom I had ordered to join me after having covered the points which might serve to besiege the enemy in the forts opposite Matamoros.

" The forces under my orders amounted to three thousand men, and twelve pieces of artillery; those of the invaders were three thousand, rather less than more, and were superior in artillery, since they had twenty pieces of the calibre of sixteen and eighteen pounds.

" The battle commenced so ardently, that the fire of cannon did not cease a single moment. In the course of it, the enemy wished to follow the road to Matamoros, to raise the siege of his troops; with which object he fired the grass, and formed in front of his line of battle a smoke so thick, that he succeeded in covering himself from our view, but by means of manœuvres this was twice embarrassed.

" General Taylor maintained his attack rather defensively than offensively, employing his best arm, which is artillery, protected by half of the infantry, and all of his cavalry, keeping the remainder fortified in the ravine, about two thousand yards from the field of battle.

" I was anxious for the charge, because the fire of cannon did much damage in our ranks; and I instructed General D. Anastasio Torrejon to execute it with the greater part of the cavalry, by our left flank, with some columns of infantry, and the remainder of the cavalry.

" I was waiting the moment when that general should execute the charge, and the effect of it should begin to be seen, in order to give the impulse on the right; but he was checked by a fire of the enemy, which defended a slough that embarrassed the attack.

" Some battalions, becoming impatient by the loss which they suffered, fell into disorder, demanding to advance or fall back. I immediately caused them to charge with a column of cavalry, under the command of Colonel D. Cayetano Montero ; the result of this operation being that the dispersed corps repaired their fault as far as possible, marching towards the enemy, who, in consequence of his distance, was enabled to fall back upon his reserve ; and night coming on, the battle was concluded, the field remaining for our arms.

" Every suitable measure was then adopted, and the division took up a more concentrated curve in the same scene of action.

" The combat was long and bloody, which may be estimated from the calculations made by the commandant-general of artillery, General D. Thomas Requena, who assures me that the enemy threw about three thousand cannon-shots from two in the afternoon, when the battle commenced, until seven at night, when it terminated, — six hundred and fifty being fired on our side.

" The national arms shone forth, since they did not yield a hand's-breadth of ground, notwithstanding the superiority in artillery of the enemy, who suffered much damage.

" Our troops have to lament the loss of two hundred and fifty-two men dispersed, wounded, and killed, — the last worthy of national recollection and gratitude for the intrepidity with which they died fighting for the most sacred of causes.

" Will your Excellency please with his note to report to his Excellency the President, representing to him that I will take care to give a circumstantial account of this deed of arms ; and recommending to him the good conduct of all the generals, chiefs, officers and soldiers under my orders, for sustaining so bloody a combat, which does honour to our arms, and exhibits their discipline."

CHAPTER IX.

At daybreak on the 9th, the rear of the enemy was seen
retiring through the chaparral towards Fort Brown, and the general belief was, that he was disposed to try his fortunes again, and
would further dispute the advance of the American army.

After their morning meal, General Taylor called a council
composed of the heads of the commands, in which some were
for marching forward ; others preferred intrenching where they
were, until reinforced by the volunteers that were expected ; while
others, again, were in favour of returning to Point Isabel. The
commanding-general reconciled all differences by declaring, that
he would be in Fort Brown before night, if he lived. Thereupon
the council closed, and orders were given to form in line, and
march forward. In passing over the battle-ground of the former
day, the terrible effects of our artillery were visible in the heaped-
up masses of dead bodies disfigured with ghastly wounds and
distained with blood, — in the dead horses scattered along the
route of the retreating cavalry, — and in the fragments of arms,

military accoutrements, and clothing strewed over the field in admirable confusion.

On reaching the edge of the chaparral, General Taylor halted the troops at a pond, and ordered forward into the chaparral an advanced corps, to feel the enemy, and ascertain his position. This consisted of the light companies of the First Brigade, under Captain C. F. Smith, 2d artillery, and a select detachment of light troops ; the whole under command of Captain A. G. McCall, 4th infantry, and numbering two hundred and twenty men. Captain Smith's party moved along upon the right of the road, the remainder of the command upon the left. In expectation of an engagement, General Taylor parked his supply-train, and fortified its position by intrenchments, and by a battery consisting of the two 18-pounders and two 12's. The artillery battalion, under Lieutenant-Colonel Childs (excepting the flank companies), was stationed as a guard to the train, some distance in advance of it.

While scouring the chaparral in search of the enemy, the American advance upon the right discovered some small parties of infantry, and one of cavalry, and immediately fired upon them. Shortly after this the head of the command, on reaching the open ground bordering upon the Resaca de la Palma, came within range of a masked battery, and received three rounds of canister, which killed one man, and wounded three others. Upon this the men broke and took to the chaparral. Shortly after, however, they rallied, and uniting with the detachment under Captain Smith, prepared to move upon the flank of the enemy and attack him.

While this was going on upon the right of the road, Lieutenant Dobbins, with a small party, encountered upon the left a large body of Mexicans. The lieutenant raised his rifle and killed the Mexican leader ; almost at the same instant his soldiers fired, killing and wounding a number of the enemy, while the remainder

Scale of one mile
½   1

Thick Chaparral

N

Mexican Camp

Infantry Reserve

To Lower Ferry

Gen.ˡ Hd. Aristas Quaters

Mexican Rancheros

Thick Chaparral

Place where the Battery was taken

Road from Tampico

Road from Tampico

Thick Chaparral

U.S. Artillery

Dragoons

Capt. C. A. May
Vanguard Dragoons

Capt. K.'s Squad: Dragoons Com.ds

2 U.S. Infantry
deployed as skirmishers

8 U.S. Infantry
Deployed as skirmishers

4 U.S. Infantry
Deployed as skirmishers

4 U.S. Infantry
deployed as skirmishers

BATTLE
of
RESACA DE LA PALMA
9ᵗʰ May 1846.

Train
300 Wagons

fell back. Soon after, a masked battery opened upon the party, and Lieutenant Dobbins was struck down by a grape-shot. He recovered himself soon after, and ordered his men to the dense chaparral, which they reached in time to escape a troop of Mexican cavalry that came dashing up in pursuit. He now ordered his men to press upon the rear of the cavalry, who, fearing they had fallen into an ambuscade, hastily retreated. After this the lieutenant, with his men, returned to the main body of the advance-guard; when Captain McCall despatched three dragoons to inform General Taylor that the enemy occupied the ravine in force, with the evident design of obstructing his march.

The position selected by the enemy was one of great natural strength. Midway between Palo Alto and Fort Brown, and in the centre of the forest of chaparral which extends for about seven miles between these points, the road crosses a ravine which is semicircular in shape, with the opening between its extremities lying towards Point Isabel. The ravine is about sixty yards broad, and is nearly breast-high. At different places along its extent are ponds, oval or of serpentine shape, which are so increased during the rainy season, as to unite and form a continuous stream that flows off towards the Rio Grande, and is hence called the Resaca de la Palma, or *Dry River of Palma*. The bed of this river, now dry, with the exception of ponds at intervals, was occupied by the enemy in double lines; one posted under the front bank, the other intrenched behind the chaparral that lined the further bank. Batteries were planted upon the right and left of the road in the centre of each line, and one upon the enemy's right, so that the fire of the whole might converge in a terrible focus upon the American column, as it advanced between the horns of the crescent which the ravine formed across the road. With these advantages of position, Arista, with seven thousand men, many of them veteran troops, awaited the approach of the American army.

20

About three o'clock in the afternoon, General Taylor received the message from Captain McCall, and instantly put his army in motion, which came up with the advance-guard about four o'clock. Lieutenant Ridgely, with his battery, was immediately thrown forward on the road. Captain Smith, with his party, was now directed to take the right of the road, while Captain McCall took the left, with orders to feel the enemy and bring on the action, after which they were to assume a position upon the enemy's flanks, and harass him. Having advanced about three hundred yards to front and flank, the advance encountered the right of the enemy's infantry, and with great gallantry brought on the action, pouring an incessant and destructive fire upon the enemy.

Ridgely's battery, in the mean time, had advanced upon the road; while the 5th infantry and one wing of the 4th, thrown into the chaparral on the left, and the 3d infantry and the other wing of the 4th upon the right, moved simultaneously upon the enemy. These corps were deployed as skirmishers, and intended to cover the battery and engage the Mexican infantry.

Moving cautiously along, Ridgely discovered the enemy in the road, about four hundred yards in advance, and almost instantaneously their artillery opened upon him. Ridgely ordered forward his battery at full speed, about a hundred yards, and returned the fire with precision and effect. The cannonade was kept up for some time on both sides with great spirit, after which, as the fire of the enemy slackened, Ridgely limbered up and advanced upon him, until at length he was within a hundred or a hundred and fifty yards of the enemy's batteries, and at this fearful proximity, galled him with rapid and terrible discharges of grape and canister.

Simultaneous with the opening roar of the artillery was heard the sharp rattle of musketry. On the left the 5th infantry, led by the gallant Lieutenant-Colonel McIntosh, rushed on towards the

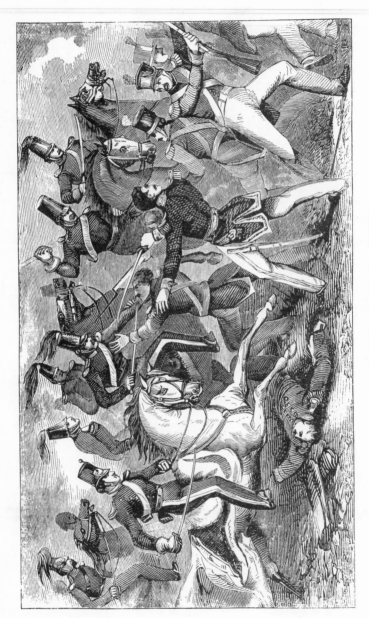

BATTLE OF RESACA DE LA PALMA.

enemy at full speed, made its way through the almost impenetrable chaparral, engaged the enemy, and for some time sustained the fire of the Mexican army, without any infantry to
support it, except the advance party, under Captain McCall.

The 4th infantry, while pressing on towards the enemy through
the chaparral, became divided. A part united with the 5th,
while the remaining portion, under Captain Buchanan, with
Lieutenants Hays and Woods, crossed the pond in the ravine,
which was waist-deep, and on surmounting the crest of the hill,
charged and took one of the enemy's pieces, though defended by
a hundred and fifty infantry; and immediately after drove the
enemy from a breastwork behind which he was intrenched.
Before the cannoneers fled, they had set fire to the priming-tube,
and the match was about to ignite the powder; Lieutenant
Woods sprang forward in time to prevent it, and with his sword
knocked off the priming. Soon after a body of cavalry came
dashing up, and made an effort to recapture the artillery; but a
part of the 3d infantry, under Captain Barbour, had arrived to
the support of the 4th. They formed in the face of the enemy,
and advanced with the utmost determination, when rapid discharges from the united force drove back the enemy in confusion.

The action now became general, and the battle raged with
fury. In various parts of the field was heard the roll of musketry,
where the infantry, divided into small parties by the intervening
chaparral, was contending with the enemy. At times the conflict
became nearer, and bayonets were crossed in the deadly
encounter. The artillerists, under Ridgely, meanwhile, were
bared like reapers to their toil, and the corses of the enemy, like
ripened grain, strewed the field of death beneath their incessant
and terrible service at the pieces. Their intrepid commander,
cool and determined, not only gave direction to the discharges
of the guns, but with his ready glass sought afterwards the evidences of the effect with which each charge was sped. The roar

of the enemy's cannon, in the mean time, was almost continuous; and had it not been that the fire was directed too high, it would have swept Ridgely's batteries, and annihilated his command.

While the battle thus raged, Lieutenant-Colonel Belknap, who commanded the First Brigade, ordered up the 8th infantry, and Duncan's artillery, which had been posted as a reserve. On arriving at the scene of action, the 8th charged the enemy on the right of the road, and after a vigorous resistance drove him from his position; but Duncan's battery, on arriving at the edge of the ravine, could not open fire on the enemy without galling his friends at the same time. He was obliged, therefore, to let it remain inactive until near the close of the action.

The battle had now continued for some time without any decided advantage on our part, and General Taylor perceived that the enemy could not be driven from his position until his artillery was silenced. He therefore ordered Captain May, who was stationed in the rear, to report himself for duty. He soon appeared, with his command, and was directed to charge and take the enemy's batteries, at whatever sacrifice. After exhorting his men to remember their regiment, the captain pointed towards the batteries and bade them follow. Striking spurs into his horse, he dashed forward, followed by his command in columns of fours.

On arriving at the place occupied by Ridgely and his brave cannoneers, May halted to learn the position of the enemy's batteries. Knowing the danger attending a charge upon their pieces when loaded, Ridgely desired him to wait until he drew the fire of their batteries. He suddenly applied the match, and, ere the reverberation of his pieces had died away, the enemy replied, and their shot swept like hail through his batteries.

Instantly the squadron of dragoons sprang forward, May in the advance, with his long hair streaming behind like the rays of a comet. The earth shook beneath the iron hoofs of their steeds, and the rays of the tropic sun flashed back in flame from their

LIEUT. COL. CHARLES A MAY.

burnished sabres, as they swept along, cheered by a shout of exultation from the artillerists and infantry.

Still foremost, May reached at length the batteries in the road, and upon the right of it; and, as his steed rose upon the enemy's breastworks, he turned to wave on his men to the charge. Closely pressing upon him, was Lieutenant Inge, who answered to the challenge with a shout, and turned in like manner to encourage his platoon, when a terrible discharge of grape and canister from the upper battery swept down upon them, and dashed to the earth, in mangled and bloody masses, eighteen horses and seven men; among them the gallant Inge and his charger. May's steed at a bound cleared the batteries, followed by Lieutenant Stevens, and the survivors of the 1st and 2d platoons. Their impetus carried them through and beyond the batteries, when charging back, they drove the enemy from the guns and silenced their fire. Captain Graham, and Lieutenants Winship and Pleasanton, with the 3d and 4th platoons, in the mean time swept to the left of the road, and at the point of the sword carried the battery situated there.

Perceiving the small force by which they were assailed, the Mexicans recovered from their panic, and rushing back to the batteries, prepared to fire them. Gathering around him a few followers, May charged upon them with irresistible force, while the terror-stricken enemy shrunk back from the blows of his sword, which descended with a flash and force like that of lightning. An intrepid officer, however, kept his place, and endeavoured to rally his men. With his own hands he seized a match and was about to apply it, when he was ordered by Captain May to surrender. Finding himself without support, he acknowledged himself a prisoner, and handed his sword to his gallant captor. It was General Vega, a brave and accomplished officer. He was placed in charge of Lieutenant Stevens, and conducted in safety to the rear, to Colonel Twiggs, though exposed to a shower of musketry.

The fire of the enemy's batteries was silenced, but a terrible struggle commenced for their possession. The 5th infantry, under the brave Lieutenant-Colonel McIntosh, though separated into masses by the chaparral, rushed on through a sweeping fire of musketry, and at length crossed bayonets with the enemy over the cannon-muzzles.

The 8th infantry, having learned that May had carried the main battery, but could not maintain it for want of support, was formed in the road, and led on in person by Colonel Belknap. While moving forward they were joined by a part of the 5th regiment, under Captain Martin Scott. Under the heavy fire of the enemy they faltered for a moment, when the gallant Belknap sprang forward, and smiting down a Mexican ensign, seized his standard, and with it waved on the troops to the charge. A shot soon carried away the flag, but with the staff he continued to cheer his men, until thrown from his horse over a pile of dead and wounded artillerists. Supposing him slain, the regiment fought with desperation to avenge his death, and, together with the 5th, engaged in a terrible conflict, hand to hand, with the Tampico battalion, composed of veterans victorious in twenty fields. Some time after, the regiment was gratefully surprised at seeing Colonel Belknap appear again at the head of his column.

The 8th, under the immediate command of Captain Montgomery, and the 5th, under Lieutenant-Colonel McIntosh, had charged up the ravine, under a sheeted fire from right and front of the enemy, and after a vigorous resistance forced him back through the dense chaparral. Lodged in different clumps of these impenetrable thickets, the enemy continued the fight, and poured a destructive fire upon the Americans, which caused the action to be varied by numberless skirmishes, in one of which

Lieutenant Chadbourne, who had distinguished himself by his bravery, was mortally wounded at the head of his command.

While Colonel McIntosh was forcing his way through a dense thicket of chaparral, lined with infantry and cavalry, his horse was struck with a shot and fell dead, and the colonel was precipitated through the chaparral into the midst of the enemy. Mounting to his feet, he encountered them sword in hand, and warded off, for the instant, both bayonets and lance-points; but he was soon overpowered by numbers, and disabled by wounds. A bayonet entered his mouth and came out at his ear; a second, aimed at his heart, pierced through his arm and terribly shattered the bone; while by a third, which passed through his hip, he was borne down, and pinned to the earth. Upon his fall the command of his regiment devolved upon Major Staniford, who with great energy and spirit followed up the advantages already obtained, and drove the enemy before him.

The 4th regiment, after carrying the battery on the right, as before described, continued to press on, increased by squads of men from the different regiments, and at length emerged from the chaparral into the camp of General Arista, of which they immediately took possession. Here was found his splendid marquée, his private carriage, his trunks, private property, and his correspondence, among which was recognised in his own handwriting the original of the disgraceful proclamation which he had caused to be distributed among the American troops to encourage desertion. In addition to the above, they took five hundred mules, with their pack-saddles, stands of small-arms, ammunition, ammunition-boxes, and military equipage of every variety.

Soon after the capture of the Mexican camp, an officer rode up, as if for the purpose of reconnoitring, and received from the captors a volley of musketry, but escaped unhurt. He returned again soon after, and was again fired on and escaped. After receiving a third fire, he came dashing back, followed by a company of lancers, who prepared to charge with headlong impetuosity. The regiment, however, steadily delivered its fire, emptying a few of the Mexican saddles, and then fell back within the chaparral. Lieutenant Cochrane, who kept his ground fearlessly, defended himself with his sword, but was borne down by the charge, and fell dead, having received seven lance-points in his breast. This was the last success of the enemy.

The intrenchments, artillery, and camp of the Mexicans, were now in possession of the Americans; yet the enemy for a time bore up against his losses with fortitude, and disputed the advance of his victorious foe by an obstinate resistance. But American valour and discipline at length were triumphant. The Tampico battalion, that, with the pride of veterans victorious in many a bloody fight, had struggled to roll back the tide of battle, was almost annihilated. Its proud tricolour, that had been rent in the iron storm of our artillery on the plains of Palo Alto, was the last Mexican flag that waved upon the field; and its stand-bearer, indignantly spurning its surrender, tore it from the flagstaff, and, concealing it about his person, attempted to escape in the general rout that had now taken place; but he was ridden down by our dragoons, and captured with his precious burden. The flag of the "Batallon Guarda Costa de Tampico" now hangs among the trophies of the American Capitol.

Just before the enemy's last struggle, the two batteries, which could not operate on account of the close contest that had been raging, were ordered across the ravine. When the rout became general, Duncan's battery, and fresh infantry, brought up for the pursuit, thundered in the rear of the panic-stricken enemy as they fled, increasing their confusion, and thinning their ranks with the iron hail poured upon their columns in full retreat.

The overthrow and rout of the enemy were complete. In the panic of uncontrollable fear, horsemen rode down the infantry before them, and all, in haste to escape from the Americans in pursuit, rushed tumultuously down to the river-side, and found, amid its boiling waves, the death they were striving to avoid from behind. At the crossings of the Rio Grande, infantry and cavalry sprang into the flats, till they sank beneath the weight of the multitude upon them. To stop this headlong rush to destruction, Father Leary, a venerable priest, in his sacred robes, with crucifix in hand, stood before them and exhorted them to patience. He succeeded for a moment in his efforts, but a troop of horse came spurring down the bank, and in an instant priest and soldiers were struggling with the waters, and perished in the stream. Many of these bodies were thrown ashore afterwards, and hung suspended among the branches of the trees by the river-side, as the Rio Grande fell. That of the priest mentioned above was found near the fort, his canonicals still upon him, and the emblem of salvation grasped tightly in his hand.

During the night, Matamoros was a scene of confusion and consternation. The inhabitants had been assured of certain victory, and preparations had been made for a festival, in honour of the occasion. Ball-rooms were decorated and hung with garlands, and music and beauty waited to welcome back the conquerors. But when the sad reverse was learned, — when the terror-stricken troops entered the city, and the groans and shrieks of the wounded were heard, as they were borne in sacks through the streets, the women rushed to the rooms, tore down and stamped upon the festal wreaths and decorations, and testified their sorrow by cries of passionate despair. The soldiery, lawless and reckless, roamed about the streets committing disorders of every kind, while the inhabitants shut themselves up in their homes in fearful apprehension, or, gathering up their goods, fled to the country, or were engaged in lamenting friends that were dead, or tending upon those that were wounded.

Ker's squadron of dragoons, the artillery battalion, under Colonel Childs, and the 3d infantry, pursued the fleeing enemy

21

to the Rio Grande, and bivouacked on its banks. May's squadron having followed also to the river, returned again to the battle-ground, and rested with the main army.

In the evening after the battle, the following brief despatch was prepared by the commanding-general. It was followed by a more detailed report on the 17th.

> " HEAD-QUARTERS, ARMY OF OCCUPATION,
> Camp at Resaca de la Palma, 3 miles from Matamoros,
> 10 o'clock P. M., May 9, 1846.

" SIR: I have the honour to report that I marched with the main body of the army at two o'clock to-day, having previously thrown forward a body of light infantry into the forest which covers the Matamoros road. When near the spot where I am now encamped, my advance discovered that a ravine crossing the road had been occupied by the enemy with artillery. I immediately ordered a battery of field-artillery to sweep the position, flanking and sustaining it by the 3d, 4th, and 5th regiments, deployed as skirmishers to the right and left. A heavy fire of artillery and of musketry was kept up for some time, until finally the enemy's batteries were carried in succession by a squadron of dragoons and the regiments of infantry that were on the ground. He was soon driven from his position, and pursued by a squadron of dragoons, battalion of artillery, 3d infantry, and a light battery, to the river. Our victory has been complete. Eight pieces of artillery, with a great quantity of ammunition, three standards, and some one hundred prisoners have been taken; among the latter, General La Vega, and several other officers. One general is understood to have been killed. The enemy has recrossed the river, and I am sure will not again molest us on this bank.

" The loss of the enemy in killed has been most severe. Our own has been very heavy, and I deeply regret to report that Lieutenant Inge, 2d dragoons, Lieutenant Cochrane, 4th infantry, and Lieutenant Chadbourne, 8th infantry, were killed on the field. Lieutenant-Colonel Payne, 4th artillery; Lieutenant-Colonel McIntosh, Lieutenant Dobbins, 3d infantry; Captain Hooe, and Lieutenant Fowler, 5th infantry; and Captain Montgomery, Lieutenants Gates, Selden, McClay, Burbank, and Jordan, 8th infantry, were wounded. The extent of our loss in killed and wounded is not yet ascertained, and is reserved for a more detailed report.

" The affair of to-day may be regarded as a proper supplement to the cannonade of yesterday; and the two taken together, exhibit the coolness and gallantry of our officers and men in the most favourable light. All have done their duty, and done it nobly. It will be my pride, in a more circumstantial report of both actions, to dwell upon particular instances of individual distinction.

" It affords me peculiar pleasure to report that the field-work opposite Matamoros has sustained itself handsomely during a cannonade and bombardment of a hundred and sixty hours. But the pleasure is alloyed with profound regret at the loss of its heroic and indomitable commander, Major Brown, who died to-day from the effect of a shell. His loss would be a severe one to the service at any time, but to the army under my orders, it is indeed irreparable. One officer and one non-commissioned officer killed, and ten men wounded, comprise all the casualties incident to this severe bombardment.

" I inadvertently omitted to mention the capture of a large number of pack-mules left in the Mexican camp.

" I am, sir, very respectfully, your obedient servant,

Z. TAYLOR,

Brevet Brig. Gen. U. S. A., commanding.

The Adjutant-General of the Army, Washington, D. C."

The day after the battle of Resaca de la Palma, was devoted to the burial of the slain; in which sad duty the heart of many a brave soldier sank within him, that the day before had rushed upon the bayonet or lance-point, or braved death at the cannon's mouth.   Their honoured remains were laid at length in their resting-places, beneath the turf on which they fought and fell, and the rolling volleys of musketry fired, that were the last sad tribute to the dead from those who had shared with them the trials and the triumphs of a soldier's life.

Nor did friends only share in this sacred duty, at the hands of the conqueror.   With a generosity and manliness of soul equal to the stern bravery of his spirit in battle, General Taylor paid the same scrupulous regard to the dead and wounded Mexicans.   Not being able to attend properly to all, he sent over to Matamoros for Mexican surgeons, to assist in taking care of their wounded left on the field, and for men to assist in burying the dead.

On the morning of the 11th, agreeably to the request of General Arista, an exchange of prisoners took place, and Captains Thornton and Hardee, and Lieutenant Kane, with the gallant little band captured by General Torrejon, were marched on foot to the battle-field, and there exchanged for an equal number of officers and men captured in the action of the 9th.   As there was an excess of Mexican prisoners, they were delivered to their countrymen, a receipt being taken for their number, to be held against future chances of capture.   General Vega was offered his parole, but declined the acceptance, as he knew his government would force him to bear arms, notwithstanding his pledge to the contrary.

After this General Taylor set out for Point Isabel, to confer with Commodore Conner respecting the reduction of Matamoros, Barita, and Camargo; while the army, under Colonel Twiggs, left the battle-ground, and took up its former position on the left of the Rio Bravo.   Before General Taylor departed he published the following order, in acknowledgment of the gallantry and good conduct of the troops:—

HEAD-QUARTERS, ARMY OF OCCUPATION,
Resaca de la Palma, May 11, 1846.

" The commanding-general congratulates the army under his command upon the signal success which has crowned its recent operations against the enemy. The coolness and steadiness of the troops during the action of the 8th, and the brilliant impetuosity with which the enemy's position and artillery were carried on the 9th, have displayed the best qualities of the American soldier. To every officer and soldier of his command, the general returns his thanks for the noble manner in which they have sustained the honour of the service and of the country. While the main body of the army has been thus actively employed, the garrison left opposite Matamoros has rendered no less distinguished service, by sustaining a severe cannonade and bombardment for many successive days. The army and the country, while justly rejoicing in this triumph of our arms, will deplore the loss of many brave officers and men who fell gallantly in the hour of combat.

" It being necessary for the commanding-general to visit Point Isabel on public business, Colonel Twiggs will assume command of the corps of the army near Matamoros, including the garrison of the field-work. He will occupy the former lines of the army, making such dispositions for defence and for the comfort of his command as he may deem advisable. He will hold himself strictly on the defensive until the return of the commanding-general.

" By order of Brigadier-General Taylor.
W. W. J. BLISS, *Act. Adj.-General.*"

General Parrode, of the department of Tamaulipas, after the actions of the 8th and 9th of May, published a manifesto to the army under his command, which is in striking contrast with the congratulatory orders of the American general to his victorious troops. It breathes a spirit of patriotism and bravery, which is honourable to a manly mind. If such sentiments had inspired the Mexicans generally, they would have been invincible, to any foe.

The Commander-in-chief of the Department of Tamaulipas to the troops under his command.

" FELLOW-CITIZENS : The afternoon of the 8th of this month our brothers of Matamoros have fought with intrepidity and enthusiasm in the Fanques del Raminero. On the 9th they charged with the same ardour. But fate has not crowned our efforts. The enemy passed from the fort, favoured by the dense smoke of a wood on fire, which protected them from our shot. Thus have our enemies escaped!

" Soldiers! another time we shall conquer. Such is the fate of war, a defeat to-day and glory to-morrow; that glory which shall be ours at the end of this holy struggle. The God of battles is trying our valour, but he has not abandoned us. We know how to conquer, and we know how to suffer.

" Soldiers! the lamentation of the soldier for the companion who dies on the field of battle ought to be a shot well-aimed at the enemy. Those are the tears which our brothers require of our love. Their tomb must be raised in the American camp. The corpses of the Yankees ought to form their mausoleums.

" Soldiers! if we have lost some of our brothers, the glory will be greater, there will be fewer conquerors; it is not the number which gives victory. There were but three hundred Spartans, and the powerful Xerxes did not cross the Thermopylæ. The celebrated army of the great Napoleon perished in Spain at the hands of a defenceless people, but they were free and intrepid, and were fighting for their liberty.

"Fellow-soldiers! shall we do less than they did? We are fighting for our liberty, our religion, our country, our cradles, our graves. Let him who does not wish to die a traitor, him who wishes to deserve the tears of his children, let him take breath and sustain his courage. He must not faint, he must not fear, but what have we to fear? The heart tells us that in it we shall find all that is requisite; and our hearts we will oppose to the enemy.

"Soldiers! vengeance for our brothers! glory for our children! honour for our country!

"We defend those cherished feelings. Do not fear. I swear to you that if the day be a laborious one, our glory will be sweeter; but glory we will have, and your general and companion will attain it with your loyalty and valour.

ANASTASIO PARRODE.

Tampico, May 13th, 1846."

CHAPTER X.

WHILE at Point Isabel, General Taylor published an order, in which he suitably recognised the merit of Major Munroe, who commanded at Point Isabel, and all the officers and men under his command, for the energy and activity which they had displayed in fortifying the place. In this praise Commodore Conner also participated. While cruising off the harbour of Vera Cruz, he had heard of the preparations of the Mexicans, at Matamoros, to attack the American army, and with great promptitude had sailed for Point Isabel, to render any assistance in his power. The five hundred marines, whom he caused to land and aid the garrison, contributed much towards putting it in a proper state of defence.

Having made his arrangements with Commodore Conner for a combined movement up the river, General Taylor set out for Point Isabel on the morning of the 13th; but on his way thither he was met by a courier, with intelligence that the enemy was receiving reinforcements, and was fortifying Barita and other points near the mouth of the river. In consequence of this, the general returned to the Point, and found that a small body of regulars, and some volunteer troops from Alabama and Louisiana, had just arrived. The volunteers were in prompt answer to his late call for additional troops.

General Taylor promptly organized a command, under Colonel Wilson, for the reduction of Barita, consisting of three hundred regulars, and three hundred and fifty volunteers. Of the latter, two companies were from Louisiana, under Captains Stockton and Tobin, and one company from Alabama, under General Desha. At one o'clock in the afternoon of the 15th, the command took up its line of march from the Brazos, while three steamers ascended the river, to transport the troops at the proper place. Commodore Conner ordered, at the same time, a part of the fleet to appear off the mouth of the river, to co-operate with them. Colonel Wilson proceeded up the river towards Barita, in momentary expectation of an attack from the cavalry, who were reported to be in the vicinity, and took possession of the town without any resistance. The inhabitants fled on his approach, without firing a gun. He immediately issued a manifesto, in which he invited them to return to their dwellings, and assured them of the peaceable enjoyment of all their civil and religious rights.

On the 14th of May, General Taylor left Point Isabel, with six hundred men, a train of artillery, and two hundred and fifty wagons, loaded with stores, and reached Fort Brown on the evening of the same day. He determined to attack Matamoros the next day, if possible. It required, however, considerable time and effort to make preparations for transporting the troops across the river, and to mount the two 16-inch mortars destined to throw shell into the city, should it not be surrendered. On the morning of the 17th, everything was ready; and it was arranged that, while General Taylor moved upon Matamoros, Colonel Wilson, at the same time, should advance from Barita. The

22

delay of General Taylor in following up the advantages of the
battles of the 8th and 9th of May, was owing to the neglect of
the War Department, to furnish him a ponton train, and heavy
mortars, as requested in his letters of the former year. The following letter presents a detailed account of the occupation of
Matamoros by the American troops:—

> "HEAD-QUARTERS, ARMY OF OCCUPATION,
> City of Matamoros, May 18, 1846.

"SIR: I have the honour to report that my very limited means
of crossing rivers prevented a complete prosecution of the victory
of the 9th instant. A ponton train, the necessity of which I
exhibited to the department last year, would have enabled the
army to have crossed on the evening of the battle, take this city,
with all the artillery and stores of the enemy, and a great number
of prisoners. In short, to destroy entirely the Mexican army.
But I was compelled to await the arrival of heavy mortars, with
which to menace the town from the left bank, and also the accu-
mulation of small boats. In the mean time, the enemy had
somewhat recovered from the confusion of his flight, and ought
still, with three thousand men left him, to have made a respectable defence. I made every preparation to cross the river above
the town, while Lieutenant-Colonel Wilson made a diversion on
the side of Barita, and the order of march was given out for one
o'clock yesterday, from the camp near Fort Brown, when I was
waited upon by General Reguena, empowered by General Arista,
commanding-in-chief the Mexican forces, to treat for an armistice
until the government should finally settle the question. I replied
to this, that an armistice was out of the question; that a month
since I had proposed one to General Ampudia, which was
declined; that circumstances were now changed; that I was
receiving large reinforcements, and could not now suspend operations which I had not invited or provoked; that the possession
of Matamoros was a *sine qua non;* that our troops would occupy

the town; but that General Arista might withdraw his forces, leaving the public property of every description.

"An answer to the above was promised in the afternoon, but none came; and I repaired at sundown to join the army, already in position at a crossing some two miles above the town. Very early this morning the bank was occupied by two 18-pounders, and three batteries of field-artillery, and the crossing commenced : the light companies of all the battalions were first thrown over, followed by the volunteer and regular cavalry. No resistance was made, and I was soon informed from various quarters that Arista had abandoned the town, with all his troops, the evening before, leaving only the sick and wounded. I immediately despatched a staff-officer to the prefect to demand a surrender; and, in the mean time, a commission was sent by the prefect to confer with me on the same point. I gave assurance that the civil rights of the citizens would be respected, and our troops at once dropped down opposite the town, and crossed at the 'Upper Ferry,' the American flag being displayed at Fort Paredes, a Mexican redoubt near the crossing. The different corps now encamped in the outskirts of the city. To-morrow I shall make suitable arrangements for the occupation of the town, and for taking possession of the public property. More than three hundred of the enemy's wounded have been left in the hospitals. Arista is in full retreat towards Monterey, with the fragments of his army.

"I deeply regret to report that Lieutenant George Stevens, a very promising young officer, of the 2d dragoons, was accidentally drowned this morning while attempting to swim the river with his squadron.

"I am, sir, very respectfully, your obedient servant,

Z. TAYLOR,

Brevet Brig. Gen. U. S. A., commanding.

The Adjutant-General of the Army, Washington, D. C."

The proposition of Arista for an armistice, was a dishonourable artifice to gain time, that he might be enabled to withdraw or destroy the public and military stores of the city. At the very moment he solicited it, his troops were busily engaged in burying artillery or throwing it into wells, and in destroying or concealing arms and ammunition.

After taking possession of the city, General Taylor, with great humanity and courtesy, adopted efficient means for the protection of the persons and property of the citizens.

A single guard was allowed in the city, the rest of the troops were distributed in the suburbs and vicinity. Colonel Twiggs was appointed governor of the city.

Arista left Matamoros on the evening of the 17th, with the remnant of his army, and fled in the direction of Camargo. He continued his retreat into the interior, and towards the close of the month arrived at the hacienda of Coma, with the shattered columns of his troops, many having died from the privations and fatigue of forced marches, and others having deserted and formed predatory bands, that plundered their defenceless countrymen. From Coma he continued his march to Monterey. While here, he was ordered to lay down his command and repair to Mexico, to answer for the reverses of the army under his orders; but, dreading the character of Paredes, he refused to appear at the seat of government.

On the 11th of May, 1846, the President of the United States announced to Congress the commencement of hostilities between the Mexican and American armies, and used the following language:—" A war exists; and, notwithstanding all our efforts to avoid it, exists by the act of Mexico herself. We are called upon by every consideration of duty and patriotism to vindicate with decision, the honour, the rights, and the interests of our country." Immediately after, Congress passed an act recognising the existence of war, and appropriating ten millions of dollars, and empowering the President to accept the services of fifty thousand volunteers for the army. The appropriations were made with great promptness and unanimity, but that part of the preamble which declared the war to exist by the act of Mexico, met with great opposition.

The proclamation of the President was immediately issued, and, with an ardour unprecedented in military annals, volunteers rushed to the call of their country. The influx of troops, however, was so great and so rapid, that General Taylor was completely embarrassed by their arrival—for they were unaccompanied by proper supplies and adequate means of transportation. This irregularity was, in part, owing to the indiscreet zeal of General Gaines; who, in his anxiety to reinforce the Army of Occupation, had exceeded his instructions.

Owing to the perplexing circumstances in which he was placed, General Taylor was unable to follow up the advantages gained over the enemy in the late battles. This will appear more particularly by an extract from a letter to the War Department, dated June 3d:—

"I am necessarily detained at this point for want of suitable transportation to carry on offensive operations. There is not a steamboat at my command proper for the navigation of the Rio Grande; and without water transportation, I consider it useless to attempt any extensive movement. Measures have been taken to procure boats of suitable draught and description, and one or two may now be expected. In the mean time, I propose to push a battalion of infantry as far as Reynosa, and occupy that town. For any operations in the direction of Monterey, it will be necessary to establish a large depot at Camargo, which I shall lose no time in doing as soon as proper transports arrive, unless I receive counter-instructions from the Department.

"I trust the Department will see that I could not possibly have anticipated the arrival of such heavy reinforcements from

Louisiana as are now here, and on their way hither. Without large means of transportation, this force will embarrass, rather than facilitate our operations. I cannot doubt that the Department has already given instructions, based upon the change in our position since my first call for volunteers."

Although General Taylor had asked but for eight regiments of men, his army was enlarged far beyond the requisition he had made, by successive arrivals of troops, while he was unable to make any forward movement for want of all the materials necessary for an·invading army. With the straight-forward policy which has always characterized his conduct, he addressed a letter to the adjutant-general of the army on the 10th of June, in which he set forth the situation in which he was placed, in plain and explicit terms.

" I beg leave earnestly to invite the attention of the Department to the following points :—

" First. The great influx of volunteers at Point Isabel. Five regiments certainly from Louisiana, numbering, say 3600 men; two regiments or battalions from Louisville and St. Louis, numbering, say 1200 more; several companies from Alabama, and I know not how many from Texas; the latter now beginning to arrive. The volunteer troops, now under my orders, amount to nearly 6000 men. How far they may be increased without previous notification to me, it is impossible to tell.

" Secondly. The entire want of the proper kind of transportation to push my operations up the river. The boats on which I depended for this service were found to be nearly destroyed by worms, and entirely unfit for the navigation of the river. At my instance, Major Thomas, on the 18th of May, required from Lieutenant-Colonel Hunt a boat of the proper description, and followed it up in a few days by a requisition for another. At the last dates from New Orleans no boat had been procured. Captain Sanders, of the engineers, was despatched by me to New Orleans, to assist in procuring suitable boats, but I have yet received no report from him.

" As I have previously reported, my operations are completely paralyzed by the want of suitable steamboats to navigate the Rio Grande. Since the 18th of May, the army has lain in camp near this place, continually receiving heavy reinforcements of men, but no facility for water transport, without which, additional numbers are but an embarrassment.

" I desire to place myself right in this matter, and to let the Department see that the inactivity of the army results from no neglect of mine. I must express my astonishment that such large reinforcements have been sent forward to join the army, without being accompanied by the means of transportation, both by land and water, to render them efficient. As matters now stand, whatever may be the expectations of the Department, I cannot move from this place ; and unless Captain Sanders shall succeed in procuring boats of the proper kind, I can give no assurance in regard to future operations."

In a letter to the same, dated a week later, General Taylor, with the frankness of a soldier, unwilling to have his character misconceived, complained of the delay of the Department to provide him with the means of offensive operations, while the country was expecting him to prosecute the campaign. He uses the following plain language :—

" No steamboats have been sent out from New Orleans for the navigation of the Rio Grande, and in the absence of all information upon that point, or respecting the views of the government, I am altogether in the dark as to our future operations. I must think that orders have been given, by superior authority, to suspend the forwarding of means of transportation from New Orleans. I cannot otherwise account for the extraordinary delay shown by the Quartermaster's Department in that city. Even the mails, containing probably important despatches from the government, are not expedited.

"Volunteer regiments have arrived from Louisville and St. Louis, making, with those from Louisiana, eight strong and organized battalions—mustering over 5000 men.

"In addition, we have seven companies of Alabama volunteers, and twelve or fifteen companies from Texas. Others from Texas are continually arriving. A portion of these volunteers has been lying in camp at this place for nearly a month, completely paralyzed by the want of transportation. Exposed as they are in this climate to diseases of the camp, and without any prospect, so far as I can see, of being usefully employed, I must recommend that they be allowed to return to their homes."

Great fears had been entertained throughout the country for the safety of General Taylor and his little army, when threatened by the legions of Arista; and the brilliant victories of the 8th and 9th of May came unexpectedly, and filled the whole country with enthusiastic admiration. In almost every city, meetings were called to express the general joy, and legislative and municipal bodies vied with each other in awarding honour to the triumphant general and his troops.

The President of the United States immediately forwarded General Taylor a commission, as Major-General by brevet; and, with great cordiality, expressed the profound sense which he entertained of the meritorious services of the gallant general, and all the officers and men under his command. On the 18th of June, Congress passed an act, promoting him to the rank of a full Major-General in the army of the United States; and shortly after, the Secretary of War forwarded his commission, with remarks of a complimentary character.

About this time, general officers were appointed to command the volunteer troops. They were, William O. Butler of Kentucky, and Robert Patterson of Pennsylvania, major-generals;

MAJ. GEN. ROBERT PATTERSON.

and Gideon J. Pillow of Tennessee, Thomas L. Hamer of Ohio, John A. Quitman of Mississippi, Thomas Marshall of Kentucky, Joseph Lane of Indiana, and James Shields of Illinois, brigadier-generals. Generals Butler and Patterson were officers in the army during the last war with Great Britain, and the former was distinguished for his good conduct at the battle of New Orleans, where he was a member of General Jackson's staff.

While waiting for boats, and other things necessary to enable him to make a forward movement with the main body of the army, General Taylor had sent detachments to occupy the different towns up the Rio Grande, whose occupation was necessary to his advance upon Monterey.

On the 1st of June, the Alcalde of Reynosa, together with many of the principal citizens of the place, tired of the depredations and ill treatment of the rancheros, waited on General Taylor, asking the protection of the American flag, and tendering the surrender of the town. Accordingly, on the 5th, General Taylor despatched Lieutenant-Colonel Wilson, with the 1st infantry, a section of Bragg's battery, under Lieutenant Thomas, and Price's Texan rangers, to take possession of the place and hold it. After a fatiguing march of four days and a half, the colonel reached Reynosa with his command, and took undisputed possession. He was ordered by the commanding-general to throw up intrenchments, and fortify the place; but he occupied with his troops the plaza, which was sufficiently protected by the heavy stone buildings that surrounded it, without additional defences.

Having determined to make Camargo his principal depot and the base of his future operations, General Taylor ordered Captain Miles, of the 7th infantry, to capture the town from the enemy. It was held at that time by about seven hundred rancheros, under General Canales. The captain's orders were, on reaching Reynosa to take two pieces of Bragg's battery, commanded by Lieu-

23

tenant Thomas, and Captain McCullough's company of Texan rangers. The latter, with three companies of the 7th infantry, were to march by land, under Captain Holmes; Captain Miles, with the other three companies, was to ascend the river in steamers. This expedition was considered an honourable testimonial to the bravery of the defenders of Fort Brown.

The progress of the boats was slow, on account of the flood; and one, with Captain Ross and company, was left behind. The other, with Captain Miles and the other two companies, continued on. About dusk, while moving on in utter ignorance of the bearings of the river, an American, named Davis, was discovered lurking in the swamp to escape from Canales, from whom they learned that the boat was just below the mouth of the river San Juan, and within two miles of Camargo. Their informant also stated, that Canales was then in town with about two hundred men, and intended fighting, if the citizens would permit him.

On approaching the town, Captain Miles sent that night to the Alcalde, General Taylor's proclamation, and his own summons for the surrender of the town. He gave notice, that he would take possession at nine o'clock the next morning. About midnight the Alcalde returned answer, that the town would be given up as demanded. The entire force under Captain Miles, officers and men, did not exceed eighty-five; yet with these he boldly advanced and took formal possession, at nine o'clock on the 11th of July. As the troops entered the town, Canales with his cavalry scampered out towards the west. This small force held the town until the morning of the 12th, when Captain Holmes arrived with his command, and on the evening of the same day, Captain Ross with his company. The whole then took possession of the grand plaza, and held the place. Soon after the planting of the American standard at this place, steamboats arrived daily, freighted with troops and government stores, and the river-banks were lined with tiers of barrels, boxes, and bales.

MAJ. GEN. WILLIAM C. BUTLER.

On the last day of July, Captain Vinton took undisputed possession of Mier, with a company of the 3d artillery, and a small party of Texan rangers, and stacked his arms in the plaza.

After the capture of Matamoros, the steady influx of volunteers from the United States, increased the strength of the army to over nine thousand men. On the 5th of August, General Taylor, having completed all his arrangements for a forward movement, left Matamoros for Camargo, which had been occupied as a main depot for provisions. On the 18th of the same month, the army was organized in two divisions.

The First Divison, under Brigadier-General Twiggs, consisted of four companies of the 2d dragoons, Lieutenant-Colonel May, and Captain Ridgely's battery; Captain Bragg's battery, 3d infantry, Major Lear, and 4th infantry, Major Allen, forming the Third Brigade of regulars, and commanded by Lieutenant-Colonel Garland; and the 1st infantry, Major Abercrombie, and the Baltimore and Washington battalion, Lieutenant-Colonel Watson, forming the Fourth Brigade, commanded by Lieutenant-Colonel Wilson. This division numbered two thousand and eighty men.

The Second Division, under General Worth, consisted of Lieutenant-Colonel Duncan's battery, the artillery battalion, Lieutenant-Colonel Childs, and 8th infantry, Captain Scrivner, forming the First Brigade, commanded by Lieutenant-Colonel Staniford; and Lieutenant Mackall's battery, 5th infantry, Major M. Scott, 7th infantry, Captain Miles, and Captain Blanchard's company of Louisiana volunteers, forming the Second Brigade, commanded by Colonel P. F. Smith, of the mounted riflemen. The whole column amounted to seventeen hundred and eighty men.

On the arrival of the volunteers, a third division was organized, under the command of Major-General Butler, consisting of the 1st Kentucky regiment, Colonel Ormsby, and 1st Ohio regiment, Colonel Mitchell, forming the first brigade, commanded by

General Hamer; and the 1st Tennessee regiment, Colonel Campbell, and Mississippi regiment, Colonel Davis, forming the Second Brigade, commanded by General Quitman. The sum total of this division was two thousand eight hundred and ten men.

The Texas Division, which arrived during the march upon Monterey, consisted of the 1st and 2d regiments of mounted volunteers, under Colonels Hays and Woods. It was commanded by Governor T. Pinckney Henderson, with the rank of major-general, and was detached, as occasion required, to co-operate with the other divisions.

The total number of effectives destined for this particular service, was, therefore, six thousand six hundred and seventy men. Besides these, a garrison of two thousand men was established at Camargo, for the protection of that important point, and small detachments at points of less significance. Of these six thousand six hundred men composing the divisions organized for marching upon Monterey, nearly four thousand were raw and undisciplined volunteers.

The march to Monterey was commenced on the 18th of August, by the Second Division, under General Worth, moving upon Seralvo, with the view of occupying that place as a depot of supplies.

The First Division, under Twiggs, followed on the 31st of the same month. The Volunteer Division was ordered to bring up the rear, as fast as the means of transportation arrived.

On the 6th of September General Taylor started for Seralvo, leaving Major-General Patterson in command at Camargo, with authority over all the troops between that place and the mouth of the Rio Grande,—some three thousand in number.

A considerable portion of these troops might have been added to the main column, under General Taylor, if sufficient means of transportation has been at his disposal. Before leaving Camargo, General Taylor addressed to the Adjutant-General of the army a letter, which, as it will relieve him from the imputation of any want of promptness in the prosecution of the campaign, we give entire :—

HEAD-QUARTERS, ARMY OF OCCUPATION,
Camargo, September 1, 1846.

" SIR : Before marching for the interior, I beg leave to place on record some remarks touching an important branch of the public service, the proper administration of which is indispensable to the efficiency of a campaign.   I refer to the Quartermaster's Department.   There is at this moment, when the army is about to take up a long line of march, a great deficiency of proper means of transport, and of many important supplies.

" On the 26th April, when first apprising you of the increased force called out by me, I wrote that I trusted the War Department would ' give the necessary orders to the staff department, for the supply of this large additional force ;' and when first advised of the heavy force of twelve-months' volunteers ordered hither, I could not doubt that such masses of troops would be accompanied, or, preferably, preceded by ample means of transportation, and all other supplies necessary to render them efficient. But such has not been the case.   Suitable steamboats for the Rio Grande were not procured without repeated efforts directed from this quarter, and many weeks elapsed before a lodgment could be made at this place, the river being perfectly navigable.

" After infinite delays and embarrassments, I have succeeded in bringing forward a portion of the army to this point, and now the steamers procured in Pittsburg are just arriving.   I hazard nothing in saying, that if proper foresight and energy had been displayed in sending out suitable steamers to navigate the Rio Grande, our army would long since have been in possession of Monterey.

" Again, as to land-transport.   At this moment our wagon train is considerably *less* than when we left Corpus Christi, our force being increased *five-fold*. Had we depended upon means from without, the army would not have been able to move from this place.   But fortunately the means of land-transport existed to some extent in the country, in the shape of pack-mules, and we have formed a train which will enable a small army to advance perhaps to Monterey. I wish it distinctly understood, that our ability to move is due wholly to means created here, and which could not have been reckoned upon with safety in Washington.

"I have adverted to the grand points of water and land transportation.   Of the want of minor supplies, the army has suffered more than enough.   The crying deficiency of camp equipage has been partially relieved by the issue of cotton tents, of indifferent quality.   Our cavalry has been paralyzed by the want of horseshoes, horseshoe-nails, and even common blacksmith's tools, while many smaller deficiencies are daily brought to my notice.

"I respectfully request that the above statement, which I make in justice to myself and the service, may be laid before the General-in-Chief and Secretary of War.

"I am, sir, very respectfully, your obedient servant,

Z. TAYLOR,

Maj. Gen. U. S. A., commanding.

The Adjutant-General of the Army, Washington, D. C."

On the 9th, the First and Second Divisions, now close up with each other, entered in admirable order the beautiful little town of Seralvo, accompanied by the General-in-Chief.   At this place, a number of proclamations from General Ampudia gave the first authentic information that the possession of Monterey would be disputed.   The information received by General Taylor respecting the force and disposition of the enemy, had been hitherto of the most meagre and contradictory character.   So late as the 31st of August, General Taylor, writing to the War Department, stated, from what he supposed reliable information, that there were "not more than two thousand or twenty-five hundred regular troops at Monterey, and a considerable number of the militia of the country." This force he estimates in all as not over six thousand, and expresses himself in a subsequent letter as doubtful whether Ampudia would attempt to hold the city. Most of the reports coincided, with regard to the number of troops at Monterey; while some Mexicans, professing to come direct from the city, asserted that the American army would meet with no opposition.

The tidings, however, gradually assumed a graver and less dubious character.

On the 11th of September, a spy came in from Monterey with far more accurate information, concerning the force of the garrison and the strength of the works, than any previously received. His relation seemed so extravagant, that many of the officers did not believe it at all. A map of the batteries reported by him to protect the town, was, however, made by a member of the staff of General Worth.

The next day the pioneers of the army, consolidated into one party, under the command of Captain Craig, were thrown forward on the route to Marin, for the purpose of making the road practicable for artillery and wagons. The operations of this party were covered by Captain Graham's squadron of dragoons, and McCullough's company of rangers.

On arriving the following day at Papagayo, the enemy appeared in considerable force; and Captain Craig, believing his party inadequate to venture an attack, despatched a courier to hasten on the First Division.

On the 14th, Captain McCullough, with forty rangers, set out on an expedition to the town of Ramas. After skirmishes with inconsiderable parties, he attacked two hundred of the enemy near the town, and after a spirited firing, charged them at full

speed and drove them through the town. He returned to the
advance after this engagement, and found that General Taylor
had arrived with the First Division.

The column of Major-General Butler having arrived, the First
Division was put in motion towards Marin on the 13th, closely
followed by the Second Division and that of the volunteers.

This march was excessively fatiguing both to men and horses:
the days were intensely hot, and the road both rocky and rugged.
But the character of the scenery along the line of route was
of a description well calculated to beguile even the wayworn
soldier of some portion of his weariness.

In front, and on either hand, magnificent mountains were piled
over one another in an ascending series, until the abrupt and fan-
tastic peaks of the highest range stood out clearly defined against
the deep blue of the cloudless sky. These mountains, clothed with
chaparral and delicate flowering shrubs, presented at every turn
of the road an ever-varying aspect, while valleys of extraordinary
beauty, broken by bold hills and precipitous chasms, lent a constant charm to scenes which the gallant little army, with its
artillery and wagons and mules stretched out for miles among
the undulations of the hills, imbued with spirit and with life.

But the pleasant emotions elicited by the loveliness of the
country through which the troops were passing soon changed to
feelings of a more stirring character, when the enemy's cavalry
were seen hovering in the distance, and reports of occasional
skirmishes were passed from lip to lip.

Slowly receding, however, as the American troops advanced,
tne swarthy lancers of Torrejon seldom suffered either the dragoons or rangers to come within easy fighting distance.

Near the dilapidated village of Marin the First Division
encamped on the 16th, until the rear divisions came up. The
village was found almost entirely deserted. The cavalry of the

enemy, in passing through it, had driven the poorer people into the chaparral, and carried with them the local authorities.

Here General Taylor concluded to remain two days, in order to concentrate his forces. Even this brief halt was of considerable service in resting his men from the fatigues of the march.

From the tower of the cathedral at Marin, the city of Monterey, though still twenty-five miles distant, was distinctly visible. Its picturesque appearance, embosomed among mountains, was the source of many an animated remark between the officers and their subordinates, as they surveyed, apparently so near, the point at which it was now ascertained a garrison of nine thousand men was assembled, protected by fortifications of the most formidable character.

The troops, at length, certainly expected to meet with a stubborn resistance; and this expectation was partially confirmed on the evening of the 17th, by a letter which the General-in-Chief received from the Spanish consul at Monterey, inquiring whether the property of foreigners in that city would be respected. The reply returned by General Taylor was, that if the town should be taken by assault, he could not be responsible for the consequences that might ensue.

On the morning of the 18th, the First Division, followed by the Second and Third, took up its line of march, and reached the town of Francisco.

At Agua Frio, eleven miles from Marin, the army was joined the same evening by a brigade of mounted Texans, under General Henderson. The well earned reputation for daring bravery which this class of soldiers had acquired, made so strong a reinforcement, when within a few hours' march of the city of Monterey, as inspiriting as it was seasonable.

At sunrise the next morning, General Taylor and his staff, accompanied by McCullough's and Gillespie's rangers, pushed

24

forward to reconnoitre the city, closely supported by Henderson's noble brigade.

The columns of Twiggs, Worth, and Butler, advancing in order of battle, followed. By nine o'clock A. M., the army had reached within three miles of the city, when the report of a cannon suddenly startled the air and echoed from mountain to mountain. This was followed by others in quick succession. It was the challenge of Ampudia. The men no longer felt weary. Inspired with new energies, and filled with the most enthusiastic ardour, they pushed rapidly forward, ready to answer at once, if need be, that daring challenge to battle, the voice of whose thunder was still reverberating among the mountains.

But General Taylor was already aware, that before the commencement of the assault a more extended knowledge of the enemy's strong points would be necessary. He saw at once that the contest, come when it might, would be fierce and sanguinary. The brief reconnoissance he had been enabled to make, showed him strong forts and batteries, surrounding a compactly built city, the thick walls of whose houses might well afford protection to a determined enemy, whose expulsion would require the utmost exercise of coolness and daring.

Quickening their pace, and shouting as they ran, the troops of the First Division soon reached the spot where the General-in-Chief, surrounded by his staff, was quietly surveying with his glass the defences of the city.

This being done, and reconnoissances ordered to commence at once, the division was countermarched until it reached the beautiful grove called Walnut Springs, where the army was encamped for the night.

These lovely and secluded woods, soon to become famous in history as the favourite camp of General Taylor, consist of a magnificent collection of pecan and live-oak trees, flourishing with the greatest luxuriance, in what must have formerly been the basin of a small oblong lake. The grounds, sloping on all sides towards the centre, are naturally beautified by numberless springs, fountains, and cascades.

The grove of San Domingo, or Walnut Springs, the pride and constant resort of the citizens of Monterey, is preserved with the most scrupulous care. It is three miles long, and about three-quarters of a mile in width. Within its sylvan recesses many a gay group had listened to the music of guitar and mandolin, and bounded through the intricate mazes of the dance with light hearts and laughing lips. Among its cool shadows, and where the silence was only broken by the lulling sounds of rivulet and waterfall, many a loving couple had given utterance, in the stately music of the Spanish tongue, to the beautiful fancies with which young passionate hearts build up the romance of the unknown future.

The scene was now changed. Guitar and mandolin had given place to the spirit-stirring sounds of trumpet-blast and drum—the neighing of war-steeds, and the clash of arms. Where the light feet of joyous dancers once bounded merrily, the heavy tramp of martial men now fell in measured stroke upon the ear; and where delighted lovers once breathed their ardent vows, the watchful sentinel now paced his solitary round. Led by a sturdy gray-haired man, quiet and unostentatious in manner, but bold in resolve, and energetic in action, the hardy warriors of the North had pitched their tents among the cool and grateful shadows of the sequestered grove, and now waited with high hopes and a quicker pulse the fierce events of that morrow which was to bring to many a hero's grave—to all, a soldier's glory.

CHAPTER XI.

MONTEREY, the capital of New Leon, is situated on the northern bank of the Arroyo Topa, in the valley of San Juan. The
Sierra Madre girdles, and in some places closely approaches it
on three sides, but receding on the North, leaves the whole extent
of the valley and its tributaries open in the direction of Marin.

The city is approached in front by the roads from Marin and
Guadalupe, and on the West through a stupendous rift of the
Sierra Madre, by the road from Saltillo.

Northward from Monterey run the roads to Monclova and Pres-
queria Grande. While on the South, across the Topa, a road
extends in the direction of Guaxuco.

West of the city, the approaches were defended by Fort Independencia, a strong work on the crest of a steep hill, and by the
Bishop's Palace, a castellated structure on the slope of the same
hill, below. South of these, on the other side of the river, was
Federacion Hill and an adjoining height, both of which were
fortified by redoubts and batteries. In front, and to the north of
the city, was the citadel, also regularly fortified.

(174)

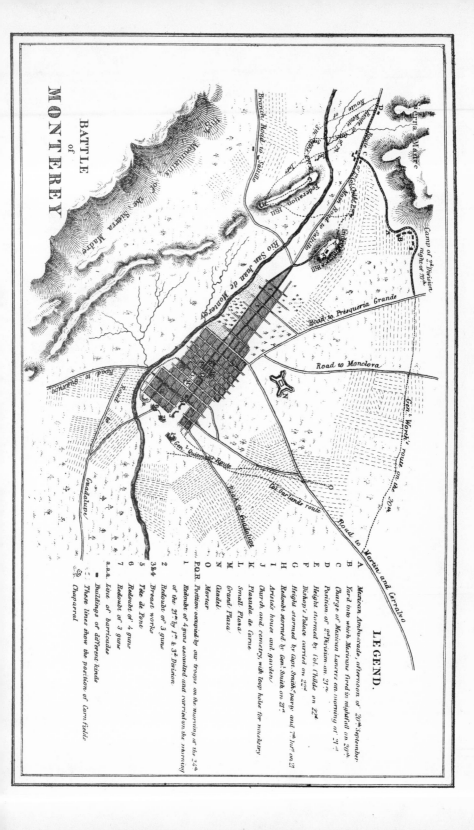

BATTLE of MONTEREY

LEGEND.

A Mexican Ambuscade, afternoon of 20th September.
B Yard into which Mexicans fired in nightfall on 20th.
C Charge of Mexican Lancers on morning of 21st.
D Position of 2d Division on 21st.
E Height stormed by 2d Division on 21st.
F Bishop's Palace carried on 22d.
G Height stormed by Col. Childs on 22d.
H Redoubt stormed by Capt. Smith's party and 7th Infty on 21st.
I Height stormed by Capt. Smith on 21st.
J Artista's house and garden.
K Church and cemetery, with loop holes for musketry.
L Plazula de Carne.
M Small Plaza.
N Grand Plaza.
O Citadel.
☉ Mortar
P.O.R. Position occupied by our troops on the morning of the 24th.
1 Redoubt of 4 guns assaulted and carried on the morning of the 21st by 1st & 3d Division.
2 Redoubt of 3 guns.
3 & 4 Breast works
5 Tête de Pont
6 Redoubt of 4 guns
7 Redoubt of 3 guns
a.a.a. Line of barricades
▪▪ Buildings of different kinds
〰 These lines show the position of Cornfields
🌿 Chaparral

In advance of the city, to the east, the works consisted of a succession of strong redoubts, mounting fourteen guns; and behind these, and within the city, were infantry breastworks supporting the redoubts. In rear of these, again, was a line of barricades, commanding all the avenues, and the terrible tête-du-pont of the Purisima bridge. Nor were these all; the houses being strongly built of stone, their flat roofs and low parapets afforded shelter to numbers of armed men, whose commanding position enabled them to direct a plunging fire upon the assailants; while the batteries, breastworks, and barricades below, were raking the streets.

The correct force of the enemy, as subsequently verified, was ten thousand men, of whom seven thousand were regular troops. Notwithstanding this large force, General Taylor felt confident of being able to carry the place by storm, by the bayonet, and by artillery.

Such were the difficulties against which the American army were preparing to contend. The reconnoissances, begun on the afternoon of the 19th, and extending to the morning of the 20th, though executed with great skill and coolness, under the repeated fire of the enemy, could obtain no information beyond what could be gathered of the works not masked by the buildings of the city. Within the city, the character of the defences remained unknown, until gradually ascertained, with great loss of life, after the assault had actually commenced.

On the morning of the 20th the troops were ordered under arms. At ten o'clock A. M., the reconnoitring parties, one of which, under Major Mansfield, had observed the western approaches, the other, under Captain Williams, the eastern, returned and reported to the General-in-Chief the result of their observations.

The possibility of reaching the western approaches of the city being ascertained by Major Mansfield, the Second Division, under Brigadier-General Worth, was directed to turn the enemy's position by making a wide sweep to the right of the Marin road; and, after joining the Saltillo road, to storm, if practicable, the detached works in that quarter.

Accordingly, at two o'clock P. M., the Second Division, reinforced by Hays's regiment of mounted Texans and McCullough's and Gillespie's companies of rangers, took up its line of march; while, in order to divert the enemy, whose attention had been already drawn to the movement, the First Division, under Brigadier-General Twiggs, and the field division of volunteers, under Major-General Butler, were ordered to form in line of battle upon the plain to the east of the city, and threaten the formidable redoubts in front. They remained in position until dark. During the afternoon, a battery was commenced for the mortar and two 24-pound howitzers, with the view of opening a fire upon the city the following morning, during the attack by General Worth's column. The infantry and the 1st Kentucky regiment covered the erection of the battery during the night. The remainder of the troops were withdrawn, after dark, to their camp at Walnut Springs. In the mean time, General Worth had succeeded, with great difficulty, in gaining the vicinity of the Saltillo road, and at six o'clock P. M. the division was halted for the night, just without range of the battery upon Independence Hill and that of the Bishop's Palace, about midway of the same slope.

Nearly opposite, on the other side of the Arroya Topa, were the forts of Federation and Soldada. These latter heights General Worth determined to carry by assault, the following morning, and despatched an express to the General-in-Chief, informing him of his intention, and requesting that a strong diversion might be made in his favour on the eastern side of the city. This had already been determined upon by General Taylor, and was promptly responded to by him.

Early on the morning of the 21st, the First and Volunteer

Divisions were ordered under arms, and, supported by the light artillery, marched towards the city. The 2d dragoons, under Lieutenant-Colonel May, and Colonel Woods's regiment of Texan cavalry, were thrown to the right, to support General Worth, and make an impression upon the upper part of the town. The loud reports of artillery and small arms to the west of the city, proved the contest in that direction already begun. The mortar, under Captain Ramsey, and the howitzers, under Captain Webster, now opened from the east upon the citadel and town, and the main battle commenced.

A portion of the First Division, under the command of Colonel Garland, and consisting of the 1st and 3d regiments of infantry and the Baltimore battalion, supported by Bragg's and Ridgely's batteries, was ordered to make a strong demonstration upon the lower part of the town, and carry, if possible, one of the redoubts. Major Mansfield and Captain Williams, topographical engineers, accompanied the column, and the most favourable points of attack were to be indicated by Major Mansfield. The column was accordingly formed, beyond reach of the guns of the enemy, when it received directions to move forward and attack battery No. 1, in advance of the north-east corner of the city. Major Mansfield, the chief engineer officer, covered by skirmishers, had already succeeded in reaching the suburbs. The remainder of the column followed, and although subjected, for a distance of five hundred yards across the plain, to the fire from battery No. 1, and a severe cross-fire from the citadel, it dashed impetuously towards the city, passed the batteries in front, and entered the streets. In an instant, without note or warning, a masked battery opened its deadly fire; and from the tops of houses, from the corners of streets, from windows, and barricades, poured down one continuous storm of bullets. Without shelter; in a narrow street; exposed to the enemy in every direction, without the possibility of effectually returning his fire — officers and men fell rapidly. Major Barbour, the first officer who fell, was killed instantly by an escopet ball passing through his heart. The assault at this point was hopeless; so the column retired into the next street, under cover of the walls and houses. Here were brought the wounded, the dying, and the dead. The men still pressed on, encouraged by Major Mansfield, who, though wounded, with indomitable courage led them forward, and pointed out places of attack.

At the head of the Baltimore battalion, here was seen the gallant Colonel Watson, cheering on his men with the courage of a veteran commander. When the stoutest hearts quailed amid the iron tempest poured upon them, dismounting from his horse he still pressed on, though followed by but few of his men. His horse was soon struck by a shot, and fell dead, and shortly after the colonel himself received a ball, which severed the jugular vein and killed him instantly.

Bragg's battery now dashed up, but could make no impression upon the barricades. The firing increased: artillery and small-arms, hurling a storm of grape, canister, and bullets, at all imaginable angles, literally swept the streets. To have remained any longer, hemmed in by batteries and barricades and superior numbers of the enemy, would have entailed a still more terrible loss of life, without any corresponding prospect of success. The command was therefore withdrawn, for the purpose of seeking a more favourable point of attack.*

During this time, Captain Backus, of the 1st infantry, with a mixed command, had possessed himself of a shed attached to a tannery. This shed faced the gorge of battery No. 1, at a distance of a hundred and twenty yards, and from behind the low parapets surmounting its roof the Americans poured a deadly and incessant fire into the battery.

Learning, however, that Colonel Garland's command, unable

* Captain Henry's Campaign Sketches.

COL. WILLIAM H. WATSON.

any longer to maintain itself within the city, was in the act of withdrawing, Captain Backus also prepared to retire. At this moment the guns of all the batteries poured out a stream of fire upon two companies of the 4th infantry, advancing across the plain to join their comrades within the city. One-third of their number fell under this galling fire, among them the gallant Lieutenants Graham, Hoskins, and Woods. Captain Backus now determined to maintain his position at all hazards, and commenced an avenging fire upon the battery No. 1, by which many of its defenders were killed, and the remainder considerably shaken.

As soon as the heavy firing within the city indicated that Colonel Garland's command had met the enemy in force, General Taylor despatched the Volunteer Division, under Major-General Butler, to his support. The general himself, with the 1st Ohio regiment, entered the town to the right, leaving Colonel Ormsby, with the Kentucky regiment, to protect the batteries.

The brigade of General Quitman, consisting of the Mississippi and Tennessee regiments, formed in front of redoubt No. 1, and marched directly upon it, almost immediately in rear of the two companies of the 4th infantry, which had been so fearfully cut up. As soon as the brigade approached near enough for a dash at the work, the two regiments, stimulated by a generous rivalry, strove with each other which should be first within the work.

The Mexicans, already staggered by the galling fire in rear, and now threatened in front by the impetuous advance of the determined brigade, precipitately retreated from the work, so that when the stormers poured like a resistless tide through the embrasures, and over the walls, but few of the enemy remained. These were quickly dispersed, leaving the battery, so long a source of terrible annoyance, with all its cannon and ammunition, in the hands of the daring victors.

25

The Mississippians entered in front, Lieut. Colonel McClung being the first to mount the parapet. He fell wounded immediately after; and, simultaneously with his fall, the Tennessee regiment carried the left, and flung their colours to the breeze.

The cannon of battery No. 1 was instantly turned upon No. 2, a redoubt which, from the constant and fearful activity of its fire, had been named *El Diablo*, and loosely translated by the troops, " *The Devil's Own.*" Captain Ridgely, who in the commencement of the action had annoyed the enemy with a section of his battery, directed one of the 12's of the fort against the enemy with great effect, until the ammunition gave out. After that he advanced against the enemy's breastworks with his own battery, but unable to accomplish anything, returned again to the work taken from the enemy.

While this heroic achievement was in the act of accomplishment, Butler entered the city to the right. Coming up shortly after with the shattered remains of Garland's noble column, General Butler was advised by Major Mansfield of the impracticability of attempting an assault in that direction. The two commands accordingly fell back, but they had scarcely reached the plain when the General-in-Chief, having learned the fall of the first battery, ordered the First Division immediately to return and hold possession of the captured work, while General Butler, with the Ohio regiment, marching to the left, should enter the city in the direction of El Diablo, and attempt to carry it by storm.

The regiment accordingly advanced across the plain, and soon came under a galling fire from El Diablo, and from two batteries on the right. On approaching nearer, a terrible fire of musketry was opened upon it from troops in rear of the redoubt, and so sheltered as to be perfectly secure from attack. At this juncture, General Butler and Colonel Mitchell both fell severely wounded; and, as the redoubt was found to be protected in front by a deep ditch, and in rear by masses of infantry, while its flank was defended by a high stone wall, the column was reluctantly ordered to fall back. No sooner was this movement observed than the Mexican cavalry, hovering under the guns of the citadel, made a sudden dash at the regiment. The charge was successfully repulsed. The lancers, however, soon returned, strongly reinforced, when Bragg's battery hastened up to the support of the regiment, and by a series of rapid discharges, which did great execution, forced the enemy to retreat in disorder.

During these operations on the left, Colonel Garland, with parts of the 1st, 3d, and 4th regiments, and of the Baltimore battalion, while remaining under cover of the captured battery, was ordered again into the city, for the purpose of carrying, if possible, a battery supposed to be but a few streets beyond. No sooner had the column left its shelter, than the terrible fire of artillery and small-arms recommenced. Covering themselves as much as possible, the men advanced from street to street steadily and in good order.

After moving cautiously along for some distance, and crossing exposed points whenever the enemy had momentarily exhausted his fire, the column suddenly found itself confronted by the *tête-du-pont* of Puente de Purisima. An awful fire now burst upon them, and after attempting to turn the work by breaking through the walls of houses, and crossing gardens and yards, they found their progress arrested by the impassable character of the stream, the opposite bank of which was lined with masses of the enemy, whose force at the bridge was at least a thousand strong. The attacking column, amounting to only a hundred and fifty men, after forcing its way thus far, finding every street barricaded, and incessant firing still kept up from every point that offered cover to an enemy, abandoned all further effort to proceed, and once more fell back to the captured battery, with the loss of many of its bravest officers and men.

This closed the engagement on the 21st. The day was now fast drawing to a close; the First Division, reinforced by one battalion of the 1st Kentucky regiment, was ordered to hold possession of the battery during the night, while the remainder of the troops, weary and dispirited, returned to the camp at Walnut Springs.

On the western side of the city, the column under General Worth had been more fortunate. Early on the morning of the 21st, the column recommenced its march for the Saltillo road. At six o'clock A. M., the advance consisted of Hays's regiment of Texans and the light companies of the First Brigade, under Captain C. F. Smith. These, while sweeping round the base of the mountain near the hacienda of San Jeronimo, came suddenly upon a strong force of cavalry and infantry, supported by a second body of cavalry in the cornfields beyond. The two foremost companies of rangers, under McCullough and Acklen, immediately dismounted and threw themselves under cover of a fence to the left of the road. The lancers now dashed forward with the utmost impetuosity, the daring gallantry of their colonel rendering him conspicuous above all others. As they swept past, the rifles of the Texans and a fire of musketry from the skirmishers under Smith and Scott, told with murderous effect upon their ranks, while two companies of the 8th regiment, and a part of the mounted rangers, under Captain Walker, dashed in amongst them and engaged them hand to hand. Finding their comrades thus severely handled, the lancers in reserve now galloped rapidly up to their support. In one minute Duncan and McCall's batteries were unlimbered, and poured a destructive fire upon the enemy over the heads of our own troops. Thus assailed in front by infantry and cavalry, on their flank by the terrible fire of skirmishers and rangers, and in rear by Duncan's and McCall's artillery, the lancers faltered, and within fifteen minutes their imposing array was broken into fragments, and fell back to the

Saltillo road, with the loss of one hundred men killed and wounded; among the former of whom was their brave colonel, Don Juan N. Najera, whose heroic conduct throughout the whole of the conflict won the unqualified admiration of all who witnessed it.

The fugitives were promptly pursued, and the column moving forward under the fire of the guns from Federacion and Soldada, secured the gorge where all the *debouches* from Monterey unite, and thus cut off not only the retreating cavalry, but all other reinforcements from entering the city in that direction.*

General Worth now turned his attention to the capture of Forts Federacion and Soldada, situated on twin heights to the south of the Topa. The occupation of these was necessary, ultimately, as commanding the city, and immediately, as restoring the communication with head-quarters, which had been broken by sending troops to occupy the Saltillo road. By noon his plans were arranged. It was decided that the battery on Federacion Hill should be the first attacked. A storming-party was accordingly organized, under Captain C. F. Smith. It consisted of three hundred men, one half regulars, the other half Texans, and was ordered to cross the Arroyo Topa at a point beyond the reach of the enemy's guns, and commence the assault immediately. Shortly afterwards, Captain Miles, with the 7th infantry, was ordered to support the stormers. This reinforcement moved in a direct line, crossed the Topa under the fire of the enemy, and finding the forces of the enemy largely increasing, Brigadier-General Smith, with the 5th regiment and Blanchard's Louisianians, was also ordered to cross the river, co-operate with, and assume command of the storming columns.

Discovering on his approach the practicability of carrying the Soldada simultaneously with Fort Federacion, Smith moved

* Worth's Official Report.

with the 5th and 7th regiments and Blanchard's company, obliquely up the hill in the direction of the former work.

During this movement the stormers, under Captain C. F. Smith, clambered up the height, and under a severe fire of artillery and musketry, swarmed over the walls, drove the enemy from the work with rifle and bayonet, turned the gun upon the opposite fort, and then leaving a small detachment to hold possession, dashed over the hill to the support of their comrades, now nearly up with Fort Soldada.

As soon as this heroic rivalry was observed, the 5th and 7th pressed on with accelerated speed, while side by side the Louisianians and rangers also contested the honour of first entering the work.

Under a fire of grape and heavy discharges of small-arms, the mixed commands struggled up the ascent with unwavering gallantry, driving in the enemy's skirmishers before them. In the course of a few minutes the fort was abandoned by its dismayed garrison, and the colours of the United States planted in triumph upon the walls. Captain Gillespie, of the Texan mounted volunteers, was the first to mount the parapet and enter the work. The forts were now garrisoned by detachments of the victors, Captain Smith retaining possession of the first, Captain Miles of the last fort taken; and this being done, the gallant division on both sides of the Arroyo Topa having tasted no food for thirty-six hours, was rested and refreshed preparatory to assaulting the opposite heights on the following morning.

The enemy, from the Bishop's Palace, commenced a fire of round-shot and shell upon the 7th infantry in Fort Soldada, which was returned by the captured gun, under Lieutenant Dana.

Independence Hill is seven or eight hundred feet high, and almost inaccessible on account of its perpendicularity, its rocky surface, and the thick and tangled bushes that cover it. With the Bishop's Palace, which it commands and overlooks, distant about three hundred and fifty yards to the south-east, it may be regarded as the key to Monterey on the western side. It was defended by artillery, and in anticipation of an attack, strengthened by a heavy detachment thrown forward from the Bishop's Palace.

Early on the morning of the 22d, the column was appointed to storm the Forts of Independencia and the Bishop's Palace. It consisted of three companies of the 8th infantry, three companies of the 3d and 4th artillery, and two hundred dismounted Texans, under Hays and Walker; all under the command of Lieutenant-Colonel Childs. This column moved at three o'clock A. M., recrossed the river, and, favoured by mist and darkness, clambered up the steep ascent, unobserved by the enemy, until it gained within a hundred yards of the crest. Here the advanced pickets were first discovered, and a skirmishing fire commenced; but so great was the panic, that when the regulars and Texans approached within a few yards of the crest of the hill, and pouring in a heavy fire upon the startled enemy, dashed forward with rifles and bayonets, the work was precipitately abandoned. During the ascent of the hill, two gallant spirits fell, Captain Gillespie and Herman S. Thomas of the rangers, the former of Texas, the latter of Harford county, Maryland. The 5th regiment, under Major Scott, and Blanchard's Louisianians now crossed the river to aid the assault of Childs upon the Bishop's Palace. A 12-pound howitzer was hauled bodily up the steep ascent of Independencia, and being placed in battery, opened upon the Palace and its outworks with decided effect. Under cover of this fire, the column moved down the hill in the direction of the enemy's last remaining defence. Here the Mexican general had concentrated a large body of troops, and rendered desperate by the loss of Independencia, he attempted a formidable sortie from the Palace, for the purpose of recovering it.

This sortie was, however, so effectually repulsed, that the troops soon gave way under the front and flank fires of the stormers, and being closely pursued, some fled past the Palace in the direction of the city, while others, seeking the protection of the works, were followed so rapidly, that fugitives and pursuers entered them together.

A brief, spirited, but unavailing resistance then ensued. In a few minutes, amidst the sharp crack of the deadly Texan rifles — the clash of swords, the dull heavy sound of clubbed muskets, mixed up with shouts and yells and imprecations — the earnest cries of supplicating men and the groans of the wounded — the Mexican flag was hauled down, and the last outwork of the enemy was forcibly wrested from him. The guns of the Palace, together with Duncan's and McCall's batteries, which came up at a gallop, were now directed upon the retreating masses of the enemy with terrible effect.

This ended the labours of the 22d.

The division was now concentrated about the Palace, and upon the morning of the 23d the assault upon the city commenced.

" Two columns of attack were organized, to move along the two principal streets in the direction of the great Plaza, composed of light troops, slightly extended, with orders to mask the men whenever practicable, avoid those points swept by the enemy's artillery, to press on to the first Plaza (Capella), get hold of the end of the streets beyond, then enter the buildings, and, by means of picks and bars, break through the longitudinal section of the walls, work from house to house, and ascending to the roofs, to place themselves upon the same, breast-high with the enemy."

Such were the graphic directions given by General Worth for the assault of the city from the west. The plan was eminently successful. By dark the men had worked their way through walls and squares, until they had reached to within one square of the Great Plaza, carried a large building commanding the principal defences of the enemy, and during the night and succeeding morning, placed two howitzers and a 6-pounder in battery upon its roof. A 10-inch mortar was also brought into the smaller square (Capella), and at sunset opened upon the main Plaza.

In the mean time, on the eastern side of the city, the severe check received on the 21st had also been amply redeemed.

During the 22d but little was attempted beyond a strong demonstration to favour the operations of General Worth; but when the morning of the 23d arrived, the successes of Worth's column offered an opportunity of renewing the assault, under advantages not heretofore enjoyed.

The enemy, too, evidently staggered by the pertinacity with which the storm was carried on, had deserted the battery of El Diablo, during the night of the 22d, and concentrated the main body of his forces nearer the heart of the city.

Immediately this was made known to the General-in-Chief, the Mississippi and Tennessee regiments were ordered to take possession of the abandoned works.

The enemy, however, holding some strong buildings close by, and a triangular work some two hundred yards off, still kept up an annoying fire through the gorge of El Diablo.

The General-in-Chief now arriving in the city, directed Quitman's brigade to move in, and force the annoying positions. It was immediately advanced, and a sharp firing once more swept the streets. Bragg's battery was also ordered up, supported by the 3d infantry. When within range of the guns of the citadel, the battery crossed the field of fire at full gallop, and escaped injury. The infantry and battery now engaged the enemy, and drove him back with repeated discharges.

While the assault was thus warmly urged by the Mississippi and Tennessee regiments, the dismounted Texans, under Henderson, entered the city, and the united commands, by breaking into houses, and crashing through walls, fought the enemy in his own manner, and in the midst of his own defences, until the defenders were forced resolutely back into the very heart of the city. This being done, the columns of Quitman and Hen-

26

derson were withdrawn to the captured works, until such time as
the General-in-Chief could concert with General Worth a combined attack upon the last remaining defences.   This attack had
been already anticipated by the latter officer ; so that by dusk of
the 23d the respective commands, moving from east and west
almost simultaneously, had each succeeded, though unknown to
each other, in reaching to within one square of the principal
Plaza.   A heavy mortar had been placed in battery, and General
Worth was ready to open upon the enemy in the morning with shell.

The next morning, while preparations were being made to
renew the attack, General Ampudia despatched a flag of truce
to General Taylor, expressing a desire to negotiate for a surrender of the city.   The assault was accordingly suspended on both
sides of the city, and commissioners having been appointed to
confer with each other, the following basis of capitulation was at
length agreed upon :—

"Terms of the Capitulation of the city of Monterey, the capital of Nuevo
   Leon, agreed upon by the undersigned commissioners, to wit: General
   Worth, of the United States Army, General Henderson, of the Texan
   volunteers, and Colonel Davis, of the Mississippi riflemen, on the part
   of Major-General Taylor, commanding-in-chief the United States forces ;
   and General Requena and General Ortego, of the Army of Mexico, and
   Senor Manuel M. Llano, Governor of Nuevo Leon, on the part of Senor
   General Don Pedro Ampudia, commanding-in-chief the Army of the
   North of Mexico.

"Art. 1. As the legitimate result of the operations before the
place, and the present position of the contending armies, it is
agreed that the city, the fortifications, cannon, the munitions of
war, and all other public property, with the under-mentioned
exceptions, be surrendered to the commanding-general of the
United States forces now at Monterey.

"Art. 2. That the Mexican forces be allowed to retain the
following arms, to wit: The commissioned officers their side-
arms ; the infantry their arms and accoutrements ; the cavalry
their arms and accoutrements ; the artillery one field-battery, not
to exceed six pieces, with twenty-one rounds of ammunition.

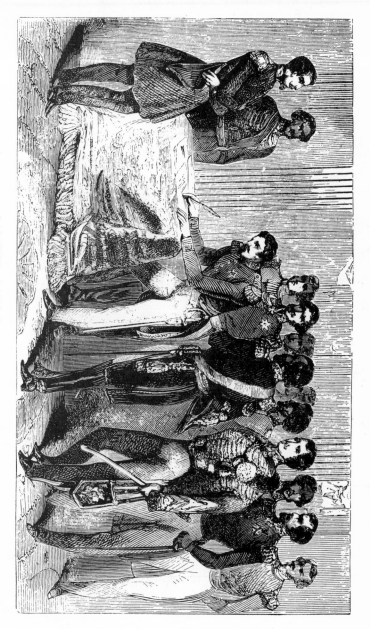

CAPITULATION OF MONTEREY.

" Art. 3. That the Mexican armed force retire within seven days from this date beyond the line formed by the pass of the Rinconada, the city of Linares, and San Fernando de Pusos.

" Art. 4. That the citadel of Monterey be evacuated by the Mexican and occupied by the American forces to-morrow morning at ten o'clock.

" Art. 5. To avoid collisions, and for mutual convenience, that the troops of the United States will not occupy the city until the Mexican forces have withdrawn, except for hospital and storage purposes.

" Art. 6. That the forces of the United States will not advance beyond the line specified in the third article before the expiration of eight weeks, or until the orders of the respective governments can be received.

" Art. 7. That the public property to be delivered shall be turned over and received by officers appointed by the commanding-generals of the two armies.

" Art. 8. That all doubts, as to the meaning of any of the preceding articles, shall be solved by an equitable construction, and on principles of liberality to the retiring army.

" Art. 9. That the Mexican flag, when struck at the citadel, may be saluted by its own battery.

W. J. WORTH, *Brig.-Gen. U. S. A.*

J. PINKNEY HENDERSON,
Major-Gen. commanding Texan volunteers.

JEFFERSON DAVIS, *Col. Mississippi Riflemen.*

J. M. ORTEGA.

T. REQUENA.

MANUEL M. LLANO.

Approved:

PEDRO AMPUDIA.

Z. TAYLOR,
Major-Gen. U. S. A. commanding.

Dated at MONTEREY, Sept. 25, 1846."

CHAPTER XII.

At ten o'clock on the 25th, pursuant to the articles of capitulation, the ceremony of the surrender took place. General Worth, who by his labours had contributed so largely to the reduction of the place, was appointed to see the execution of the stipulations. Two companies of each regiment in the second division, with a section of each battery, the whole under the immediate command of Colonel Persifer F. Smith, were appointed to take possession of the citadel. These troops were drawn up on the road leading to the citadel, the Texans on one side, and the regulars on the other, while the imposing display was graced by the presence of General Taylor and staff, and all the principal officers of the army in splendid military costume.

With a parting salute from the shrill bugle and the booming cannon, the Aztec eagle fluttered down from its airy height, while the " stars and stripes" floated upward on the gentle breeze, and unfolded from the citadel amid the strains of martial music and the

(190)

united cheers of the victorious troops. From the other eminences, in like manner, the Mexican colours disappeared, and were replaced by the national ensign of the conquerors. The Mexicans then marched out from the citadel, between the two lines of the Americans, and the latter moved into the place they had quitted. The first division of the enemy marched out of the city on the 26th, the second on the 27th, and the remainder on the 28th. General Ampudia accompanied the second division and proceeded with his troops to Saltillo. He wished to fortify the place, but since he had been unable to defend Monterey, a position having much greater advantages, the inhabitants refused their consent, whereupon he retired to San Luis Potosi, which became, shortly after, the head-quarters of the northern army. He, himself, soon became a prisoner in the castle of Perote, by order of Santa Anna, who had returned from exile, as will hereafter be related.

The terms of the capitulation, though favourable to the Mexicans, displayed not merely an exalted humanity on the part of General Taylor, but great military prudence, and sound policy. A brief consideration of the circumstances will serve to show this view of the capitulation to be correct.

Without siege-artillery, or intrenching tools, General Taylor could not have carried the citadel without great loss to his troops, who were less than one-half the forces of the enemy. If he had carried the citadel, he could not have prevented the escape of the enemy, for he had not sufficient troops to invest the city; nor had he means of transportation, so that he could have pursued him after he had compelled him to evacuate the city. If beaten, the Mexican general could still have retired with his troops, small-arms, and ammunition.

How much better and wiser was it in General Taylor, to gain, without sacrificing the lives of his troops, all the advantages which could have been ultimately obtained, with this additional circumstance in his favour, that the moral effect upon the enemy was much greater than if he had retired, as he could otherwise have done, without the consent of the Americans.

The government at Washington, however, and a small portion of the administration party, did not approve of the terms of the capitulation, and especially the armistice. Accordingly, General Taylor was instructed by the President " to give the required notice, that the armistice was to cease at once, and that each party was at liberty to resume and prosecute hostilities without restriction." The reply of the general to this order, addressed to the Adjutant-General at Washington, is so full and satisfactory upon these points, that we insert it entire :—

" CAMP NEAR MONTEREY, ⎞
        November 8, 1846. ⎠

" SIR : In reply to so much of the communication of the Secretary of War, as relates to the reasons which induced the convention resulting in the capitulation of Monterey, I have the honour to submit the following remarks.

" The convention presents two distinct points: *First*, the permission granted the Mexican army to retire with their arms, &c. *Secondly*, the temporary cessation of hostilities for the term of eight weeks. I shall remark on these in order.

" The force with which I marched on Monterey was limited, by causes beyond my control, to about six thousand men. With this force, as every military man must admit, who has seen the ground, it was entirely impossible to invest Monterey so closely as to prevent the escape of the garrison. Although the main communication with the interior was in our possession, yet one route was open to the Mexicans throughout the operations, and could not be closed, as were also other minor tracks and passes through the mountains. Had we, therefore, insisted on more rigorous terms than those granted, the result would have been the escape of the body of the Mexican force, with the destruction of its artillery and magazines, our only advantage being the capture of a few prisoners of war, at the expense of valuable lives and much damage to the city. The consideration of humanity was present to my mind during the conference which led to the convention, and outweighed, in my judgment, the doubtful advantages to be gained by a resumption of the attack upon the town. This conclusion has been fully confirmed by an inspection of the enemy's position and means, since the surrender. It was discovered that his principal magazine, containing an immense amount of powder, was in the Cathedral, completely exposed to our shells from two directions. The explosion of this mass of powder, which must have ultimately resulted from a continuance of the bombardment, would have been infinitely disastrous, involving the destruction not only of Mexican troops, but of non-combatants, and even our own people, had we pressed the attack.

"In regard to the temporary cessation of hostilities, the fact that we are not at this moment, within eleven days of the termination of the period fixed by the convention, prepared to move forward in force, is a sufficient explanation of the military reasons which dictated this suspension of arms. It paralyzed the enemy during a period when, from the want of necessary means, we could not possibly move. I desire distinctly to state, and to call the attention of the authorities to the fact, that with all diligence in breaking mules and setting up wagons, the first wagons in addition to our original train from Corpus Christi (and but one hundred and twenty-five in number), reached my head-quarters on the same day with the secretary's communication of October 13th, viz: the 2d instant. At the date of the surrender of Monterey, our force had not more than ten days' rations, and even now, with all our endeavours, we have not more than twenty-five. THE TASK OF FIGHTING AND BEATING THE ENEMY IS AMONG THE LEAST DIFFICULT THAT WE ENCOUNTER—the great question of supplies necessarily controls all the operations in a country like this.

At the date of the convention, I could not of course have foreseen that the Department would direct an important detachment from my command without consulting me, or without waiting the result of the main operation under my orders.

" I have touched the prominent military points involved in the convention of Monterey. There were other considerations which weighed with the commissioners in framing, and with myself in approving the articles of the convention. In the conference with General Ampudia, I was distinctly told by him that he had invited it to spare the further effusion of blood, and because General Santa Anna had declared himself favourable to peace. I knew that our government had made propositions to that of Mexico to negotiate, and I deemed that the change of government in that country since my instructions, fully warranted me in entertaining considerations of policy. My grand motive in moving forward with very limited supplies had been to increase the inducements of the Mexican government to negotiate for peace. Whatever may be the actual views or disposition of the Mexican rulers, or of General Santa Anna, it is not unknown to the government that I had the very best reason for believing the statement of General Ampudia to be true. It was my opinion at the time of the convention, and it has not been changed, that the liberal treatment of the Mexican army, and the suspension of arms, would exert none but a favourable influence in our behalf.

" The result of the entire operation has been to throw the Mexican army back more than three hundred miles, to the city of San Luis Potosi, and to open the country to us, as far as we choose to penetrate it, up to the same point.

" It has been my purpose in this communication, not so much to defend the convention from the censure which I deeply regret to find implied in the Secretary's letter, as to show that it was not adopted without cogent reasons, most of which occur of themselves to the minds of all who are acquainted with the condition of things here.   To that end I beg that it may be laid before the General-in-chief and Secretary of War.

"I am, sir, very respectfully, your obedient servant,

Z. TAYLOR,

Maj. Gen. U. S. A., commanding.

The Adjutant-General of the Army, Washington, D. C."

An extract from a letter of General Taylor's, of the date of November 5th, still further shows that the armistice was of no disadvantage, because being without proper transportation he was not then in a condition to move further into the enemy's country.

"In regard to the armistice, which would have expired by limitation in a few days, we lost nothing by it, as we could not move even now, had the enemy continued to occupy Saltillo; for, strange to say, the first wagon which has reached me since the declaration of war was on the 2d instant, the same day on which I received from Washington an acknowledgment of my despatch announcing the taking of Monterey; and then I received only one hundred and twenty-five, so that I have been, since May last, completely crippled, and am still so, for want of transportation. After raking and scraping the country for miles around Camargo, collecting every pack-mule and other means of transportation, I could bring here only eighty thousand rations (fifteen days' supply), with a moderate supply of ordnance, ammunition, &c., to do which, all the corps had to leave behind a portion of their camp equipage necessary for their comfort, and in some instances, among the volunteers, their personal baggage.   I moved in such a way, and with such limited means, that, had I not succeeded, I should no doubt have been severely reprimanded, if nothing worse.   I did so to sustain the administration."

We will now turn our attention for a moment to the affairs of Mexico.

In January, Paredes, by a revolution which had been jointly projected by the army and clergy, gained the executive chair on

27

the downfall of Herrera. Instead of conciliating discordant parties by moderation and gentle measures, he changed both the letter and the spirit of the constitution acknowledged by his predecessors, abridged the privileges of the people, trampled upon the press, and arrogated to himself a power nearly absolute.   In the embarrassed state of the treasury he appealed to the priesthood for alienation of a part of the church fund, which disaffected in a measure a part of that influential body from him.

The popular discontent was fomented by factious chiefs, until it broke out into open rebellion.   There was a defection, not only of military bodies, but of cities, and provinces.   Local governments were overthrown, and the central power assailed.   Vera Cruz pronounced in favour of Santa Anna on the 31st of July, and the capital, three days afterwards, followed the movement.   A provisional government was declared, with General de Salas and other military chiefs at its head, which denounced all opposition to them as traitorous, and invited the return of all political exiles, especially Santa Anna, desiring him to assume the command of all the forces raised against the army of the United States of the North.   A short conflict took place between the revolutionists and the troops of Paredes, when the latter abandoned his power and fled from the city.

Thus recalled by his countrymen, Santa Anna sailed from Cuba, and arrived at Vera Cruz on the 16th of August, passing without molestation through the United States' squadron then blockading the place.   This was done by express permission of the President of the United States, in the vain expectation that Santa Anna, so coming into power, would favour negotiations for peace.   Instead of this, however, after a triumphal entry into the city of Mexico on the 15th of September, he united opposing factions, and with singular energy and ability prepared to prosecute the war against the invaders with the utmost vigour.   So far from answering the expectations of President Polk, Santa Anna promptly replied to General Taylor, when inviting propositions for peace some time after: " You ought to discard every idea of peace while a single North American treads in arms the territory of this republic, or while hostile squadrons remain in front of her ports." With these views and feelings, Santa Anna hastened to San Luis Potosi, the head-quarters of the northern army, and on the 8th of October, commenced to supply and equip the new levies for vigorous operations against the invaders of his country. For this end he not merely exerted his talents, but contributed much of his private fortune, and succeeded in raising and organizing a large and powerful army.

While General Taylor remained at Monterey, he received from Washington a letter containing instructions to terminate the armistice, and accordingly promptly notified Santa Anna that it would cease on the 13th of November. By a previous letter from the Secretary of War, General Taylor had been informed of the plan of the government in the prosecution of the war, and that it contemplated taking " possession of the department of Tamaulipas, or some of the principal places in it," by means of a column advanced from the Rio Grande, which should have communication with the ships then in the gulf, and derive assistance from them. Tampico was particularly specified as a prominent point to be occupied by the American troops; and Major-General Patterson was named by the Secretary as the choice of the government to command the expedition, assisted by Brigadier-Generals Pillow and Shields. A simultaneous movement upon San Luis Potosi was also suggested.

In reply to the letter of the Secretary, General Taylor showed the impracticability of moving upon San Luis Potosi with the forces and means of transportation at his disposal; but advised holding Monterey, with the places already in his possession, with advances pushed forward to occupy Saltillo, and detachments at Monclova, Linares, Victoria, and Tampico. He pointed to Vera

Cruz or Alvarado as the proper base of operations against the city of Mexico, and advised the landing there of twenty-five thousand men, ten thousand to be regulars, if the government desired to strike a decisive blow at the power of Mexico.

General Taylor considered Saltillo as a necessary outpost of the main body of his army at Monterey, because it covered the great defile leading from the low country to the table-land, and controlled the fertile region around Parras, while, as the capital of Coahuila, its occupation would be important in a political point of view. Accordingly, on the 12th of November, a division of the army under General Worth, consisting of two regiments of infantry, one company of volunteers, a field-battery of eight pieces, and eight companies of artillery, marched from Monterey to Saltillo.   On the next day, General Taylor followed Worth's division, accompanied by two squadrons of dragoons.   When he passed the boundary of the state of Coahuila, on his way to Saltillo, the governor of the state, José Marie de Aguirre, sent him a written protest, in which he remonstrated against the march of the Americans, and the usurpation of the territory, " with all the outrages and damages likely to accrue to the defenceless inhabitants." Without replying to this manifesto, General Taylor proceeded on to Saltillo, which he reached on the 16th, and encamped with his dragoons a little beyond the city.   General Worth occupied the plaza.

Reconnoissances were now ordered into the interior for about twenty-five miles, and the two principal routes in this direction covered by troops.   The one towards San Luis Potosi was covered by General Worth's command, the other, towards Parras, through a fertile country, by the " Army of the Centre" under General Wool, which had arrived at Monclova on the 29th of October, and was now ordered by General Taylor to move upon Parras.   We will now bestow attention upon this division of the forces invading Mexico.

BRIG. GEN. JOHN E. WOOL

Immediately after the passage of the act of May 13th, 1846, recognising war between the republics, General Wool was ordered to muster into service the volunteers of Ohio, Illinois, Indiana, Kentucky, Tennessee, and Mississippi. After organizing and sending to the seat of war about ten thousand men to reinforce General Taylor, he was ordered with the remainder to San Antonio de Bexar, where Colonel Harney of the 2d dragoons was stationed with a small force of regular cavalry, and some companies of Texan volunteers. During the month of August all the regiments and detachments arrived at the place of rendezvous, and were employed some weeks in learning the different military evolutions before taking the field. The Central Division, under General Wool, consisted of four companies of the 2d dragoons, Colonel Harney; one company of the 4th artillery, Captain Washington, with eight pieces, two 12-pounders, and the remainder 6-pounders; battalion of 6th infantry, Major Bonneville; Colonel Yell's regiment, Arkansas mounted volunteers; 1st Illinois infantry, Colonel Hardin; 2d Illinois, Colonel Bissell; and one company of Kentucky cavalry, and one of Texan volunteers. Total strength, 2,829.

The advance of the army of the centre, under Colonel Harney, left San Antonio on the 26th of September, and was followed by the head-quarters on the 29th. Colonel Hardin, with the 1st Illinois regiment, marched on the 2d of October; and the rear, under Colonel Churchill, followed some days after, comprising the 2d Illinois, and various other detachments.

From San Antonio, their route lay westward to Presidio, where they crossed the Rio Grande, through a country diversified by prairies, sandy deserts, and forests of chaparral. From Presidio, General Wool led his army through Nava and San Fernando to Santa Rosa, taking peaceable possession of the towns upon his route. On arriving at the latter place, he found his further march upon the city of Chihuahua, his ultimate destination, prevented by the impassable peaks of the Sierra Gorda. He turned aside, therefore, to Monclova, the ancient capital of Chihuahua, from which he reported to General Taylor at Monterey, who directed him to remain where he was, until ordered otherwise. General Wool, therefore, remained at Monclova until after the occupation of Saltillo, when he moved forward to Parras, and occupied the Alameda. At both these places he and his troops were treated with great kindness by the inhabitants. Having thus disposed his troops so that in case of further operations they could be thrown upon Zacatecas, Durango, or San Luis, as occasion might require, General Taylor returned to Monterey on the 23d of November.

On the 14th of November, Tampico was taken without opposition, by a portion of the Gulf squadron, and was garrisoned by a force under General Shields, consisting of eight companies of artillery, under Lieutenant-Colonel Belton, and a regiment of Alabama volunteers. Immediately after Tampico fell into the hands of the Americans, General Taylor determined to occupy Victoria, the capital of Tamaulipas. Situated at the debouchée of a pass through the mountains, threatening the flank of the Mexican army, should it advance from San Luis Potosi, and with Soto la Marina convenient as a depot, its occupation was considered of great importance. Accordingly, General Taylor ordered General Patterson to march on Victoria, with three regiments of volunteers of his division, one of them Tennessee horse, while he himself, with the regular troops under Brigadier-General Twiggs, except those in garrison, and the regiments of General Patterson's division under General Quitman, would proceed to Montemorelos, and, after uniting with the column the 2d Tennessee regiment, under orders for that place, to effect a junction with Major-General Patterson, before Victoria.

When, in prosecution of this plan, General Taylor reached Montemorelos, a despatch arrived from General Worth, in command at Saltillo, with the intelligence, that Santa Anna was about making a rapid movement upon Saltillo, and, after carrying that position, intended to attack Wool's forces at Parras. In consequence of this news, General Taylor ordered the volunteers, under Quitman, reinforced by a field-battery, to continue their march to Victoria, while he returned with Twiggs's division to Monterey, and immediately set out for Saltillo. General Wool, in the mean time, had moved up from Parras to reinforce General Worth; and Major-General Butler, who was in command at Monterey, advised in like manner of the threatened attack, had proceeded with reinforcements to Saltillo, and assumed command of the forces. On his way to Saltillo, General Taylor learned that Wool's column had joined Worth, and that no demonstration was likely to be made by the Mexican commander; whereupon he considered Twiggs's division as unnecessary, and determined to proceed with it to Victoria, which place he reached on the 4th of January, where he was met on the same day by Major-General Patterson, with troops from Matamoros. General Quitman had reached the place six days before. Upon his approach, the enemy occupying the town with a force of fifteen hundred cavalry, fell back to Jaumaze, in the direction of the Tula Pass.

From Montemorelos, on his way to Victoria, General Taylor despatched a party of engineers, protected by May's squadron of dragoons, to reconnoitre the mountain passes from that to Labradores and Linares, and on their return, ten men of the rear-guard were cut off by the enemy.

While proceeding to Victoria, General Taylor learned the arrival of General Scott in Mexico, to assume the command of an expedition against Vera Cruz, with the view of making it the base of a new line of operations, having for their ultimate design the reduction of the Mexican capital.

General Taylor had received intimations of this design some time before, and now awaited, at Victoria, despatches from the General-in-chief in relation to it. These arrived on the 14th of January, and contained a demand for the greater part of his army, embracing nearly all his regulars, with the volunteer divisions of Generals Worth and Patterson, and the brigade of Quitman and Twiggs. The forces of the latter generals were already at Victoria ; the troops, under Worth, marched from Saltillo back to Camargo, and thence to Matamoros, and joined General Scott at the Brazos.

On parting with the troops, endeared to him by long and faithful services, the commanding-general gave expression to his feelings in the following orders :—

" It is with deep sensibility that the commanding-general finds himself separated from the troops he so long commanded. To those corps, regular and volunteer, who have shared with him the active services of the field, he feels the attachment due to such associations, while to those who are making their first campaign, he must express his regret that he cannot participate with them in its eventful scenes. To all, both officers and men, he extends his heartfelt wishes for their continued success and happiness, confident that their achievements on another theatre will redound to the credit of their country and its arms."

After thus withdrawing nearly all his forces, it was the wish of the government, in which General Scott concurred, that General Taylor should withdraw his troops from Saltillo and fall back to Monterey, but as he considered the occupation of the place important for the procuring of supplies, and essential to the due defence of the line he held, he not only continued to hold Saltillo, but advanced with his main force to Agua Nueva, eighteen miles beyond. He deemed this prudent, because the place had a large plain to drill his troops in, and held in observation the road from San Luis, and the different passes in the vicinity ; and while there, he would be in position to attack the enemy at a disadvantage after advancing over a barren waste that afforded neither water nor food of any kind.

On the 22d of January, a party of Arkansas and Kentucky cavalry, seventy in number, under Majors Borland and Gaines, was surprised and captured at the hacienda of Encarnacion, forty-eight miles from Saltillo, by the cavalry under General Minon. A party of seventeen of the Kentucky volunteers under Captain Heady, was also captured on the 27th of the same month, and the advanced pickets were frequently driven in by the enemy. These occurrences, with the frequent rumours of the march of Santa Anna against the American army, disposed General Taylor to believe an attack would soon be made. He therefore left Monterey on the 31st of January, with a reinforcement of five hundred men for General Wool's column, and proceeded to Agua Nueva, on the San Luis road, where he remained encamped until the 21st of February.

Lieutenant-Colonel May, with a strong reconnoitring party, consisting of four companies of the 1st and 2d dragoons, a section of Washington's battery under Lieutenant O'Brien, and some volunteer cavalry, making an entire force of four hundred mounted men, was sent on the 20th to Hedionda to ascertain the presence of General Minon, who had been hovering near with his cavalry for some time, and whether the enemy under Santa Anna might be advancing. At the same time, Major McCullough with a party of Texan spies was sent to Encarnacion for the same purpose.

On reaching Hedionda in the afternoon, Colonel May sent out pickets in every direction through the valley in which it was situated, to gain intelligence of the enemy, and shortly after saw at the extremity of the valley, near the hacienda of Potosi, signal fires lighted on several peaks, and clouds of dust, indicating the march of troops. These clouds of dust appeared to move around the hills in the neighbourhood of Guachuchil, whence he inferred that Minon's brigade was marching around, to gain a position between him and the main army, and thus cut him off.

28

Having to await the return of his pickets, and expecting an attack, he prepared for a defence, by placing bales of cotton at each end of the street running through the rancho.

About ten o'clock, by which time the pickets had all returned except one, a deserter from the Mexican army came to Colonel May with the intelligence that General Minon was in the neighbourhood, and that Santa Anna was at Encarnacion that morning with 30,000 men, and intended attacking General Taylor the next day at Agua Nueva. Colonel May, knowing the importance of his detachment, which contained all the regular cavalry of the army, immediately left Hedionda, and rejoined the main column under General Taylor by daybreak, having made a march of sixty miles in twenty hours. Contrary to expectation, he did not encounter General Minon on the march. Instead of intersecting the San Luis road at Encantada, as May had expected, Minon continued on to San Antonio, and through the pass of Palomas, in the rear of Saltillo.

Major McCullough with his party had proceeded to Encarnacion, and managed to gain a position where he could see the whole force of the enemy, which he estimated at upwards of twenty thousand, with a large proportion of artillery and cavalry. He returned by twelve o'clock on the 21st, and reported his observations to the commanding-general.

The position of the camp at Agua Nueva, though a good one, and possessing many advantages, could easily be turned on either flank. Because of this, and the great disparity of the Mexican and American forces, General Taylor determined to fall back about twelve miles to a place of great natural strength called Angostura, near the hacienda of Buena Vista, and particularly suited to a small army resisting the advance of superior numbers.*

" The road [from San Luis Potosi to Saltillo] at this point

---

* General Taylor's Report.

becomes a narrow defile, the valley on its right being rendered quite impracticable for artillery by a system of deep and impassable gullies, while on the left a succession of rugged ridges and precipitous ravines extends far back toward the mountain which bounds the valley. The features of the ground were such as nearly to paralyze the artillery and cavalry of the enemy, while his infantry could not derive all the advantage of its numerical superiority."

This place had been selected some time before by General Wool, and approved by General Taylor. Besides, the commanding-general believed that by his falling back a day's march, Santa Anna would mistake the movement for a precipitate flight, and urge on his forces, already exhausted by a march of thirty-five miles from Encarnacion to Agua Nueva, over a barren desert that afforded neither water nor food of any kind ; and the Americans would thus be able to engage their enemy under all the disadvantages of a forced march, want of food, and general disarray.

On the 21st, at noon, General Taylor broke up his encampment and fell back to Buena Vista, leaving Colonel Yell, with a part of the Arkansas mounted volunteers, to superintend the removal of the stores. The 1st Illinois regiment, under Colonel Hardin, was halted at Angostura, where General Taylor intended to give battle; the main body, under General Wool, encamped a mile and a half in the rear ; so that, instead of passively awaiting the enemy, the troops might feel the moral effect of marching forward to meet him. General Taylor, with May's dragoons, two batteries of the 3d artillery, under Captains Sherman and Bragg, and the Mississippi rifles, under Colonel Davis, proceeded to Saltillo, to put it in a better state of defence, and prepare for the expected battle.

Santa Anna left Encarnacion at noon on the 21st of February, after mass had been said in front of the several divisions. General Ampudia commanded the advance-guard of four battalions of light infantry. A brigade of artillery of 16-pounders followed, with a regiment of engineers and their train, and after them a park of the regiment of hussars. Next came the first division of heavy infantry, with five 12-pounders and their park, under General Lombardini. The second division, with eight 8-pounders and their park, followed under General Pachecho; then the divisions of cavalry under General Juvera. Lastly came the remainder of the cannon, the general park and baggage, with a rear-guard consisting of a brigade of lancers, under General Andrade, making in the aggregate a force of upwards of twenty thousand men.

About midnight on the 21st, Colonel Yell was reinforced by two companies of the 1st dragoons, and a part of the Kentucky mounted volunteers; and immediately after their arrival, the Mexican light infantry, under Ampudia, attacked Colonel Yell's advance piquet, stationed in the pass of Cornero, about five miles south of Agua Nueva. The whole train of wagons was now moved off with speed towards Buena Vista, while the troops remained to destroy the stores that had not yet been removed. In pursuance of an order, the buildings and some stacks of wheat were fired, and the flames filled the whole valley of the Encantada, and illumining the rugged mountain peaks, and flashing back from the glittering appointments of armed men and steeds, produced a picture wonderfully sublime, whose impression was heightened by the rumbling of the wagons in retreat, the random shots of the advanced parties, and the sounds of signal trumpets startling the midnight air.

After destroying the stores that remained, the Americans returned to Buena Vista, which they reached about day-break. In the mean time, Santa Anna had put his heavy forces in motion, and emerging at length from the mountain gorge, above Agua Nueva, was surprised to find the forces gone, which he had expected to surprise and cut up. Supposing the American army in full retreat, and intercepted in the rear by Minon's brigade, he hurried forward his exhausted and nearly famished troops, after a meagre repast, and a single draught of water, cheering them with the assurance that they would soon enjoy abundance from the American supplies at Saltillo.

In the morning of the 22d of February, a day hallowed to every American as the birthday of Washington, General Wool, in the absence of the commanding-general, who had not yet returned from Saltillo, ordered the troops under arms. The banners were unfurled to the breeze amid the inspiring strains of " Hail Columbia" from the bands, and the talismanic words " The memory of Washington," passed from corps to corps.

The following was the disposition of the troops. Captain Washington, with his battery, was posted so as to command the road at Angostura, supported by the 1st regiment of Illinois volunteers, under Colonel Hardin, which partly occupied a ridge of land extending from Angostura to the plateau or high table-land, running back to the mountains. The 2d Illinois volunteers, and a company of Texans, commanded by Colonel Bissell, were on its left, and the 2d regiment of Kentucky volunteers occupied the crest of a ridge by the roadside. On the extreme left, and near the base of the mountains, was the Arkansas regiment of mounted volunteers, under Colonel Yell, and the Kentucky regiment, under Colonel Marshall. The Indiana volunteer brigade, under General Lane, composed of the 2d and 3d regiments, under Colonels Bowles and Lane, the 1st regiment of Mississippi riflemen, under Colonel Davis, Colonel May's squadron of the 2d dragoons, Captain Steen's squadron of 1st dragoons, and the batteries of Sherman and Bragg, constituted the reserve, and were stationed on the ridges in the rear of the right of the plateau. Shortly after the troops were placed in position, General Taylor returned from Saltillo, and riding along the lines, was received with enthusiastic cheers. General Wool also rode along, and inspirited the troops, especially his own column, by brief, yet stirring remarks.

In the mean time, a cloud of dust was seen rising over the distant hills, and soon after the enemy's cavalry advance came thundering down the valley of Encantada, and, coming in sight of Washington's battery, sounded a halt with their bugles just out of cannon-range. The advanced squadrons now filed off towards the mountains on the American left, while others came up and formed, till nearly the whole space from the road to the mountains was covered by the serried legions, with all their blazonry of banners and panoply of armour gleaming in the sun.

While the engineers of both armies were busily employed in learning the disposition of the forces of their antagonist, and providing for their own, a white flag advanced from the Mexican front, and its bearer presented the following letter:—

" CAMP AT ENCANTADA,
February 22, 1847.

"God and Liberty!

" You are surrounded by twenty thousand men, and cannot, in any human probability, avoid suffering a rout, and being cut to pieces with your troops ; but as you deserve consideration and particular esteem, I wish to save you from a catastrophe, and for that purpose give you this notice, in order that you may surrender at discretion, under the assurance that you will be treated with the consideration belonging to the Mexican character, to which end you will be granted an hour's time to make up your mind, to commence from the moment when my flag of truce arrives in your camp.

" With this view, I assure you of my particular consideration.

ANTONIO LOPEZ DE SANTA ANNA.

To General Z. TAYLOR,
   Commanding the forces of the U. S."

To this summons General Taylor immediately despatched the following answer:—

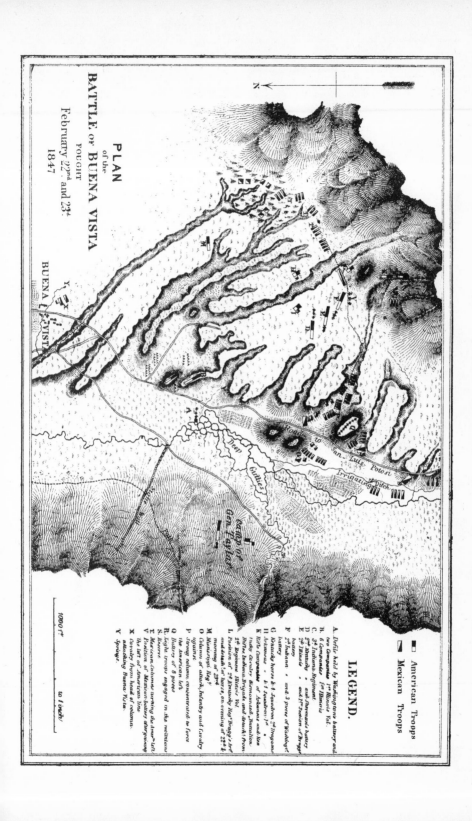

PLAN
of the
BATTLE OF BUENA VISTA
FOUGHT
February 22nd and 23d
1847

N

BUENA VISTA

LEGEND.

A. Defile held by Washington's battery and
   two Companies 1st Illinois Vol.
B. 6 Companies 1st Illinois
C. 3d Indiana Regiment.
D. 3d Kentucky . and Sherman's battery
E. 2d Illinois . and 1st section of Bragg's
   battery
F. 2d Illinois . and 3 piece of Washingt.
   battery
G. Kentucky horse & 1 Squadron 2d Dragoons
H. Arkansas . & 1 Squadron 1st
K. Rifle Companies of Arkansas and Ken
   tucky Cavalry dismounted, dismation
   Rethe Indiana Brigade and detacht from
   2d Regiment Illinois Vol.
L. Position of 2d Kentucky Reg't Troop's 1st
   and detacht of horse, on evening of 22d &
   morning of 23d
M. Mississippi Reg't
O. Column of attack, infantry and cavalry
   against
P. Strong column concentrated to force
   the American left
Q. Battery of 8 piece
R. Light troops engaged in the mountains
S. Reserve
T. Mexican column turning the American left
V. Position of Mexican battery after gaining
   the left of American line
X. Cavalry from head of column.
Y. Sprague

1000 Ft   to 1 inch)

American Troops
Mexican Troops

" Head-Quarters, Army of Occupation,
Near Buena Vista, February 22, 1847.

" Sir : In reply to your note of this date, summoning me to surrender my forces at discretion, I beg leave to say that I decline acceding to your request.

" With high respect, I am, sir, your obedient servant,

Z. TAYLOR,

Major-Gen. U. S. A. commanding.

Senor Gen. D. Antonio Lopez de Santa Anna,
Commander-in-chief, La Encantada."

Soon after this the whole Mexican army had come up, and was arranged as follows :—

On the second ridge, in front of the American army, the enemy stationed the first and second divisions of infantry, one behind the other. On the right of this, upon a higher point, was stationed a battery of 16-pounders, supported by the regiment of engineers. Upon their left, and near the road, were two other batteries of 12 and 8-pounders and a large howitzer. In rear of the two wings was the cavalry ; in rear of the centre was the head-quarters of Santa Anna, and the regiment of hussars, his body-guard. In the rear of all was the general park, protected by the brigade of General Andrade.

The first movement of the enemy was an attempt to get possession of one or two gradual slopes of the mountain upon the left of the plateau, occupied by the American reserve. To check this, Colonel Marshall was sent up the other slope with a battalion from the Indiana brigade under Major Gorman, and a portion of the Arkansas and Kentucky volunteers, dismounted. While these hostile bodies approached each other, both with the design of outflanking, General Taylor sent Captain Bragg's battery and the 2d Kentucky regiment of volunteers under Colonel McKee, to occupy the slope of the eminence on the right of Washington's battery at Angostura, and a little in advance of it, for the purpose of checking a demonstration made upon the enemy's left. Three pieces of artillery had also been detached by Captain Washington up to the left of the plateau and placed under Lieutenant O'Brien, who was supported by the 2d Indiana regiment.

These dispositions being made, the Americans calmly awaited the attack of the enemy.

The signal for the opening strife was given at three o'clock by a shell from the enemy's howitzer, and soon after the light division under Ampudia was hotly engaged with the American riflemen. The former fired with rapidity and in continuous vollies; the latter with cool deliberation and terrible effect, while they sheltered themselves from the fire of the enemy behind the crest of the ridge, which they occupied. This and an occasional cannonade directed at our troops on the plateau, comprised the action of the 22d, which was suspended about dark by a signal shell thrown into the air by the enemy. The American loss was but four men wounded, while that of the enemy in killed and wounded was over three hundred; * so deadly was the aim of the American rifle!

During the day, the 1st regiment of Illinois volunteers had formed a parapet along its front, and, directed by the engineers, had dug a ditch, and thrown up an epaulement with a traverse, before Washington's battery at Angostura, to occupy which Colonel Hardin detached a supporting force of two companies of his regiment, under Lieutenant-Colonel Weatherford.

At sunset, General Taylor left General Wool in command of the forces, and proceeded to Saltillo, with May's dragoons and the Mississippi regiment, to complete arrangements for its defence, and prepare for the reception of his wounded after the main attack by Santa Anna, expected on the morrow. The defences were arranged as follows : Two companies of the 1st Illinois volunteers,

* Santa Anna's account.

under Captains Morgan and Prentiss, and two companies of the 2d Illinois volunteers, under Captains Hacker and Wheeler, the whole commanded by Major Warren, occupied the town. The field-work commanding its approaches was garrisoned by Captain Webster's company, 1st artillery, with two 24-pound howitzers; while the train and head-quarters camp was defended by a 6-pounder from Bragg's battery under Lieutenant Shover, supported by two companies of Mississippi riflemen under Captain Rogers.

After the close of the battle, Santa Anna made a spirited address to his troops, which was received with enthusiastic cries, distinctly heard in the American lines. After this the band of the Mexican chief struck up, and strains of surpassing sweetness floated down the mountain sides, and died away in faint echoes along the narrow gorge. Silence and darkness now succeeded, and amid the gloom, the troops in general sank down to slumber on their arms, without covering and without fires, exposed to the chill night-winds and occasional gusts of rain; but on the mountains, where the cold was extreme, the light troops of both armies gathered the trunks of dwarfish trees, and the stalks of shrubs, and kindled fires, around which they gathered in shivering groups during the night.

29

CHAPTER XIII.

Action of the 23d—Commencement on the American left—Enemy's Columns of Attack—Advance of Lombardini's and Pachecho's Divisions—O'Brien, with his Artillery and 2d Indiana Regiment, ordered to repulse them—Retreat of the 2d Indiana Regiment—American Reserve ordered up—Second Column of Attack repulsed at Angostura—Troops on the Plateau reinforced by Artillery and Infantry—Arrival of General Taylor on the Field—Confidence restored—The gallant Mississippi Regiment—The Enemy driven back on the American left—The contest on the Plateau—Movement of the Cavalry on the Enemy's right checked—Batteries of Sherman and Bragg—Baggage-train threatened by Cavalry—Dangerous Position of the Enemy's Cavalry — *Ruse* of Santa Anna — Mexican Reserve ordered up—Terrible Service of O'Brien's Artillery—Slaughter of the Illinois and Kentucky Regiments—Deaths of Colonels Hardin, McKee, and Clay—Washington's Battery—Gallantry of Lieutenant O'Brien—Repulse of Minon's Cavalry—Close of the Battle—American and Mexican Losses.

AT two o'clock on the morning of the 23d, the advanced pickets of the American army were driven in by those of Ampudia, whose light division was reinforced towards day-break by two thousand men from the divisions of Lombardini and Pachecho, with the view of gaining the American left and rear upon the mountains. Here the action commenced at dawn on the 23d, and was maintained with great spirit by Colonel Marshall's command, holding themselves under cover, and contending against nearly eight to one, until reinforced by Major Trail, 2d Illinois volunteers, with three companies of riflemen, including Captain Conner's Texas volunteers. About sunrise, Lieutenant O'Brien, who was stationed at the upper edge of the plateau with a 12-pound howitzer, and two guns—one a 6-pounder, the other a 4-pounder—came to their aid, and advancing his howitzer, threw with great accuracy and terrible effect six or eight shells among the troops of Ampudia, now pouring down the

(212)

slope of the mountain that intervened between them and the American riflemen. The precision of the firing elicited the most enthusiastic cheering from the whole American line.

By this time, the chief of Santa Anna's staff, General Micheltorena, had planted his battery of 8-pounders on the high ridge lying between the contending forces, and commenced a plunging fire on the plateau, which was more especially directed against O'Brien's pieces, but with little success, on account of the great distance intervening. For this reason O'Brien did not attempt to answer the fire of the enemy, as his guns were of lighter metal than the pieces of their battery. He remained silent, therefore, until subsequently ordered by General Lane to meet the advance of Pachecho's division.

The enemy had now arranged three columns of attack. The first, to be led by General Mora y Villamil, and destined to force the pass of La Angostura, was composed of the 2d regiment of engineers, the 12th regiment, the *figo de Mexico,* and the battalions of Puebla and Tampico. The second column was composed of the divisions of Lombardini and Pachecho. The former division was to move across the ridge mentioned above, to the left of their 8-pounder battery, while the division of Pachecho advanced up the ravine in front of the plateau; and thus, both uniting near the mountain, together with their supporting forces of cavalry, turn the left of the American troops stationed on the plateau. The light troops, under Ampudia, were the third column of attack, and were to turn the extreme left on the mountains, and attack the American rear in conjunction with the second column, under Generals Lombardini and Pachecho. Besides these three columns, a reserve, under General Ortega, was stationed on the ground occupied by the two lines of the enemy, when first displayed on coming in sight of the American army.

While the third column was hotly engaged with the American riflemen upon the mountains, and the rattle of musketry and the rifle was intermingled with the roar of the 8-pounders directed against the left of the plateau, Lombardini's division was moving along the ridge to unite with Pachecho, in view of the American army; his men in full uniform, his horses in gay caparison, their burnished weapons and appointments flashing in the sunlight, and every standard, colours, and guidon unfurled to the breeze.

While this pageant was passing in review, Major Mansfield, of the engineers, about nine o'clock came with the intelligence that Pachecho's division, which had moved along screened from sight, was coming up the ravine with the evident design of gaining the plateau by way of the ridge adjoining the third principal gorge, which scalloped the plateau. At this time General Wool was at Angostura, having gone thither to give some directions about the defences in that quarter. General Lane, therefore, the next in command, ordered Lieutenant O'Brien, with his three pieces of artillery, and the 2d Indiana regiment, to take position just beyond the head of the third gorge, and repel the enemy.

By the time the guns were in battery and the regiment displayed, the Mexican infantry was ascending the ridge, and, forming in lines, opened upon it at a distance of two hundred yards. Their fire was returned immediately and effectively; and, simultaneously with it, O'Brien's guns poured their deadly discharges upon the columns of the enemy. Though struggling against a superiority of ten to one in front, and enfiladed by a cross-fire of grape and canister from the 8-pounder battery on his left, General Lane gallantly maintained the contest for twenty-five minutes; during which he swept down whole platoons at a time, and repeatedly broke the front lines of the enemy, which were as often re-formed. So murderous was the fire, that the corps of Guanajuato, which constituted the advance, was totally destroyed.

With the view of getting out of range of the enemy's guns, and driving back Pachecho's troops into the ravine, General Lane ordered O'Brien to advance about fifty yards to the front, which was immediately done, and his pieces served, as before, with

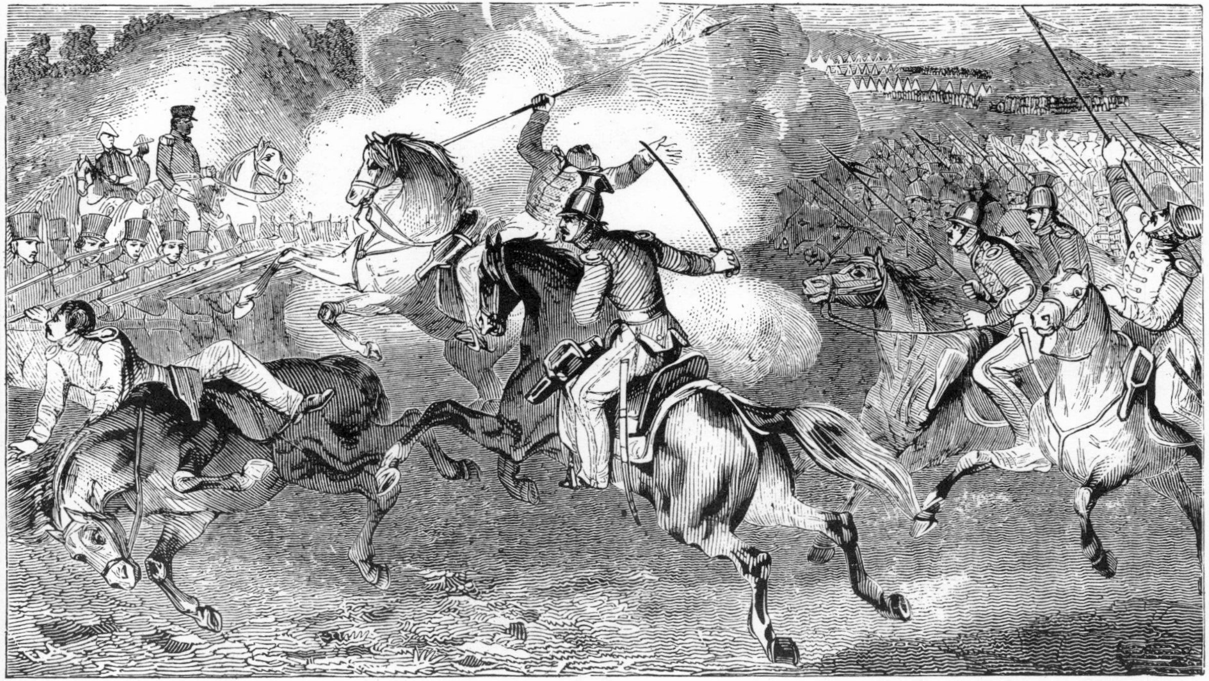

BATTLE OF BUENA VISTA.

terrible effect.   And had he been promptly sustained by his supporting force, he would have defeated this division of the enemy,
and driven it back into the ravine.*   But, instead of moving up
to his support, the 2d Indiana volunteers hesitated and staggered
under the severe fire of the enemy, and then, breaking off by
companies from the right, fled in utter confusion, leaving the
gallant O'Brien to bear the contest alone.   Exertions were made
to rally them, by General Lane and his staff, but without effect;
and in the effort, the brave Captain Lincoln lost his life.   A few
of them joined the Mississippi regiment, and did good service
during the day; some retired to Buena Vista, and others to Saltillo, where they assisted in defending the depot.   It may at
least be mentioned to their credit, that before flying, they had
fired twenty rounds of cartridge at the enemy.   In the flight,
four companies of the Arkansas volunteers, which had been dismounted and ordered into action, participated, having delivered but
a single fire after coming into action.   By the giving way of the
2d Indiana regiment, the riflemen, under Colonel Marshall, were
cut off from the centre, and, unable to withstand the overwhelming
force of the enemy on this flank, retreated in good order, in the
direction of Buena Vista.   They were pursued by the Mexican
cavalry and a part of the light forces under Ampudia.   This
force was held in check for a time by the spirited conduct of the
Arkansas and Kentucky cavalry, under Colonels Yell and Marshall.

Left without support, and exposed to a continuous sheet of fire,
O'Brien and his brave artillerists struggled for a time against the
fearful odds; and before their pieces, charged with double canister, the enemy fell in scores, like grass before the scythe.   But,
overpowered by numbers, he was compelled at length to limber
up and fall back, yielding the 4-pounder to the enemy, after
every horse and man that belonged to it had been killed or dis-

* Mexican Engineer's Report.

abled.   Pachecho immediately advanced, with his cavalry on the right of his infantry, and, united with Lombardini's forces, now emerging from the ravine.   The entire column, moving across the plateau, concentrated its fire upon the 2d Illinois, under Colonel Bissell, the squadron of 1st dragoons, under Captain Steen, and the first section of Sherman's battery, under Lieutenants Thomas and French; all of which had been ordered to advance just before the 2d Indiana regiment gave way.   The service of the artillery was terrible, and cut avenues through the dense masses, while the storm of musketry strewed the ground with the dead and dying of the enemy.   The cavalry, unable to attempt anything by charging into the overwhelming masses, fell back to the ravine in the rear.   The enemy continued to advance in the teeth of the deadly engines, and their right to pass around the American left; and shortly after, the Illinois troops and the battery were assailed in front and rear, and upon each flank. The iron storm was resistless; and before its fury, the Americans faltered and fell back.   But the pieces were soon in battery again, supported by the Illinoians, and the enemy's flank severely galled as he passed to the left of the plateau to gain the rear.

At this time the heavy first column of attack, under General Mora y Villamil, came within range of the guns at Angostura, when Washington's pieces opened upon it with signal effect. Nothing could stand up against the storm that assailed it.   The enemy soon wavered, and was thrown into confusion, and sought shelter in the third gorge of the plateau and in the great ravine beyond, nor renewed the attack in that direction.

About this time Captain Sherman gained the plateau with the second section of his battery, and, on reaching the head of the first gorge, opened fire upon the enemy.

The 2d Kentucky volunteers, under Colonel McKee and Captain Bragg, with two pieces of his battery, soon after arrived from their position beyond Washington's battery, at Angostura.

A line of artillery was now formed from the head of the gorge
to the ravine, which was soon driving its masses of iron and lead
into the Mexican ranks.   The 1st Illinois regiment, under the
gallant Colonel Hardin, now came up from Angostura, after the
repulse of Villamil, and with the squadron of 1st dragoons, the 2d
Illinois and the 2d Kentucky regiment, constituted the supporting force of the artillery, and poured its leaden hail upon the
serried masses of the enemy.

When these reverses had taken place, and while the fate of
the battle seemed decided—the American left forced—the enemy
almost in entire possession of the plateau—and the Americans
despairing of the issue—General Taylor arrived upon the field
from Saltillo, and restored confidence.   He was accompanied by
May's dragoons, the Mississippi riflemen, under Colonel Jefferson Davis, Captain Pike's squadron of Arkansas horse, and a
piece of artillery, under Lieutenant Kilburn.   After some orders
relative to the battle, General Taylor immediately attempted
restoring the American left, and bringing into action again the
2d Indiana fugitives.

The Mississippians under the gallant Colonel Davis were immediately led into action, while General Wool himself started to
bring up to their support the third Indiana regiment stationed
upon the left and in the rear of Washington's battery, at Angostura.   Near the head of a small ravine which intersects the third
large ravine in rear of the plateau, Colonel Davis intercepted the
pursuing forces of Ampudia.   A tremendous fire smote the head
of the enemy's column, yet he still passed on over dead and dying—successive discharges checked his advance and caused his
fire to slacken—when the Mississippians, with a loud hurrah,
rushed on the enemy, passed the ravine, and clambering up
the bank, after a murderous fire drove back his routed ranks
upon the reserves.   This accomplished, they made a dash at the
enemy's cavalry on the flank, and after a few volleys, turned it

back to join the infantry. Soon after the 3d Indiana volunteers and Lieutenant Kilburn's piece of artillery arrived, and the united force compelled the enemy to fall back still farther.

While these things were going on upon the American left, the battle was still raging upon the plateau, where the advantage was rather in our favour, when Santa Anna brought upon the plateau with a heavy battery the battalion of San Patricio, consisting of Irish renegades who had basely deserted the American colours which they had sworn to support. The fire of this battery enfiladed the plateau, and was effective, but the American batteries still kept the advantage, and at length broke the attacking column. A part moved off in a direction to reinforce Ampudia, while the other, under Santa Anna, fell back to take shelter in the ravine. Perceiving this, the forces under Hardin, Bissell, and McKee, pressed on and drove back the enemy precipitately. After this advantage Captains Sherman and Bragg were despatched, with two pieces each, to sustain the American left, where the strife was obstinate and sanguinary. The plateau was still defended by four pieces—two under the intrepid O'Brien, and two under Lieutenants Thomas and Garnet.

In the mean time, upon the enemy's extreme right, beyond Ampudia's forces and along the base of the mountains, cavalry was moving down towards Buena Vista, whose advance was impeded by the mounted volunteers, under Colonels Yell and Marshall. To reinforce this small body of troops, General Taylor despatched Colonel May with the regular cavalry, and Captains Preston and Pike's mounted volunteers. The united force immediately stopped the progress of the enemy's cavalry, and caused it to return along the base of the mountain, where the fire from the detachments of the batteries of Sherman and Bragg was concentrated upon it with decisive effect.

Soon after, a powerful brigade of cavalry, principally lancers, under General Torrejon, had crossed the ravines in the rear, and

threatened a descent upon the baggage-train parked near Buena
Vista. They charged in columns of squadrons the Arkansas and
Kentucky volunteers, who gallantly received them, and maintaining the contest with great spirit, repulsed them with the aid of parties of troops in that vicinity, that had fled in the morning. Colonel
May with the dragoons and other cavalry, and Lieutenant Reynolds
with two pieces of artillery, had been ordered to their support.
The former came up too late to participate in the fight; the other
wheeled his section into battery, and played upon the retreating
columns of cavalry with precision and effect. In this charge of
cavalry, the gallant Colonel Yell fell at the head of his regiment,
and by his side the brave Captain Porter, with many of their
men.

After this failure, a fresh brigade of cavalry with supporting
infantry, the chivalry of the Mexican army, attempted to drive
the Mississippi regiment and 3d Indiana volunteers, and thus
force a passage to the road nearer the plateau. On they came at
a gallop, in close columns of squadrons, their flags and pennons
flying, and their lance-points flickering in the sun, while the
Mississippi regiment was in line to receive them, and the Indiana
troops in like manner, with their left resting on the right of Colonel
Davis's regiment, the two lines forming an obtuse re-entrant angle
to receive the enemy. A howitzer from Sherman's battery was
on the left. Arrived within eighty yards, the brigade received a
murderous fire from the faces of the angle, which struck down
the front ranks of the column. The deadly discharges of musketry
and the rifles rapidly delivered, increased the confusion of the
enemy, while the howitzer of Sherman, charged with canister
and grape, strewed the earth with the dead and wounded. The
iron tempest poured upon him was resistless, and the dismayed
enemy turned and fled for shelter to the mountains.

Following up this advantage, General Taylor sent Lieutenant-
Colonel May, with the troops lately returned from the engagement
30

at the hacienda, to drive in the enemy's right along the base of the mountains. As the cavalry under May forced the troops to fall back, Lieutenant Reynolds with his two pieces kept following on, and poured destruction upon their ranks. Bragg also advanced upon them with his three pieces of artillery, and Sherman with his howitzer, supported by the Mississippi and Indiana regiments. As the enemy continued to retreat along the base of the mountains, he came at length within range of the guns upon the plateau, which prevented further retreat.   Hemmed in now upon all sides, and exposed to the fire of nine pieces of artillery, whose shot and shells went crashing through their crowded masses––Reynolds's pieces on their right, Sherman's and Bragg's in front, and the pieces of O'Brien and Thomas on the plateau upon their left— their destruction seemed inevitable, when they were relieved from their dangerous position by a dishonourable *ruse* of Santa Anna. That treacherous chief sent a white flag to General Taylor, *desiring to know what he wanted,* and during the suspension of the fire ordered upon the advance of the flag, the enemy's forces which were so sorely pressed, amounting to five or six thousand, cavalry and infantry—escaped from their perilous situation.   On arriving, however, near the head of the plateau, a heavy fire from O'Brien's and Thomas's pieces, which were advanced to meet them, and from the Illinois and Kentucky troops, that had also moved up, caused great destruction to their confused ranks.

But while thus engaged, the Mexican reserve, composed of the best troops, with the veteran regiments in front, was entering the plateau at the head of the third gorge. The retreating party joined the reserve, making the column about twelve thousand. Before this irresistible force, the Kentucky and Illinois troops were compelled to retire and seek cover in the second gorge. O'Brien in the mean time served his pieces, charged with canister, with terrible effect; but the enemy still pressed on, until they

LIEUT COL HENRY CLAY, JR

reached the head of the second gorge. The one half continued
to move across the plateau, resisted only by O'Brien's guns;
while the other half occupied each side of the gorge, and marched
down upon the American troops there crowded together, and
scarcely able to stand on account of the inclined position which
they occupied. The slaughter was great, and the Americans
pressed down the gorge, to escape by its mouth to the road, while
the whole line of their retreat was strewed with the dead and
dying.

On reaching the opening of the gorge, they found a large body
of cavalry just closing up the door of escape. Some endeavoured
to force their way through, but sank beneath the lance-points of
the enemy ; while the work of destruction went rapidly on among
the densely-crowded masses in the ravine. In this fearful
moment was heard the thunder of Washington's battery, and
spherical case-shot falling amid the enemy's cavalry, exploded
with signal effect, causing confusion, dismay, and rout—and
upon their rapid retreat, the remnants of the Illinois and Kentucky
regiments escaped to the road, leaving hundreds of their brave
companions behind them in death—among them the gallant
Colonels Hardin and McKee, and Lieutenant-Colonel Clay.

After the escape of the enemy's right, consequent on Santa
Anna's stratagem, General Taylor ordered the troops from the
American left to the plateau, where he expected a strong demonstration. While these were coming up, the American infantry had
been driven, as related, by a part of the Mexican reserve, and
O'Brien and Thomas, with their artillery, were endeavouring to
hold in check the other portion, which kept steadily advancing.
At every discharge avenues were made through the enemy's column, but the men soon closed up, and moved firmly on, while they
assailed the battery with a steady fire. Nearly all his horses
and cannoneers were killed and wounded, as O'Brien saw Bragg's
battery coming into action, and Davis and Lane, with their brave

troops, ascending the plateau. The enemy by this time was quite upon him,—he gave a final and murderous fire, and, with the few crippled companions that remained, fell back from the contest. The guns thus obtained by the enemy for want of horses to bring them away, were subsequently recaptured by Captain Drum, 4th artillery, at Churubusco.

Bragg's battery now opened upon the enemy, with terrible fury; Sherman's battery soon united its fire, and the Mississippi riflemen and Indiana volunteers poured a severe enfilading fire upon his flank. Still raged the iron tempest, and still, as the front ranks of the enemy fell, others succeeded to their places, who in their turn were shot down. To advance against such a storm was impossible—the enemy at length began to falter—confusion spread through their ranks, and they retreated to the great ravine, leaving the ground covered with the dead and dying, in fearful evidence of the severity of the contest.

It was now about five o'clock, and the batteries moved up a few hundred yards, and opened a destructive fire upon the battalion of San Patricio, supported by the Mississippi regiment and other troops, while General Taylor despatched the cavalry under Lieutenant-Colonel May to the left, to guard against any attempt again to turn our flank in that direction.

General Minon with his cavalry had advanced against Saltillo during the day, but was received by a heavy fire from the redoubt occupied by Captain Webster's company, which caused him to move off with rapidity. Towards the close of day he renewed the attempt, when, galled by a severe fire from two pieces of artillery, under Captain Shover and Lieutenant Donaldson, and a mixed command of volunteers, he hastily fled up the base of the mountains to his encampment.

As the sun set, the firing on both sides slackened, and at length ceased, and darkness and comparative silence settled down upon the two armies. Expecting a renewal of the attack,

General Taylor made due preparations for the next day, but when the morning dawned, the dense masses of the enemy were nowhere to be seen, and shouts of victory went up from the American host that shook the very hills around. The Mexicans had fallen back upon Agua Nueva, and subsequently retreated to Encarnacion, strewing the desert between with the dead bodies of men and horses, who had perished for lack of food. Indeed the great physical exertions, and, in a measure, the success of the Americans, may be attributed to the fact that during the pauses in the fight they were regularly refreshed, while the enemy passed three days with no more than a single meal.

The battle of Buena Vista may be considered the crowning glory of the brave old chief, who had already covered himself with imperishable renown upon the fields of Palo Alto and Resaca de la Palma, and at the heights of Monterey. The exultation of victory, however, was saddened by the loss of the many valorous spirits, who had gone down amid the storm of battle, in the vigour of manhood or the full honours of years. The American loss in killed, wounded, and missing, was seven hundred and forty-six; that of the Mexicans upwards of two thousand.

The battle of Buena Vista left General Taylor in undisputed possession of the whole line of the Sierra Madre. Nothing was afterwards attempted by the enemy in that quarter, beyond the depredations of small parties of guerillas. For the purpose of strengthening General Scott's line, further drafts were made the following August upon his forces, which had been considerably increased. Having made proper disposition of the remaining portions for the maintenance of his own line, General Taylor obtained leave of absence in November, and returned home, having left General Wool in command of all the forces.

CHAPTER XIV.

THE story of the recent conquest of New Mexico and California is one of rare and romantic interest. Yielding the pre-eminence in brilliancy of achievement and blood-bought triumph to the operations in southern and central Mexico, it takes no second place in the importance of its results, while it asserts for the force employed, skill, valour, devotion, and endurance, unsurpassed in military annals, and has crowned our arms with the truest and most abiding fame.

On recognition of war between the United States and Mexico, the American land forces designed to operate against the latter formed three divisions, with distinct points of attack. The " Army of Occupation," under Major-General Taylor, was instructed to move forward from its position on the Rio Grande, and subjugate and hold Coahuila, New Leon, and Tamaulipas. Brigadier-General Wool, with the "Army of the Centre," was to rendezvous at San Antonio de Bexar, and move on the city and state of Chihuahua; while at Fort Leavenworth, on the Missouri, was concentrated the "Army of the West" under Colonel Kearny, of the 1st regiment United States dragoons. His primary instructions were to march upon Santa Fé, the capital

(224)

of New Mexico, and effect the conquest and occupation of that
state or department, but they were subsequently enlarged so as
to embrace the conquest of California.

Mounted troops were considered best for the expedition; and
agreeably to the requisition of Governor Edwards of Missouri,
companies began to arrive at Fort Leavenworth in the early part
of June, 1846. They were immediately mustered into service,
and instructed and drilled in military exercises. Horses, mules,
wagons, ordnance, subsistence—all the necessary *materiel* for an
invading army were collected with prudent haste, and before the
end of June, the expedition, fully organized, was on its route
for Mexico.

The little army under Colonel Kearny numbered 1658 men,
with sixteen pieces of ordnance, twelve 6-pounders, and four 12-
pound howitzers. It consisted of the following corps:—Five
companies 1st regiment United States dragoons, under Major
Sumner, three hundred men, and the only regulars in the army;
Captain Hudson's company of St. Louis dragoons, the "Laclede
Rangers," one hundred and seven men; two companies of flying
artillery, under Captains Fischer and Weightman, two hundred
and fifty strong, with Major Clark as field-officer; a battalion of
infantry, numbering one hundred and forty-five men, under Captains Angney and Murphy; with eight companies, composing the
1st regiment of Missouri mounted volunteers, eight hundred and
fifty-six men, with the following field-officers—William Gilpin,
Major; C. F. Ruff, Lieutenant-Colonel; Alexander W. Doniphan,
Colonel, and second in rank to the commander of the whole
column. A gallant band of field and topographical engineers
accompanied the expedition, consisting of Lieutenants Emory,
Warner, Abert, and Peck. They received their orders at the
seat of government, on the 5th of June, and within twenty-four
hours thereafter were on their way, and having expeditiously
completed their equipment at St. Louis, reported to Colonel

Kearny at Fort Leavenworth, in time to take their line of march across the prairies ahead of the main column.

A short time previous to his departure, Colonel Kearny received a communication from the Secretary of War, covering additional instructions and extended command. After the conquest and occupancy of Santa Fé, he was to press forward to California, and co-operate with the fleet there in conquering and holding that province. Besides one thousand men added to his column, he was empowered to call for additional troops, and was directed to secure the aid of a large body of Mormon emigrants, *en route* for that distant region. His orders in relation to the route, and many other things appertaining to the expedition, were discretionary, and he was informed that the rank of Brigadier-General would be conferred on him as soon as his movement to California should be commenced.

In the last days of June, the army, broken into divisions, and preceded or accompanied by long trains of baggage and provision wagons, set forth on its toilsome westward march. Health, hopeful impatience, confidence in their chief and in each other, gave nerve to every limb, and to every bosom soldierly pride. For some days their wholly pathless route lay over elevated and rolling plains, covered with tall luxuriant grass and matted vines, and traversed by many deep ravines and steep-banked streams, the tributaries of the Kansas, or " Kaw," and its sovereign, the Missouri. The country, rich in picturesque beauty and fertility, presented the general appearance of " vast, rolling fields, enclosed with colossal hedges." The army, on the 1st of July, struck upon the great Santa Fé road. The earliest rays of the morrow's sun glanced brightly back from the long lines of polished arms and streaming banners that already moved across the broad, level plain, or rose over the gently-heaving hills, which here and there diversified the boundless sea of green. Out upon the silence of the mighty solitudes, with nought but plain and sky on every side, burst forth the mirthful shout and spirit-stirring strains of martial hymns, on Independence Day. The afternoon of the 5th brought the advanced battalion of the army to the well-known Council Grove, the general rendezvous for union, rest, and repair, of all caravans and hunting companies, and prized deservedly for its hospitable pasturage and shade, its copious springs of most delicious water, and its abundance of serviceable timber of various kinds. Here, at a distance of about one hundred and fifty miles from the western borders of Missouri, runs the line that limits the eastward roamings of the savage tribes of Pawnees, Osages, and Sioux. The intermediate country is in the hands of Indians who own allegiance to, and receive stipends from, the United States; and who, having abandoned nomadic life, dwelling in log-houses, rearing cattle, cultivating the soil, and pursuing some of the other arts of peace, "form the connecting link between the savage of the plains and the white man of the States." Pawnee Fork was reached on the 14th; and here Colonel Kearny, with the rear division, overtook the advance, and formed a junction of forces with Colonel Doniphan. The waters of this creek, swollen by recent rains, were so high as to be then impassable; "the trees along the sides of the banks were half hidden; the whirling eddies were rushing along with great velocity; the willows that grew on the bank were waving under the strong pressure of the water, and brush and large logs were hurriedly borne along on the turbid bosom of the stream." Having encamped beside the river, whose angry condition is thus described by Lieutenant Abert, the men were promptly set to work on the construction of a raft. The energy of the commander was rivalled by the cheerful labours of his soldiers, and a wild excitement marked their struggles with, and triumph over, the fiercely rapid current that presumed to obstruct their onward way. In the forenoon of the 16th, immense toil and resolution had accomplished the passage across, and on the 17th, the whole

31

column was again in motion, the Arkansas river route having
been chosen as the most practicable. Here commenced that portion of the prairies that may justly be considered as the outskirt
of the Great Desert. A scanty vegetation sprang from the soil of
these plains of granite sand, over which the eye wanders in search
of trees, but wanders in vain. In all directions lay the short,
curly buffalo-grass, with thistles and endless varieties of cactus.
Wild horses, large and well-proportioned, stood in groups watching the approach of the troops, then dashed off into their native
wilds in wonder and alarm. The ground was darkened and the
horizon lined with herds of buffaloes ; and in close proximity to
these prowled gray wolves, eagerly watching the opportunity of
prey. Along the margin of the Arkansas, a strip of luxuriant
bottom-land afforded suitable places for encampment, and here
occasionally scattered clumps of the cotton-wood extended an
irresistible invitation to the wearied and sunburnt soldier, after his
march over the sandy plains, whose monotony was sometimes
relieved by the villages of prairie dogs that dotted the solitudes.
Bois de vache and wild sage was the only fuel to be procured.
Sickness assailed the troops. On the 20th, the severe illness of
Colonel Kearny caused general anxiety, while the doctors' lists
exceeded one hundred men. The anxiety respecting the leader
of the column was, however, quickly relieved, nor was the sickness generally, though extremely harassing and debilitating,
attended with fatal results. By the 24th, many of the gallant
steeds that had thus far borne their owners over the wilderness of
the strange land, failed, and were reluctantly abandoned on the
prairie. Still with unabated vigour was the march continued,
while the sun came hotly and witheringly down upon arid plains,
that marked further entrance on the desert, and the buffalo
ceased by his presence to give somewhat of life and interest to
the scene. On the 28th, the troops first caught glimpses of the
enemy's country, and every heart beat responsive to the challenge

of the clarion, ringing out its joyous intimation that the struggle
was now at hand. Crossing the Arkansas on the 29th, the army
encamped on the Mexican territory, on a spot chosen for the convenience of grazing, about nine miles below Bent's Fort, a small
post on the north bank of the Arkansas, in longitude 103° 25′
45″ west, and latitude 38° 2′ 53″ north. Thither large stores of
supply had previously been forwarded ;—here was the appointed
general rendezvous, and here, on the appointed day, August the
1st, with admirable precision, was concentrated the whole force,
regular and volunteer, having accomplished a journey of about
six hundred miles.

To recruit his men, after the fatigues and distresses of their
long march, as well as to make necessary provision for onward
progress, Colonel Kearny detained the army three days in their
regular and strictly-guarded encampment. During these days
intelligence of various kinds was brought in. Three Mexicans,
having upon their persons blank letters addressed to the American
commander, for the supposed purpose of diverting suspicion of
their character as spies, were apprehended, and by the colonel's
command so conducted through the camp, as to leave upon their
minds the liveliest impressions of the strength of the army ; then
allowed to retire in peace—their known propensity to exaggerate
being relied on, to give a sufficiently satisfactory account of what
they had seen to the people and the governor of New Mexico.
Rumour contradicted rumour as to the resolves and proceedings
of the latter. By some it was announced that our forces would
meet with no opposition ; by others, that Governor Armijo was at
the head of a formidable army, that Santa Fé and Taos were
being strongly fortified, and that everywhere throughout New
Mexico there would be resistance to the death. Lieutenant De
Courcy was, with twenty men, ordered to proceed directly through
the mountain passes to the valley of the Taos, to ascertain the
feelings and disposition of the people ; and on the same day,

July 31st, was issued the following proclamation, bearing date as above, at the camp at Bent's Fort :—

" The undersigned enters New Mexico with a large military force, for the purpose of seeking union with, and ameliorating the condition of its inhabitants.   This he does under instructions from his government, and with the assurance that he will be amply sustained in the accomplishment of this object.   It is enjoined on the citizens of New Mexico to remain quietly at their homes, and to pursue their peaceful avocations.   So long as they continue in such pursuits, they will not be interfered with by the American army, but will be respected and protected in their rights, both civil and religious.   All who take up arms or encourage resistance against the government of the United States will be regarded as enemies, and will be treated accordingly.

S. W. KEARNY,
Colonel 1st Dragoons."

From the Fort, on the 2d of August, an American flag threw out its wide folds to the breeze from the desert, in salutation to the Army of the West, again *en route* for Santa Fé.   The ordnance train had not arrived, neither had the new levies ordered in Missouri; but the colonel desired, by the celerity of his movements, to embarrass and frustrate any attempts at combined resistance by the enemy.   For several days the road lay across the Great American Desert, and men and animals suffered much, the horses, especially, falling off in an alarming manner.   This arid waste being left behind, they ascended the Raton or Mouse, a chain of ragged mountains that separates the waters of the Arkansas from those of the Canadian.   The ascent of the pass was arduous; but the views from the summit, seven thousand five hundred feet above the level of the sea, were inexpressibly beautiful and sublime.   To the north-west rose Pike's Peak; to the south and south-west, the Wattahyah, or Twin Hills, and the

spurs that run southward from the Wattahyah ; to the east towered
up the singularly formed summits of the Raton, presenting the
appearance of a succession of castles, with time-worn and storm-
stained battlements, now glistening in the sunshine, now seeming
to frown upon the small adventurous host that threaded upward
the defile.

The descent was found more rapid, and much more difficult
than the ascent, the road passing over many sharp spurs formed
by the channel of the mountain stream, resolutely working its
way to the Canadian ; on the main branch of which latter river,
a day's halt, with abundant supplies of water, wood, and grass,
was gladly enjoyed after the fatigues of crossing the mountains.
Here commenced a hardship incidental to such expeditions, but
infinitely more harassing and annoying to the volunteer just fresh
from the abundance and comforts of home, than any toil of the
road, or any effort of Mexican military skill and prowess.   The
army was put on half rations, and so continued, until their arrival
in Santa Fé.   But after a few good-humoured benedictions on
the provoking *contre-temps*, the men calmly accommodated themselves to the sacrifice, and even merrily discussed the diminished
fare.

Spies were daily captured, but upon the information elicited
from them, little reliance could be placed.   On the 10th, Mr.
Towle, an American citizen, came into camp, reporting himself
just escaped from Taos, and stating that on the previous day
had been received there the proclamation of Governor Armijo,
calling all the citizens to arms, and placing the whole country
under martial law; that Armijo had assembled the Pueblo Indians,
numbering about two thousand, and all the citizens capable of
bearing arms ; that on the day this proclamation was issued, three
hundred Mexican dragoons had arrived in Santa Fé, and that
twelve hundred more were hourly expected ; that the Mexicans
were every man eager for a fight, but the Indians generally not

so bellicose.   Each day now brought its quota of increasing interest.   On the persons of several Mexicans captured on the 11th,
were found copies of the proclamation of the Prefect of Taos,
based on that of Armijo, summoning the people to arms to repel
the American invaders, who were coming to "destroy their
property and liberties," and ordering an enrolment of all citizens
between the ages of fifteen and fifty.   The 13th brought the
advance of the column to the valley of the Moro creek, and the
first settlements they had seen in their march of seven hundred
and eighty miles.   Bent's spy company brought in an ensign and
three privates, sent forward by the enemy to reconnoitre.   From
them it was learned that the Mexicans were assembling in force
to do battle at Las Vegas.   And at the halting-place this evening
a Mr. Spry came into camp, on foot, and nearly destitute of
clothing, having been furtively despatched from Santa Fé on the
previous night, to communicate to Colonel Kearny the stirring
intelligence, that Armijo was energetically assembling his forces
in preparation for a vigorous resistance, and that the Cañon, a
well-known pass or defile, narrow, and easily defended, was now
being fortified, that from this vantage-ground, and with overwhelming numbers, the further progress of our army might be
disputed and stayed.

Early in the march of the 14th a lieutenant, accompanied by
a sergeant and two privates, of Mexican lancers, all respectably
clad and accoutred, but miserably mounted, presented themselves.
The officer proved to be the bearer from Governor Armijo of a
letter, which, says Lieutenant Emory, was a sensible, straight-
forward missive, and if written by an American or Englishman,
would have meant this :—" You have notified me that you intend
to take possession of the country I govern.   The people of the
country have risen *en masse* in my defence.   If you take the
country, it will be because you prove the strongest in battle.   I
suggest to you to stop at the Sapillo, and I will march to the

Vegas. We will meet and negotiate on the plains between them."
After a delay of some hours, during which the artillery was
passed over the Sapillo, and the troops brought within sight of
Las Vegas, a village on the creek of the same name, the messenger and his escort were dismissed with a verbal reply from Colonel
Kearny, " Say to General Armijo, that I shall meet him soon, and
I hope it will be as friends." This day the face of the country
had begun greatly to improve, indications of culture and comfort
presented themselves, herds and flocks dotted the valleys, the
stately pine and cedar adorned the hills, and gardens and waving
corn for the first time greeted the soldiers' weary eyes. The
village, at a short distance, looked like an extensive brick-kiln.
On nearer approach, its outline presented a square with some
arrangements for defence, within which the inhabitants are, not
unfrequently, compelled to retreat with all their stock, for protection against the attacks of the predatory Eutaws and Navajoes.
In sight of the little town, and away for a mile down the valley
of the beautiful creek, extended the American camp. On one
side rushed the clear mountain stream, on the other, unprotected
by any interposing hedge or fence, lay the broad fields of luxuriant
grain, irrigated from the creek by numerous artificial canals.
The sweet water was free, but a closely-posted chain of sentinels
strictly guarded those tempting fields from intrusion or injury by
the hungry animals, and the men with jealous honour obeyed
the orders given to respect the persons, properties, and feelings
of the inhabitants.

At midnight, news was brought that the enemy was in considerable force in one of the formidable gorges of the mountain,
distant two miles from the camp, and that here battle would be
given. By seven in the morning of the 15th, the troops were
in motion ; and, as they neared the town, they were overtaken by
Major Swords, from Fort Leavenworth, with Captain Weightman
and Lieutenant Gilmer, who, hearing there was to be a fight, had

ridden sixty miles during the night to be in for the fray. Major Swords was bearer to Colonel Kearny of his commission as Brigadier-General of the army of the United States.

A halt was called close to the village, while the general addressed, from the broad roof of one of the low adobé houses in the public square, the alcalde and people. He came, he said, by orders of his government, to take possession of the country, and extend over it the laws of the United States. They came amongst the people as friends — not as enemies ; as protectors — not as conquerors ; to confer benefits — not to commit injuries. Henceforth they were absolved from all allegiance to the Mexican government, from all obedience to General Armijo. The latter was no longer their governor—he (General K.) was their governor. Active partisanship on their part was not expected. Those who remained peaceably at home should be amply protected in their properties, persons, and religion ; and not a pepper, not an onion, should be taken or disturbed by the troops, without pay and the consent of the owner. Submission would insure safety—resistance was useless.

The general then, in a solemn manner, administered the oath of allegiance to the United States, to the alcalde and two captains of militia ; one of the latter swallowing it with a ludicrous ill-grace. He then shook hands with the alcalde, whom he continued in office, and through him with all the people, whom he hailed as good citizens of the United States, to which a general shout and grimaces of satisfaction were the ready response.

" To horse, and onward !" was now the cry; the foe were waiting in the pass. Banners and guidons were unfurled, and streaming out to the dazzling sun — the officers dashed eagerly along the lines — each great gun was ready, and every rifle charged. Nerved to the utmost was every arm, and the flash of stern joy in every eye. The gorge is neared—the walk quickens to a lively trot—the trot breaks into a gallop. The pass is entered

—it is cleared—no enemy is seen. Even the horses droop their heads in disappointment, as sullenly, and one by one, the guidons are furled, and all things assume the ordinary tameness of the march. Noon brought the army to the village of Tacoletè, and to the people there, the same change of government, with the same ceremonies, as had metamorphosed Las Vegas. San Miguel, another of these adobé villages, situated on the river Pecos, witnessed a repetition of the same drama, on the 16th. And here again expectation was on tiptoe, for every few minutes brought in additional reports, that Armijo was collecting an overwhelming force, to contest the army's further march, at the celebrated Cañon, the Pecos pass, fifteen miles from Santa Fé.

The 17th saw the banner of the Union passing proudly by the interesting ruins of the ancient, and once strongly fortified, town of Pecos, standing on a rocky eminence. Built, as it is alleged, before the conquest by the Spaniards, it presents the blended features of Pagan and Catholic architecture. Here, until within the last seven years, had burned the eternal holy fire, whose incense had ceaselessly ascended for centuries before the conquest, and whose sacredly fatal flame was watched and fed with unwearied fidelity by the Indian, even after his conversion to the faith of the Cross. But gradually the devoted tribe diminished in number, until at last too few were left to maintain the undying flames in the vast "estuffa;" then yielding to the sore necessity, the remnant abandoned the holy spot, and passed over the mountains to the south, to mingle with a kindred tribe of their original race, and there still keep up the eternal fire of Montezuma. Some few years it yet may burn; but the toil, the unceasing watchfulness, and the exposure to continued heat, consequent upon their faithful adherence to the old delusion, is with steady progress diminishing the already thin numbers of the tribe, and ere long, in all human probability, the holy fire, and the breath of the last of Montezuma's race, will go out together.

32

Santa Fé was still distant nine-and-twenty miles, on the morning of August the 18th, and between it and the army lay the formidable Cañon, which, fifteen miles from the town, contracts into a narrow gorge, some forty feet in width, above which rise hills many hundred feet on either side. "It is a gateway," says Colonel Emory, "which in the hands of a skilful engineer and one hundred men, would have been perfectly impregnable." Here Governor Armijo had taken up his position, with four thousand men and six pieces of artillery, and had thrown up an abattis. But even here our troops were destined to find no foe in arms. Whether owing to dissensions among his followers and officers, or from some other cause, Armijo had abandoned this commanding position without firing a single gun, and with his artillery and an escort of one hundred dragoons, had fled in hot haste towards Chihuahua. The army passed on. Vigil, the lieutenant-governor, with other leading citizens, received the general and his companions at the palace, and tendered to them the hospitalities of the place. With the setting of the sun, our guns, from an eminence overlooking the town, saluted the flag of the United States, floating over the capital of New Mexico. In fifty days the Army of the West had marched, from Fort Leavenworth, eight hundred and eighty-three miles, over solitudes and arid wastes, and subjugated, without striking a blow, a province containing a hundred thousand inhabitants, and in its commercial and military aspect a possession all-important to these United States.

On the morning of the 19th, the general, through his interpreter Robideaux, addressed the assembled people at considerable length, distinctly and firmly claiming henceforth the whole of New Mexico for his country, while giving the strongest assurances to all, of the peaceable and friendly intentions of his government, and of his army, and pledging the national faith to the protection of person, property, and religion. He declared them absolved from all allegiance to the government of Mexico, and promised the speedy promulgation of a civil government, similar to those in his own country, and under which the people would enjoy freedom and happiness hitherto unknown. The acting governor and other magistrates then took the oath of allegiance to the United States, and the people at large saluted the general with shouts, vivas, and huzzas.

The same energy and skill that had conducted the army through difficulties of no ordinary kind to bloodless victory, and the quiet occupation of the capital, now marked the measures taken for the permanent securing of the conquest. A fort, suited for a competent garrison, was immediately commenced on a site selected by Lieutenants Emory and Gilmer, within six hundred yards of the heart of the town, and from sixty to one hundred feet above it. Under the superintendence of these officers, and by the cheerful labours of men detailed from the several corps, quickly arose a substantial structure, named, in compliment to the Secretary of War, Fort Marcy. A proclamation was issued announcing to the people of New Mexico the capture of Santa Fé, and the general's intention to hold the province, or department, with its original boundaries on both sides the Del Norte, as a part of the United States, and under the name of the territory of New Mexico;—reiterating and confirming the promises heretofore given of the fullest protection in religion, property, and person ; and urgently recommending peaceful submission and allegiance to the United States. Interviews were had with those who had held authority under the Mexican government, with the clergy, and others, and the most conciliatory efforts used to win public confidence and attachment. With the chiefs and wise men of the Pueblo Indians, a large and formidable tribe, but among the most peaceable and best citizens of the department, conferences were had, in which their minds were fully disabused of the terrors sought to be impressed by the Mexican priests, regarding the barbarous treatment to be expected from the "Americanos," and they, and the several tribes of half-breeds, were made fast friends for ever. The savage Navajoes were warned to desist henceforth from their predatory and murderous inroads, and menaces of immediate and effective vengeance held forth in case of their disobedience. From Taos and its neighbourhood, deputations arrived, charged with the duty of giving in the popular allegiance and adhesion, and soliciting protection from the Indians. Their words and demeanour manifested the most friendly disposition; subsequent events proved them adepts in duplicity.

The last day of August brought with it reports, apparently well authenticated, that Armijo, having been joined by Colonel Ugarte with a force of five hundred regulars and some artillery, was now rallying the people to the south, and with daily increasing strength, advancing on the capital. To quiet the public apprehensions, and promptly suppress any symptoms of an insurrectionary kind, General Kearny, on September 2d, marched out of Santa Fé with seven hundred men, on a reconnoissance down the valley of the Rio Grande. He passed through Santo Domingo, San Felipe, Albuquerque, and many other villages, to Tomé, distant one hundred miles from Santa Fé. Everywhere the troops were received with hospitality, and manifestations of friendly welcome. The last sixty miles of this route, from Algodones to Tomé, presented the appearance of one continued straggling village, so closely clustered towns, hamlets, and farm-houses, along both banks of the river; while the inhabitants, especially the women, as well as the soldiers, enjoyed what seemed rather an excursion of pleasure among friends, than a military demonstration in a hostile land. Returned to Santa Fé by the 13th, General Kearny busied himself in making arrangements for the civil government of the province, for the military occupation of the capital and outposts, and for the prosecution of the further object intrusted to him, the expedition to California. A collection of laws for the administration of the territory, prepared by Colonel Doniphan,

with the aid of Mr. Willard P. Hall, then serving as a private in
the Missouri dragoons, and afterwards, while still so serving,
elected by his district as representative in Congress, was promulgated on the 22d ; and simultaneously therewith the following
appointments were made by the general, under authority from
the president :—Charles Bent, to be governor; Donaisano Vigil,
to be secretary; Richard Dallam, marshal; F. P. Blair, United
States district attorney; Charles Blumner, treasurer; Eugene
Leitzendorfer, auditor of public accounts; Joab Houghton, Antonio
José Otero, Charles Baubian, judges of the superior court, of the
newly subjugated territory. In this list of officials, it will be
seen, Americans and Mexicans were combined.

The conquest was complete, tranquillity was perfectly restored,
law and order succeeded to oppression and anarchy ; everything
wore the aspect of peacefulness and content. By letter to the
adjutant-general, the chief now communicated his resolution of
departing for the shores of the Pacific on the 25th of September,
in the hope of reaching his destination by the end of the following
month ; assuring the department, that no exertions would be
wanting on the part of any one attached to the expedition in
insuring to it full and entire success.

The little army, whose triumphant progress we have hitherto
followed from the borders of Missouri to the capital of New
Mexico, was now divided into three columns, destined to operate
in districts far apart, and never to reunite on foreign soil. Colonel Doniphan, with his own regiment, and Captain Weightman's
battery of artillery, was directed to remain in New Mexico, until
the arrival, now daily expected, of the 2d Missouri mounted volunteers, under Colonel Price, and, on being relieved by that
officer, to proceed southward and effect a junction with General
Wool at Chihuahua. The infantry battalion, under command
of Captain Angney, and Fischer's company of artillery, were to
remain in Santa Fé. The force designated to march on Califor-

nia consisted of the little corps of topographical engineers, and three hundred of the 1st United States dragoons, under Major Sumner, with two mountain howitzers.

Of the vast territories which lay between our western borders and the broad Pacific, and the acquisition of which has added more than a fourth to the national domain, little was accurately known, previous to the visit of the United States expedition under Lieutenant Wilkes, in 1841, and the subsequent explorations by land of Colonel Fremont. At intervals of frequent recurrence in the history of this continent, the name of California had attracted attention, and rumour had spread abroad vague and varying ideas of its extent, capabilities, and resources; but, while the coast of that distant region was imperfectly and even erroneously laid down, the great interior of the two provinces was an unexplored land, from which only the adventurous trader or daring hunter occasionally brought back scant and contradictory information. The peculiarities, however, of its position, as regarded these states; its commercial and political importance, in relation to a not far distant future; had not failed to be appreciated, either by our own statesmen, or by those of foreign countries: and the necessary, self-protecting policy of America was plainly indicated by the precautionary seizure and temporary occupation of Monterey, in 1842, by our squadron, under Commodore Ap Catesby Jones, acting upon information of a contemplated surrender of California to Great Britain.

After the conquest of New Mexico, and the establishment of civil government at Santa Fé, General Kearny made a proper disposition of his forces, and prepared for his second and more arduous enterprise. Leaving orders for the officer commanding the Mormon battalion, five hundred strong, upon arriving at Santa Fé, to take up the line of march in his rear, General Kearny, on the 25th of September, set out for California with the corps of topographical engineers, and the three hundred United

States dragoons, under Major Sumner. For several days the route lay over ground previously traversed, and through villages visited before, during the military reconnoissance as far as Tomé. The Rio Grande was crossed at Albuquerque, sixty-five miles below Santa Fé, where the depth of the river was about thirty inches, and its width some five-and-twenty yards. The valley of the Rio Grande presents thus far down, bottom lands, about a mile and a half wide, and elevated but a few feet above the level of the running stream, which is rapid and regular, and affords the greatest facilities for irrigation, by means of zequias, or little artificial canals. These are indispensible aids to cultivation in a country, the lowlands of which are seldom, if ever, visited by rains. West of this belt of bottom land lies a succession of rolling sand-hills, amid which are the hiding-places during day of the Navajoes, whence, in small companies, these predatory lords of New Mexico descend at night to the valley, to bear off from the settlements motley plunder of fruit and cattle, as well as children and women. When united in more numerous bands, they boldly come down by day and levy their blackmail, then quickly retire to their far distant, and apparently inaccessible, retreats in the mountains, whither Mexican vengeance has never yet essayed pursuit.

At Tomé, reached October the 1st, the river was found to measure thirty yards in width, its depth still continuing about thirty inches. Below this, for a distance of some miles, the valley widens, the soil improves, and the cultivation is of a superior kind. But after passing the pretty village of Sabinal, " the settlements became very few and far between." In their encampment at the bend of the river, opposite La Joya, the column awaited during the 3d, the wagons which had fallen in the rear. Here an express from Colonel Price announced the arrival of that officer at Santa Fé. And at noon a Mexican on panting steed rode into camp, claiming instant aid and protection against the

Navajoes, on the part of the alcalde and people of Pulvidera.
Captain Moore's company was forthwith despatched to the
rescue: while orders were sent to Colonel Doniphan to march
his regiment into the Navajo country, for the purpose of effectually repressing their incursions.   A march of twelve miles on the
4th brought the column to the appropriately named village of
Pulvidera, at which place the dragoons had arrived too late on
the preceding day to render any assistance.   The Indian assailants, in number about one hundred well mounted men, had
descended rapidly on the town, and driven off the horses and
cattle, while the terrified inhabitants took refuge in their mud
houses.   The people of Lamitas, a village two miles below, rose
to the rescue of their neighbours, and seized upon the pass, or
gorge, by which alone retreat with all the plunder could be made
good.   The Indians, thus in part foiled, slaughtered wantonly on
the spot as many as they could of the captured oxen and goats,
and with the larger number of the horses and mules scrambled
away over the hills and cliffs beyond pursuit.   No wounds had
been given or received.   A more disastrous foray had been made
by the same band upon the settlements higher up the river, ere
yet the American army had reached Santa Fé, and when Armijo
had called for a levy *en masse*.   Then, in addition to other varied
plunder, fifteen or sixteen of the prettiest women had been borne
away.   " Women," says Colonel Emory in his extremely interesting Notes,—" women, when captured, are taken as wives by
those who capture them, but they are treated by the Indian wives
of the capturers as slaves, and made to carry wood and water;
if they chance to be pretty, or receive too much attention from
their lords and masters, they are, in the absence of the latter,
unmercifully beaten, and otherwise maltreated.   The most unfortunate thing which can befall a captive woman, is to be claimed
by two persons.   In this case she is either shot, or delivered up
for indiscriminate violence."   To the people of New Mexico

assuredly the change in government ought to be welcome, even were it attended by no other benefit, than absolute security in the future against outrages such as these.

Pursuing his route along the bank of the Rio Grande, on the 6th of October, General Kearny was met by the celebrated adventurer, trapper and guide, Kit Carson, sent with an escort of sixteen men, including six Delaware Indians, as bearer of express despatches from Commodore Stockton and Lieutenant-Colonel Fremont, at Monterey, to the authorities at Washington. The information brought by Mr. Carson, who had left Ciudad de los Angelos on the 1st of September, represented the Californias as already in possession of the above-named officers; that in the space of some ten days the upper country had been revolutionized, and placed under the American flag, which now floated in undisputed sovereignty from every important position; that there the war was ended, and peace and harmony established among the people.

If this unlooked-for intelligence shot a momentary chill through the bosoms of the gallant little band, that had in loyal brotherhood of hope threaded its way through toils and trials to such a distance from home, and saw now even the chance of honourable trophy from the battle-field denied, the patriotic and the brave will know how to appreciate and to pardon the soldier's disappointment. How much more ready to acknowledge and estimate aright the purer, sterner patriotism, that quickly swallowed up the lingerings of self-love and soldierly ambition in the pride of American success, and with cheerfulness resumed the dull routine of duty ever faithfully performed, while sighing as it thought of laurels which it might have shared!

Under these circumstances, it seemed to the general unnecessary to take with him the whole of his present force, a portion of which might be more serviceably employed in the already subjugated province. Accordingly, three companies of the dra-

33

goons and the principal part of the baggage-train, under Major Sumner, were ordered to retrace their steps, to winter at Albuquerque, or operate as might be found expedient. The reduced column for advance now comprised the general and his personal staff, Major Swords, Captains Johnson and Turner, Assistant-Surgeon Griffin, Lieutenants Emory and Warner, with their assistants and attendants, and Captain Moore, with Lieutenants Hammond and Davidson, and one hundred men of the 1st dragoons. Mr. Robideaux accompanied as interpreter; and Mr. Carson, yielding to the urgent representations of General Kearny, who insured the safe delivery in Washington of the despatches, by a trust-worthy and expeditious messenger, and took on himself the whole responsibility, consented to forego his cherished hopes of soon rejoining his family, and undertook the piloting of the column through the mountains and the deserts, the difficulties and the dangers of which he had, with his faithful followers, just overcome. The two mountain howitzers went with the advancing force, and the returning command was put under requisition to supply the best outfits for these, and the six wagons, drawn each by eight stout mules, that followed the dragoons.

Soon the last settlements were past, and thenceforth a new road was to be explored. The valley began to narrow, and the table-land, over which they were compelled to make their way, was rugged, and obstructed by thick bushes, rendering the toilsome services of a pioneer force indispensable, and progress consequently slow. Worse, they were informed, awaited them in front. On the 9th, the teams came blown and staggering into camp, after a journey of less than twelve miles, and some of the wagons were broken. It was therefore determined to send back the wagons and resort to mules with pack-saddles, for the transportation of the baggage and provisions. Awaiting these new modes of conveyance, for which messengers had been sent to Major Sumner, the four following days were spent in camp.

Here a cross section of the river gave a width of one hundred and eighteen feet, with an average depth of fourteen inches, the water flowing over large round pebbles, making it unsuitable for navigation with any kind of boats; the fall is estimated at four feet and a half in the mile.

On the 13th, Lieutenant Ingalls arrived with a mail, the last communication that could be expected with the United States. On the evening of the same day, the pack-saddles came up, and on the morrow, the wagons having been sent back, under charge of Lieutenant Ingalls, the march was resumed. Two hundred and thirty miles below Santa Fé, the army took its final departure from the Rio Grande del Norte, on October 15th, marching westward over a table-land, deeply cut by the now dry channels of the mountain streams. The approach to the Sierra de los Mimbres was over " a beautiful rolling country, traversed by small streams of pure water, fringed with a stunted growth of walnut, live oak, and ash," and through the delightful and rich, though here narrow, valley of the Mimbres river. The 18th brought them to the celebrated copper-mines, which are extremely rich in that ore and in gold, but have been abandoned in consequence of the Apache Indians cutting off all supplies from the operators, destroying the mining town, and manifesting jealous and determined hostility. On the morning of the 20th, a party of these Indians, headed by their chief, Red Sleeve, came into camp, mounted on small, but fine and well-cared horses, and fantastically attired, mostly in habiliments plundered from the Mexicans. Beautiful helmets decked with black feathers covered the heads of some, but the most were bare-headed and bare-legged, with buskins, waist-belt, and cartridge-box. Variously armed as attired, some bore guns, others lances and bows and arrows, in the use of all of which they are exceedingly expert. A nomad race, whose temporary dwellings are formed of interwoven twigs, they roam the fair hills and pleasant rolling lands that over-

hang the Del Norte between the 31st and 32d parallels of
latitude, and plunder without compunction any weaker bands
that fall in their way. Now they vowed before the general
eternal peace and friendship with the *white* men, and everlasting
hatred to the Mexicans. Carson placed little value on their
vows.

Resuming the march at noon, they slowly descended the
narrow valley of Night Creek, overhung on each side by huge
masses of volcanic rock, that with their ragged and precipitous
walls much impeded the road. A descent of five miles brought
them to the bank of the famous Gila, a bold, clear stream, fifty
feet wide and about two feet deep, running swiftly over a pebbly
bed, bordered with trees, and closed in by mountains.

Hence the route wound through the wild and bewildering fastnesses of the savage Indian tribes, who hold in terrified subjection the once flourishing states of Chihuahua and Sonora. Still
fertile and abounding in natural resources, they are rapidly
declining in wealth and population; and if the incessant devasta-
tions and alarms of these, their uncivilized mountain lords, be
not stayed, the country must soon become a wide, luxuriant
waste. An almost impracticable labyrinth of mountain-spurs
and valleys; ascents and descents narrow, tortuous, and paved
with sharp fragments of basalt and of trap; rocks, precipices, and
ravines, in which every aspect of nature and of life was strange,
imposed on men and beasts an incredible amount of painful
exertion and incessant toil. Ruins, connected by tradition with
the ancient race of Montezuma, and manifesting a civilization
now lost in its antiquity, were frequently encountered; these
were generally surrounded by heaps of broken pottery, and in
some instances traced with hieroglyphics, no key to which has
yet been discovered. Interviews were repeatedly had with
smaller or larger groups from the Apache and kindred tribes;
but treacherous and cruel themselves, they obstinately declined

such intercourse as could be beneficial. Vain were all efforts made to procure from them a supply of mules, to replace those which had in numbers foundered and died under the toils of the road. Their promises were abundant, their anxiety to barter manifest, and their desire of gain strong, but stronger than all these were their cowardly doubts and habitual duplicity. Centuries had formed the roots of that deep, undying hate, which they bore the Mexican; the wrongs of their forefathers were vaguely remembered, but shapeless as these memories were, they exercised over the now savage race a resistless sway, and made them look upon all whites with that most deadly of hatreds, the hatred of revenge and of fear.

The rugged mountains were left on the 9th of November, and the valley of the Gila extended its width. This river had been crossed times innumerable by the army, so often frequently as from ten to fifteen times in a single day's march, so jealously do the craggy spurs and precipitous cañons obstruct the progress of an intruding force. On the 10th, a march of six miles over a plain, giving, in its now unused zequias, ruins, and thickly strewed fragments of pottery, evidences of having once sustained an industrious and dense population, brought them to the remains known as the " Casa de Montezuma." Portions of the walls of four buildings exist, and piles of earth testify to the site of many others. The one which was found most nearly entire, was a building of some fifty or sixty feet square, of four stories in elevation; the walls, built of a sort of whitish earth mixed with pebble, were four feet thick, pierced for doors and windows, smoked outside, and plastered, or glazed, within. No traces of steel implements were left upon the timbers, which were round and unhewn. Fire had evidently destroyed the whole interior, and no specimens of household furniture or domestic art were to be found—with the exception of marine shells cut into ornaments, and the corn-grinder commonly met among all the ruins on the plains. About two hundred yards from the chief ruin, a terrace, about three hundred feet in length, and five in height, was surmounted by a pyramid, eight feet high, which commanded a view of the vast plain, stretching to north-east and west, on the left bank of the Gila; the whole extent of which, for many miles, seemed to have been at one time irrigated by water from the river.

Along this plain now graze the cattle of the peaceful and interesting Indian tribes, the Pimos and Maricopas; tribes distinct, but not dissimilar, living as neighbours in cordial amity. To the army they accorded a frank welcome, and ready hospitality. An industrious, intelligent, and virtuous people, they occupy a beautiful and fertile valley, from which they procure many of the comforts and even little luxuries of life, remote from the busy world, and seldom visited by whites, and then only by those who in distress confidently seek aid, that is ever generously bestowed. Their religion consists simply in a belief in one supreme and benevolent spirit. "It was a rare sight," we quote from Colonel Emory, "it was a rare sight to be thrown in the midst of a large nation, of what is termed wild Indians, surpassing many of the Christian nations in agriculture, little behind them in the useful arts, and immeasurably before them in honesty and virtue." Even by the Mexican government the worth of this people, numbering several thousand souls, has been uniformly appreciated, while the Apaches have ever found them superior in battle, and have even in their own retreats suffered severe chastisement for thefts and other outrages, whenever hazarded against men that are as peaceful as they are brave.

A two days' rest in this pleasing neighbourhood having much refreshed the men and recruited the animals, at noon of the 13th, a farewell watering was given to the horses, ere they set out on the Tesotal Jornada. Across a plain of granitic sand, which rose almost imperceptibly to the summit of a hill range, running south-east, and which was wholly destitute of vegetation, and down the opposite slope of similar character, they made a two days' journey, during which the mules suffered dreadfully for lack of food and water. Many perished, and those which survived gave little promise of future service. Rest in camp, in the Gila bottom-land, was necessary during the 15th, as on the morrow they were to set out on the most distressing part of the journey, a distance of three hundred miles, reported to be without grass. For many days the march was over parched valleys and table-lands, dreary beyond description, where a few stunted growths of the Larrea Mexicana, gave almost the only sign of vegetation. This bitter and offensive shrub, even mules when most hungry refuse to touch. The cane and willow found here and there in the low grounds, afforded these poor animals a scanty subsistence. By the 22d, most of the men were on foot, and the general's horse having given out, he was obliged to have recourse to his mule. This day they reached the junction of the Gila with the Colorado, where the united streams force a cañon through a butte of feldspathic granite, and flow due magnetic west. As the column approached the end of its day's march, they encoun-tered a trail, indicating the recent passage of a mounted force of probably one thousand men. Reports which had reached the Pimo villages strengthened the first supposition, that it was General Castro on his return from Sonora, with a cavalry force, to regain California. If so, he could not be far distant; the column numbered only one hundred and ten men, that was a force too small to await an attack; promptly therefore did the general resolve, should the conjecture prove correct, to assail the enemy's camp the moment night set in, and beat them before they could have time or light to discover the disparity of numbers. Lieutenant Emory was ordered to reconnoitre, and soon ascertained that their neighbours were a party of Mexicans, on their way from Cali-fornia to Sonora, with five hundred horses for the use of Castro's command.   On the person of one of these intercepted Mexicans was found a mail; the letters, suspected of being on public affairs, were of course opened, and from them it was ascertained that a counter-revolution had taken place in California, that the Americans were expelled from Santa Barbara, Puebla de los Angelos, and other places, and that Captain Flores commanded as general and governor in the country, which had thrown off "the detestable Anglo-Yankee yoke." From the horses, General Kearny levied a much needed supply.

Ten miles below the mouth of the Gila they forded the Colorado, there five hundred yards wide, and in mid-channel about four feet deep.   Along the river bottom they marched thirty miles further, then, at dawn of day on November 25th, each man with a bundle of the river-grass tied to the cantle of his saddle, turned their course across the formidable desert.   This dreary waste of floating sand lay in their route ninety miles from water to water; in crossing it, during three days and nights, much suffering was endured, and numbers of the horses and mules sunk on the heavy sands, to die of hunger and thirst.

Refreshed by the waters of the Cariso creek, they slowly pursued a scarcely less toilsome road, partly through thickets of the centennial plant, the Agave Americana, the countless spears of which sadly tore the dismounted and wearied men, whose feet and legs were now almost bare; partly over rugged rocks, amid hills where barrenness and desolation held sovereign sway.   The flesh of the jaded horses, poor and tough, supplied no palatable food, and the howl of the wolves no cheering lullaby, as the ferocious creatures battled over the carcasses of the deserted beasts.

December the 2d, the frontier settlement of California, Warner's Rancheria, in the beautiful valley of the Agua Caliente, burst upon their delighted view.   Here they rested, and made some slight amends for their long-continued abstinence.   This rancho,

or farm, was sixty miles from San Diego, now in possession of
Commodore Stockton, and eighty miles from Los Angelos. Despatching a letter to Commodore Stockton, requesting him to send
out a party to open a communication between them, the general
pushed cautiously forward, and on the 5th was met, about forty
miles from San Diego, by Captain Gillespie, with an escort of
thirty-five men, sent out by the commodore. This little force
consisted of California volunteers, with some carbineers from the
ship Congress, under Lieutenant Beall, and was accompanied by
a field-piece.

From Captain Gillespie were learned the main facts of the
attempted revolution and the then existing state of affairs.
Thinking his conquest complete, and all things secure, Commodore Stockton, on the 2d of September, withdrew his force of
sailors and marines from Ciudad de los Angelos to San Francisco, where he designed to make arrangements for an attack on
Mazatlan and Acapulco, in conjunction with Lieutenant-Colonel
Fremont. The latter joined him on the 12th of October with the
main strength of his battalion, leaving Captain Gillespie, with
nineteen volunteers and a few pieces of ordnance, to garrison the
capital. The departure of the great body of the American forces
from the vicinity of Los Angelos, was the signal for revolt, incited
by the Mexican officers still lingering in the territory. The
insurgents, several hundred strong, took the field under Flores,
and hourly gathering force, compelled Captain Gillespie to capitulate, on terms highly honourable to him and his little band, and
to retire from the presence of overwhelming numbers, on board
the Savannah, Captain Mervine, then lying off San Pedro. Meantime, Lieutenant Talbot, a young, but most gallant and meritorious officer, who had been left as military commandant at Santa
Barbara, a pretty place about one hundred miles north of Los
Angelos, with his little force of nine men, was hotly besieged by
above two hundred insurgents, under Don Manuel Gaspar.
    34

Having effected his escape from the town, Talbot took post in the neighbouring hills, to await the return of the troops. Being discovered in his retreat, the Californians burned him out, and, with infinite peril and difficulty, he and his band escaped into the mountains, and thence, after a month's travel over some five hundred miles, enduring much hardship and suffering, they effected a junction with Colonel Fremont at Monterey, where the latter was recruiting for the expedition to the south.

Informed of the revolt, Commodore Stockton had sent down the "Savannah" to San Pedro. He followed himself in the "Congress," and took up his march for Los Angelos, dragging along by hand six of the ship's guns. Now he was in possession of San Diego, with his noble force of sailors and marines, doing duty merrily on shore, as horse, foot, and artillery.

Having further learned from Captain Gillespie, that an armed band of the enemy, with an extra supply of horses, was encamped at the Indian village of San Pasqual, nine miles distant from his present position, General Kearny sent out Lieutenant Hammond with a party to reconnoitre. This party saw, and was seen by, the foe. The *reveille* sounded at two o'clock on the morning of the 6th December, and at three the march was resumed in order of battle. The enemy, one hundred and eighty fresh, well-armed, and well-mounted men, under Colonel Andreas Pico, were already in the saddle, prepared for an attack. Here then, at length, the little section of the army, weary and worn from its perilous and most harassing march over the half of a mighty continent, ill clad, ill mounted, and ill fed, was to grapple for the first time, and at his own door, with the foe.

General Kearny, with Lieutenants Emory and Warner at his side, rode immediately in rear of Captain Johnson and the advanced guard of twelve dragoons, mounted on the best horses that remained. Then followed Captain Moore, with about fifty of the dragoons, mounted, with few exceptions, on the jaded and

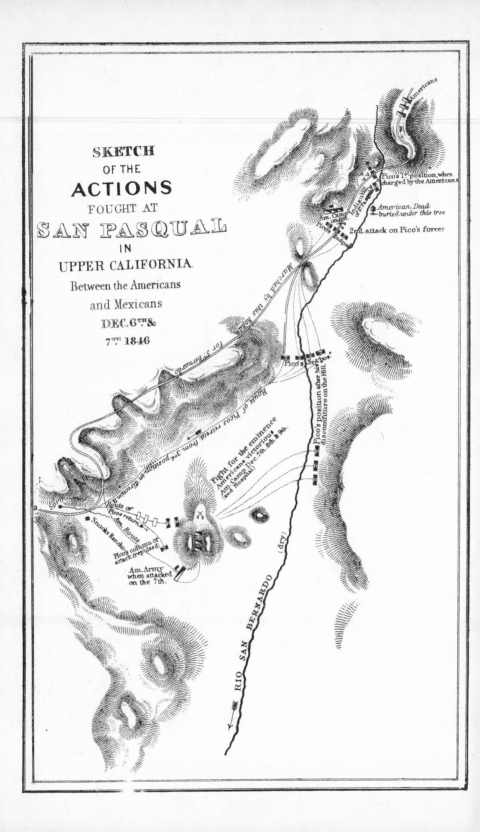

SKETCH
OF THE
ACTIONS
FOUGHT AT
SAN PASQUAL
IN
UPPER CALIFORNIA.
Between the Americans
and Mexicans
DEC. 6TH &
7TH 1846

Americans

Pico's 1st position, when
charged by the Americans

American Dead
buried under this tree

2nd. attack on Pico's forces

Indian village
of S. Pasqual

Am. Camp
on 6th.

Pico's 3rd. pos.

Marched to the Road

Route of Pico's retreat from his 3rd. position to his 1st.

Pico's 3rd. pos.

Pico's position after his
discomfiture on the Hill

Fight for the eminence
Americans victorious
Am. Camp Dec. 7th. 8th. & 9th.
(and Hospital)

Route of
Pico's return

Am. Route

Snooks Rancho

Pico's column of
attack repulsed

Am. Army
when attacked
on the 7th.

RIO SAN BERNARDO (dry)

famished mules they had ridden, over one thousand and fifty miles, from Santa Fé. Next came Captains Gibson and Gillespie, with twenty of their volunteers: Lieutenant Davidson, with the two howitzers, managed by dragoons, brought up the rear. The remainder of the force, dragoons, volunteers, and citizens, were left to protect and bring on the baggage, under command of Major Swords, the quartermaster of the expedition.

Drawn nigh to the enemy, Captain Johnson made a furious charge upon them with his advanced guard, promptly supported by General Kearny and Captain Moore. The Californians withstood not the shock, but pouring in a continual fire, gave way and retreated to an open plain about half a mile distant. Eagerly Captain Moore, with the few dragoons on horseback, pursued; the tired mules slowly seconded the ardour of their riders, and soon an interval was left between the hot pursuers and these thus retarded in their support. Well mounted, and among the most expert horsemen in the world, the enemy rallied in full force, took advantage of the interval, charged with desperation on the advance, and from their overwhelming superiority in numbers, made dreadful havoc with their long lances. For five minutes they furiously held the ground, for five minutes the rapidly thinning handful around the general bore up against the storm: the support came up, hand to hand the fierce but unequal fight continued for half an hour; then the outnumbering foe was repulsed, and fled from the field, to which they returned not again. The affrighted and wholly unmanageable mules had refused to bring their howitzers into the fight.

With the dawning of the day, the smoke cleared off from the battle-field, permitting the victors to collect their wounded and their dead. Of officers and men, sixteen wounded and nineteen slain, gave melancholy evidence of how hardly the victory had been won. The killed were Captains Johnson and Moore, Lieutenant Hammond, Sergeants Moore and Whitehurst, Corporals Clapin and West, and ten privates of the 1st dragoons, one private of the topographical corps, and one volunteer. The wounded included General Kearny, Captains Gibson and Gillespie, Lieutenant Warner, Mr. Robideaux, Sergeant Cox, and ten privates of the dragoons. On the next day, the gallant Sergeant Cox died of his wounds. Many of the survivors had from two to ten lance-wounds; Captain Gillespie and Lieutenant Warner had three each; the general two, and these so serious, that during the remainder of the day, Captain Turner assumed the command. The loss of the enemy was not ascertained, they having carried off in their final retreat all the wounded and the dead, excepting six; but it must have been severe.

Having been assured that the dead, wherever buried, would be dug up, that the bodies might be stripped of their clothing, the sorrowing victors bound on mules the remains of their fallen companions, with the intention of taking them to San Diego, there to be decently interred; but the number of mules required for conveyance of the wounded, caused this intention to be abandoned, and the men were engaged in fortifying the camp for the night. During the whole of the 6th, the enemy hovering around, kept the camp in constant and harassing excitement. Early in the day three of Captain Gillespie's volunteers were despatched to San Diego, thirty-nine miles distant, to procure conveyances for the wounded. As night closed in, under a willow that grew beside the battle-field, were laid to rest, in all possible silence and secrecy, the departed brave. Thus to lay down for ever in the strange land, far away from kindred and from home, those whom a march together of two thousand miles, common hopes and hardships, common dangers, enjoyments and privations, had familarized and endeared, was to the survivors of this little band of brothers no common grief.

On the ground where they were forced to encamp, rocks and cacti afforded scarcely so much of level space as to accommodate the wounded during the damp, cold night, and sleep was denied even after thirty hours of ceaseless exertion and fatigue. The dawn of the 7th called to new efforts and new endurance; the column was now reduced to one-third of its number, worn down with toil, ragged and emaciated, with mules fast falling away, horses dead, and provisions exhausted. By the skill and untiring assi-duities of Dr. Griffin, the only surgeon of the party, the wounded men were now capable of being removed in rudely formed ambu-lances, and General Kearny was enabled to resume the command. Pursuing the San Barnardo road towards San Diego, they found the enemy occupying the hills in their front, but retiring as they approached. At the rancheria of San Barnardo, they watered their horses and procured refreshments for the sick, then moving towards the bed of the river, drove before them many cattle, a much needed supply. These, however, had soon to be aban-doned, for the enemy debouching from the hills in the rear, sent forward a party in full gallop to seize a hill commanding the road, and these it became necessary to dislodge. To accomplish this, was but the work of a few moments, and the task of the advance. The Californians had five or six killed and wounded in the skirmish, which entailed on the victors no other loss than that of the cattle, one sufficiently serious under the circumstances. Against a force so numerically superior and so splendidly mount-ed, it was impossible to move, while the ambulances required the services of half the effective men; and even with the tender-est care in transporting them, the sufferings of the sick were exceedingly distressing. Here, therefore, the general encamped, to wait until the wounded could be carried on horseback, resolved then to cut his way to San Diego.

A flag of truce sent in by Pico on the morning of the 8th, led to a conference; he wishing to exchange four Americans, whom he had captured, for an equal number of Californians. Unfor-tunately there was but one Californian prisoner in camp; but this one was well exchanged for Burgess, who was one of those despatched to Commodore Stockton on the 6th. He and his companions had arrived safely in San Diego, and on their return had, previously to their capture, concealed their letters under a tree ; but on subsequent examination, it was found that these had been abstracted. That night, Lieutenant Beall of the navy, Mr. Carson, and an Indian, voluntarily went forth, on the perilous attempt of reaching San Diego, nine-and-twenty miles distant, and every pass towards which was now occupied by the enemy.

During four days' rest in this camp, as for many days before, their food was the meat of the poor worn-down horses and mules ; but the wounded were going on well, and on the evening of the 10th all save two were declared by the surgeon ready for the saddle. Orders were given to resume the march next morning. Before daybreak, they were joyously surprised by the arrival in camp of Lieutenant Gray, of the navy, sent out from San Diego by Commodore Stockton, with an escort of one hundred tars and eighty marines. Beall, Carson, and the Indian, had safely arrived in San Diego. The gallant new-comers found glad employment until day, in distributing among the naked and famished soldiers their own clothing and provisions.

By ten in the forenoon of the 11th December, the united force was on its route. Before them the enemy precipitately fled, leaving behind most of the cattle, for which they had so eagerly contested. This day first burst upon their view, from one of the hills, the broad Pacific, henceforth to be their country's western boundary. On the 12th they entered San Diego, having thus terminated the arduous march of one thousand and ninety miles from Santa Fé.

The preparations for the contemplated expedition against Ciudad de los Angelos, distant one hundred and forty-five miles, having been steadily pushed forward, at the request of Commodore Stockton, who had in September assumed the title of Governor of California, General Kearny assumed the command, and went forth from San Diego, on the 29th of December, at the head of about five hundred men. The force was constituted thus: sixty dismounted dragoons consolidated into one company, under Captain Turner; fifty Californian volunteers, commanded by Captain Gillespie; the remainder, sailors and marines, acting as infantry and artillery, with six great guns of various calibre; Lieutenant Emory acted as assistant adjutant-general, and Commodore Stockton accompanied the army.

Progress was slow, the oxen used in the wagons being poor, and the wagons themselves of the miserable construction of the country. No enemy was seen until January the 8th, when they showed themselves in full force, under their acting governor and captain-general, Flores, occupying with six hundred men and four pieces of artillery the heights in front commanding the San Gabriel, and evidently prepared to dispute the passage of that river. The troops were immediately disposed in the order best adapted to meet a wholly mounted force, a strong party of skirmishers being thrown forward to cover the front, the wagons and baggage occupying the centre, and the remainder of the command protecting the flanks. The position of the enemy was highly favourable. A ridge fifty feet high ran parallel with the bank on his side of the river, on which he posted his artillery, and just behind this hill, on either flank, a squadron of his cavalry awaited the favourable moment for a charge. As the leading battalion, deploying as skirmishers, reached the middle of the stream, the battery on the hill opened upon them, and made the water fly around with grape and round-shot. The artillery tars were now ordered forward, the guns were quickly unlimbered, pulled over cheerily by the men, and planted in counter battery on the enemy's side. And soon, and briskly, they sent forth their thundering replies to the hill, making the fire from the latter

wild and uncertain.   Thus covered, the baggage and cattle were
with great toil, forced across the river, which flowed one hundred
yards wide and about twenty inches deep, over a bottom of quick-
sand.   Under a natural banquette, breast-high, on the right bank,
the troops deployed into line, while a heavy shower of round-shot
and of grape passed chiefly over their heads.   In an hour and
twenty minutes the baggage-train had all crossed, the artillery
of the enemy was silenced, and the troops were in full charge
upon the hill.   Half way between the bank and the hill, the foe
made a furious charge on the left flank, while the right was
menaced at the same moment.   A volley or two repulsed the hot
assailants, and in ten minutes more the heights were carried, and
our troops masters of the field.   Pursuit was impossible, from the
wretched condition of the wagon-train, which, bearing provisions
for the garrison intended to be left in the city of Los Angelos,
could not be abandoned.   On the battle-field the army encamped
that night.

Next morning, the cattle but little refreshed, the route was
leisurely pursued across the Mesa, a wide plain, lying between
the San Gabriel and the stream, called indifferently the Rio San
Fernando, and the Rio de los Angelos.   The enemy hung continually on the front and flanks for a distance of about six miles,
then concentrated their force at a crest and ravine, that commanded the road on the right.   Here General Flores addressed
his men, urging them to make one more bold and determined
charge, to which he promised certain success.   Deviating to the
left of the road, to deprive him of the vantage-ground for his
artillery, the army steadily pursued its march, disregarding the
fire which the enemy opened with his artillery from a distance.
Flores now deployed his force, making a horse-shoe in the
column's front, and opening with his nine-pounders a galling
fire on the right flank.   A halt was called to silence this annoyance,
which was a fifteen minutes' work, and the order was again

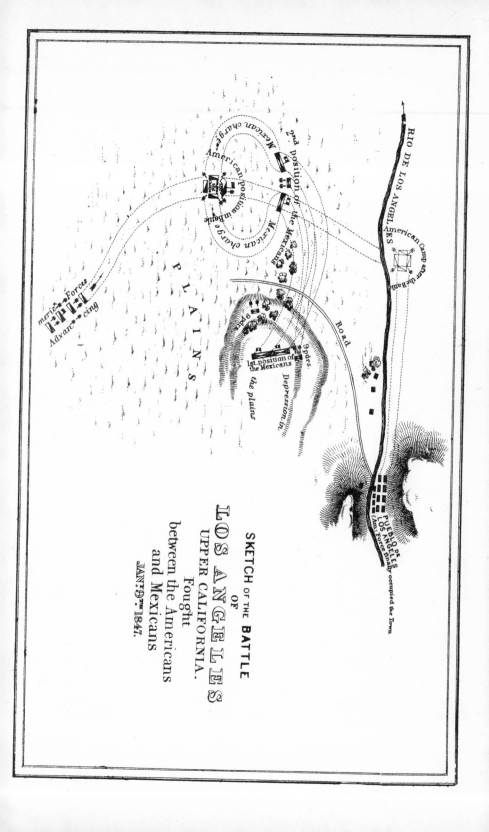

SKETCH OF THE **BATTLE**
OF
𝕷𝕺𝕾 𝕬𝕹𝕲𝕰𝕷𝕰𝕾
UPPER CALIFORNIA.
Fought
between the Americans
and Mexicans
JANY 9TH 1847.

given to move forward, when down came the enemy at once on the left flank and the rear in menacing charge.   One volley from the small-arms brought them to a check; a round of grape completed their repulse.   The accoutrements of their fallen horses, with their dead and wounded, they bore away on horseback to the hills.   Now, three o'clock in the afternoon, the town was distant only four miles.   It was known to abound in wine and *agua ardiente;* with wise precaution, therefore, the general led his little army of conquerors across the stream, and encamped some three miles below the town.

During these two days, the loss on the part of the Americans was small.   In the spirited battle of the 8th, one seaman, acting artilleryman, was killed, one volunteer and eight seamen wounded, of whom two subsequently died.   In the continued skirmishing and annoying affairs of the 9th, one dragoon and two seamen were severely wounded; Capt. Gillespie of the volunteers, and Lieutenant Rowan of the navy, were slightly contused by spent balls.   Their extraordinary expertness on horseback, enabled the enemy to carry off all their dead and wounded, and so conceal their loss, but it must have been comparatively great; it was estimated at eighty-five.

Next morning the army entered, without encountering opposition, the City of the Angels, the capital of California, and hitherto the centre of the wealth and population of that province, as well as the focus of revolution, and the point of military power.   On the 14th, Colonel Fremont, with four hundred volunteers raised in the neighbourhood of the Sacramento, reported himself at the capital.   With him a portion of the enemy had on the preceding day entered into terms of capitulation, among them Andreas Pico, second to Flores in command of the insurgents, who had by breaking his parole forfeited his life, but by this capitulation procured pardon.   Don José Mariana Flores made good his

35

escape to Sonora.   The revolt was now effectually quelled, and the country peaceably submitted to American authority.

At the meeting of these three distinguished officers, Kearny, Stockton, and Fremont, each of whom had so materially contributed to the success and the glory of their country's arms, difficulties unhappily arose, as to their relative powers and position in the conquered territory.   About the 16th of January, Commodore Stockton, acting, according to his own opinion, in strict conformity with the instructions received by his predecessor in the naval command, and by himself, proceeded to organize a temporary civil government for California, and nominated Colonel Fremont as governor.   Against this procedure General Kearny protested, and in writing assured the commodore, that to him (General K.) the President had confided the sole right of erecting a civil government in California.   Commodore Stockton, relying on his instructions, refused to acknowledge General Kearny's authority.   Colonel Fremont abided by the decision of the commodore.

The instructions, under which General Kearny claimed his right to sole authority in the territorial government of the conquest, have been materially embodied in the preceding chapter.   For the more ready comprehension of the counter-claim, a brief retrospect may be desirable.

By a "secret and confidential order" from the Navy Department, bearing date June 24, 1845, Commodore Sloat, then commanding the United States naval forces in the Pacific, was instructed, so soon as he should ascertain beyond a doubt that Mexico had declared war against the United States, to "at once employ the force under his command to the best advantage," "to at once possess himself of the port of San Francisco, and blockade or occupy such other ports as his force may permit."   In subsequent orders from the same department, under date respectively, May 13th, May 15th, and June 8th, 1846, those instructions were confirmed, and the commodore was expressly directed to exercise all the rights that belonged to him as commander-in-chief of a belligerent squadron; while in every communication the importance was urged of establishing friendly relations with the people of California, and making the occupation of the ports a benefit to the inhabitants.

On the 7th of June, Commodore Sloat, then at Mazatlan, in the Savannah, received intelligence of the actual outbreak of hostilities, and properly considered these as justifying his commencing offensive operations on the west coast, under the order of June, 1845. Immediately he set sail for Monterey, landed the necessary force of seamen and marines, entered that town, hoisted the standard of the United States, without bloodshed or strenuous opposition, and issued his proclamation, declaring, among other things, California henceforth to be a portion of the United States. Other ports were similarly occupied, and possession of the coast, with its bays and harbours, secured.

About the same time, Lieutenant-Colonel Fremont, then near the settlement of Sonoma, on the bay of San Francisco, with his topographical corps, had been compelled in self-defence to hoist the American flag and raise a volunteer force, in consequence of the extraordinary, unprovoked, and faithless conduct of De Castro, governor of Upper California. The design of the latter was avowed, to attack and destroy, not only Fremont's party, but all the American settlers. Hemmed in by a treacherous foe, more than tenfold his number, Fremont turned on his pursuers, defeated them in fiercely contested engagements, and on the 4th of July, at Sonoma, headed the American and foreign residents in a declaration of independence, and war against De Castro and his troops, as the only means of safety. A few days afterwards an officer from Commodore Sloat brought intelligence of his capture of Monterey. Colonel Fremont, then leaving some fifty men in garrisons behind him, set forth in pursuit of De Castro with one

hundred and sixty riflemen, when he received instructions from
Commodore Sloat to march upon Monterey.

On the 29th July Commodore Stockton succeeded to the naval
command, and therewith to the authority conveyed in the instructions from the Naval Department.   He declared the whole coast
of California to be in a state of blockade, proclaimed himself
governor and commander-in-chief of all the forces by sea and
land, and claimed by right of conquest the whole territory of
Upper and Lower California as a territory of the United States, a
form of government for which he forthwith caused to be promulgated.   He next organized the " California Mounted Riflemen,"
of the men who had followed Fremont, received them as volunteers into the service of the United States, appointing Captain
Fremont their major, and Lieutenant Gillespie, of the marines,
their captain.   Directing Major Fremont to proceed to San Diego
in the sloop-of-war Cyane, with his one hundred and sixty riflemen and seventy marines, for the purpose of intercepting or capturing De Castio, the commodore himself set sail for San Pedro,
and uniting their forces, on the 13th of August, both these commanders marched upon, and took without opposition, Ciudad de
los Angelos.

Thus unvarying success had already crowned the arms of the
republic, and the whole country was under dominion of her flag,
ere yet the despatch of the 13th of May, and the President's proclamation in reference to the war, had reached the officers
engaged.

Two subsequent despatches from the Secretary of the Navy,
bore date July 12th and August 13th.   They embodied the substance of previous instructions, and added, that the object of the
United States was, under its rights as a belligerent nation, to possess itself entirely of Upper California.   That object had reference to ultimate peace with Mexico ; and if, at that peace, the
basis of the *uti possidetis* should be established, the government

expected, through the forces under the commodore, to be found
in actual possession of Upper California. This would bring with
it the necessity of a civil administration. Such a government
should be established under the commodore's protection.

Under all these instructions, directed at various times to the
commander of the naval forces in the Pacific, Commodore Stockton now asserted his superior authority in California; and, disregarding the protest and representations of General Kearny, per-
sisted in confirming the appointment, as governor, of Colonel
Fremont.

General Kearny withdrew to San Diego, where on the 29th of
January he was joined by the Mormon battalion, four hundred
strong, under Lieutenant-Colonel Cooke, of the 2d U. S. dragoons. This corps arrived in excellent condition and fine health,
having had no serious loss during their long march, and in their
appearance, conduct, and discipline, reflecting the highest honour
on their military chief.

On the 23d of January, Commodore W. B. Shubrick, in the
razee Independence, arrived at Monterey, and assumed command
of all the naval forces, and on the 1st of February issued his first
general order. General Kearny, leaving the Mormons at San
Diego, went on board the Cyane, and arrived at Monterey on the
8th of February. The interview and arrangements between
these two officers proved perfectly harmonious. Commodore
Shubrick, and subsequently Commodore Biddle, his senior, cor-
dially supported the views of the general, and co-operated with
him in carrying out his instructions. In consequence, the following *general order* was by them jointly promulgated :—

"To all whom it may concern, be it known—That the President of the United States, desirous to give and secure to the
people of California a share of the good government and happy civil
organization enjoyed by the people of the United States, and to

protect them at the same time from the attacks of foreign foes, and from internal commotions, has invested the undersigned with separate and distinct powers, civil and military; a cordial co-operation in the exercise of which, it is hoped and believed, will have the happy results desired. To the commander-in-chief of the naval forces, the President has assigned the regulation of the import trade, with conditions on which vessels of all nations (our own as well as foreign) may be admitted into the ports of the territory, and the establishment of all port-regulations. To the commanding military officer, the President has assigned the direction of the operations on land, and has invested him with administrative functions of government over the people and territory occupied by the forces of the United States. Done at Monterey, capital of California, this 1st day of March, A. D. 1847.

W. BRANDFORD SHUBRICK,

Commander-in-chief of the Naval Forces.

S. W. KEARNY,

Brig. Gen. U. S. A. and Governor of California."

On the same day the general issued his proclamation as governor, promising respect and protection to person, property, and religion, absolving the inhabitants from all ties of allegiance to Mexico, assuring the people of the early establishment of a free government, and earnestly urging peace and union, and combined efforts to promote the prosperity and happiness of the country.

Early in February Captain Tompkins and his company of the 3d United States artillery arrived in the transport Lexington, with 24-pounders, mortars, ordnance stores, and intrenching tools: the company was stationed in Monterey. On the 6th of March, Colonel Stevenson arrived at San Francisco, in the ship T. H. Perkins, with two hundred and fifty men of the New York California volunteers—and a few days after, other transports brought the remainder of that regiment, numbering, in full, eight hundred men, and including many mechanics: they brought with them, in addition to six pieces of artillery and a supply of small-arms, machinery for saw and grist-mills, mechanics' tools, and other *materiel* of industry. With these forces little fears could be entertained that the peace of the territory would again be easily disturbed. Settlements were made and towns founded, confidence was restored, and industry, released from terror and doubt, was now active, under the impartial and wise protection of the American flag.

The work which had been assigned to General Kearny was completed—the object of his government fully achieved—the honour of his country maintained and exalted—his name and the fame of his little army written imperishably on the brightest pages of that country's history. On the 31st of May, 1847, having transferred to Colonel R. B. Mason the authority and duties of governor and commander-in-chief, the general, with his staff and a small party of officers, set out on his return to the United States. Difficult and hazardous was his route of two thousand two hundred miles across the continent. On the 22d of August he arrived at Fort Leavenworth. A little more than one year had sped by since last its flag saluted him — the story of those intervening twelve months has yet in military annals to find a parallel.

CHAPTER XV.

FULFILMENT of the promises of protection made to the people
of New Mexico by their conquerors, was neither forgotten, nor
delayed. From La Joya, on his route to the Pacific, General
Kearny addressed to Colonel Doniphan at Santa Fé an express,
instructing him to defer his contemplated movement on Chihuahua, and to proceed with his regiment into the hill country of the
Navajoes, to effect the restitution of all prisoners and property
taken by stealth or violence from the newly-subjugated people,
and to exact from that half-civilized, fierce, and powerful tribe,
ample security for their future good conduct. These warlike
Indians have, for full two centuries, been the terror and the
scourge of the New Mexican border. From the range of mountains bounding the valley of the Del Norte, their country stretches
away down the tributaries of the Colorado, and towards the settlements of California on the west, the Cordilleras, and the highlands beyond, affording them strongholds and almost inaccessible
retreats. Without towns or permanent abodes, they live chiefly
on horseback, and in the open air, wealthy in countless herds of
horses, cattle, and sheep ; yet, ever at the dictate of wild caprice,
or in the spirit of a long-cherished hate, descending on the villages and settlements of the valley, plundering and destroying

(266)

wherever they come.   In their latest incursion they had slain
seven or eight men, taken off captive as many women and children, and driven away into their highlands ten thousand head of
sheep, cattle, and mules.

Leaving the town of Santa Fé, on the 26th of October, Colonel
Doniphan divided his command into separate detachments, and
invaded the Navajo country by three routes.   The season was
far advanced, and winter had set in with more than usual
severity.   For artillery and wagons the country was wholly impracticable; mules with pack-saddles, therefore, alone accompanied the force, which, without tents, almost destitute of shoes and
clothing, and stinted in provisions, pursued over snow-clad
mountains, and through precipitous ravines, barricaded by stupendous cliffs, and paved with huge masses and sharp fragments
of the living rock, its strangely perilous way.   Their daily march
was through snows gathered deeply in the gorges, up mountain
walls pendent with icicles, along narrow ledges overhanging
appalling chasms, where an error or a stumble would have hurled
horse and man among jagged and pointed rocks, hundreds of
feet below.   As the days passed on, the cold became intense;
yet frequently at night, the adventurous soldiers laid down their
weary bodies, wrapped in blankets and skins, on the rugged
earth or the frozen snow, and rose in the morning from beneath
a newly-fallen coverlet of snow, with limbs benumbed, and
icicles pendent in clusters from beard and hair.   Even when
they reached the diversified table-lands and the rich valleys, the
snow continued equally deep, and the cold no less severe.   Success crowned such fearless resolution.   The Mexicans looked
with undisguised amazement on what they considered the extreme
of temerity; the braver Indians, with respect upon the strangers
whose skill and courage they could appreciate, a respect soon
deepened into reverence by the generous confidence, the fairness
and fidelity in every instance displayed.   Every portion of their

36

country was visited, and with incredible toil about three-fourths of the adult males of their tribe, including all the head chiefs, were collected to a conference at the *Ojo Oso*, the Bear Spring, situate in the Navajo country.   And here, after two days' delibe-rations, was made a permanent treaty of peace and amity between the American people—in which term were specially included the New Mexicans and the Pueblo Indians—and this hitherto irre-concileable and tameless race.   To the memorandum of this treaty, signed on the 22d of November, by Colonel Doniphan, Lieutenant-Colonel Jackson, and Major Gilpin, fourteen Indian chiefs appended their marks.

Returning through the large and singularly built town of Zuni, situate about two hundred miles west of the Del Norte, and con-taining an interesting, intelligent, and honest population of about six thousand persons, who look upon the New Mexicans as an inferior race, and are said to have preserved to this day the ancient Aztec character, arts, and habits, Colonel Doniphan was enabled by skilful diplomacy to effect a reconciliation and treaty of peace between them and the Navajoes, hitherto mutual foess Thus, in despite of physical privations, in the face of the obstacle. of nature, and the incessant hostility of the elements, the import-ant object of the expedition was accomplished.   By different routes, each rivalling each in dreariness, difficulty, and danger, and all by the Mexicans declared to be impracticable, the several detachments of the force arrived, between the 8th and 12th of De-cember, at Valverde, on the Del Norte, the appointed rendezvous.

The advance, consisting of three hundred men under command of Major Gilpin, took up the line of march southward from Val-verde, on the 14th of December.   Lieutenant-Colonel Jackson followed, with two hundred men, on the 16th.   While yet Colonel Doniphan was in the Navajo country, Lieutenant-Colonel Mitchell, accompanied by Captain Thompson, of the United States 1st dragoons, had been despatched by Colonel

Price from Santa Fé with an escort of between ninety and one hundred men, volunteers from the 2d mounted regiment, and the light artillery of Missouri, with the view of opening a communication with General Wool. This force having passed down the valley of the Del Norte, joined the column of Colonel Doniphan, who, thus strengthened, left Valverde, with the remainder of his command, on Dec. 18th. The whole force was eight hundred and fifty-six effective men, armed with rifles—no artillery. Before leaving Valverde, information of the advance of the enemy to the defence of El Paso, on the Chihuahua road, induced Colonel Doniphan to send orders to Santa Fé for Major Clarke, of the Missouri artillery, to join him at the earliest possible moment, with one hundred men, and a battery of howitzers. That union could not be effected until the 1st of February following.

The march lay along the Rio Grande to Fra Christobal, and thence across the dreary and dreaded desert, known by the appropriately ominous name *El Jornada del Muerto*, "the journey of the dead." On the 22d, at Doña Anna, the whole force was consolidated, and a number of traders, with over three hundred wagons, fell in with the baggage and provision trains in the rear. Certain intelligence now came that seven hundred men and six pieces of cannon had reached the pass of the river, sixty miles below. The column moved forward in gay anticipation on the 23d.

About three o'clock in the afternoon of Christmas-day, after a merry march of eighteen miles, the advance of five hundred men was called to a halt, at the Brazito, or little arm of the river, for the purpose of encamping. The horses were unsaddled and let loose to graze, and the men, scattered in all directions, were busy in quest of wood and water. Suddenly a thick cloud of dust arose and moved towards them from the direction of El Paso, and soon one of the advanced guard in full speed announced that the enemy was at hand. To the call of the bugle the men hastily collected; time to horse there was not; in open order, and on foot, the troops formed as skirmishers, the extremes of the wings thrown towards the river to protect the flanks, the baggage, and the traders' wagons. The enemy, under General Poncé de Leon, numbered twelve hundred and twenty men, of whom five hundred and thirty-seven were well-mounted and splendidly equipped lancers and dragoons, from Vera Cruz and Chihuahua; the remainder, infantry from Chihuahua and El Paso, with one 2-pound howitzer. To the east, within half a mile of the American troops, they drew up their line in gallant and imposing array, the Vera Cruz dragoons on the right, the Chihuahua Activo battalion on the left, the infantry and militia, with the howitzer, in the centre.

From their marshalled ranks rode forward briskly a lieutenant bearing a *black* flag: he halted at a distance of about one hundred paces, and through the American interpreter delivered his presumptuous message, and received an approriate response. He came to demand that the commander of the column should go over to confer with his general, menacing, at the same time, that, unless the demand was complied with, they would charge and take him, adding that *they gave no quarter and asked none.* Receiving in reply a scornful defiance, he gracefully waved his black flag, and galloped back to the Mexican lines.

Instantly and boldly their charge commenced, the Vera Cruz dragoons riding in firm array down on the left of the American line. The charge was coolly met, and when within a few rods a deadly volley, again repeated and again, rained in among them dreadful execution. The remainder of their force pressed forward simultaneously, and under cover of the intervening chaparral three rounds were fired by their whole line, seconded by the howitzer, before a single rifle was discharged in return. Colonel Doniphan had directed his men to lie down on their faces, and reserve their fire until the foe came within sixty paces. The manœuvre fully succeeded. The Mexicans, supposing they had caused great destruction in the quickly dropping ranks, pushed forward exultingly, when, suddenly rising, the whole centre and right wing sent forth a volley so terribly unerring, that the foe reeled, turned, and fled in irredeemable confusion, while the Howard county company, dashing into the melée, captured and bore away the cannon. Meantime, the ever vigilant and intrepid Captain Reid gallantly led up against the Vera Cruz dragoons, rallying on the left, twenty of his regiment who had succeeded in regaining the saddle. Furiously this little squad charged on, and into the force more than threefold their number, broke their ranks, and with their sabres hewed destructively around. Here, for full twenty minutes, the desperate fight continued. Another division of the enemy's horse, having outflanked the left of the line, and attacked the commissary and baggage train, were met by a well directed fire from the steady soldier-wagoners—and soon over every part of the field the foe was in disorderly flight. In the contiguous mountains they found refuge.

The volunteer force in this engagement was under five hundred, the rear, under Lieutenant-Colonel Jackson, not having arrived until the battle was entirely ended; their loss, none killed —seven wounded, all of whom recovered to participate in future struggles and renown. The strength of the enemy has been already given: their loss, so far as could be ascertained, exceeded seventy killed, and a hundred and fifty wounded, including their commanding officer, General Poncé de Leon. Besides the howitzer, a number of carbines, several stands of colours, a large quantity of ammunition and baggage, with ample store of provisions and delicious wines, were among the spoils. The latter supplied the victors no unwelcome feast for their merry Christmas night.

Such was the battle of Brazito, the first in which the volunteers of the West crossed weapons with the foe. With troops fresh and vigorous, and outnumbering them in the proportion of five to two, their struggle was brief, their victory brilliant. Brighter laurels were none, than Missouri won that day.

Proceeding with military precaution, in anticipation of another attack, the army entered without opposition the populous town of El Paso, on the 27th. Here it was ascertained that General Wool had not as yet advanced on Chihuahua. A forward movement under these circumstances was judged extremely hazardous, and therefore Colonel Doniphan resolved to await at this point the arrival of the artillery ordered from Santa Fé.

The beautiful and fertile valley of El Paso extends along the Rio Grande about two-and-twenty miles, by an average breadth of ten, and is occupied by a peaceable population, whose settlements present the appearance of a continuous farm, thickly intervalled by orchards and vineyards. The fruits and wines of the valley are of unsurpassed excellence, the produce in grain abundant. By the capture of the town, Colonel Doniphan was placed in possession of more than twenty thousand pounds of powder, lead, musket and great-gun cartridge, grape and canister shot, and of five hundred stands of small arms, four hundred lances, four pieces of cannon, and several stands of colours.

Finding that, contrary to representations industriously circulated among them, and unblushingly put forward even by their chief officers and clergy, the Americans behaved themselves in the captured city with the greatest forbearance, order, respect, and humanity, the inhabitants soon abandoned their doubts and hostility, and gratefully repaid such unexpected conduct by friendly and generous hospitality. The men now fared sumptuously every day, purchasing in the well supplied markets the more substantial food they desired, and having kindly pressed upon them the rich fruits, luscious wines, and other luxuries of the place. Hours of reasonable relaxation, and the intercourse of amity with the citizens, alternated with company and regimental drills and other military exercises, and the preparation of supply and outfit for the march on Chihuahua.

Events in New Mexico caused the detention for several weeks of the artillery. At length Colonel Price found himself in a position to comply with Colonel Doniphan's order, and despatched Major Clark with one hundred and seventeen men, and six pieces of cannon, which, after extraordinary exertion and toil through the deserts and deep snows, reached El Paso on the 1st of February. On the 8th, the column was on march for Chihuahua. It was an enterprise pre-eminently perilous; and the national heart beat more quickly in suspense for the fate of the heroic army, thus thrown out upon their own unaided resources, in the very centre of innumerous foes, and encompassed by natural obstacles still more to be dreaded.

We must not stay to record the hardships they endured, and the dangers they encountered from the deserts, the flinty cañons, and fire on the prairie. The force consisted of nine hundred and twenty-four effective men; of whom one hundred and seventeen officers and privates were of the artillery, ninety-three of Colonel Mitchell's escort, and the remainder of the 1st mounted volunteers, all of Missouri. The merchant-train under their escort numbered three hundred and fifteen wagons; and, at the recommendation of Colonel Doniphan, the merchants and teamsters organized themselves into a well-armed and highly efficient corps of about one hundred and fifty men, in two companies, commanded respectively by Captains Skillman and Glasgow, with Samuel C. Owens elected their major. On the 25th, they reached the shallow, brackish Laguna de Encenillas, about twenty miles long and three miles wide, two hundred and seven miles below El Paso, and seventy-four from Chihuahua. Previous rumours now shaped themselves into intelligence, that about twenty-five miles in advance, and near the margin of the lake, the enemy was in force at Inseneas, the country-seat of Don Angel Trias,

governor of Chihuahua. Arrived at Inseneas on the evening of
the 26th, they found it evacuated by the military; and on the
following evening, at the Fort of Sans, they learned from their
spies that the enemy, in great force, had fortified the pass of the
Sacramento river, about fifteen miles north of the city.

By the authorities of Chihuahua the approach of the American
troops had been for a long time expected, and extensive preparations made to obstruct their advance. In full confidence of the
result, the legislature of the department had in session determined that Doniphan's men, when captured, should be stripped
of arms and money, and sent bound, on foot, to the city of
Mexico; and that no delay might occur, a quantity of cord was
provided, and cut into suitable lengths, for tying the prisoners.
Governor Frias strenuously promoted the arrangements made
under direction of Don José A. Heredia, commandant-general of
Durango, Chihuahua, Sonora, and New Mexico, aided by Generals Garcia Condé, Justiniani, and Uguarté.

The position commanding the road and pass was well chosen.
Two rivulets, rising in the mountains westward of the valley of
the Sacramento, cross the valley in an easterly direction; then
the northern of these streams, the Arroyo Seco, bending to the
south, meets the other, the Arroyo Sacramento, and with it forms
the Rio Sacramento, which flows into the Conchas, a tributary
of the Rio Grande del Norte. Across the peninsular plateau
formed by these rivulets, the main road leads from north to south:
on its left the ground abruptly rises in a bench, sixty feet high,
sloping upwards from all directions to the north-east corner, where
it is crowned by the rocky height of the Cerro Frijoles, one hundred and fifty feet above the plain. The sierras south of the
Arroyo Sacramento come at right angles in upon that stream,
their easternmost advance, the Cerro Sacramento, narrowing the
valley to a breadth of one mile. From the Cerro Frijoles along
the northern front of the eminences, and thence southwardly

along the whole bench overhanging the road, was erected a continued line of redoubts and intrenchments, under the superintendence of General Condé, formerly Mexican Minister of War, and a man of science and skill. On the Cerro Sacramento also there was a strong battery, commanding the road as it approached the ferry below. In this seemingly secure position, the enemy, under command of the experienced officers before named, awaited the approach of the American troops. Their infantry was protected behind the redoubts and intrenchments; their cavalry was drawn up in front of the redoubts four deep, and in rear of the redoubts two deep, so as to mask them as far as practicable. Their force consisted of twelve hundred cavalry from Durango and Chihuahua, with the Vera Cruz dragoons, twelve hundred infantry from Chihuahua, three hundred artillerists, and fourteen hundred and twenty rancheros, badly armed with lassos, lances, and machetoes, or corn-knives; ten pieces of field-artillery, and six culverins, or rampart-pieces.

At sunrise, on the 28th of February, Colonel Doniphan took up the line of march. The traders' commissariat, and company wagons, more than three hundred in number, were arranged in four parallel columns, with intervals of fifty yards. In the central interval marched the artillery, the first battalion in the interval on the right, the second battalion in that on the left. In advance of all rode two hundred cavalry proper. Thus was the force rendered more compact, and its numbers effectually concealed, while the wagons could be at a moments notice converted into a cáral, to encompass and bulwark the troops. When arrived within one mile and a half of the formidable intrenchments, Colonel Doniphan, pushing still further forward the cavalry in advance, suddenly diverged to the right, so as to gain the easier though narrow ascent to the west. This the enemy perceived, and promptly endeavoured to prevent, by pushing forward in that direction one thousand cavalry, masking four pieces of cannon in their rear.

37

These were, however, anticipated, and by a rapid movement the
elevation was gained and the line formed before the enemy came
within reach of the guns.   The American line was now parallel
with the main road, and fronting the enemy's defences on the west
of the heights, with a marsh protecting its rear.   Embarrassed by
this well-conceived and quickly executed movement, the enemy
halted, and a brisk fire from the now unmasked American battery, at the distance of nine hundred and fifty yards, commenced
the action.   The enemy unmasked his guns and replied.   Then
rapidly deploying into line, he brought up additional artillery
from his trenches, and opened a heavy fire, mainly directed
against the battery under Major Clark, but with little effect.   Not
so with the fire from the American line — that proved effective,
killing fifteen, wounding many, and dismounting one of the
enemy's guns.   At length, thrown into confusion and driven
from his position, he slowly retreated behind his intrenchments,
while Colonel Doniphan moved forward his whole line obliquely
to the right, to obtain a more advantageous position.   In this
way they reached the southern edge of the plain, and within five
hundred yards of the Mexican army, posted in a round battery
and trenches, extending along the crest of the bench to the right.
From this bench three trenches and a stone câral completed the
connexion with the ford, and with the fortified rancho on the
southern bank, beneath the Cerro Sacramento.   Between the two
armies, and beneath the Mexican works on the height in front, ran
a deep gully, impassable for cannon, and greatly strengthening
their position.   To the right of the advancing American line, on
an abrupt bench of the Sacramento Hill, a strong fort was occupied by a battery supported by cavalry, the balls and grape from
which raked with a plunging fire the flank of the line, the whole
of the passage down to the ford, and the ravine in front of the
trenches.

And now with greater fierceness the hot battle is renewed;

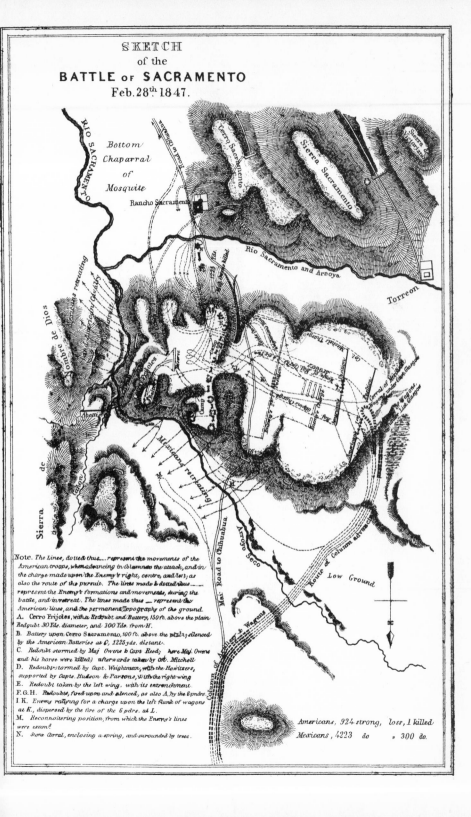

SKETCH
of the
BATTLE OF SACRAMENTO
Feb. 28th 1847.

RIO SACRAMENTO

Bottom
Chaparral
of
Mosquite

Rancho Sacramento

Cerro Sacramento

Sierra Sacramento

Sierra Sacramento

Rio Sacramento and Arroya.

Torreon

Sierra de Lombre de Dios

Sierra de Cohera

Abott

Camp

Mexicans retreating

Corral of Mezquite

Mar Road to Chihuahua

Arroyo Seco

Route of Column advanced

Low Ground

Column of Artillery & Wagons

Note. The Lines, dotted thus .... represent the movements of the American troops, when advancing in Columns to the attack, and in the charge made upon the Enemy's right, centre, and left; as also the route of the pursuit. The lines made & dotted thus .... represent the Enemy's formations and movements, during the battle, and in retreat. The lines made thus ___ represent the American lines, and the permanent Topography of the ground.

A. Cerro Frijoles, with a Redoubt and Battery, 150 ft. above the plain Redoubt 30 Yds. diameter, and 100 Yds. from H.
B. Battery upon Cerro Sacramento, 100 ft. above the plain, silenced by the American Batteries at O, 1225 yds. distant.
C. Redoubt stormed by Maj. Owens & Capt. Reed; here Maj. Owens and his horse were killed) afterwards taken by Cpt. Mitchell.
D. Redoubt stormed by Capt. Weightman, with the Howitzers, supported by Capts. Hudson & Parsons, with the right wing.
E. Redoubt taken by the left wing, with its entrenchment.
F.G.H. Redoubts, fired upon and silenced, as also A, by the 6 pndrs.
I.K. Enemy rallying for a charge upon the left flank of wagons at K., dispersed by the fire of the 6 pdrs. at L.
M. Reconnoitering position, from which the Enemy's lines were exam'd.
N. Stone Corral, enclosing a spring, and surrounded by trees.

Americans, 924 strong,   loss, 1 killed
Mexicans, 4223   do   „ 300 do.

security and honour, ruin and shame, are dependent on its issue.
On either side there is scornful resolve. With fourfold odds,
embattled vantage-ground, and on their country's soil, these
must not think of less than crushing victory. Those are American
volunteers; they have no time nor will for counting odds; that
victory must be theirs. There is glory to be won this day. A
series of rapid movements and of brilliant charges divide the
fight; artillery, cavalry, and dismounted men press emulously
forward. On the main central battery of the foe the foremost
onset is directed; there Weightman with his two howitzers, and
Reid, Hudson, and Parsons, are ordered to charge. By some
mischance the order reaches not the latter two; Reid is already,
where he ever is, in front, and on the foe. Weightman's guns
come full gallop to the gully, turn it by the left, and unlimbering
within fifty yards of the well-manned intrenchment, open their
effective salutation of canister and grape. The courtesy is
warmly returned. The horsemen, some leaping the gully, and
others riding round it, have charged up the slope. Their impulse
is resistless, and for a moment the battery is silenced; but the
numbers of the enemy are as yet overwhelming, and Reid's
gallant men, met by dense masses thronging the breastworks,
and sending forth a ceaseless hail of bullets, are forced to oblique
to the left, and seek the intervals of the redoubts through which
to charge. Here many are wounded, Reid is unhorsed, and the
chivalrous Owens, who had volunteered in this charge, is slain.
Hudson, anticipating his commander's order, and Parsons,
demanding permission to charge, are now up the slope and in
the hottest of the fray. Gilpin, with the second battalion, has
deployed to the left at a gallop, his men have dismounted, and
are running up the hill to the support of their brethren in arms.
Mitchell with his mounted riflemen have advanced on the right;
having reached the ravine, they too dismount, and charge as
skirmishers on the Mexican position, which is with much gallantry

maintained, until, within five-and-twenty yards, the rifle tells on every head raised above the breastworks, with fatally unerring aim. Weightman presses on the intrenchments, regardless of obstacles; and within a few feet of the ditches, and in the midst of a cross-fire from three directions, opens his fire to the right and to the left. The work is furious now. Doniphan is there to order, to encourage, and to lead. No officer, no man fails, or falls short of the leader's hopes. From right to left along the whole line of redoubts, the brisk and deadly fire of the American rifles is poured in. Horse, howitzers, and foot, in one simultaneous charge they dash upon the works of the enemy; to the very brink of the strong redoubts they advance and attack with their sabres. Long and obstinately are the works defended; now they are cleared, and the foe is sent whirling in flight across the plain. Meantime, under a heavy cross-fire from the battery on the Cerro Sacramento, Clark is bringing up, as fast as practicable, the main battery of four 6-pounders, followed by the wagon-train under escort of its own staunch companies. He opens upon the enemy's extreme right, from which an incessant fire had hitherto been kept up; and soon two of their guns are dismounted, the battery silenced, and the enemy dislodged from the redoubt on the Cerro Frijoles. A body of Mexican lancers attempt to outflank the left of the American line, and attack the wagon-train; on them, Clark again opens his untired battery, and a destructive fire of grape and spherical case-shot has cleared them away. Bravely the enemy has fought, and gallantly have Heredia and Condé striven for victory. Before the volunteers they are borne headlong down, their intrenchments are abandoned, their guns deserted, and by both wings of the conquering force, with the merciless howitzers, they are hotly pursued towards the mountains beyond the Frijoles height, and away down the ravine of the Arroyo Seco. Repeated discharges of Clark's guns disorder, while they expedite this retreat.

But all is not over yet. The main battery on the mountain bench beyond the Arroyo Sacramento, consisting of six of their best and heaviest guns, supported by eight hundred cavalry, continues, as it has done during the heat of the engagement, to pour down a constant and heavy fire. Mitchell and Jackson, obeying the order to remount their men, and accompanied by the howitzers, charge across the main road, and round the rancho, up the ascent to the rear of this position. Gilpin, with his second battalion, on foot, crosses the Sacramento rivulet higher up, and scales the rough mountain, to come down on the enemy from the other side; while Clark, occupying that one of the enemy's deserted intrenchments nearest the Cerro Sacramento, twelve hundred and twenty-five yards distant, tries upon it the effect of his well-used battery. His first fire has dismounted one of the enemy's guns. They are of greater calibre, and their elevated position gives them a plunging fire into the intrenchment, but a third shot from below has cut in two one of their ammunition wagons. Brisk and precise is the discharge of the American guns, and their horsemen are now seen ascending the hill in full gallop. Further struggle is vain. Their guns and ammunition are abandoned, their colours flung down: as men astounded by the force of an incredible calamity, they fly in wild disorder, they are pursued for a short distance—they have disappeared.

Thus ended the battle of the Sacramento, which had lasted above three hours, was resolutely contested, and most nobly won. For the skill of the commanders, the discipline of the men, the brilliant daring and resistless energy of all, it tells its own tale.

The Mexican force in the engagement numbered upwards of four thousand two hundred men; their loss was three hundred and four killed on the field, a still larger number wounded, many mortally, and above forty prisoners, together with a large quantity of provisions, all their artillery and mules, wagons, ammunition, imple-

ments, small-arms, and colours. The American loss was one
killed, and eleven wounded—three of them mortally.

A detachment of the American army took possession of the city
of Chihuahua on the 1st of March, and the following day the
whole army entered it and took quarters. On the 25th of April
Colonel Doniphan resumed his march, and on the 22d of May,
1847, reported to General Wool at Saltillo. On the 27th they
reported to General Taylor at Monterey, and reached St. Louis
on the 2d of July following, after a march which in interest and
incident far transcended the famous "Retreat of the Ten Thousand."

The route from Chihuahua to Saltillo was no less arduous, no
less toilsome and dangerous, than those through which we have
already accompanied the men of Missouri. For details of their
progress we have not time. The brilliant affair of El Poso must
alone detain us for a moment in our rapid survey.

The good people of the rich and beautiful city of Parras had
received with hospitality, and treated with kindness, the soldiers
of General Wool's command, and to his sick especially extended
generous attentions. Just now they were thrown into general
gloom by an incursion of the robbing and murderous Camanches,
who had descended from their mountain-holds on the fair valley,
cruelly slaughtered several of the people, plundered and desecra-
ted many abodes, driven off some five hundred head of cattle, and
hurried away into captivity nineteen young persons, of both sexes,
but mostly females. Ere yet they had made good their retreat to
the mountains, and while meditating new outrages to add to
their spoil, they found themselves face to face with a foe, other
than they had ever met. Thus far had reached on the advance
of the army, our gallant Captain Reid, ever present, whenever
wanted. To him the injured people related the cause of their
distress. The appeal was irresistible. The kindness shown to

their sick and wounded compatriots, the volunteers could not forget; and among the captives not a few were of that sex that always finds in the American arm a sure defence, of that sex that in Parras had been, as everywhere, the tenderest, most assiduous, most considerate, by the couch of pain. With fifteen of his men, Reid proffered to intercept the barbarous marauders at El Poso. Near this place, on the morning of the 13th of May, he met Lieutenant Gordon, sent forward with fifteen men from the main body, to provide water. United, they formed a band of some three or four-and-thirty men. By a skilful feint they drew the Indians, intent on further spoil, towards a hacienda, where Reid had concealed his force. The Camanches were sixty-five, well mounted and armed, elate with success, and strangers to defeat. When they had come within half a mile of the friendly hacienda, the order was given to Reid's band, to charge. Like the lightning flash, they were in among the surprised, but nothing-daunted foe. With desperate determination not to lose their rich booty, the latter fiercely fought for full two hours, yielding each foot of ground, only as it was made slippery in the blood of some newly fallen of their number. Reid was himself severely wounded in the face, and in the shoulder, in both places by steel-tipped arrows. Of his gallant corps of supporters, none was materially injured. The Indians lost seventeen killed on the field, including their chief, and had full five-and-twenty dangerously wounded. Thus severely chastised, the remnant found protection in the high grounds, leaving behind all the spoil they had lately acquired. The restoration of the captive youths and maidens to the bosoms of their delighted families, was more than compensation to the generous deliverers. Through the Prefect of the department of Parras, Don José Ignacio Arrabe, a letter of graceful acknowledgment and thanks was conveyed to the chivalrous leader and his corps of worthy brothers.

WE turn now to take a hasty glance at events occurring in
New Mexico, while thus the troops under Doniphan were passing
in triumph through the centre of the enemy's country. Mr.
Charles Bent, it will be remembered, had been by General
Kearny constituted governor of New Mexico; on the departure
of Colonel Doniphan, the command of the troops remaining in
the subjugated province devolved on Colonel Sterling Price.
They consisted of his own regiment, the 2d Missouri mounted
volunteers; an extra battalion, under Lieutenant-Colonel Willock;
the Laclede rangers, under Lieutenant Elliott; two hundred of the
U. S. 1st dragoons, commanded by Captain Burgwin; Angney
and Murphy's battalion of infantry; Fischer's company of light
artillery, and some additional artillery and miscellaneous troops,
under Lieutenants Dyer and Wilson, of the U. S. Army; making
an aggregate of nearly two thousand men. Of these a considerable number was sent out, in separate detachments, to stations
throughout the province, for the threefold purposes of preserving
health and activity among the men, securing forage for their
beasts, and maintaining tranquillity. The large proportion of the
troops, however, was detained to garrison Santa Fé. For such
service the volunteers were little fitted; and notwithstanding the
strenuous efforts of the officers, deviations from good order, disregard of discipline, and fatal excesses and indulgences, were
frequent.

At the time of General Kearny's departure, all things at Santa
Fé and throughout New Mexico wore the aspect of acquiescent
tranquillity. Smiles and gaiety, and professions of cordial amity,
were, however, but the skilfully assumed covering of deep discontent, jealousy, and hate, in the bosoms of very many. Early
in December, the leading malcontents, including officers who
had held rank under Armijo, displaced officials, and those
generally to whom the old and corrupt system was gain, in midnight conclaves began to plot the overthrow of the existing

government. Their plans were craftily laid, and approaching towards maturity—their several departments for action assigned, and consequent duties commenced—on the 19th of December, the church-bells at Santa Fé were to give the signal for a simultaneous revolt. The time was subsequently postponed, to insure more complete organization and more effective action, and the night of Christmas-eve was finally fixed on for the rising, which was to be universal and instantaneous. Counting on certain success, they had already nominated from among themselves Don Tomas Ortiz, as governor, and Don Diego Archuleta, as commander of the forces. By a female the whole plot was discovered, and revealed to Colonel Price. Several of those supposed to be implicated were at once arrested, and ample evidence obtained of the existence, character, and objects of the conspiracy. Ortiz and Archuleta by timely flight escaped arrest, and, from motives of politic clemency, the other arrested persons were discharged. But the contemplated rebellion seemed utterly crushed. This appearance was deceptive.

With embittered determination, and with closer secrecy, the conspiracy was renewed. To it were committed the most influential men of the state; the priests especially, bigoted in proportion to their ignorance, using all their authority to excite the people against the "heretic Americanos." Their teachings and exhortations were but too successful. The suppression of the embryo rebellion had been followed by a proclamation from Governor Bent, in which he addressed himself to the good sense as well as to the honour of the people, seeking to disabuse their minds of the absurd impressions which designing factionists had busied themselves to make, showing the folly and hopelessness of insurrection, and urgently inviting the co-operation of the people themselves in the peaceful struggle for common prosperity.

Meantime the organization of the government in its inferior departments had gone on, and *pari passu* the enjoyment and

38

relaxation of the soldiery in Santa Fé. Imprudence and excess counted many victims among the troops, and increasing familiarity with the city revellers and their habits, brought with it increase of sickness. To all this the conspirators were unceasingly awake. On the 14th of January, 1847, Governor Bent, accompanied by several officials, left Santa Fé for San Fernando de Taos, in which place he had previously to his installation resided, and where he still had a house and estate. On the 19th, the refusal to release two Indians, incarcerated for some misdemeanour, was followed by the murder, in the most cruel manner, of the governor; the sheriff, Lee; the district-attorney, Leal; the prefect, Vigil, a Mexican; a son of Judge Baubian; and Harvimea, also a Mexican. In these inhuman murders Mexicans and Pueblo Indians were common actors. Nor was this the result of any sudden or unpremeditated outbreak. On the same day, seven Americans were in cold blood butchered at the Arroya Hondo, four others at the Moro town, and two at the Rio Colorado. By the alcalde of Moro, and the faithful gallantry of a Frenchman of Cañada, letters were intercepted, in which, with revelations of the plot, were contained earnest invitations to the inhabitants along the Rio Abajo, and the northern portion of New Mexico, to strike for revenge, in union with their brethren of the other districts. From these letters it was further ascertained that the enemy, bent upon the extermination of the Americans and of all Mexicans in their confidence and friendship, was approaching Santa Fé, gathering in his advance upon this city accessions of force. In this movement the leaders were Tafoya, Pablo Chavez, Pablo Montoya, Cortez, and Tomas, a Pueblo Indian.

Prudently anxious to meet the foe, ere yet increased by their anticipated reinforcements along their line of march, Colonel Price, leaving Lieutenant-Colonel Willock with a comparatively strong force in garrison at Santa Fé, went forth to meet the insurgents, on the morning of January 23d, at the head of three hun-

dred and fifty-three men, rank and file, supported by four mountain howitzers, in charge of Lieutenant Dyer, United States
Army. The weather was then merciless, but action was necessary. Captain St. Vrain's company, the only mounted men of
the force, formed the advance, and early in the afternoon of the
24th discovered the enemy in considerable strength, occupying
the high grounds commanding, and close to, the little town of
Cañada, situated on a tributary of the Rio Grande.

Two thousand strong, under command of Tafoya, Chavez, and
Montoya, the foe had taken advantageous ground on both sides
of the Chicito stream, and in three houses at the base of the hills.
Promptly forming such line of battle as his force and circumstances directed, Colonel Price threw forward and across the
creek his four howitzers, from which, about two o'clock in the
afternoon, Lieutenant Dyer opened a brisk fire upon the houses
and the more distant height, occupied by the enemy. Meantime
the dismounted men were moved up to a position, in some degree
protected by the bluff bank of the stream from the Mexican fire;
while Captain St. Vrain was despatched to protect and bring up
the wagon-train, already menaced by a large party. This service
satisfactorily effected, Angney and Murphy's infantry battalion
charged, and dislodged the enemy from the house opposite the
American right flank. This gallantly accomplished, a general
charge was ordered; the same infantry battalion, supported by
two companies of the 2d Missouri, moved rapidly up one of the hills,
while St. Vrain by a circuit turned it, so as to cut off retreat.
The artillery, supported by the remaining three companies of
Price's regiment, drove the enemy from some houses and a
densely wooded coral, and from the heights beyond. Till sunset the struggle continued; then the enemy, routed at all points,
was seeking safety by flight. The nature of the ground rendered
pursuit hopeless, and the troops were for the night quartered in
the town. Next morning, they hesitatingly showed themselves

on the distant heights; but on the first intimation of a disposition to renew the intercourse of the preceding afternoon, they most unceremoniously decamped. The American loss in this affair of Cañada was two killed and seven wounded. Of the latter was Lieutenant Irvine. The Mexicans acknowledged a loss of thirty-six killed and forty-five wounded.

On the 27th, Colonel Price resumed his march towards Taos, whitherward the enemy had retreated, as to their stronghold. Next morning he was joined by Captain Burgwin with his own company of the 1st U. S., and Lieutenant Boone's company of the 2d Missouri, dragoons, all dismounted, and by Lieutenant Wilson, with a 6-pounder brought up from Cañada. His whole force was now four hundred and seventy-nine rank and file, with whom he proceeded to La Joya, and there learned, on the 29th, that the gorge leading to Embudo was held in command by the enemy. The road by Embudo being impracticable for artillery or wagons, Captain Burgwin pushed forward with his own company, St. Vrain's, and White's, accompanied too by Adjutant Walker of the 2d Missouri, and Lieutenant Wilson—their conjoined force numbering one hundred and eighty men.

The enemy, some six or seven hundred strong, was discovered occupying a formidable position on the mountain slopes, over-hanging each side of the road, just where the gorge was so narrow, as scarcely to admit of the passage of three men abreast, and still further protected by dense brushwood and large fragments of detached rock. From the gallant force so numerically inferior, flanking parties were thrown out on either side, while St. Vrain, dismounting his men, advanced up the rugged and precipitous hill-face, whose trees lent aid to the climbing men. The brisk contest was still going on, when Captain Slack, with twenty-five mounted men, came up from La Joya, to lend aid. Another half hour, and the battle was decided—the pursuit of the foe occupied two hours. One killed and one severely wounded, bought this victory; defeat cost the Mexicans and their Indian allies full twenty killed and sixty wounded. A white flag greeted Captain Burgwin's entry into the town of Embudo.

The march resumed led over the Taos Mountain, covered to a depth of two feet with snow, through which the troops, with admirable constancy and patience, trampled down a road for the artillery and wagons. On the 3d of February Colonel Price marched, without meeting any show of resistance, through San Fernando de Taos, and there ascertained that the enemy had posted himself advantageously in the Indian village, Pueblo de Taos, a strongly protected place a short distance in advance. Walls of adobé, or sun-dried bricks, with strong pickets, and flanked by projecting buildings, supplied whatever was wanting to the means of defence afforded by the large church, two other large structures rising in an irregular pyramid to the height of seven or eight stories, and a number of smaller edifices. These were now occupied by Mexicans and Indians, numbering between six and seven hundred. On the evening of the 3d, a warm fire was opened on the western flank of the church, from Lieutenant Dyer's battery of two howitzers and one six-pounder, and kept up for about two hours and a half; when, as the ammunition wagons had not yet come up, and the men were suffering severely from cold and fatigue, the colonel commanding withdrew them for the night to San Fernando.

Early on the morning of the 4th, the troops were in station for attacking the town. From the north and the west, a cross-fire was briskly opened from the artillery under Lieutenants Dyer and Hassendaubel, the former supported by Captain Angney's battalion and two companies of the 2d Missouri; the latter by Captains Burgwin and McMillen; while Captains St. Vrain and Slack, with the mounted men, moved round to the east of the town, to intercept any attempt at flight. Two hours' cannonading having proved it impossible to breach the strong walls of the church with the 6-pounder and howitzers, the troops were ordered forward to storm. Most gallantly was the service performed, and most manfully was the building defended by its occupants, who poured out a continual and destructive fire. Establishing themselves close under the western wall, the troops now endeavoured to breach it with axes; and by means of a temporary ladder the roof was fired. Meanwhile Captain Burgwin with a small party, leaving the cover of the wall, entered the coral in front of the church, and essayed to effect an entrance at the great door. This attempt was found fruitless, and in making it, the daring Burgwin received his death-wound. About 4 P. M. the 6-pounder, brought within sixty yards, enlarged into a practicable breach one of the holes made by the axes. The gun was then run up within ten yards, a shell and three rounds of grape were poured through the breach, and now the storming-party burst in. On the north the charge was equally successful; the long and hotly contested fight resulted in the utter discomfiture and disordered flight of the foe. It was now night, and the troops were quietly quartered in the houses on the west side of the town, abandoned by the enemy. Early next morning, the old men, the matrons, and the priest, bringing with them the children and the altar images, humbly implored mercy and peace. Their supplication was granted, on the condition that Tomas should be given up, that chief having been an instigator and actor in the cruel murder of Governor Bent and his party. In this battle the enemy's ascertained loss was about one hundred and fifty killed—his wounded unknown. The American loss was seven killed and forty-five wounded. Of these many afterwards died.

In the earlier days of the revolt, Captain Hendley, than whom Missouri counted among her bravest none more brave, fell, while endeavouring to suppress the insurrection in the valley of the Moro. He was in command of the grazing detachment on the Pecos, but hearing of the insurrection, on the 20th of January, promptly

ordered the different grazing parties to assemble, and took possession of Las Bagas, where a concentration of the forces of the
insurgents had commenced. These were readily dispersed by
the captain and his command, which was soon increased to the
number of two hundred and twenty-five men, by the arrival of
different parties. Leaving the main body of his force to preserve
tranquillity at Las Bagas, he set out on the 22d to the Moro,
where the insurgents had embodied two hundred men. Upon
arriving before the place, on the 24th, he found the Mexicans
under arms. While preparing for an attack, he perceived a small
party of insurgents running from the hills. A detachment which
he sent out to cut them off, encountered the main body of the
enemy, and soon brought on a general engagement. After a
few volleys the enemy gave way, and sought their houses, from
the windows and loopholes of which they fired upon the Americans. The latter hotly pursued them in their flight, rushing into
the houses with them, shooting, and running through many with
the bayonet. A part of the insurgents gained an old fort and
commenced a fire on the American troops. Captain Hendley,
with a small party, forced his way into one of the apartments,
and, while preparing to fire the fort, received a ball, from which
he died in a few minutes. Being without artillery, the Americans
considered the fort impregnable under present circumstances,
and abandoned the place, having killed twenty-five of the enemy,
and taken seventeen prisoners. The American loss was Captain
Hendley killed, and three wounded. His body was taken to
Santa Fé, and buried with military honours. Subsequently his
remains were conveyed to Fort Leavenworth, and thence to Richmond, where they were interred on the 23d of September, 1847.
On the 1st of February, his death, and the fall, too, of other gallant
men, was avenged by the complete demolition of the Moro
village, by the troops under Captain Morin.

By those prompt exertions the insurrection was effectually suppressed. Of the leaders in the revolt, Tafoya fell at Cañada, Chavez at Pueblo; Montoya was hanged as a traitor, at San Fernando; and Tomas was, in a quarrel, shot by a private, while a prisoner in the guard-room of the latter town. Sanction of General Kearny's assumed power to transfer the allegiance of the New Mexicans from their own government to the United States, was refused by the latter. Consequently the charge of treason alleged against the revolters was not to be sustained, and the military executions under this supposed right were very promptly stopped.

In May, marauding bands of Mexicans and Indians made desultory attacks on supply-trains and grazing-parties. On the 26th of this month, at the Red River Cañon, after a sharp conflict, Major Edmondson, with a detachment of about two hundred men, severely punished the largest of these bands, killing forty-one of their number, and wounding a still greater proportion. In June, Lieutenant Brown, with two of his men, in an effort to recover horses stolen from his command, was cruelly murdered. Major Edmondson hastily marched from Las Vegas in pursuit of the murderers, shot down a few, and took forty prisoners. In July, rumours of an intended renewal of the insurrection were rife. But the increased vigilance of the troops, and the presence of an additional force from the States, checked the contemplated outbreak.

On the 20th of July, all now seeming more permanently tranquil, Colonel Price was raised to the rank of brigadier-general, and appointed still to command at Santa Fé.

Here we take leave of the Army of the West—an army whose sufferings and whose deeds alike entitle it to the admiration and boundless gratitude of its country.

GEN. W. SCOTT.

Winfield Scott

CHAPTER XVI.

WITH the capture of Monterey ended the campaign of 1846.

But before this brilliant achievement took place, it became evident to the government, that another and even more effective column of invasion would be required to operate from a point affording a nearer approach to the Mexican capital.

General Santa Anna, whose return from exile had been connived at by our government, so far from distracting the Mexican people by internal dissensions, or inclining them to more peaceful views, had succeeded in allaying the feuds of opposing parties, and in rousing and uniting all classes to a more vigorous prosecution of the war.

Finding all hope of reasonable accommodation cut off by this untoward state of things, a new and shorter line was determined on, striking into the heart of the enemy's possessions. While the

line of the Sierra Madre was to be held by General Taylor with
diminished forces, the city of Vera Cruz was selected as the base
of a new line of operations, for the assault of which preparations
were made on a scale commensurate with the formidable character of the undertaking.

Vera Cruz, the only commercial city of importance belonging
to the republic of Mexico, is situated in latitude 19 deg. 11
min. 52 sec. N.; longitude 19 deg. 10 min. W. of Washington,
and has an average temperature of 77 degrees Fahrenheit.

Founded about the year 1560 by the Count of Monterey, and
upon the exact spot which witnessed the landing of Cortez, forty
years before, it became, in 1600, the capital of the department of
Vera Cruz.

It contains about one thousand and sixty-three houses, built
mostly of stone, two stories high, and of a square shape, with flat
roofs and parapets.   The population, which in the year 1804 was
computed at 16,000, has fallen off gradually to about 5000 souls,
which is believed to be about its present number.

The city is surrounded by a stone wall, 3124 varas or yards in
circumference, which is defended by nine bastions, capable of
supporting 100 guns.

Vera Cruz is small but regularly laid out, well paved, and
well lighted.   Its police regulations are admirable.   It contains
a Cathedral, to which are attached the two chapels of Del Pastora
and Del Loreto.   It has also five convents and three hospitals.
The Cathedral occupies the south side of the principal Plaza.
On the east is the Government House, dignified by the title
of Palace, and on the west and north are ranges of porticoes.
The more modern erections for public offices, near the wharf, are
among the finest in the city. ·

Although Vera Cruz itself is situated upon an arid plain, surrounded by billowy sand-hills of various heights, and intervening
clusters of thick chaparral, the country at a little distance inland

is fertile and productive. Game, fish, fruit, and vegetables are abundant; and there are few cities in which the necessaries or even the luxuries of life, can be obtained with greater facility.

The harbour or roadstead is a very insecure one, and, from the anchorage being among shoals, affords but little protection during the prevalence of "Northers."

But the pride of the republic, as it was formerly the boast of Old Spain, is the famous fortress of San Juan d'Ulloa.

This almost impregnable structure was commenced in the year 1582, and the immense sum of forty millions of dollars was expended by the Spaniards upon its erection.

It is built upon an island in front of the city, and at a distance from it of one thousand and sixty-two " varas," or yards. This island had been visited by Don Juan di Orijalva, as early as the year 1518, and from him received the name by which the fortress is now known.

The foundations of this immense structure are laid in the sea, and with a solidity that has defied alike the furious storms of that latitude, and the encroachments of the fierce element by which it is surrounded.

The length of the exterior polygon towards Vera Cruz, is three hundred yards; on the north channel two hundred yards, while the fire upon both the northern and southern channels can be doubled by the use of the additional batteries of Santiago and San Miguel. The stone used in the construction of the fortress, is the *Madrepora Astrea*, a species of soft coral, the walls and exposed points being further defended by a facing of stone of a harder quality. The complement of guns which it is capable of mounting, is said to be three hundred and seventy. When the Castle was taken by the French in 1838, its batteries were found to contain one hundred and seventy-seven guns of various calibre.

Notwithstanding the formidable character of its works, San

Juan d'Ulloa had been captured three times, previous to its investment by the American forces.   It was surprised in 1668,
by Juan Aguinas Acle, a well known buccaneer, who was,
however, expelled shortly afterwards by Don Francisco di Lujan,
supported by a fleet of twenty-three vessels.

The second capture is a remarkable one in the annals of Vera
Cruz.   It was made on the night of the 17th of May, 1693, by
the pirate Lorencillo, who, after defeating the garrison, sacked
the city at his leisure, retaining possession of both for two weeks ;
when, having secured an immense amount of plunder, he retired
without molestation.

The third capture, that by the French naval forces under Ad-
miral Bodin, has already been alluded to.

It was upon this point, already blockaded by our squadron, that
the greater proportion of the military force in actual service, or in
the progress of enlistment, was directed by our government to be
concentrated.   By a despatch, dated the 22d of October, 1846,
General Taylor was notified by the Secretary of War to hold himself in readiness to meet a requisition upon him for four thousand
of his best officers and men ;—while, by a subsequent letter, he was
informed that a still greater number, amounting to one-half of his
whole force, would be required.   Nine new regiments of volunteers
were called for, and the President proposed to ask at the next
meeting of Congress for permission to organize ten additional regiments of regulars.   This authority he expected to receive early
in the session, but the bill was not passed until near its close.

On the 23d of November, General Scott, having been previously put in possession of the views of the Executive, received
the following order from the Secretary of War :—

" WAR DEPARTMENT,
Washington, Nov. 23, 1846.

" SIR :—The President, several days since, communicated in
person to you his orders to repair to Mexico, to take command

of the forces there assembled, and particularly to organize and set on foot an expedition to operate on the Gulf coast, if, on arriving at the theatre of action, you shall deem it practicable. It is not proposed to control your operations by definite and positive instructions, but you are left to prosecute them as your judgment under a full view of all the circumstances shall dictate. The work is before you, and the means provided for accomplishing it, are committed to you, in the full confidence that you will use them to the best advantage.

"The objects which it is desirable to obtain have been indicated, and it is hoped that you will have the requisite force to accomplish them. Of this you must be the judge, when preparations are made, and the time for action arrived.

"Very respectfully, your obedient servant,

W. L. MARCY,
Secretary of War.

General WINFIELD SCOTT."

Under these instructions, General Scott left Washington the next day for New York, from which place he sailed on the 30th, and reached the Rio Grande on the 1st day of January, 1847. Here he was met by the divisions of Generals Worth, Twiggs, Quitman, and Pillow. These, after a brief delay at the mouth of the river, with the forces here collected, were embarked on board the transports waiting to receive them. Their destination was the island of Lobos.

This island, as described by an eye-witness, " is a lovely little spot, formed entirely of coral, about two miles in circumference, twelve miles from the Mexican shore, sixty from Tampico, and one hundred and thirty from Vera Cruz.

" It was covered, before the Americans made it their rendezvous, with a variety of trees and shrubs, the highest of the former probably some twenty-five feet, and these so thickly covered with vines that one can hardly get through them. Almost all the trees are of strange growth. Banyan-trees speading over large spaces of ground, their limbs forming props as they pierce into the earth and take root; while the tops, thickly thatched with evergreen vines, form most beautiful arbours. Lemon, lime, fig, palm, cane, and an hundred other species of wood, are growing with all the freshness and beauty of the Indies. There is plenty of water to be had by digging from four to six feet. It is blackish and sweet, and about the quality of ship-water. Fish and sea-fowl we have in profusion. With these we have a sea air that, fourteen hours out of the twenty-four, makes the place delightfully pleasant."

By the 15th of February, thirty-six hundred volunteers and four hundred regulars had already concentrated here, together with eighteen vessels of the first class.

Shortly after, the transports arrived from the Rio Grande; and the commander-in-chief, having at length increased his forces to about twelve thousand men, embarked them on board one hundred ships and transports, and sailed for Anton Lizardo.

On the 5th of March, in the midst of the violent "norther," look-outs on board the squadron lying at the latter place, descried the long-expected armament bearing down upon them, and whitening the horizon with a wall of canvass. Spurning the fierce waves in triumph, ship after ship came dashing into the harbour, and, casting anchor, presented at the close of the day a perfect forest of masts.

On the 7th, General Scott, accompanied by Commodore Conner, commanding the naval forces stationed in the Gulf, proceeded on board the steamer Petrita, for the purpose of reconnoitring the city and castle, and choosing a point best calculated to facilitate the landing of the troops

The beach west of the island of Sacrificios was selected; but the anchorage being very contracted, it was decided, in order to avoid the confusion which would necessarily follow the crowding of so many vessels, to transfer most of the troops from the transports to the vessels of war.

And now all delays and impediments having been overcome, the eventful day at length arrived which was to witness the disembarkation of the invading force upon Mexican soil, and within sight of the heroic city, and the renowned castle of San Juan d'Ulloa.

It was the 9th of March. The sun rose bright and beautiful. The fierce "norther," the terror of those latitudes, had given place to a gentle breeze from the south-east, and a sea as smooth as if it had never known a ripple, and every heart beat high with eager expectation. About an hour before noon, the squadron got under way, the Princeton leading, with the Raritan in tow. About mid-day those on board the steamer New Orleans, just arrived with six hundred and fifty additional men, while casting anchor beheld the steamer Massachusetts pass, and upon her deck the tall and stately form of the Commander-in-chief. He was saluted with deafening cheers. The remainder of the transports followed in their turn; and then was exhibited a spectacle which for magnificence has seldom, if ever, been equalled. The ships of war moving under easy sail, were packed closely with warlike men, whose bayonets, flashing in the sunlight, flickered up continually like innumerable tongues of flame. Following the vessels, and attached to them, were the numerous surf-boats destined to convey the troops ashore.

Steamers and other vessels brought up the rear, crowded with spectators, anxious to witness the landing. The ships of war of three European nations looked on — their masts, rigging, and every point of vantage crowded with eager faces. Inspiriting strains of martial music were heard from afar, and at intervals rose, subdued by distance, the shouts and joyous outbursts of the soldiers, who, weary of a life of inaction, welcomed with enthusiasm the fierce excitement of the hour. But the crowning glory of the scene was yet to come.

In about three hours the frigates and transports dropped anchor opposite the island of Sacrificios. Quietly and in admirable order, each ship took up its appointed station. The steamers Spitfire and Vixen, and five gun-boats, were detailed to cover the landing. The immense surf-boats, sixty-five in number, each capable of holding one hundred men, were hauled to the gangways of the various ships; and, by four o'clock, freighted with four thousand five hundred men, were seen drawn up abreast of each other, in a single line extending for nearly a mile. This was the first division, under General Worth.

The Massachusetts fired the signal for landing, and then, simultaneously, the bristling flotilla, filled to the gunwales with its human freight, was seen under way; and, amid the hearty cheers of those who were left behind, to the spirit-stirring strains of martial music, and within sight of the gray old walls of Vera Cruz, and the terrible armature of its almost impregnable fortress, the dauntless soldiers neared the shore.

As the boats touched ground, the foremost men of each sprang into the water waist deep, and dashed up the sandy beach, followed by their equally impetuous comrades; the stars and stripes were rapidly flung to the breeze, and the setting sun cast for a few minutes a lingering radiance among its folds. Thus was achieved the landing of the first division.

The second, under command of Major-General Patterson, speedily followed. The reserve of regulars under Brigadier General Twiggs succeeded, and by ten o'clock, P. M., the men-of-war and transports were relieved of the remaining troops.

The facility, directness, and precision with which this important object was accomplished, reflect great credit upon Commodore Conner and the officers of the squadron. All the necessary arrangements had been made with so much skill and forethought, that nearly twelve thousand men were thus disembarked without confusion, disturbance, or a solitary accident of any kind. Never, perhaps, in the annals of warlike operations, was a disembarkation completed in which skill and science were more successfully combined. The able and effective manner in which the naval dispositions were carried out, proved how fully that arm of service participated in the enthusiasm animating the faces of those destined to operate on shore.

The toils and hardships performed by the squadron in the performance of thankless and inglorious duties, have never been sufficiently appreciated by the country at large. The more brilliant achievements of the army have had the effect of casting the less imposing, but equally arduous services of the navy into the shade. Time alone can do justice to the incessant caution, diligence, and watchfulness required of both officers and seamen, in an exceedingly unsafe position, and constantly exposed to the terrible effects of the fierce winds called " northers," so prevalent in the Gulf during eight months of each year.

That the navy panted to share in the successes of their companions in arms, and that they could be equally zealous in maintaining the honour of their country's flag, the best evidence was given in the manner in which the marine batteries were worked during the subsequent operations of the siege, and in the eagerness with which all the officers and men of the squadron availed themselves of this only opportunity for distinction.

The landing of the troops, which all expected to have been met by a most bloody and determined resistance, was effected, to the great disappointment of the ardent spirits of our men, without any demonstration being made on the part of the enemy, further than the firing of roundshot and shells from the long guns of the fortress. The enemy lost here, as at the passage of the Arroya Colorado, the best opportunity of resistance to the army of the United States.

During the night the line of investment was partially taken up,

40

and by the 12th, the entire army had assumed the positions previously assigned them in general orders, which were minute in particulars, based on information carefully obtained and thoroughly studied by the Commander-in-chief, and pointed out everything with the utmost precision.

It must not be supposed, however, that this was achieved without difficulty, or an attempt at opposition; on the contrary, the labours of both officers and men were unusually severe.

The character of the country around Vera Cruz—loose hills of light shifting sand, varying from twenty to two hundred feet in height, interspersed with dense and almost impenetrable forests of chaparral—and the limited means of land transportation, was only to be overcome by the most excessive exertions on the part of the men, upon whom the conveyance of the ordnance, munitions of war, and the necessary provisions for subsistence, was almost entirely devolved.

Their labours, sufficiently severe at any time, were rendered still more so by the prevalence of violent " northers," which blew away whole hills of sand, added to and created others, blinding and stifling the men with the minute and penetrating particles.

On the morning of the 10th the firing of heavy ordnance commenced from the city and castle; and, except during the fury of the storm, was kept up night and day without any intermission, though with but little effect upon the lines of investment.

By eleven o'clock General Worth succeeded in taking up his position on the right of the line. The division of General Patterson followed, Pillow's brigade being in the advance. After passing Worth, Pillow was detached with the 1st and 2d Tennessee, and 1st and 2d Pennsylvania regiments, to dislodge the enemy, who were in possession of an old building near the head of the Laguna Malibran, while Lieutenant French, with one field-piece of Taylor's battery, was ordered to open fire upon a stone magazine also occupied by the enemy, and situate in the rear of the city. Both these orders were successfully accomplished. The Mexicans evacuated the magazine, and Pillow's detachment, after driving their antagonists from the field, with the loss of one officer and three men on the part of the latter, cut their way through the chaparral, and with the 1st Tennessee regiment took possession of the magazine. Leaving Colonel Campbell with his brave Tennesseans at this point, Pillow again pressed forward, encountered the enemy near the Medellin road, and drove them rapidly thence to the hills south-east of the city. Here they again attempted to rally, but eventually fell back within shelter of the city guns.

Upon these hills Pillow rested his command for the night. In the morning, General Quitman, while in the act of relieving Pillow, was fired upon simultaneously by the enemy's infantry and the batteries of the city. A detachment of riflemen under Captain Davis was instantly thrown forward, supported by Lieutenant Colonel Dickinson and Major Gladden with two companies, each of the South Carolina regiment, and after a brief but spirited engagement the enemy was repulsed. Two skirmishes subsequently ensued, in which separate detachments of the New York regiment distinguished themselves, and with the same successful result.

The same day, Brigadier-General Twiggs commenced the march of his division, the position laid down for him being the village of Vergara, and the left of the line.

Nothing but the well known energy and perseverance of this veteran commander, enabled him to overcome the numerous difficulties which beset him at every step. The ground was rugged and broken—the sandhills high and loose, and utterly impassable for artillery—the chaparral required to be pierced at many points to allow the passage of the troops, and the guns to be hauled and lifted over high ridges, the successful accomplishment of which demanded the utmost exercise of physical force.

The men had also to sustain the burden of carrying their provisions and munitions of war, and were besides annoyed oy incessant attacks from skirmishing parties of the enemy, who, repeatedly driven back at one point, reappeared at another, and kept the Mounted Rifles, under the command of the gallant Major Sumner, 2d dragoons, continually on the alert.

The enemy lost two commissioned officers, and it was during these operations that Brevet Captain Alburtis, an officer highly distinguished in the Florida war, was killed by a cannon-bal: from the city.

On the 13th the line of investment was complete, and from this time until the 18th, when the trenches were opened, the men were kept constantly busy in throwing up breastworks, erecting batteries, planting mortars, landing supplies, and beating off the light troops of the enemy.

Commodore Perry, who on the 21st succeeded to the command of the Home Squadron, rendered efficient aid to General Scott. On the 22d, simultaneously with the opening of the batteries in the rear of Vera Cruz, he directed the fire of his flotilla of steamers and gun-boats upon the city with good effect. By permission of the General-in-chief, he also established under the direction of Captain Aulick a marine battery, of three Paixhan guns, and three long thirty-two pounders, which bore an important part in the demolition of the city.

From the 18th, until the final surrender, the progress of events is best marked by the following official despatches.

> "HEAD-QUARTERS OF THE ARMY,
> Camp Washington, before Vera Cruz,
> March 23, 1347.

" SIR :—Yesterday, seven of our 10-inch mortars being in battery, and the labours for planting the remainder of our heavy metal being in progress, I addressed, at two o'clock, P. M., a summons to the Governor of Vera Cruz, and within the two hours

COMMODORE M. C. PERRY

limited by the bearer of the flag, received the Governor's answer. Copies of the two papers (marked respectively A and B) are herewith enclosed.

" It will be perceived that the Governor, who, it turns out, is the commander of both places, chose, against the plain terms of the summons, to suppose me to have demanded the surrender of the castle and of the city; when in fact, from the non-arrival of our heavy metal — principally mortars — I was in no condition to threaten the former.

" On the return of the flag with that reply, I at once ordered the seven mortars, in battery, to open upon the city. In a short time the smaller vessels of Commodore Perry's squadron—two steamers and five schooners—according to previous arrangement with him, approached the city within about a mile and an eighth, whence, being partially covered from the castle — an essential condition to their safety—they also opened a brisk fire upon the city. This has been continued uninterruptedly by the mortars, and only with a few intermissions, by the vessels, up to nine o'clock this morning, when the Commodore, very properly, called them off from a position too daringly assumed.

" Our three remaining mortars are now (12 o'clock, A. M.) in battery, and the whole ten in activity. To-morrow, early, if the city should continue obstinate, batteries Nos. 4 and 5 will be ready to add their fire: No. 4, consisting of four 24-pounders, and two 8-inch Paixhan guns, and No. 5 (naval battery), of three 32-pounders, and three 8-inch Paixhans — the guns, officers, and sailors, landed from the squadron — our friends of the navy being unremitting in their zealous co-operation, in every mode and form.

" So far, we know that our fire upon the city has been highly effective, particularly from the batteries of 10-inch mortars, planted at about 800 yards from the city. Including the preparation and defence of the batteries, from the beginning — now many days—and notwithstanding the heavy fire of the enemy, from city and castle, we have only had four or five men wounded and one officer and one man killed in or near the trenches. That officer was Captain John R. Vinton, of the United States 3d artillery, one of the most talented, accomplished, and effective members of the army, and who was highly distinguished in the brilliant operations at Monterey. He fell last evening in the trenches, where he was on duty as field and commanding officer, universally regretted. I have just attended his honoured remains to a soldier's grave—in full view of the enemy and within reach of his guns.

" Thirteen of the long-needed mortars—leaving twenty-seven, besides heavy guns, behind—have arrived, and two of them landed. A heavy norther then set in (at meridian), that stopped that operation, and also the landing of shells. Hence the fire of our mortar batteries has been slackened since two o'clock to-day, and cannot be reinvigorated until we shall again have a smooth sea. In the mean time I shall leave this report open for journalizing events that may occur up to the departure of the steamship-of-war, the Princeton, with Commodore Conner, who, I learn, expects to leave the anchorage of Sacrificios, for the United States, the 25th inst.

" *March* 24.—The storm having subsided in the night, we commenced this forenoon, as soon as the sea became a little smooth, to land shot, shells, and mortars.

" The naval battery, No. 5, was opened with great activity, under Captain Aulick, the second in rank in the squadron, about ten A. M. His fire was continued to two o'clock, P. M., a little before he was relieved by Captain Mayo, who landed with a fresh supply of ammunition, Captain Aulick having exhausted the supply he had brought with him. He lost four sailors, killed, and had one officer, Lieutenant Baldwin, slightly hurt.

" The mortar batteries, Nos. 1, 2, and 3, have fired but languidly during the day, for want of shells, which are now going out from the beach.

" The two reports of Colonel Bankhead, chief of artillery, both of this date, copies of which I enclose, give the incidents of those three batteries.

" Battery No. 4, which will mount four 24-pounders and two 8-inch Paixhan guns, has been much delayed in the hands of the indefatigable engineers by the norther, that filled up the work with sand nearly as fast as it could be opened by the half-blinded labourers. It will, however, doubtless be in full activity early to-morrow morning.

" *March* 25.—The Princeton being about to start for Philadelphia, I have but a moment to continue this report.

" All the batteries, Nos. 1, 2, 3, 4, and 5, are in awful activity this morning. The effect is, no doubt, very great, and I think the city cannot hold out beyond to-day. To-morrow morning, many of the new mortars will be in a position to add their fire, when, or after the delay of some twelve hours, if no proposition to surrender should be received, I shall organize parties for carrying the city by assault. So far, the defence has been spirited and obstinate.

" I enclose a copy of a memorial received last night, signed by the consuls of Great Britain, France, Spain, and Prussia, within Vera Cruz, asking me to grant a truce to enable the neutrals, together with Mexican women and children, to withdraw from the scene of havoc about them. I shall reply, the moment that an opportunity may be taken, to say—1. That a truce can only be granted on the application of Governor Morales, with a view to surrender. 2. That, in sending safeguards to the different consuls, beginning so far back as the 13th inst., I distinctly admonished them — particularly the French and Spanish consuls — and of course, through the two, the other consuls, of the dangers that have followed. 3. That, although at that date I had already refused to allow any person whatever to pass the line of investment either way, yet the blockade had been left open to the consuls and other neutrals, to pass out to their respective ships of war, up to the 22d instant; and, 4. I shall enclose to the memorialists a copy of my summons to the Governor, to show that I had fully considered the impending hardships and distresses of the place, including those of women and children, before one gun had been fired in that direction. The intercourse between the neutral ships of war and the city was stopped at the last-mentioned date by Commodore Perry, with my concurrence, which I placed on the ground that that intercourse could not fail to give to the enemy *moral aid and comfort.*

"It will be seen from the memorial, that our batteries have already had a terrible effect on the city (also known through other sources), and hence the inference, that a surrender must soon be proposed. In haste,

"I have the honour to remain, sir, with respect, your most obedient servant,

WINFIELD SCOTT.

Hon. WM. L. MARCY, Secretary of War."

The naval battery which opened its fire on the 24th, under the command of Captain Aulick, was erected within 700 yards of the walls of the city, and such was the secrecy and celerity with which the work was performed by the night labours of two thousand men, that its proximity was not discovered by the besieged until the intervening chaparral was suddenly cut away from before it by some daring volunteers headed by Midshipman Allan McLane, a descendant of the brave Revolutionary officer of the same name, and, to the great astonishment of the enemy, it stood boldly developed with its guns mounted, and the men at their stations.

Then commenced its destructive fire, which was vainly attempted to be silenced by turning on it, as upon a terrible focus, the fire of all the batteries in town.

The marine battery opened the succeeding morning, and it was here that, within a few hours, fell Midshipman Shubrick, while watching the effects of his shot.

" The effect of this battery," writes an eye-witness, " was awful. The walls were breached, a number of guns dismounted, and the red battery completely silenced.

" Equally brave and determined were the Mexicans. Three times the flag-staff was shot away, and three times a Mexican leaped to the battlements and held it aloft amid the cheers of the assailants. In the afternoon a flag of truce arrived, requesting six hours to bury their dead. It was accorded, and the firing ceased."

While the siege was thus vigorously pressed, two affairs occured with the enemy without the walls, which are well worthy of record.

The first took place on the 23d, when tidings having been received, that a number of Mexicans were in the vicinity of the Puebla road, Colonel Persifor F. Smith detached from his command Lieutenant Roberts, with company C, of the Mounted Rifles, with orders to reconnoitre and return. Near the Puente del Medio, six men were discovered, who displayed a white flag and summoned them to surrender. Then it was that he discovered several hundred men on the heights, commanding the bridge, the former being entrenched, and the latter barricaded with abbatis. Finding his force too small to act with effect, he sent back for reinforcements. Two hundred men, commanded by Colonel Smith in person, soon arrived.

Lieutenant Roberts was now directed to display in the chaparral to the right; and, crossing below, turn the left of the enemy; while Captain Pope, with two companies, crossed above, and

41

turned their right, the remainder advancing by the road and bridge.

These orders were gallantly carried out. Roberts, from his previous knowledge of the ground, was the first to reach the enemy. He succeeded in facing their position, when, finding themselves charged on all sides, they broke in confusion, and were pursued until sunset. In this skirmish Lieutenants Roberts, Maury, and Hatch, were particularly distinguished.*

The second affair was of a far more important character, and may be justly regarded as one of the most brilliant actions of the war.

Learning on the 25th that a considerable force of the enemy were in the neighbourhood of the Medellin river, Colonel Harney advanced to meet him, taking with him Thornton's dragoons under Major Sumner, and some fifty dismounted men, commanded by Captain Ker.

On reaching the stone bridge of the Morena, he found it fortified, and all further passage disputed by two thousand men and two pieces of artillery. Small parties of lancers were also occasionally seen. On approaching the bridge, a heavy fire was poured upon our skirmishers, by which one man was killed and two wounded. Harney then fell back, and waited for two pieces of artillery, with which he determined to force the bridge. Meanwhile he was joined by Captain Hardee with forty men, a company of the 1st Tennessee regiment under Captain Cheatham, and part of four companies of the 2d Tennessee regiment under Colonel ·Haskell. As soon as the two pieces of artillery under Lieutenant Judd arrived, preparations were made for the attack. Captain Ker, with the dismounted dragoons, was stationed on the left of the road leading to the bridge, the volunteers on the right, while Captain Hardee and Lieutenant Hill supported the artillery, and held themselves in readiness to charge. Major

* Smith's Report.

Sumner with the mounted men were kept in reserve. Lieutenant Judd was directed to approach with caution, as the road was circuitous, and the bridge not visible until within fifty yards of the fortification. No sooner was he discovered than the whole fire of the Mexicans was concentrated upon him. To divert this, the detachments to the right and left of the road were ordered to fire, while Lieutenant Judd, nothing daunted, opened upon the fortification ; and, after six or eight well directed rounds, the heads of the enemy were no longer to be seen above the parapet.*

At this moment Harney ordered a charge, and forward rushed the volunteers under Haskell and Cheatham ; and, following with a shout, came the bold dragoons. Haskell was the first man to clear the parapet. The enemy fell back, and re-formed beyond the bridge. Sumner's command now came galloping up, and with a wild hurrah they leaped the fortification, and charged across the bridge. The Mexican infantry broke and fled, some towards Medellin, some into the chaparral. The lancers stood, and a hand-to-hand conflict ensued. Sumner and Lieutenant Sibley, in the thickest of the melee, several times measured strength with the enemy, killing or dismounting their antagonists. Harney was seen everywhere; his tall form and gallant bearing, his coolness, and his audacity, won the admiration of his command, and struck terror into the enemy. The 2d dragoons, the bravest and best disciplined corps in the whole army, parried the quivering lance-points with the easy grace and expert swordsmanship for which they are renowned. The lancers faltered, gave way, fled, and were routed so utterly, that Lieutenants Lowry and Oaks, with three men, pursued a party of thirty, and sabred or dismounted all but five.

The pursuit was urged to the village of Medellin, where another party of lancers were found ;—these, too, soon partook of the general panic, and were pursued by Lieutenant Neill, outstripping

* Harney's Report.

his three companions; but his daring had near cost him his life. The flying foe, ashamed of being chased by one man, turned suddenly, and by dint of numbers succeeded in lancing him in the breast and arm. The pursuit was urged for two miles beyond this, and then the victors rode back to the village. After halting to refresh both men and horses, Harney returned with his command to camp, which they reached on the morning of the 26th, after a warlike episode which, in its chivalric character, has nothing to compare with it but the series of dashing heroic exploits we have yet to record, and of which the action at Medellin was a fitting forerunner.

But we have now to notice events of greater magnitude. The siege of Vera Cruz was approaching its close. On the same day which witnessed the return of Harney, General Scott received in answer to his reply to the consuls, overtures of surrender by General Landero, upon whom, owing to the sickness of General Morales, the chief command of both city and castle had been devolved.

The Mexican general invited the appointment of three commissioners on each side, to meet at some intermediate point, and treat upon the terms of accommodation.

Generals Worth and Pillow, and Colonel Totten, were accordingly appointed on the part of the Americans; and Colonels Villanueva and Herrera, and Lieutenant-Colonel Robles, on the part of the Mexicans. After a considerable discussion, and a rejection of several of the articles first proposed, articles of capitulation were agreed upon and assented to by the respective Commanders-in chief. On the 27th the ratification took place. The following are the articles of capitulation:—

"Generals W. J. Worth and G. J. Pillow, and Colonel J. G. Totten, Chief Engineer, on the part of Major-General Scott, General-in-chief of the armies of the United States; and Col. Jose Gutierrez de Villanueva, Lieutenant Colonel of the Engineers, Man-

SURRENDER OF VERA CRUZ.

uel Robles, and Colonel Pedro de Herrera, commissioners appointed by General-of-brigade Don Jose Juan Landero, commanding in chief Vera Cruz, the castle of San Juan d'Ulloa, and their dependencies—for the surrender to the arms of the United States of the said forts, with their armaments, munitions of war, garrisons, and arms.

" 1. The whole garrison, or garrisons, to be surrendered to the arms of the United States, as prisoners of war, the 29th inst., at ten o'clock, A. M. ; the garrisons to be permitted to march out with all the honours of war, and to lay down their arms to such officers as may be appointed by the General-in-chief of the United States, and at a point to be agreed on by the commissioners.

" 2. Mexican officers shall preserve their arms and private effects, including horse and horse furniture, and to be allowed, regular and irregular officers and also to rank and file, five days to retire to their respective homes, on parole, as hereinafter prescribed.

" 3. Coincident with the surrender, as stipulated in article one, the Mexican flags of the various forts and stations shall be struck, saluted by their own batteries ; and, immediately thereafter, forts Santiago and Conception and the castle of San Juan d'Ulloa, occupied by the forces of the United States.

" 4. The rank and file of the regular portion of the prisoners to be disposed of, after surrender and parole, as their general-in-chief may desire, and the irregular to be permitted to return to their homes. The officers, in respect to all arms and descriptions of force, giving the usual parole, that the said rank and file, as well as themselves, shall not serve again until duly exchanged.

" 5. All the *materiel* of war, and all public property of every description found in the city, the castle of San Juan d'Ulloa, and their dependencies, to belong to the United States ; but the armament of the same (not injured or destroyed in the further prosecution of the actual war) may be considered as liable to be restored to Mexico by a definitive treaty of peace.

"6. The sick and wounded Mexicans to be allowed to remain in the city, with such medical officers of the army as may be necessary to their care and treatment.

"7. Absolute protection is solemnly guarantied to persons in the city, and property, and it is clearly understood that no private building or property is to be taken or used by the forces of the United States, without previous arrangement with the owners, and for a fair equivalent.

"8. Absolute freedom of religious worship and ceremonies is solemnly guarantied."

On the 29th, the ceremony of surrender occurred. The spot chosen for this purpose, was a plain in the rear of the city walls, and extending back towards Malibran. The American army was drawn up in two lines facing inwards, and extending nearly a mile.

General Worth, who had been appointed to superintend the ceremony of capitulation, appeared upon the ground in full uniform. About ten o'clock, the Mexican troops marched out to the sound of music, and in their customary military costume and equipments; women and children bearing burdens followed. Halted between our lines, the conquered army stacked their arms, laid down their colours and equipments, and marched into the interior as our troops entered the city.

Simultaneously with the act of surrender, the American flag floated over the plaza, and was saluted by the guns of the city and squadron.

On this memorable day, Scott dated from the Palace of Vera Cruz the following despatch to the Secretary of War:

"HEAD-QUARTERS OF THE ARMY, ⎱
            Vera Cruz, March 29, 1847. ⎰

"SIR: The flag of the United States of America floats triumphantly over the walls of this city and the castle of San Juan d'Ulloa.

" Our troops have garrisoned both since ten o'clock: it is now noon. Brigadier-General Worth is in command of the two places.

" Articles of capitulation were signed and exchanged at a late hour night before last. I enclose a copy of the document.

" I have heretofore reported the principal incidents of the siege up to the 25th instant. Nothing of striking interest occurred till early in the morning of the next day, when I received overtures from General Landero, on whom General Morales had devolved the principal command. A terrible storm of wind and sand made it difficult to communicate with the city, and impossible to refer to Commodore Perry. I was obliged to entertain the proposition alone, or to continue the fire upon a place that had shown a disposition to surrender; for the loss of a day, or perhaps several, could not be permitted. The accompanying papers will show the proceedings and results.

" Yesterday, after the norther had abated, and the commissioners appointed by me early the morning before had again met those appointed by General Landero, Commodore Perry sent ashore his second in command, Captain Aulick, as a commissioner on the part of the navy. Although not included in my specific arrangement made with the Mexican commander, I did not hesitate, with proper courtesy, to desire that Captain Aulick might be duly introduced and allowed to participate in the discussions and acts of the commissioners who had been reciprocally accredited. Hence the preamble to his signature. The original American commissioners were Brevet Brigadier-General Worth, Brigadier-General Pillow, and Colonel Totten. Four more able or judicious officers could not have been desired.

" I have to add but little more. The remaining details of the siege — the able co-operation of the United States squadron, successively under the command of Commodores Conner and Perry — the admirable conduct of the whole army, regulars and volunteers—I should be happy to dwell upon as they deserve; but the steamer Princeton, with Commodore Conner on board, is under way, and I have commenced organizing an advance into the interior. This may be delayed a few days, waiting the arrival of additional means of transportation. In the mean time, a joint operation, by land and water, will be made upon Alvarado. No lateral expedition, however, shall interfere with the grand movement towards the capital.

"In consideration of the great services of Colonel Totten, in the siege that has just terminated most successfully, and the importance of his presence at Washington, as the head of the engineer bureau, I intrust this despatch to his personal care, and beg to commend him to the very favourable consideration of the department.

"I have the honour to remain, sir, with high respect, your most obedient servant,

WINFIELD SCOTT.

Hon. Wm. L. Marcy, Secretary of War."

The expedition upon Alvarado determined upon between Scott and Perry, was entirely superseded by that vexatious little town having surrendered in the meanwhile to Lieutenant Hunter, who, in the steamer Scourge, had boldly undertaken on his own responsibility the capture of a place which had twice baffled the efforts of our navy, owing to the difficulty of crossing the bar, and the shallowness of the river upon which it is situated.

This gallant act of disobedience entailed upon Lieutenant Hunter the censure of his superior officers, while it raised him in the estimation of the American people.

The fruits of the capture of Vera Cruz, were five thousand prisoners, as many stand of arms, four hundred pieces of ordnance, and a large quantity of ordnance stores.

The prisoners were all set at liberty upon their "parole" not to serve again during the war, with the exception of a few who had especially distinguished themselves. These General Scott, with the chivalric sympathy of a kindred mind, released, not only without conditions of any kind, but with high encomiums upon their valour.

When the American troops entered Vera Cruz, they became for the first time eye-witnesses of the terrible effects of their shot and shells.

There was scarcely a building in the whole city which had escaped the unerring precision of our artillery. Many houses were totally destroyed, some by fire, some by the bursting of the destructive missiles that had fallen upon them. Roofs were crushed in, walls rent to their foundations, and the massive stones, hurled forcibly from their places, lay in confused heaps, mingled with broken shells, and the dead carcasses of horses and mules.

An intolerable stench pervaded the place, which required the incessant efforts of General Worth and his successor Colonel Wilson to even partially subdue.

42

ON the 15th of March, two days subsequent to the complete
investment of Vera Cruz, Scott received information of the wonderful victory of Buena Vista, and immediately issued a general
order apprising his troops of the same. In this order, after congratulating the army upon this glorious achievement, he hazards
the opinion, that Santa Anna having already fallen back upon
San Luis Potosi, would probably not stop short of the capital.

In this opinion he was correct; but even his sagacity could
scarcely have imagined the fatal tenacity with which, notwithstanding his late disastrous expedition, the war party in Mexico
still clung to the fortunes of its favourite chief.

The false bulletin issued by Santa Anna immediately after that
great battle, could scarcely have deceived his most credulous adherents. All must have been aware that, while claiming a victory, he retreated in such confusion that his wounded were left to
the tender mercy of the victor, while his troops were so utterly
discomfited and disorganized, that thousands deserted by the way.

Meanwhile, as if under the influence of that madness which the
ancients imputed to those forsaken of the Gods, while Taylor held

316

undisputed possession of the country from Matamoros to Saltillo, and Scott was surrounding Vera Cruz with a belt of fire, civil war broke out in the capital.

Gomez Farias, the acting President, having with the authority of Congress attempted, by a proposed sale of church property, to levy the sum of five millions of dollars for the purpose of carrying on the war, found himself thwarted by the resistance of the priesthood, and their adherents among the masses, supported by the " guarda nacional," or enrolled militia. These latter raised the standard of revolt, and for three weeks the city of Mexico was the theatre of one of those disgraceful scenes which have so often shamed that turbulent republic.

Houses were fortified—convents and public offices seized as barracks and places of defence—the stones of the streets were torn up, and barricades erected; and then both parties, as if unwilling to test their strength in bold and open encounter, retired behind their defences, and kept up for many days a desultory firing upon each other, with unfortunately less loss to themselves than to the unoffending citizens, whom duty or necessity compelled to be abroad.

At this juncture, all eyes were again turned upon Santa Anna, as to the only man who could reunite the shattered fragments of the nation, and perhaps retrieve, by the prestige of a single victory, some portion of that glory which seemed to have departed for ever.

How far that able but unscrupulous chief might himself have assisted in bringing about this state of things, we have no means of knowing. Well versed in all the chicanery which belongs to political intrigue, the use of base means, where his own purposes were to be served, was not uncommon to Santa Anna; and to act as mediator between parties in a storm of his own raising, was a species of diplomacy for which he is known to be well qualified.

We may therefore regard it as certain that he was at least kept well advised of the progress of things at the capital, and was prepared, at any moment, to act as circumstances might dictate.

That moment at length arrived. Finding that both parties now looked to him for the adjustment of their mutual differences, he took leave of his troops, and quitting San Luis Potosi on the 14th of March, proceeded to the city of Mexico. His progress was hailed by the people with enthusiasm. Addresses of confidence from various states met him by the way. Deputations from Congress were sent out to conciliate him. His march was as the march of a conqueror, binding and forgiving, dictating and dispensing.

He entered the capital on the 20th, amid the acclamations of the multitude; and, on the 23d, was formally installed President of the Republic, at Guadalupe Hidalgo.

In the general joy elicited by his presence, party animosities were hushed, at least for a time, and all seemed disposed to unite once more in a vigorous attempt to revive the drooping fortunes of the republic.

Money was subscribed, arms and munitions of war collected, the city and its immediate environs placed in a state of the most formidable defence, and all the principal points of the route between Vera Cruz and the capital—points in themselves offering great natural advantages—were so strongly entrenched and fortified as to become almost impregnable.

In addition to this, the citizens enrolled themselves for home service, and a new army was rapidly organized under approved leaders; while a partisan warfare of guerilla bands was authorized, in which no quarter was to be given to those who fell into their hands, and the plunder of our trains was to be divided among the victors.

All things being thus satisfactorily arranged, General Santa

Anna assumed command of the army, and previous to leaving the capital issued the following address to the Mexican people:

"*Antonio Lopez de Santa Anna, President ad interim of the Mexican Republic, to his compatriots.*

"MEXICANS: Vera Cruz is already in the power of the enemy. It has succumbed,—not under the influence of American valour, nor can it ever be said that it has fallen under the impulses of their own good fortune. To our shame be it said, we ourselves have produced this deplorable misfortune by our own interminable discords.

" The truth is due to you from the government; you are the arbiters of the fate of our country. If our country is to be defended, it will be you who will stop the triumphant march of the enemy who occupies Vera Cruz. If the enemy advance one step more, the national independence will be buried in the abyss of the past.

" I am resolved to go out, and encounter the enemy. What is life worth ennobled by the national gratitude, if the country suffers under a censure the stain of which will rebound upon the forehead of every Mexican!

" My duty is to sacrifice myself, and I well know how to fulfil it! Perhaps the American hosts may proudly tread the Imperial Capital of Azteca. I will never witness such an opprobrium, for I am determined first to die fighting.

" The momentous crisis is at length arrived to the Mexican Republic. It is as glorious to die fighting, as it is infamous to declare oneself conquered without a struggle, and by an enemy whose rapacity is as far removed from valour, as from generosity.

" Mexicans! you have a religion—protect it! you have honour —then free yourselves from infamy! You love your wives, your children—then liberate them from American brutality. But it must be action—not vain entreaty nor barren desires—with which the enemy must be opposed.

"The national cause is infinitely just, although God appears to have abandoned us; but His ire will be appeased, when we present as an expiation of our errors the sentiments of a true patriotism, and of a sincere union.

"Thus the Almighty will bless our efforts, and we will be invincible! for, against the decision of eight millions of Mexicans, of what avail are the efforts of eight or ten millions of Americans, when opposed by the fiat of Divine Justice?

"Perhaps I speak to you for the last time! I pray you to listen to me! Do not vacillate between death and slavery, and if the enemy conquer you, at least they will respect the heroism of your resistance. It is now time that the common defence should alone occupy your thoughts! The hour of sacrifice has sounded its approach! Awaken! A tomb opens itself at your feet! Conquer a laurel to repose on it.

"The nation has not yet lost its vitality! I swear to you, I will answer for the triumph of Mexico, if unanimous and sincere efforts on your part second my desires. Happy will have been—a thousand times happy—the unfortunate event at Vera Cruz, if the destruction of that city may have served to infuse into the Mexican breast the dignity and generous ardour of a true patriotism!

"Thus will the country have been indubitably saved; but if the country succumb, she will bequeath her opprobrium and her censure to those egotists who were not ready to defend her—to those who traitorously pursued their private turmoils to trample upon the national banner!

"Mexicans! Your fate is the fate of the nation! Not the Americans, but you will decide her destiny! Vera Cruz calls for vengeance!—follow me, and wash out the stain of her dishonour.

ANTONIO LOPEZ DE SANTA ANNA.

Mexico, March 31, 1847."

CHAPTER XVIII.

Scott commences his March for the Capital—Twiggs thrown forward in advance
—Reaches Plan del Rio—Is joined by the General-in-chief—Description of
Cerro Gordo—Scott determines upon turning the Position—A new Road cut—
Twiggs ordered to take up his Position—Is met by the Enemy—Gallantry of 7th
Infantry—Dashing Charge of Harney's Brigade—They capture a Hill in the rear
of Cerro Gordo—Mount a Battery in the Night—Wonderful Exertions of the Men
—Morning of the 18th of April—Scott's celebrated Order—Position of the Mexi-
cans—Battle of Cerro Gordo—Storming of the Heights—Operations of Shields's
Brigade—Shields dangerously wounded—Defeat of the Enemy—Fruits of Victory
—Scott's Despatch to the War Department—Worth enters Puebla.

In the face of the formidable obstacles arrayed against him,
Scott commenced his march for the interior.

On the 8th of April, Twiggs left Vera Cruz, taking up the line
of march by the Jalapa road, and arrived at Plan del Rio on the
11th. The next day he was reinforced by the brigades of Generals Pillow and Shields, and subsequently joined by a portion of
the volunteers, under Major-General Patterson.

Meanwhile, having received information that the enemy, to the
number of sixteen thousand men, under the immediate command
of Santa Anna, were in the neighbourhood of Cerro Gordo, he ordered a reconnoissance. The report of the officers showed that
a succession of heights, each commanding the other, had been
entrenched and fortified, and the road cut up and barricaded.

In the face of these formidable obstacles, Twiggs determined
to advance : and preparations were made to commence the attack on the morning of the 13th, but the morning of the 14th was

321

afterwards adopted at the solicitations of Generals Pillow and Shields, whose commands, though desirous of engaging the enemy, were yet too weary from their march, to do it with spirit and effect.

At this juncture, Major-General Patterson, who had been on the sick list, reported himself for duty, and assuming the command, suspended all further offensive operations until the arrival of the General-in-chief.*

The division of Worth had come up in the meanwhile, and shortly afterwards Scott himself reached Plan del Rio, when a second and more extended reconnoissance being made, it was discovered that a front attack, even if successful, would occasion the sacrifice of an immense number of lives, and might possibly result in the almost total annihilation of our army. The position opcupied by the Mexicans was indeed almost impregnable.

" The road, as it passes the Plan del Rio, which is a wide, rocky bed of a once large stream, is commanded by a series of high cliffs, rising one above the other, and extending several miles, and all well fortified.

" The road then debouches to the right, and curving round the ridge passes over a high cliff, which is completely enfiladed by forts and batteries.

" This ridge is the commencement of the ' Tierra Templada,' the upper or mountainous country.

" The high and rocky ravine of the river protected the right flank of the position, and a series of abrupt and almost impassable mountains and ridges crowned their left.

" Between these two points, running a distance of two or three miles, a succession of strongly fortified forts bristled at every turn, and seemed to defy all bravery and skill." †

* Twiggs's Report, April 19, 1847.
† Correspondent of the New Orleans Delta.

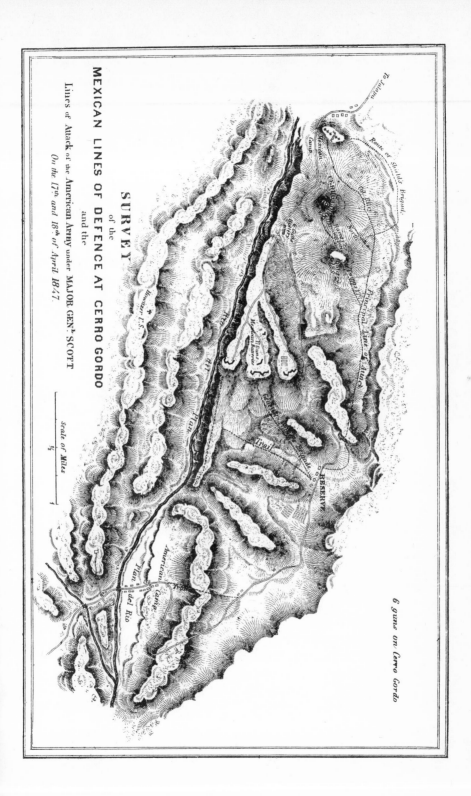

SURVEY
of the
MEXICAN LINES OF DEFENCE AT CERRO GORDO
and the
Lines of Attack of the American Army under MAJOR GEN.ˡ SCOTT
On the 17ᵗʰ and 18ᵗʰ of April 1847

Scale of Miles

6 guns on Cerro Gordo

" On the other side, the lofty and difficult height of Cerro Gordo commanded the approaches in all directions. "[*]

Under these circumstances, Scott determined to turn the position of the enemy by cutting a road which, diverging from the main road, and descending abruptly a deep ravine, should skirt the base of the mountains, over rough ground and chaparral, " along difficult slopes and over chasms, out of the enemy's view, but reached by his guns when discovered,"[†] until it should debouch on the Jalapa road, and in the rear of the main body of the Mexican army.

This road, after incredible labour, was only partially completed. For three days, the working parties succeeded in pushing forward unknown to the enemy; but on the 17th, while approaching the Mexican lines, they were discovered and fired upon. Their labours, however, had been crowned with success, as the Jalapa road, though not entirely reached, was known to be within easy distance.

The division of Twiggs was accordingly ordered to advance by the new route, and, supported by Shields's brigade of volunteers, turn the enemy's left, and take up the position previously designated. In doing this it was necessary to occupy the heights in the vicinity of Cerro Gordo.

Lieutenant Gardner was accordingly detached with a company of the 7th infantry, to a height on the left, for the purpose of reconnoitring the enemy. Upon observing this movement, a strong party of Mexican skirmishers were advanced towards him, supported by a reserve of some two thousand men. Under this severe fire he gallantly maintained his position, until Harney advanced to his support with the Rifles under Major Sumner, and the Artillery under Colonel Childs.

Moving rapidly up in line, these regiments reached the summit of the hill, drew the fire of the enemy, and charged. For a while the ground was obstinately disputed, but nothing could

---

[*] Scott's official report, April 23, 1847.   [†] Ibid.

43

withstand the impetuosity of our troops.   Animated by the voice and the example of Harney, and led by Sumner and Childs, they forced the Mexicans down the steep, and up and over the neighbouring heights.

On the height in front of Cerro Gordo, and under cover of its guns, the enemy again made a desperate stand.   Here they imagined themselves secure ; but, through a fierce storm of grape and canister, and amid a heavy fire of musketry, the Artillery and Rifles dashed forward, stormed the hill and carried it with severe loss.

Three times the Mexicans rallied, and attempted to retake the height, and each time they were successfully beaten back, until at length they gave way, thoroughly disorganized, and were pursued by Colonel Childs, with a portion of the 1st artillery, till they sought shelter within the Tower of Cerro Gordo.

Such was the reckless enthusiasm with which this chase up the steep of Cerro Gordo had been conducted, that upon halting his command within one hundred and fifty yards of the Tower, Colonel Childs found that he had urged the daring pursuit with only sixty followers.

At this juncture, Major Sumner, while hastening to the support of the brave little band, fell severely wounded.   Captain Magruder was more fortunate ; he gallantly dashed through a shower of bullets, and with nine of his men succeeded in reaching Colonel Childs, when, the recall being sounded, they withdrew from their perilous position, and retiring slowly, rejoined the remainder of their command, with only men enough to carry back the wounded.*

But there was yet a work to be accomplished, which was destined to tax the physical energies of the men to the point of exhaustion.   Upon the height thus gallantly captured, a height commanding all others with the single exception of Cerro Gordo,

* Childs's Report, April 20, 1847.

a battery consisting of one 24-pounder and two 24-pound howitzers was ordered to be planted.

For this arduous service a thousand men were detailed, and although the work was commenced at dusk, it occupied the greater portion of the night.

The guns were of immense weight, and had to be lifted up the rugged and almost precipitous sides of the mountain by dint of main force, the men being divided into two parties of five hundred men each, and relieving each other by turns.

At length, however, the work was successfully accomplished; and pickets being placed, the weary soldiers threw themselves down upon the rocky crest of the captured hill, and sought a brief, but imperfect repose.

Thus far, then, the admirable arrangements of the General-in-chief had been successfully carried out, and the division of Twiggs being reported in position, Scott now issued the following confident and prophetic order:

"GENERAL ORDERS, No. 111.

"HEAD-QUARTERS OF THE ARMY. }
Plan del Rio, April 17, 1847. }

" The enemy's whole line of entrenchments and batteries will be attacked in front, and at the same time turned, early in the day, to-morrow—probably before ten o'clock, A. M.

" The second (Twiggs's) division of regulars is already advanced within easy turning distance towards the enemy's left. That division has instructions to move forward before daylight to-morrow, and take up a position across the national road in the enemy's rear, so as to cut off a retreat towards Xalapa. It may be reinforced to-day, if unexpectedly attacked in force, by regiments —one or two taken from Shields's brigade of volunteers. If not, the two volunteer regiments will march for that purpose at daylight to-morrow morning, under Brigadier-General Shields, who will report to Brigadier-General Twiggs, on getting up with him, or to the General-in-chief, if he be in advance.

"The remaining regiment of that volunteer brigade will receive instructions in the course of this day.

" The first division of regulars (Worth's) will follow the movement against the enemy's left at sunrise to-morrow morning.

" As already arranged, Brigadier-General Pillow's brigade will march at six o'clock to-morrow morning along the route he has carefully reconnoitred, and stand ready as soon as he hears the report of arms upon our right, or sooner if circumstances should favour him, to pierce the enemy's line of batteries at such point— the nearer the river the better—as he may select.   Once in the rear of that line, he will turn to the right or left, or both, and attack the batteries in reverse ; or, if abandoned, he will pursue the enemy with vigour until further orders.

" Wall's field battery and the cavalry will be held in reserve on the national road, a little out of view and range of the enemy's batteries.   They will take up that position at nine o'clock in the morning.

" The enemy's batteries being carried or abandoned, all our divisions and corps will pursue with vigour.

" This pursuit may be continued many miles, until stopped by darkness, or fortified positions towards Xalapa.   Consequently, the body of the army will not return to this encampment, but be followed to-morrow afternoon, or early the next morning, by the baggage-trains of the several corps.   For this purpose, the feebler officers and men of each corps will be left to guard its camp and effects, and to load up the latter in the wagons of the corps.   A commander of the present encampment will be designated in the course of this day.

" As soon as it shall be known that the enemy's works have been carried, or that the general pursuit has been commenced, one wagon for each regiment and battery, and one for the cavalry, will follow the movement, to receive, under the direction of the

BRIG. GEN. DAVID E. TWIGGS

medical officers, the wounded and disabled, who will be brought back to this place for treatment in general hospital.

" The Surgeon-General will organize this important service and designate that hospital, as well as the medical officers to be left at it.

" Every man who marches out to attack or pursue the enemy, will take the usual allowance of ammunition, and subsistence for at least two days.

By command of Major-General Scott,

H. L. SCOTT, *A. A. A. General.*"

The morning of the 18th rose bright and beautiful. The sun rode up the clear, deep, cloudless blue, ascending through an atmosphere of such transparent purity, as rendered remote objects sharply distinct, and confounded to unaccustomed eyes the idea of distance.

A gentle, cooling breeze swept over the hill-tops, and fanned the parched lips of the fevered watchers of both armies, whose eyes were now bent eagerly upon each other, waiting the signal which should impel them from the opposing heights, to meet in close and deadly conflict.

The division of Twiggs, whose gallantry on the preceding day had elicited that old veteran's unqualified admiration, was now to go forth again into the hottest of the battle.

To the brave regulars of the First Brigade was committed the perilous duty of storming the tower of Cerro Gordo, the success or failure of which enterprise would stamp the orders of the General-in-chief with the spirit of prophecy, or cause them to appear in the annals of history as the vainglorious production of an over-confident man.

During this attack upon the key position, the Second Brigade under Riley, and the volunteers under Shields, were to press forward in the direction of the enemy's left, over rough and rugged ways, and through the thorny chaparral which intervened between the newly cut road, and the plain in the rear of the mountain.— The object of this movement was to seize the Jalapa road, and prevent the escape of the fugitives.

The division of Worth was ordered to support the storming party, while that of Pillow operated upon the strong river batteries upon the right. Upon the columns of Twiggs and Pillow, therefore, the fiercest brunt of the battle would necessarily fall; but, upon the results achieved by the former mainly depended the fortune of the day. Cerro Gordo was the key position, overtopping and commanding all others, and, that once taken, the river batteries to be assaulted by Pillow, though almost impracticable when attacked in front, were comparatively valueless as means of defence, whenever the position should be effectually turned, and Cerro Gordo in possession of its conquerors.

But the effect of the capture of Cerro Gordo did not end here. Not only would the river batteries be rendered ineffective, but also the ascending series of forts and breastworks, all of which were commanded by the tower.

The movement of Pillow was more for the purpose of diverting the attention of the enemy from the storm of Cerro Gordo, than from any great result which was likely to ensue otherwise; and, if this succeeded, the object of the General-in-chief would be gained, even though Pillow should be beaten back with severe loss, as happened to be subsequently the case.

Through the desertion of a German soldier from our ranks, on the evening of the 17th, General Santa Anna obtained early information of the plan of attack as arranged for the morrow, and strengthened his left accordingly. In order to protect his front and right, General La Vega, previously known as a most gallant and efficient officer, supposing Cerro Gordo secure from assault, exchanged command of the latter with General Vasquez, and sought, by his presence in the river batteries, to animate the defenders to a successful resistance.

Throughout the night of the 17th, there were eight thousand Mexicans lying upon and around the different heights, protected by breastworks and fortifications, and further secured from direct assault, by deep ravines, and almost precipitous rocks, up whose steep sides they imagined a man would scarcely dare to climb.

In addition to the force thus formidably posted, there was a reserve of six thousand men encamped upon the plain in the rear of Cerro Gordo, and close to the Jalapa road.

These troops, under the immediate command of General Santa Anna, were posted so as to be within supporting distance of any point upon or among the heights, that might be most exposed to danger from a vigorous assault.

The American force did not exceed eight thousand men.

At break of day, the second division was ordered to prepare for battle, and the command was obeyed with a quiet fearlessness that augured well for the success of their heroic efforts.

The battery planted with so much difficulty upon the crest of the captured hill now opened its fire upon Cerro Gordo, which was returned by a plunging fire of grape and canister.

Meanwhile, Harney was organizing his storming party. This consisted of the 7th infantry under Lieutenant-Colonel Plympton, the Rifles under Major Loring, four companies of the 1st artillery under Colonel Childs, and six companies of the 3d infantry under Captain Alexander.

All of these, composing the forlorn hope, were regulars; picked men, daring and resolute. Many of them were veterans who had passed not unscathed through the desperate battles of Palo Alto and the Palm Ravine, and the still more deadly storm of Monterey. Now they were about to wrestle with a danger, perhaps more imminent than any they had hitherto encountered.

They were to advance in the face of an enemy confident in the strength of his defences—in the face of a plunging fire from the Tower of Cerro Gordo—in defiance of the enemy's reserve thrown forward as a succouring force—over barricades bristling with musketry, up steep rocks, several hundred feet in height, and over and into the Tower of Cerro Gordo, itself filled with armed men outnumbering their assailants, and protected by a well directed fire from guns served by the ablest artillerists of the nation, yet not a man faltered.

Forming the 7th Infantry on the right, the 3d on the left, and the Artillery in the rear, Harney detached the Rifles to check a large force of the enemy hastening to the support of Cerro Gordo, and, without waiting for the fire of his skirmishers, ordered the charge to sound.

And now, down rushed those daring men through a storm of grape and canister, and musketry.

They descended the hill—they crossed the ravine; and, with a shout, commenced clambering the terrible height. Looking back from its base, they recognise on the crest of the hill they have so lately quitted, the tall form of the General-in-chief. He has come to witness the exploit which is to determine the fate of the day, and, as he beholds the men clinging to, and surmounting the rocks, in every direction—each eager to be first, regardless of his exposure to the fierce fire continually poured upon them; as he sees a part of them form a little distance from the base of the hill; and, led by the intrepid Harney, carry the interposing breastwork at the point of the bayonet, in defiance of its resolute defenders; and as he hears, in the ravine below, the brave Rifles, already baptized in blood, sustaining, with a courage never surpassed, a galling fire in front and upon both flanks from entrenchments and batteries, and yet keeping the succouring force at bay, while their comrades ascend the height, he feels that the agonizing suspense which intervenes between the projecting of a perilous exploit and its successful execution, is gradually sub-

BATTLE OF CERRO GORDO.

siding into a calm confidence that with such men, and led by such officers, victory is as certain as that the sun shines, or the water flows.

Nor was this confidence misplaced. Onward they rushed, impelled by the double consciousness, that the eyes of the General-in-chief were upon them, and of the terrible consequences that would follow a disastrous issue. Harney led the way, — conspicuous above all others by his full military uniform, and his commanding stature. Waving his sword, and calling on his men to follow, he rapidly ascended, in full view of the enemy, while his cheering voice infused into the breasts of his command the same energy and dauntless enthusiasm which animated his own.

It was a race for glorious renown, wherein each strove to be foremost. The front ranks fell, but the survivors still pressed on; and still, above the thunder of the war, rose high, distinct, and clear, the voice of their intrepid leader.

Near the crest of the hill, and encircling the Tower, another breastwork was to be carried. It was done;—and then, swarming up the walls of the fort, they bayoneted the artillerists at their guns, and drove the desperate enemy from his central defence down the steep sides of the hill, in utter and irremediable rout.

Lieutenant Ewell, the first to mount the breastworks, here fell mortally wounded. Lieutenant Van Dorn killed two Mexican soldiers with his own hands. Captain Magruder promptly turned the captured guns upon the flying foe. Sergeant Henry of the 7th infantry hauled down the Mexican standard, — while almost simultaneously with the scaling of the walls, the colours of the 1st artillery and the 3d and 7th infantry were planted upon them amidst the deafening cheers of the conquerors. Such was the famous storming of Cerro Gordo.

In a little while, having been delayed by the rugged character

44

of the route it had to traverse, Worth's division arrived, and shortly afterwards, the nearest batteries below surrendered.

The remainder of the division of Twiggs was equally successful.

The Second Brigade, under Riley, after moving some distance on the enemy's left, cleared the foot of the ridge, which was infested with their skirmishers, and then attacked the reverse of Cerro Gordo, gaining the crown of the hill at the same moment that the First Brigade reached it from the front. After the capture, both brigades joined in the pursuit.

The volunteers, under Shields, were moving upon the extreme left of the enemy. Upon approaching the Jalapa road, a battery of five pieces was discovered, in front, supported by a large force of cavalry and infantry.

While forming his men for the attack, Shields fell dangerously wounded, and Colonel Baker of the Illinois regiment assuming the command, charged the enemy's lines, supported by the 3d and part of the 4th Illinois volunteers, under Harris and Falman, and the New York regiment, under Colonel Burnett, when the enemy, already disheartened by the fall of Cerro Gordo, and being threatened at the same time by a detachment of the 2d infantry, upon his right, after a few-random shots scattered in all directions, leaving his guns, baggage, specie, provisions, and camp equipage, in the hands of the victors.

On the enemy's right, Pillow was less fortunate. After encountering many obstacles and delays, he took up his position in front of the river batteries, and attempted to carry them by assault; but a murderous enfilading fire opening upon him, he was compelled to fall back with considerable loss.

A second time he attempted the assault, with a storming force composed of the 2d Tennessee regiment, and a company each from Pennsylvania and Kentucky, all under the command of Colonel Haskell, an officer already distinguished by his gallant

BRIG. GEN JAMES SHIELDS.

conduct in the affair at Medellin. This column, after having sustained itself under a galling fire of grape and musketry until the Tennessee regiment was nearly annihilated, and the supporting companies proportionably shattered, was also withdrawn beyond the range of the enemy's guns.

Pillow then organized his command for a third attack; but in the meanwhile Cerro Gordo had fallen, and General La Vega, finding himself threatened from the Tower, and cut off from all support, surrendered himself, with three thousand men, prisoners of war.

The battle was now ended. On the other side of the mountain Generals Santa Anna, Almonte, and Canalizo, with eight thousand men, were already in full retreat, and the pursuit of the fugitives commenced.

Harney's dragoons, with Worth's division of regulars, dashed forward in advance. The brigades of Twiggs, Shields, and Riley soon followed, and from mid-day until set of sun the pursuit was urged with an energy that not only left the flying Mexicans no time to rally, but broke and dispersed them utterly.

At length the wearied victors halted at various distances along the national road, the furthest in advance being within ten miles of the beautiful city of Jalapa, and fifteen from the scene of action.

The fruits of this glorious victory were three thousand prisoners, between four and five thousand stand of arms, forty-three pieces of splendid bronze artillery of large calibre, mostly manufactured at the Royal Foundry of Seville, and a large quantity of fixed ammunition of superior quality.

Our loss during the two days, was sixty-three killed, and three hundred and ninety-eight wounded. That of the enemy was supposed to be, in killed and wounded, nearly twelve hundred.

The appearance of the battle-field, as described by an eye-witness, was appalling to the sight.

" A dragoon we encountered on the way kindly offered to be

our guide, and from him we learned the positions of the different armies, their divisions and subdivisions. As winding around the hills by the national road, the enemy's entrenchments, their barricaded heights, strong forts, and well defended passes came in view, we halted, and gazed for several moments in mute amazement. No one, from reading the newspaper accounts or the reports of the generals, can form a proper idea of the advantages possessed by the enemy in his chosen position. The battle, I knew, had been fought and won by our troops; yet it seemed, in its bare, still reality, a dream. I could not shake off this feeling as I rode along the enemy's lines of entrenchments, entered his dismantled forts and magazines, and looked from his chosen heights upon the paths up which our troops rushed into the jaws of death.   *   *   *   *   *   *

" Passing down the ravine where the National Guard had three times attempted to dislodge the mounted riflemen, who, supported by the howitzer battery, literally rained death among their ranks, I was obliged to turn back and retrace my steps. The gorge was choked up with the mangled bodies of the flower of the Mexican army. The wolf-dog and the buzzard howled and screamed as I rode by, and the stench was too sickening to be endured. Returning to the national road, we passed a large number of cannon taken by our troops, and saw piles of muskets, charred with fire, in heaps, where they had been heaped and burned.   *   *   *   *

" All along the road were the bodies of Mexican lancers and their horses, cut down by Colonel Harney's dragoons, when these fire-eaters chased Santa Anna and his retreating troops into and beyond Jalapa. Almost every man's skull was literally split open with the sabres of our horsemen, and they lay stretched upon the ground in ghastly groups."

From the old camp at Plan del Rio, where he had established his hospital for the sick and wounded, Scott forwarded to the Department of War the following despatch :—

" HEAD-QUARTERS OF THE ARMY,
Plan del Rio, 50 miles from Vera Cruz,
April 19, 1847.

" SIR: The plan of attack, sketched in General Orders, No. 111, forwarded herewith, was finely executed by this gallant army, before two o'clock, P. M., yesterday. We are quite embarrassed with the results of victory—prisoners of war, heavy ordnance, field batteries, small arms, and accoutrements.

" About 3,000 men laid down their arms, with the usual proportion of field and company officers, besides five generals, several of them of great distinction—Pinzon, Jarrero, La Vega, Noriega, and Obando. A sixth general, Vasquez, was killed in defending the battery (tower) in the rear of the whole Mexican army, the capture of which gave us those glorious results.

" Our loss, though comparatively small in numbers, has been serious. Brigadier-General Shields, a commander of activity, zeal, and talent, is, I fear, if not dead, mortally wounded. He is some five miles from me at the moment. The field of operations covered many miles, broken by mountains and deep chasms, and I have not a report, as yet, from any division or brigade.

" Twiggs's division, followed by Shields's (now Colonel Baker's) brigade, are now at or near Xalapa, and Worth's division is in route thither, all pursuing, with good results, as I learn, that part of the Mexican army—perhaps six or seven thousand men—who had fled before our right had carried the tower, and gained the Xalapa road.

" Pillow's brigade alone, is near me at this depot of wounded, sick, and prisoners; and I have time only to give from him the names of 1st Lieutenant F. B. Nelson, and 2d C. G. Hill, both of the 2d Tennessee foot (Haskell's regiment), among the killed, and in the brigade 106, of all ranks, killed or wounded.

" Among the latter, the gallant brigadier-general himself has a smart wound in the arm, out not disabled; and Major R. Farqueson, 2d Tennessee, Captain H. F. Murray, 2d Lieutenant G.

T. Sutherland, 1st Lieutenant W. P. Hale, Adjutant, all of the same regiment, severely, and 1st Lieutenant W. Yearwood, mortally wounded.   And I know, from personal observation on the ground, that 1st Lieutenant Ewell, of the Rifles, if not now dead, was mortally wounded in entering, sword in hand, the entrenchments around the captured tower.

   " 2d Lieutenant Derby, topographical engineers, I also saw, at the same place, severely wounded, and Captain Patten, 2d United States infantry, lost his right hand.*   Major Sumner, 2d United States dragoons, was slightly wounded the day before, and Captain Johnston, topographical engineers (now lieutenant-colonel of infantry), was very severely wounded some days earlier, while reconnoitring.   I must not omit to add, that Captain Mason, and 2d Lieutenant Davis, both of the Rifles, were among the very severely wounded in storming the same tower.

   " I estimate our total loss, in killed and wounded, may be about 250, and that of the enemy at 350.†   In the pursuit towards Xalapa (25 miles hence), I learn we have added much to the enemy's loss in prisoners, killed, and wounded.   In fact, I suppose his retreating army to be nearly disorganized, and hence my haste to follow, in an hour or two, to profit by events.

   " In this hurried and imperfect report I must not omit to say, that Brigadier-General Twiggs, in passing the mountain-range beyond Cerro Gordo, crowned with the tower, detached from his division, as I suggested the day before, a strong force to carry that height, which commanded the Xalapa road at the foot, and could not fail, if carried, to cut off the whole, or any part of the enemy's forces from a retreat in any direction.

   " A portion of the 1st artillery, under the often-distinguished Brevet-Colonel Childs; the 3d infantry, under Captain Alexander;

---

* The General is in error; it was a portion of his left hand Captain Patten lost.

† A very inaccurate estimate—our loss was 431, killed and wounded; that of the enemy nearly 1200. See data.

MAJ. GEN. GIDEON J. PILLOW.

the 7th infantry, under Lieutenant-Colonel Plymton; and the Rifles, under Major Loring, all under the temporary command of Colonel Harney, 2d dragoons, during the confinement to his bed of Brevet Brigadier-General P. F. Smith, composed that detachment. The style of execution, which I had the pleasure to witness, was most brilliant and decisive.

" The brigade ascended the long and difficult slope of Cerro Gordo, without shelter, and under the tremendous fire of artillery and musketry, with the utmost steadiness, reached the breast-works, drove the enemy from them, planted the colours of the 1st artillery, 3d and 7th infantry—the enemy's flag still flying—and, after some minutes' sharp firing, finished the conquest with the bayonet.

" It is a most pleasing duty to say that the highest praise is due to Harney, Childs, Plymton, Loring, Alexander, their gallant officers and men, for this brilliant service, independent of the great results which soon followed.

" Worth's division of regulars coming up at this time, he detached Brevet Lieutenant-Colonel C. F. Smith, with his light battalion, to support the assault, but not in time. The general reaching the tower a few minutes before me, and observing a white flag displayed from the nearest portion of the enemy towards the batteries below, sent out Colonels Harney and Childs to hold a parley. The surrender followed in an hour or two.*

" Major General Patterson left a sick-bed to share in the dangers and fatigues of the day; and after the surrender went forward to command the advanced forces towards Xalapa.

" Brigadier-General Pillow and his brigade twice assaulted with great daring the enemy's line of batteries on our left, and though without success, they contributed much to distract and dismay their immediate opponents.

" President Santa Anna, with Generals Canalizo and Almonte,

* These were the batteries commanded by General Pinzon, a mulatto officer.

and some six or eight thousand men escaped towards Xalapa just before Cerro Gordo was carried, and before Twiggs's division reached the national road above.

"I have determined to parole the prisoners—officers and men —as I have not the means of feeding them here beyond to-day, and cannot afford to detach a heavy body of horse and foot, with wagons, to accompany them to Vera Cruz. Our baggage-train, though increasing, is not half large enough to give an assured progress to this army.

"Besides, a greater number of prisoners would, probably, escape from the escort, in the long and deep sandy road, without subsistence—ten to one—than we shall find again, out of the same body of men, in the ranks opposed to us. Not one of the Vera Cruz prisoners is believed to have been in the lines of Cerro Gordo. Some six of the officers, highest in rank, refuse to give their paroles, except to go to Vera Cruz, and thence, perhaps, to the United States.

"The small-arms and accoutrements, being of no value to our army here, or at home, I have ordered them to be destroyed; for we have not the means of transporting them. I am, also, somewhat embarrassed with the —— pieces of artillery,* all bronze, which we have captured. It would take a brigade, and half the mules of our army, to transport them fifty miles.

"A field-battery I shall take for service with the army; but the heavy metal must be collected, and left here for the present. We have our own siege-train and the proper carriages with us.

"Being much occupied with the prisoners, and all the details of a forward movement, besides looking to the supplies which are to follow from Vera Cruz, I have time to add no more—intending to be at Xalapa early to-morrow. We shall not, probably, again meet with serious opposition this side of Perote—certainly not, unless delayed by the want of the means of transportation.

* Forty-three.

JALAPA.

"I have the honour to remain, sir, with high respect, your most obedient servant,

WINFIELD SCOTT.

Hon. WM. L. MARCY, Secretary of War."

The complete rout at Cerro Gordo opened the way to Jalapa. The partially completed defences of the La Hoya pass, offered no molestation to the march of our troops. On the 19th, the day succeeding the battle, the division of Twiggs was in undisputed possession of Jalapa, while Worth's division pushed on to Perote, and captured the town and castle without resistance; receiving at the hands of Colonel Velasquez, the commissioner appointed to surrender them by the Mexican government, the following arms and munitions of war:—"Fifty-four guns and mortars, iron and bronze, of various calibres, in good service condition,— eleven thousand and sixty-five cannon-balls, fourteen thousand three hundred bombs and hand-grenades, and five hundred muskets."*

Here Worth rested, and recruited his command. After remaining for about two weeks, he again resumed his line of march, and on the 15th of May, accompanied by Quitman's brigade of volunteers, entered the city of Puebla, with no more opposition than a slight skirmish, near Amosoque, distant about twelve miles from the city. There his progress had been threatened by a force of about three thousand cavalry, under General Santa Anna; but a few discharges from the light artillery, dismounting some ninety of the enemy, sufficed to clear the way, and by ten o'clock the next morning, the division, numbering four thousand men, stacked their arms in the Grand Plaza.

* Worth's Report, Perote, April 22, 1847.

45

CHAPTER XIX.

NOTHING could exceed the astonishment of the citizens of Puebla, at witnessing the entrance of the small force of four thousand American troops, one-half of whom were raw, and only partially disciplined volunteers, into the midst of a hostile population of eighty thousand souls.

The false and exaggerated reports which had been circulated throughout the interior of Mexico, in regard to the ferocious prowess of the North Americans,—their gigantic stature—their cannibal propensities, and their wonderful skill in arms, had disposed the more imaginative of the Pueblanos to expect the arrival of a body of men far different in personal appearance from those who marched with quiet confidence into their midst. Great, indeed, was the wonder of the citizens to find, that in stature and apparent physical strength, the conquerors were not superior to the conquered ; that the arms of the Anglo-Americans were plain and unpretending, their equipments indifferent in the extreme, and themselves apparently worn down with the fatigue of a long march, the sickliness of the country through which they

340

had passed, and the alternations of heat and cold to which they had been constantly exposed.

The undaunted courage, and indomitable resolution, which had made every man a hero, could not be exaggerated. The commonest soldier in our armies fought as if the fate of the battle and the fortunes of his country rested upon his single arm.

The battles won by Taylor and Scott, from Palo Alto to Cerro Gordo, are as much instances of individual daring, as of fine military skill.

To us it appears as if they present a new and terrible feature in warfare—terrible from its very effectiveness—the combination of the individual heroism of the old chivalric era, with the warlike science of modern times.

In European warfare, men are still considered as mere machines, to be impelled or withdrawn as the science of the commander shall dictate. The sentiments of a pure patriotism, as acting upon and stimulating the gallantry of the soldier, are but little regarded, while thought, genius, ability, or a quick perception in the masses, are considered as obstacles to success rather than calculated to promote it. The perfection of the art has been hitherto supposed to consist in a blind unreasoning obedience— the accuracy of mechanism in military evolutions, and a perfect knowledge of the manual.

But, unfortunate indeed would that general be, who should attempt to snatch a victory from the grasp of the Anglo-American by means of the present continental system of military tactics.

Enthusiastic in temperament, and elastic under reverses—accustomed to a life of hardihood and adventure—familiar from childhood with the use of arms—pressing forward continually to the outskirts of civilization, whence he has often to repel savage incursions, and often obliged to maintain his own rights by his own hand, in states and territories thinly settled, where the force of law is many times administered with difficulty or inefficient in its operation, the Anglo-American has learned, in a severe school, the benefits of self-reliance, and the good results which never fail to follow the strong will, supported by a corresponding energy.

The system of volunteer training has also been of service ; so that, while retaining much that is really useful in modern military science, and acting when necessary under its strictest rules, he still maintains an independence of thought and action which enables him to cope successfully with dangers from which no mere skill could extricate him, and to win battles after science has pronounced them irrecoverably lost.

While Worth took possession of the hills commanding Puebla, and accumulated supplies, the General-in-chief, still at Jalapa, found himself placed in a situation of the utmost embarrassment.

Of the twenty-three regiments of twelve months volunteers called out by the President in May and June 1846, seven regiments were with Scott, and the period for which they enlisted was now about to expire.

By the abstraction of these forces, honourably discharged and amounting to nearly three thousand men, the army was so greatly reduced that the General-in-chief found himself compelled to await for reinforcements before he could resume offensive operations.

It is true, that the spirit of the Mexican army appeared to have become completely paralyzed by the terrible defeat of Cerro Gordo, but the main body, which escaped with Santa Anna and Almonte, amounting to eight thousand men, still remained as a nucleus around which many yet eager and untried spirits might rally.

The prospects of peace also seemed further off than ever. Indignant under their repeated disasters, the cry of the Mexican people was still for vengeance. The chief papers of the capital and departments of Mexico, teemed with appeals to the honour and patriotism of the nation, and every effort which a feeble government could exert, was made to induce the people to rise " *en masse*" and exterminate their invaders.

On the 20th of April, the Mexican Congress passed a series of resolutions, the preamble to which is as follows :—

" The Sovereign Constitutional Congress of Mexico, in use of the full powers with which it has been invested by the people of the republic for the sacred object of preserving its nationality, and faithful interpreters of the firm determination of their constituents to carry on the war which the government of the United States is waging against the nation, without losing courage at any kind of reverses, and considering that in these circumstances, the first public necessity is to preserve a centre of union, to direct the national defence with all the energy which the state of things demands, and to avoid even the danger of a revolutionary power arising to dissolve the national union and destroy its institutions, or to consent to dismember its territory, has decreed the following."

The first resolution asserts the power of the supreme government " to take the necessary measures to carry on the war, defend the nationality of the republic, and to save the republican form of government, popular and federal, under which the nation is constituted."

The second resolution, in explanation of the true intent and meaning of the first, states that " the foregoing article does not authorize the Executive to make a peace with the United States, conclude negotiations with foreign powers, nor alienate the whole or a part of the territory of the republic."

The fourth article declares null and illegal " all treaties and arrangements made between the United States and any authority who should substitute itself for the supreme powers legally established."

And in the fifth, every individual is denounced as a traitor, " who, either in his private capacity or as a public officer, either privately, or invested with any incompetent authority, or of revolutionary origin, shall treat with the government of the United States."

It is sufficiently evident from the above action of Congress, that great distrust had entered the public mind after the repeated reverses which the nation had suffered. The sincerity of Santa Anna was doubted, and fears were entertained that he would make peace with the invaders, on terms which should not only yield Texas to the conquerors, but dismember a portion of the republic.

Congress also entertained a suspicion that the priesthood, alarmed by their attempt to appropriate to the uses of the government a portion of the revenues of the church, were engaged in intrigues, which had for their object the overthrow of the government and the establishment of royalty, either in the person of Santa Anna himself, Paredes, or some continental prince. Fearful of these attempts, they sought to intimidate them by a course of action which showed they were cognizant of the designs entertained, and which should check them if attempted.

In strict accordance with the defiant resolves of Congress, on the following day General Salas issued a proclamation to the citizens, in which he exhorts them to unite at general head-quarters, and enroll themselves as guerrilleros for the purpose of attacking and destroying the invaders in every manner imaginable. " War without pity unto death!" he continues, " will be the motto of the guerrilla warfare of vengeance."*

On the first of May, Anaya, the President ad interim, declared the city of Mexico in a state of siege, assigning as his reason the necessity of providing for the defence of the capital and the common defence of the nation against the enemy.

On the 6th, following out the above proclamation, General Bravo, Commander-in-chief of the Army of the Centre, issued a decree, wherein all Mexicans between the ages of sixteen and sixty are

* Extracts from El Monitor.

called upon to enroll themselves for the defence of the capital, under the penalty of being considered as traitors, and treated as such, in the event of evasion or refusal.

Nor was this exhibition of energy confined to the capital only.

The states of San Luis, Mexico, Zacatecas, Jalisco, and Queretaro, bound themselves, by a solemn league and covenant, to preserve the unity of the republic ; and in their address to the Mexican people, they protest, " that never will they consent to, nor be bound by any convention or treaty of peace with the North American enemy, so long as he threatens or occupies the capital or any part of the Mexican republic ; they also will not recognise any general suspension of arms which should compromise all the belligerent forces of the nation ;" and they close by asserting their determination to aid with their private resources the general government, independent of the assistance they are bound by law to give ; so that the one cause — common to them in its disgraces and its perils — may be sustained, the national credit and honour re-established, and all possible opposition and resistance made to every attack upon the popular federal representative system."*

Had these various resolutions been as firmly carried out as they were pertinaciously insisted upon, it is possible that victory might yet have inclined to the Mexican standard ; but there is a vast difference between the energy which can be exhibited in fiery denunciations, and the spirit necessary to meet in successful conflict even a mere handful of resolute men.

In an equally firm, but far more moderate tone, was the proclamation of General Scott, addressed also to the Mexican nation, and dated Jalapa, May 11th, 1847. It is a paper which proves him to be as accomplished in diplomacy, as in the art of war. In this admirable document, after briefly alluding to the causes which precipitated the war, and the successes that had in every

* New Orleans Bulletin.

battle attended the American arms—successes which he attributes
more to the unskilfulness of the Mexican generals than to the
want of valour in their troops—he concludes by saying:—

"Again, Mexicans of honourable pride—contemplate the lot
of peaceful and laborious citizens, in all classes of your society.
The possessions of the church menaced and held out as an in-
citement to revolution and anarchy; the fortunes of rich proprietors pointed out for plunder to the ill-disposed; the merchant and
the artisan, the labourer and the manufacturer, burdened with
contributions, excises, monopolies, taxes upon consumption,
surrounded with restrictions and charged with odious internal
customs; the man of letters and the statesman, the man of
liberal knowledge who dares to speak, persecuted without trial
by some faction, or by the rulers who abuse their power; crimi-
nals unpunished and set at liberty, as were those of Perote—is
this, then, Mexicans, the liberty which you enjoy?

"I will not believe that the· Mexicans of the present day are
wanting in courage to confess errors which do not dishonour
them, and to adopt a system of true liberty, of peace, and union
with their brethren and neighbours of the north; neither will I
believe that they are ignorant of the falsity of the calumnies of
the press, intended to excite hostility. No! public sentiment is
not to be created or animated by falsehood. We have not pro-
faned your temples, nor abused your women, nor seized your
property, as they would have you believe.

"We say this with pride, and we confirm it by your own
bishops, and by the clergy of Tampico, Tuspan, Matamoros, Monterey, Vera Cruz, and Jalapa, and by all the authorities, civil and
religious, and the inhabitants of every town we have occupied.

"We adore the same God: and a large proportion of our army,
as well as of the people of the United States, are Catholics, like
yourselves. We punish crime, wherever we find it, and reward
merit and virtue.

"The army of the United States respects, and will always respect private property, of every description, and the property of the Mexican church.

"Mexicans! the past cannot be remedied, but the future may be provided for. Repeatedly have I shown you, that the government and people of the United States desire peace, desire your sincere friendship.

"Abandon, then, rancorous prejudices; cease to be the sport of individual ambition, and conduct yourselves like a great American nation; leave off at once colonial habits, and learn to be truly free, truly republican, and you will become prosperous and happy, for you possess all the elements to be so. Remember that you are Americans, and that your happiness is not to come from Europe.

"I desire, in conclusion, to declare, and with equal frankness, that, if necessary, an army of one hundred thousand Americans could promptly be brought, and that the United States would not terminate their differences with Mexico (if compelled to do so by force of arms) in any manner uncertain, precarious, or dishonouring to yourselves. I should insult the intelligent of this country if I had any doubt of their acquaintance with this truth.

"The order to form guerrilla parties to attack us, I assure you can procure nothing but evil to your country, and no evil to our army, which will know how to proceed against them; and if, so far from conciliating, you succeed in irritating, you will impose upon us the hard necessity of retaliation, and then you cannot blame us for the consequences which will fall upon yourselves.

"I am marching with my army upon Puebla and Mexico—I do not conceal it; from those capitals I shall again address you. I desire peace, friendship, and union—it is for you to select, whether you prefer war; under any circumstances, be assured I shall not fail my word.

WINFIELD SCOTT."

46

That the government of the United States was really desirous of peace there cannot be the least doubt. It had originally contemplated nothing more than a small border war, in which the Mexican troops, being beaten, would retire from the frontier line, and, by the conclusion of an armistice, leave the existing difficulties to be settled by negotiation.

In this expectation, however, our government was deceived. It had not sufficiently considered the pride and obstinacy which have always formed the two most prominent elements of the Spanish character. The revolt of Texas, and the establishment of its independence, were sufficiently mortifying to Mexican pride. With the mortification was coupled hatred of the United States, from which the original settlers of Texas came; that increased on the incorporation of the latter with the states of the Northern Confederacy, and became an implacable hostility, when the Army of Occupation, not content with Texas, carried its aggressive banner to the banks of the Bravo.

The hatred with which an American was regarded in all parts of the Mexican republic, was by no means of recent origin. The unexampled prosperity of the United States, and its consequent rapid increase in power; its energetic character, and the wonderful vitality which able legislation had infused into every part of the body politic; had long been viewed by the Mexicans with feelings of ill suppressed jealousy and distrust.

A presentiment natural to a weak nation watching the advancing and gigantic strides of a powerful neighbour, seems to have constantly stimulated this feeling of antagonism. This presentiment was, that a collision must some day take place, and upon the results which followed would depend the question of Mexican nationality. Hence, in some respects, arose the early anxiety to measure their strength with that of the "barbarian of the north," and the disasters that followed repeated trials, wounded still deeper a self-love, which attributed its defeats to every other than the true cause—the manifest superiority of our men in courage, tenacity, and the use of arms; and the great military skill and undaunted resolution of the officers by whom they were conducted.

Had but a single victory crowned the arms of Mexico, it is possible that from the vantage ground thus obtained, and with her national honour soothed by an unwonted triumph, she might have consented to open negotiations; but, defeated in every battle, pride, shame, and a galling sense of the presence of a victorious enemy, goaded her on to new offorts, only to end in more terrible disasters.

As early as the 15th of April, Mr. Buchanan wrote to the Minister of Foreign Affairs, in answer to a previous communication, in which the latter declined, according to an earlier proposition made by our government, to send commissioners to Jalapa, Havana, or any other point that might be agreed upon, unless the blockade of the Mexican ports should be first raised, and our army withdrawn beyond the limits of the Mexican territory.

In reply, Mr. Buchanan states, that the President holds such a preliminary condition to be wholly inadmissible, both as calculated to prolong the war, and as contrary to the usages of nations; and that he will not make further overtures for the opening of negotiations, at least until he shall have reason to believe that such will be accepted by the Mexican government. Devoted, however, to honourable peace, he is determined that the evils of war shall not be protracted one day longer than shall be rendered absolutely necessary by the Mexican republic.

Mr. Buchanan then announces, that, to carry this determination into effect, the President has sent in the quality of commissioner, to the head-quarters of the army in Mexico, Mr. N. P. Trist, First Clerk in the State Department, with full powers to conclude a definitive treaty of peace with the United Mexican States, and recommends him as eminently worthy the confidence and consideration of the Mexican government.*

* Washington Union.

This letter, after numerous vexatious delays, was referred by General Santa Anna to the Mexican Congress, that body being convened for the especial purpose of deliberating upon its contents.

On the 13th of July, a quorum of seventy-four members being present, the question as to whether the commissioner should be received and negotiations opened, was considered, when the committee on Foreign Affairs, upon whom the primary consideration of the subject was devolved, offered a report and resolutions to the effect, "that it belonged to the Executive under their constitution to receive all ministers and public agents, and to make treaties of peace, alliances, &c.; that the functions of Congress were limited to the approving or disapproving these treaties when made, and that consequently, until a treaty should be submitted in form, it could take no constitutional action on the subject.*

The report being submitted, it was accepted by a vote of fifty-two to twenty-two; and the letter having been ordered to be returned to General Santa Anna, the Congress adjourned the same day, as if desirous of avoiding any further action upon it.

The resolutions thus adopted might be considered expressive of a determination to continue the war, inasmuch as it was well known that the Executive was effectually prevented from taking the initiative in any negotiations for peace by the fifth section of the law passed on the 20th of April, 1847, in which every public officer is declared a traitor who should enter into any treaty or arrangement with the government of the United States.†

The numerical weakness of the American force in Mexico at this time, may have had its effect in sustaining the determination of the Mexican government, to prolong the war at all hazards. Something, too, they doubtless hoped from the effects of climate upon men unaccustomed to its changes, and unprepared by a sufficiency of clothing to sustain the great contrast between the cool

---

* Synopsis of the Washington Union, August 23d, 1847.   † See *ante.*

temperature of the mountainous region in which they were then garrisoned, and the excessive heat of the plains.

The Mexicans well knew that sickness and disease had hitherto been infinitely more fatal to our troops, on the route between Vera Cruz and Puebla, than all the battles in which they had been engaged since the commencement of the war.

Weak indeed was the condition of our gallant army at that time. On the 4th of June, Scott wrote to the Secretary of War, stating that the strength of the army had been surprisingly reduced. That in addition to the discharge of seven regiments, and two independent companies of volunteers, there was left in hospital at Vera Cruz about one thousand men—a like number of sick and wounded at Jalapa; two hundred at Perote (afterwards increased to nearly a thousand), and in the hospital at Puebla, one thousand and seventeen. In all, three thousand two hundred, in the short space of two months, or nearly one-fourth of the whole force that disembarked at Vera Cruz. If we add to these the three thousand discharged volunteers, and the killed at Cerro Gordo, we shall not wonder that, after deducting the garrisons of Vera Cruz, Jalapa, and Perote, there remained but the small force of five thousand eight hundred and twenty effective non-commissioned officers, artificers, musicians, and privates.*

Thus situated, Scott determined to abandon Jalapa, and withdraw its garrison, together with a portion of the garrison at Perote, in order to place him in a more favourable condition for advancing upon the capital.

But the reinforcements, long looked for, and almost despaired of, were at this time fairly on their way. By the 8th of July, in addition to the garrison of Puebla, the brigades of Pillow and Cadwalader reached the head of the army, increasing the number of effectives—rank and file, to eight thousand and sixty-one men, and swelling the sick list, by the addition of the hospitals from

* Scott's Official Despatch, No. 29.

Jalapa, to the fearful extent of two thousand two hundred and fifteen men, and eighty-seven commissioned officers.*

About this time, Scott heard that Brigadier-General Pierce had arrived at Vera Cruz with twenty-five hundred recruits, and the General-in-chief determined to delay his march until they also should join him.   After various delays, arising from the want of transportation, Pierce reached Puebla on the 6th of August, with twenty-four hundred and twenty-nine men; and the next day Scott commenced his march for the capital, with an army composed of ten thousand seven hundred and thirty-eight, rank and file.

* Scott's Official Papers, No. 29.

BRIG. GEN. FRANKLIN PIERCE.

CHAPTER XX.

THE numerous delays by which a portion of our troops was detained so long at Puebla, were at least beneficial in one point of view, by enabling the new levies, as they came up, to acquire that perfect discipline and thorough knowledge of their officers, without which it is doubtful whether they would have achieved those signal victories which have since made the Anglo-Saxon name a terror to the hearts of the inhabitants of the valley of Mexico.

It must be remembered, that of the force which left Puebla for the Mexican capital, nearly one-half was new and untried. Most of them were men suddenly called from the occupations of civil life, from the plough, the loom, the desk, and the anvil; and though perhaps there were none among them wholly unaccustomed to the use of arms, there were, yet, very few indeed who were expert in the manual, or who could have performed with precision the numerous and complicated manœuvres, the knowledge of which is always requisite in the presence of an enemy, and so often essential to the success of a battle.

The rigid system of military instruction instituted at Puebla, made every man a soldier who arrived early enough to participate

353

in it, so that, before the army left that city, it had acquired the high distinction of being the best disciplined of any which had yet been sent forth by the American nation on the road to conquest. Its subsequent deeds fully proved that this estimate of its character was not less just than true.

One of the most remarkable features of the war, was the unbounded confidence which animated the American army on all occasions. No matter by how many obstacles surrounded, or by what numbers opposed, the possibility of defeat never seems to have been entertained for a single moment. To anticipate a battle was to anticipate a victory; and that the city of Mexico would be reached, in despite of the difficulties which were known to beset the way, was entertained with so undoubting a belief, that the possession of the Aztec capital was assured from the very moment that Puebla was left in the rear.

Leaving the meagre force of three hundred and ninety-three men under Colonel Childs to garrison the latter city, and charged with the protection of eighteen hundred sick in its hospitals, the army advanced towards the capital in four divisions, preceded by a cavalry brigade.

These divisions had been previously arranged as follows:

CAVALRY BRIGADE.
COLONEL HARNEY.

1st Dragoons, Captain Kearney.
2d   do.   Major Sumner.
3d   do.   Captain McReynolds.

FIRST DIVISION.
GENERAL WORTH.

First Brigade,
COLONEL GARLAND.
{
2d Artillery.
3d   do.
4th Infantry.
Duncan's Battery.
}

Second Brigade,
COLONEL CLARKE.
{ 5th Infantry.
6th   do.
8th   do.

SECOND DIVISION.

GENERAL TWIGGS.

First Brigade,
GENERAL SMITH.
{ Mounted Rifles.
1st Artillery.
3d Infantry.
Taylor's Battery.

Second Brigade,
COLONEL RILEY.
{ 4th Artillery.
2d Infantry.
7th   do.

THIRD DIVISION.

GENERAL PILLOW.

First Brigade,
GENERAL PIERCE.
{ 9th Infantry.
12th   do.
15th   do.
Magruder's Battery.

Second Brigade,
GENERAL CADWALADER.
{ Voltigeurs.
14th Infantry.
11th   do.

FOURTH DIVISION.

GENERAL QUITMAN.

First Brigade,
GENERAL SHIELDS.
{ New York regiment.
South Carolina do.
Marines.
Steptoe's Battery.

Second Brigade,
COLONEL ROBERTS.
{ 2d Pennsylvania regiment.

But though the above was the arrangement of the divisions, the order of march was different. Twiggs's division, preceded by

47

Harney's cavalry, was in advance; then followed Quitman's division; to this succeeded the division of Worth; and the division of Pillow brought up the rear.

These divisions left Puebla on four successive days, beginning on the 7th of August, and ending on the 10th, but were at no time beyond five hours' march, or supporting distance, apart. On the 8th, the General-in-chief overtook and continued with, the leading division.*

The route by which the troops marched was over a rolling road, gradually ascending towards the Sierra Nevada. During the first day of their departure from Puebla, the country through which they passed, was of great natural beauty and fertility. It was well-watered, and bore evidences of the most careful cultivation. In the midst of the magnificent estates before them, were to be seen the haciendas of wealthy proprietors, embosomed in foliage, each with its appropriate chapel gleaming white through the trees, and surrounded by the numerous habitations of the labourers. Upon the left, at the distance of many miles, though seemingly close by, rose high, clear, distinct, and sharply defined in the pure atmosphere of the mountains, the mighty summits of Popocatapetl and Iztaccihuatl, clothed densely around their bases with the dark verdure of forest trees, but crowned with everlasting snows; while nearer yet, and between the road and the mountains, were to be seen the ruins of the pyramid of Cholula, the only vestige remaining of the populous city of the Aztecs, which in the days of Cortez numbered two hundred thousand souls.

During the morning of the second day, the face of the country began to wear a more rugged aspect; the signs of cultivation gradually grew less, and, after passing a few miles beyond the village of San Martin, terminated altogether.

The road now became wilder, winding about and over a suc-

* Scott's Official Despatches, No. 31.

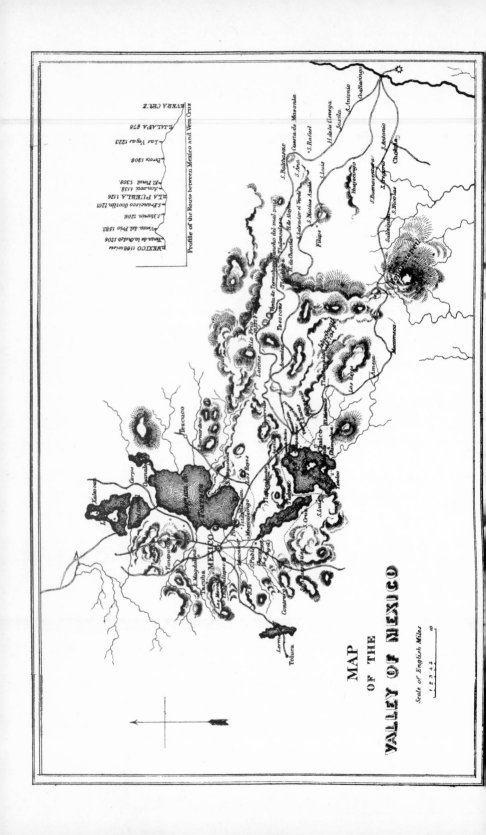

MAP
OF THE
VALLEY OF MEXICO

Scale of English Miles

Profile of the Route between Mexico and Vera Cruz

VERA CRUZ
XALAPA 678
Las Vegas 1223
Ivrea 1308.
El Pinal 1308.
Arcoeti 1138.
LA PUEBLA 1126
S.Francisco Ocotlan 1201
S.Martin 1206
Venta del Pino 1583
Venta de la Cañada 1206
MEXICO 1164

cession of mountain ranges, each higher than the ctner, until it reached at Rio Frio its greatest elevation.

Here the advance expected to have been met by a formidable resistance, and such had evidently at one time been the intention of the Mexicans; but, from some cause or other, the design was abandoned after they had thrown up a few breastworks, and felled a considerable quantity of timber.

From the time of leaving Puebla until they reached Rio Frio— a distance of about fifty miles—the troops had been constantly gaining in ascent, so that they now stood two thousand nine hundred and twenty-two feet above the former city, and ten thousand one hundred and twenty-two feet above the level of the ocean.

But they were soon to be compensated for the toils of the march by one of the loveliest sights that ever greeted the eyes of a traveller. A few miles further was a sudden turn of the road, and then first burst upon the astonished vision, with the splendour of an enchantment, the glorious valley of Mexico—clothed with rich verdure—traversed by silver streams—dotted with lakes, villages, and haciendas,—and the whole enclosed by an amphitheatre of mountains hundreds of miles in extent, many of them extinct volcanoes, green with forests or white with eternal snow,—with other mountain barriers, rising beyond them and blending in the far distance, with the soft blue sky above.

On the 10th, the leading division encamped for the night at the base of the mountain, surrounded on all sides by the enemy's scouts.

The next day, Twiggs reached Ayotla, fifteen miles from the capital. Here he halted until the other divisions came up.*

On the 12th, the different divisions, as they approached the base of the mountains, drew more closely towards each other. Twiggs's division halted at Ayotla, and Worth's at the village of Chalco, five miles distant across the lake in a straight line, but double

* Letter to the New York Courier.

that distance by the road; between Twiggs and Worth were encamped the divisions of Pillow and Quitman.

The National or Vera Cruz Road, by which the troops had
hitherto advanced, is approached on the left at Ayotla, by the
margin of Lake Chalco, and at a distance of seven miles further
on and to the right, is bounded by Lake Tezcuco, which extends
to within three miles of the city. The road is a causeway running
for a considerable portion of the space intervening between the
lakes by marshy and boggy grounds.

At a distance of seven miles, or about midway between Ayotla
and the capital, rises the lofty mound called El Peñon. " This
hill or mound completely enfilades and commands the National
Road, and had been fortified and repaired with the greatest care
by Santa Anna. One side was inaccessible by nature, the rest
had been made so by art. Batteries mounting in all fifty guns of
different calibres had been placed on its sides, and a deep ditch
twenty-four feet wide and ten deep, filled with water, had been
cut connecting the parts already surrounded by marshes."*

Such was the information gained by a reconnoissance of the
work, which was decided to be impracticable, and a second reconnoissance was directed, the next day, the 13th, upon Mexicalcingo, a village at a fortified bridge across the canal leading from
Lake Xochimilco. The reconnoitring party, consisting of the
regiment of Mounted Rifles and three companies of cavalry—in all
about four hundred men—discovered a road leading from Los Reyes
to the left, and followed its windings until within five miles of the
city, when they were halted by coming suddenly upon five strong
batteries on the hill which commanded the road. Rapidly countermarching, the party quickly discovered that in avoiding one
danger they had laid themselves open to another still more terrible.
El Peñon, with its three tiers of works, and its fearful array of
cannon, lay directly between them and their camp at Ayotla.

* Letter to the New York Courier.

Expecting every instant an attack, they dashed forward at their utmost speed, and arrived safely at camp about midnight. This brilliant reconnoissance was pronounced by the General-in-chief "the boldest of the war."[*]

Of the route by Mexicalcingo, General Scott thus wrote to the Secretary of War :—

"It might have been easy—masking the Peñon—to force the passage ; but, on the other side of the bridge, we should have found ourselves four miles from this road on a narrow causeway, flanked to the right and left by water or boggy grounds. These difficulties, closely viewed, threw me back upon the project, long entertained, of turning the strong eastern defences of the city, by passing around south of Lakes Chalco and Xochimilco at the foot of the hills and mountains, so as to reach San Augustine, and hence to manœuvre on hard though much broken ground to the south and south-west of the capital, which has been more or less under our view since the 10th instant."[†]

The attempt, therefore, to advance by the National Road was abandoned, and the strength of the defence upon and near the Acapulco road was now to be tested. These consisted of San Antonio, Contreras, and Churubusco. Reversing the order of march, Worth's division now took the lead, Pillow and Quitman followed, while the division of Twiggs brought up the rear, after remaining one day longer at Ayotla, in order to mask the new movement as long as possible, by threatening the Peñon and Mexicalcingo.

On the 16th, Twiggs commenced his march. Upon reaching the village of Buena Vista, he found his train threatened by a force of cavalry and infantry to the number of five thousand men, under General Valencia ; the skirmish and subsequent march is thus described :—

"On our left were large fields of half-grown barley, through

---

[*] Letter to the New York Courier.   [†] Official Despatches.

which was seen advancing in splendid order the enemy's column. It was the most splendid sight I had ever witnessed. The yellow cloaks, red jackets and caps of the lancers, and the bright blue and white uniforms of the infantry, were most beautifully contrasted with the green of the barley-field. Our line of battle was soon formed, and we deployed through the grain to turn their left, and cut them off from the mountains. A few shots, however, from the battery, showed them that they were observed; and countermarching in haste, they left their dead on the field. Thus ended our fight of Buena Vista. That night we stayed at Chalco.

" The next day we made a long and toilsome march over a horrible road, through which, with the utmost difficulty, we dragged our wagons, by the assistance of both men and mules. The next was nearly the same, except that the road, if possible, was worse than before, as the Mexicans had blocked it up with large stones, rolled down from the neighbouring hills."[*]

The route thus laboriously traversed, lay on the left, along the base of a mountain range, whose sides, often precipitous, would have afforded an enterprising enemy frequent opportunities of annoyance, or the road itself might have been effectually obstructed by blocking up the way with rocks rolled from the summits of the hills, a task of easy accomplishment; for, on the right of the road, the ground was frequently marshy and insecure, and occasionally bounded by the actual waters of the lakes.

The bed of the road was covered with loose rocks and rugged land, and intercepted by ravines, over which, in many places, the artillery had to be dragged by hand; and slow, and painful, and fatiguing in the extreme, was the toil by which these difficulties over a circuitous route of twenty-seven miles were at length successfully overcome.

On the 18th, all the divisions were again concentrated in the vicinity of San Augustine and the Acapulco road.

* Letter to the New York Courier.

By changing the line of march from the Vera Cruz or National Road to the Acapulco road, the formidable defences of the Peñon and Mexicalcingo were avoided altogether; but there were yet many fortifications to be turned, or taken by assault, and an army of thirty thousand Mexicans to be routed before either of the approaches to the capital would be open to the advance of the American troops.

CHAPTER XXI.

THE defences of the three great roads which approach the city of Mexico, were as follows :—

On the Vera Cruz or National Road, was the mound of El Peñon with its three tiers of works, containing twenty batteries that mounted fifty-one guns, and commanding the causeway by which the Americans were expected to advance, and at its base were fifteen infantry breastworks. It was also, as we have seen, surrounded by a deep ditch filled with water, while the causeway beyond, though broad, was flanked to the right by the waters of Lake Tezcuco, and to the left by marshy grounds.

As there was a road turning off to the left of the National Road at Los Reyes, leading to a causeway at Mexicalcingo, five miles from the city, the approach to the capital in that direction was defended by eight batteries for thirty-eight guns, and one infantry breastwork; and the difficulty of an advance beyond, was still great, from the causeway being narrow, and flanked to the right and left by water.

The movement upon the capital by the National Road, either by storming El Peñon and following the direct route, or by passing to the left at Los Reyes and forcing the batteries at Mexicalcingo

362

and the causeway beyond, was found too hazardous to attempt with so small an army, and was therefore most wisely abandoned.

The Acapulco road was then selected, as being protected by defences of somewhat inferior strength, and as affording a better opportunity for our troops to manœuvre with advantage.

The defences upon this road were those of San Antonio, Churubusco, and Contreras. San Antonio was a village approachable only in front by a causeway flanked by wet ditches or by difficult grounds, composing the outskirts of a field of broken lava, called the Pedregal.

Its works consisted of seven batteries for twenty-four guns, and two breastworks for infantry.

Churubusco was a strongly fortified hacienda, surrounded on all sides by a high and thick wall, within which was also a strong stone church.

In front of the hacienda, without the wall, and embracing two sides of it, was a field-work mounting seven pieces of cannon, which commanded the approach in all directions. Besides these, at a distance of five hundred yards, and directly across the causeway by which it is approached, was a *tete-du-pont*, or bridge-head, at the crossing of a canal: this was defended by a deep ditch, and mounted three large pieces of cannon.

To the left of San Augustine, and distant from it about four miles, was the hill of Contreras, a strongly fortified position commanding a difficult pass through which, by means of a cross road through San Angel and Cuyoacan, the fortifications of San Antonio might have been turned, and those of Churubusco more favourably approached. Upon this hill were twenty-two pieces of cannon, surrounded by a breastwork.

On the third approach to the capital, the Toluca road, where the mountains most closely approach the city, were the works of Molino del Rey, and the fortress of Chapultepec.

The first consisted of the strong stone buildings of the maga-

48

zine, called "*Casa Mata*," and the foundry of Molino del Rey, protected by a field-battery, the guns of Chapultepec, and infantry breastworks.

The second, of the hill of Chapultepec, crowned with the military college, an immense building well fortified; surrounded at its base by a thick stone wall fifteen feet high, protected at different points by seven batteries mounting nineteen guns, and seven infantry breastworks; and further defended by mines which perforated the hill in all directions, and by broad and deep wet ditches.

Such, then, were the exterior defences commanding all the approaches to the capital.

The interior defences, or those more immediately round the city, were of a slighter character, and consisted mainly of the narrow causeways flanked by water, or wet ditches, and upon which breastworks had been hastily thrown up. At the head of these causeways were the Garitas, or small forts immediately protecting the entrance to the capital.

Of the positions and force of the Mexican troops, by which these various works were to be defended, we shall now take occasion to speak.

General Valencia occupied the hill of Contreras with seven thousand men, the best and bravest of the Mexican army.

A corps of reserve, consisting of twelve thousand men under the immediate command of General Santa Anna, was stationed in front of the village of Contreras, an intermediate point between the hill of Contreras and Churubusco, and so situated as to be able to reinforce the one or the other as circumstances might require.

Three thousand troops under General Bravo garrisoned San Antonio, while at the hacienda and the tete-du-pont of Churubusco were from seven to nine thousand men under General Rincon.

On the 18th, Worth's division and Harney's brigade of cavalry, after reaching San Augustine, were thrown forward to reconnoitre San Antonio, and, if possible, to carry or mask it.*

Advancing on the direct road to within a mile of that village, they found its front thoroughly fortified with heavy guns, which at various angles commanded the approach through the whole length of the route.†

The approach was by a causeway, flanked to the right by marshy grounds, while on the left, extending to the mountains a distance of five miles, was the field of volcanic rocks called the Pedregal. This singular field is in shape an irregular oval—it is skirted occasionally by patches of dense chaparral, and on passing these is found cut up in all directions by deep ravines, and covered with huge masses of rock and rugged lava.

The Mexicans believed it opposed an effectual barrier to any attempt which might be made to turn their position in that direction; but the skilful and daring reconnoissances of the 18th and continued on the morning of the 19th, proved, that by the exercise of great energy, perseverance, and severe toil, the Pedregal might be penetrated, and, by a semicircular sweep, the main road beyond San Antonio be gained.

By this means, the double purpose would be effected of turning the enemy's position, and cutting off his retreat towards the capital.‡

Meanwhile, also on the 18th, another reconnoissance was ordered from San Augustine, the head-quarters of the General-in-chief, over the left of the Pedregal and at the opposite side from San Antonio, with the view of avoiding, if possible, the works at the latter place (the assault of which would have involved an immense loss of life), and at the same time reaching Churubusco through the villages of San Angel and Cuyoacan by a road which was known to exist beyond the Pedregal.

* Worth's Official Report.   † Ibid.

‡ Scott's Official Despatch, No. 31.

In doing this, however, the entrenched camp upon the hill of Contreras would have to be carried by assault; but as it was supposed to be less capable of sustaining a defence than San Antonio, this route, if practicable at all, would be preferable to the latter.

The reconnoissance continued over the morning of the 19th, when a route was discovered, through which, however, it was found that a road would have to be opened for the passage of artillery. Pillow's division was accordingly sent forward for that purpose.

The division of Twiggs arriving at San Juan, a small village within two miles of San Augustine, was ordered to the front to cover the working parties. The men were directed to sling their blankets across their shoulders, leave their knapsacks behind in the wagons, and put bread and beef for two days in their haversacks. From this order they knew that a battle was impending; and though somewhat fatigued already with a rugged march of seven miles, they met the requisition with their accustomed alacrity. The distance they had yet to march before reaching the San Angel road, was nearly seven miles more, a considerable portion of which lay through thick chaparral, and over loose rocks and lava, intermingled with prickly pear and cactus, and cut up by deep ditches and ravines.

About two o'clock P. M., Smith's brigade reached the summit of a hill, dragging with it Magruder's battery of three pieces, and two mountain howitzers, under Lieutenant Callender, when even the boldest of the advance were suddenly startled at finding themselves within two hundred yards of Valencia's fortifications upon the hill of Contreras.

Now it was that the great strength of the Mexican works became distinctly visible. Twenty-two pieces of artillery, mostly of large calibre, commanded the road, between which and the works in front and to the left, was a deep and almost impassable ravine. " The camp and ravine were closely defended by masses of infantry, and these again supported by clouds of cavalry at hand and hovering in view;"* while between Contreras and Churubusco, and within supporting distance of both, was the reserve of twelve thousand men, under General Santa Anna.

From an elevated position in San Augustine, many of the movements of the enemy beyond the volcanic field could be plainly seen, and at an earlier hour heavy reinforcements having been discovered approaching Contreras from the capital, Cadwalader's brigade was pushed forward to support Riley, and Pierce's brigade was subsequently despatched to sustain Smith.†

Without pausing upon the eminence from which the fortifications had been discovered, Smith ordered the batteries forward, and threw out the Rifles to protect them. The enemy's pickets were soon driven in, and the batteries dashed past at a gallop under a severe fire from the hill. Gaining a position about four hundred yards from the Mexican works, Magruder and Callender opened their fire; but though the pieces were served with wonderful precision and rapidity, they were opposed by so great a superiority, both in the number of guns and weight of metal — twenty-two against five — that the contest was too unequal on our side to be maintained with any hope of success. Accordingly, after the lapse of two hours, during which, at every discharge from the hill, our troops threw themselves flat upon the ground, to avoid the balls, and then sprang up to serve the guns, the batteries were withdrawn, with the loss of fifteen artillerists and thirteen horses, killed and wounded.‡

During this time repeated charges of lancers had been repulsed both by Smith's brigade supporting the batteries, and by the Second Brigade, under Riley.

In attempting to gain the San Angel road in the rear of the

* Scott's Official Despatch, No. 31.

† Kendall's Letter to the New Orleans Picayune.

‡ Letter to the New York Courier.

enemy, Riley became separated from support by the difficult character of the ground. Taking advantage of his isolated position, two or three thousand Mexicans sallied out from the camp, and threw themselves between him and Smith's brigade ; a large body of cavalry also bore down upon him in two successive charges, while the reserve of Santa Anna was discovered closing upon his rear.

Notwithstanding the perilous array thus opposed to him, Riley, though hemmed in on all sides, gallantly maintained his ground, beat back both the infantry and cavalry, and by a series of well conducted manœuvres, executed in the face of the enemy, succeeded, late in the evening, in joining Smith's brigade at the village of Contreras.

In the meanwhile the General-in-chief had arrived upon the ground; and observing, from an eminence overlooking the field of battle, that large reinforcements of the enemy were advancing from the city by the road which, passing through the villages of San Angel and Contreras, led to the entrenched camp, he ordered Morgan's regiment, the 15th, to push forward and occupy Contreras, and the brigade of Pierce, just arrived from San Augustine, to follow and sustain Morgan. The brigades of Smith and Riley were already moving in that direction, and Cadwalader's brigade, despatched at an earlier hour upon the same point, was found already in position, though much in need of assistance.*

For the first time in the history of the war, no impression had been made upon the enemy : and, as the day was drawing to a close, the General-in-chief, accompanied by General Twiggs, who was disabled from following his division, returned to San Augustine, leaving General Smith in command.

On approaching Contreras, that active officer discovered the immense reserve of Santa Anna forming on the slope on the

---

* Scott's Official Despatch, No. 31.

STORMING OF CONTRERAS.

opposite side of the village, and threatening the brigade of Cadwalader, already there and in position.

" The village lay entirely on the other side of the main road, and was divided from it by a small stream running through a deep ravine. On the road, and between it and the stream, was a garden and house surrounded by a high and tolerably strong stone wall. The village was intersected by narrow lanes lying between high dikes enclosing gardens full of trees and shrubbery —the lanes affording cover and the trees concealment for the men. In the centre stood an old stone church."*

Forming Cadwalader's brigade on the outer edge of the village, flanked on the right by the 3d infantry and Rifles, Smith occupied the church with the Engineer company, while the 11th regiment took up its position in the garden on the road, to protect that avenue and the rear.

The enemy now formed opposite in two lines, the infantry in front, the cavalry in the rear and about ten thousand strong.

Riley's brigade having arrived in the mean time, Smith determined upon an immediate and energetic attack; but the troops were disengaged from among the ravines and chaparral with so much difficulty, that it grew dark before his order of battle was perfected, and the design was abandoned.

The men now bivouacked for the night. The brigades of Smith and Riley occupied a narrow road running through the centre of the village, while Cadwalader resumed his former position. The brigade of Shields, which came up later in the evening, lay in an orchard near by.

But sleep visited not the eyelids of the weary troops on that eventful night, for the indecisive result of the day was succeeded by prospects gloomier still. They were surrounded by a force of eighteen thousand Mexicans, within range of the batteries upon the hill of Contreras, completely cut off from all reinforcements,

* Smith's Official Report.

and without even the possibility of hearing from General Scott, whose messengers, repeatedly despatched across the Pedregal, returned, one after another, foiled by the darkness of the night and the difficulties of the route.

To add to the discomfort of their situation, the rain fell in torrents. The rush of waters choked up the bed of the road where they lay. Drenched and benumbed, they sprang to their feet, and huddling closely together, awaited with desperate resolution the events of the morrow.*

But while the ill success of the day, the terrible storm by which they were now assailed, and the threatening aspect of the enemy by whom they were surrounded, all contributed to infuse a feeling of despondency among the troops, an unexpected discovery stirred their drooping spirits with hopeful animation.

A route, barely practicable for infantry, had been found by Lieutenant Tower, of the Engineers, leading from the village through a ravine to the rear of Valencia's fortifications; and Smith instantly determined upon the daring project of carrying them by storm.

Dangerous as the execution of this design was, while hemmed in by masses of the enemy's troops, who might at any moment become the assailants, it was instantly acquiesced in by his subordinate officers, and Smith had actually matured his plans before the arrival of Shields.

That brave officer, though then the senior upon the ground, and, as such, entitled to the command, not only delicately waived his right to interfere, but took upon himself the perilous duty of holding the village against the overwhelming force of the enemy posted opposite, and of cutting off the retreat of the fugitives in the event of Smith proving successful.

The plan of attack having been arranged, Captain Lee, of the Engineers, volunteered to cross the Pedregal, for the purpose of

* Letter to the New York Courier.

requesting that a powerful diversion might be made from San Augustine upon the front of the works, while Smith assaulted them in the rear.

The hour of three A. M. had been agreed upon as the time when the troops should move forward to the attack; but, though the march commenced at the hour appointed, it was near daylight before the head of Cadwalader's brigade succeeded in getting out of the village.

Riley's brigade led, followed by that of Cadwalader, while Smith's brigade brought up the rear.

The rain still fell, and it was so dark that the men were required to keep touch of each other, to prevent their going astray. The path was narrow, and the ground a stiff muddy clay full of rocks, and the difficulties of the march were greatly enhanced by the necessity of advancing by a flank which extended the command to thrice its length.* Eventually, however, the troops succeeded in attaining a point of the ravine from which it was supposed possible to reach the rear of the enemy; the advance then halted until those behind closed up. It was now about four o'clock on the morning of the 20th.

Forming in line, the wet loads were drawn; and, with Riley's brigade in two columns on the right, the march recommenced.

They were yet about a quarter of a mile from the enemy's camp. Wending their way through a thick orchard, which, together with the darkness, effectually concealed their approach, they debouched into a deep ravine which, running within five hundred yards of the work, led directly in rear and out of sight of the batteries, being screened from them by an intervening hill.†

Up to this time it was evident that Valencia was utterly ignorant of the movement which so seriously threatened his position. Prepared for, and anticipating only an attack in front, he seems to have relied upon the vigilance of the main army stationed in

---

* Smith's Official Report.　　　† Letter to the New York Courier.

front of the village of Contreras, for intercepting any demonstration which might be made upon his rear.   Flushed with the
temporary success he had gained on the preceding evening, he
distributed promotions among his officers with a lavish hand, and
impatiently awaited the renewal of the attack, in full confidence
that from so small a body of assailants, operating without either artillery or cavalry, there was nothing to fear, and everything to hope.

But he was soon to be sternly undeceived.   With celerity and
in profound silence, the gallant Riley drew up his noble brigade
just under the brow of the hill.

The entrenched camp was upon another and rather lower
eminence, in front of the one upon which our troops now were ;
from the crest of the latter a smooth slope descended directly to
the work.

The position of Smith's command was now as follows:—
Riley's brigade was under the brow of the hill facing the rear of
Valencia's camp, and awaiting the command to storm.   Cad-
walader was pressing forward to support Riley.

Major Dimmick with Smith's brigade, following in the same
direction, changed the march of his command to meet a large
body of Mexican cavalry discovered on the left flank.

Ransom, with a temporary brigade sent from San Augustine
under the guidance of Captain Lee, crossed the ravine in front
of the works, to divert the attention of the enemy from the meditated point of attack.   These arrangements were completed
about sunrise, and then Smith, walking slowly up to Riley's brigade and finding all was ready, gave the word of command—
" Men, forward !"

In an instant, with a wild fierce yell, they sprang up and dashed
over the brow of the hill—the Rifles, previously thrown forward to
the foot of the slope, protected the storming-party by throwing in
a deadly fire upon the startled enemy, and then gallantly rushed
forward to participate in the assault.

The Mexican fire overshot the stormers, and, before the pieces could be depressed, the men clambered over the earthen parapet with deafening cheers, and attacked the garrison hand to hand. A brief but terrific conflict ensued. Intermingled with the firing, the clash of swords and the crashing blows from musket and rifle stocks could be distinctly heard. Valencia himself suddenly disappeared, while his officers and men, taken by surprise—compacted together into a confused struggling mass—assaulted in their midst, in front and in rear at one and the same moment—were perfectly paralyzed, and suffered themselves to be cut to pieces with dreadful slaughter, while the survivors, unable to resist the impetuous avalanche of intrepid Americans, animated as by one heart, threw down their arms in vast numbers, and took to flight in all directions. Some fled to the mountains, others across the Pedregal, and others again, in the direction of Contreras and San Angel. Five hundred fugitives jammed up in a narrow pass, were headed by thirty men, and surrendered themselves prisoners of war.

The road was literally strewn with the dead and dying; nor did the pursuit pause until it received a check, near the village of San Angel, from the fire of the Mexican reserve.

So fierce had been the assault, that the brunt of the action lasted only seventeen minutes, and in that brief space of time the fort had been captured, and its defenders completely routed.

During the storm of the hill, the other portions of Smith's command had not been idle. Cadwalader had ably supported Riley. Smith's brigade under Major Dimmick met the large body of Mexican cavalry, and drove them at the point of the bayonet; then, turning back, rushed up the slope in front of the work, and fell upon the enemy outside, just as he was escaping from Riley's furious attack from the rear.

In the mean time, completely deceived by the masterly arrangements of Smith and Shields, the Mexican reserve remained perplexed and inactive before the village of Contreras, until the disastrous defeat of Valencia compelled it to fall back upon San Angel and Churubusco, leaving Shields at leisure to cut off the fugitives, numbers of whom, coming under the fire of the South Carolina regiment, broke away in utter despair, and took refuge among the rocks and ravines of the Pedregal.

The victory being achieved before the detachments from Worth's and Quitman's divisions arrived in sight, they were ordered back to their former positions; Worth to attack San Antonio in front with his whole force, while Pillow's and Twiggs's divisions—so lately led by Smith, but now each under its appropriate commander—moving from Contreras through San Angel and Cuyoacan, approached it in the rear.

To the skill and bravery of General Persifor F. Smith and his intrepid subordinates, is the American nation indebted for the great victory of Contreras. Its results were, seven hundred of the enemy killed; eight hundred and thirteen taken prisoners, among whom were four generals—Salas, Mendoza, Garcia, and Guadalupe—and eighty-eight inferior officers; many colours and standards, twenty-two pieces of brass ordnance, thousands of small arms and accoutrements, an immense quantity of shot, shells, powder, and cartridges, besides seven hundred pack-mules and many horses.*

Our loss was one officer killed, and one wounded, and about fifty men killed and wounded.†

Among the ordnance captured, were the two guns lost by the 4th artillery—but without dishonour—at the battle of Buena Vista. By a singular and pleasing coincidence, these were first recognised by Captain Drum, of the same regiment, and the tidings of their recovery so exhilarated the spirits of the men under his command, that they sprang rapturously forward, and, amidst deafening cheers, caressed and embraced them as objects of affection long mourned as lost, but now suddenly and unexpectedly restored.

* Scott's Official Report.   † Letter to the New York Courier.

BRIG. GEN. PERSIFER F. SMITH.

CHAPTER XXII.

VIEWED in every aspect, the victory of Contreras was productive of the most important consequences to the American army.

It was the first victory gained in the valley of Mexico.

It cut the line of the enemy's defences, and rendered no longer a matter of doubt the advance of our troops upon Churubusco; the only remaining exterior defence, and the last obstacle protecting the causeway by which the Garitas, or small forts at the gates of the city, could be easily approached.

It broke down the confidence of the Mexicans in the strength of their fortifications, by exhibiting in the most impressive manner their inability to successfully defend them, and it reinvigorated the spirit of the Americans, to whom the change of route, from the National to the Acapulco road, had been ominous of the difficulties by which they were beset, and upon whom the check received on the 19th before both San Antonio and the hill of Contreras, was calculated to conjure up the most fearful presentiments of evil, while it encouraged the enemy to increased exertions.

While the operations which led to the indecisive results of the afternoon of the 19th, were going on over the left of the Pedregal, Worth, on the right of the same field, was pushing vigorously his reconnoissances. These, as we have already related, were at length crowned with success, by the discovery of a dubious route, over which it was hoped that by a semicircular sweep, the main road to Churubusco might be gained, and the batteries of San Antonio left in the rear.

But though San Antonio might possibly be thus effectually turned by the infantry, the advance of the heavy ordnance composing the siege train was opposed by obstacles on both sides of the Pedregal, which were almost if not entirely insuperable ; San Antonio was, therefore, ordered to be forced, as, by its capture, a short and excellent road would be open to the artillery.

Accordingly, on the morning of the 20th, Worth's detachment was countermarched from the neighbourhood of Contreras, and his two divisions being again concentrated near each other, the movement upon San Antonio commenced.

In order to fully understand the operations of the American troops, on the 19th and 20th of August, it must be borne in mind, that from San Augustine, the head-quarters of General Scott, a road swept round the skirts of the Pedregal in an almost continuous circle, ending at Churubusco, on the main road to the capital. To the right of San Augustine the road led to San Antonio, and thence to Churubusco.

To the left of San Augustine the road advanced to the Pedregal, ended there in a trail, or mule-path, and again becoming wide after the Pedregal was passed, tapped at right angles the Magdalena road in front of the hill of Contreras, and from thence passing through the villages of San Angel and Cuyoacan, also terminated in the main road at Churubusco.

It will therefore be perceived, that, if the latter road could be opened by taking the works at Contreras,—the object being to reach Churubusco,—the strong position of San Antonio need not be attacked at all. Or, if San Antonio could be taken or turned, it would not have been so necessary to have carried Contreras. But when Contreras *was* taken, the General-in-chief decided to attack, by a combined movement, the works of San Antonio in front and in rear, so as to open to his advance the road on both sides of the Pedregal, and afford a good passage for his artillery. By this means he would be enabled to approach Churubusco in the rear, through the villages of San Angel and Cuyoacan, and in front by the causeway leading through San Antonio.

Churubusco thus became the final and most important point of defence; and, as a good road led from thence to the city, it was heavily and continually reinforced from that quarter, besides receiving large accessions of fugitives from Contreras, subsequently increased by the addition of fifteen hundred men from San Antonio, until within, and in the rear of the hacienda, the field-work in front, and the tête-du-pont at the crossing of the canal, the Mexican force amounted to twenty-seven thousand men, while the Americans in all parts of the field numbered only nine thousand strong.

The work at Contreras being taken, those of San Antonio and Churubusco were next to be attacked.

Accordingly, at eight o'clock, A. M., the divisions of Twiggs and Pillow, under the immediate command of the latter, marched from Contreras to Cuyoacan, followed closely by the General-in-chief in person.

At this village, one mile from Churubusco, and five from Contreras, several roads meet, one of which, stretching off to the right, leads to the rear of San Antonio, two miles distant.

At Cuyoacan, Scott arranged his plan of battle, and the disposition of his force was briefly as follows:—

Worth, already on the San Antonio road, was to storm that work in front, supported by Cadwalader's brigade (Pillow's division), which was directed to march from Cuyoacan and attack it simultaneously in the rear.

When the work was carried, the two divisions were to unite and press forward upon Churubusco, the distance of the latter from San Antonio by the causeway being but little more than two miles.

In the mean time, Twiggs was to move upon Churubusco, and attack the works nearest to Cuyoacan. These proved to be the hacienda and convent of San Pablo.

Shields, in command of his own brigade (Quitman's division) and that of Pierce (Pillow's division), was to leave Cuyoacan by a third road further to the left, cross the Churubusco river, and, upon reaching the causeway between Churubusco and the city of Mexico, was directed to attack the enemy's right and rear, divert his attention from the movement upon the hacienda, and endeavour to intercept the retreat towards the capital of the garrison from Churubusco, in the event of the attack upon that point proving successful.

Quitman, with the remainder of his division, was to remain at San Augustine to guard the hospital, and the siege, supply, and baggage trains.

The orders rapidly given to Pillow, Twiggs, and Shields, were as promptly followed up by the march of their respective commands upon the point indicated.

Twiggs moving first, with Smith's brigade in advance supported by Riley's, soon reached the vicinity of San Pablo de Churubusco.

The works at this point were of the most formidable description. " They consisted of a fortified hacienda which was surrounded by a high and thick wall on all sides," forming a large square. " Inside the wall was a stone building, the roof of which was flat and higher than the walls. Above all this was a stone church, still higher than the rest, and having a large steeple. The wall was pierced with loopholes, and so arranged that there were two tiers of men firing at the same time. They had thus four different ranges of men firing at once, and four ranks were formed on each range and placed at such a height that they could not only overlook all the surrounding country, but at the same time they had a plunging fire upon us.

"Outside the hacienda, and completely commanding the avenues of approach, was a field-work extending around two sides of the fort, and protected by a deep wet ditch, and armed with seven large pieces of cannon. It was garrisoned by about two thousand men. This hacienda is at the commencement of the causeway leading to the western gate of the city, and had to be passed before getting on the road.

"About three hundred yards in rear of this work, another field-work had been built where a cross-road meets the causeway at a point where it crosses a river, thus forming a "tête-du-pont," or bridge-head. This also was very strong, and armed with three large pieces of cannon. The works were surrounded on every side by large corn-fields which were filled with the enemy's skirmishers, so that it was difficult to make a reconnoissance. It was therefore decided to make the attack immediately, as they were full of men, and extended for nearly a mile on the road to the city, completely covering the causeway."*

Lieutenant Stevens, of the Engineers, having reported a one-gun battery across the road leading up from Cuyaocan, the 1st artillery was detached to turn it by its left. This movement being met by a vigorous fire from the work, Taylor's battery, supported by the 3d infantry, took up a position fronting the buildings about the church. The tremendous fire which immediately opened from that quarter, indicated not only the presence of a strong force of the enemy, but that the works were more considerable than had been at first reported.

What was supposed to be a one-gun battery proved afterwards

* Letter to the New York Courier.

50

to have been the right salient angle of the field-work which flanked the hacienda, and enfiladed the road to Cuyoacan, so that when the 1st artillery attempted to turn it, they found themselves in front of the work, and exposed to a terrible and plunging fire from the musketry, poured through the embrasures of the walls beyond. Gallantly standing their ground, they took such cover as they could get, and picked off the Mexican infantry at the loops whenever an opportunity offered.

Taylor's battery, though assailed by a most fearful fire of grape, canister, musketry, round-shot, and shell, which struck down two officers, twenty men, and thirteen horses, not only maintained its position, but, for upwards of two hours, was served with a destructive precision and regularity which won the admiration of all who witnessed it.*

While Twiggs was thus actively engaged before the convent and hacienda, Shields, on the extreme left, found his command confronted by the Mexican reserve, consisting of four thousand infantry and three thousand cavalry, drawn up in rear of Churubusco, and on the road towards the capital. Finding it impossible to outflank the enemy, owing to the superior character of the ground occupied by the latter, and Pierce's brigade being hard pressed in consequence, Sibley's troop of 2d dragoons and the Rifles, both under command of Major Sumner, were ordered to his support.

Shields now withdrew his men, and under cover of the Hacienda de los Portales, determined to attack the enemy upon his front.†

From this time the battle gradually deepened; the resolution of the Mexicans seemed at length to have caught something of the heroic spirit of their Spanish progenitors, and, animated by the knowledge of their superior numbers, and confident in the strength of their position, they kept up an incessant fire of artillery and

* Smith's Official Report.   † Shields's Official Report.

small arms, until the shouts of their assailants and the cries of the wounded were drowned in the thunder of the conflict.

Then it was that the indomitable courage of the American soldiers shone conspicuous. The South Carolina and New York regiments, while forming for the charge, endured with unflinching intrepidity a fire as terrible as ever man witnessed,* while further to the right, from the walls of San Pablo, tier above tier, from the roof of the hacienda, and from the steeple of the convent, the enemy's infantry poured down such rapid volleys of musketry, that for three hours, the sound of their firing was one continuous roll.†

Deadlier still was the service of the artillery from the field-work in advance. Three of the pieces were manned by deserters from our own army, commanded by the traitor Riley. Knowing that if taken the penalty of their crime was an ignominious death, and that their only safety lay in a victory over their own countrymen, these men fought with the courage of despair, picking off, with the malignity of private revenge, several of the American officers whom they recognised, and, at a subsequent period of the battle, pulling down the white flag of surrender no less than three times.‡

It was about mid-day when the battle became general. An hour earlier Worth commenced his movement upon San Antonio.

The Second Brigade, under Colonel Clarke, advanced up the causeway to within five hundred yards of the works, and then striking off to the left, across the Pedregal, by the route previously reconnoitred, turned the enemy's right, and regained the road, a short distance in rear of the village, and between it and Churubusco.

During this time the First Brigade, under Colonel Garland, remained in front of San Antonio, but masked by an angle of the causeway from the direct fire of the batteries. This position was

---

* Shields's Official Report.   † Letter to the New York Courier.   ‡ Ibid.

assumed with a view to a direct assault as soon as Clarke's fire was opened in rear.

But the enemy, already shaken by the fall of Contreras, and fearful of being intercepted in his retreat, as soon as Clarke's brigade threatened his rear, commenced precipitately evacuating his position, for the purpose of falling back upon Churubusco. This intention, however, was partially frustrated by the rapidity with which Clarke dashed forward to gain possession of the road. Finding the Mexican garrison in full retreat, two companies of the 3d infantry, under Captains Morrill and McPhail, and commanded by Lieutenant-Colonel Scott, precipitated themselves furiously upon the column and cut it nearly in the centre, the advance portion of it moving upon Churubusco, and the remainder, some two thousand strong, under General Bravo, retreating upon Dolores.

As soon as Clarke was known to be engaged, Garland's brigade moved to the assault of the works in front, but, the enemy being found to have already deserted them, it passed quickly through, and the two brigades were soon united and in hot pursuit.

Approaching Churubusco, the hacienda and convent of San Pablo were discovered in advance and to the left of the road, crowded with Mexican troops. At a distance of three hundred yards to the right, and still further in advance, was the field-work, or tête-du-pont, garnished with heavy guns and filled with troops. Between the two a continuous line of infantry, and on the left and rear the enemy was also seen in force, as far as the eye could reach.*

Twiggs had already been engaged for upwards of an hour, when Worth, previously joined on the causeway by Pillow with Cadwalader's brigade, arrived before Churubusco close on the heels of the fugitives from San Antonio.

* Worth's Official Report.

BATTLE OF CHURUBUSCO.

The whole of Worth's division, as soon as it came within musket-shot of the works, was thrown to the right of the road, with the exception of the 6th infantry.

The latter, moving to the assault in front, was exposed to a torrible fire of grape, canister, and musketry, which raked the road and momentarily checked its advance, but the 5th and 8th infantry, marching by a flank parallel to the road, drove the enemy's skirmishers, and in defiance of a tremendous fire from the tête-du-pont, dashed across the deep wet ditch surrounding the work, carried it at the point of the bayonet, and instantly turned the captured cannon upon the hacienda and convent, before which Twiggs was still hotly engaged.

Duncan's battery of light artillery, no longer exposed to the effects of the heavier metal of the tête-du-pont, now galloped up the main road, and opened upon the field work surrounding San Pablo. " Seizing the prolongation of a principal face, in a space of five minutes, by a fire of astonishing rapidity, the enemy was driven from his guns in that quarter and the infantry from their intrenchments."*

The battery was now directed upon the convent. At this time Duncan's battery, upon the San Antonio causeway; Taylor's battery, further to the left and in front of the field-work; and the captured guns of the tête-du-pont, were all turned upon San Pablo, and within half-an-hour from the storm of the tête-du-pont, the enemy's fire visibly slackened under this terrible combination. As soon as this was perceived by Smith, the 3d infantry, already advanced under cover of some huts near the right bastion, was ordered to charge; and, as soon as the brave fellows had partially cleared the ramparts by a fire of musketry, they dashed dauntlessly over, led by Captain J. M. Smith and Lieutenant Sheppard, when the garrison, throwing out several white flags, surrendered themselves prisoners of war, General Rincon, its brave com-

* Worth's Official Report.

mander, appearing at the balcony with Captain Alexander, just as a staff officer despatched by Worth to receive the surrender, arrived within the works.

After the storm of the tête-du-pont, and the surrender of San Pablo, that portion of the enemy engaged with Garland's and Clarke's brigades, to the left and rear of the former work, gave way precipitately.

Still further to the rear, Shields, operating against the reserve, having determined upon an assault in front, formed his command accordingly. Selecting the Palmetto regiment as the base of his line, the New York and 12th and 15th were deployed to the right, and the 9th to the left; the whole then gallantly advanced, under a withering discharge of small arms, opening their fire as they came up and moving steadily forward. As soon as the enemy was observed to waver, the order to charge was given, and the men rushed upon him with the bayonet, broke his ranks, and put him to the rout, just as the fugitives from Churubusco came wildly up the road, closely pursued by the head of Worth's division *

All was now confusion. The Mexican cavalry, putting spurs to their horses, fled panic-struck; while the infantry, throwing away their arms by thousands, either knelt down by the wayside, and with uplifted hands prayed for quarter, or scattered with the speed of fear in every practicable direction.

Harney's bold dragoons were now let loose upon the fugitives, and, galloping along the high road to the capital, sabring as they went, dashed into the enemy's intrenchments at the very gate of the city; but this impetuosity laid them open to a severe fire of grape from one of the batteries in that quarter, whereby Major Mills, of the 15th infantry, a volunteer in the charge, was killed. Captain Kearney, who led the squadron, lost his left arm;

* Shields's Official Report.

Captains McReynolds and Duperu were severely wounded, and several of the dragoons placed " *hors du combat.* "

Thus ended the famous 20th of August, a day upon which the American troops, in three separate and distinct actions, upon the same field, assaulted and signally defeated an enemy from three to five times their own number; captured no less than three strong positions, protected by ten batteries, prepared for sixty-one guns, and within which thirty-eight guns were taken, together with an immense quantity of small arms and ammunition, sufficient to supply a large army.

In these actions the Mexicans suffered a loss in killed and wounded of three thousand two hundred and fifty; and in prisoners two thousand six hundred and twenty-seven, among whom were eight generals, and one hundred and ninety-seven subordinate officers.

The American loss was, in killed, sixteen officers, and one hundred and twenty-three rank and file; and in wounded, sixty officers, and eight hundred and sixteen rank and file.

But, though these brilliant events occurred within a few miles of each other, the storm of Contreras and the turning of San Antonio were but subordinate parts of the main action at Churubusco. Here General Santa Anna concentrated all his forces for a final and determined resistance ; and it is but justice to the Mexicans to say, that, at this point, the severe loss on both sides affords the strongest evidence that they fought with greater intrepidity than had been exhibited in any previous engagement.

The battle was indeed most obstinate and bloody, and that a crowning triumph should at length have been obtained over a resolute enemy, numbering from twenty-seven to thirty thousand men, by a force of nine thousand Americans, exhausted by fighting, marching, and countermarching for thirty-six hours, is a significant proof of the indomitable courage, energy, and perseverance by which the latter were animated.

CHAPTER XXIII.

AFTER the victory of Churubusco, and while the American
troops were hotly pursuing the discomfited enemy, Scott proceeded to Tacubaya, and established his head-quarters in the
bishop's palace.

The next morning, while on his return to Cuyoacan, he was
met by commissioners to propose a truce, the terms of which were
promptly rejected; but, previous to this, an intimation having been
received from reliable sources, that an armistice for the purpose
of opening negotiations for peace would be eagerly accepted,
Scott despatched from Cuyoacan the following note :—

"HEAD-QUARTERS, ARMY U. S. AMERICA,
    Cuyoacan, August 21, 1847.

"To his Excellency the President and General-in-chief of the Republic of
Mexico.

"SIR : Too much blood has already been shed in this unnatural war between the two great Republics of this continent. It
is time that the differences between them should be amicably and
honourably settled, and it is known to your Excellency that a
commissioner on the part of the United States, clothed with full
powers to that end, is with this army.

386

" To enable the two republics to enter on negotiations, I am willing to sign, on reasonable terms, a short armistice.

" I shall wait with impatience until to-morrow morning for a direct answer to this communication, but shall, in the mean time, seize and occupy such positions outside of the capital as I may deem necessary to the shelter and comfort of this army.

" I have the honour to remain, with high consideration and respect, your Excellency's most obedient servant,

WINFIELD SCOTT."

This letter met with an immediate reply from the Mexican Secretary of War, in which he stated that the proposition for an armistice with the view of an honourable termination of the war, had been received with pleasure, by his Excellency the President and Commander-in-chief, and that Brigadier-Generals Villamil and Quijano, were appointed commissioners to agree upon the terms of the armistice.

The commissioners subsequently appointed on the part of the United States, were Major-General Quitman, and Brigadier-Generals Smith and Pierce. Shortly afterwards, articles of agreement were drawn up, and, after some slight modification, received the signatures of Generals Scott and Santa Anna.

The terms of the armistice were as follows:—

" The undersigned, appointed respectively, the first three by Major-General Winfield Scott, commander-in-chief of the armies of the United States, and the last two by his Excellency D. Antonio Lopez de Santa Anna, President of the Mexican Republic, and commander-in-chief of its armies, met with full powers, which were fully verified in the village of Tacubaya, on the 23d day of August, 1847, to enter into an armistice for the purpose of giving the Mexican government an opportunity of receiving propositions

51

of peace from the commissioners appointed by the President of the United States, and now with the American army, when the following articles were agreed upon :

" Art. 1. Hostilities shall instantly and absolutely cease between the armies of the United States of America and the United Mexican States, within thirty leagues of the capital of the latter States, to allow time to the commissioners appointed by the United States and the commissioners to be appointed by the Mexican Republic, to negotiate.

" 2. The armistice shall continue as long as the commissioners of the two governments may be engaged on negotiations, or until the commander of either of the said armies shall give formal notice to the other of the cessation of the armistice for forty-eight hours after such notice.

" 3. In the mean time, neither army shall, within thirty leagues of the city of Mexico, commence any new fortification or military work of offence or defence, or do anything to enlarge or strengthen any existing work or fortification of that character within the said limits.

" 4. Neither army shall be reinforced within the same. Any reinforcements in troops or munitions of war, other than subsistence now approaching either army, shall be stopped at the distance of twenty-eight leagues from the city of Mexico.

" 5. Neither army, nor any detachment from it, shall advance beyond the line it at present occupies.

" 6. Neither army, nor any detachment or individual of either, shall pass the neutral limits established by the last article, except under a flag of truce, bearing the correspondence between the two armies, or on the business authorized by the next article ; and individuals of either army, who may chance to straggle within the neutral limits, shall, by the opposite party, be kindly warned off, or sent back to their own armies under flags of truce.

" 7. The American army shall not, by violence, obstruct the

passage from the open country into the city of Mexico, of the ordinary supplies of food necessary to the consumption of its inhabitants, or the Mexican army within the city; nor shall the Mexican authorities, civil or military, do any act to obstruct the passage of supplies from the city or country, needed by the American army.

" 8. All American prisoners of war remaining in the hands of the Mexican army, and not heretofore exchanged, shall immediately, or as soon as practicable, be restored to the American army, against a like number, having regard to rank, of Mexican prisoners captured by the American army.

" 9. All American citizens who were established in the city of Mexico prior to the existing war, and who have since been expelled from that city, shall be allowed to return to their respective business or families therein, without delay or molestation.

" 10. The better to enable the belligerent armies to execute these articles, and to favour the great object of peace, it is further agreed between the parties, that any courier with despatches that either army shall desire to send along the line from the city of Mexico or its vicinity, to and from Vera Cruz, shall receive a safe conduct from the commander of the opposing army.

" 11. The administration of justice between Mexicans, according to the general and state constitutions and laws, by the local authorities of the towns and places occupied by the American forces, shall not be obstructed in any manner.

" 12. Persons and property shall be respected in the towns and places occupied by the American forces. No person shall be molested in the exercise of his profession; nor shall the services of any one be required without his consent. In all cases where services are voluntarily rendered, a just price shall be paid, and trade remain unmolested.

" 13. Those wounded prisoners who may desire to remove to

some more convenient place, for the purpose of being cured of their wounds, shall be allowed to do so without molestation, they still remaining prisoners.

" 14. The Mexican medical officers who may wish to attend the wounded shall have the privilege of doing so, if their services be required.

" 15. For the more perfect execution of this agreement, two commissioners shall be appointed, one by each party, who, in case of disagreement, shall appoint a third.

" 16. This convention shall have no force or effect, unless approved by their Excellencies, the commanders respectively of the two armies, within twenty-four hours, reckoning from the sixth hour of the 23d day of August, 1847.

> A. QUITMAN, *Maj. Gen. U. S. A.*
> PERSIFOR F. SMITH, *Brig. Gen.*
> FRANKLIN PIERCE, *Brig. Gen. U. S. A.*
> IGNACIO DE MORA Y VILLAMIL,
> BENITO QUIJANO.

" A true copy of the original.

> G. W. LAY, *U. S. A.*,
> *Military Secretary to the General-in-chief.*"

> " HEAD-QUARTERS OF THE ARMY U. S.
> Tacubaya, August 23, 1847.

" Considered, approved, and ratified, with the express *understanding* that the word " *supplies*," as used the second time, without qualification, in the seventh article of this military convention —American copy—shall be taken to mean (as in both the British and American armies) arms, munitions, clothing, equipments, subsistence (for men), forage, and in general, all the wants of an army. That word " supplies," in the Mexican copy, is erroneously translated " viveres," instead of " recursos."

> WINFIELD SCOTT,
> *General-in-chief of the U. S. A.*"

[Translation.]

" Ratified, suppressing the ninth article, and explaining the fourth, to the effect that the temporary peace of this armistice shall be observed in the capital and twenty-eight leagues around it; and agreeing that the word *supplies* shall be translated *recursos ;* and that it comprehends everything of which the army may have need, except arms and ammunition.

ANTONIO LOPEZ DE SANTA ANNA."

"HEAD-QUARTERS ARMY U. S. OF AMERICA,
Tacubaya, August 24, 1847.

" I accept and ratify the foregoing qualification, added by the President-general of the Mexican Republic.

WINFIELD SCOTT."

" A true copy of the original.

G. W. LAY, U. S. A.,
Military Secretary to the General-in-chief."

"HEAD-QUARTERS ARMY U. S. OF AMERICA,
Tacubaya, August 23, 1847.

"To his Excellency the President and General-in-chief of the Mexican Republic:

" SIR: Under a flag of truce, I send Lieutenant Semmes, of the United States navy, who will have the honour to exchange with such officer as may be appointed for the purpose, the ratification of the military convention that was signed yesterday, by commissioners from the American and Mexican armies.

" I particularly invite the attention of your Excellency to the *terms* of my ratification, and have the honour to remain, with high consideration and respect, your Excellency's most obedient servant,

WINFIELD SCOTT,
General-in-chief of the U. S. army."

[Translation.]

"NATIONAL PALACE OF MEXICO,
August 23, 1847.

" I have the note of your Excellency, of this date, in which you are pleased to say that Lieutenant Semmes, of the navy of the United States, will exchange, with another officer named for that purpose, the ratification of the military convention which was signed yesterday by commissioners of the Mexican and American armies, and calls particular attention to the terms of the ratification.

" The most excellent President orders the undersigned to say to your Excellency, as he has the honour to do, that he orders its ratification within the time agreed in the armistice ; and he is also charged to direct the attention of your Excellency to the terms of ratification by his Excellency the President.

" I have the honour to be, &c.,

LINO JOSE ALCORTA,
Minister of State, and of War and Marine.

To his Excellency, the General-in-chief of the U. S. Army."

The policy of this armistice has been doubted by many.

The disorganization of the Mexican army was so complete after the battle of Churubusco, that it is well known the Americans, by pushing forward the same evening, might have entered the capital, almost without resistance.

Whether they were in a condition to advance, after the severe fatigues of the 19th and 20th, or whether they could have maintained possession of the city with so many of the surrounding defences still held by the enemy, are questions which have acquired importance from the events that subsequently transpired, and the diversity of opinions hitherto prevailing.

To improve a victory to its fullest extent, by grasping all the advantages that victory offers, is at all times the surest way to bring an antagonist to terms ; while, to stop short at the moment of success, enables the enemy to recover from the paralysis of defeat, and but too often jeopards results which might otherwise have been considered certain.

The American army being then avowedly in the most favourable position at this time for entering, with comparatively small loss, the city of Mexico, we incline to the belief that the wisest policy would have been to have pressed on, to have taken the opportunity which the panic of the enemy presented, and allowed him no time to recover from his fears, and rally behind new defences.

The adventurous Kearney, with the small but daring squadron under his command, did actually penetrate to the very gates of the city; and, had a sufficiently strong supporting force moved rapidly upon the heels of the fugitives, the small number of defenders behind the breastworks being operated upon by the presence of a victorious array, and their confidence weakened by that vague but powerful sense of terror, which the experience of an overwhelming disaster so certainly creates, would have soon given way, and the network of obstacles, which subsequently compelled the General-in-chief to advance by a different road, being thus easily cut through, perhaps the serious losses which afterwards befell the American troops before the Molino del Rey and Chapultepec, might have been avoided altogether.

The reasons given by General Scott for offering an armistice at this juncture were,

First: The information of intelligent and disinterested men, that the Mexican Government were prepared to listen favourably to the project of a treaty of peace, amity, and lasting boundaries, of which Mr. Trist, as the agent of the Executive of the United States, was known to be the bearer.

Secondly: That it was feared if the capital was entered by force of arms and the government dispersed, a spirit of national desperation would be engendered, and the hope of accommodation indefinitely postponed.

Thirdly: A humane desire to shield the Mexicans from the crowning dishonour of beholding a victorious enemy in possession of the chief city of their republic.

The argument of others is, that the severe marches and battles of the 19th and 20th left the Americans too much shaken by losses and fatigue to advance immediately; but, as they subsequently took possession of the city with only six thousand men, after storming the formidable heights of Chapultepec, and forcing the well defended Garitas of San Cosmé and Belen, it cannot be questioned that the same result could have been at least as readily achieved at a time when the effective force of the army numbered eight thousand men, and while the causeway of San Antonio lay comparatively open to their advance, the few troops at that Garita being already terribly shaken by the victory of Churubusco.

But, as the General-in-chief admits the ease with which the capital might have been taken on the evening of the 20th, it may not be amiss to examine how far his own reasons justified either the proposal or the acceptance of an armistice, taking into consideration the commanding position he occupied, with the capital avowedly within his grasp.

There is no doubt that the American residents and intelligent neutrals who cautioned General Scott against precipitancy, sincerely believed the Mexicans at length desired peace; but, as the interior line of defences surrounding the city still afforded the latter a further means of resistance, were time allowed them to reunite their shattered forces, the sincerity of their seeming readiness to treat—taking in view their characteristic pride and obstinacy—might well have been doubted.

Every hour's delay was of eminent service to them, by reviving their drooping courage, and by infusing, with increase of numbers, new hopes of eventual success.

To the Americans the pause was pregnant with danger, not only by closing the avenues easily accessible at present, but by threatening their future safety.

A large body of the enemy was known to be in their rear, and their reinforcements were too far back to be available in the event of an emergency; while in their front it was soon to be shown how little regard was paid by the enemy to the solemnly ratified articles of the armistice, by the Mexican population being seen openly engaged in the erection of breastworks, and in still further obstructing, in various ways, the approaches to the city.

The forcible entrance into the capital, the effect of which it was supposed would jeopard the prospects of peace, was also subsequently made; and the absolute quiet that ensued was sufficient evidence that the possession of the city and the dispersion of the government, so far from rousing the people to a more clamorous outcry in favour of the further prosecution of the war, was the first event which brought home to them the reality of their condition, and seriously inclined them to listen to terms of accommodation.

But, though the armistice may have been impolitic, there is not the slightest reason to suppose that General Scott, in granting it, was actuated by any other feeling than that of the most exalted humanity. The forlorn situation of the Mexican people, proud, obstinate, and unreasoning as they had proved themselves, could not have been witnessed by him without a chivalric desire to spare them the last and bitterest scene of degradation—the sight of a victorious enemy within the very walls of a capital which the valour of their ancestors had surrounded with so many heroic associations. Nor could his frank nature have easily imagined them so lost to all sense of moral obligation, as to seek to take advantage of the humane forbearance of the conqueror, by using

52

the respite allowed them, not for the stipulated purpose of terminating existing difficulties by an honourable peace, but with the
treacherous view of improving the interval in strengthening themselves for a continuance of the war.

A sterner soldier would have pushed on, regardless of the piti-
able condition of the enemy; a humane one would have paused,
as Scott did, and, in trusting to the honour of such an enemy,
would have found himself in like manner deceived. Although,
perhaps, by a wiser policy, war with Mexico might have been
avoided, it will redound to the eternal honour of our country, that
we conducted it agreeably to the dictates of an exalted humanity;
and that we were ready at all times to terminate a contest which
was prolonged by the indomitable obstinacy of the Mexican
people.

The armistice, however, being ratified, the American troops
were quartered in different villages, within supporting distance
of each other, leaving Mr. Trist, on the part of the United States,
to open negotiations for peace with the Mexican government.

Accordingly, on the 25th of August, that gentleman wrote to
Mr. Pacheco, the Mexican Minister for Foreign Affairs, informing
him of his readiness to treat, and on the succeeding day received
answer that the Mexican commissioners, then in the act of being
appointed, would meet at the village of Atzcopozalco, on the
morning of the 27th; and, in accordance therewith, Generals Herrera, Conto, and Villamil, Don Miguel Atristain, and Don Jose
Miguel Arroyo, were accredited on the part of the Mexican government, to confer with Mr. Trist, at the place designated.

Negotiation now commenced, but from the lofty attitude
assumed by the Mexican commissioners, under the instruction of
their government, it soon became apparent that the peace which
America so earnestly sought, could only be obtained by sacrifices
incompatible with her honour.

The preliminary condition insisted upon by the Mexicans, that the treaty should be made upon the basis that they had triumphed and were yet in a situation to successfully prosecute the war, might have been accorded by the United States with a smile of contempt for the weakness that dictated an assumption so well known to be utterly at variance with the facts; but when Mexico refused to recognise the Rio Grande, which had been claimed by the United States government as the boundary of the two republics, and pertinaciously insisted upon the line of the Nueces, though professing herself willing to stipulate that the interval between the two rivers should remain uninhabited, the impression soon became general, that President Santa Anna had hailed the armistice rather as a means of delaying the advance of General Scott until he was again prepared to oppose him, than as affording an opening for the ratification of a permanent peace.

It is true that the " project of a treaty," of which Mr. Trist was the bearer from his government, was discussed by the Mexican commissioners, and it is equally true that they offered in return a counter-project; but, as Mr. Trist was clothed with no powers to treat for peace upon any other terms than those stipulated in the instrument he had been delegated to present, it could hardly have been supposed that he would assume the responsibility of altering boundaries already strictly defined by his government.

The question of boundaries involved a cession of territory by Mexico to the United States, for which the latter offered an equivalent in money.

These boundaries, as proposed by the fourth article of the project submitted by Mr. Trist, were as follows : That the boundary line of the two republics should commence at the mouth of the Rio Grande ; follow the middle of that river until it reached the southern boundary of New Mexico ; thence west with that line to the western boundary ; thence north with the river Gila, and through the mouth of that river down the middle of the Gulf of California into the Pacific.

By this article it will be seen that the United States demanded the acknowledgment of the Rio Grande as her true boundary, and required the cession by purchase of about ten degrees of thinly inhabited territory, including within its limits the department of New Mexico and Upper and Lower California. In addition to this, a free right of way for ever across the isthmus of Tehuantepec was demanded by a subsequent article.

In their counter-project the Mexican commissioners proposed to commence the boundary line of the two republics in the bay of Corpus Christi, thence to the mouth of the Nueces, thence with the middle of the latter river to its source, thence west to the eastern boundary of New Mexico, thence north with that boundary to the 37th degree of latitude, thence west to the Pacific.

In other words, they claimed the disputed territory between the Nueces and the Rio Grande, and declined ceding the greater part of New Mexico, the southern portion of Upper California, or any of Lower California.

The commissioners also declared their inability to grant a free right of way across the isthmus of Tehuantepec, on the plea that the Mexican government had, some years before, divested itself of the power to do so, by granting a privilege with reference to this object to a private contractor, by whom it had been transferred, with the authority of the Mexican government, into the hands of English subjects, of whose rights Mexico could not dispose.

In an effort to adjust these differences, and finding the Mexican commissioners resolute in adhering to the boundary of the Nueces, as the condition "*sine qua non*" of peace, Mr. Trist did eventually so far depart from the letter of his instructions, as to offer to refer the question of that boundary to his government, and to abandon the claim to Lower California altogether; but at the same time he insisted upon the cession of New Mexico, and upon this latter point neither party being willing to yield to the other, the negotiations fell through.

However sincere the Mexican commissioners may have been, personally, in their efforts to promote a peace, the instructions by which they were fettered showed that their government was far from desirous of participating in such a result. Perhaps, indeed, peace might have been obtained, had the United States been willing to yield all the points of controversy, and further agreed to surrender the line of the Rio Grande and fall back upon the Nueces; but such a retrogression, even had the Mexican proposition been referred by Mr. Trist, would never have been acceded to by his government.

But, long previous to the close of the armistice, the warlike temper of the Mexican people had made itself apparent. Independent of their almost undisguised efforts to fortify the approaches to the city, the representatives of the states of Mexico, Jalisco, and Zacatecas united in a protest in which they asserted that "the city of Mexico would not allow the necessary freedom in its discussions and deliberations, if Congress should assemble in that city."

They declared also, that any arrangement made in relation to foreign affairs, unless ratified by Congress, would be unconstitutional, and that their only motive for protesting against the negotiation then pending, was to save the republic "from the ignominy of a treaty concluded and ratified under the guns of the enemy, and on the day succeeding unlooked-for reverses."

In addition to this, a circular was sent by the Secretary of State to the states of Puebla and Mexico, exhorting the people to grasp whatever arms they could conveniently obtain, and by fire and sword, and every other practicable means, endeavour to annihilate the invaders.

Matters were now drawing to a crisis. On the 6th of September, the day before the failure of the negotiations was fully ascertained, Scott addressed a letter to the Mexican General-in-chief, complaining of repeated violations of the armistice, and threatening a resumption of hostilities, unless full satisfaction was accorded before twelve o'clock of the following day.

To this General Santa Anna replied in a letter of the same date, indignantly denying the charges specified, and accusing his antagonist of similar infractions of the truce. This closed the correspondence; on the 7th, the negotiations were publicly declared to be abortive, and both parties entered into active preparations for the renewal of the war.

During the pending of the armistice, an event occurred which produced emotions of painful regret among many of the Mexican people. This was the trial of the deserters from the American army, taken in arms against their own countrymen at the battle of Churubusco.

These men, after clandestinely quitting the colours of the United States, had enrolled themselves in the service of the enemy, by whom they had been formed into two companies, under the title of the companies of St. Patrick, commanded by the notorious Riley, a man whose undaunted courage won the admiration even of those who abhorred his treason. They had fought long and desperately in the field-work before the convent of San Pablo, and were not taken prisoners until their Mexican comrades had fled, and their own ammunition was entirely exhausted.

At a general court-martial, over which Colonel Bennett Riley presided, twenty-nine of these deserters were tried and found guilty, sixteen of whom were hung on the 10th of September, at San Angel, and four the day following, at Mixcoac.

At a subsequent general court-martial, of which Colonel Garland was president, thirty-six more were tried and convicted, thirty of whom were also executed at Mixcoac, on the 13th of September.

The remainder on both occasions, amounting to fifteen in number, owing to mitigating circumstances, had their sentences commuted to lashing and branding; among the latter was the commander, Riley, who escaped the extreme penalty of the law by having deserted previous to the formal declaration of war by the United States.

Thus ignominiously perished, by the hands of their indignant comrades, fifty convicted traitors, whose weapons at Buena Vista and at Churubusco had been wantonly turned against the colours they had sworn to defend, and the nation to which they owed allegiance. It was a terrible spectacle, and only to be justified by the enormity of the crime, which had, however, been provoked, throughout the whole war, by the allurements with which the Mexican generals basely tempted them.

CHAPTER XXIV.

Hostilities recommenced—Reconnoissances—Valley of Mexico—Defences around the City—Description of Chapultepec—Molino del Rey—Casa de Mata—Strength of the Mexican Lines—Storm of Molino del Rey—Capture of the Mexican Battery—Repulse of the Victors—The Battery retaken—Storm of Casa de Mata—Terrible Fire of the Mexicans—McIntosh's Brigade repulsed—Duncan's Battery—Surrender of Casa de Mata—Mexican Loss—American Loss.

DURING the period of the truce, the head-quarters of General Scott were established at Tacubaya, a delightful village about two and a half miles distant from the city of Mexico, and within point-blank range of the guns of Chapultepec. There Worth's division and Harney's cavalry brigade were also quartered. The remainder of the army occupied the surrounding villages; Pillow's division head-quarters being at Mixcoac, that of Twiggs at San Angel, and Quitman's at San Augustine.

On the 7th of September, hostilities were recommenced on the part of the United States, by a reconnoissance of the enemy's interior line of defences immediately around the capital. These defences will be best elucidated by a brief description of the topography of the valley.

The view of the valley of Mexico, as displayed from the eminence on which the Archbishop's Palace at Tacubaya is situated, exhibits the city of Mexico as built on a slight elevation, in the centre of a level plain, hemmed in for two hundred miles around by lofty mountains.

The immense expanse of this lovely valley, which the transparency of the atmosphere renders distinctly visible, is chequered

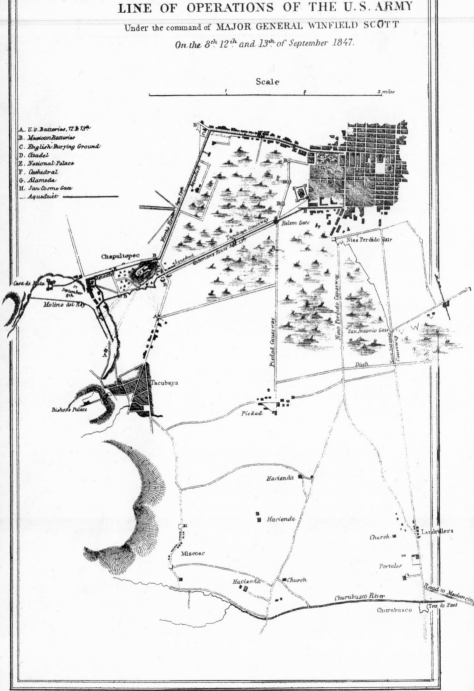

BATTLES OF MEXICO,
LINE OF OPERATIONS OF THE U.S. ARMY
Under the command of MAJOR GENERAL WINFIELD SCOTT
On the 8th 12th and 13th of September 1847.

Scale

3 miles

A. U.S. Batteries, 12 & 13th
B. Mexican Batteries
C. English Burying Ground
D. Citadel
E. National Palace
F. Cathedral
G. Alameda
H. San Cosme Gate
___ Aqueduct ___

Chapultepec

Casa de Mata

Molino del Rey

Tacubaya

Bishops Palace

Belem Gate

Niño Perdido Gate

San Antonio Gate

Ditch

Piedad

Hacienda

Hacienda

Church

Ladrillera

Portales

Mixcoac

Hacienda

Church

Churubusco River

Road to Mexicaltzingo

Churubusco

Tête de Pont

in the vicinity of the city by numerous lakes, the borders of which are beautified by the residences of wealthy Mexicans, gleaming whitely from the midst of groves and gardens, while, interspersed throughout its whole extent to the base of the furthest mountains, are seen wide stretches of cultivated land, diversified by noble orchards and evergreen forests, and intersected by the silver threads of many fair rivers. The imposing haciendas of large landed proprietors, and villages and hamlets innumerable, are scattered all about, some boldly relieved by back-grounds of luxuriant foliage, and others partly hidden by intervening trees, or the swells and undulations of the plain. The central attraction of this beautiful valley, the city of Mexico, is approached from the plain on various sides by five great or main roads, terminating in eight causeways, elevated some six feet above the marshes and soft grounds by which the city is partially surrounded. These marshes render any approach to the city impracticable, except by the causeways, each of which " presents a double roadway on the sides of an aqueduct of strong masonry and great height, resting on open arches and massive pillars, and flanked by ditches of unusual dimensions."* At the end of these causeways, Garitas are built over arches, through the gates of which all persons are compelled to pass before they can enter the city ; and at this time the gates were defended by a system of strong works, and the passage of the causeways protected by numerous batteries and breastworks for infantry.

But the causeways of Belen and San Cosmé — the routes by which General Scott proposed to advance—had other and more formidable defences still. These were the works of Molino del Rey, Casa de Mata, and the castle of Chapultepec.

•Chapultepec, or " the hill of the grasshopper," is famous in tradition as the favourite resort of the unfortunate Montezuma, and the princes of the old Aztec empire, whose wealth and semi-

<hr>

Scott's Official Reports, Nos. 33 and 34.

barbaric taste are strikingly attested by the gardens and cypress groves, and the ruins of tanks and grottos which yet remain scattered around.

This natural isolated mound, composed of porphyritic rock, is of considerable height, and commands from its summit an extensive prospect of the beautiful valley below and of the mountains encircling it. The western side, its most accessible point, is clothed for some distance upwards with a stately grove of cypress; beyond this the face of the hill presents a series of abrupt ascents over rocks and chasms. The summit is crowned with an imposing and strongly fortified structure, originally erected by the Viceroy Galvez as a palace. It was subsequently converted under the republic into a military college, and, at the period of the resumption of hostilities, was garrisoned in part by the cadets of that institution.

At the western foot of the hill, adjoining the grove, is a group of stone buildings, known as El Molino del Rey, or the King's Mill; and, as the only practicable approach to the fortress above was on this side, El Molino del Rey was heavily garrisoned to defend it, and in return was itself protected by Chapultepec, being directly under the guns of the latter.

About five hundred yards still further to the west, and at the foot of the ridge that slopes gradually from the heights above Tacubaya to the plain below, is an old Spanish work, called Casa de Mata, consisting of a strong stone citadel, recently repaired and enlarged, and surrounded with bastioned intrenchments, and impassable ditches. El Molino del Rey was supposed to be used by the enemy for the founding of cannon, and the Casa de Mata as a magazine.

As Molino del Rey defended the only access to the fortress of Chapultepec, and as the latter commanded the approaches to the city from Tacubaya, it was necessary to take Molino del Rey, before Chapultepec could be effectually assaulted, and afterwards

Chapultepec, before the south-western avenues either of Belen or San Cosmé could be traversed with any possible hope of success.

Another reason for the reduction of Molino del Rey, was the impression entertained that certain church-bells had been sent out from the city for the purpose of being cast into cannon; and this impression was the more probable, inasmuch as the immense number of guns already captured from the enemy had not left him with sufficient remaining to arm, all at the same time, the strong works at each of the eight Garitas.* The destruction of the powder in the magazine of Casa de Mata was also considered of primary importance.

Accordingly, on the 7th of September, after a personal reconnoissance of Molino del Rey and Casa de Mata by Generals Scott and Worth, the latter was ordered to attack the following morning those lines and defences with his division reinforced by Cadwalader's brigade of Pillow's division, three squadrons of dragoons under Major Sumner, and some heavy guns of the siege-train under Captain Huger of the ordnance and Captain Drum of the 4th artillery. Worth's division, and the reinforcements detailed for this perilous service, amounted in all to only three thousand one hundred men.

The instructions given by the General-in-chief to Worth, limited his operations to carrying Casa de Mata and Molino del Rey, capturing the enemy's artillery, and after destroying the machinery and *materiel* supposed to be in the foundry, he was to immediately withdraw his command to its former position in the village of Tacubaya,† until certain contemplated reconnoissances upon the southern gates should enable the former to decide upon the most favourable point for his future operations.

Fully sensible of the importance of maintaining these posts, the Mexican general occupied the lines with his troops in great force.

* Scott's Official Despatch, No. 33.

† Worth's Official Report, September 10th, 1847.

A daring reconnoissance, made on the morning of the 7th, by Captain Mason, of the Engineers, subsequently verified by the enemy's own statement, determined the Mexican left as resting upon and occupying the group of stone buildings called Molino del Rey. This wing, commanded by General Leon, was composed of National Guards, and consisted of the battalion of Mina, those of Union and La Patria or Oaxaca, with a few companies from Puebla and Queretaro.

The right wing, the brigade of Perez, rested on Casa de Mata, and was composed of regulars, fifteen hundred strong.

Midway between these was a field-battery, supported on each side by lines of infantry, amounting to ten thousand men. These were under the immediate command of General Santa Anna.

A second reconnoissance was made by Captain Mason and Colonel Duncan on the afternoon of the same day, and the results of both alike indicated the centre as the weak point of the enemy, and that his left flank on Molino del Rey was stronger than his right.[*]

As the orders of General Scott had reference only to the defences at the foot of Chapultepec, the storm of the latter remaining yet to be determined on, Worth found it necessary, in disposing his forces for the attack, to isolate the works below from the fortress above.

Accordingly, Garland's brigade, with two pieces of Drum's battery, was ordered to take position on the enemy's left, for the purpose of watching Molino del Rey and any supporting force that might be sent down from Chapultepec. This position was also to be within sustaining distance of the assaulting column, and of Huger's battery of 24-pounders, the latter being placed on the ridge sloping from Tacubaya, some five or six hundred yards from El Molino.

An assaulting column of five hundred men, under Brevet Major

* Worth's Report.

STORMING OF MOLINO DEL REY.

Wright, was posted on the same ridge, to the left of Huger's battery, for the purpose of forcing the enemy's centre.

Clarke's brigade, commanded by Colonel McIntosh, and strengthened by Duncan's battery, was stationed still further up the ridge, opposite the enemy's right—Casa de Mata—with instructions to look to the left flank, sustain the storming party if necessary, or to attack the enemy, as circumstances might dictate.

Cadwalader's brigade was held in reserve in a position yet further up the ridge, between Huger's battery and Clarke's brigade, and within easy support of either.

Sumner's cavalry enveloped the extreme left, with orders to act in any manner that commander might think best.[*]

Accordingly, under cover of the darkness, at three o'clock on the morning of the 8th the troops were put in motion, and at early dawn were found as accurately posted as if for review.

The battle commenced by Huger's guns opening upon Molino del Rey, which was actively continued until that part of the enemy's line was sensibly shaken, when the storming column, guided by Captain Mason and Lieutenant Foster of the Engineers, dashed forward to the assault. Undismayed by a tremendous fire of artillery and small-arms, they rushed upon the artillerymen and infantry, drove them at the point of the bayonet, took the battery, and turned the captured guns upon the retreating masses.

But this success was only temporary. On discovering the smallness of the force by which his position had been stormed, the enemy rallied and made a desperate effort to regain it. Assisted by the infantry which covered the house-tops and had a plunging fire upon the battery, his whole line poured a terrific fire of musketry upon the stormers, which struck down eleven out of the fourteen officers composing the command, among whom Major Wright, Captain Mason, and Lieutenant Foster fell severely wounded. Staggered by this unexpected revulsion, the stormers

* Worth's Report.

were falling back, when the light battalion under Captain E. Kirby Smith moved rapidly up to their support, and, precipitating themselves upon the enemy, shattered his advancing ranks, and recaptured the position, and held it.

In the mean while, Garland's brigade, supported by Drum's artillery, bore down upon Molino del Rey, and although every inch of the ground was obstinately disputed by the enemy, succeeded in driving him from that strong hold, when Drum's section and Huger's battery immediately advanced, and adding the guns captured from the enemy to their own pieces, poured a destructive fire upon his retreating masses until they were beyond reach.

During the time these intrepid and successful assaults were being made on the left and centre, Duncan's battery opened upon Casa de Mata and continued its fire with terrible activity, until Molino del Rey and the enemy's centre were pierced and taken; when, being masked by McIntosh's brigade as it moved to the assault, and observing a large force of cavalry and infantry rapidly moving to the support of Casa de Mata, it dashed forward promptly to meet them, in concert with Andrews' voltigeurs of Cadwalader's brigade, and opening fire upon the cavalry as they came up, shattered their ranks and drove them back in confusion; Sumner's dragoons now dashed gallantly up and completed the discomfiture, while the battery returned to its former position.

During the progress of this brilliant affair, McIntosh's brigade, animated by the successes of their comrades, moved intrepidly to the attack of Casa de Mata; and now, for the first time, its great strength, which had hitherto been skilfully concealed, became fearfully apparent. The reconnoitring parties had mistaken for an ordinary field-work what proved to be a regular fortification, garrisoned by the choicest troops in the Mexican service.

Notwithstanding this ominous developement, the brigade resolutely pressed forward.

The enemy waited quietly until it approached within one hundred yards of his first position, when he poured in a terrible fire of musketry; but finding the Americans, though much cut up, still undauntedly advancing, he retreated to his second position behind the walls of Casa de Mata and the breastworks in front. From this shelter, he continued to pour volley after volley upon the devoted column of assailants, who, staggering on under a murderous fire, at length reached the slope of the parapet.

Their heroic bravery could carry them no further. Colonel McIntosh and Major White had already fallen severely wounded, and Lieutenant-Colonel Martin Scott was killed in the act of urging his men across the ditch which separated them from the enemy. With their muskets foul and unserviceable, their ammunition nearly expended, and with one-third of the noble brigade, including one-half of the officers, killed and wounded, they fell slowly and reluctantly back in rear of Duncan's battery. These guns, no longer masked by the movements of the brigade, now opened a retributive fire upon Casa de Mata; and so terrible was the effect of the rapidity and precision with which the pieces were served, that the enemy, unable to endure the avenging storm, precipitately abandoned the post he had hitherto so obstinately defended, and sought securer refuge under the guns of Chapultepec.

Thus, in the terse language of General Worth, was "fought and won" the battle of Molino del Rey, in which his command of three thousand one hundred men, after two hours' severe fighting, carried the strong works at the foot of Chapultepec; routed fourteen thousand of the enemy, led by General Santa Anna in person; killed and wounded twenty-two hundred, among the former of whom were Generals Valdarez and Leon, the second and third in command; took over eight hundred prisoners, including fifty-two commissioned officers; and captured a battery of four pieces, together with a large quantity of ammunition and small-arms.

In this terrible contest, the American loss was seven hundred and eighty-seven killed and wounded, fifty-eight of whom were officers.

The enemy being dispersed at all points, in obedience to the instructions of the General-in-chief, Casa de Mata was blown up, and the cannon-moulds and useless ammunition destroyed; after which Worth returned with his command to Tacubaya, to await the result of future reconnoissances.

CHAPTER XXV.

THE dearly-bought victory of Molino del Rey was promptly followed up by the reconnoissances already projected, with the view of ascertaining the most practicable route by which the city could be approached.

The result of a close and daring scrutiny, principally towards the gates of the Piedad, Niño Perdido, San Antonio, and Paseo de la Viga, showed that a navigable canal, both wide and deep, and very difficult to bridge in the presence of an enemy, stretched along the southern front of the city, while the causeways, running for the most part through wet meadows and boggy grounds, were not only flanked by broad ditches filled with water, but were cut up in numerous places, to impede the progress of the troops, who would be exposed at the same time to severe cross fires from the Garitas, and from batteries and infantry breastworks, thrown up at every available point.

The impracticability of these approaches being determined, Scott concluded to storm Chapultepec, and force an entrance into the city by the causeways either of San Cosmé or Tacubaya.

The prospects of success even here were scarcely less problematical; for, notwithstanding the destruction of Molino del Rey and Casa de Mata, the hill of Chapultepec still presented an array of obstacles of the most formidable description.

The base of the hill was girdled by a stone wall some four feet thick, and about twenty feet in height. Inside of this lay a considerable body of troops, protected by breastworks and the immense trunks of ancient cypresses.

The lower slope of the hill was mined in all directions, with the trains laid ready to be fired at any moment. Beyond the mines, and about midway of the ascent, was a strong redoubt, clasping the entire front. This also was filled with troops. Above this redoubt was an inner wall, enclosing the crest of the hill, with a wide and deep ditch and counterscarp. Inside this wall was the main citadel or fortress of Chapultepec, filled with troops, with eleven pieces of cannon, some of them of the largest calibre, and these commanded the approaches on all sides—the causeways leading to the city, and even the city itself.

In order to economize the lives of his troops, by deceiving the enemy as to the real point of attack, Scott arranged a movement upon a different point than that which he intended as the true one. Following out the orders of the General-in-chief, Quitman's division marched by daybreak on the 10th, to join the division of Pillow before the southern gates, and after this open exhibition of strength in that quarter, the two divisions proceeded by night secretly to Tacubaya, to operate upon Chapultepec, leaving only Twiggs, with Riley's brigade and Steptoe's and Taylor's batteries, in front of the southern gates, to maintain the deception by a series of menacing manœuvres and by false attacks.

This admirably executed stratagem was completely successful. Fully convinced that an attack was contemplated upon the southern gates, the enemy heavily reinforced his troops in that direction, and increased the strength of his defences by additional breastworks and batteries; nor was he undeceived until the evening of the 13th, when it was too late to repair his error.

As soon as the divisions of Pillow and Quitman reached Tacubaya on the night of the 11th, they were ordered into position before Chapultepec. In the course of the same night four batteries were established within easy range of that point; and, as it was the intention of the General-in-chief to delay the assault until the fortifications were well crippled by his artillery, Pillow and Quitman were ordered to remain passive until that object was effected.

On the morning of the 12th the batteries opened their fire upon Chapultepec and its outworks, under the direction of Captain Huger, and the bombardment and cannonade were continued with marked effect during the whole of that day, and down through the evening, until it became too dark to distinguish objects.

During this time, Twiggs, on the San Angel road, was holding a considerable part of the Mexican army in check, and his batteries were heard again in full activity, when Huger's guns reopened upon Chapultepec on the morning of the 13th.

The period for closer and more determined action having at length arrived, the plan of attack, which was in two columns, commanded by Generals Quitman and Pillow, was ordered to be simultaneously commenced on the west and south-east sides of the works.

An assaulting party of two hundred and fifty picked men, commanded by Captain McKenzie of the 2d artillery, was furnished by Worth's division to precede the column under Pillow, and a similar one, led by Captain Casey of the 2d infantry, was supplied by the division of Twiggs, to aid the column of Quitman. The remainder of Worth's division was held in reserve near Molino del Rey, with orders to support Pillow's attack, while that of Quitman was sustained in like manner by Smith's brigade, which had moved up for the purpose that morning from the village of Piedad.

At eight o'clock on the morning of the 13th, the momentary cessation of the heavy batteries gave the preconcerted signal for the assaulting columns to advance. Pillow, who had occupied the buildings of Molino del Rey ever since the night of the 11th, promptly threw out his skirmishers to clear a sand-bag breast-work protecting a breach in the wall, through which it was necessary to pass. The enemy being driven from this position, McKenzie's storming party advanced, supported by four compa-nies of voltigeurs under Colonel Andrews, and preceded by four other companies of the same under Colonel Johnstone. These eight companies, acting as skirmishers, soon took the lead and kept it; for the assaulting column of McKenzie, being encumbered with the scaling-ladders, were compelled to move less rapidly.

Protected by the cypresses, the enemy fell back slowly, dis-puting the ground inch by inch. Pillow being wounded at the base of the hill, the command of the column fell upon Brigadier-General Cadwalader, and that gallant officer proved himself fully equal to the occasion.

Terrible indeed was the struggle of these brave men, through the cypress forest, where every tree hid an enemy; amidst the sheeted fire and thunder of the guns of Chapultepec, and an in-cessant storm of musketry from behind trees and rocks and breast-works; and over mines, the trains of which were laid ready for ignition, shooting down the soldier appointed to fire them, as he stood at his post with the match lighted in his hand, ready to hurl them to destruction.

Thus it was the intrepid skirmishers pressed forward, followed by the stormers and the remainder of the assaulting column, and by Clarke's brigade of Worth's division, which had hastened up at a critical moment to their support.

From behind the redoubt, midway of the ascent, the enemy

again made a desperate stand, and at this point, by a most fearful fire of musketry, checked the impetuous advance of the voltigeurs. Then, for the first time during that eventful day, hope animated the Mexican heart. But that hope was illusive. A single act of gallantry converted the momentary indecision of the assailants into an irresistible enthusiasm.

At this awful crisis, when to pause was to risk annihilation, for the ground was mined beneath them, Captain Chase, of the 15th infantry, dashed towards the right flank of the work, and bade his company follow—supported instantly by Lieutenant Beach of the same regiment with his company and by the voltigeurs and the 9th regiment of infantry, the work was stormed at all points, and the enemy, unable to withstand an onset so terrible and so determined, fell back to within the enclosure surrounding the fortress, with the daring stormers pressing rapidly upon his rear. Reaching the crest of the counterscarp and enveloping it, these three regiments, joined soon after by Clarke's brigade, and portions of Quitman's command, awaited under a severe fire of artillery and small-arms the arrival of McKenzie's party with the scaling-ladders. These soon came up, and another brilliant display of courage ensued. The ladders were quickly planted, and many of those who first scaled the wall fell back either killed or wounded. Nothing daunted, however, others promptly took their places, and as these fell, the ladders were thronged by spirits equally daring. Of McKenzie's storming party, Lieutenants Rogers of the 4th and Smith of the 5th infantry were killed while gallantly leading their men,—and Lieutenant Selden of the 8th infantry, one of the first to mount the scaling-ladder, fell back severely wounded. But in spite of this resistance by the enemy, a foothold was at length obtained, and the stormers, swarming up the ladders and over the wall, rushed into the fortress and carried it. Captain Barnard, though twice wounded in the act, seized the colours of his regiment and unfurled the first American flag upon the captured work, while Major Seymour, of the 9th infantry, entered the fortress sword in hand, and himself struck down the Mexican flag.*

In the mean time, Quitman, marching by the Tacubaya road, approached the works on the south-east, over a causeway obstructed by intersecting ditches and batteries, and further defended by an army strongly posted outside and to the east of the works.

Moving in reserve on the right flank of the assaulting column, Smith's brigade took a sweep across the meadows, turned the two batteries at the foot of Chapultepec, and presented a front against the enemy outside.

While the column, thus ably supported, was pressing boldly on towards the batteries, ready for a dash at them as soon as opportunity offered, the South Carolina and New York regiments, under Brigadier-General Shields, and the 2d Pennsylvania regiment, under Lieutenant-Colonel Geary, by an oblique movement to the left, crossed the low grounds at the foot of Chapultepec, and in the face of a terrible fire of artillery and musketry, effected a lodgment at the wall. Major Gladden, with his regiment, immediately penetrated the enclosure, through a breach made by the artillery; and the Pennsylvania and New York regiments as quickly effected a like entrance by climbing over a deserted battery further to the south.

As soon as this was achieved, the storming parties precipitated themselves upon the batteries and breastworks protecting the causeway; and, after a desperate conflict, in which Major Twiggs was killed and Captain Casey severely wounded at the head of their respective commands, captured the works and completely routed the enemy. This gallant attack was nobly seconded by Smith, whose daring Rifles were as usual among the foremost. The batteries being taken, and within them seven pieces of cannon and a large number of prisoners, the stormers, now united with

* Pillow's Report.

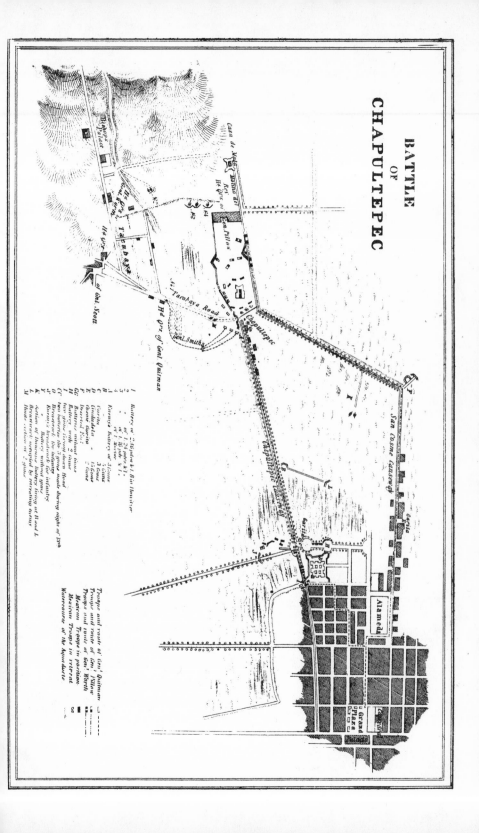

BATTLE
OF
CHAPULTEPEC

Smith's brigade, pursued the fugitives to the causeway leading to the Garita Belen, and then, turning to the left, clambered up the steep ascent of Chapultepec, with the view of assisting in the assault of the fortress; but the immense crowds of the enemy, whom they soon met flying down the hill in all directions, showed that Pillow had already anticipated them.

Part of Quitman's command, however, shared in the honour of its capture. Following rapidly upon the heels of Pillow's column, the New York, Pennsylvania, and South Carolina regiments struggled up the rugged acclivity, driving the enemy before them, and two active companies, one from the New York regiment, and one of marines, led by Lieutenant Reid, succeeded in reaching the crest of the hill in time to take part in the final assault. The daring gallantry which was then displayed in scaling the walls surrounding the fortress has been already related; but even when that gallant feat was successfully accomplished, the fortress itself still frowned defiance on its assailants.

Animated by the presence of the veteran General Bravo, the National Guards and the cadets of the institution contested the possession of this, their last stronghold, with the most heroic resolution; but their efforts to retrieve the fortunes of the day could avail but little when directed against men who had fought, a forlorn hope, from the steeps of Cerro Gordo to the walls of Mexico. The struggle, though fierce and sanguinary, was brief. The fortress was carried, its artillery captured, and a large number of its defenders, including fifty general officers, made prisoners of war.

But another and still more imposing event was now about to take place. The city of Mexico, whose almost unparalleled system of defences had so long baffled the advance of the Americans, at length lay open to attack. The garitas and the works protecting the causeways were the only remaining obstacles. These were now to be overcome.

Worth, who, during the storming of Chapultepec, had passed around the base of the hill, and with Garland's brigade, Smith's light battalion, and Duncan's battery, had defeated the right wing of the enemy, was already moving in the direction of the San Cosmé Garita, while Quitman, equally energetic, had concentrated his command and was fighting his way over the causeway leading to the Garita Belen.

Leaving only the 15th regiment of Pillow's division to garrison Chapultepec, Scott despatched the brigades of Clarke and Cadwalader to support Worth's attack, and subsequently ordered up Riley's brigade from before the southern gates for the same purpose. The latter, however, did not arrive until after the Garita of San Cosmé had been carried and the action was over for the day.

The column of Quitman, consisting of his own division and the noble brigade of Smith, received no additional assistance, with the exception of Steptoe's battery, and two regiments of Pierce's brigade.

The advance upon the Garita Belen being intended by the General-in-chief merely as a manœuvre to favour the main attack by Worth, Quitman was ordered only to threaten the works in that quarter; but, being nobly seconded by his gallant subordinates, he determined to advance, notwithstanding the severe direct and enfilading fires from the enemy's batteries, which threatened to gall and impede his progress. Smith's brave Rifles led the way; and a brilliant little episode, which occurred shortly afterwards, considerably facilitated Quitman's future movements.

While struggling with masses of the enemy, and suffering dreadfully under the severe cross-fires from batteries in the low grounds to his left, a daring and chivalric exploit achieved by a section of Duncan's battery, covered by the light battalion of Lieutenant-Colonel Smith, both attached to Worth's command, materially assisted in clearing his front.

Worth, while operating on the San Cosmé road, observing a cross route over the meadows to the right and in the direction of the works which were annoying Quitman's advance, promptly threw out a section of Duncan's battery to within four hundred yards of the enemy's line, which opened a destructive fire, first upon the battery, and then upon the troops obstructing the causeway. This unexpected support enabling Quitman to advance with greater freedom, the artillery with its covering force then fell back to the San Cosmé road, and rejoined the column of Worth.

Clarke's brigade coming up at this time from the support of Pillow's attack upon Chapultepec, Worth dashed forward, in the face of a terrible fire from two batteries, and carried them both. He had now reached the Campo Santo, or English burying-ground, a little in advance of which, the causeway and aqueduct incline to the right. At this point the General-in-chief came up, and ordered the garita carried, and that the column should endeavour to penetrate the city as far as the Alameda, a spacious green park, some fifteen hundred yards within the gate.

Accordingly, after leaving Cadwalader's brigade, which had just reached him in position at Campo Santo, with instructions to look to the left and rear, Worth advanced in a direct line upon another battery, distant about two hundred and fifty yards from the San Cosmé Garita, and protected by it. The firing now became terrible in the extreme. The causeway was literally raked by grape, canister, and shells, from the battery, while from the tops of the neighbouring houses, from churches, and from every point of vantage, the enemy poured down an incessant storm of musketry. To equalize the position of the combatants, and check this fearful fire, another mode of operations became necessary. Garland's brigade was accordingly thrown to the right, under cover of the arches of the aqueduct, with orders to dislodge the enemy from the buildings in his front, and turn the left of the garita; while Clarke's brigade, breaking open the building to

55

the left of the causeway, were to work their way with bars and picks from house to house, and carry the right of the garita.*

Favoured by the fire of two mountain howitzers, which had been placed upon conspicuous buildings, these orders were slowly, but, in the end, successfully accomplished. At five o'clock in the afternoon, both columns had gained the required positions.

The enemy soon after abandoned the battery, and fell back upon the garita. A most dangerous service was now required to be executed. This was the advance of a piece of artillery to the evacuated battery in the face of the direct fire from the garita. This duty fell upon Lieutenant Hunt, and was performed with a gallantry that extorted the admiration of all who witnessed it.

Followed by nine men, he traversed with his piece a distance of one hundred and fifty yards, and, though moving at full speed, he lost in killed and wounded five of his command. With the remaining four he met the enemy at the breastwork, muzzle to muzzle, conquered his position, and successfully opened a fire upon the garita and the intermediate force of infantry.

During this time the brigades of Garland and Clarke, preceded by a company of sappers and miners, under Lieutenant G. W. Smith, and the storming party of Captain McKenzie, had succeeded in approaching undiscovered to within easy range of the works at the garita, when, the signal being given for attack, they sprang up suddenly to the tops of the houses on each side of the causeway, and poured a destructive fire upon the astonished enemy. One terrible volley sufficed. The gunners were killed at their pieces; and, before the supporting force could recover from their consternation, the two brigades charged the garita with a wild hurrah! and carried it. The next instant the shouts of the victors announced their entrance into the city of Mexico.

On the Tacubaya causeway, the column of Quitman had been equally successful.

* Worth's Report.

STORMING OF CHAPULTEPEC.

Preceded by an eight-inch howitzer under the direction of Captain Drum, the Mounted Rifles, supported by the South Carolina regiment, and followed by the remainder of Smith's brigade, advanced under shelter of the arches of the aqueduct towards a strong battery thrown across the causeway, nearly midway between Chapultepec and the Garita Belen.

Sustained by flanking batteries, and a large force of the enemy stationed on a cross-road to the left, the defence at this point was of the most obstinate character. The interposition of a section of Duncan's battery from the San Cosmé road, and the effective fire of Drum's howitzer, having at length partially cleared the way, the Rifles dashed forward with a yell, and, by an exhibition of the most daring courage, carried the work by assault. The command was now halted and reorganized for an attack upon the garita.

The Rifle and South Carolina regiments were still thrown in advance, but intermingled—three rifles and three bayonets being placed under each arch. These regiments were closely sustained by the residue of their respective brigades, under Smith and Shields.

Winding round the pillars of the aqueduct, and creeping from arch to arch, the whole column worked its way onward, though assailed incessantly by a tremendous direct fire from the garita, and by cross-fires from the Paseo and from the Piedad road. These terrible fires, though they cut up the column to a fearful extent, did not check for a single instant its determined advance. The flank fires sweeping through the arches being at length silenced by Drum's howitzer and a sixteen-pounder which had been brought up by Lieutenant Benjamin, the Rifles and the South Carolinians succeeded about noon in getting close to the garita. Immediately after this was accomplished, they sprang from the sheltering arches, and, with their accustomed yell, charged the garita—drove the enemy, and at twenty minutes past one, P. M., nearly the whole column had passed the gate and was within the limits of the city.

But the victory was not yet complete. The Ciudadela, or Citadel, a work of immense strength, mounting fifteen pieces of cannon, now opened upon the column at only three hundred yards distance. The slaughter was terrible, and, to add to the peril of their position, the ammunition of the heavy pieces worked by Captain Drum and Lieutenant Benjamin was soon entirely expended, without the possibility of obtaining another supply under the heavy fire that raked the causeway.

The loss at the guns was also most disastrous. The brave South Carolina regiment had twice supplied additional men to work the pieces, when Quitman was called upon to mourn the loss of two of his bravest and most efficient subordinates. Captain Drum, one of the ablest artillery officers in the service, fell mortally wounded by the side of his gun; and within a few minutes afterwards Lieutenant Benjamin shared the same fate. The command of the battery then devolved upon Lieutenant Porter. No sooner did the enemy find the battery silenced for want of ammunition, than he made the most desperate efforts to force back the column, and recover his position. Under cover of a terrific fire of artillery and small-arms, from the Citadel, from the Paseo, and from the buildings in front and upon the right, he made several sallies on both flanks of the column, but was each time repulsed with loss.

Finding it impossible to bring forward a supply of ammunition during daylight, Quitman determined to shelter his command and hold his position until the darkness should afford a more favourable opportunity for crossing the causeway.

During the night, the firing of the enemy having ceased, two batteries for heavy guns and a breastwork for infantry were erected within the garita, under the superintendence of Lieutenant Beauregard, the requisite supply of ammunition obtained, and the guns mounted ready to open at daylight.

When the morning of the 14th of September dawned, and while the undaunted column was preparing to recommence the attack, the defenders of the Citadel, finding all further resistance useless, despatched to General Quitman a white flag of surrender.

Before this, however, as early as four o'clock on the same morning, General Scott had been waited upon by a deputation of the city council, who, after reporting the evacuation of the capital by the Mexican government and army, demanded terms of capitulation in favour of the church, the citizens, and the municipal authorities. To this Scott replied, that, as the city had been virtually in his possession ever since the forcing of the garitas, he intended not to accept but to impose such terms as were consistent with the honour of the army, the dignity of the United States, and the spirit of the age.*

Upon this the Ayuntamiento retired, and orders were shortly afterwards given to Worth and Quitman to advance cautiously and take up commanding positions within the city.

Acting under these instructions, Worth promptly moved forward his command, and at six o'clock, A. M., occupied two sides of the Alameda, while Quitman, after leaving Smith's brigade and the South Carolina regiment to garrison the Citadel, marched with the remainder of his column through the principal streets, and took possession of the Grand Plaza, where the colours of the United States were for the first time flung abroad from the National Palace.

Soon after were seen the waving plumes and commanding person of the General-in-chief, as he rode into the Plaza, escorted by the 2d dragoons; and a deafening hurrah greeted the gallant hero, who, amid so many difficulties and disappointments, and with means totally inadequate, had, by prudent arrangements, and that military skill in which he is unsurpassed by any commander

* Scott's Official Despatch.

of modern times, triumphed over every difficulty, and established his head-quarters in the very palace of the enemy's capital.

But the daring victors were not yet to enjoy that repose which their protracted and arduous services so imperiously demanded. While in the act of occupying the city, a fire was opened upon them from the roofs of houses, from the windows and loops, and from the corners of streets. This insurrection of the *leperos* and liberated convicts, instigated by many Mexican soldiers in the dress of citizens, occasioned a desultory contest of twenty-four hours' duration, when it was effectually put down, and on the morning of the 16th of September, 1847, the army of the United States of North America, after a series of victories untarnished by a single defeat, was in complete and unmolested possession of the Capital of the Republic of Mexico, from the National Palace of which, General Scott addressed the following despatch to the Secretary of War:—

> "HEAD-QUARTERS OF THE ARMY,
> National Palace of Mexico, Sept. 18, 1847.

" SIR :—At the end of another series of arduous and brilliant operations of more than forty-eight hours' continuance, this glorious army hoisted, on the morning of the 14th, the colours of the United States on the walls of this palace.

" The victory of the 8th, at the Molino del Rey, was followed by daring reconnoissances on the part of our distinguished engineers—Captain Lee, Lieutenants Beauregard, Stevens, and Tower —Major Smith, senior, being sick, and Captain Mason, third in rank, wounded. Their operations were directed principally to the south—towards the gates of the Piedad, San Angel (Niño Perdido), San Antonio, and the Paseo de la Viga.

" This city stands on a slight swell of ground, near the centre of an irregular basin, and is girdled with a ditch in its greater extent—a navigable canal of great breadth and depth—very diffi-

VIEW OF THE CITY OF MEXICO.

cult to bridge in the presence of an enemy, and serving at once for drainage, custom-house purposes, and military defence; leaving eight entrances or gates, over arches—each of which we found defended by a system of strong works, that seemed to require nothing but some men and guns to be impregnable.

"Outside and within the cross-fires of those gates, we found to the south other obstacles but little less formidable. All the approaches near the city are over elevated causeways, cut in many places (to oppose us), and flanked on both sides by ditches, also of unusual dimensions. The numerous cross-roads are flanked in like manner, having bridges at the intersections, recently broken. The meadows thus checkered are, moreover, in many spots, under water or marshy; for, it will be remembered, we were in the midst of the wet season, though with less rain than usual, and we could not wait for the fall of the neighbouring lakes and the consequent drainage of the wet grounds at the edge of the city—the lowest in the whole basin.

"After a close personal survey of the southern gates, covered by Pillow's division and Riley's brigade of Twiggs'—with four times our numbers concentrated in our immediate front—I determined on the 11th to avoid that net-work of obstacles, and to seek, by a sudden diversion to the south-west and west, less unfavourable approaches.

"To economize the lives of our gallant officers and men, as well as to insure success, it became indispensable that this resolution should be long masked from the enemy; and again, that the new movement, when discovered, should be mistaken for a feint, and the old as indicating our true and ultimate point of attack.

"Accordingly, on the spot, the 11th, I ordered Quitman's division from Cuyoacan, to join Pillow, by daylight, before the southern gates, and then that the two major-generals, with their divisions, should, by night, proceed (two miles) to join me at

Tacubaya, where I was quartered with Worth's division. Twiggs, with Riley's brigade and Captains Taylor's and Steptoe's field batteries—the latter of 12-pounders—was left in front of those gates, to manœuvre, to threaten, or to make false attacks, in order to occupy and deceive the enemy. Twiggs' other brigade (Smith's) was left at supporting distance, in the rear, at San Angel, till the morning of the 13th, and also to support our general depot at Mixcoac. The stratagem against the south was admirably executed throughout the 12th and down to the afternoon of the 13th, when it was too late for the enemy to recover from the effects of his delusion.

" The first step in the new movement was to carry Chapultepec, a natural and isolated mound, of great elevation, strongly fortified at its base, on its acclivities, and heights. Besides a numerous garrison, here was the military college of the republic, with a large number of sub-lieutenants and other students. Those works were within direct gun-shot of the village of Tacubaya, and until carried, we could not approach the city on the west, without making a circuit too wide and too hazardous.

" In the course of the same night (that of the 11th) heavy batteries, within easy ranges, were established. No. 1, on our right, under the command of Captain Drum, 4th artillery (relieved late next day, for some hours, by Lieutenant Andrews of the 3d), and No. 2, commanded by Lieutenant Hagner, Ordnance—both supported by Quitman's division. Nos. 3 and 4 on the opposite side, supported by Pillow's division, were commanded, the former by Captain Brooks and Lieutenant S. S. Anderson, 2d artillery, alternately, and the latter by Lieutenant Stone, Ordnance. The batteries were traced by Captain Huger and Captain Lee, Engineer, and constructed by them with the able assistance of the young officers of those corps and the artillery.

" To prepare for an assault, it was foreseen that the play of the batteries might run into the second day; but recent captures had not only trebled our siege-pieces, but also our ammunition; and we knew that we should greatly augment both by carrying the place. I was, therefore, in no haste in ordering an assault before the works were well crippled by our missiles.

" The bombardment and cannonade, under the direction of Captain Huger, were commenced early in the morning of the 12th. Before nightfall, which necessarily stopped our batteries, we had perceived that a good impression had been made on the castle and its outworks, and that a large body of the enemy had remained outside, towards the city, from an early hour to avoid our fire, and to be at hand on its cessation, in order to reinforce the garrison against an assault. The same outside force was discovered the next morning, after our batteries had reopened upon the castle, by which we again reduced its garrison to the minimum needed for the guns.

" Pillow and Quitman had been in position since early in the night of the 11th. Major-General Worth was now ordered to hold his division in reserve, near the foundry, to support Pillow; and Brigadier-General Smith, of Twiggs's division, had just arrived with his brigade from Piedad (two miles), to support Quitman. Twiggs's guns, before the southern gates, again reminded us, as the day before, that he, with Riley's brigade and Taylor's and Steptoe's batteries, was in activity, threatening the southern gates, and there holding a great part of the Mexican army on the defensive.

" Worth's division furnished Pillow's attack with an assaulting party of some two hundred and fifty volunteer officers and men, under Captain McKenzie, of the 2d artillery; and Twiggs's division supplied a similar one, commanded by Captain Casey, 2d infantry, to Quitman. Each of those little columns was furnished with scaling-ladders.

" The signal I had appointed for the attack was the momentary cessation of fire on the part of our heavy batteries. About eight

56

o'clock in the morning of the 13th, judging that the time had arrived by the effect of the missiles we had thrown, I sent an aid-de-camp to Pillow, and another to Quitman, with notice that the concerted signal was about to be given. Both columns now advanced with an alacrity that gave assurance of prompt success. The batteries, seizing opportunities, threw shots and shells upon the enemy over the heads of our men, with good effect, particularly at every attempt to reinforce the works from without to meet our assault.

"Major-General Pillow's approach, on the west side, lay through an open grove, filled with sharp-shooters, who were speedily dislodged; when being up with the front of the attack, and emerging into open space, at the foot of a rocky acclivity, that gallant leader was struck down by an agonizing wound. The immediate command devolved on Brigadier-General Cadwalader, in the absence of the senior Brigadier (Pierce), of the same division—an invalid since the events of August 19. On a previous call of Pillow, Worth had just sent him a reinforcement—Colonel Clarke's brigade.

"The broken acclivity was still to be ascended, and a strong redoubt, midway, to be carried, before reaching the castle on the heights. The advance of our brave men, led by brave officers, though necessarily slow, was unwavering, over rocks, chasms, and mines, and under the hottest fire of cannon and musketry. The redoubt now yielded to resistless valour, and the shouts that followed announced to the castle the fate that impended. The enemy were steadily driven from shelter to shelter. The retreat allowed not time to fire a single mine, without the certainty of blowing up friend and foe. Those who at a distance attempted to apply matches to the long trains, were shot down by our men. There was death below, as well as above ground. At length the ditch and wall of the main work were reached; the scaling-ladders were brought up and planted by the storming-parties; some of the daring spirits first in the assault were cast down—killed or wounded; but a lodgment was soon made; streams of heroes followed; all opposition was overcome, and several of our regimental colours flung out from the upper walls, amidst long-continued shouts and cheers, which sent dismay into the capital. No scene could have been more animating or glorious.

" Major-General Quitman, nobly supported by Brigadier-Generals Shields and Smith (P. F.), his other officers and men, was up with the part assigned him. Simultaneously with the movement on the west, he had gallantly approached the south-east of the same works, over a causeway with cuts and batteries, and defended by an army strongly posted outside, to the east of the works. Those formidable obstacles Quitman had to face, with but little shelter for his troops or space for manœuvring. Deep ditches flanking the causeway, made it difficult to cross on either side into the adjoining meadows, and these again were intersected by other ditches. Smith and his brigade had been early thrown out to make a sweep to the right, in order to present a front against the enemy's line (outside), and to turn two intervening batteries near the foot of Chapultepec. This movement was also intended to support Quitman's storming-parties, both on the causeway. The first of these, furnished by Twiggs's division, was commanded in succession by Captain Casey, 2d infantry, and Captain Paul, 7th infantry, after Casey had been severely wounded; and the second, originally under the gallant Major Twiggs, marine corps, killed, and then Captain Miller, 2d Pennsylvania volunteers. The storming-party, now commanded by Captain Paul seconded by Captain Roberts, of the Rifles, Lieutenant Stewart, and others of the same regiment, Smith's brigade, carried the two batteries in the road, took some guns, with many prisoners, and drove the enemy posted behind in support. The New York and South Carolina volunteers (Shields's brigade) and the 2d Pennsylvania volunteers, all on the left of Quitman's line, together with portions of his storming-parties, crossed the meadows in front, under a heavy fire, and entered the outer enclosure of Chapultepec just in time to join in the final assault from the west.

"Besides Major-Generals Pillow and Quitman, Brigadier-Generals Shields, Smith, and Cadwalader, the following are the officers and corps most distinguished in those brilliant operations: The voltigeur regiment in two detachments, commanded respectively by Colonel Andrews and Lieutenant-Colonel Johnstone—the latter mostly in the lead, accompanied by Major Caldwell; Captains Barnard and Biddle, of the same regiment—the former the first to plant a regimental colour, and the latter among the first in the assault; the storming-party of Worth's division, under Captain McKenzie, 2d artillery, with Lieutenant Seldon, 8th infantry, early on the ladder and badly wounded; Lieutenant Armistead, 6th infantry, the first to leap into the ditch to plant a ladder; Lieutenant Rodgers of the 4th, and J. P. Smith of the 5th infantry —both mortally wounded; the 9th infantry, under Colonel Ransom, who was killed while gallantly leading that gallant regiment; the 15th infantry, under Lieutenant-Colonel Howard and Major Woods, with Captain Chase, whose company gallantly carried the redoubt, midway up the acclivity; Colonel Clarke's brigade (Worth's division), consisting of the 5th, 8th, and part of the 6th regiments of infantry, commanded respectively by Captain Chapman, Major Montgomery, and Lieutenant Edward Johnson—the latter specially noticed, with Lieutenants Longstreet (badly wounded, advancing, colours in hand), Pickett, and Merchant, the last three of the 8th infantry; portions of the United States marines, New York, South Carolina, and 2d Pennsylvania volunteers, which, delayed with their division (Quitman's), by the hot engagement below, arrived just in time to participate in the assault of the heights—particularly a detachment under Lieutenant Reid, New York volunteers, consisting of a company of the same, with one of marines; and another detachment, a portion of the storming-party (Twiggs' division, serving with Quitman), under Lieutenant Steele, 2d infantry, after the fall of Lieutenant Gantt, 7th infantry.

"In this connexion, it is but just to recall the decisive effect of the heavy batteries, Nos. 1, 2, 3, and 4, commanded by those excellent officers, Captain Drum, 4th artillery, assisted by Lieutenants Benjamin and Porter of his own company; Captain Brooks and Lieutenant Anderson, 2d artillery, assisted by Lieutenant Russell, 4th infantry, a volunteer; Lieutenants Hagner and Stone of the Ordnance, and Lieutenant Andrews, 3d artillery; the whole superintended by Captain Huger, chief of Ordnance with this army—an officer distinguished by every kind of merit. The mountain-howitzer battery, under Lieutenant Reno of the Ordnance, deserves, also, to be particularly mentioned. Attached to the voltigeurs, it followed the movements of that regiment and again won applause.

"In adding to the list of individuals of conspicuous merit, I must limit myself to a few of the many names which might be enumerated: Captain Hooker, Assistant Adjutant-General, who won special applause, successively, in the staff of Pillow and Cadwalader; Lieutenant Lovell, 4th artillery (wounded), chief of Quitman's staff; Captain Page, Assistant Adjutant-General, (wounded), and Lieutenant Hammond, 3d artillery, both of Shields's staff, and Lieutenant Van Dorn (7th infantry), aid-de-camp to Brigadier-General Smith.

"Those operations all occurred on the west, south-east, and heights of Chapultepec. To the north, and at the base of the mound, inaccessible on that side, the 11th infantry, under Lieutenant-Colonel Hebert; the 14th, under Colonel Trousdale, and Captain Magruder's field-battery, 1st artillery — one section advanced under Lieutenant Jackson—all of Pillow's division—had, at the same time, some spirited affairs against superior numbers, driving the enemy from a battery in the road, and capturing a gun. In these, the officers and corps named gained merited

praise.   Colonel Trousdale, the commander, though twice
wounded, continued on duty until the heights were carried.

" Early in the morning of the 13th, I repeated the orders of the
night before to Major-General Worth, to be, with his division, at
hand to support the movement of Major-General Pillow from our
left.   The latter seems soon to have called for that entire division,
standing momentarily in reserve, and Worth sent him Colonel
Clarke's brigade.   The call, if not unnecessary, was at least, from
the circumstances, unknown to me at the time ; for, soon observing that the very large body of the enemy, in the road in front of
Major-General Quitman's right, was receiving reinforcements
from the city—less than a mile and a half to the east—I sent
instructions to Worth, on our opposite flank, to turn Chapultepec
with his division, and to proceed cautiously, by the road at its
northern base, in order, if not met by very superior numbers, to
threaten or to attack, in rear, that body of the enemy.   The movement, it was also believed, could not fail to distract and to intimidate the enemy generally.

" Worth promptly advanced with his remaining brigade—
Colonel Garland's—Lieutenant-Colonel C. F. Smith's light battalion, Lieutenant-Colonel Duncan's field-battery—all of his division—and three squadrons of dragoons, under Major Sumner,
which I had just ordered up to join in the movement.

" Having turned the forest on the west, and arriving opposite
to the north centre of Chapultepec, Worth came up with the
troops in the road, under Colonel Trousdale, and aided, by a flank
movement of a part of Garland's brigade, in taking the one-gun
breastwork, then under the fire of Lieutenant Jackson's section
of Captain Magruder's field-battery.   Continuing to advance, this
division passed Chapultepec, attacking the right of the enemy's
line, resting on that road, about the moment of the general retreat
consequent upon the capture of the formidable castle and its outworks.

" Arriving some minutes later, and mounting to the top of the castle, the whole field to the east lay plainly under my view.

" There are two routes from Chapultepec to the capital—the one on the right entering the same gate, Belen, with the road from the south, via Piedad ; and the other obliquing to the left, to intersect the great western, or San Cosmé road, in a suburb outside of the gate of San Cosmé.

" Each of these routes (an elevated causeway) presents a double roadway on the sides of an aqueduct of strong masonry and great height, resting on open arches and massive pillars, which together afford fine points both for attack and defence. The sideways of both aqueducts are, moreover, defended by many strong breastworks at the gates, and before reaching them. As we had expected, we found the four tracks unusually dry and solid for the season.

" Worth and Quitman were prompt in pursuing the retreating enemy—the former by the San Cosmé aqueduct, and the latter along that of Belen. Each had now advanced some hundred yards.

" Deeming it all-important to profit by our successes, and the consequent dismay of the enemy, which could not be otherwise than general, I hastened to despatch from Chapultepec—first Clarke's brigade, and then Cadwalader's, to the support of Worth, and gave orders that the necessary heavy guns should follow. Pierce's brigade was, at the same time, sent to Quitman, and, in the course of the afternoon, I caused some additional siege-pieces to be added to his train. Then, after designating the 15th infantry, under Lieutenant-Colonel Howard—Morgan, the colonel, had been disabled by a wound at Churubusco—as the garrison of Chapultepec, and giving directions for the care of the prisoners of war, the captured ordnance and ordnance stores, I proceeded to join the advance of Worth, within the suburb, and beyond the turn at the junction of the aqueduct with the great highway from the west to the gate of San Cosmé.

"At this junction of roads, we first passed one of those formidable systems of city defences, spoken of above, and it had not a gun!—a strong proof, 1. That the enemy had expected us to fail in the attack upon Chapultepec, even if we meant anything more than a feint; 2. That, in either case, we designed, in his belief, to return and double our forces against the southern gates—a delusion kept up by the active demonstrations of Twiggs and the forces posted on that side; and, 3. That advancing rapidly from the reduction of Chapultepec, the enemy had not time to shift guns—our previous captures had left him, comparatively, but few —from the southern gates.

"Within those disgarnished works, I found our troops engaged in a street-fight against the enemy posted in gardens, at windows, and on house-tops—all flat, with parapets. Worth ordered forward the mountain-howitzers of Cadwalader's brigade, preceded by skirmishers and pioneers, with pickaxes and crowbars, to force windows and doors, or to burrow through walls. The assailants were soon in an equality of position fatal to the enemy. By eight o'clock in the evening, Worth had carried two batteries in this suburb. According to my instructions, he here posted guards and sentinels, and placed his troops under shelter for the night. There was but one more obstacle—the San Cosmé gate (custom-house), between him and the great square in front of the cathedral and palace, the heart of the city; and that barrier it was known could not, by daylight, resist our siege-guns thirty minutes.

"I had gone back to the foot of Chapultepec, the point from which the two aqueducts begin to diverge, some hours earlier, in order to be near that new depot, and in easy communication with Quitman and Twiggs, as well as with Worth.

"From this point I ordered all detachments and stragglers to their respective corps, then in advance; sent to Quitman additional

MAJ. GEN. JOHN A. QUITMAN.

siege-guns, ammunition, intrenching tools; directed Twiggs's remaining brigade (Riley's) from Piedad, to support Worth, and Captain Steptoe's field-battery, also at Piedad, to rejoin Quitman's division.

" I had been, from the first, well aware that the western, or San Cosmé, was the less difficult route to the centre, and conquest of the capital, and therefore intended that Quitman should only manœuvre and threaten the Belen or south-western gate, in order to favour the main attack by Worth, knowing that the strong defences at the Belen were directly under the guns of the much stronger fortress, called the Citadel, just within. Both of these defences of the enemy were also within easy supporting distance from the San Angel (or Niño Perdido) and San Antonio gates. Hence the greater support, in numbers, given to Worth's movement as the main attack.

" These views I repeatedly, in the course of the day, communicated to Major-General Quitman; but being in hot pursuit— gallant himself, and ably supported by Brigadier-Generals Shields and Smith, Shields badly wounded before Chapultepec, and refusing to retire, as well as by all the officers and men of the column—Quitman continued to press forward, under flank and direct fires, carried an intermediate battery of two guns, and then the gate, before two o'clock in the afternoon, but not without proportionate loss, increased by his steady maintenance of that position.

" Here, of the heavy battery (4th artillery), Captain Drum and Lieutenant Benjamin were mortally wounded, and Lieutenant Porter, its third in rank, slightly. The loss of those two most distinguished officers the army will long mourn. Lieutenants J. B. Morange and William Canty, of the South Carolina volunteers, also of high merit, fell on the same occasion, besides many of our bravest non-commissioned officers and men, particularly in Captain Drum's veteran company. I cannot, in this place, give

57

names or numbers; but full returns of the killed and wounded of all corps, in their recent operations, will accompany this report.

"Quitman within the city—adding several new defences to the position he had won, and sheltering his corps as well as practicable—now awaited the return of daylight under the guns of the formidable citadel, yet to be subdued.

"About four o'clock next morning (Sept. 14), a deputation of the *Ayuntamiento* (city council) waited upon me to report that the federal government and the army of Mexico had fled from the capital some three hours before; and to demand terms of capitulation in favour of the church, the citizens, and the municipal authorities. I promptly replied, that I would sign no capitulation; that the city had been virtually in our possession from the time of the lodgments effected by Worth and Quitman the day before; that I regretted the silent escape of the Mexican army; that I should levy upon the city a moderate contribution, for special purposes; and that the American army should come under no terms not self-imposed : such only as its own honour, the dignity of the United States, and the spirit of the age, should, in my opinion, imperiously demand and impose.

"For the terms so imposed, I refer the department to subsequent General Orders, Nos. 287 and 289 (paragraphs 7, 8, and 9 of the latter), copies of which are herewith enclosed.

"At the termination of the interview with the city deputation, I communicated, about daylight, orders to Worth and Quitman to advance slowly and cautiously (to guard against treachery) towards the heart of the city, and to occupy its stronger and more commanding points. Quitman proceeded to the great plaza or square, planted guards, and hoisted the colours of the United States on the National Palace, containing the halls of Congress and executive departments of federal Mexico. In this grateful service, Quitman might have been anticipated by Worth, but for my express orders, halting the latter at the head of the Alameda (a green park), within three squares of that goal of general ambition. The capital, however, was not taken by any one or two corps, but by the talent, the science, the gallantry, the prowess of this entire army. In the glorious conquest, all had contributed early and powerfully, the killed, the wounded, and the fit for duty, at Vera Cruz, Cerro Gordo, Contreras, San Antonio, Churubusco (three battles), the Molino del Rey, and Chapultepec, as much as those who fought at the gates of Belen and San Cosmé.

" Soon after we had entered, and were in the act of occupying the city, a fire was opened upon us from the flat roofs of the houses, from windows and corners of streets, by some two thousand convicts, liberated the night before by the flying government, joined by, perhaps, as many Mexican soldiers, who had disbanded themselves, and thrown off their uniforms. This unlawful war lasted more than twenty-four hours, in spite of the exertions of the municipal authorities, and was not put down till we had lost many men, including several officers, killed or wounded, and had punished the miscreants. Their objects were to gratify national hatred, and, in the general alarm and confusion, to plunder the wealthy inhabitants, particularly the deserted houses. But families are now generally returning; business of every kind has been resumed, and the city is already tranquil and cheerful, under the admirable conduct (with exceptions very few and trifling) of our gallant troops.

" This army has been more disgusted than surprised, that by some sinister process on the part of certain individuals at home, its numbers have been, generally, almost trebled in our public papers, beginning at Washington.

" Leaving, as we all feared, inadequate garrisons at Vera Cruz, Perote, and Puebla, with much larger hospitals; and being obliged, most reluctantly, from the same cause (general paucity of numbers) to abandon Jalapa, we marched (August 7–10) from Puebla with only 10,738 rank and file. This number includes

the garrison of Jalapa, and the 2,429 men brought up by Brigadier-General Pierce, August 6.

"At Contreras, Churubusco, &c. (August 20), we had but
8,497 men engaged—after deducting the garrison of San Augustin (our general depot), the intermediate sick and the dead; at
the Molino del Rey (September 8) but three brigades, with some
cavalry and artillery—making in all 3,251 men—were in the
battle; in the two days—September 12th and 13th—our whole
operating force, after deducting, again, the recent killed, wounded,
and sick, together with the garrison of Mixcoac (the then general
depot), and that of Tacubaya, was but 7,180; and, finally, after
deducting the new garrison of Chapultepec, with the killed and
wounded of the two days, we took possession (September 14th)
of this great capital with less than six thousand men. And I
reassert, upon accumulated and unquestionable evidence, that, in
not one of those conflicts was this army opposed by fewer than
three-and-a-half times its numbers—in several of them, by a yet
greater excess.

"I recapitulate our losses since we arrived in the basin of
Mexico:—

"AUGUST 19, 20.—Killed, 137, including 14 officers. Wounded,
877, including 62 officers. Missing (probably killed), 38 rank
and file. Total, 1,052.

"SEPTEMBER 8.—Killed, 116, including 9 officers. Wounded,
665, including 49 officers. Missing, 18 rank and file. Total, 789.

"SEPTEMBER 12, 13, 14.—Killed, 130, including 10 officers.
Wounded, 703, including 68 officers. Missing, 29 rank and file.
Total, 862.

"Grand total of losses, 2,703, including 383 officers.

"On the other hand, this small force has beaten on the same
occasions in view of their capital, the whole Mexican army, of
(at the beginning) thirty-odd thousand men—posted, always, in
chosen positions, behind intrenchments, or more formidable

defences of nature and art; killed or wounded, of that number, more than seven thousand officers and men; taken 3,730 prisoners, one-seventh officers, including thirteen generals, of whom three had been presidents of this republic; captured more than twenty colours and standards, seventy-five pieces of ordnance, besides fifty-seven wall-pieces, twenty thousand small-arms, an immense quantity of shots, shells, powder, &c. &c.

" Of that enemy, once so formidable in numbers, appointments, artillery, &c., twenty-odd thousand have disbanded themselves in despair, leaving, as is known, not more than three fragments— the largest about 2,500—now wandering in different directions, without magazines or a military chest, and living at free quarters upon their own people.

"General Santa Anna, himself a fugitive, is believed to be on the point of resigning the chief-magistracy, and escaping to neutral Guatemala. A new President, no doubt, will soon be declared, and the federal Congress is expected to reassemble at Queretaro, a hundred and twenty-five miles north of this, on the Zacatecas road, some time in October. I have seen and given safe-conduct through this city, to several of its members. The government will find itself without resources; no army, no arsenals, no magazines, and but little revenue, internal or external. Still, such is the obstinacy, or rather infatuation, of this people, that it is very doubtful whether the new authorities will dare to sue for peace on the terms which, in the recent negotiations, were made known by our minister.

* * * * * * *

" In conclusion, I beg to enumerate, once more, with due commendation and thanks, the distinguished staff officers, general and personal, who, in our last operations in front of the enemy, accompanied me, and communicated orders to every point and through every danger. Lieutenant-Colonel Hitchcock, acting Inspector-General; Major Turnbull and Lieutenant Hardcastle, topographical engineers; Major Kirby, chief paymaster; Captain Irwin, chief quartermaster; Captain Grayson, chief commissary; Captain H. L. Scott, chief in the Adjutant's-General's department; Lieutenant Williams, aid-de-camp; Lieutenant Lay, military secretary; and Major J. P. Gaines, Kentucky cavalry, volunteer aid-de-camp; Captain Lee, engineer, so constantly distinguished, also bore important orders from me (September 13), until he fainted from a wound and the loss of two nights' sleep at the batteries. Lieutenants Beauregard, Stevens, and Tower, all wounded, were employed with the divisions, and Lieutenants G. W. Smith and G. B. McClellan, with the company of sappers and miners. Those five lieutenants of engineers, like their captain, won the admiration of all about them. The ordnance officers, Captain Huger, Lieutenants Hagner, Stone, and Reno, were highly effective, and distinguished at the several batteries; and I must add that Captain McKinstry, assistant quartermaster, at the close of the operations, executed several important commissions for me as a special volunteer.

" Surgeon-General Lawson, and the medical staff generally, were skilful and untiring, in and out of fire, in ministering to the numerous wounded.

" To illustrate the operations in this basin, I enclose two beautiful drawings, prepared under the directions of Major Turnbull, mostly from actual survey.

" I have the honour to be, sir, with high respect, your most obedient servant,

WINFIELD SCOTT.

The Hon. WM. L. MARCY, Secretary of War."

Thus ended a campaign, perhaps the most wonderful in modern military annals. A mere handful of enthusiastic men, under the guidance of skilful and brave officers, had dared to penetrate into the heart of an enemy's country, and occupy his capital, in defiance of the great natural and artificial obstacles that impeded their way, and the immense superiority of hostile numbers by which those obstacles were strengthened and defended. Useless defence! The descendants of the heroic Cortez, though proud, obstinate, and vainglorious, enervated by a luxurious climate, had neither the physical strength nor mental firmness which might have enabled them to successfully measure swords with those whom they contemptuously designated as "the barbarians of the North."

In the short space of eighteen months, the armies of the United States had penetrated various parts of the Mexican Republic from the Atlantic Gulf to the Pacific Ocean; and neither castles, hitherto called impregnable, nor rugged fortified passes, nor walled cities, though defended by immense quantities of artillery, nor the bristling bayonets of innumerable infantry, nor the flickering lance-points of a cavalry admirably equipped and thoroughly versed in the use of their particular arm, could offer more than a temporary resistance to men whose fixed determination was never to yield, but with life, one single foot of ground over which they had already advanced, and never to turn aside from their march upon any point towards which their efforts had been directed.

Nor is the glory of these achievements lessened when we reflect that the brilliant victories in Mexico were not gained by regularly disciplined soldiers, but by men who a few months before were quietly engaged in the various avocations which distinguish the business of civil life, and by men in all grades of society. The sons of the greatest statesmen of the republic and those of the humblest tillers of the soil strode side by side into the thickest of the combat, and each rivalled the other in the exhibition of courage and conduct. Each man fought as if the eye of his country was upon him, and the victories that ensued, apart from the plans of the general in command, were the result of individual heroism in the aggregate, rather than of collective bravery.

The battles of Palo Alto and the Palm Ravine were fought by regulars only; and perhaps a nice analysis would find that, from these initial successes by the organized troops of the republic, arose subsequently that tremendous enthusiasm by which the volunteers, emulating the renown of their better disciplined companions-in-arms, more than rivalled them in acts of individual daring, and stood coequal with them in the splendour of their successes.

How seemingly inadequate the force was by which these great results were obtained, will be best shown by the following statement:—

August 19th and 20th, before Contreras and Churubusco,   8497
September 8th, Molino del Rey,   3251
September 13th and 14th, Chapultepec and the Garitas,   7180

And the city of Mexico was finally entered, after deducting the garrison of Chapultepec and the killed and wounded, by less than 6000 men.

The intermediate losses in killed, wounded, and missing, were as follows:—

	Killed.	Wounded.	Missing.
Contreras and Churubusco,	137	877	38
Molino del Rey,	116	665	18
Chapultepec, the Garitas, and within			
the city,	130	703	29
	383	2245	85

Of the number of killed, 33 were officers and 350 rank and file.

The Mexican losses in these engagements, were

Killed and wounded,   7000
Prisoners,   3730

or 10730,

equal to the whole number of the American troops that marched from Puebla upon the capital. The trophies consisted of more than 20 colours and standards, 75 pieces of ordnance, 57 wall-pieces, and 20,000 stand of arms.

After the capture of the capital, the disorganization of the Mexican army was so complete, that out of an array of 20,000 men, but three fragments remained, the largest of which did not contain more than 2500 men.*

* Scott's Official Despatch, September 18, 1847.

CHAPTER XXVI.

Isolated condition of the American Army—Guerrilla Warfare—Attack on McIn-
tosh's Train—Reinforced by Cadwalader—Skirmish at the National Bridge—
Arrival at Jalapa—Battle of La Hoya—Gallantry of Captain Walker—Cadwa-
lader's Report—Pillow's Reinforcement—General Pierce's—Attack on Lally's
Train—Skirmish at Paso de Ovejas—At the National Bridge—At Cerro Gordo
—At Las Animas—Arrival at Jalapa—American Loss.

FROM the time the army of the United States left Puebla, on
the 7th of August, to the 14th of September, when it entered the
city of Mexico, Scott did not receive a single reinforcement, and
for the most part of that period his communication with the coast
was completely cut off by the activity of the guerrilleros, who had
thrown themselves between the inadequate garrisons established
along the line.

These garrisons were themselves frequently threatened, and it
required the most incessant vigilance on the part of the commanders both at Perote and Puebla, to avert the designs of the
enemy. Puebla was indeed eventually besieged, and its weak
but heroic garrison maintained a noble defence until it was relieved by reinforcements under General Lane.

But it was upon the trains, which containing, besides the usual
army supplies, large amounts of specie for the use of the disburs-
ing officers, that the attacks of the guerrilleros were most frequently
made. The long stretch of wagons and mules of which these
trains were composed, and the utterly inadequate force by which
they were usually guarded, offered irresistible temptations to
roving bands of the enemy, whose knowledge of the country

58   **443**

enabled them to appear suddenly at any designated point, and to disappear with equal rapidity, if the chances of success promised to be unfavourable. The distance between Vera Cruz and Perote is so great, and the points of attack so many, that, notwithstanding the exertions of a company of Mounted Rifles, under the celebrated Captain Samuel H. Walker, which for a time kept the route tolerably clear, there was scarcely a train that ventured up to Perote which did not meet with interruption by the way.

Had there been at this time a subsidiary force sufficient to have maintained posts, such as were subsequently established at the National Bridge, Plan del Rio, and the city of Jalapa, much of the annoyance and loss incident to a line of route continually blocked up and reopened might have been avoided.

On the 4th of June, 1847, a train of wagons left Vera Cruz, under the command of Lieutenant-Colonel J. S. McIntosh. This brave and gallant officer had already gloriously distinguished himself at the battles of Palo Alto and Resaca de la Palma, where he fell pierced with wounds, from which he had not fully recovered when he sought to rejoin his regiment at Puebla.

Subsequently, after enduring the perils of the march and distinguishing himself at the battle of Churubusco, he was again seriously wounded while leading the brigade of Clarke to the terrible assault of Molino del Rey, of which wound, aggravated by those previously received, he shortly afterwards died.

The train of which he assumed the command, was in every respect inefficient. The drivers were bad, the teams unbroken, and the troops, new volunteers from the northern states of the Union, exceedingly debilitated by the heat and unhealthiness of the climate.

The train consisted of one hundred and twenty-eight wagons, loaded with specie and ammunition, and its conducting force amounted in all to six hundred and eighty-eight men, of whom six hundred and six were reported on the 7th of June as fit for duty.

By the evening of the second day, owing to accidents which had befallen them, four wagons were abandoned.   On the morning of the 6th the troops broke up their camp on the San Juan, and after proceeding a few miles, were attacked for the first time by the guerrilleros, while ascending a hill.   The hills in the distance being also seen covered with the enemy, the wagons were parked, and, after a short contest, the assailants were dislodged with some loss.   The march was then resumed, but the train had not proceeded more than a mile when the firing, which was previously in front, now opened in rear.   As soon as the enemy was beaten off, the march was again resumed.   Half a mile further on he made another and more desperate attack, but was eventually dispersed by a vigorous charge, and his force driven back into the recesses of the forest.   It being now dark, and the firing having ceased, the train was halted at this point, and the troops rested upon their arms all night.

The next day, on the route to Paso de Ovejas, the train was again harassed, when finding himself scantily supplied with provisions and forage, and learning that more serious attacks were to be apprehended at the National Bridge and the passes beyond, Colonel McIntosh determined to send back his mules to Vera Cruz for a supply of provisions, and at the same time despatched a communication to General Cadwalader, then at that place, requesting an additional force.   In the mean time he encamped at Paso de Ovejas, with the loss of twenty-four wagons, and of twenty-five men killed and wounded.

On the 11th, General Cadwalader joined him with a reinforcement of five hundred men, and assumed command of the whole.

On the afternoon of the 12th the march was continued, and late in the day the column reached the National Bridge.

Here the enemy was discovered strongly posted in occupation

of the fort to the left of the road, and beyond the bridge upon the heights to the right. The bridge was barricaded, and the positions of the enemy were such that it could only be crossed under a raking fire.

A simultaneous attack upon the fort and barricade was accordingly ordered, and as soon as the howitzers, under Lieutenant Prince, had breached the barricade, one company of cavalry and two of infantry dashed forward amid a plunging storm of musketry, and succeeded in crossing the bridge. No sooner was this accomplished than Pittman's company of the 9th infantry, supported by a detachment from other companies, led by Brevet Captain Hooker, rapidly ascended the heights beyond, and after a sharp skirmish drove the enemy from his position and held it.

In this affair the loss of Cadwalader was thirty-two, killed and wounded.

No further interruption of consequence occurred until after leaving the city of Jalapa. From this place the column, being joined by the garrison under Colonel Childs, continued its march on the 18th, and on the 20th approached the pass of La Hoya, where the enemy was known to be already posted in considerable numbers.

The necessary dispositions were accordingly made to repel his attack; but, on nearing the pass, he was found to have been already successfully assailed from the opposite end by Walker's Rifles, supported by five companies of the Pennsylvania regiment, under the command of Colonel Wynkoop, who, being aware of the approach of the train, and of the force by which it was threatened, had marched out from Perote to meet it.

In the battle of La Hoya, great credit is due to Colonel Wynkoop for his promptitude in marching from Perote to assist in disengaging the column of Cadwalader from the apprehended difficulties of the pass; but the honour of dispersing the guerrilleros assembled at that point belongs almost exclusively to the heroic Walker.

The detail from the 1st Pennsylvania regiment reached the pass before midnight of the 19th, when, finding the enemy in force, Wynkoop refrained from making an attack until Walker's Rifles should come up. These had been detained in an examination of the village of Las Vegas, and did not arrive at the pass until three o'clock on the morning of the 20th. As soon as they moved to the front, they were ordered to advance and dislodge the enemy. This, during the darkness, was more properly the duty of infantry; but observing by the light of his picket-fires that a considerable number of the enemy were thrown across the front of the pass, Walker gave the order to charge, and galloping impetuously through the midst of a random and harmless fire, drove the guerrilleros to their fastnesses among the hills. The pursuit was urged with the most daring impetuosity, but was suddenly arrested by the advance encountering a fence at a turn of the road, over which Walker and seven of the foremost were precipitated, with the loss of their horses.

Finding it impossible to render further service against an unseen enemy, and ignorant of what obstacles might yet remain to be overcome, Walker withdrew his men and rested them on their arms until daylight.

The next morning, Colonel Wynkoop, finding the guerrilleros occupying the heights in great numbers, and fearful of being himself surrounded, determined to fall back upon Perote. This ill-timed resolution, the result of an excessive prudence rather than of any lack of courage, might have been productive of the most unfortunate consequences to the column of Cadwalader, had not Walker, stung to the quick with the dishonour of a retrograde movement, separated his command from that of the infantry, and galloping back in the direction of La Hoya, commenced the action with the Mounted Rifles alone.

About two miles from the pass, some fifty of the enemy being discovered, Walker threw out his skirmishers on foot, with orders to bring on the engagement, and immediately afterwards dismounting the rest of his command, he posted them under cover of a low stone fence. In a few minutes the skirmishers were driven in by overwhelming numbers, and the action commenced.

After a sharp and well contested firing, which lasted half an hour, the enemy fell back, with the loss of forty killed and wounded. The Rifles now sprung to their horses and charged.

In the mean time, Cadwalader's artillery had been heard to open at the other end of the pass. Wynkoop's detachment returned at this juncture to the support of Walker, and the guerrilleros, finding themselves pressed on all sides, fled precipitately. Shortly afterwards the train was brought through without loss. In this brilliant affair the command of Walker consisted of only fifty-one men, while the enemy had three hundred men actually engaged, and a like number hovering in view.

The following report, by General Cadwalader, presents a connected view of the incidents of the march after he came to the relief of the train :—

"HEAD-QUARTERS, FIRST BRIGADE, THIRD DIVISION, }
Puebla, Mexico, July 12, 1847. }

"SIR : In reply to your letter dated the 11th instant, requesting to be furnished with a report of the incidents which occurred on my march from Vera Cruz to this place, including combats with the enemy, I respectfully submit the following for the information of the General-in-chief.

"On the 7th of June, whilst awaiting at Vera Cruz the arrival of a portion of the troops of my brigade, I received a letter by express from Colonel McIntosh, dated the 6th June, eleven P. M., at Paso de Ovejas, stating that he had been ' constantly attacked since ten A. M., to-day, and that the immense train under the escort of my (his) troops is so extensive, that it is impossible without a considerable additional force to guard it and proceed.' A copy of the letter is herewith enclosed.

BRIG. GEN. GEORGE CADWALADER.

"Immediately orders were communicated for so many of the troops as could be provided with transportation, to be put in marching order; and early on the morning of the 8th, one company of the 3d dragoons, one section of the howitzer battery from the regiment of voltigeurs, and a detachment of infantry, in all about five hundred, were *en route* to reinforce the column awaiting support.

"On coming up with Colonel McIntosh, which was on the 10th of June, it was found that we would be unable to proceed without delay, in consequence of the crippled condition of his train, while, at the same time, the scarcity of forage and the limited supply of provisions for the troops to Jalapa, rendered it necessary for me to direct that every effort should be made to put the train in marching condition, and for the troops to be in readiness to leave at the earliest practicable moment.

"On the following afternoon the column resumed its march Before leaving Paso de Ovejas, we had reason to believe that the enemy, in considerable numbers, were occupying the commanding positions in our front, at the National Bridge, and were prepared to resist us at that point.

"On approaching the bridge, they were found to be in possession of the fort on the left of the road, from which they could deliver their fire with effect upon the train at several points, from the circuitous course of the road in its descent to the bridge before reaching the foot of the ravine. The enemy were also in possession of the heights on the opposite side of the bridge, from which point they would have a raking fire upon our columns during the passage of the river. These heights I found it impracticable to reach, except by crossing the bridge.

"The bridge itself was barricaded. Under these circumstances it appeared to be necessary to detach a sufficient infantry force to drive the enemy from the fort overhanging the road, before reaching the bridge; and, simultaneous with that movement, to order forward the howitzers to breach the barricade, and a company of cavalry and two of infantry to force the bridge as soon as a passage was prepared for them. Lieutenant and Adjutant Henry Prince, of the 4th infantry, who had been assigned to command the howitzers, rendered me highly valuable service at this critical moment. He advanced with the battery, and succeeded in breaching the barricades, and preparing the way for our troops to charge, which was made under a heavy fire from the enemy. The heights upon the right, after crossing the bridge, were carried by Captain Pitman's company of the 9th infantry, and a small detachment from other companies, under a fire from the enemy, handsomely led by Brevet Captain Hooker, the chief of my staff. Having thus gained possession of the points on which it was necessary for us to encamp, both on account of water and the security of the train, the latter was ordered forward and parked for the night. I have to regret the loss of thirty-two officers and men, killed and wounded, belonging to the service, with others employed with the train whose names are not known. We have reason to believe that the enemy suffered severely, although no positive information has been communicated to me with regard to their loss, or the numbers engaged. In consequence of our delay in marching from Paso de Ovejas, we were compelled to accomplish a part of our work under cover of the night, and to this I mainly attribute the limited loss we sustained. Had those positions been forced by daylight, the list of killed and wounded would have been, unquestionably, greatly augmented.

" On the 13th, after sending back the wounded with a suitable escort, we proceeded to Plan del Rio, with no other interruption or annoyance than an occasional discharge of escopets at small portions of our troops and train. The discharges usually proceeded from behind dense thickets, almost impracticable for our flankers to penetrate, and not unfrequently resulted in the loss of men, horses, and mules.

"We passed Cerro Gordo the 14th, having previously taken possession of the commanding positions, and on the 15th reached Jalapa, where we were joined by the brigade under Colonel Childs. Before leaving that city on the 18th, information reached us that the enemy were in force at La Hoya, prepared to resist our advance in so strong a position, and we encamped at the village before entering the pass on the 19th. On approaching it on the 20th, at an early hour, our advance found it occupied with a considerable force, apparently determined to dispute the passage of the train. Four companies, under Captain Winder, of the 1st artillery, were sent in advance, with written instructions to occupy the successive heights in the pass. On gaining the mountain on the left with two companies, he reported the enemy to be also in force upon the intermediate height that he had already gained, from which only the other height, which commanded the road, could be approached. Major Dimick, with two companies, was sent to reinforce him. The approach of this detachment upon the rear of the enemy was unexpected, and they were driven precipitately from the mountains across the road. Captain Winder succeeded in killing four, and taking three prisoners, and three prisoners were taken by Major Dimick. The enemy falling in with a portion of the first regiment Pennsylvania volunteers, and Captain Walker's company of mounted riflemen, under the command of Colonel Wynkoop, a brisk fire was opened by both parties. The advance of the Second Brigade, under Colonel Childs, drove the enemy in confusion for more than two miles, they leaving seven or eight dead upon the field, several who were wounded having made their escape, the enemy admitting a loss of over thirty men. The force of the enemy seen by us, was estimated at about seven hundred, although it was said to have been much greater. The command encamped that night at Rio Frio, and on the 21st reached Perote, at twelve o'clock, M.

"I refer you to the report of Colonel Thomas Childs, in com-
59

mand of the Second Brigade of the division under my command, herewith enclosed, from whom I received valuable assistance from the time he joined me.

" The miserable mustang ponies, by which our train was drawn, rendered it difficult, over a mountainous country, to keep the train closed up, and to afford proper protection to it in the face of an enemy, without attention to the management of the train by the proper officers, and the assistance of persons of experience and industry.

" At Perote, it became necessary to purchase a number of mules for the train, and on the 23d June, as I was about to march for Puebla, I received an order from Major-General Pillow, by express from Vera Cruz, directing me not to proceed beyond Perote until his arrival at that place.

" On the 1st July, General Pillow arrived at Perote, and assumed the command previously to our march to this place. Enclosed you will find a return of the killed and wounded during the march from Paso de Ovejas to Perote.

" I have the honour to be, very respectfully, your obedient servant,

GEO. CADWALADER,

Brigadier-General U. S. Army, commanding.

Captain H. L. Scott,
    Act'g Ass't Adjutant-General, head-quarters of the army."

On the 17th of June, General Pillow left Vera Cruz for Puebla, with a reinforcement of one thousand men, and arrived safely at the head-quarters of the army, with scarcely the loss of a single man.

General Pierce, who left Vera Cruz in July, to join General Scott, with twenty-five hundred men, one hundred and fifty wagons, seven hundred mules, and a million of dollars in specie, was less fortunate.   When he had reached the National Bridge, with his command, he was attacked by fourteen hundred Mexicans, when a spirited engagement took place, in which the Mexicans were defeated with a loss of one hundred and fifty men. The American loss in killed and wounded was thirty. General Pierce found it necessary, after this, to return to Vera Cruz for artillery and reinforcements. With these advantages he marched forward, and reached Puebla the day before General Scott marched on the capital.

But a train of wagons, guarded by a force of one thousand volunteers, which started from Vera Cruz on the 6th of August, under the command of Major Lally, met with serious and continual interruptions.

Under the impression that this train conveyed a large amount of specie, the guerrilleros assembled from all quarters, in numbers varying, at different points along the line of route, from twelve hundred to two thousand men.

The first attack, made on the 10th of August, at Paso de Ovejas, was repulsed by Lally, after a severe skirmish which lasted an hour and a half. The American loss was eleven men killed and wounded.

On the 12th, a second and far more serious attempt upon the train was made by the enemy at the National Bridge. The bridge itself was found to be barricaded, and the hills in front and on the right of the town, and the castle on the left, were all occupied by large numbers of guerrilleros.

By the exertions of the Artillery, under Lieutenant Sears, those positions were eventually forced and the guerrilleros compelled to retire. The contest at this point had been unusually obstinate and protracted; and the American loss was correspondingly severe, the number of killed and wounded amounting to fifty-one, of whom thirteen were killed and seven wounded mortally.

On the 15th, leaving his train behind him at Plan del Rio, Lally determined to force the passes of Cerro Gordo with the main body of his command, before advancing his wagons. This was successfully accomplished on the 16th, by a dashing assault upon the batteries enfilading the road. The storming-party, consisting of a detail of one hundred and thirty men from various companies, was led with great gallantry by Lieutenant Ridgely, of the 4th infantry, the enemy being rapidly driven from all his defensive positions, and two guns and a large amount of ammunition captured. Lally's loss at this point was two killed and eleven wounded.

On the 19th, at Las Animas, within a mile and a half of Jalapa, the enemy made a final attempt upon the train; but after receiving a few rounds of canister, he was effectually dispersed by a charge of infantry, and the train entered Jalapa a short time afterwards, having sustained a loss, including the skirmishes already mentioned, and desultory attacks along the line of route, amounting in killed, wounded, and missing, to one hundred and five men.

On the 13th, an expedition left Vera Cruz to reinforce Major Lally's command. It was composed of Captain Wells's company of the 15th infantry, Captain Haile's company of the 14th infantry, and Captain Fairchild's company of the Louisiana Rangers, all under command of Captain Wells. They proceeded as far as the National Bridge, where they expected to overtake Major Lally's command, but he had proceeded on and carried his train in safety beyond Jalapa. The guerrilleros occupied the heights about the bridge, and opened a heavy fire upon the command of Captain Wells as it came up, killing nearly all the mules, and forcing the whole party to retire. The enemy captured all the wagons save one, the baggage of the officers, and the knapsacks of the men. Before the final affair at the bridge, Captain Wells had five successive engagements with the enemy. The repulse of his command was owing to the advantage of artillery, possessed by the Mexicans, from which they fired grape with good effect.

To restrain the depredations of the guerrilleros, it was deemed advisable to obtain possession of the National Bridge. Colonel Hughes was despatched for that purpose with two pieces of artillery, and some companies of infantry. He succeeded readily in dislodging the enemy, and by his promptitude held them in check in that vicinity. Soon after his occupation of the place, his command was strengthened by some recruits for the 2d infantry, which were brought up by Captain Heintzelman. The captain left Vera Cruz on the 11th of September with a battalion of six companies, and a train of wagons with provisions and money for the army. On reaching the Paso de Ovejas, about nightfall, he anticipated an attack from the enemy, and placed sentinels around his camp, and posted a picket of forty men upon the heights to prevent any sudden surprise.

During the night the enemy made a descent upon them, drove in the party posted upon the heights, and poured a destructive fire into the camp which disconcerted the raw troops. Captain Hays, who had seen considerable service, perceived the danger of leaving the enemy in possession of the heights, and advanced to dislodge them from their position. He took with him about two hundred men, and after a sharp conflict, in which many of the enemy fell, succeeded in repelling them and regaining the lost position. Checked by the loss which they met, the enemy fell back and did not again attempt to molest the picket, which was now reinforced to the number of a hundred. This was the first conflict in which the battalion was engaged, and the result in killed and wounded evinced their bravery under a first fire, while it afforded an opportunity to its newly-appointed surgeon, Dr. R. T. Spence, for the exercise of his skill and humanity.

In the morning the army proceeded onward, and reached the National Bridge; from which place it did not move until the 25th, when it proceeded on with the army of General Lane, of

Indiana. It had arrived from Vera Cruz on the 23d, and consisted of twenty-eight hundred infantry, horse, and artillery.

In the mean time, Lally, who had reached Jalapa, did not venture out upon the road, but remained at that place until the arrival of Lane with his command.

Thus, by active parties of guerrilla bands, the road between Vera Cruz and Puebla was continually infested, and no one could travel without a powerful escort. The most active and daring of the partisan leaders of these bands was Father Jarauta, a priest, who had laid aside the pastoral crook of the ministry of peace for the sword of strife and the sanguinary spear.

CHAPTER XXVII.

THE American army having at length obtained undisputed possession of the city of Mexico, General Scott established his head-quarters at the National Palace.

His first act was to issue an order, dated September 14th, cautioning his troops against excesses of every kind, and urging the importance of the strictest military discipline. By the same order Major-General Quitman was appointed civil and military Governor of the city.

On September, the 16th, he promulgated a second order, in which he " calls upon his brethren-in-arms to return, both in public and private worship, thanks and gratitude to God for the signal triumphs" which he had vouchsafed to the American arms. In this order, he reiterates the necessity of the strictest discipline, lest the discomfited enemy, reuniting with the populace, should attempt to make himself once more master of the capital.

The following day he caused to be republished, with additions, the General Orders of February 19th, 1847, declaring martial law, and imposing a contribution of one hundred and fifty thousand dollars upon the city of Mexico, to be paid by the corporate

(457)

authority in four weekly instalments of thirty-seven thousand five-hundred dollars each.

Of this levy, twenty thousand dollars were appropriated to the purchase of extra comforts for the wounded and sick, ninety thousand dollars to the gratuitous distribution of blankets and shoes among the rank and file, and forty thousand dollars reserved for other military purposes.*

On the 18th of September the army was ordered to be quartered over the city as early as practicable, in the following manner:—

" The first division on or near the direct route from the gate of San Cosmé, towards the Cathedral, and extending a little beyond the east end of the Alameda.

" The second division about the Plaza Mayor, extending towards the gate of San Lazaro, or the Peñon.

" The third division on or near the direct route from the gate of Peravilla, or Guadaloupe, towards the Cathedral.

" The volunteer division on or near the direct route from the gate of San Antonio, towards the Cathedral."

On each of these gates a competent guard was ordered to be detailed from the respective divisions, protected by two pieces of artillery.

From this time, up to the second week in October, General Scott was busily engaged in preparing his despatches, detailing the operations around the capital. This appears to have been— particularly at this time—a task of great labour. Not only were discrepancies to be reconciled, and errors corrected, but the more delicate office of discriminating between rival claims, and award- ing to each gallant soldier his due share of honour, imposed the necessity of much material investigation. These labours resulted, as is generally the case, in the disappointment of many aspirants for military fame.

As if to imbitter still more this unpleasant state of feeling, the

* General Orders, 287.

republication of some letters from the United States, professing to give an account of the battles of the 19th and 20th of August, and most unjustly claiming for Major-General Pillow the chief honour of those victories, widened the breach between the General-in-chief and some of his nearest subordinates, and led to charges and recriminations as dangerous to the " *morale*" of the army, as they were injurious to its efficiency.

By the middle of October, having learned unofficially that reinforcements ranging in number between four thousand and seven thousand men, were on their route from Vera Cruz towards the capital, General Scott issued a circular to the commanders of posts along the line, directing three military posts to be established between Vera Cruz and Jalapa, the regarrisoning of the latter city with twelve hundred men, and the garrison at Puebla to be strongly reinforced. The line of communication was still further strengthened by the establishment of a new post at the pass of Rio Frio, about midway between Puebla and the city of Mexico.

Nothing now remained to be done until the arrival of additional troops at the capital. In the meantime, the duties of the military and civil government of the city were ably fulfilled by Major-General Quitman.

The most perfect order was rigorously maintained, and a quiet courtesy and decorum strictly enforced towards the citizens generally. By this generous course of conduct, the wealthy were induced to return to the homes they had timidly abandoned, and the customary pleasures and avocations of a luxurious city were resumed, with a spirit and confidence which the presence of the American flag floating from the walls of the national palace seemed rather to heighten than subdue.

The prospects of peace, however, were still clouded. Some faint hopes, indeed, were entertained from the Congress about to assemble at Queretaro, but the elements of discord among the

60

rival candidates for power were as yet too much disturbed to allow of any calculation as to what would be the result of the session.

The recall of Mr. Trist about this time, and the revocation of his powers by his own government, were a source of regret to many who were pacifically disposed; and, had that gentleman implicitly obeyed his instructions, by returning home at once, it is doubtful whether any subsequent attempt at negotiation might not have been seriously embarrassed by those malcontents whose official existence depended upon maintaining a belligerent attitude on the part of the Mexican people.

The reinforcements gradually drawing towards the capital, and the activity of General Lane in routing the guerrilla bands from their fastnesses and occupying the towns which had hitherto afforded them protection, by proving even that system of warfare of little avail against American troops, also predisposed many influential Mexicans to a favourable termination of hostilities; but they were fearful of giving voice to their desires while the possibility remained of the war party regaining their former ascendancy.

The imposing position, however, which General Scott was enabled to assume by the occupation of the Mexican capital, the increase of his garrisons along the line, and the strong force which it was contemplated he would soon have at his disposal for operating against the states of the interior, began to make an impression even upon those defiant spirits who, residing hitherto remotely secure from the actual scene of warfare, were at length threatened with an actual participation in its evils.   This favourable state of feeling was still further enhanced by a noble act of clemency on the part of General Scott.

After the capture of Vera Cruz and the victory of Cerro Gordo, the prisoners of war, both officers and rank and file, were released on parole.   Unfortunately, this generosity was in many instances abused; and men of all stations were known to have dishonoured themselves by immediately resuming arms against their former conquerors. To correct this evil, those prisoners taken in the battles around Mexico were held in durance. These amounted to about eight hundred men, and the deplorable condition to which the families of many were reduced in consequence moved the venerable Archbishop of Mexico to intercede in their behalf. A correspondence alike honourable to both parties was accordingly opened between that prelate and the General-in-chief, and resulted favourably.

The letter of the Archbishop, and the reply of General Scott, are equally worthy of preservation, as indicating the esteem in which the American commander was held by the Mexican Church, and the frank and generous conduct by which this good opinion had been won :—

ECCLESIASTICAL GOVERNMENT OF THE ARCHBISHOPRIC OF MEXICO,
Mexico, November 5, 1847.

" MOST EXCELLENT SIR: The respect which your Excellency has manifested to the Mexican church (of which I am the unworthy head), in calling upon me, has induced me to take advantage of the favourable disposition of your Excellency to ask a favour which will perpetuate your memory, and will make known to the faithful members of my diocess the feeling of benevolence which you entertain towards them.

" A multitude of fathers, wives, children, brothers, and other relations of the prisoners who are now confined, under the order of your Excellency, loudly entreat their liberty ; and the prisoners themselves vehemently lament the many evils which their confinement has brought down upon their families, who depend upon them for subsistence, and who, consequently, are reduced to misery, and in many cases to an absolute state of indigence. Were there any important political reason why these prisoners should not be liberated, I should not have been so bold as to ask it ; but their

number is small, and distributed, as they will be, in different
parts of the republic, their importance must be insignificant.

"I ask their liberty, not only because it is a duty of my office,
but my heart also impels me to solicit some real consolation for
these unfortunate men whom the fates of war have reduced to
so lamentable a condition.   And, as if they were sheep of the
flock most especially intrusted to my care, I considered myself
called upon to use my utmost endeavours in their favour, because
in that character they have a right to demand my pastoral and
most tender care.   For the same reason, I wish to imitate the example of so many illustrious prelates, who, before now, have lent
their good offices (not without success) in cases of the same nature.
Neither would I hesitate to constitute myself a prisoner in their
stead, and willingly I would be the ransom of their liberty, as my
faith obliges me even to be anathematized for the sake of my
brethren.   In our days, the brave General Lamoriciere, by the
mediation of the bishop of Algiers, obtained the liberty of a considerable number of French prisoners from the barbarous Abdel
Kader, and I take the liberty to recall to your Excellency this
notable trait of benevolence and magnanimity on the part of a man
who is ignorant of the duties of Christian charity.   General
Scott, doubtless, has a heart equally noble and generous; nor to
his Christian character, will be indifferent the mediation of a
Catholic archbishop who entreats your Excellency, in the name of
the church which he governs, to grant this favour.   It is difficult
to believe that after so many proofs of philanthropy, your Excellency
will not lend yourself to an act of clemency and generosity which
the church will remember as a great favour, and the annals
of history as one of those noble actions peculiar to republican
countries.

"I entreat God Almighty to preserve your Excellency many
years, and to incline your heart to grant to the Mexican prisoners
the precious gift of liberty.

"I am, with respect, the servant of your Excellency, who loves you in Jesus Christ.

JUAN MANUEL,

Archbishop of Cesarea.

To the most excellent DON WINFIELD SCOTT,
    Major General and Commander-in-chief of the Army
        of the United States of the North, in Mexico."

The reply of General Scott, a few days afterwards, was as follows :—

"HEAD-QUARTERS OF THE ARMY OF THE U. S.
Mexico, Nov. 10, 1847.

"SIR: The request of your grace, on the part of the holy church of which you are the head, that I should release, on parole, the prisoners of war remaining in the hands of the American army, is entitled to the highest consideration.

"I beg to state what have been, heretofore, my practice and endeavours on the subject of prisoners in this unhappy war between the United States and Mexico.

"At Vera Cruz, I very willingly stipulated that the Mexican garrison should be permitted to return to their respective homes *on parole*, although I had it in my power to reduce the garrisons to unconditional submission.

"At Cerro Gordo, the Mexican prisoners who surrendered at discretion to the army under my command, were voluntarily and promptly paroled by me.

"I am sorry to say, that many of the officers and men released on those occasions, encouraged by the late Mexican authorities, are known to have violated their paroles.

"Of the prisoners captured by the army in the basin of Mexico, not an officer remains in confinement, except one, who openly avowed his intention to resume arms against us, if left at large. Several of the general officers, who happened to be members of the Supreme Congress, I voluntarily discharged without exchange and without parole.

"July 12, from Puebla, I addressed a communication to the Mexican Minister of Foreign Relations, demanding th ˋ release of certain American prisoners of war, taken from the army ɔf the Rio Grande, who had been exchanged by agreement between Generals Taylor and Santa Anna, immediately after the battle of Buena Vista, or Angostura, but who were still held in close confinement contrary to that agreement; and, at the same time, I proposed that commissioners should be appointed on the part of the two armies, to agree upon a cartel for the general treatment and exchange of all prisoners of war in future. To this communication I received an evasive reply, when I addressed another to that minister, dated the 29th of the same month. It is singular that the only reply received to my second communication I found here, in the palace, enveloped, sealed, and addressed to me, bearing date August.

"In the armistice agreed upon by the belligerents, in August, there was a stipulation (article 8) for the immediate release of the same American prisoners mentioned above. But this stipulation was also evaded and wholly neglected by the Mexican government; and I have since, on terms very disadvantageous to the United States, been obliged to exchange for the officers of that party who were confined at Toluca. The rank and file of the same party were, at the time, confined at some place far in the direction of Tampico. I learn, unofficially, that they have been recently permitted to return home by the way of that port.

"But the application of your grace comes to me under sanctions too high to be neglected.

"I therefore beg to say, that if your grace will have the goodness to appoint some dignitary of the church to visit the Mexican prisoners of war (rank and file, or common men) now confined in this capital, and explain to them the customs and usages of war in such cases, viz: that prisoners, released on parole, are always put to death, if taken in arms against the same belligerents before being duly exchanged; and add the solemn admonition of the church against the violation of their paroles, I will, immediately, under that holy sanction, cause the said prisoners to be released *on parole*, so that they may return to their respective families, friends, and peaceful occupations.

I have the honour, &c.,

WINFIELD SCOTT.

To the most illustrious ARCHBISHOP OF MEXICO."

By a second letter, dated the 16th of December, the Mexican Archbishop professed himself willing to accept and fulfil all the conditions stipulated by General Scott, and also volunteered personally to administer the oath to the prisoners. This he satisfactorily performed on the 22d of the same month, and followed it by a brief but dignified address, in which he pointed out the heinousness of the crime of perjury, and the consequences, both eternal and temporal, which were likely to ensue. Each man then received a paper attesting the fact of his release on parole, and his obligation not to take up arms against the United States unless exchanged in the manner customary in such cases. The policy of this act on the part of General Scott cannot be doubted; and the prompt manner in which he responded to the appeal of the Archbishop doubled the obligation, while it exhibited a grateful contrast to the evasive duplicity of the Mexican government in similar circumstances.

The American army was now in a condition to assume the offensive. The columns of Major-General Butler and Lieutenant-Colonel Johnston reached the city of Mexico about the 17th of December. As soon as the General-in-chief was aware of their proximity, he caused a general order to be published, in which it was stated that the army was about to recommence active operations against the enemy, and that immediately on the occupation of the principal point or points in any state, the payment of all taxes and dues usually collected by the Mexican government would be absolutely prohibited. These revenues were henceforth to be demanded of the proper civil authorities for the support of the army of the United States. The states already occupied by American troops were held as immediately liable, and the amount assessed to the several states of the Mexican republic, as respectively brought under the control of the forces of the United States, was distinctly defined in a supplemental order bearing date the 31st of December.

The first movement towards the collection of dues beyond the limits of the city of Mexico, was made by despatching Colonel Withers, with a detachment of the 9th infantry, to Pachuca, for the purpose of preventing the Mexican officers from seizing the assay duties constantly accruing at that place, from its being in the vicinity of the silver mines of Real del Monte.

Another detachment, under the command of Brigadier-General Cadwalader, was subsequently sent to Toluca, the capital of the state of Mexico, while Colonel Clarke, with a small brigade, was ordered to occupy Cuernavaca. All these officers were directed to treat the Mexican authorities with courtesy, and to await a reasonable time for the payment of the amount assessed, and if gentle means failed, they were then to resort to forced levies. The same instructions were forwarded to the military commanders of Puebla, Perote, Jalapa, Vera Cruz, and Tampico.

Other and more extensive operations were contemplated in the direction of Zacatecas and San Luis Potosi; but, owing to vexatious delays and disappointments, these movements were obliged to be postponed. In the mean time, however, these active preparations were producing a corresponding effect upon the enemy. The result of the elections was decidedly favourable to peace. General Santa Anna, deprived of his command, and but too severely visited with the scorn and contumely of those by whom he was previously idolized, was now a wanderer, anxiously desiring

the passport that should guaranty him safe-conduct until beyond
the limits of the republic. The adherents of that party, so long
clamorous for a continuance of the war, dropped off, one by one ;
while those who, from fear of the consequences, had heretofore
remained silent, were now emboldened to deprecate any further
prosecution of hostilities.

The accession of General Herrera to the Presidential chair,
and the negotiations which followed, will be more fully developed
hereafter.

The brilliant career of General Scott was now drawing to a
close, the war was virtually ended, when he was superseded in
command of the army he had so gloriously led, by Major-General
Butler. How far party feeling entered into this act of the American
government, must be left for posterity to judge; the chronicler of
the present day could scarcely be expected to hold an even balance while weighing the dry acts of the politician against the
splendid achievements of the soldier. One thing, however, is
certain : that both before assuming the command of the army, and
afterwards, General Scott laboured under the impression that there
did not exist, on the part of the War Department, a feeling of
kindness towards him, or even of justice. An investigation of the
whole matter would carry us beyond the limits prescribed for our
work, if it even came within the legitimate province of the historian rather than the biographer.

61

CHAPTER XXVIII.

AFTER the capture of Vera Cruz, the naval operations along the
Mexican coast, though marked by none of those imposing events
which distinguished the progress of the army, were yet of a
character well calculated to test the efficiency of the seamen,
and the ability of the officers by whom they were commanded.

The services of the squadron were both important and hazardous. The Mexican coast was effectually blockaded; Alvarado,
Tuspan, Laguna, Fronteira, and all the towns of any note were
taken and garrisoned, and the multifarious duties pertaining to
the service performed with that skilful celerity which is only to
be acquired by means of the most perfect discipline.

Alvarado was taken by Lieutenant Hunter, as described in a
former part of our narrative, and Commodore Perry resolved to
fit out an expedition to reduce and occupy Tuspan. The fleet
employed consisted of the steamer Mississippi, frigate Raritan,
sloop-of-war Albany, ships John Adams, Germantown, Decatur,
Spitfire, Vixen, Scourge, Vesuvius, Hecla, Etna, Bonita, Reefer,
and Petrel. Among the vessels were distributed one hundred and
fifty men belonging to the Potomac, and three hundred and forty
men belonging to the Ohio. After some delay at the island of

Lobos, and derangement at sea in consequence of the prevalence of a norther, arrangements were made for landing on the morning of the 18th of April. The Mississippi was anchored off the bar of the river near the town, while, to enable them to ascend, the other steamers were relieved of their masts and lightened in every possible way. While the other vessels of the squadron remained at anchor under Tuspan shoals, the steamers took in tow the gunboats and barges, which carried twelve hundred men and two pieces of artillery.

The steamers, with each a gun-boat in tow, soon ploughed their way across the bar, and gained the entrance of the river amid all the difficulties presented by the breakers. Having gained an entrance by twelve o'clock, the gallant Perry hoisted his broad pennant on board the Spitfire, and led the rest of the vessels. As they proceeded, two forts from the right bank opened on the squadron, when all the boats were manned with storming-parties, and while the gun-boats and steamers briskly returned the fire of the enemy, the storming-parties rushed on and into the forts, while the enemy in terror fled from before them. Continuing to press on towards the town, they were assailed by a fire from another fort and troops posted in the chaparral. The fort was soon carried, and simultaneously a division entered the town and took possession of it, while the enemy fled in every direction. After holding the place for some time, Commodore Perry demolished the forts, and retired, leaving the Albany and gun-boat Reefer to garrison the place.

Previous to the month of June, 1847, all the Mexican ports upon the gulf had now been captured, with the exception of the city of Tabasco; and, as the latter was in commercial importance second only to Vera Cruz, Commodore Perry determined upon its speedy reduction.

Accordingly, leaving the frigate Potomac before Vera Cruz, and a small naval force at Tuspan, Alvarado, and Laguna, for the protection of those places, Perry sailed on his proposed expedition, and on the 13th of June anchored off Tabasco bar with the following vessels of his squadron: Flag-Steamship Mississippi, Commander Adams; Albany, Captain Breese; Raritan, Captain Forrest; John Adams, Commander McCluney; Decatur, Commander Pinckney; Germantown, Commander Buchanan; bomb brig Stromboli, Commander Archer; bomb brig Vesuvius, Commander Magruder; brig Washington, Lieutenant-Commanding Phillips Lee; Steamer Scorpion, Commander Bigelow; Steamer Spitfire, Lieutenant-Commanding Smith Lee; Steamer Vixen, Lieutenant-Commanding William Smith.

By one o'clock, P. M., of the 14th, the flotilla selected for the expedition was fairly under way. The steamers Scourge, Scorpion, Spitfire, and Vixen, had towed over the bar the brigs Stromboli, Washington, and Vesuvius; and the three divisions of surf-boats, launches, and cutters, carrying seven field-pieces, and filled with officers and men detailed for service from the vessels of the squadron left behind. The city being situated seventy-five miles up the river, Tabasco could only be approached by vessels of the lightest draft. At Fronteira, the bomb brig Etna, Commander Van Brunt, and the schooner Bonita, Lieutenant-Commanding Berrien, joined the expedition.

Here the flotilla was reorganized, and after being formed into divisions, the ascent of the river was begun in the following manner:—

Perry in the Scorpion took the lead, with the brigs Vesuvius and Washington in tow, and the boats containing the detachments of officers and men from the Mississippi, Potomac, and John Adams.

The Spitfire towed the Stromboli and Bonita; and the Vixen towed the Etna, and detachments from the Germantown, Raritan, and Decatur.

In ascending the river, the commodore kept under way all

night.   At a distance of ten leagues from its mouth, the river was found to be contracted so much, that an enemy stationed in the thick chaparral covering the banks, could command the opposite shore with musketry alone.

It was not, however, until the evening of the 15th, that the enemy made any attempt to oppose the progress of the flotilla. General Bruno, who had posted himself with a strong detachment behind a breastwork in the chaparral, at the bend of the river where the channel ran close to the right bank, suddenly poured a plunging but ineffectual fire upon the deck of the Scorpion.   This attack, though totally unexpected, was instantly replied to by a fire of grape and canister from the Vesuvius and Washington, and by rapid volleys of musketry from their tops and from the Scorpion and the boats in tow.   These volleys effectually silenced the enemy, who shortly afterwards abandoned his breastwork with some loss, and the remainder of the divisions swept past without any molestation whatever.

By sunset the flotilla had arrived at the Seven Palms, a noted landmark two leagues below the city; and though it had been occasionally annoyed by desultory firing from the chaparral, the loss amounted to only one man wounded.

Near the landmark the enemy was found to occupy the right bank of the river in considerable numbers.   Night was now approaching, and as the channel by nearing that side subjected his men to a galling fire from the chaparral, Perry ordered the rigging to be barricaded with cots, hammocks, and bags; and thus sheltered, after making his preparations for a movement upon the city by land and water, the ensuing morning, he cast anchor, and rested his men against the toils of the morrow.

On the morning of the 16th, the boats of the flotilla, filled with their complement of men, were arranged in three divisions, under the respective commands of Captains Breese, Forrest, and

McCluney. The artillery formed a fourth division, under the command of Captain A. Slidell Mackenzie.

The schooner Bonita was now towed into position, for the double purpose of covering the landing and protecting the sounding-party under Lieutenants Alden and May.

Just as the latter had discovered an insufficiency of water for the brigs, the enemy opened a heavy fire of musketry from a concealed breastwork, called by them "Calmena," by which one officer and three men were wounded.

A raking fire of grape, canister, and musketry was promptly thrown from the flotilla along the bank and into the chaparral, by which that of the enemy was checked; and then Commodore Perry, standing erect in his barge in front of the first division, gave the spirit-stirring order, "Three cheers, and land!" Then burst forth the loud hurrahs! from over a thousand manly voices, and the sinewy rowers, bending simultaneously to their oars, impelled the numerous boats towards the right bank. Commodore Perry and Captain Mayo were the first to reach it, and in ten minutes afterwards, clambering up the steep bank and lifting the cannon rapidly to the top, the whole of the detachment, consisting of nine hundred seamen, including officers, and two hundred and twenty marines, were safely landed without hindrance or impediment.

While the little army, thus boldly debarked in the face of the enemy, were preparing to march upon the city, "the light-draft steamers Spitfire, Vixen, and Scourge, picked up all the boats, took them and the Bonita in tow, and stood for the city, followed by the Scorpion, who forced her way over the obstruction under a heavy head of steam."

These movements by land and water had the effect of disconcerting the enemy, who, expecting an attack by water only, found his strong works turned by a movement for which he was not prepared.

No sooner was the landing effected, than the enemy abandoned the position of " Calmena," and fell back to a breastwork nearer the city, where Colonel Hidalgo had stationed himself in force.

The naval army, led by the gallant commodore in person, now moved forward over a narrow trail, preceded by a pioneer party under Lieutenant Maynard. The distance to be traversed was about seven miles. The route lay for the most part through dense chaparral, with occasional cane-brake and marshy ground.

About one o'clock, the advance came within sight of Hidalgo's breastwork at Acachapan. This was a strong position, defended by cavalry and infantry, and strengthened by a battery mounting two guns. Here the enemy opened a harmless fire at long range, which being returned by the field-pieces under Mackenzie, Hidalgo was soon thrown into confusion; and the men, dashing forward with loud shouts, possessed themselves of the work just as the last of the enemy had evacuated it. The command was now halted to refresh. An hour previous to this, the steamers had been seen to pass up the river, and firing was afterwards heard in the direction of the city. This soon ceasing, it was conjectured that the city had surrendered; a supposition which was verified some three hours later by discovering the American flag displayed from the walls of Fort Iturbide, a work of considerable strength, erected on the skirts of the city, and commanding a long reach of the river below.

It was now ascertained that the Scorpion, having no boats in tow, passed the Spitfire and was the first to come within range of the guns of the fort.

The steamers soon silenced the fort, and when the Mexican flag was hauled down, the Scorpion passed up and received from the alcalde an offer for the surrender of the city. In the mean time, as the enemy had treacherously reopened a fire from the fort upon the Spitfire, Lieutenant Porter was despatched with a small force to storm the work. This duty was gallantly performed, and resulted in driving the enemy, and capturing two brass field-pieces and three long 28-pounders, with a considerable quantity of small arms and ammunition.

No sooner had Perry entered the city with his command, than, stationing the artillery and marines in the plaza, so as to command the principal streets, he drew off the rest of his men and quartered them on board the steamers for the night. At eight o'clock on the morning of the 17th, the colours of the United States were hoisted over the city of Tabasco, and a national salute fired.

The armory and magazine were then taken possession of by one detachment, while another party under Captain Mackenzie, dismantled Fort Iturbide, and removed the large guns to the river ready for embarkation. The arms were burnt; and the captured powder, not being of good quality, was destroyed, together with the magazine.

The next day, the mud walls of Fort Iturbide were mined and blown up, and then, the object of the expedition being successfully accomplished, the flotilla prepared to return, leaving Commander Van Brunt to hold possession of the city, with the bomb brig Etna, the steamers Spitfire and Scourge, and a detachment of seventy marines.

CHAPTER XXIX.

Consequences of the Occupation of the Capital—Condition of the Mexican Government—Disorganization of its Army—Santa Anna retires to Guadaloupe Hidalgo—Circular of Señor Alcorta to the Commandants-General—Resignation of the Presidency by General Santa Anna—His Letter to the Mexican People—Circular of Señor Pacheco—Reasons for abandoning the Capital—The future intentions of the Government developed—Santa Anna sets out for Puebla—Reflections upon his Reverses.

THE occupation of the capital by General Scott was an event from which the peace party in Mexico were soon to reap the most beneficial results.

The advocates for a continuance of the war still, indeed, predominated, both in numbers and in authority, but day by day the chiefs of this faction found their adherents grow more lukewarm, as their confidence of redemption by means of the national prowess gave way before the stern reality of the Anglo-Saxon conqueror quietly reposing himself in their very midst, and by his lion port frowning down all opposition.

It was now for the first time that the government began to feel the effects of its own treachery in regard to the unfortunate armistice. Grown bold in the strength of the defences by which the capital was surrounded at all points, and fully aware that the final struggle must take place long before any additional troops could arrive to strengthen the meagre force of their antagonist, the Mexican rulers were so inflated with the hope of a final and glorious success that the possibility of so disastrous a contingency as the loss of their capital seems scarcely to have been entertained at all.

62 (475)

When, therefore, it was found that the heroism of the Americans, rising with the occasion, had forced all the obstacles to the
city, and at length penetrated the city itself, the government dispersed in dismay, and all concert of action was lost in the general
confusion that ensued.

Of that boasted army, which on the morning of the 12th of
September numbered upwards of twenty thousand men, within
two days afterwards a few fragments alone remained; and though
the defection was glossed over in the official reports, and the disorganization systematized into imaginary divisions under different
military chiefs, it was well known that the orderly retirement
from the capital degenerated into a complete rout, long before the
remains of the panic-stricken troops reached the appointed place
of rendezvous.

At Guadaloupe Hidalgo, General Santa Anna concentrated
about his own person the few cavalry that yet were faithful to
their colours.   From this place also, the government commenced
the first of a series of spasmodic efforts, ostensibly to sustain the
flagging zeal of its adherents, but in reality for the purpose of
retrieving its own waning popularity, and of defending the General-in-chief from the fierce denunciations by which his civil
policy and military skill had been relentlessly assailed.

On the 14th of September, Señor Alcorta, immediately after
reaching Guadaloupe Hidalgo, addressed a circular to the commandants-general of the departments, in which he informed them
that, after the events which had taken place, it was found necessary to abandon the capital in order that other means might be
adopted and pursued for harassing the enemy.

He further notified them that the General-in-chief was still
firmly resolved to prosecute the war, and, whatever might be the
consequences, to wage it by all possible means; expressing at
the same time a hope that each commandant would endeavour to
preserve and reanimate the public spirit in his particular depart-

ment, in order that the war might be carried on with that vigour and energy so imperiously demanded by the national honour.

But the fatal reverses which had attended his efforts to beat back the invaders, had so weakened the popularity of the Mexican chief, that, foreseeing he should be unable to control the storm of indignation now boldly launched against him, General Santa Anna sought to shield himself from its fury by formally resigning, on the 16th of September, the presidency of the republic. By the same document he transferred the executive power into the hands of General Herrera and Señor Alcorta, and appointed Queretaro as the seat of government, subject to the decision of the National Congress, which was then about to meet.

On the same day he addressed the following letter to the Mexican people :—

" *The President of the Integral Republic of Mexico to his fellow-countrymen :*

" With the most poignant and profound grief do I announce to you that it was after repeated and extraordinary efforts, and after fifteen hours' incessant fighting, I saw myself under the necessity of abandoning the capital, with my ranks considerably thinned by the projectiles of the enemy, which penetrated our nearest lines, strewing the way with their bodies and with those of the noble Mexicans who so gloriously defended, inch by inch, the rights and honour of their country.

" You have been witnesses that I have created resources at a time when there were none ; that I laboured day and night; that I erected fortifications around Mexico ; that I organized and assembled a powerful army, in order that I might wrest some favour from fortune, which has been so adverse to us.

" The insubordination of one general subverted my entire plan of operations—a thing which you already know. In the convent and bridge of Churubusco the enemy received some very severe lessons, which were thrice repeated afterwards, in the fort of Chapultepec, the suburbs of Belen and San Cosmé, and finally in the Citadel.   But the valour of many of our soldiers of the guard and of the army was not always supported, yet it was only by fire and sword that the enemy, in a day most fatal to the nation, made himself master of the capital.   I have anxiously sought death in all parts, because a loss so great has occasioned me the most profound despair.   In Chapultepec I received a contusion, in Belen my clothes were pierced by the balls of the enemy, and around me disappeared the best soldiers of the republic.

" What remains to me, then, in the midst of the woe and anguish which assail me?   The unprofitable consciousness that I have personally sustained the combat to the very last extremity, and that I have sold dearly to the enemy his astonishing victory. He has seen me in the front at Angostura, Cerro Gordo, Churu-busco, Chapultepec, Belen, San Cosmé, and the Citadel, and he shall find me, I swear to you, wherever it shall be useful and glorious for me to combat.

" I ought also to announce to you that I have spontaneously resigned the Presidency of the Republic, calling to assume it, according to the Constitution, the President of the Supreme Court of justice, with the associates, who will be the depositaries of power until the National Congress can decide who is he to whose guidance shall be intrusted its future destinies.

" When power was intrusted to me under the most trying cir-cumstances, I accepted it in order that I might combine the elements of resistance existing in the country ; and, upon the enemy's advance towards the capital, I resumed military com-mand, that I might oppose to him a force of considerable strength, and concentrate all our resources for its defence.   But after the fall of the capital, circumstances have been altered, and now a division of the command is requisite to promote the same object —to attack the enemy in his line of communication from Vera

Cruz to the capital is imperiously urgent, and I alone must take upon myself that responsibility, because I feel it incumbent on me ever to place myself in that quarter in which there is the most peril.   The supreme magistracy cannot be exposed to the hazard of war, and it is necessary to locate it amid population and wealth, in order that it be not given over to anarchy, and in order that it may again arise with power and with glory.

" For this reason have I surrendered an authority, to me so laborious and so bitter, and in whose reception and laying down I have aspired to nothing more than the welfare of my beloved country.   I may have committed some errors in the discharge of my civil obligations, but be assured that my desires and my hopes have known no other stimulus than the noble one of sustaining the rank of the nation in which I first saw the light, and which has laden me with honours and with favours.

" I have said it before, and I here repeat it, that I never despair of the fate of my country.   If faction be silent and will listen to the sovereign voice ; if we be unanimous in our desires and in our yearnings, there is yet time to hurl the enemy from the soil which he pollutes by his presence.

" It is known to you that I rejected a peace which would reduce the republic to a nullity the most absurd and complete. The nation has desired and still desires war.   Let us continue it, then, with the greatest intrepidity, and my example shall be a most ardent one.

" Factions cannot now dispute with me concerning the power which with pleasure I abandon.   If they would dispute with me, let them come to the field of battle.   There they will find me serene, and firmly consecrated as ever, to the most generous and holy of causes.   What do we care for misfortunes?   Misfortune is the crucible of nations, and never is the Mexican nation grander than when she strives to force from destiny the victory which God and justice promise us.

"Mexicans! Thirty years have passed over since you proclaimed your independence amid perils and privations. Sustain
it for ever!

ANTONIO LOPEZ DE SANTA ANNA.

GUADALOUPE HIDALGO, Sept. 16, 1847."

In the above well written, but occasionally overstrained appeal,
General Santa Anna made use of the same arguments which he
had so often heretofore found available in moving and moulding
the Mexican mind; but the ears which had so frequently listened
favourably, were now deaf to the voice of the charmer.

This appeal was followed up, on the 18th, by a circular under
the signature of Señor Pacheco, Secretary of State, and addressed
to the governors of the different states.

In this document, the secretary enters into an elaborate defence
of the policy by which General Santa Anna had been guided in
the conduct of the war.

The disasters which attended the Mexican army in the various
conflicts around, and immediately before, the capital, he likewise
attributes mainly to the insubordination of General Valencia and
to his subsequent loss of the important position of Contreras. In
regard to the evacuation of the capital, he avers that it was decided
at a meeting of the generals held in the Citadel on the night of
the 13th, that a continued resistance would only expose the city
to pillage and to all the acts of immorality to which a savage
enemy abandons himself. It was this latter misfortune, he avers,
which General Santa Anna sought at all hazards to avoid, by
causing, at the commencement, all his fortifications to be made at
advanced points.

The result at which the generals arrived in their midnight conference was, that, in order to retain all their armament and the
means to continue the war, it was necessary to abandon the city
that very night; that the whole army should retire to Guadaloupe

Hidalgo, ready to take the road to Puebla, the next day, for the purpose of redeeming that city out of the hands of the Americans, and cutting off all communication with the coast.

This intent being, however, frustrated by the want of means, it was finally resolved to divide the army into sections, under the command of tried officers who were directed to make their way into the states of the interior, where each division might serve as a nucleus to be increased or shaped as subsequent circumstances might prove most beneficial.

The partition of the army accordingly took place, General Santa Anna retaining about his own person a portion of the cavalry only, proposing to unite these with the troops already before Puebla under General Rea, and carry out, as far as possible, his original design.

The exposition of Secretary Pacheco is valuable in two things; as explaining the reasons which led to the desertion of the capital, and elucidating the events which followed soon after. We therefore give it entire :—

" Toluca, Sept. 18, 1847.

Circular by Dr. Jose Ramon Pacheco, Secretary of State, to the Governors of the different States.

" Your Excellency: After having sent to your Excellency from the city of Guadaloupe Hidalgo the manuscript decree issued from that city under yesterday's date, by his Excellency the President *ad interim*, I have now the honour of sending you (blank) copies printed in this city, in order that your Excellency may circulate them in the state which you so worthily govern, and that the nation may be informed that it is not left without a head, as his Excellency, General Don Antonio Lopez de Santa Anna, previous to his march to commence his military movements against the base of the enemy's operations, has devolved the government upon the authority designed by the constitution.

His Excellency, by virtue of the extraordinary powers conferred on him, took the responsibility of ordering some details, which, from the force of circumstances, could not be done in conformity with the tenor of the constitution, none of the bodies in whom these attributes are vested being in existence. On this account he has dispensed with one of the necessary qualifications in one of the colleagues of the Executive, in order to give this additional guarantee to the nation. It is also desirable that the place fixed upon as the residence of the Supreme Government should be generally known, in order that all the functionaries and servants of the General Government should regulate their actions according to our political system as provided by the laws.

"Impartial history will some day record, whatever fate Providence may have decreed, the causes which brought about the events which have just occurred in the capital, in consequence of which it is now, to our astonishment, indignation, and grief, in the power of the enemy. These causes are known to thousands of witnesses, and well understood by those only who truly feel its immense loss to their country. The fact is that one of the points which defended the entries to the city having been abandoned without any orders, and another point having been taken at the end of the day on the 13th, after a combat of fifteen hours, it was decided by a meeting of the generals, held that night in the citadel, that a continued resistance would only expose the city to pillage, and to all the acts of immorality to which a savage enemy abandons himself. This latter was a misfortune which his Excellency wished to avoid at all hazards, and with a view to which he had at the very commencement caused the fortifications to be made at far advanced points. In order to retain on the other hand all his armament and the necessary means to continue the war, without owing them to a humiliating capitulation, it was resolved to evacuate the city that very night, conducting the whole army to the city of Guadaloupe de Hidalgo, in order to take the next day, according to the intentions of his Excellency, the road to Puebla, to redeem that city out of the power of the enemy, cutting off at the same time all communication with Vera Cruz.

"The troops having already commenced the march, and having made some progress on the road, it became known, as much to our satisfaction as surprise, that the people, who the day before, although supported by the army and the valiant National Guards, had taken no part in the struggle, had undertaken on their own account the extermination of the invaders. Immediately the army was countermarched, and two columns, one under the command of his Excellency and the other under General Don Juan Alvarez, penetrated as far as the streets of Santo Domingo, and La Cerca, lancing some of the Americans. Subsequently, after some measures and other circumstances which it is unnecessary to mention, the heroic people of the capital were disarmed.

"In undertaking to carry out his first intent, the most formidable obstacle to be encountered was the entire want of means. The troops had been five days without any support. His Excellency the President had exhausted all his personal resources. From the 19th of August, the date of the misfortune at Padierna, to which our present situation is to be ascribed, up to that day—that is, in twenty-six days—not a man nor a dollar had been sent from any part. How could it be exacted, or even expected, that the city of Mexico, which had already made so many sacrifices, should alone carry on the war and bear the weight of the burdens which are destroying the nation? To the evils of the war, caused by the invaders, it would not have become the government to add those of making the army live at the expense of the people; and yet to disband the troops, in order that they might devastate the roads and villages, would have been a still greater evil. The difficulty was insuperable, as there

63

was no food on that day for the soldiers, and the situation was dreadful.

" His Excellency the President, since his return to the republic, has above all had to contend with difficulties of this nature, and to them is to be attributed the greater part of our misfortunes; but rather than destroy a force which, after being purified and organized in a different manner, could still be rendered serviceable to the nation, he embraced the middle course, of dividing the army into sections, under the command of tried officers, giving them instructions as to the roads they were to take, his Excellency reserving for himself a part of the cavalry. In this manner were obviated the great evils of a disbandment of the army: the burden was distributed so as not to weigh on a single district, and above all it furnished to the States of the Interior a nucleus which they could increase or shape as they might like, in order to carry on the war, which they have all demanded, without listening to any propositions of peace from the enemy.

" As regards political organization, his Excellency saw the extreme of perplexity of another kind in which he was placed by his determination to continue, personally, the defence of the independence of his country until one of the reverses of which so many have fallen upon us, through the will of God and our own dissensions, and under which we are suffering, should put an end to his existence. His Excellency did not wish to be invested with the character of President of the Republic, in conformity with the resolution of August of last year, his desire being to devote himself exclusively to carrying on the war against the invaders; and if he has since assumed that power, it was to put down a civil war which was raging in the capital, and, finally, to raise the necessary resources to place it in a state of defence.

" His Excellency saw that there was no one before whom he could make his resignation, in order to release himself from that onerous charge which prevented him from pursuing the only object of his

ardent desires, and which had drawn upon him so many annoy-
ances; that all his efforts and repeated orders had been in vain
to bring about a meeting of the Congress, composed of a hundred
and forty members, which never held its regular sessions for
want of numbers, and of which hardly twenty-six members could
be assembled on occasions when he applied to it to discharge the
mission which had been confided to it, and in order that the Executive might do no more than to carry out the will of the representatives of the nation. His Excellency saw that, for the new
operations which he meditated, it would be necessary that he
should be personally absent from the centre; and that, moving
with his forces in different directions, the very uncertainty of his
movements would occasion great difficulties in the administration
of the government; he saw, finally, the consummation of the
triumph of the enemy by abandoning these questions to the views
of designing partisans. Under these circumstances, his Excellency determined to issue the decree which I communicated to
your Excellency, and of which I have the honour to annex a
printed copy, by which his Excellency, the President *ad interim*,
endeavoured to consult not only the observance of the fundamental law in a great crisis, but also the spirit of the law and the
will of the nation, manifested on former occasions.

"His Excellency only intends by this decree to fill a vacuum
in the present circumstances, to preserve a representation of the
unity and nationality of the republic—the capital of which is in
possession of the enemy—but by no means to impose his will
upon his fellow-citizens. Far from this, he has on this occasion
only taken upon himself the solution of the difficulty, because,
neither at the capital, which is its legal residence, nor in any
other part of the republic, is there a legislative body, and he is
ready to abide by whatever it may decide.

"After acts so pure, originating in intentions so honourable,
there will not be wanting vile passions that always will accuse

after a misfortune, and upon that very account they are the more reprehensible. His Excellency the President carries in his garments, in the death of individuals allied to his person, and in his own person, irrefragable testimonials of his self-denial to devote himself to his country. General Santa Anna does not despair on account of these misfortunes, nor on account of ingratitude, which is still worse. His Excellency renounces power, and yet it is possible that stupidity may join with malice to add absurd calumnies to his other immense disasters. He abandons power, and with it consigns three facts to history for his eternal honour.

" First, that at the north, at the east, and at the capital, although with various fortune, he has been found confronting the enemies of his country, appearing at all points of the battle, and in those most exposed to danger ; secondly, that in all the States their respective authorities, as well individuals as corporations, remain in the free exercise of their functions and in the enjoyment of their respective laws; thirdly, that the nation, and the government which may be called to preside over it, will have absolute liberty to act as may seem proper with regard to the question of war or peace with the United States, since it has been proved that neither the presence of their cannon nor the approach of a danger which has since become a reality, have had any influence on what was due by the government of his Excellency General Santa Anna to the divinity of his country nor to his own honour. The government has not taken a step, nor has it had a single communication with the enemy but what is within the reach of all his compatriots, nor has it been bound by any compromise, past, present, or future. If in the publications which have been made it may have excited surprise, and not without reason, not to have found the discussions which were expected from the general and the commissioner of the government of the United States, it was that the contempt with which they treat us, and the unblushing determination which they have taken to carry on a war the most infamous and sanguinary, for their simple diversion and pleasure, no other answer could be given, except through the cannon's mouth and death.

"His Excellency the President *ad interim* orders the undersigned to communicate to your Excellency the preceding exposition, at the time transmitting to you the decree of his resignation, reserving to himself to give at a proper time to his fellow-citizens a circumstantial manifesto; he has also enjoined him particularly to state in his name to the new Constitutional Government, that he will not lay down his arms against the enemy of his country, until this government, or whatever government may be nominated by the nation or Congress, shall order him to lay them down; that he will be its firmest support against any revolution, as also in every matter which may be determined as to the American question, be it peace or war; that he will comply in his quality of subject with the national will legitimately expressed, as he always has done in his capacity of First Magistrate, and that his Excellency wishes to be the first to give an example of submission to the authority of the laws.   God and liberty!

"I have the honour to be, with distinguished consideration,

PACHECO.

"His Excellency the Governor of ——."

There is something at this period of the war in regard to the condition of General Santa Anna which commands our pity, even while the knowledge of his former duplicity forbids our esteem. Suddenly fallen from the topmost height of national honour; deserted by his former friends and parasites; anathematized by many of his own countrymen; and soon to experience that even remote and secluded cities offered no secure refuge from the untiring pursuit of his warlike and energetic foes, he exhibited the sad spectacle of a once goodly ship shorn of the white and expansive adjuncts by which she was formerly impelled in graceful and imposing state, and rolling helplessly, a shattered hulk, upon a stormy sea, subject to the sport of every wind and the treachery of every wave.

The fact that General Santa Anna had made great personal sacrifices for the Mexican nation, even to the impairment of his private fortune ; that he had succeeded in organizing three large armies; that he had raised unexpected, though limited supplies; that he infused an unwonted energy and uniformity of action into the complex machinery of government; that he had stilled the unnatural feud existing between opposite factions in the republic ; that he had blended, for a time, the heterogeneous elements of which parties are composed in that unhappy land; that he had built admirable fortifications, at points judiciously selected for defence, and that he had offered a steady and continuous, though unavailing resistance to the American arms, wherever resistance promised success, should at least have shielded him from many of the calumnies to which his ill-success had exposed him, and should have taught the Mexican people to look leniently even upon his errors.   No other man in the republic possessed either the power or the ability to have achieved as much in its defence ; and though his frequent manifestoes exhibit an absence of that modesty so becoming in a great man, there is little doubt the peculiar idiosyncrasy of the Mexican mind had often before mistaken the vapourings of Ancient Pistol for the self-sacrificing spirit of Leonidas.

CHAPTER XXX.

City of Puebla threatened by General Rea—Situation of the Garrison—Loss of an American Detachment—Puebla invested—Summons of General Santa Anna to Colonel Childs—His noble Reply—Operations of the Besiegers—General Santa Anna leaves the city to intercept General Lane—Successful Sortie from the Garrison—The Besiegers Reinforced—Severe Street-fight—Approach of General Lane—The Siege raised.

In the mean time the city of Puebla was seriously threatened by General Rea. No sooner was this active partisan chief aware that the divisions under General Scott had left Puebla, and were fairly on their march towards the capital, leaving behind them only a weak garrison to hold the former city, than he moved down from his fastnesses, and after hovering about Puebla for some time in the hope of cutting off foraging-parties from the garrison, he commenced its investment on the 13th of September. Left entirely isolated, without communication with the coast, or the possibility of aid from General Scott, the situation of Colonel Childs as Governor of Puebla was in every respect a critical one.

With a slender command, amounting in all to only three hundred and ninety-three men, exclusive of convalescents from the hospitals under his charge, he had to garrison the grand depot of San José within the city, and the forts of Loreto and Guadalupe, two tolerably strong works crowning the heights to the east of Puebla, and distant from it about a mile.

The first open act of hostility by which the presence of General Rea was signalized, resulted in a loss to the Americans, which, considering the weakness of the respective garrisons, may be considered serious.

489

On the morning of the 26th of August an express arrived at San José, with the tidings that the guerrilleros had broken into the stock-yard near Fort Loreto, and driven off in the direction of Camargo seven hundred and fifty mules.

Five teamsters immediately started in pursuit; but after a slight skirmish, in which one Mexican was killed, this small party were driven in by superior numbers. Unable to dispense with the services either of the cavalry or infantry, which constituted the effective force of the already too limited garrison of San José, Colonel Childs consented to the formation of an irregular force of mounted men for the purpose of pursuing the guerrilleros and recovering the stolen animals. This little detachment, consisting of thirty-three men under the command of Captain Blanchard, of the Quartermaster's department, followed the tracks of the mules for some miles, until they were lost in the bed of a ravine.

With the reckless impetuosity of the American character, the advance guard clambered across the ravine closely followed by their companions, and were in the act of dashing over the crest of the hill beyond, when they were fired upon from a clump of trees, and a few guerrilleros were seen in full flight towards an old stone building at the foot of the hill.

Unconscious of the trap which had been laid for him, Blanchard gave the order to charge upon the fugitives, when the chase was suddenly arrested by the appearance of the main body of the guerrilleros darting out from their hiding-places among the willows beyond.

Finding himself thus drawn into an ambuscade, with bodies of lancers increasing on all sides, until their numbers, including the infantry afterwards discovered, amounted to eight hundred men, Blanchard ordered his men to retreat in the direction of the city. In an instant the whole array of the enemy was let loose upon them, and, like a pack of famished wolves panting for blood, they sprang from all points of the compass, and with screams and *vivas* darted towards the common centre formed by the devoted band they had so successfully decoyed.

On approaching the ravine so lately crossed with impunity, the opposite bank was found lined with the enemy, holding their lances ready couched for the attack. As the ravine only admitted the passage of a single man at a time, it would have been madness to have attempted its passage in the face of an enemy possessing the advantage both of position and numbers.

Hemmed in on all sides by a force continually increasing, Captain Blanchard, who had hitherto kept his little command well together, now gave the mournful order for every man to look to himself, and sell his life as dearly as possible.

In an instant his command scattered in all directions; some forced their way across the ravine, and precipitating themselves upon the enemy died hardily, pierced with innumerable wounds; others dashed along the bank of the ravine in search of a more favourable outlet, but the quivering lances met them at every point. A few sought the tempting refuge of a neighbouring cornfield, but were forced back by finding it filled with infantry. Tossed to and fro, the little band of victims turned daringly upon their pursuers, and fighting desperately, died literally hacked to pieces. Of thirty-three men only eleven, more fortunate than their comrades, succeeded in cutting their way through the dense ranks of the enemy, or in outstripping pursuit by the superior fleetness of their horses. Among the victims was the brave Captain Blanchard.

During the three following weeks, the enemy, as if satisfied with his bloody achievement, remained inactive, or contented himself merely with cutting off such straggling soldiers as chanced to fall in his way. This interval was improved by Colonel Childs, who, confining his defence to the principal squares around the Plaza, threw up breastworks across the principal streets that

64

led to it, and by the energy of his foraging-parties was enabled to obtain a small but much needed supply of provisions.

On the night of the 13th the investment commenced in earnest. Emboldened by the cautious policy to which Colonel Childs prudently restricted his command, the guerrilleros entered the city, and combining with a portion of the citizens, seized such positions as could be made available, and opened a heavy fire upon San José from the tops of houses and churches, from balconies, and from the corners of the various streets leading to the Plaza.

As the safety of the posts of Loreto and Guadaloupe depended upon the successful defence of San José, the immediate command of the latter was intrusted to Lieutenant-Colonel Black, of the 1st Pennsylvania regiment, with Captain Ford's company of cavalry, Captain Miller's company of 4th artillery, and four companies of the 1st Pennsylvania regiment, together with such convalescents from the hospital under his charge as were enabled from time to time to do duty.

The point of attack being San José, the enemy, in constantly increasing force, kept up an incessant firing upon that post by day and night, in the vain hope of breaking down the courage of its defenders through the effects of utter physical exhaustion.

On the 23d of September, a joyous ringing of bells throughout the city announced the arrival of General Santa Anna; but the melodious congratulations were speedily silenced by a discharge of shot and shells from Loreto into the heart of the city.

On the 25th, General Santa Anna, having united his force with that of General Rea, and assumed command of the whole, despatched the following message to Colonel Childs, in which he informed him he was surrounded by eight thousand men, and demanded his evacuation of the city and of the posts of Loreto and Guadaloupe within a certain and peremptory time.

"HEAD-QUARTERS, PUEBLA,
September 25, 1847.

" Having taken possession of this city with the forces under
my command, to operate against the points occupied by you,
and for the purpose of restoring to full liberty the citizens who
have suffered so much from the troops of the United States, I
deem it proper, before making any movement, and for the sake
of humanity, to intimate to your Excellency that you shall have
leave, within a limited time, to abandon the places you now
occupy in this city, and march out with the honours of war, either
to join General Scott, or to proceed to Perote, as may be most
convenient for you. But if this moderate proposition be not
accepted by your Excellency, I shall, in that case, with the deepest feeling, proceed to act in a military manner, and assault all
of your positions, and from the consequences of which your troops
must suffer, inasmuch as there is in the vicinity of your Excellency an army of eight thousand men, determined to cause the
rights of this nation to be respected. God and liberty!

ANTONIO LOPEZ DE SANTA ANNA,
General-in-chief, Mexican Army.

Señor Colonel CHILDS,
Commander of the United States forces in this city."

To this demand Colonel Childs immediately replied by the
following letter, in which, after indignantly denying that any
outrages had been committed upon the citizens of Puebla, as was
insinuated in the message of the Mexican general, he proceeded
to contrast the conduct of the Mexican with that of the American
troops, and concluded with a quiet defiance worthy of all honour.

"HEAD-QUARTERS, CITY OF PUEBLA, MEXICO,
September 25, 1847.

" I had the honour to receive this day (2 o'clock, P. M.) the
note of your Excellency, of this date, notifying me that you had

taken possession of this city, and ' for the purpose of restoring to full liberty the citizens who have suffered so much from the troops of the United States,' and also offering the garrison certain terms in case they would, in a limited time, abandon the points occupied by the same.

" In regard to the first point, I deem it necessary and just, in vindication of the good name of the military forces of the United States—which they have earned by the humanity, good order, and discipline which have at all times distinguished their conduct, and more particularly while holding military possession of the city of Puebla—to deny the imputation conveyed in your Excellency's communication; but, on the contrary, would assert that the rights of persons and property have been most scrupulously respected, and maintained to a degree unparalleled in warfare; and would willingly leave the question for the decision of the intelligent and impartial portion of the population of this city, by whom have they suffered most violence, from their own people, or from troops of the army of the United States.

" As for the other portion of your Excellency's communication, demanding a surrender, within a limited time, of the places held by the troops under my command, I have but this reply to make to your Excellency: that having been honoured with the custody and safe-keeping of these places, it is alike my desire and my duty to maintain them to the last, feeling fully confident in the means at my disposal to accomplish that purpose.

" With considerations of high respect, I have the honour to be, your Excellency's most obedient servant,

THOMAS CHILDS, *Col. U. S. A.*,

Civil and Military Governor.

To his Excellency Señor DON LOPEZ DE SANTA ANNA,
 Commander-in-chief of the Mexican army before this city."

No sooner was this reply transmitted to General Santa Anna, than Colonel Childs rode to the different posts and informed his

GENERAL THOMAS CHILDS.

troops of the demand which had been made and the tenor of his reply. The hearty and enthusiastic cheers with which his information was greeted on all sides, showed that he had not miscalculated the courage and the spirit of his men.

Few in numbers, and beset by a large army and a hostile population, with but a scanty store of subsistence and a slender supply of ammunition, weakened already with continuous watching, and without hope of any immediate relief, these heroic little garrisons looked forward to renewed and painfully wearying exertions with a serenity unshaken by the hazard of their position, and a resolute determination to endure all things rather than stain the American name with the ignominy of having surrendered a post of such vital importance to the safety of their victorious comrades in the capital, and the reinforcements which might be hastening up from below.

On the 27th, the Mexicans having taken possession of the strong stone monasteries and convents of San Juan de Dios, San Juan, Santa Monica, and Santa Rosa, opened from these points a fire of artillery and small-arms upon San José, which was vigorously responded to by the latter, and by the guns of Fort Loreto. Late in the evening the cannonading ceased, but was resumed the next morning, and continued throughout the day with equal spirit on both sides.

During the night of the 29th, the enemy succeeded in establishing two 6-pounders in position above the Tivoli, from which he opened with vigour on the morning of the 30th; but, anticipating this movement, Colonel Childs, by a wise forecast, had thrown up a traverse across the Plaza, and withdrawn a 12-pounder from Loreto, by which he was enabled to answer the fire.

Towards night his battery ceased; and, failing in all his attempts to force the Americans from their position, General Santa Anna transferred the conduct of the siege into the hands of General Rea, and set out on the 1st of October, with four thousand men, and three pieces of artillery, for the purpose of intercepting the reinforcements which were understood to be approaching under General Lane.

Taking advantage of this reduction in the strength of the enemy, Colonel Childs directed a sortie to be made against those barricades and buildings by which the garrison at San José had been most annoyed. One of the expeditions was confided to Captain Small, of the 1st Pennsylvania volunteers. "Passing through the walls of an entire square with fifty men, he succeeded, after an incessant labour of twenty-four hours, in gaining a position opposite the barricade, and drove the enemy with great loss, they leaving seventeen dead on the ground. The barricade, consisting of one hundred and fifty bales of cotton, was consumed."* Other prominent buildings were also blown up and demolished by parties commanded by Lieutenant Laidley, of the Ordnance, and Captain Herron, of the 1st Pennsylvania regiment.

From the 2d of September, until the 8th, the firing on the part of the enemy was of a more desultory character; but on the last-mentioned day, the besiegers having been strongly reinforced, attempted a closer investment, but were eventually driven back with loss.

From this time their efforts began to relax, and, on the morning of the 12th, they were discovered in the act of retiring from the positions they had so long and so unavailingly occupied.

A severe fire being still kept up from the corner of a street upon the breastwork, Colonel Black moved down with two companies for the purpose of silencing it. Seeing the enemy retire at his approach, he directed Captain Herron, with one company, to move round the plaza, and, if possible, cut off their retreat, while an attack was being made in front by the remaining company.

After a short time, firing was heard in the direction by which Captain Herron had advanced, and on hastening to his support,

* Report of Colonel Childs.

Colonel Black found the company enveloped by clouds of lancers, and fighting desperately. The timely reinforcement saved the remains of the gallant little detachment from being utterly annihilated ; the enemy was driven back and the company rescued, after having experienced a loss of thirteen killed, and four severely wounded. But relief was now near at hand ; for, while the firing still continued, the worn-out garrisons were cheered by the welcome sight of reinforcements under General Lane. This brave and energetic officer, after beating at Huamantla the strong force under General Santa Anna, hastened to the relief of Puebla.

As soon as he reached the city, and found that the contest was still raging, he dashed without pause upon the besiegers, and, aided by the now liberated garrisons, drove them from their breastworks and other positions, and effectually broke up an investment which had kept the besieged almost incessantly harassed for thirty days and nights.

This memorable siege is remarkable as developing a novel and important phase in the character of the American soldier. Hitherto the qualities of energy, spirit, determination, and unexampled daring, had been most conspicuously displayed. He was now to exhibit the higher faculty of passive endurance. Weak in point of numbers, surrounded by watchful enemies, and deprived for thirty days and nights of that necessary repose from incessant toil, by which the physical powers are recruited and sustained, like the ancient Roman soldier at the Pompeian gate, he remained firmly at his post, choosing rather to die, if need be, amidst the fiery storm than desert a trust confided to him by his superiors.

CHAPTER XXXI.

Communication with the Coast reopened—Steady increase of Reinforcements from the United States—The Guerrilleros driven from their Strongholds—Advance of General Lane—Battle of Huamantla—Heroism of Captain Walker—Repels the Lancers in repeated charges—Hemmed in by the Enemy—His daring Stratagem —His Death—Chivalric Character of Walker—Official Tribute to his Memory— Lane marches to Puebla.

THE communication between Vera Cruz and the capital, which had so long been cut off by intervening parties of the enemy, was at length effectually opened.

The steady increase of reinforcements from the United States, permitted the establishment of posts at the long-neglected points of the National Bridge and Plan del Rio, whilst the reoccupation of Jalapa by a competent garrison, and the possession of the castle of Perote, and of the forts commanding the city of Puebla, completed the links in the chain of communication which were never afterwards severed.

Thus driven from their strongholds, and divested in a certain degree of those powers of annoyance, which, arising from the numerical weakness of their adversary, declined with his strength, the guerrilleros congregated in various small towns, remotely situated, and of difficult access to any but those who were acquainted with the topography of the country.

Broken up into hills and ravines, intersected by water-courses, the roads themselves were mule paths, winding through rugged passes whose precipitous sides offered a safe protection to the enemy above or beyond ; and these paths also, often obstructed by loose masses of lava, or broken up by cavities and fissures,

498

the impracticable character of the ground, was in every respect suited to the nature of guerrilla warfare, and well calculated to set at defiance the efforts of any troops, less energetic and determined than those of the United States.

But the cities of Huamantla, Atlixco, Orizaba, and Matamoros, places, which had hitherto swarmed with guerrilla bands, were no longer to afford them a secure refuge. The duty which Captain Walker was refused permission to undertake, was soon to be effectually performed by a much stronger force, under General Lane.

Leaving Vera Cruz with a considerable train, and with reinforcements to the number of two thousand men, this gallant officer succeeded in reaching Perote almost entirely unmolested. Learning at this place of the investment of Puebla, he marched promptly to the relief of that garrison, taking with him Brough's regiment of Ohio volunteers, Captain Simmon's battalion of three companies, and Lieutenant Pratt's battery; these were subsequently detached, to guard the train at San Antonio Tamaris. The remainder of his command consisted of Colonel Wynkoop's battalion from Perote; Colonel Gorman's battalion of Indiana volunteers; Captain Heintzelman's battalion of six companies; Major Lally's regiment of four companies of mounted men, under command of Captain Samuel H. Walker, and five pieces of artillery under Captain George Taylor.

At various points along the road, tidings came to General Lane, that a large force of the enemy was concentrating between Perote and Puebla, for the purpose of disputing his advance.

Nothing definite, however, was received until the evening of the 8th of October, when the train reached San Antonio Tamaris. While halting to rest at this hacienda, certain spies brought in word, that General Santa Anna, with a force of four thousand men and six pieces of artillery, was at the city of Huamantla, but was preparing to leave it, for the purpose of occupying the

65

Black Pass, six miles distant; and from that impregnable position holding the American force at bay, until the garrison of Puebla, already reduced to the last extremity, should be compelled to surrender to General Rea.*

To avert the possibility of this disaster, and, by falling upon the enemy unawares, to seize his artillery before it could be removed to positions too difficult of access, General Lane determined to commence his march at once, and endeavour to bring on an engagement at Huamantla.

Parking his train at the hacienda, under guard of the troops already mentioned, he pressed on with the rest of his command, in the hope of coming up with the enemy before he should have left the city.

On approaching within five miles of Huamantla, Captain Walker was directed to push on quickly with his cavalry, and, by making an intrepid dash at the enemy, keep him engaged until the infantry could come up. His orders were also to secure the artillery at all hazards.†

These instructions were promptly obeyed. Throwing in advance a couple of his own men, with orders to feel the enemy and ascertain if possible the position of his artillery, Walker himself, at the head of his command, kept on at an easy pace until he reached the outskirts of the city.

Before entering a narrow lane thickly lined on each side with overarching maguey bushes, the squadron was closed compactly up, moving by twos and fours, as the nature of the ground admitted.

In the mean time, this advance-guard being driven in, reported

---

* When General Lane entered the city of Puebla on the 13th of October, such was the haggard and exhausted condition of its defenders, that it was supposed to have been almost physically impossible for them to have held out two days longer.

† This differs materially from the official report; but, as it comes from the lips of one who heard distinctly the orders given, it is but just to rescue the memory of the intrepid Walker from the charge of rashness implied in the report.

the enemy still in force in the plaza and adjacent streets, but evidently preparing to retire.

Throwing these men again in front, Walker rapidly seized the opportunity which the confusion of the enemy offered, and as soon as his command neared the plaza, he ordered the trumpet to sound a charge. Of the four companies under his command, only his own company of seventy-five men responded to the call of their heroic leader.* These, spurring forward with enthusiastic shouts, gallopped into the plaza, seized the cannon from the affrighted artillerists, and then precipitated themselves upon the supporting force of some four hundred lancers.

Foremost of all in this noble charge was the gallant Walker. Firing his revolvers with a cool, steady, equable movement, his unerring hand brought down an enemy with every shot. And then, closing up, looking neither to the right hand nor the left, nor turning once back to see by whom he was supported, he kept his place in the advance, and wherever the enemy attempted to make a stand, dashed upon him with a cry of triumph, and tore a bloody pathway through.

The fierce impetuosity of such a charge no enemy could long withstand. Closely followed by his own daring company, the lancers were soon put to rout, and pursued out of the city and beyond it for more than a mile.

Flushed with success, Walker returned to the plaza, and while the rest of his command was coming slowly in from the pursuit, those that remained about him were engaged in securing the

---

* None of the other companies of cavalry were in the engagement at all; nor did they make their appearance until the infantry was near at hand and their services no longer of any paramount importance. The terrific conflict at Huamantla was borne by Walker's Rifles only: had these been properly supported, they would have been saved from almost utter annihilation, and the fate of their heroic commander might have been different.

From this censure a part of the officers must be relieved. Captains Lewis and Besancon, and Lieutenants Anderson and Waters rode off from their commands, and, joining the Rifles, fought most gallantly.

cannon already captured. But the triumph of the daring victors was destined to be of short duration. While thus busily employed, to the number of twenty-five men only, the look-out stationed in the steeple of the church opposite, warned Captain Walker that the fugitive lancers, powerfully reinforced, were gallopping impetuously towards the plaza.

Sheltering his horses behind the wall of a convent-yard, Walker stationed his dismounted men at the windows of the house adjoining, and coolly awaited the expected charge. Riding fiercely up the streets, with that triumphant confidence which the knowledge of their immense superiority inspired, the lancers dashed into the plaza.

In an instant the whole front rank, as if simultaneously struck by the same lightning-flash, fell dead. For one moment—it was only for one moment—their comrades continued to advance ; but a plunging fire from the first and second stories of the house, and from behind the parapet of the roof, drove them back in huddled-up confusion.

Retreating out of rifle-shot, they could yet be seen hanging irresolutely about the edges of the streets leading to the plaza, while the movements and gesticulations of their officers indicated that they were endeavouring to urge the men to make another attack.

But the fear of the deadly and unerring rifle made them for a time hold back. At intervals, indeed, the numerous trumpets would blow a charge, and then the enemy, as if lashed into firmness, would move out for a short distance, but after settling themselves in their saddles, their brief stimulus seemed to desert them ; they would move on, then hesitate, then halt altogether, and at length, overcome by their fears, wheel round and return to their starting-place.

But this hesitation and timidity, though affecting in a like degree some of the Mexican officers, did not extend to all. A few brave men were seen riding across the front, urging, imploring, commanding, and even threatening, but all in vain. At last, one heroic spirit, as if determined to excite the courage of his command by his own brilliant example, gallopped out from their midst, and dashed alone across the plaza, waving his sword and calling upon his men to follow. The gallant fellow succeeded in reaching the gate of the convent-yard, and there fell riddled with balls.

The Mexicans were now seen for some time in earnest consultation, but after a while this ended, and then they scattered in various directions, swept round interior streets, and reappeared, choking up every avenue leading to the plaza.

The object of this movement was soon discovered. Two-thirds of the Rifles, who had been carried away by the ardour of pursuit, or were sent out in search of the missing artillery, were now seen by the look-out hovering beyond the dense masses of lancers, vainly endeavouring to find some break in the hostile circle by which they might rejoin their companions. It was, therefore, to cut off these men from all hope of succour that the lancers had occupied all those streets by which they might have succeeded in reaching the plaza.

No sooner, however, was Captain Walker made acquainted with the situation of his men, than he adopted a daring stratagem for their release.

Leaving behind him a few men under Lieutenant Claiborne to garrison the house and protect the artillery from recapture, he mounted the rest of his command, and sallying into the plaza, commenced what seemed to be a retreat. Immediately he left the protection of the enclosure, the lancers darted out from the different streets and bore down upon him in converging line. The avenues being thus partially cleared, and many of his stragglers having succeeded in passing through, Walker now suddenly wheeled his little command, and furiously charging the enemy, attempted to cut his way back to the convent yard.

His whole command numbered at this time scarcely more than twenty men, while the intervening space was literally crammed with the dense masses of the enemy.

In front, and by successive leaps, rather than by regular progression, he plunged upon the nearest of the enemy, and won by a length at a time the ground occupied by his foes. Standing erect in his stirrups, with his clenched teeth gleaming white from beneath the tightly-drawn upper lip and its long red overshadowing moustache, those who saw the gallant soldier at this fearful time, still call to mind with terrible distinctness how the blood trickled down from his uplifted sword, and, falling across his hand, died with crimson streaks the white mane of his horse; and they remember, too, with what surpassing coolness his commands were uttered, even while the incessant attacks of the lancers were gradually lessening the number of his devoted followers.

Swayed to and fro by the pressure of accumulating numbers, now dashing onward a few paces, and now forced back to the wall, the little band of twenty, finally reduced to only seven men, succeeded at length in reaching to within a few yards of the convent gate. But they could proceed no further. Their former spirited attacks were now changed to incessant yet hopeless parryings of the lance-points thrust at them from all sides. But, at the moment when all seemed lost, the captured gun in front of the gateway was turned upon the lancers by some of the slender garrison, and Lieutenant Claiborne made the attempt to fire it with his pistol. The lancers, on seeing this, gave way, and Captain Walker, followed by his sorely diminished troop, dashed at the gate, and entered it with a loss of thirteen men.

These, with the stragglers, who had succeeded in getting through, soon commenced a destructive fire from the windows and roof, and the baffled enemy once more fell back and occupied the neighbouring streets.

It was at this time, when the enemy had entirely deserted the plaza, that Captain Walker stepped out a few paces from the gateway, and was in the act of directing his men to draw the captured cannon nearer to the yard; when, in the midst of the most profound silence, the report of a single gun was heard, and those who looked across the square, saw the smoke issue from a window of the house opposite, and from which a white flag had been flying during the whole engagement. In another instant a sharp agonizing cry arose, and then passed from lip to lip of the bereaved garrison the fearful words: " Captain Walker is killed!" It was but too true; the treacherous ball fired from behind, had entered the shoulder, and passing obliquely downwards came out on the side. He fell instantly and was carried within the yard. In half an hour he was dead.

With his last breath, his heroic exhortation to his sorrowing command was: " Never surrender!"

Thus fell, in the very vigour of manhood, one of the most remarkable men of the age. As a partisan soldier, he had not, perhaps, his equal in any service—prompt, daring, and energetic, his fiery ardour was yet tempered in the midst of danger by the most imperturbable coolness.

With a constitution confirmed and strengthened by a life of toil and hardship—a life full of romantic incidents and terrible episodes, he was able to endure the vicissitudes of climates and hunger and thirst and prolonged fatigue, to an extent, and with an apparent insensibility, that was a theme and a wonder to all who knew him.

To a most thorough knowledge of the cunning, treacherous, and cruel character of the enemy, he united an intense personal hatred, the result of foregone and painful experiences. But yet, fierce as he at all times proved himself, both in the random fight and in the headlong charge, no man was more humane, even to the enemy he despised, when the brunt of the battle was over, and the wounded lay about him.

To disabled men and defenceless women, he was at all times a sure friend and a protector. Even in the last fatal battle of Huamantla, he was seen to alight from his horse in the midst of the street, tie up with his own hands the dislocated jaw of a stricken enemy, and remove him to the wall, lest he should be trampled upon by advancing horsemen.

His conduct towards his own command was a happy compound of decision and kindness. To all the duties of a well disciplined soldier, he exacted the most implicit obedience. His discipline, both as respects the cavalry exercise and rifle practice, was of the most rigid character; but at the same time, his thoughtful regard for the comfort of his men was so well known, and his attention to their requirements so steady and unremitting, that the strict disciplinarian was soon forgotten in the kind-hearted man, and a love sprang up between himself and his command, that, with the few who yet survive, will remain a tender and a tearful memory for ever.

Nor was his loss mourned by his own company only, it was felt by the whole army. One with whom he had been at variance, a gallant, generous, open-hearted man, when he heard of his death, burst into tears and exclaimed : " I would have given two years of my life, but for fifteen minutes' speech with Captain Walker;" and even the official report of the commanding general rises into a mournful dignity, when announcing the event. With a brevity that approaches the sublime, it says :—

" This victory is saddened by the loss of one of the most chivalric, noble-hearted men that graced the profession of arms— Captain Samuel H. Walker, of the mounted riflemen. Foremost in the advance, he had routed the enemy when he fell mortally wounded."

How otherwise than so gloriously, should an heroic spirit like his desire to die ?

After the death of Captain Walker, the command devolved upon Captain Lewis. The enemy made one more attempt upon the convent-yard and the house adjoining, but was again repulsed with loss.

Finding all further effort useless, and the infantry under General Lane coming up at this time, the guerrilleros rapidly abandoned the city, leaving two pieces of artillery and a large quantity of ammunition in the hands of the victors. The Mexican loss in the engagement was one hundred and fifty, killed and wounded.

But brilliant as the event had been to the American arms, and although the victory of Huamantla prevented General Santa Anna from intercepting the train at the Black Pass, according to his original plan, the success was dearly won. Of all that splendid company of mounted riflemen, constituting the immediate command of Captain Walker, and which numbered seventy-five men at the commencement of the engagement, only seventeen were able to keep the saddle at its close.

That same evening, General Lane took up his line of march for Puebla, and reached his destination about one o'clock on the afternoon of the 13th. His presence having speedily relieved the exhausted garrison of that city from an obstinate and long-protracted investment, he rested his men for a few days, and then turned his attention to those secluded towns, which were yet daring enough to afford refuge and protection to the guerrilleros.

66

CHAPTER XXXII.

Battle of Atlixco—Running Fight with the Guerrilleros—Atlixco taken—Expedition to Matamoros—Its Capture—Lane returns to Puebla—Is attacked—Daring Bravery of Colonel Hays—Peace Prospects—Anaya elected President—Secret Expedition to Tehuacan—Escape of General Santa Anna—Orizaba captured—Garrisoned.

LEARNING, on the 18th of October, that a considerable body of guerrilleros was at Atlixco, a town about ten leagues from Perote, General Lane marched from Puebla, on the morning of the 19th, for the purpose of attacking them.

His force consisted of the 4th Ohio and the 4th Indiana regiments, Major Lally's and Captain Heintzelman's battalions, Colonel Wynkoop's battalion of four companies of the 1st Pennsylvania regiment, Taylor's and Pratt's batteries of light artillery, and a squadron of dragoons under Captain Ford.

The advance-guard of the enemy was first discovered near Santa Isabella about four o'clock in the afternoon. General Lane then halted his force, and waited until the cavalry should come up. In the mean time, the enemy came down to the foot of the hill where he was posted, and invited the attack by the firing of escopets, and waving of lances. As soon as the cavalry came up, the column moved forward. Lally's battalion led the advance, while the Ohio regiment made a wide sweep to the left of the road, for the purpose of flanking a deep ravine on that side.

No sooner were these arrangements observed by the enemy than he began to exhibit signs of irresolution. The cavalry was

508

accordingly ordered to charge at once, and keep the enemy engaged until the infantry should have time to come up.

Pratt's battery was ordered to follow at a gallop, but owing to a previous change in its position was unable to do so; and the opportunity which then presented itself of taking prisoners the entire force of the enemy, was consequently lost.

The cavalry, however, pursued the retreating enemy, and a brisk running fight ensued. On arriving at a small hill, another stand was made, but the appearance of the infantry and a few shots from the artillery, soon caused the flight to be renewed. The dragoons followed the fugitives closely for about four miles, when the main body of the enemy was discovered strongly posted on a side-hill, round which the road curved in the form of a horse-shoe. It was on the opposite side of the curve that the enemy had stationed himself, and the fire from his escopets commanded the entire sweep of the road; but the cavalry by a bold dash gallopped round the circuit under a heavy and continuous fire, and, dismounting at the base of the hill, charged the chaparral on foot, and commenced a desperate engagement which lasted until the infantry made their appearance, when the enemy fled to Atlixco, a distance of about a mile and a half. The cavalry being too much exhausted to head the pursuit any further, the infantry now took the lead; but, before they reached the town, night had already set in. As they approached the town several shots were fired at them; and General Lane, deeming it unsafe to risk a street-fight by such imperfect light as the moon alone afforded, halted his command and ordered the artillery to take possession of a hill overlooking the town and open its fire.

This was promptly done. After pouring a rapid and well directed fire into the most populous parts of the town, for three-quarters of an hour, General Lane silenced his artillery, and directed Major Lally and Colonel Brough to advance with their commands into the town. It was immediately surrendered by the authorities. But the guerrilleros had already dispersed.

The Mexican loss on this occasion was very severe : between Santa Isabella and Atlixco, no less than five hundred and nineteen of the enemy were killed and wounded, while the Americans lost only two men.*

Routed from Atlixco, the remainder of the guerilleros, under General Rea, retreated upon Matamoros, which became, in the course of a short time, the head-quarters of all those predatory bands who were yet held together by various chiefs, though actuated far less by patriotic considerations than the hope of occasional plunder.

Forming, however, a nucleus around which many disaffected men began to rally, the Mexican government affected to recognise these insubordinates as a part of the army which yet remained available for future operations. A military depot was consequently established at Matamoros, and the mixed force there assembled well supplied with artillery and munitions of war. In order to break up this organization, and seize the public stores, General Lane determined to make a sudden descent upon the town.

He accordingly started from Puebla, on the night of the 22d of November, taking with him only one hundred and sixty men and one piece of artillery. These, however, were all choice troops, and well fitted to move with that celerity which the nature of the service demanded. They consisted of twenty-five men under the command of Lieutenant Field, 3d artillery, and one hundred and thirty-five men, part of whom were Texan rangers under Colonel John C. Hays, and part Louisiana dragoons under Captain Lewis.

Notwithstanding the incessant rain, which continued from ten o'clock on the evening of the 22d until five o'clock the following

---

* Lane's Official Report synopsized.

morning, they reached Matamoros by seven o'clock A. M. of the 23d, "accomplishing a march of fifty-four miles in twelve hours."

Charging the advance-guard of the enemy as they approached the town, they drove it back upon the main body within the city, and by a dashing attack upon the combined force of the enemy, dispersed it with scarcely a shadow of resistance.

In this short action, from sixty to eighty of the enemy were killed or wounded, while the Americans did not lose a single man. Among the killed was Colonel Piedras, commanding at Matamoros, two artillery and several other officers. Twenty-seven American soldiers, who had been captured at various places, were discovered and set free. Three pieces of bronze cannon were captured, together with a considerable supply of ammunition of all kinds, and large quantities of public stores.

After resting his men at Matamoros during the whole of the 23d, Lane set out on his return to Puebla on the morning of the 24th.

While moving with difficulty through a long mountainous pass, called the Pass of Galaxra, the train became considerably extended, the artillery, and four wagons containing captured property, having fallen far in the rear. At this time the advance-guard, consisting of some thirty mounted riflemen, under Captain Roberts, were driven in, pursued by two hundred lancers. Colonel Hays was instantly ordered to the front, to unite with the advance-guard, and engage the enemy. His movement was gallantly executed. The lancers were charged with such impetuosity, that they broke, and were pursued "across an extended plain, and towards the mountain, from which they had made the attack."

When about midway of the hill the enemy attempted to rally, but falling rapidly before the rifles of Hays, again broke and was pursued across the crest of the mountain.

Here the enemy were reinforced by five hundred lancers under General Rea, and the mounted men under Hays not carrying sabres, being armed only with revolvers and rifles, which had been already discharged, he gave the order to fall back to their original position. This was performed in fine style, and in the face of a charge of five hundred lancers. Hays himself fell to the rear of his command, and halting as the enemy advanced, deliberately shot dead two of the foremost, and then covered his own retreat until within supporting distance of the artillery and dragoons.

As soon as the former unlimbered, the enemy retired to the mountains; and, although he hovered for some hours afterwards along the line of march, he did not again venture an attack. The Mexican loss in this affair was fifty killed and wounded, that of the Americans two men killed and two wounded; one of the former was Lieutenant Henderson Ridgley, a young officer of much promise, who was lanced mortally while charging by the side of Colonel Hays.

After visiting Atlixco and refreshing his men at that place, General Lane returned to Puebla, which he reached on the afternoon of the 25th, after an absence of sixty hours.* On his return, he heard at Cholula that the Mexicans had just finished two pieces of artillery at Guexocingo; these he determined to destroy, and, proceeding thither with a part of his forces, he found that the guns had been removed, but destroyed the carriages, which had been left behind.

Information having reached General Lane that a train of thirty-six wagons, containing merchandise belonging to merchants in Puebla and the capital, had been captured at San Martin by guerrilleros under Generals Rea and Torrejon, he started in pursuit of the marauders with a party of cavalry and infantry, and overtook them at Tlascala on their way to Queretaro with the booty. Captain Roberts, with the Mounted Rifles, first came up with them, and attacking them with headlong impetuosity,

*Official Report of General Lane.

scattered them in every direction. Seventeen of the enemy were killed, and fourteen officers taken prisoners, without loss to the Americans. The wagons and nearly their entire contents were recaptured.

These repeated incursions being followed up by others of a like character, the condition of the guerilleros was soon reduced to the extreme of weakness.

Hunted from their hiding-places in the mountains, and timidly refused admittance into those towns which had usually afforded them protection, they had no alternative left but to disband as quietly as possible, or to take refuge in states as yet remote from the American arms.

This routing of the guerrilleros had also another and equally beneficial effect. It carried the terrors of war into those small but wealthy towns, to which, at the commencement of the campaign, most of the better class of Mexicans had retired. These having experienced none of the evils which accompany the presence of a hostile soldiery, had been hitherto most clamorous for a continuance of the war. But when they found themselves unexpectedly exposed to the effects of sudden and uncertain irruptions, and their quiet abiding-places in daily danger of being crushed in by shot or shells, they became sudden, but very decided converts to the blessings of peace, and wondered at the obstinacy of the people of more distant states, who, being exempt from the calamities experienced by those nearer the scene of action, still cried out lustily against any negotiation with " the barbarians of the North."

But the cry gradually grew fainter and fainter. The election for deputies to the new Congress took place, and resulted in a large majority favourable to peace.

A considerable party yet remained, it is true, who sought, by artful appeals to the passions of the people, to keep alive those hostile elements by which alone they could hope to prosper.

Generals Santa Anna, Paredes, Gomez Farias, and their adherents, still shouted war; but the more sensible portion of the nation began to see, in its further prosecution, the eventual absorption of the Mexican republic, and its annexation as a conquered province to the republic of the United States. Reinforcements were already flocking in by thousands, and emigration might soon be expected to follow. The question was reduced, therefore, to a sacrifice of territory, or that of separate independence; and, with becoming patriotism, they inclined to the former. In leaning to this decision, they were doubtless influenced by the fact that the United States already held, by conquest, the territories for the cession of which she offered to pay an equivalent in money; and that, if this offer was again refused, she might determine to keep possession without any remuneration at all, and defy recapture.

Amid the anarchy and confusion that prevailed, Santa Anna was intriguing for restoration to the supreme power, which he had abandoned; and Paredes, who had returned from exile, was active and persevering for the establishment of a monarchy, of which he expected to be constituted head. But the government and the people began to see the selfish designs of these chieftains, and not only discountenanced, but thwarted their designs. Peña y Peña, upon whom the supreme power of the government had devolved, ordered General Santa Anna to surrender his forces to General Rincon, in the following letter of his Secretary of State:

" OFFICE OF HOME AND FOREIGN RELATIONS,)
                S. W. Department.)

"EXCELLENT SIR: His Excellency the Señor Provisional President of the republic, feeling profoundly his duties to his country, convinced of the necessity of establishing in the nation public morality, and of giving more energy to the discipline of the army, almost extinguished by civil dissensions—desiring, moreover, to manifest to the people of the city of Mexico, and other points now in the enemy's possession, that their lot is not indifferent to his Excellency — considering, in fine, that in every country, well organized, the generals of an army answer before a tribunal for the faults which they have committed, and even for the misfortunes which may have befallen them in their campaigns — has resolved that your Excellency deliver up the chief command of the army to his Excellency the General of Division, Don Manuel Rincon; and until this chief may present himself to receive it, temporarily to his Excellency Señor General Don Juan Alvarez.

"The President orders that your Excellency establish headquarters wherever you may see fit, in agreement with the supreme government, and there await, under the guarantees of its word and honour, the orders you may receive regarding the formation of a council-of-war, who may judge your Excellency for the loss of the actions which your Excellency, as Commander-in-chief in the present war, has directed, and particularly for the loss of the capital of the republic.

"His Excellency the President believes that it is due to your own honour that, by a council-of-war, your conduct should be cleared of all blame, and he entertains the hope that the result will be favourable for your Excellency. I have the honour of communicating to you this supreme order, and have the honour of offering you my distinguished consideration. God and liberty!

ROSAS.

To His Excellency Señor General, well deserving of his country, Don ANTONIO LOPEZ DE SANTA ANNA."

Refusing to obey this order, Santa Anna directed the chief part of his troops to join General Alvarez, in Oajaca, and the remainder, with the exception of a small body-guard for himself, to repair to Queretaro. The fallen general attempted to find his way out of the country through Oajaca; but, changing his intention, he returned to Tehuacan, from which place he addressed a protest to the new government, in which he asserted that he had

67

only divested himself temporarily of executive authority, that he might be able to oppose the enemy with more vigour. He published, also, an appeal to the people, complaining of the treatment he had received, and magnifying his services in the cause of his country. But he had now lost the power of moving and moulding the people to his will.

On the 11th of November, General Anaya was elected President of the Mexican republic, until the 8th day of January, 1848; this being the remainder of the constitutional term yet unexpired. His opponent was General Almonte, who was warmly supported by the adherents of Santa Anna, who sought by this means to raise the fallen fortunes of their chieftains.

The choice of this distinguished man, more than any event which had yet occurred, justified the opinion that the war was now drawing to a close. Friendly to peace, and at the same time acknowledged to be devoted to the best interests of his country, the inaugural address of President Anaya was looked forward to with an anxiety heightened by the solemn urgency of the occasion, and the importance of the subject upon which it would necessarily treat.

In this address, which is remarkable for its mildness and brevity, General Anaya rather hints, than openly asserts, his own prepossession in favour of a peace; but the favourable manner in which even this slender intimation was received by the assembled deputies, emboldened the new government, the leading members of which, Peña y Peña, Secretary of State, and Mora y Villamil, Minister of War, were avowed friends of peace, to immediately organize a commission for the purpose of reopening negotiations with Mr. Trist. But, as the powers with which the latter gentleman had been intrusted by his government had been subsequently revoked, it became doubtful whether the favourable opportunity which now presented itself might not be lost altogether.

With a happy daring, which under other circumstances would have been censured severely, Mr. Trist determined to assume the responsibility of still acting as the agent of the United States, provided the negotiation could be conducted upon the basis of the project formerly refused.

One great obstacle to negotiation was felt to be the presence of General Santa Anna. His adherents, though few in number, were yet strong enough to disturb harmonious action; and the knowledge that the vanquished general was still in Orizaba, watching an opportunity to regain his popularity, withheld many from joining the advocates of peace, who would otherwise have ranked themselves among its supporters.

An expedition undertaken by General Lane on the 18th of January, tended materially to hasten a pacific result. His command, consisting of dragoons, rifles, and Texan rangers, all well mounted, and numbering three hundred and fifty men, left the city of Mexico on the day already mentioned, taking the National Road in the direction of Vera Cruz. Colonel Hays was in chief command of the rangers, and Colonel Polk led the mounted riflemen and dragoons. The column reached Venda de Chalco by four o'clock the next morning, and by nine o'clock the same evening reached the Rio Frio Pass. The next day it entered Puebla. On the evening of the 21st the column again started, and at the village of Amazoque diverged from the National Road, and pursued one to the left for a distance of ten or twelve miles, when the direction of the column was again changed. The road now taken was a mere mule-path, winding among the mountains, and for ten miles presented nothing but a rough bed of jagged limestone rock. On gaining a hacienda near the village of Santa Clara, at the foot of the mountains, the general halted for the day. Then it was he first informed his command, that the expedition had been organized for the purpose of attempting the arrest of General Santa Anna, who was known to have taken refuge at Tehuacan, a town some forty miles distant.

At night the column was again put in motion, the inmates of the hacienda, and all persons previously met, having been put under strict surveillance, to prevent any tidings from reaching Tehuacan ; but the deepest and wisest plans often prove abortive when success is nearest.

Shortly after leaving the hacienda, a party of armed Mexicans were encountered escorting a carriage. These were immediately arrested, when the traveller stepped from the vehicle and presented a passport from General Smith, authorizing him to proceed from Mexico to Orizaba and back, accompanied by eight armed servants. The cortege was permitted to proceed.

No sooner, however, had the column passed out of sight, than the traveller, surmising the object of the expedition, despatched one of his servants by a shorter route across the country towards Tehuacan, who apprised General Santa Anna of the approach of the Americans. He immediately fled ; and when the excited rangers dashed into the plaza some two hours afterwards, with their revolvers cocked and their eyes roving from window to parapet in the hope of resistance, the expected captive was far beyond reach of pursuit.

It appears by a letter of Santa Anna's to the Minister of War, dated at Cascatlan, February 1st, 1848, that while Santa Anna was engaged in writing a note, requesting a passport to leave the country, that he learned of Lane's advance and hastily retired. After leaving Tehuacan, he took refuge in the town of Teotitlan del Camiro, where there were troops from Oajaca. He was subsequently permitted to leave the country, and embarked on the 4th of April at Antigua, near Vera Cruz, in a Spanish brig, destined for Kingston, Jamaica.

After resting for a day and a night at this place, General Lane determined to push on to Orizaba, a beautiful town situated in the valley of that name, and containing from twenty to twenty-five thousand inhabitants. Near the village of Acalcingo, the column was met by the curate and ayuntamiento, by whom they were furnished with good quarters for the night. The next morning General Lane was waited on by the authorities of the city of Orizaba, who desired to know upon what terms he would accept the surrender of the city. His reply was, they should know when he had possession.

When within about three miles of the city, he was approached by a larger and more imposing deputation, who accompanied the column to the gates, and there formally surrendered the keys without making any stipulation whatsoever.

Having thus quietly obtained possession of the city, General Lane appointed Major Polk its civil and military governor, and intrusted to Colonel Hays the chief command of the troops. A few days afterwards, Colonel Bankhead arrived with large reinforcements, and the possession of the city was thus effectually secured by the presence of a competent garrison.

CHAPTER XXXIII.

On the 8th of January, 1848, General Herrera was elected constitutional President of the Mexican republic. This was another advance made by the peace party, and showed that the nation had at length become thoroughly alarmed at the situation of affairs.

Never, indeed, had the independence of Mexico been in so great a danger as at this period. Her armies beaten and dispersed, her arsenals and forts in the possession of the enemy, her stores and resources exhausted; she lay prostrate at the feet of her victorious foe. The probability of absorption into the republic of the United States, became, therefore, every day less doubtful; and had the Mexican government refused much longer those overtures for peace, which it had been repeatedly and so earnestly urged to accept, it is certain that the course of conduct thus forced upon the Executive of the United States, would have ended in the annihilation of the separate independence of the sister republic.

Fortunately the Mexican people, while standing upon the

(520)

very brink of destruction as a nation, saw, with at least partial distinctness, the consequences which inevitably awaited them, if they advanced but a single step further. That step was not taken. The perilous position was slowly abandoned, and those negotiations commenced, which, with the loss of that portion of the republic which they were too weak to defend, were to insure the independence of what yet remained.

It has been already stated, that shortly after the election of Anaya to the temporary occupancy of the Presidency, a commission had been appointed to confer with the American agent, Mr. Trist, and that the latter, conscious that his powers were annulled by his own government, hesitated for a while as to what step he should take in the emergency, but at length decided to meet the commissioners, as if he was still clothed with powers to treat, from the American Executive. This was a rash assumption of authority, which, under other circumstances, might have entailed serious consequences upon the nation which he professed to serve. But Mr. Trist knew his countrymen: he was conscious that, to the majority of the American nation, peace was desirable upon any terms not incompatible with its honour. Constant success had cloyed the public appetite; and the possibility of a long-continued war affecting the financial condition of the country, began to be weighed seriously by those upon whom the burden would fall most heavily.

He knew also that an act of successful daring, even when performed in defiance of the express commands of those whose position entitles them to implicit obedience, has always been regarded with a lenient eye by the people of the United States. With them the success cancels the obligation. How far a less favourable result would have excused the temerity of the offence, Mr. Trist was happily not called upon to experience.

The negotiations opened harmoniously by concessions on both sides. The old issues were surrendered. Mexico abandoned her claim to the Nueces as her frontier, while Mr. Trist waived the cession of Lower California, and the right of way across the isthmus of Tehuantepec. The consideration in money, which he had previously offered for the transfer of New Mexico and Upper California, he professed himself still willing to allow, also to pay to citizens of the United States the amounts of their claims upon the Mexican republic, under the conventions of April 1839 and January 1843. The definition of boundaries, as originally drawn up by the government of the United States, subject to the exceptions already mentioned, was then discussed and finally accepted by the Mexican commissioners ; and on the 2d of February, at the city of Guadalupe Hidalgo, a treaty of peace, elaborated in due form, was unanimously adopted and signed by Señors Conto, Cuevas, and Atristain, as commissioners on the part of the Mexican government, and by Mr. Trist on that of the United States, subject to the ratification of their respective governments.

Four days afterwards, Señor Rosas, the Mexican Minister of Foreign Relations, notified the governors of the different states that the treaty had been concluded, and urged upon them the necessity of using their influence in insuring its prompt acceptance by the deputies, then about to be assembled in special session. These deputies soon after met, and the treaty, having received their sanction, was instantly despatched to the government of the United States. Immediately on its receipt, it was submitted by the Executive to the action of the Senate, then in session, by whom, after a few unimportant amendments, it was solemnly ratified on the 9th of March, 1848.

The Mexican Congress having ratified the treaty as amended by the Senate of the United States, the ratifications thereof were exchanged on the 30th of May, 1848, at Queretaro, by the American commissioners, Ambrose H. Sevier and Nathan Clifford, and Señor Rosas, minister of Internal and Foreign Relations.

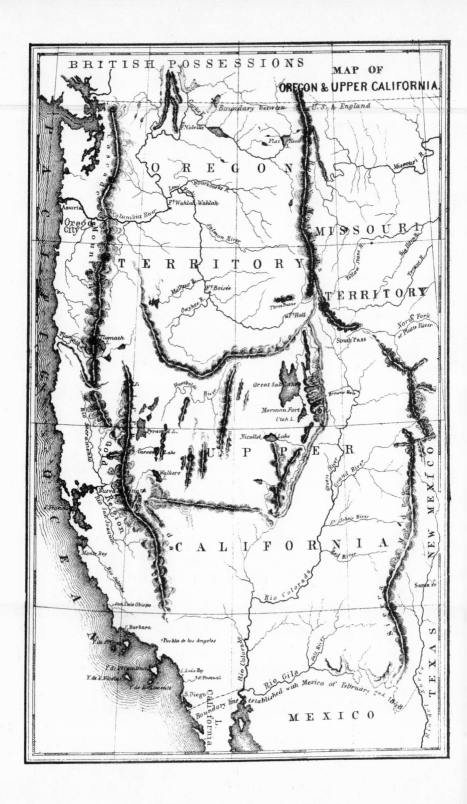

Immediately thereafter, the American troops began to evacuate the country. On the 12th of June the last division left the capital. The American flag descended from the National Palace, after a complimentary salute by the Mexican artillery, in command of General La Vega, while the Mexican colours were run up amid a salute from the battery of Lieutenant-Colonel Duncan.

The treaty of Guadalupe Hidalgo ceded to the United States territories extending from the eastern base of the Rocky Mountains to the shores of the Pacific, in breadth over ten degrees of latitude, and containing an area of far more than half a million of square miles. This vast region, exceedingly diversified in features, in climate, and in soil, has been usually comprehended under the rather vaguely applied names of Upper California and New Mexico. Between these two acknowledged, though greatly unequal, divisions, no boundary-line seems ever to have been definitely fixed. They meet and melt into each other; and, so far at least as Mexican geographers enlighten us, while Nuevo Mexico implies the country extending from the easternmost range of the Northern Cordilleras, towards the west, by Alta California, on the other hand, may be understood, the region reaching from the coast of the Pacific far away towards the rising sun.

This indefiniteness of boundary being premised, we shall not be surprised to find the area of New Mexico estimated at one time as covering two hundred thousand, and at another time as embracing only forty-four thousand square miles. For any practical purpose, we shall not, perhaps, materially err, in considering the name applicable strictly to the irregularly shaped basin of the Upper Rio Grande. This extensive district is on all sides hemmed in, and in all directions crossed and chequered, by bleak and barren mountains, whose summits rise from ten to thirteen thousand feet above the level of the sea. Its table-lands, forming part of the great Mexican plateau, are everywhere strewed with large angular fragments of basalt, trap, lava, and amygdaloid.

68

The valleys alone offer inducements to cultivation. These, however, are numerous, of various sizes and running at various angles into the main valley of the Rio Grande. The latter is described as being magnificent in scenery and rich in soil, traversed by mountain streams paying tribute to the broad bright river, whose whole course is dotted by towns, villages, and farms. The whole country enjoys a bland and salubrious climate.

New Mexico is divided into three departments, the Northern, the Middle, and the South-eastern: these are subdivided into counties or districts; and these again into townships. Of the principal divisions, that lying furthest south is incomparably the richest, the valley of the Del Norte in this part containing the main agricultural wealth of the state, and sustaining a population of about fifty thousand, most of whom are in easy circumstances, and many possess wealth in land, stock, and gold dust. From official documents found at Santa Fé, Lieutenant Abert calculated the population of the whole state at one hundred thousand; others raise the estimate to one hundred and sixty thousand. In either number is included the Pueblo Indian population. The mountains are said to contain immense mineral treasures, and when even imperfectly, and under great difficulties, worked, to have bountifully repaid the labour. Gold, silver, lead, and copper, with coal and brimstone, gypsum and salt, are all said to abound. Nor can there be much doubt of the correctness of these representations. The products of the valleys are grain, pulse, pepper, and onions, and, most valuable of all, the grape. In the latter the Rio Grande possesses a source of revenue, unsurpassed by any region in Europe. Even now many hundred thousand gallons of excellent wine are manufactured yearly, while to American energy the means are at hand for a tenfold increase. Immense herds of cattle, horses, and mules find sustenance on the mountain slopes; and when, under new policy and ample protection, the countless hillsides shall have been thickly dotted over with sheep, the mildness of the climate gives promise that New Mexico may, in the abundance and fineness of her fleeces, outrival Old Spain. Nor can we believe that the thousand unfailing mountain streams, that leap invitingly down to the valley, will be very long permitted to exhaust their unappreciated powers, strangers to American enterprise and manufacturing skill.

Independent of its intrinsic value, as the future abode of a numerous and happy branch of the great republican family, New Mexico is, in a commercial and in a political view, an important and even necessary possession to the United States. Holding it, the latter will effectually suppress the ruinous incursions of the savage Indian tribes, and thus protect and nurse into prosperity, not only New Mexico itself, but, what true policy equally dictates, the adjoining provinces of the sister republic also. From Santa Fé to the city of Mexico, and to the several capitals and leading towns of the central states, the common table-land affords all facilities for travel. From Santa Fé to Fort Leavenworth, the authority of Colonel Emory demonstrates that there are few obstacles for a railway, no obstacle insurmountable or of exceeding difficulty. Pursuing the route followed by Major Cooke, from the Rio Grande, across the great table-land, there is the all but established certainty, that such railway may be easily continued to the Pacific. Thus will be opened easy routes for the introduction of immense quantities of merchandise from the United States, into the then thriving and populous states of Durango, Sonora, and Lower California; while the most desirable means of connexion shall have been secured between the new Great West, with its ocean tributary, and the teeming valley of the Father of Waters.

The region which, under the name of Upper California, has passed under dominion of the American flag, lies between the 32d and 42d degrees of north latitude, extending from Sonora and Lower California in the south, to Oregon in the north; and reaching from the Pacific, over successive mountain ranges, basins, and table-lands, to the uncertain limits of New Mexico. The most eastern and central portions of this vast extent have been, until lately, wholly unknown, and are still unoccupied, save by a few wandering tribes of Indian savages. Its average length, and average breadth, are each about seven hundred miles. The natural diversities of such an extent of country, it may be anticipated, must render any general description unsatisfactory and fallacious. But here those differences are greater than usually met with in tracts of even equal extent.

The exceedingly interesting observations of Colonel Fremont, afford us the most satisfactory and reliable information in regard to the whole region. From these principally we must abbreviate, recommending the perusal of his memoir to those who desire fuller and more detailed accounts.

The universally prevailing opinion has been, that the strip of country lying along the Pacific, and between that ocean and the Sierra Nevada, in length about seven hundred, and in breadth about an average of one hundred and twenty-five miles, was the only portion of Alta California capable of being cultivated and occupied by a civilized population. Exploration has ascertained the ground-lessness of this opinion. The Sierra Nevada—a part of that great range which, under different names and with different elevations, runs nearly parallel and nigh to the coast, from the Californian peninsula to Russian America—divides Upper California into two parts, exercising a decided influence on the climate, soil, and productions of each. Its appellation, " The Snowy," as applied in Spanish geography, ascertains the fact that its summits ever dwell in snow. " Stretching along the coast, and at a general distance of one hundred miles from it, this great mountain wall receives the warm winds, charged with vapour, which sweep across the Pacific Ocean, precipitates their accumulated moisture in fertilizing rains and snows upon its western flank, and leaves cold and dry winds to pass on to the east. Hence the characteristic differences of the two regions— mildness, fertility, and a superb vegetable kingdom on one side; comparative barrenness and cold on the other." The state of vegetation, as well as thermometrical observations, have established and illustrated the fact, that the two sides of the Sierra exhibit two distinct climates, varying by about twenty degrees. Thus, December on one side of the mountain was winter; on the other it was spring.

East of the Sierra Nevada, and between it and the Rocky Mountains, is that anomalous feature in our continent, the Great Basin; some five hundred miles in diameter every way, between four and five thousand feet above the level of the sea, shut in all around by mountains, with its own system of lakes and rivers, and having no connexion whatever with the sea. Partly arid and sparsely inhabited, the general character of the basin is that of a desert, but with great exceptions, there being parts of it very fit for the residence of a civilized people; and of these parts, the Mormons have lately established themselves in one of the largest and best. The predominating features of the interior are mountains rising abruptly from narrow bases to heights of from two to five thousand feet above the level of the country, having their summits, for the greater part of the year, capped with snow, their sides wooded and grassy, and their bases, ere they meet the level, girt with belts of rich alluvium, while streams, varying in breadth from two to fifty feet, hurry down their slopes, and lose themselves, some in lakes, some in the loose and light alluvial belts, and some in the dry plains that isolate these mountains from each other.

The Great Salt Lake—a saturated solution of common salt— of very irregular outline, and about seventy miles in length, and the Utah, a lake of fresh water, are situated in this basin towards its eastern rim. The Salt Lake is four thousand two hundred feet above the level of the sea; the Utah, about one hundred feet above the level of the Salt, is connected with the latter by a strait, or river, thirty-five miles long. Both united drain an area of ten or twelve thousand square miles, and have on the east, along the base of the mountain, the usual bench of alluvion, which extends to a distance of three hundred miles, with wood and water, and abundant grass. Along the connecting strait the Mormons have established themselves, where arable land for a large settlement abounds.* The Utah and its numerous tributaries afford large trout and other fish in abundance. In the Salt Lake no fish or animal life of any kind is found; every evaporation from it leaves an incrustation of salt, and a covering like ice forms over the waters which its waves throw over the rocks.

Other lakes there are within this basin, many of them deep and clear, and abounding in excellent fish. There are also several considerable rivers, the most important, perhaps, of which, is that named by Colonel Fremont " *Humboldt*," but sketched sometimes on maps as " Mary's" or " Ogden's." Rising in two streams from the mountains west of the Great Salt Lake, and bearing nearly due west towards the Sierra Nevada, it presents a narrow valley of rich alluvion, beautifully covered with nutritious grasses, and is tracked through the plain by a line of willow and cotton-wood trees. Lying on the present line of travel to California and Oregon, furnishing a level, unobstructed way for nearly three hundred miles, and terminating in a marshy lake within fifty miles of the base of the Sierra Nevada, and opposite to the Salmon-Trout pass, which leads over the mountain into the valley of the Sacramento, some forty miles north of Nueva Helvetia, this river is certainly an object of interest and importance. There are very many other streams of various lengths, up to two hun-

---

* In the spring of 1848, these settlers had three thousand acres in wheat, seven saw and grist-mills, seven hundred houses in a fortified enclosure of sixty acres, with stock and other suitable accompaniments. Intelligence from them up to May of the present year, indicates continued prosperity. They have commenced the erection of a city on a grand scale, to include a council-house, bridges, baths, schools, colleges, and all the institutions of a great metropolis.

dred miles, but similar in their general character, and all obeying
the general law of terminating their course within the basin, in
some one of the modes before mentioned.

The climate of the Great Basin does not present the rigorous
winter that might be expected from its elevation and mountainous
structure. The summer appears to linger long, the winter to be
open, pleasant, and clear. In fact, there is nothing in the
climate of this great, and hitherto maligned region, to prevent
civilized man from making it his home, and finding in its arable
parts a comfortable subsistence.

The words of Colonel Fremont will best and most briefly
describe the second great division of this vast territory. "West
of the Sierra Nevada, and between that mountain and the sea, is
the second grand division of California (Upper), and the only
part to which the name applies in the current language of the
country. It is the occupied and inhabited part, and so different
in character—so divided by the mountain wall of the Sierra from
the Great Basin above—as to constitute a region to itself, with a
structure and configuration—a soil, climate, and productions—
of its own; and as Northern Persia may be referred to as some
type of the former, so may Italy be referred to as some point of
comparison for the latter. East and west from the Sierra Nevada
to the sea, it will average, in the middle parts, one hundred and
fifty miles, in the northern parts two hundred, giving an area of
above one hundred thousand square miles. Lateral ranges,
parallel to the Sierra Nevada and the coast, make the structure
of the country, and break it into a surface of valleys and mountains, the valleys a few hundred, and the mountains two to four
thousand feet above the sea. Stretched along the mild coast of
the Pacific, with a general elevation in its plains and valleys of
only a few hundred feet above the level of the sea—and backed
by the long and lofty wall of the Sierra—mildness and geniality
may be assumed as the characteristics of its climate. The

inhabitant of corresponding latitudes on the Atlantic side of this continent can with difficulty conceive of the soft air and southern productions under the same latitudes in the maritime region of Upper California. The singular beauty and purity of the sky in the south of this region, is characterized by Humboldt as a rare phenomenon, and all travellers realize the truth of his description. The present condition of the country affords but slight data for forming correct opinions of the agricultural capacity and fertility of the soil. At present, but little remains of the high cultivation which had been attained at the "Missions" (successively under the control of the Jesuits, the Franciscans, and Dominicans). Only in some places do we see the evidences of what the country is capable of. At San Buenaventura we found the olive-trees in January, bending under the weight of neglected fruit; and the mission of San Luis Obispo (latitude 35°), is still distinguished for the excellence of its olives, considered finer and larger than those of the Mediterranean. The productions of the south differ from those of the north and the middle. Grapes, olives, Indian corn, have been its staples, with many assimilated fruits and grains. Tobacco has been recently introduced, and the uniform summer heat which follows the wet season, and is uninterrupted by rain, would make the southern country well adapted to cotton. Wheat is the first product of the north, where it always constituted the principal cultivation of the missions. This promises to be the grain-growing region of California. The moisture of the coast seems particularly suited to the potato, and to the vegetables common to the United States, which here grow to an extraordinary size. Perhaps few parts of the world can produce in such perfection so great a variety of fruits and grains, as the large and various region enclosing the bay of San Francisco, and drained by its waters. The climate of maritime California is greatly modified by the structure of the country, and under this aspect may be considered in three divisions—the *southern*, below

Point Conception and the Santa Barbara Mountain, about latitude 35° ; the *northern*, from Cape Mendocino, latitude 41°, to
the Oregon boundary ; and the *middle*, including the bay and
basin of San Francisco, and the coast between Point Conception
and Cape Mendocino.   Of these three divisions, the rainy season
is longest and heaviest in the north, and lightest in the south.
Vegetation is governed accordingly, coming with the rains,
decaying where they fail.   Summer and winter, in our sense of
the terms, are not applicable to this part of the country.   It is
not heat and cold, but wet and dry, which mark the seasons ;
and the winter months, instead of killing vegetation, revive it.
The dry season makes a period of consecutive drought, the only
winter in the vegetation of this country, which can hardly be said
at any time to cease.   In forests, where the soil is sheltered, in
low lands of streams, and hilly country, where the ground remains
moist, grass continues constantly green, and flowers bloom in all the
months of the year.   In the southern half of the country, the long
summer drought has rendered irrigation necessary, and the experience of the missions, in their prosperous day, has shown that in
California, as elsewhere, the dryest plains are made productive, and
the heaviest crops produced by that mode of cultivation.   With
irrigation, a succession of crops may be produced throughout the
year.   Salubrity and mildness characterize the climate, there
being no prevailing diseases, and the extremes of heat during
the summer being checked by sea-breezes during the day, and
by light airs from the Sierra Nevada during the night.   The
nights are generally cool and refreshing, as is the shade during
the hottest day."

Thus largely we have borrowed, by selection and condensation,
from the official memoir of Colonel Fremont, whose observations
are, almost to the letter, confirmed and corroborated, if confirmation and corroboration be deemed necessary, by all competent
and trustworthy authorities, both of earlier and later date.   And

69

such distinct and satisfactory evidence, as to the character and
general capabilities of that distant region, can scarcely be omitted,
in view of the accumulating farrago of confusion and contradic-
tion, that forms the burden and the refrain of the ephemeral press.

A historical and geographical memoir of the country our limits
forbid ; nor are the materials for the latter portion of such a work
as yet sufficiently comprehensive and ample.   From the exceedingly interesting, and, under the circumstances, wonderfully
accurate work of M. de Mofias, giving an account of the country
in 1842; from Humboldt and Greenhow; from Sir George Simpson's " Overland Journey ;" and from the notes of the exploring
expeditions by sea and land, under Wilkes and Fremont, as well
as from many comparatively unpretending documents from various adventurers, military and commercial, a large mass of information has been accumulated.   To those we must refer for
details.

Some notice, however brief and imperfect, will be expected
from us, of the discovery, position, and prospects of that extraordinary mineral wealth, which during the past twelve months
has caused feverish excitement, not only throughout our own
dominion, and the countries adjacent, but even in Europe, and
the islands of the Pacific, while it has roused from his torpor even
the sluggish Asiatic.   The gold mines—rather let us call them,
in the homely, and certainly, so far as experience has yet taught,
more appropriate term of the *once Far West*, the gold diggings—
independently of all that unwholesome, and not unnatural pertur-
bation which they have caused, are an object of very great, though
not, in our opinion, primary or overwhelming importance.

The belief has long prevailed, that California teemed with
mineral treasure ; more especially with the most insinuating and
beloved of metals.   To the Jesuit Fathers, even in the earliest
period of their benevolent labours, the existence of this source of
wealth was not unknown ; but, either from a belief in the insuffi-

ciency of reward to be reaped by the time, labour, and expenditure supposed to be required—or from the desire of directing the main attention of their reclaimed children of the wilds to the more unfailing mine of steady industry, they extended no countenance, no encouragement to the search for gold. The discovery then, or re-discovery of these layers of wealth, bears date in the early part of 1848.

At the western base of the Sierra Nevada, betweeen it and the coast range, and stretching across the head of the spacious bay of San Francisco, lies the continuous valley of the Sacramento and San Joaquin rivers, which, rising at its opposite ends, and receiving in their course many tributaries from the mountains, flow towards each other, the Sacramento from the north, the San Joaquin from the south, meet about half-way, and send their united waters by a delta into the bay. This long valley, extending some five hundred miles, is the garden of California. On the Sacramento is the settlement of Nueva Helvetia, founded by Captain Sutter, a native of Switzerland, who having held a commission in the Swiss Guards of Charles X. of France, and being released from that employment by the revolution of 1830, emigrated first to Western Missouri, and thence, in 1838–9, to the country in which he has so fortunately established himself, under a grant from the Mexican government. By well-timed conciliation and decision, he speedily acquired over the Indians all desirable authority, and converted them into a peaceable and industrious people. By their labour, with the aid of American, French, and German mechanics, he constructed various works. Around him, others, allured and taught by his example, settled on the Rio de los Americanos, or American Fork, a tributary of the Sacramento, and like him prospered in their industry. For the protection of his settlement, he has had a large fort, mounting twelve cannon, and capable of containing one thousand men, but garrisoned by forty trained and uniformed Indians.

Ascending the south branch of the American Fork, the country becomes broken and mountainous, the hills rise to about one thousand feet above the valley, and at a distance of some fifty miles from his fort, Captain Sutter resolved to locate a saw-mill in the centre of a growth of pine. For the erection of such a mill he contracted with a Mr. Marshall, in September 1837. In the course of the winter and ensuing spring, the building was completed, and a dam and race constructed; but the tail-race having been in the first instance found too narrow to permit the sufficiently rapid escape of the water, the latter was, to save labour, allowed to run with a strong current directly into the race, so as to wash it wider and deeper. This purpose effected, a bed of mud and gravel was carried to the foot of the race. Some glittering particles lying on the upper edge of this deposit attracted Mr. Marshall's attention. They were gathered, their value ascertained, and Captain Sutter made acquainted with the discovery. These gentlemen naturally wished to keep the matter secret, at least for a time, but it leaked out and spread with lightning velocity.

The first explorers—and daily did they increase in numbers—were amply repaid for their labours. On the banks of the streams, and in the dry ravines, the precious metal was found, principally in particles of greater or less coarseness, mixed with gravel and sand from which it was easily washed. As search was extended, the adjoining and even more distant streams and ravines proved equally wealthy. In three months full four thousand persons were engaged in gold-hunting. In scales it was usually found, but sometimes lumps of extraordinary size startled with delight some toiling explorer, and even at this period from thirty to forty thousand dollars' worth of gold was daily obtained.

The discovery of these vast deposits of gold, says Colonel Mason, in a despatch to his government, has entirely changed the character of Upper California. Its people, before engaged in cultivating their small patches of ground, and guarding their herds of cattle and horses, have all gone to the mines. Labourers and mechanics abandoned their pursuits, traders forsook their stores, and sailors their vessels. Even from the garrisons soldiers deserted, unable to resist the strong temptation. In all quarters of the states the news of the discovery and the success attendant on adventure, summoned forth thousands, ready to forsake home and all its allurements to try their fortunes in the mines. The influx of new comers lessened not the wealth of any; ample room for all was found, and each day but showed that almost limitless along the Sierra, was the extent of the region of gold.

On the 8th of December, 1848, the first deposit of gold from California was received at the U. S. Mint in Philadelphia. It had been brought by Mr. David Garter, from San Francisco, over the isthmus, and weighed 1804.59 ounces Troy. On the 9th another deposit was made of 228 ounces. The gold was of two sorts in external character, though apparently not differing in quality. That from the dry diggings was in grains, averaging from one to two penny-weights; that from the swamps or margins of the streams in spangles of much smaller bulk. Assays of this gold, when melted, showed an average fineness of 894, being thus slightly below the standard fineness, which is 900. The average value per ounce of the bullion, before melting, is stated at 18.05\frac{1}{3}$; in bars, after melting, $18.50. Further assays by various professional persons, have ascertained that the California gold is in fineness fully equal to any found on this continent, and within half a carat of the quality of English and American standard coin.

The history of these mines, during the last few months, we cannot venture to trace. Ship after ship from the American ports has borne away expectant hundreds, and many hundreds more have sought the distant treasure-ground by land. The latest intelligence more than confirms early accounts. Marvellous as were deemed the stories respecting the abundance of the metal, they have been found to fall far short of the reality. New discoveries have almost daily enlarged the region in which gold is found; and the most substantial evidence of the riches of the region, is supplied in the arrival at various ports in the States, of vessels bearing large consignments of the metal. The " *Crescent City*" steamer reached New Orleans on the 11th of June, with dust on board to the amount of one million of dollars.

During the winter, gold-washing had been carried on with varied success. At the dry diggings snow fell to the depth of three feet, and remained on the ground several days after each storm. Little gold was procured. At Culloma, however, or the saw-mill, where first the gold was discovered, the season was uniformly gentle, and the labours of the persevering explorer attended with partial success. On the Middle Fork, the average return was about two ounces per day to each man, but high water retarded the work, and was likely so to do until the end of May.

Fair success, with a like average, rewarded operations on the Yuba. The same may generally be said of Feather River, Bear Creek, Dry Creek, Mohelumne and Cosumne rivers. But the great attraction has been the Stanislaus, whose waters are said to wash out the beautiful ore in size and quantity unequalled. The borders of this stream form an inexhaustibly rich portion of the *placer*.

The abundance of the gold, and the facility with which it is accumulated, very naturally have had the effect of raising the price of labour enormously. One hundred dollars a month fail to induce the services of ordinary seamen, and numbers of ships in the bay are deserted by their crews. The town of San Francisco is crowded with constantly arriving immigrants, and about the beginning of May, it was calculated some eight thousand persons were at work in the various mines. In the town, accommodations of any kind could be procured only at enormous rents. Good provisions were equally scarce and dear. Other prices may be inferred from that of board, which stood, exclusive of lodging, at $20 per week. Dates from San Francisco to the 18th of May, in the main corroborated the previously received intelligence, and represent the tide of immigration as unceasing and undiminished. "In a few days," says the "Alta California," a newspaper published at San Francisco, "this place will resume its wonted business bustle, when rare times are anticipated. We will have but little rain from this time until the setting in of another winter. A cloudless sky is above us, verdant plains and woodlands stretch for leagues away in the distance; but, in the interval of another year, what changes shall be rung in the beautiful valley before us! The flood-gate to fortune is opened with the balmy breath of spring, but in the resistless torrent pouring in, how great must be the sacrifice of health; how many shall 'by the way-side fall and perish' in the struggle for wealth—many, very many who are now setting out strong in hope and heart, and buoyant in youth's full vigour!"

Hitherto all comers, foreigners from every clime, as well as American citizens and inhabitants of the Californias, have participated without hindrance in the abundant wealth of this region, nor does any effort seem as yet to have been made to assert the undoubted rights of the nation over the soil purchased by national blood and treasure. At length the American citizens in the country begin to murmur, and question the right of those foreign intruders, for such, under every aspect of international law, they must be considered. It is hoped that a grievance so manifest and so detrimental to the interests and just rights of our citizens, will speedily be removed; and that, as a next step, means will be adopted of securing to the nation at large some benefits, at least, from that which is national property alone.

A few words on the advantages of the maritime region, before this chapter is brought to a close. From the time of its earliest discovery until the present, the bay of San Francisco has been considered one of the finest in the world, and is fully entitled to that high character, viewed even only as a harbour. To this fact all visiters of all nations have borne unanimous testimony. But far beyond its value as a mere harbour, is its geographical position in relation to the commercial and political interests of the United States, and not only of the States, but of also the opposite extremes of the old world. The other harbours are, proceeding southwardly, Monterey, Santa Barbara, San Pedro, and San Diego. All these are of secondary importance. San Diego is, next to San Francisco, the safest and best in the province, being land-locked, with deep water and a good bottom. Thus, at its opposite extremities, Upper California possesses two of the best ports on the Pacific, while each of them is greatly enhanced in value by the distance of any other harbour worthy of the name, San Francisco being nearly a thousand miles from Port Discovery, to the north, and San Diego, nearly six hundred miles from the Bay of Magdalena, to the south. Add to these commanding advantages the fertility of the large district west of the Sierra Nevada, the mildness and salubrity of the climate, the vast resources for ship timber, grain, and cattle, and we can the better appreciate the admiring language of Sir George Simpson, in his " *Overland Journey*," " What a splendid country, whether we regard its internal resources or its commercial capabilities !"

But thoughts here arise, on which we must not now permit ourselves to dwell. A future of almost overwhelming interest is before the nation, which now grasps the two great world oceans, and invites Asia and Europe to meet and draw closer together the ties of common humanity on her mediating soil. Through her broad dominions the wealth of Asia and the civilization of Europe pass one another, to leave their riches deposits on the way; and to both she is called on to become the exemplar and the guide in the higher civilization that awaits the species—in the moral and social progress that is to bring with it the happiness of mankind.

Whether the sudden and immense influx of the precious metals from the new territory will enervate or strengthen the North American Republic, time alone can determine. Too often is it found inimical to national virtue; and it may well be doubted, whether the eager search for gold by a promiscuous crowd of unsteady adventurers, will not be hostile to the industry, frugality, and virtue, for which, as a nation, we are proverbial. At present the fear and the hope are so intimately intermingled, that the sincere patriot trembles while he glows. One advantage from the discovery will necessarily arise—the rapid settlement of the newly-acquired territory.

In another point of view the war with Mexico has been productive of the most beneficial consequences. It has given our country a prominent rank among the nations of the earth. It has displayed to the eyes of doubting monarchists the existence of a majestic power and energy, a youthful freshness of spirit combined with a manly vigour, which are well calculated to insure prolonged peace, by the respect which her ability has inspired, and the admiration which has been elicited by the heroic conduct of her sons. The United States has not merely shown her ability for defensive war, but has successfully solved the problem of the capacity of a republic to engage in a foreign war. She has demonstrated that, without the expense of a standing army, she can at any time bring into the field a force of one hundred thousand men drawn from the body of the people, able to endure fatigue, surmount obstacles, and achieve victories, under circumstances which would have broken the spirits, and quelled the courage, even of troops inured to war.

The consequences of the Mexican war must necessarily be favourable to the inhabitants of the territory ceded to the United States. Under a fixed and stable form of government, relieved from former exactions, with ample guaranties for the protection of person and property, they will have additional inducements

70

to industry and enterprise, and by the example of their northern neighbours, who may settle among them, will be stimulated to generous exertions, which will raise them from their present ignorance and degradation, to all the blessings of rational liberty and a higher civilization.

Mexico herself, being brought into more immediate connexion with the republic of the United States, and enjoying a freer intercourse with its citizens, will participate in these advantages. Enervated by dependence on her mines, long distracted by internal dissensions, and a prey to the intrigues of military despots, she will at length rise to an appreciation of real liberty, learn that her true policy is industry and peace, and, beating her " swords into ploughshares, and her spears into pruning-hooks," find her chief wealth and happiness in peaceful, health-inspiring toil. Relieved from the exorbitant exactions of her military and priesthood, her expenditures will be diminished, while increased attention to agriculture and manufactures will develop and augment her resources; and institutions of learning, after the manner of those of her northern sister, diffuse knowedge and virtue among her ignorant and half-civilized multitudes.

Nor is this all. The light of liberty and civilization, from where our flag is now planted on the shores of the Pacific, will illumine not only the adjacent countries, but the far-off islands of the watery waste. From the bay of San Francisco, our white-winged ships will visit the shores of Asia and Africa, and each green isle that gems the Southern Ocean, freighted for their heathen inhabitants not merely with perishable merchandise, but the " true riches," civilization, and the knowledge of the one God, causing the " isles to be glad," and the " desert to smile and blossom as the rose."

APPENDIX.

TREATY

Of Peace, Friendship, Limits, and Settlement, between the United States of America, and the Mexican Republic, concluded at Guadalupe Hidalgo, on the Second Day of February, with Amendments by the American Senate, March 10th, 1848, and by the Mexican Senate, May 25th, 1848.

THE TREATY.

In the name of Almighty God:

The United States of America and the United Mexican States, animated by a sincere desire to put an end to the calamities of the war which unhappily exists between the two republics, and to establish on a solid basis relations of peace and friendship, which shall confer reciprocal benefits on the citizens of both, and assure the concord, harmony, and mutual confidence wherein the two people should live as good neighbours, have, for that purpose, appointed their respective plenipotentiaries; that is to say, the President of the United States has appointed N. P. Trist, a citizen of the United States, and the President of the Mexican republic has appointed Don Luis Gonzaga Cuevas, Don Bernardo Conto, and Don Miguel Atristain, citizens of the said republic, who, after a reciprocal communication of their respective powers, have, under the protection of Almighty God, the author of peace, arranged, agreed upon, and signed the following treaty of peace, friendship, limits, and settlement, between the United States of America and the Mexican republic.

ART. I.—There shall be a firm and universal peace between the United States of America and the Mexican republic, and between their

541

respective countries, territories, cities, towns, and people, without
exception of places or persons.

Art. II.—Immediately on the signature of this treaty, a convention
shall be entered into between a commissioner or commissioners
appointed by the general-in-chief of the forces of the United States,
and such as may be appointed by the Mexican government, to the
end that a provisional suspension of hostilities shall take place; and
that in the places occupied by the said forces, constitutional order
may be re-established, as regards the political, administrative, and
judicial branches, so far as this shall be permitted by the circumstances
of military occupation.

Art. III.—Immediately upon the ratification of the present treaty
by the government of the United States, orders shall be transmitted to
the commanders of their land and naval forces, requiring the latter
(provided this treaty shall then have been ratified by the government
of the Mexican republic) immediately to desist from blockading any
Mexican ports; and requiring the former (under the same condition)
to commence, at the earliest moment practicable, withdrawing all
troops of the United States then in the interior of the Mexican republic,
to points that shall be selected by common agreement, at a distance
from the sea-ports not exceeding thirty leagues; and such evacuation
of the interior of the republic shall be completed with the least possible
delay: the Mexican government hereby binding itself to afford every
facility in its power for rendering the same convenient to the troops,
on their march, and in their new positions, and for promoting a good
understanding between them and the inhabitants. In like manner,
orders shall be despatched to the persons in charge of the custom-
houses at all ports occupied by the forces of the United States, requiring them (under the same condition) immediately to deliver possession
of the same to the persons authorized by the Mexican government to
receive it, together with all bonds and evidences of debt for duties on
importations and on exportations, not yet fallen due. Moreover, a
faithful and exact account shall be made out, showing the entire
amount of all duties on imports and on exports, collected at such
custom-houses, or elsewhere in Mexico, by authority of the United
States, from and after the day of the ratification of this treaty by the
government of the Mexican republic; and also an account of the
cost of collection; and such entire amount, deducting only the cost
of collection, shall be delivered to the Mexican government, at the

city of Mexico, within three months after the exchange of ratifications.

The evacuation of the capital of the Mexican republic by the troops
of the United States, in virtue of the above stipulation, shall be completed in one month after the orders there stipulated for shall have
been received by the commander of said troops, or sooner if possible.

ART. IV.—Immediately after the exchange of ratifications of the
present treaty, all castles, forts, territories, places and possessions,
which have been taken and occupied by the forces of the United
States during the present war, within the limits of the Mexican
republic, as about to be established by the following article, shall be
definitely restored to the said republic, together with all the artillery,
arms, apparatus of war, munitions, and other public property, which
were in the said castles and forts when captured, and which shall
remain there at the time when this treaty shall be duly ratified by the
government of the Mexican republic.   To this end, immediately upon
the signature of this treaty, orders shall be despatched to the American
officers commanding such castles and ports, securing against the
removal or destruction of any such artillery, arms, apparatus of war,
munitions, or other public property.   The city of Mexico, within the
inner line of intrenchments, surrounding the said city, is comprehended
in the above stipulations, as regards the restoration of artillery,
apparatus of war, &c.

The final evacuation of the territory of the Mexican republic by the
forces of the United States, shall be completed in three months from
the said exchange of ratifications, or sooner if possible : the Mexican
republic hereby engaging, as in the foregoing article, to use all means
in its power for facilitating such evacuation, and rendering it convenient
to the troops, and for promoting a good understanding between them
and the inhabitants.

If, however, the ratification of this treaty by both parties should
not take place in time to allow the embarkation of the troops of the
United States to be completed before the commencement of the sickly
season, at the Mexican ports on the Gulf of Mexico, in such case a
friendly arrangement shall be entered into between the general-in-
chief of the said troops and the Mexican government, whereby healthy
and otherwise suitable places, at a distance from the ports not exceeding thirty leagues, shall be designated for the residence of such troops
as may not yet have embarked, until the return of the healthy season.

And the space of time here referred to as comprehending the sickly season, shall be understood to extend from the first day of May to the first day of November.

All prisoners of war taken on either side, on land or on sea, shall be restored as soon as practicable after the exchange of the ratifications of this treaty. It is also agreed that if any Mexicans should now be held as captives by any savage tribe within the limits of the United States, as about to be established by the following article, the government of the said United States will exact the release of such captives, and cause them to be restored to their country.

ART. V.—The boundary line between the two republics shall commence in the Gulf of Mexico, three leagues from land, opposite the mouth of the Rio Grande, otherwise called Rio Bravo del Norte, or opposite the mouth of its deepest branch, if it should have more than one branch emptying directly into the sea; from thence up the middle of that river, following the deepest channel, where it has more than one, to the point where it strikes the southern boundary of New Mexico; thence, westwardly, along the whole southern boundary of New Mexico (which runs north of the town called *Paso*) to its western termination; thence northward along the western line of New Mexico, until it intersects the first branch of the river Gila; (or if it should not intersect any branch of that river, then to the point on the said line nearest to such branch, and thence in a direct line to the same;) thence down the middle of the said branch and of the said river, until it empties into the Rio Colorado; thence across the Rio Colorado, following the division line between Upper and Lower California, to the Pacific Ocean.

The southern and western limits of New Mexico, mentioned in this article, are those laid down in the map, entitled " *Map of the United Mexican States, as organized and defined by various acts of the Congress of said republic, and constructed according to the best anthorities. Revised edition. Published at New York, in* 1847, *by J. Disturnell.*" Of which map a copy is added to this treaty, bearing the signatures and seals of the undersigned plenipotentiaries. And in order to preclude all difficulty in tracing upon the ground the limit separating Upper from Lower California, it is agreed that the said limit shall consist of a straight line, drawn from the middle of the Rio Gila, where it unites with the Colorado, to a point on the coast of the Pacific Ocean—distant one marine league due south of the southernmost point of the port of San Diego, according to the plan of said port, made in the year 1782, by Don Juan Pantojer, second sailing-master of the Spanish fleet, and published at Madrid in the year 1802, in the atlas to the voyage of the schooners *Sutil* and *Mexicana*, of which plan a copy is hereunto added, signed and sealed by the respective plenipotentiaries.

In order to designate the boundary line with due precision, upon authoritative maps, and to establish on the ground landmarks which shall show the limits of both republics, as described in the present article, the two governments shall each appoint a commissioner and a surveyor, who, before the expiration of one year from the date of the exchange of ratifications of this treaty, shall meet at the port of San Diego, and proceed to run and mark the said boundary in its whole course to the mouth of the Rio Bravo del Norte. They shall keep journals and make out plans of their operations : and the result agreed upon by them, shall be deemed a part of this treaty, and shall have the same force as if it were inserted therein. The two governments will amicably agree regarding what may be necessary to these persons, and also as to their respective escorts, should such be necessary.

The boundary line established by this article shall be religiously respected by each of the two republics, and no change shall ever be made therein, except by the express and free consent of both nations, lawfully given by the general government of each, in conformity with its own constitution.

ART. VI.—The vessels and citizens of the United States shall, in all time, have a free and uninterrupted passage by the Gulf of California, and by the river Colorado, below its confluence with the Gila, to and from their possessions situated north of the boundary line defined in the preceding article ; it being understood that this passage is to be by navigating the Gulf of California, and the river Colorado ; and not by land, without the express consent of the Mexican government.

If, by the examinations that may be made, it should be ascertained to be practicable and advantageous to construct a road, canal, or railway, which should, in whole or in part, run upon the river Gila, or upon its right or its left bank, within the space of one marine league from either margin of the river, the governments of both republics will form an agreement regarding its construction, in order that it may serve equally for the use and advantage of both countries.

Art. VII.—The river Gila, and the part of the Del Norte lying below the southern boundary of New Mexico, being, agreeably to the fifth article, divided in the middle between the two republics, the navigation of the Gila and of the Bravo, below said boundary, shall be free and common to the vessels and citizens of both countries; and neither shall, without the consent of the other, construct any work that may impede or interrupt, in whole or in part, the exercise of this right—not even for the purpose of favouring new methods of navigation. Nor shall any tax or contribution, under any denomination or title, be levied upon vessels, or persons navigating the same, or upon merchandise, or effects, transported thereon, except in the case of landing upon one of their shores. If, for the purpose of making the said rivers navigable, or for maintaining them in such state, it should be necessary or advantageous to establish any tax or contribution, this shall not be done without the consent of both governments.

The stipulations contained in the present article shall not impair the territorial rights of either republic, within its established limits.

Art. VIII. — Mexicans now established in territories previously belonging to Mexico, and which remain, for the future, within the limits of the United States, as defined by the present treaty, shall be free to continue where they now reside, or to remove, at any time, to the Mexican republic, retaining the property which they possess in the said territories, or disposing thereof, and removing the proceeds wherever they please, without their being subjected, on this account, to any contribution, or tax, or charge, whatever.

Those who shall prefer to remain in said territories, may either retain the title and rights of Mexican citizens, or acquire those of citizens of the United States. But they shall be under the obligation to make their selection within one year from the date of the exchange of ratifications of this treaty; and those who shall remain in the said territories, after the expiration of that year, without having declared their intention to retain the character of Mexicans, shall be considered to have elected to become citizens of the United States.

In the said territories, property of every kind, now belonging to Mexicans not established there, shall be inviolably respected. The present owners, the heirs of these, and all Mexicans who may hereafter acquire said property by contract, shall enjoy, with respect to it, guaranties equally ample as if the same belonged to citizens of the United States.

Art. IX.—The Mexicans who, in the territories aforesaid, shall not preserve the character of citizens of the Mexican republic, conformably with what is stipulated in the preceding article, shall be incorporated into the union of the United States, and admitted as soon as possible, according to the principles of the federal constitution, to the enjoyment of all the rights of citizens of the United States. In the mean time, they shall be maintained and protected in the enjoyment of their liberty, their property, and the civil rights now vested in them according to the Mexican laws. With respect to political rights, their condition shall be on an equality with that of the inhabitants of the other territories of the United States, and at least equally good as that of the inhabitants of Louisiana and the Floridas, when these provinces, by transfer from the French republic and the crown of Spain, became territories of the United States.

The same most ample guaranty shall be enjoyed by all ecclesiastics and religious corporations or communities, as well in the discharge of the offices of their ministry as in the enjoyment of their property of every kind, whether individual or corporate. This guaranty shall embrace all temples, houses, and edifices dedicated to the Roman Catholic worship, as well as all property destined to its support, or to that of schools, hospitals, and other foundations for charitable or beneficent purposes. No property of this nature shall be considered as having become the property of the American government, or as subject to be by it disposed of, or diverted to other uses.

Finally, the relations and communication between the Catholics living in the territories aforesaid, and their respective ecclesiastical authorities, shall be open, free, and exempt from all hindrance whatever, even although such authorities should reside within the limits of the Mexican republic, as defined by this treaty; and this freedom shall continue, so long as a new demarkation of ecclesiastical districts shall not have been made, conformably with the laws of the Roman Catholic church.

[Article IX. was expunged, and in its stead the Senate adopted and inserted substantially the third article of the treaty with France, of 1803, for the cession of Louisiana, to the effect *that inhabitants of the ceded territory shall be incorporated in the Union of the United States, and admitted as soon as Congress shall deter-*

71

mine, according to the principles of the federal constitution, to the enjoyment of all the rights, advantages, and immunities of citizens of the United States ; and in the mean time, they shall be maintained and protected in the full enjoyment of their liberty, property, and the religion which they profess.]

ART. X.—All grants of land made by the Mexican government, or by the competent authorities, in territories previously appertaining to Mexico, and remaining for the future within the limits of the United States, shall be respected as valid, to the same extent that the same grants would be valid if the said territories had remained within the limits of Mexico. But the grantees of lands in Texas, put in possession thereof, who, by reason of the circumstances of the country, since the beginning of the troubles between Texas and the Mexican government, may have been prevented from fulfilling all the conditions of their grants, shall be under the obligation to fulfil the said conditions within the periods limited in the same, respectively ; such periods to be now counted from the date of the exchange of ratifications of this treaty ; in default of which, the said grants shall not be obligatory upon the State of Texas, in virtue of the stipulations contained in this article.

The foregoing stipulation in regard to grantees of land in Texas is extented to all grantees of land in the territories aforesaid, elsewhere than in Texas, put in possession under such grants ; and, in default of the fulfilment of the conditions of any such grant, within the new period, which, as is above stipulated, begins with the day of the exchange of ratifications of this treaty, the same shall be null and void.

The Mexican government declares that no grant whatever of lands in Texas has been made since the second day of March, one thousand eight hundred and thirty-six ; and that no grant whatever of lands, in any of the territories aforesaid, has been made since the thirteenth day of May, one thousand eight hundred and forty-six.

[The above article was expunged by the Senate.]

ART. XI.—Considering that a great part of the territories which, by the present treaty, are to be comprehended for the future within the limits of the United States, is now occupied by savage tribes who will hereafter be under the control of the government of the United States, and whose incursions within the territory of Mexico would be prejudicial in the extreme, it is solemnly agreed that all such incursions shall be forcibly restrained by the government of the United States, whensoever this may be necessary; and that when they cannot be prevented, they shall be punished by the said government, and satisfaction for the same shall be exacted—all in the same way, and with equal diligence and energy, as if the same incursions were committed within its own territory, against its own citizens.

It shall not be lawful, under any pretext whatever, for any inhabitant of the United States to purchase or acquire any Mexican, or any foreigner residing in Mexico, who may have been captured by Indians inhabiting the territory of either of the two republics, nor to purchase or acquire horses, mules, cattle, or property of any kind, stolen within Mexican territory by such Indians: nor to provide such Indians with fire-arms or ammunition, by sale or otherwise.

And in the event of any person or persons captured within Mexican territory by Indians, being carried into the territory of the United States, the government of the latter engages and binds itself in the most solemn manner, so soon as it shall know of such captives being within its territory, and shall be able to do so, through the faithful exercise of its influence and power, to rescue them and return them to their country, or deliver them to the agent or representative of the Mexican government. The Mexican authorities will, as far as practicable, give to the government of the United States notice of such captures; and its agents shall pay the expenses incurred in the maintenance and transmission of the rescued captives; who, in the mean time, shall be treated with the utmost hospitality by the American authorities at the place where they may be. But if the government of the United States, before receiving such notice from Mexico, should obtain intelligence, through any other channel, of the existence of Mexican captives within its territory, it will proceed forthwith to effect their release and delivery to the Mexican agent, as above stipulated.

For the purpose of giving to these stipulations the fullest possible efficacy, thereby affording the security and redress demanded by their true spirit and intent, the government of the United States will now and hereafter pass, without unnecessary delay, and always vigilantly enforce, such laws as the nature of the subject may require. And finally, the sacredness of this obligation shall never be lost sight of by the said government when providing for the removal of Indians from any portion of said territories, or for its being settled by the citizens of the United States; but, on the contrary, special care then shall be taken not to place its Indian occupants under the necessity of seeking new homes, by committing those invasions which the United States have solemnly obliged themselves to restrain.

ART. XII. — In consideration of the extension acquired by the boundaries of the United States, as defined in the fifth article of the present treaty, the government of the United States engages to pay to that of the Mexican republic the sum of fifteen millions of dollars, in the one or the other of the two modes below specified. The Mexican government shall, at the time of ratifying this treaty, declare which of these two modes of payment it prefers; and the mode so elected by it shall be conformed to by that of the United States.

First mode of payment: Immediately after this treaty shall have been duly ratified by the government of the Mexican republic, the sum of three millions of dollars shall be paid to the said government by that of the United States, at the city of Mexico, in the gold or silver coin of Mexico. For the remaining twelve millions of dollars, the United States shall create a stock, bearing an interest of six per centum per annum, commencing on the day of the ratification of this treaty by the government of the Mexican republic, and payable annually at the city of Washington; the principal of said stock to be redeemable there, at the pleasure of the government of the United States, at any time after two years from the exchange of ratifications of this treaty; six months' public notice of the intention to redeem the same being previously given. Certificates of such stock, in proper form, for such sums as shall be specified by the Mexican government, and transferable by the said government, shall be delivered to the same by that of the United States.

Second mode of payment: Immediately after this treaty shall have been duly ratified by the government of the Mexican republic, the sum of three millions of dollars shall be paid to the said government by that of the United States, at the city of Mexico, in the gold or silver coin of Mexico. The remaining twelve millions of dollars shall be paid at the same place, and in the same coin, in annual instalments of three millions of dollars each, together with interest on the same at the rate of six per centum per annum. This interest shall begin to run upon the whole sum of twelve millions from the day of the ratification of the present treaty by the Mexican government, and the first of the instalments shall be paid at the expiration of one year from the same day. Together with each annual instalment, as it falls due, the whole interest accruing on such instalment from the beginning shall also be paid. Certificates in proper form, for the said instalments, respectively, in such sums as shall be desired by the Mexican government, and transferable by it, shall be delivered to the said government by that of the United States.

[The second mode of payment was accepted by the Mexican government.]

Art. XIII.—The United States engage, moreover, to assume and pay to the claimants all the amounts now due them, and those here-after to become due, by reason of the claims already liquidated and decided against the Mexican republic, under the conventions between the two republics severally concluded on the 11th day of April, eighteen hundred and thirty-nine, and on the 30th day of January, eighteen hundred and forty-three; so that the Mexican republic shall be absolutely exempt for the future, from all expense whatever on account of the said claims.

Art. XIV.—The United States do furthermore discharge the Mexican republic from all claims of citizens of the United States, not heretofore decided against the Mexican government, which may have arisen previously to the date of the signature of this treaty; which discharge shall be final and perpetual, whether the said claims be rejected or be allowed by the board of commissioners provided for in the following article, and whatever shall be the total amount of those allowed.

Art. XV.—The United States, exonerating Mexico from all demands on account of the claims of their citizens mentioned in the preceding article, and considering them entirely and for ever cancelled, what-ever their amount may be, undertake to make satisfaction for the same, to an amount not exceeding three and one quarter millions of dollars. To ascertain the validity and amount of those claims, a board of commissioners shall be established by the government of the United States, whose awards shall be final and conclusive; provided, that in deciding upon the validity of each claim, the board shall be guided and governed by the principles and rules of decision prescribed by the first and fifth articles of the unratified convention, concluded at the city of Mexico on the twentieth day of November, one thousand eight hundred and forty-three; and in no case shall an award be made in favour of any claim not embraced by these principles and rules.

If, in the opinion of the said board of commissioners, or of the claimants, any books, records, or documents in the possession or power of the government of the Mexican republic, shall be deemed necessary to the just decision of any claim, the commissioners, or the claimants through them, shall within such period as Congress may designate, make an application in writing for the same, addressed to the Mexican minister for foreign affairs, to be transmitted by the secretary of state of the United States; and the Mexican government engages, at the earliest possible moment after the receipt of such demand, to cause any of the books, records, or documents, so specified, which shall be in their possession or power (or authenticated copies or extracts of the same) to be transmitted to the said secretary of state, who shall immediately deliver them over to the said board of commissioners; Provided, that no such application shall be made by, or at the instance of, any claimant, until the facts which it is expected to prove by such books, records, or documents, shall have been stated under oath or affirmation.

ART. XVI.—Each of the contracting parties reserves to itself the entire right to fortify whatever point within its territory it may judge proper so to fortify, for its security.

ART. XVII.—The treaty of amity, commerce and navigation, concluded at the city of Mexico on the 5th day of April, A. D. 1831, between the United States of America and the United Mexican States, except the additional article, and except so far as the stipulations of the said treaty may not be incompatible with any stipulation contained in the present treaty, is hereby revived for the period of eight years from the day of the exchange of ratifications of this treaty, with the same force and virtue as if incorporated therein; it being understood that each of the contracting parties reserves to itself the right, at any time after the said period of eight years shall have expired, to terminate the same by giving one year's notice of such intention to the other party.

ART. XVIII.—All supplies whatever for troops of the United States in Mexico, arriving at ports in the occupation of such troops previous to the final evacuation thereof, although subsequently to the restoration of the custom-houses at such ports, shall be entirely exempt from duties and charges of any kind; the government of the United States hereby engaging and pledging its faith to establish, and vigilantly to enforce, all possible guards for securing the revenue of Mexico, by preventing the importation, under cover of this stipulation, of any articles other than such, both in kind and in quality, as shall really be wanted for the use and consumption of the forces of the United States during, the time they may remain in Mexico. To this end, it shall be the duty of all officers and agents of the United States to denounce to the Mexican authorities at the respective ports any attempts at a fraudulent abuse of this stipulation which they may know of or may have reason to suspect, and to give to such authorities all the aid in their power with regard thereto ; and every such attempt, when duly proved and established by sentence of a competent tribunal, shall be punished by the confiscation of the property so attempted to be fraudulently introduced.

ART. XIX.—With respect to all merchandise, effects, and property whatsoever, imported into ports of Mexico whilst in the occupation of the forces of the United States, whether by citizens of either republic, or by citizens or subjects of any neutral nation, the following rules shall be observed :

1. All such merchandise, effects, and property, if imported previously to the restoration of the custom-houses to the Mexican authorities, as stipulated for in the third article of this treaty, shall be exempt from confiscation, although the importation of the same be prohibited by the Mexican tariff.

2. The same perfect exemption shall be enjoyed by all such merchandise, effects, and property, imported subsequently to the restoration of the custom-houses, and previously to the sixty days fixed in the following article for the coming into force of the Mexican tariff, at such ports respectively ; the said merchandise, effects, and property being, however, at the time of their importation, subject to the payment of duties, as provided for in the said following article.

3. All merchandise, effects, and property described in the two rules foregoing shall, during their continuance at the place of importation, or upon their leaving such place for the interior, be exempt from all duty, tax, or impost of every kind, under whatsoever title or denomination. Nor shall they be there subjected to any charge whatsoever upon the sale thereof.

4. All merchandise, effects, and property, described in the first and second rules, which shall have been removed to any place in the interior whilst such place was in the occupation of the forces of the United States, shall, during their continuance therein, be exempt from

all tax upon the sale or consumption thereof, and from every kind of impost or contribution, under whatsoever title or denomination.

5. But if any merchandise, effects, or property, described in the first and second rules, shall be removed to any place not occupied at the time by the forces of the United States, they shall, upon their introduction into such place, or upon their sale or consumption there, be subject to the same duties which, under the Mexican laws, they would be required to pay in such cases if they had been imported in time of peace, through the maritime custom-houses, and had there paid the duties conformably with the Mexican tariff.

6. The owners of all merchandise, effects, or property described in the first and second rules, and existing in any port of Mexico, shall have the right to reship the same, exempt from all tax, impost, or contribution whatever.

With respect to the metals, or other property, exported from any Mexican port whilst in the occupation of the forces of the United States, and previously to the restoration of the custom-house at such port, no person shall be required by the Mexican authorities, whether general or state, to pay any tax, duty, or contribution upon any such exportation, or in any manner to account for the same to the said authorities.

ART. XX.—Through consideration for the interests of commerce generally, it is agreed, that if less than sixty days should elapse between the date of the signature of this treaty and the restoration of the custom-houses, conformably with the stipulation in the third article, in such case all merchandise, effects, and property whatsoever, arriving at the Mexican ports after the restoration of the said custom-houses, and previously to the expiration of sixty days after the day of the signature of this treaty, shall be admitted to entry; and no other duties shall be levied thereon than the duties established by the tariff found in force at such custom-houses at the time of the restoration of the same. And to all such merchandise, effects, and property, the rules established by the preceding article shall apply.

ART. XXI.—If, unhappily, any disagreement should hereafter arise between the governments of the two republics, whether with respect to the interpretation of any stipulation in this treaty, or with respect to any other particular concerning the political or commercial relations of the two nations, the said governments, in the name of those nations, do promise to each other that they will endeavour, in the most sincere and earnest manner, to settle the differences so arising, and to preserve the state of peace and friendship in which the two countries are now placing themselves; using, for this end, mutual representations and pacific negotiations. And if, by these means, they should not be enabled to come to an agreement, a resort shall not, on this account, be had to reprisals, aggression, or hostility of any kind, by the one republic against the other, until the government of that which deems itself aggrieved shall have maturely considered, in the spirit of peace and good neighbourship, whether it would not be better that such difference should be settled by the arbitration of commissioners appointed on each side, or by that of a friendly nation. And should such course be proposed by either party, it shall be acceded to by the other, unless deemed by it altogether incompatible with the nature of the difference, or the circumstances of the case.

ART. XXII.—If (which is not to be expected, and which God forbid!) war shall unhappily break out between the two republics, they do now, with a view to such calamity, solemnly pledge themselves to each other and to the world, to observe the following rules, absolutely, where the nature of the subject permits, and as closely as possible in all cases where such absolute observance shall be impossible.

1. The merchants of either republic then residing in the other shall be allowed to remain twelve months, (for those dwelling in the interior,) and six months (for those dwelling at the seaports,) to collect their debts and settle their affairs; during which periods, they shall enjoy the same protection, and be on the same footing, in all respects, as the citizens or subjects of the most friendly nations; and, at the expiration thereof, or at any time before, they shall have full liberty to depart, carrying off all their effects without molestation or hindrance; conforming therein to the same laws which the citizens or subjects of the most friendly nations are required to conform to. Upon the entrance of the armies of either nation into the territories of the other, women and children, ecclesiastics, scholars of every faculty, cultivators of the earth, merchants, artisans, manufacturers, and fishermen, unarmed and inhabiting unfortified towns, villages, or places, and in general all persons whose occupations are for the common subsistence and benefit of mankind, shall be allowed to continue their respective employments unmolested in their persons. Nor shall their houses or goods be burnt or otherwise destroyed, nor their cattle taken, nor

their fields wasted, by the armed force into whose power, by the events of war, they may happen to fall; but if the necessity arise to take any thing from them for the use of such armed force, the same shall be paid for at an equitable price. All churches, hospitals, schools, colleges, libraries, and other establishments, for charitable and beneficent purposes, shall be respected, and all persons connected with the same, protected in the discharge of their duties, and the pursuit of their vocations.

2. In order that the fate of prisoners of war may be alleviated, all such practices as those of sending them into distant, inclement, or unwholesome districts, or crowding them into close and noxious places, shall be studiously avoided. They shall not be confined in dungeons, prison-ships, or prisons, nor be put in irons, or bound, or otherwise restrained in the use of their limbs. The officers shall enjoy liberty on their paroles, within convenient districts, and have comfortable quarters; and the common soldiers shall be disposed in cantonments, open and extensive enough for air and exercise, and lodged in barracks as roomy and good as are provided by the party in whose power they are for its own troops. But if any officer shall break his parole by leaving the district so assigned him, or any other prisoner shall escape from the limits of his cantonment, after they shall have been designated to him, such individual, officer, or other prisoner, shall forfeit so much of the benefit of this article as provides for his liberty on parole or in cantonment. And if an officer so breaking his parole, or any common soldier so escaping from the limits assigned him, shall afterwards be found in arms, previously to his being regularly exchanged, the person so offending shall be dealt with according to the established laws of war. The officers shall be daily furnished by the party in whose power they are, with as many rations, and of the same articles, as are allowed, either in kind or by commutation, to officers of equal rank in its own army; and all others shall be daily furnished with such ration as is allowed to a common soldier in its own service; the value of all which supplies shall, at the close of the war, or at periods to be agreed upon between the respective commanders, be paid by the other party, on a mutual adjustment of accounts for the subsistence of prisoners; and such accounts shall not be mingled with or set off against any others, nor the balance due on them be withheld, as a compensation or reprisal for any cause whatever, real or pretended. Each party shall be

allowed to keep a commissary of prisoners, appointed by itself, with every cantonment of prisoners, in possession of the other; which commissary shall see the prisoners as often as he pleases; shall be allowed to receive, exempt from all duties or taxes, and to distribute, whatever comforts may be sent to them by their friends; and shall be free to transmit his reports in open letters to the party by whom he is employed.

And it is declared that neither the pretence that war dissolves all treaties, nor any other whatever, shall be considered as annulling or suspending the solemn covenant contained in this article. On the contrary, the state of war is precisely that for which it is provided; and during which, its stipulations are to be as sacredly observed as the most acknowledged obligations under the law of nature or nations.

ART. XXIII.—This treaty shall be ratified by the President of the United States of America, by and with the advice and consent of the Senate thereof; and by the President of the Mexican republic, with the previous approbation of its General Congress; and the ratifications shall be exchanged in the city of Washington, in four months from the date of the signature hereof, or sooner if practicable.

In faith whereof, we, the respective plenipotentiaries, have signed this treaty of peace, friendship, limits, and settlement; and have hereunto affixed our seals respectively. Done in quintuplicate, at the city of Guadalupe Hidalgo, on the second day of February, in the year of our Lord one thousand eight hundred and forty-eight.

N. P. TRIST,	[L. s.]
LUIS G. CUEVAS,	[L. s.]
BERNARDO CONTO,	[L. s.]
MIG. ATRISTAIN,	[L. s.]

Additional and secret article of the treaty of peace, friendship, limits, and settlement, between the United States of America and the Mexican republic, signed this day by their respective plenipotentiaries. (Expunged.)

In view of the possibility that the exchange of the ratifications of this treaty may, by the circumstances in which the Mexican republic is placed, be delayed longer than the term of four months fixed by its twenty-third article for the exchange of ratifications of the same, it is hereby agreed that such delay shall not, in any manner, affect the force and validity of this treaty, unless it should exceed the term of eight months, counted from the date of the signature thereof.

This article is to have the same force and virtue as if inserted in the treaty to which this is an addition.

In faith whereof, we, the respective plenipotentiaries, have signed this additional and secret article, and have hereunto affixed our seals, respectively. Done in quintuplicate, at the city of Guadalupe Hidalgo, on the second day of February, in the year of our Lord one thousand eight hundred and forty-eight.

N. P. TRIST,	[L. S.]
LUIS G. CUEVAS,	[L. S.]
BERNARDO CONTO,	[L. S.]
MIG. ATRISTAIN,	[L. S.]

THE END.

COMPLETE HISTORY OF THE

LATE MEXICAN WAR!!

Battle of Churubusco

CONTAINING

AN AUTHENTIC ACCOUNT

OF ALL THE

Battles Fought in that Republic

TO THE

CLOSE OF THE WAR,

WITH A LIST OF THE KILLED AND WOUNDED:

TOGETHER WITH

A BRIEF SKETCH OF THE

LIVES OF GENERALS SCOTT AND TAYLOR

INCLUDING THE

TREATY OF PEACE.

ILLUSTRATED WITH FIFTEEN BEAUTIFUL ENGRAVINGS.

NEW YORK.

F. J. DOW & Co., 139 Nassau St.

1850.

GRAND PLAZA IN THE CITY OF MEXICO.

UNITED STATES VOLUNTEERS ADVANCING TO THE ATTACK OF THE FORTIFICATIONS AND HALLS AT CHAPULTEPEC

CITY OF MEXICO

NORTHERN EXTREMITY OF PUEBLO DE LOS ANGELAS

CAPTURE OF THE BISHOP'S PALACE

COMPLETE HISTORY

OF THE

LATE MEXICAN WAR.

CONTAINING AN AUTHENTIC ACCOUNT

OF

ALL THE BATTLES FOUGHT

IN THAT REPUBLIC

INCLUDING THE

TREATY OF PEACE:

WITH A LIST OF THE KILLED AND WOUNDED.

TOGETHER WITH

A BRIEF SKETCH OF THE

LIVES OF GENERALS SCOTT AND TAYLOR.

ILLUSTRATED WITH FIFTEEN BEAUTIFUL ENGRAVINGS.

BY AN EYE-WITNESS.

NEW YORK.

F. J. DOW & Co., 139 Nassau St.

1850

SANTA ANNA

GENERAL SCOTT

GENERAL TAYLOR

STORMING OF MONTEREY

BATTLE OF PALO ALTO

PREFACE.

The following pages are designed to record, in a brief manner, those facts in reference to the war in Mexico, worthy of preservation. It comprehends the substance of larger works, and is more convenient for reference. Lists of killed and wounded are given as fully and accurately as the official and authoritive reports would admit.

It is painful to contemplate, and especially describe the scenes of the battle field—the streams of blood—the groans of the wounded and dying—the hundreds or thousands slain—the gasp of death—the crushed hopes—undying spirits thus ushered suddenly and awfully into the presence of their Judge, perhaps unprepared—it is apalling! and we would turn away and weep for poor, depraved humanity. Still it is desirable that the facts should be laid before the public. How many wives, at the commencement of the war, parted with their companions never to meet again in this world, and are now eager to know all the circumstances connected with the war! How many parents, bereft of dear children, how many brothers and sisters, deprived of those whom they loved, are intensely anxious to hear all the particulars of each battle!

We present these pages to the public hoping the tragical scenes here described may deter others from imbibing a war spirit. We exhort them not to be influenced by the martial array, the din of battle and the clash of arms, and all the exciting parapharnalia of war.

BATTLE OF SIERRA GORDO

BATTLE OF BUENA VISTA

BRIEF SKETCH OF THE LIFE OF GENERAL SCOTT.

WINFIELD SCOTT was born June 13th, 1786, near Petersburgh, Virginia. His grandfather was a Scotchman, who fled to this country in consequence of being involved in the rebellion of 1847. His only son was William, who died in 1791, leaving two sons, the youngest of whom was *Winfield*.

His mother was a very amiable lady and endowed with superior intellectual and other accomplishments. She died in 1803, when the subject of this notice was only seventeen years of age.

At this time Winfield was noted for energy, stability of character, a high sense of honor, and warm social feelings. He studied one year in the High School at Richmond, and spent two years at William and Mary College, attending law lectures.

At the age of twenty years he was admitted to the bar as a lawyer.

In 1807 he emigrated to South Carolina, intending to practise law at Charleston; but in 1808 Congress determined to increase the army on account of English aggressions, and young Scott was appointed Captain of a company of Light Artillery by President Jefferson. In July, 1812, he was promoted to Lieutenant-Colonel, and was ordered to the Niagara frontier, as war between the United States and England had been declared. He soon distinguished himself by recapturing a British brig in Niagara river. In October, 1812, he proceeded to Lewiston, and with six hundred men repulsed a large force of the enemy. Finally, after several severe conflicts, the enemy being reinforced (having 1300 men), and Scott's band being reduced to 300, they were obliged to surrender to the British.

The American prisoners were sent to Quebec, and thence to Boston. Scott was soon exchanged, and joined the army at Fort Niagara in May, 1813, as Adjutant-General. He soon led on the advanced guard in an attack on Fort George, and with great bravery repulsed the British, and captured the fort.

March 9th, 1814, he was promoted to the rank of Brigadier-General. In July his brigade and a corps of artillery crossed Niagara river and captured Fort Erie, and then advanced to

Chippewa, and, with 1900 men, entirely routed 2100 of the enemy.

July 25th, Scott advanced towards Niagara and again met a large force of the enemy. The battle was fierce, and Scott manifested the greatest bravery, having two horses shot under him. He was wounded in his side, and finally disabled by a musket ball passing through his left shoulder. At midnight the Americans gained possession of the field, after a loss of 860, while the British lost 878.

Scott, immediately after this celebrated battle, was appointed Major-General, at the age of 28.

In 1816 he visited Europe, and on his return married Miss Maria Mayo, of Richmond, Va. He has several daughters, but no son living.

In 1831-2 he engaged in the " Black Hawk war," and finally terminated it by a treaty with the Indians.

When nullification in South Carolina threatened the country with civil war, Scott by his cunning yet peaceful and friendly proceedings, calmed the impending storm.

January 20th, 1836, he was ordered to take the command of the army in Florida and carry on the Seminole war. He had many skirmishes; but was recalled by the grumbling of enemies.

He made peace when there was a threatened invasion of Canada by Americans on the frontier in 1837. The steamer Caroline was burned by the British ; but the olive branch was finally accepted.

In 1838 he prevented a probable war with the Cherokee Indians.

He was the great " Pacificator" in the adjustment of the North-eastern boundary. It was undoubtedly by his wise management that a dreadfully severe war was prevented. Perhaps there is no man living who has so distinguished himself as a *brave general and kind pacificator.*

His achievements in the Mexican war are described in the following pages.

BRIEF SKETCH OF THE LIFE OF GENERAL TAYLOR.

THIS distinguished General was a native of " The Old Dominion." He was born in Orange County, Va., November 24th, 1784. His father, Richard Taylor, was somewhat noted as a military man in that State. Zachary is now (1847) 63 years old.

In 1785 his father moved to Kentucky, near Louisville, where Zachary spent most of his childhood.

As good schools were scarce at that time in Kentucky, his education was neglected. He was brought up on a farm ; but had a taste for military glory, and in May, 1808, President Jefferson appointed him a Lieutenant in the army at the age of 14 years. His first wreath of glory was won at " *Tippecanoe*," in a desperate battle with the Indians. May 7th, 1811. In consequence of his bravery in this conflict, President Madison gave him a Captain's commission.

In the spring of 1812 he was placed in command of Fort Harrison on the Wabash. War with England had been declared, and Tecumseh, with his Indian warriors, was resolved to exterminate the whites. Taylor had only 50 men in the fort, and half of them disabled by fever. September 4th, 1812, the indians attacked the fort about midnight. The sentinels were driven in, the block-house of the fort was on fire, and destruction seemed to be their inevitable lot. Taylor ordered a part of his men to extinguish the flames, and the remainder to return the fire. For seven hours the conflict was severe, and the savage yells terrific ; but the Indians were obliged to retire.

After this brave defence Taylor was promoted to the rank of brevet-Major. At the close of the war, by the influence of enemies, he was reduced to the rank of Captain. and, resenting the insult, he retired to his farm.

In 1815 he was reinstated by President Madison, and proceeded, in 1816, to Green Bay. He was soon appointed Lieutenant-Colonel, and, until 1832, was on the Western and North-western frontiers, performing important services.

General Jackson, in 1832, appointed him Colonel, and sent him into the " Black Hawk war." In July General Atkinson arrived at the scene of action with 2500 men, including 400 under Colonel Taylor. When the Indians retreated into the wilderness, 1300 men under Taylor were ordered in pursuit. They overtook them near the junction of the Mississippi and Iowa rivers, where a desperate conflict ensued, in which the savages were totally routed. Taylor soon captured Black Hawk and ended the war.

Taylor was afterwards ordered to Fort Crawford, at Prairie du Chien, and remained there until 1836, when he was called to assist in the Seminole war in Florida, which commenced in 1835. All efforts failed to bring the savages to subjection until December, 1837, when Colonel Taylor, with 1100 men, left Fort Gardner in pursuit. December 25th, he was attacked by a large body of Indians with rifles in ambuscade. The battle was fierce and bloody. The volunteers, at first, began to give way as their leaders fell, but the regulars pressed on. This battle of " Okee-cho-bee" continued an hour, when the Indians retired, but were hotly pursued. The savages exhibited the greatest bravery. Our loss was 14 officers and 120 privates killed or wounded.

This broke the power of the war. Many Indians surrendered to our men, and the scene of bloodshed gradually terminated. Taylor soon received the rank of Brevet-Brigadier-General, and in April, 1838, was appointed to the command of our troops in Florida. He remained two years longer, and then, at his request, was recalled.

Afterwards he was appointed to the command of the First Department of the U. S. Army in the South-west. His headquarters were at Fort Jesup until 1841, when he was ordered to Fort Gibson. He remained there about five years, when, in 1845, he was ordered to Texas, in anticipation of her annexation to the United States.

The remainder of General Taylor's triumphant career is described in the following pages. He has proved himself to be one of the bravest and most skilful generals of modern times

BATTLES OF MEXICO,

Various circumstances contributed to produce this war. In the first place the government of the U. S. had certain claims against Mexico, acknowledged by the latter, but not cancelled. Next, the people of Texas, having formed themselves into an independent government maintained that independence eight years, were desirous of being annexed to the United States. In order to accomplish this object, as Mexico was opposed to it, it was agreed between our government and that of Texas, that the former should send upon the borders of Texas, an armed force sufficient to put down any opposition from Mexico. Accordingly Zachary Taylor, Col. of the 6th Regiment of Infantry, was appointed to take command of these forces. He repaired to Fort Jessup, Louisana, and found that post garrisoned by seven companies of the 2d regiment of Dragoons, under the command of Col. D. E. Twiggs. May 10th, 1844, eight companies of the 3d Regiment of Infantry, stationed at Jefferson Barracks, Missouri, repaired to the same place, commanded by Lieutenant Col. E. A. Hitchcock. Their encampment was called Camp Wilkins. Eight companies of the 4th Regiment from Jefferson Barracks, went, May 13, to Grand Ecore on the Red River, under the command of Colonel Vose. Z. Taylor, with the title of Brevet Brigadier General, arrived at Fort Jessup about the middle of June. April, 1845 two companies arrived from Fort Leavenworth, making 25 companies in all of what was called the " army of observation." It having been voted by Congress (Feb. 1845), to annex Texas to the United States, and as the people of that State in convention, would meet, and probably accept the proposition of annexation in July, it was thought best for the army of observation to be prepared to move to the western frontier of Texas if necessary. Accordingly it proceeded to New Orleans in July 1845, ready to embark to any requisite point.

While at that city Col. J. H. Vose of the 4th Infantry died in a fit, which cast a gloom over his associates in arms. July 23d a part of the force set sail for Corpus Christi, (generally called Kinney's Ranch," situated on the western shore of Corpus Christi Bay) and arrived July 31. Many interesting incidents and some spirited battles have occurred at this military post, between the Mexicans and Texans, in which Santa Anna acted a prominent part; but we must not tarry to describe them here. The army now was no longer called "army of observation;" but the "army of occupation." In August the aspect of affairs began to be menacing, and it was expected that Mexico would soon declare war. General Arista, was at Monterey with a considerable Mexican force, and there was another at Matamoras. In the mean time new companies from the United States occasionally arrived.

Sept. 12th, the steamer Dayton, having on board several officers and soldiers, burst her boilers, on her way to St. oseph's Island, and eight lost their lives in a most distressing manner. In September General Worth with six companies, and Major Ringgold with his company of horse and others, arrived at the camp. By the middle of October 1845 the army of occupation consisted of 251 officers 3671 privates, total 3922. These were on the coast, and there were about 150 in the interior.

Texas claimed the land to the River Rio Grande. anc General Taylor was ordered, in Feb. 1846, to move th army to some point on that river. In March it accordingl, started, having been at Corpus Christi seven months anc eleven days. March 16th Col. Twiggs met the advances guard of the enemy and was ordered to advance no fur ther. He returned to the army and reported. Nothing however, was seen of the enemy again until our forces reached the banks of the Colorado, the passage of which was strongly disputed. The Mexican forces were drawn up on the opposite bank, and declared that they would fire upon our forces if they attempted to cross. General Taylor told them, that as soon as the bank was cut down for the train to pass, the first Mexican that he saw after our men entered the river would be shot. At this they fled. The Adjutant general, Gen. Mejia, the commanding officer at Matamoras, handed a paper to General Taylor informing him, that if he crossed they would have a fight; but no opposition appeared. The order of march as our army drew nearer Point Isabel was in four columns, the Dragoons on the right and the 3d Brigade on the left. Before arriving, however, it was ascertained that the place was deserted by the enemy and that all the buildings but one were burned. Our army were then ordered to direct their march towards Matamoras and General Worth encamped 12 miles from that place. General Taylor proceeded to point Isabel and the steamers and provisions arrived at the same time. While a deputation of fifty armed citizens of Matamoras, protesting

there against our occupying the country. The general told
them that he would answer them at Matamoras. Defences
were ordered to be constructed at the Point and Major Monroe appointed Commander of the port. March 25th, General
Worth proceeded three miles farther, to Palo Alto and waited for General Taylor. March 28th, the army moved towards Matamoras, which is on the Rio Grande, arriving op
posite the city about 11 A. M. Two of our advanced
guard were taken prisoners by the Mexicans, and the horse
of a boy who was a bugler; which excited our men considerably. About two hundred Mexicans were to be seen
and their colours flying in various places. General Worth
was ordered to answer the deputation which visited Gen.
Taylor at Point Isabel. The Mexicans for some time
would not send a boat across the river: but at last one came
with an officer. General Worth sent him back saying that
he wished to see the commanding officer. Gen. Mejia
said that he would neither receive General Worth or General Taylor's communication. Mejia sent General La Vega
and Worth crossed the river and the interview took place
on the Mexican side. La Vega said that the Mexicans
considered us as invaders. Nothing of importance was accomplished by the interview. A flag was soon raised by
our army on the banks of the Rio Grande. It was thought
that the Mexican force, at this post was fifteen hundred.
March 26th it was feared that our forces would be attacked at night and they were ordered to sleep upon their
arms. Capt. May with a squadron of the 2nd Dragoons
marched to Point Isabel (27 miles) in four hours to reinforce
the garrison. On the first of April Gen. Taylor demanded
the release of the captured Dragoons and they were returned with their equipments. It is surprising that several of
our men deserted and went over to the enemy. Some of

them were shot, who attempted to swim the river. News arrived, April 9th that Mr. Slidell, United States minister to Mexico having given up all hope of opening negotiations had left the city and returned to the U. S.

BATTLE OF MATAMORAS.

General Ampudia, who had superseded Arista, arrived from the South the 11th of April and ordered General Taylor to leave in 24 hours or he should consider us as having declared war against Mexico. Taylor answered that he did not wish for 24 hours but would return an answer at 10 o'clock the next day. He told Ampudia that he was sent there by his government in a peaceful attitude and he *intended to remain*, and warned Ampudia against firing the first gun. Lieutenant Porter, while out in pursuit of Col. Cross, who was supposed to be killed was attacked by some Mexicans and slain. Col. Cross was afterwards found murdered. April 26th an ambush was laid for a company of our men and 2 sergeants and 8 privates were killed in an engagement with the enemy.

There was every appearance of a general and speedy attack. General Taylor sent a requisition on the governors of Louisiana and Texas for 5000 men. April 25th General Arista arrived at the scene of action. April 28th Capt. Walker's camp was attacked by Generals Torrejon and Canales, being stationed midway between Point Isabel and Matamoras. 5 of his men were killed and 4 missing, he having gone out with some of his force on a scout. April 29th it was thought that the Point was attacked as cannon was heard in that direction, and a portion of the army marched immediately in that direction.   The report was false as there had been no attack.

May 3rd the batteries from Matamoras opened upon our camp at day-break with great energy.   The battle was fierce for a while and in 30 minutes all the heavy gun batteries of the enemy were silenced by our artillery. The enemy threw many shells; but without effect.

————

BATTLE OF PALO ALTO.

Most of our forces were at Point Isabel and in that vicinity though some were opposite Matamoras.   General Taylor, May 7th directed the army to march in the direction of Matamoras.   It started at 3, P. M. having a valuable train of provisions and munitions of war.   Six twelve-pounders were in the wagons and a battery of two eighteen pounders was drawn by oxen.   The forces were under the command of Lieut. Churchill.   On the morning of the 8th the enemy were observed less than a mile distant, occupying a front of about a mile and a half.   The general formed his men in column of attack and permitted them to go half at a time and get water to fill their canteens, as they had marched twelve miles that day and suffered from heat and thirst.   Our army moved on with firmness to meet the enemy, and when within 700 yards the enemy opened their fire from a battery on the right.   The right wing of our army

was composed of the fifth Infantry on the right, Ringgold's Artillery, the 3rd Infantry, Churchill's eighteen
pound battery and 4th Infantry and commanded by Col.
Twiggs. The left wing composed of Duncan's Artillery and the 8th Infantry was commanded Brevet Lieutenant-Colonel Belknap. Ringgold's and Duncan's batteries
advanced and commenced firing. The enemy fired continually but not with much precision. Their cavalry
move on the left and then three batteries placed in a line
at a considerable distance from each other and bodies of
infantry between, making a long line of battle. Ring-
golds battery made dreadful havoc, cutting down almost
whole platoons at once. The two eighteen pounders
roared tremendously and the cavalry of the enemy soon
began to retire, at first in a trot and then in a gallop.
A movement of the enemy's flank, composed of Cavalry
one thousand strong, endangered our train and was
promptly met by a section of Ringgold's battery under
Lieut. Ridgeway and the fifth and third Infantry. They
were received by 5th in a square and twenty of them
were killed from the fire of an angle. When the enemy
saw the 3rd Infantry advancing in column by division,
they fled with rapidity. On the left Duncan cut them
down in great numbers and the shout of our men could be
heard above the cannon's roar. Our left wing, particularly
the 8th Infantry, suffered from the fire of the enemy, being
in a column instead of being deployed in a line. In the
midst of the battle the prairie took fire and enveloped the
armies in smoke. The firing commenced at 3 P. M.
and ceased for a time at 4 P. M. Then Ringgold's battery and the eighteen pounders were pushed round to the
left flank of the enemy and the 4th Infantry and 1st Brigade moved up to their aid. the firing soon commenced

again and the enemy were obliged to change their line or battle. At this moment Duncan poured a tremendous fire into their right flank and threw it into the greatest confusion. As night approached the firing gradually ceased on both sides. The enemy had been driven from his position and forced to retire, and our army were left victors upon the battle ground. We had only nine killed, forty-four wounded and two missing. Major Ringgold, Captain Page, Lieutenants Luther, 2nd Artillery and Wallen, 4th Infantry were wounded. Major Ringgold received a shot while sitting on his horse, which carried away the flesh on his legs from his knees up and passed through the withers of his horse. The lower jaw of Capt. Page was shot off. Lieut. Wallen received a slight wound in the arm and Lieut. Luther in the calf of the leg. The Assistant Adjutant General, Capt. Bliss and Lieut. Daniels had their horses shot under them. Our wounded suffered much during the night. General Arista commanded the enemy having 6000 men and our force consisted of 2211. Thus ended the famous battle of Palo Alto.

May 9th the enemy, at day break, moved along the borders of the chaparral and it was supposed that they intended to occupy the road and prevent our farther progress. It was decided that we should attack them, and after the train was suitably guarded, our army moved forward soon after sunrise. It was found that the enemy were rapidly retreating. In going over the battle field the scene was awful. There were at least five hundred of the enemy killed and wounded. It would seem that enough had already been done to settle the difficulty between the two nations but a nation's pride is not easily satisfied. This war but the commencement of bloody scenes. Gen. Taylor ordered our men to take care of the wounded among the enemy

wherever found, as carefully as our own wounded.   At
1 P.M. our army moved on.

BATTLE OF RESACA DE LA PALMA.

Capt. G. A. McCall was sent forward with one hundred picked men to reconoitre.   He found that the enemy
had selected a favorable postion and were waiting for our
advance.   McCall had a slight brush with them and returned.   Our forces were deployed to the right and left of
the road as skirmishers.   Capt. Mc Call's command were
ordered to advance and draw the fire of the enemy.   The
latter were on the opposite bank of a ravine concave towards us and their batteries were so arranged as to sweep
the road and every approach through the chaparral.   Mc
Call received the fire of the enemy and Lieut. Ridgely,
successor to Ringgold, was ordered forward with his battery.   The battle commenced with fury.   Frequently
were bayonets crossed, they were in such close proximity,
The enemy gave way slowly, but fought like tigers, for
every inch of ground.   The chaparral was so thick that
our regiments were mixed ; but fought not the less bravely.
Ridgely at one time, had a body of lancers come done
upon him, with tremendous force, when he had but one
piece unlimbered.   Sergeant Kearnes put a load of cannister on the top of a shell and fired which scattered all
but four.   Then Ridgely charged them in person and
drove them back, exhibiting the greatest bravery.
Capt. May rode back and asked the general if he should
charge the enemy on the opposite side of the ravine.

The answer was " *Charge, Captain, nolens, volens* !"
As May dashed on by Ridgely, the latter cried" *hold
on Charley till I draw their fire* !" Down the ravine
they went. Lieut. Inge soon fell and many others ;
but the rest drove furiously on, crossed the ravine
and captured the battery. Capt. Graham's company
was with May's in this charge. General La Vega
stood by his battery to the last and was taken prisoner by Capt. May. The 3rd were deployed on the
right of the road ; but met no enemy and not being able to
get through the thick, dense chaparral, were obliged to
return to get into the action and arrived after the enemy
were completely routed. Duncan then took the advance
with his battery, the Dragoons, 3rd Infantry and Smith's
command being ordered to support the artillery. We
dashed on after the enemy who were in full retreat, pouring upon them a very destructive fire. Our men soon
came up with the enemy's camp and found it deserted
and captured by the brave Barbour, who with his company
of the third Infantry had resisted a formidable charge of
cavalry. Mules, packs, provisions, and other trophies
were left by the enemy. Our men pursued the enemy,
shouting as they went, to the river. Many of the enemy
were drowned endeavoring to swim across, and were scattered in every direction. The rout was general and complete, though our force consisted of 1700 men, the others
being required to guard the train. 2000 of the best of
Mexico's troops came over to join in this battle of the 9th,
called "*Resaca de la Palma.*" Our loss was three officers
and thirty-six men killed, twelve officers and fifty-nine
men wounded. The officers killed were Lieut. Z. Inge,
2nd Dragoons ; Lieut. R. E. Cochrane, 4th Infantry ; and
Lieut. T. L. Chadbourne, 8th Infantry. The wounded

officers were Colonel M. M. Payne, 4th Artillery, acting Inspector-General; Col. J. S. Mc'Intosh, 5th Infantry; Capt. A. Hooe, 5th Infantry; Lieut. S. H. Fowler, 5th Infantry; Capt. W. R. Montgomery, Lieut. J. Selden, R. P. Maclay, C. F. Morris, C. R. Gates, J. G. Burbank and C. D. Jordan, 8th Infantry; and Lieut. S. D. Dobbins, 3rd Infantry. We captured eight pieces of artillery, 2000 stand of arms, 200 mules, one hundred and fifty thousand rounds of musket cartridges, and all the baggage and camp equipage of the army. Arista's private papers and baggage fell into our hands. One General, one Colonel, one Lieut, Colonel, four Captains and five Lieutenants, were taken prisoners. Three Captains and four Lieutenants of the enemy were buried on the field, and forty-eight officers besides were acknowledged by the Mexicans to be missing. The killed, wounded, and missing of the enemy could not have been less than 2000.

Gen Taylor was sitting upon his horse in the hottest of the battle, and the balls were rattling all around him. An officer remarked to him that he was exposing himself too much, and proposed that he should retire. The General said, " Let us ride a little nearer, the balls will fall behind us."

During the bombardment of Fort Brown (opposite Matamoras), Major Brown the commanding officer was wounded by a shell May 6th and died on the 9th much lamented. The enemy fired 2700 shells at this fort killing one officer, one sergeant, and wounding thirteen privates. They were repeatedly ordered by the enemy to surrender; but would not. Major Ringgold died at Point Isabel May 11th and was buried with funeral honors on the 12th. May 17th our army were ordered to cross the Rio Grande and take possession of Matamoras. General Arista sent over

and wished for an armistice until he could hear from th
Capital, but Old Rough and Ready said, " No !'' Taylo.
was asked if he intended to take the city, "Yes," was the
reply, "if he had to batter it down. Tell General Arista,
said he, " that the city must capitulate, all public property, amunition, provisions &c. must be given up, and then
the army may march out and retire. Arista was ordered
to give an answer by 3 P. M. In the mean time our
army marched three miles up the river, where there was a
suitable place for crossing. No deputation came from
Arista and we crossed May 18th. By a sad accident
Lieut. Stephens was drowned. It was found that the Mexican army precipitately left the city and the authorities
invited General Taylor to take possession. The battle-
field of Resaca de la Palma presented a sad spectacle—
such vast numbers of the slain and now the hospitals
were filled with the wounded ! Near one poor wounded
man, sat a beautiful girl of seventeen keeping off the flies.
She was his wife. There the mother and her children were
seated by the wounded father. Colonel Twiggs was appointed to the chief command of the city.

Colonel Garland was sent out with two companies on
the 19th to follow the enemy. After he had gone 27 miles
he came up with them, had a skirmish, and returned the
22d. Two of his men were wounded. He killed two,
wounded two of the enemy and captured twenty men with
their baggage. Barita, a small town near by, was taken
May 17, by Colonel Wilson. When the Congress of the
U. S. heard of the capture of Capt. Thornton and his command, that body made declaration of war May 13th, and
voted to raise fifty thousand volunteers and to appropriate
ten milions of dollars for the expense of the war. War
was declared by Mexico, April 23rd. Our Congress ap-

pointed General Taylor Brevet Major General, after the battles of Palo Alto and Resca de la Palma.

Numerous reinforcements soon came in and the army moved forward. Monterey, Reynosa, Camargo, Mier and other towns were soon taken without resistance. When our army left Matamoras, Lieutenant Colonel Clark was appoined to the command of the city. Poor Page after suffering intensely, died July 12th.

The U. S. army proceeded up the Rio Grande as far as Mier and then left that noble river and turned to the south towards Monterey.

Sept. 14th, Capt. McCullough, with thirty-five men, had a brush with two hundred Mexicans, near Ramos. Two of the enemy were wounded, and the Capt. lost one horse. Reports seemed to be confirmed that the enemy were pre. paring for a hard battle at Monterey. It was expected that we should have a fight at Marin, where the enemy under General Torrejon were seen, just before our army entered the town. When we arrived the enemy had left. At this place the mountains at the foot of which Monterey stands, were distinctly visible, about twenty-five miles distant.

Sept. 17th General Taylor was addressed by the Spanish Consul at Monterey inquiring whether the property of foreigners would be respected. Taylor replied that he could not be responsible for anything if the city was taken by assault.

Sept. 19th at 9 P. M. the advance of our forces arrived within three miles of Monterey. Some heavy cannon were heard and our men pushed forward : but before they came within reach of the guns General Taylor ordered them to halt. It seems that some lancers came out of the city and endeavored to draw our men within reach of the shot When our advance halted the enemy opened upon us it

earnest.   The third shot went directly over General Taylor's
staff, coming very near him.   Our troops encamped three
miles from the city.   The city seemed to be well fortified
and it was feared that our small guns would not be effectual
against the large ones of the enemy.   It was concluded
that our men must take the big guns of the enemy and
turn them against themselves.   The town was thoroughly
reconnoitered on all sides and our men were frequently
fired upon.   General Taylor decided to send Genera.
Worth to take possession of the road to Saltillo, and storm
the heights at the west part of the city.   This division, including Colonel Hay's regiment, and Captains McCullough's and Gillepie's rangers, moved off according to order.

————

BATTLE OF MONTEREY.

Sept.20th, (1846), about noon.   The works commanding
the approaches to the city, are the Bishop's Palace and a
fort on a height commanding it on the west; the citadel
on the north and several detached redoubts on the east.
The streets were barricaded.   In the afternoon a battery
was commenced for the mortar, and during the night the
mortar and two twenty-four pound howitzers were established.   An express from General Worth arrived the same

night, stating that he had arrived at his position, and would storm two heights southwest of the castle before storming the heights directly west of it.

Sept. 21st at 7 A. M., the first and volunteer divisions were ordered to advance towards the city. Our mortar and howitzer batteries opened ; but did not have much effect. Taylor directed the first division to move to the east of the city to support Major Mansfield in reconnoitering the enemies' works. The division was under the command of Colonel Garland, 4th Infantry, and went into action with the 3rd Infantry under Major Lear, 4th Brigade under Colonel Wilson consisting of the 1st Infantry under Major Abercrombie and the Baltimore division under Colonel Watson, and Bragg's and Ridgeley's batteries. Major Mansfield was the first to commence the action. Company C., 3rd Infantry, under Lieutenant Hazlitt, was reinforced by company H., 3d Infantry, under Capt. Field. The division was formed in line of battle out of reach of the guns of the enemy, and was then ordered to advance by Lieutenant Pope and Colonel Kinney, and go into the city and storm battery No. 1, at the eastern end. The battery opened upon the division and the first shot struck in front of our line and ricoched over us. We were fired upon from the citadel. Our men in the midst of these shots, pushed rapidly onward five hundred yards and rushed into the streets. Not turning soon enough to the left an unperceived battery opened upon us a deadly fire and balls flew from house-tops, yards, and from every direction upon us. Many of our men were cut down. Major Barbour was the first officer who fell. An escopet ball passed through his heart. Our men retired into another street, under cover of some walls and houses. Lieutenant Bragg's battery now arrived and came into the street but could not effect much. Finally we

SIEGE OF MONTEREY

were directed to retire in order and make an attack from some other point. Capt. Backus of the 1st Infantry, succeeded, with fifty men, in stationing himself in a tan yard about a hundred and thirty yards in the rear of the battery No. 1, and nearer the town. There was a shed with a wall which served as a breast work for our men. Twenty yards southwest of the battery was a distillery with thick walls, on the top of which were sand bag embrasures. Capt. Backus drove the enemy from this. Two companies of the 4th Infantry (90 strong) moved forward under a terrible fire, and determined to storm a work defended by five hundred men.

Now the Mississippi and Tennessee regiments, under General Quitman, advanced and finally took possession of the battery, after great loss. This was severe fighting. Major Lear was severely wounded, Lieut. D. S. Irwin killed, Capt. G. P. Field killed by lancers, Lieutenants Hoskins and Woods were killed and Lieutenant Graham mortally wounded. Major Abercrombie and Capt. La Motte were slightly wounded. Lieut. Dillworth lost a leg and Lieut. Ferret was taken prisoner.

The division was ordered to the captured battery to support Ridgely's battery, about to advance into the city. Our men had the mortar and three twenty-four-pound howitzers playing upon the city and one of them having been taken to the captured work was firing upon Fort Diablo. A body of men, from the 3rd and 4th Infantry, of one hundred and fifty, were now ordered to enter the city and take possession of a work of the enemy, apparently a few streets distant. They were exposed to a most destructive fire; but moved on, taking advantage of every shelter in their way. Capt. L. N. Morris, 3rd Infantry was commander. Our men crossed one street and were fully exposed to the guns

mounted in barette of a "tete de pont," commanding the
passage of El Puente Purissima. We passed through several gardens and streets and finally reached a slight shelter.
There was a stream before us and the enemy in force with
three pieces of artillery on the opposite bank, so that we
could not go any farther.   All the streets seemed to be
blockaded and every house fortified. Capt. Morris received
a mortal wound at the bridge and Capt. W. S. Henry took
the command. Lieutenant Hazlitt soon fell.   At last, our
cartridges being nearly exhausted, we were commanded to
retire, in order. to our captured works. At one time, after
day-light, we were obliged to lay flat nearly an hour, the
balls came so thick. Lieutenant Ridgely, with a section of
his battery, advanced to the street leading to the "tete de
pont," but finding his fire entirely ineffectual, retired. Lieut.
Bragg put to flight, with his battery, a show of a charge of
lancers.   Our men had not been able to take any dinner or
supper and the night was cold and rainy.   We had mounted
on battery No. 1, one twelve pounder, one nine, two sixes,
and one howitzer, in all, five pieces.

While these scenes were transpiring under the eye of General Taylor, Gen. Worth was moving towards the Saltillo
road.   A large body of cavalry and Infantry opposed him,
and charged upon our men. They were met by the battalion of light troops under Capt C. T. Smith and Capt.
McCulloughs company of Rangers. The first squadron of
the enemy were mixed in with our advance when the second came furiously rushing on. Lieut. Hays, of Duncan's
battery, poured in among them round shot, which passed
over the heads of our men, and the enemy were dispersed
with a loss of about one hundred, and among them, one
Colonel. Our men marched round nearly two miles to the
west end of the town, under a heavy fire from "Indepen-

dence Hill," situated west of the palace and from "Federacion Hill," between which heights, the Saltillo road runs. Now General Worth determined to storm Federacion Hill, and Capt. C. F. Smith, 2d Artillery with three hundred men, half regulars and the rest Texans, under Major Chevalier, undertook the dangerous enterprise. Capt. Miles with the 7th Infantry marched soon after to his support. As Capt. Miles' command advanced, it was not observed by the enemy until it had reached the small stream (Arroyo Topa) south of the city, along the base of the hill on which the battery is situated. As soon as discovered, they were continually fired upon by the enemy, but without much effect. Our men crossed the river and formed on a point of rock out of reach of the enemy. Detachments were then sent forward under Lieutenants Grant, Little, and Gardner to divert the enemy from Capt. Smiths' command. Colonel Smith of the 2d brigade, came up with the 5th Infantry and ordered Capt. Miles with the 7th to assist him in an attack on Fort Soldado, a temporary breastwork a little south east of Federacion Hill. They moved on and found that Capt. Smith had already got possession of it. The 2d Brigade formed and advanced amid a shower of balls, and when within a hundred yards, made a charge at double quick step. The enemy fled in all directions. The left wing of the 7th entered the redoubt with that of the 5th. Many of the Louisiana volunteers under Capt. Blanchard, and the Texan Rangers were up with the advance, all fearlessly striving to be the first to meet the enemy. Colonel Smith appointed Capt. Smith to retain possession of the first height stormed, and Capt Miles with the 7th, the last. Capt. Scott with the 5th Infantry, was to move on the same ridge farther east. The second Brigade held their position during the afternoon and night of the 21st. The 7th In fantry were exposed to the fire from the Bishop's Palace several hours but Lieut. Dana of the 7th infantry, with his captured gun, returned the fire with some effect.

Those who occupied battery No. 1, at the eastern extremity of the city, at day-break, (Sept. 22d,) were obliged to lie flat in the mud to shield themselves from the sharp firing from Fort Diablo. Shells, fired from the citadel, fell all around our men, though none burst in the work. Lieut. Scarrett was laboring to put the battery and distillery in a better state of defence. Capt. Bainbridge had command of the 3rd Infantry in the morning. A portion of Colonel Davis's regiment, under General Quitman, relieved the 1st, 3rd and 4th Infantry, and the Kentucky regiment. In returning to camp, our men received a destructive fire from the batteries of the enemy, crosswise. One poor fellow, a corporal in the 4th Infantry, was cut in two. Gen. Worth's attack upon the height, commanding the, Bishop's Palace, at day-break, (Sept. 22d.) was fierce and successful. The force consisted of artillery and infantry under Colonel Childs and some Texans under Colonel Hays. The party moved up the hill and at the same time Capt. Miles, with a small force, descended towards the palace and gave three cheers to divert the enemy. In return they received a shower of grape. The enemy, at the castle, being checked so that they could not aid their flying forces, the height was carried with little loss. Capt. Gillespie first entered the breastwork and fell mortally wounded. General Worth soon sent the 5th Infantry, Capt. Smith's command and Capt. Blanchard's Louisiana volunteers, to reinforce Colonel Childs. Lieut. Roland soon placed a howitzer in position and blazed away at the castle with much effect. A light corps of artillery, under Capt. Vinton, Blanchard's company and some Texans were on the left of the hill, and fired continually. The fire was briskly returned by the enemy.

About noon, the Mexican cavalry deployed before the palace and endeavored to charge upon our skirmishers. Our men pursued them, under Vinton, with terrible effect. Many of the enemy were kept from entering the castle again, as our men rushed in through every opening, and drove the enemy before them. Lieutenant Ayers was the first to enter, pull down the Mexican flag, and raise the star spangled banner.

After the castle was taken, General Worth moved down his forces from the hill and the amunition train the ranch of the Saltillo road and remained in the castle during the night of Sept. 22nd. He, however, ordered the 5th Infantry and Blanchard's company to return to the redoubt on the hill where were stationed the 7th Infantry.

Sept. 23d, at 7 o'clock in the morning General Worth opened upon the town, from the castle, with the enemy's own guns, as he intended to do when he first approached the city. A report was raised that the enemy were endeavoring to escape and the whole command were out immediately marching towards them.

It was now expected every moment, that the city would capitulate; but they held out and fought like tigers. At the east end of the city the firing commenced briskly, the same morning at day-break. The Texan cavalry under Colonel Woods, had dismounted, and with the Mississippians, under Colonel Davis, were engaged with the enemy. The Mississippians very early took possession of Fort Diablo, without any opposition, as the enemy had abandoned it the preceding evening. This was the place from which, on the 21st and 22d, our men had received such a destructive fire. This force under General Quit man, drove the enemy before them from house to house, shooting them wherever they saw one of their heads pro jecting.

Bragg's battery was now ordered into the city and tne 3rd Infantry ordered to support it. They moved forward, and when they came within range of the enemy's guns of the citadel, they crossed the field of fire at full gallop and were unharmed. The 3d went under cover, in a circuitous route. On their arrival in the city they found it cleared of the enemy on a line with the cathedral, and within two squares of it. This edifice was in the main plaza, where the enemy had been concentrated. Much bravery was manifested by General's Quitman, Henderson, Lamar, and Colonels Wood and Davis. Several were wounded and a few killed. Bragg's battery was in action with them during the remainder of the day. The fighting was not so severe as it was on the 21st, except in the street running directly from the cathedral. It could not be crossed without passing through a shower of bullets. One of Bragg's pieces had little effect in this street as the weight of metal was too light. Bragg's first sergeant by the name of Weightman, was shot while pointing the gun. Our men could only cross, without great danger of being shot, excepting when our piece was pointed at the enemy. Then the Mexicans would fall behind their barricade and our men would cross in squads. As soon as our piece was fired the balls of the enemy came down the street like a shower af hickory nuts.

General Taylor was in town entirely regardless of his person in the midst of danger. This was very imprudent nd wrong. He even crossed the street where so many balls were continually passing, and crossed in a walk. A commanding officer ought to look out for himself and

army better than that. Taylor was brave to the back
bone, but imprudent. Capt Henry reminded him that he
ought to retire to a safer position; but he said "TAKE
THAT AXE AND KNOCK IN THAT DOOR." Our men commenced
on the door and the occupant unlocked and opened it, and
behold it was an extensive apothecary shop. The doctor
(San Juan) treated his visitors to ripe limes and cool water.
He said that Ampudia was in the Plaza with four thousand
men, and that two thousand were in the citadel. One door
was burst open and we saw five genteel looking women who
were on their knees with crucifixes pleading for mercy.
They were very grateful when they found that their throats
were not to be cut. General Taylor expected that General Worth would commence throwing shells into the city,
in the afternoon, and perceiving that the field pieces were
of little use, ordered these forces to retire to camp. During
the day (23rd) the enemy sent in a flag of truce, requesting
a cessation of hostilities, that the women and children
might be removed. Old Rough and Ready said, "No, it
was too late." It was reported that some of the enemy
were leaving on pack mules, and undoubtedly many others
would have left, had not General Worth taken possession of
the Saltillo Road. General Worth on the west side of the
city, ordered a heavy gun under Capt. Chapman's company
to open on the city. This firing drove the enemy from
their lines bordering on the river. About 10 A. M. the 7th
Infantry left the redoubt and joined Gen. Worth, at the
palace, for the purpose of entering the city. The enemy
did not make so great a resistance at the west part of the
town as at the east where they were in a larger body, and
our men did not suffer so much in the former as in the latter
position. There was some loss, however. Capt. M. Kavett,
of the 8th Infantry, while marching around the base of the

hill, on the morning of the 21st, was killed. Lieut. Potter 7th Infantry, while storming the redoubt, was wounded. Lieut. Rossell was wounded in the attack upon the palace. Major Brown's company of artillery, Capt. Blanchard's company and some Texan Rangers, with a piece from McKall's battery, were ordered to march under Brown and take possession of a mill on the road to Saltillo, in order to cut off retreat. The city had been reconnoitered by Lieutenant, Meade and Capt. McCullough. They found that the city had been cleared of the enemy as far as the Plaza in which was the cemetery. Capt. Miles, with three companies was ordered to take possession of the street nearest the river. Colonel Stanniford was to take posession of the next street north. Both parties, the first under the direction of Capt. Holmes, and the second, under Capt. Scriven, moved on and took possession of the cemetery, without a shot from the enemy. Loop holes had been made in the walls and they had been prepared for defence. A piece of artillery followed each of these commands. Then came Colonel Childs with the Artillery Battalion and Capt. Miles with the remainder of the 7th and a company of the 8th Infantry. The last was designed to protect the amunition train sent round by Gen. Taylor. Major Monroe and Lieut. Lovell soon placed the mortar in position. Captains Holmes and Scriven, with their forces marched through the same streets to a square in advance of the cemetery and soon commenced with the enemy. Colonel Childs followed the street upon which was situated a large Plaza. Capt. Gatlin of the 7th was now wounded. Our troops were soon under cover of walls and were reinforced by two companies of the 5th under Capt Merrill, and finally by three more under Major Scott. The column in the next street under Colonel Smith were now shortly engaged with the enemy. Capt. Holmes was aided by Texans under Walker, and found his way through gardens and houses until he came very near the enemy in Cathedral Plaza. Lieut. Colonel Duncan was sweeping the street with his battery. Major Brown was ordered to join the Texans in the Plaza and aid Col. Childs. They worked their way towards the enemy with pickaxes, and soon came up with them, and cracked away. Night came on and our men kept possession of the houses taken, excepting Capt. Holmes who thought best to go back a little as he was far in advance and had many wounded. Our troops in the Plaza took possession of the houses on both sides and rested till morning. Lieutenant Lovell threw shells into the city during the night with great effect, and the enemy returned the compliment from their howitzers. Lieutenant Gardner of the 7th, manifested much bravery in leading the advance with ladders and pickaxes. At one time nearly all of his men were killed or wounded.

After reveille, on the morning of Sept. 24th, General Ampudia sent Colonel Murino into our camp with a flag of truce, and an offer to surrender the city, if General Taylor would allow him to march out with his troops and all the public property. Of course when the city was nearly in our hands, such an offer was declined· But General Taylor sent back his terms, saying that an answer would be received at General Worth's headquarters at 12 M. Murino said that he had been informed that commissioners had been appointed to negotiate for peace and that no reinforcements would be sent them, and that it would cost us two thirds of our command to take the city, if we could do it at all. The action was to commence again if terms were not agreed upon.

The commissioners on our side were Generals Worth and Henderson and Colonel Davis. On the other side they were, Manuel M. Llano, T. Requena, and Ortega. The following are the terms:

Terms of the Capitulation of the City of Monterey, the Capital of Nueva Leon, agreed upon by the undersigned Commissioners, to-wit: General Worth, of the United States army ; General Henderson, of the Texan Vol unteers ; and Colonel Davis of the Mississippi Riflemen, on the part of Major-general Taylor, commanding in chief of the United States forces ; and General Requena and General Ortega, of the army of Mexico, and Senor Manuel M. Llano, Governor of Nueva Leon, on the part of Senor General Don Pedro Ampudia, commanding in chief of the army of North Mexico.

ARTICLE 1. As the legitimate result of the operations before this place, and the present position of the contending armies, it is agreed that the city, the fortifications, cannon, the munitions of war, and all other public property, with the undermentioned exceptions, be surrendered to the commanding general of the United States forces now at Monterey.

ARTICLE 2. That the Mexican forces be allowed the fol lowing arms, to-wit: The commissioned officers, their side arms ; the Infantry, their arms and accoutrements ; the cavalry, their artillery, one field battery, not to exceed six pieces, with twenty-one rounds of amunition.

ARTICLE 3. That the Mexican armed forces retire within seven days from date, beyond the line formed by the pass of the Rinconada, the city of Linares, and San Fernado de Pusos.

ARTICLE 4. That the citadel of Monterey be evacuated by the Mexican and occupied by the American forces to-morrow at 10 o'clock.

ARTICLE 5. To avoid collisions, and for mutual convenience, that the troops of the United States will not occupy
the city until the Mexican forces have withdrawn, except
for hospital and storage purposes.

ARTICLE 6. That the force of the United States will not
advance beyond the line specified in the third article before
the expiration of eight week, or until the orders of the respective governments can be received.

ARTICLE 7. That the public property to be delivered shall
be turned over and received by the commanding generals
of the two armies.

ARTICLE 8. That all doubts as to the meaning of any of
the preceding articles shall be solved by an equitable construction, and on the principles of liberality to the retiring
army.

ARTICLE. 9. That the Mexican flag, when struck at the
citadel, may be saluted by its own battery.

W. J. WORTH,
Brigadier General United States Army.

J. PINKNEY HENDERSON,
Major-General com'g Texan Volunteers.

JEFFERSON DAVIS,
Colonel Mississippi Riflemen.

J. M. ORTEGA,
T. REQUENA,
MANUEL M. LLANO,

Approved, { PEDRO AMPUDIA,
           { Z. TAYLOR, Maj. Gen. S. A. com'g.

Dated at Monterey, September 24th, 1846.

Our troops were commanded during the imposing cere
mony by Colonel P. F. Smith. When the Mexican flag
was lowered, they fired a salute of eight guns. When
our flag was raised twenty-eight guns were fired from the

Bishop's Palace. Our troops marched into the city to the tune of Yankee Doodle. Thus ended one of the severest battles ever fought on the continent. The Mexicans, in all of the battles with us have fought more desperately, 'rom the fact that our forces were so very few, compared with theirs. They were ashamed to be beaten by such an inferior force. We have believed from the first that an army of fifty thousand men could have marched to the capital of Mexico without shedding a drop of blood. How awful the idea of ushering such multitudes of immortal souls into the presence of their Maker, in such a manner! General Ampudia had about ten thousand men in action, seven thousand of whom were regulars. Our force consisted of four hundred and twenty-five officers and six thousand two hundred and twenty men. We lost twelve officers and one hundred and eight men killed; twenty-six officers, and three hundred and seven privates were wounded. The loss of the enemy was thought to have exceeded ours. Our men captured forty-two pieces of artillery and one eighteen-pounder. The munitions of war captured from the enemy were immense. The following is a list of the officers killed.

Captain Williams Topographical Engineers; 1st Infantry, Lieutenant J. C. Terrett, Lieutenant R. Dilworth; 3d Infantry, Captains L. N. Morris, G. P. Field, and Brevet Major P. N. Barbour, Lieutenants D. S. Irwin and R. Hazlitt; 4th Infantry, Lieutenant C. Hoskins, Brevet Lieutenant J. S. Wood, 2d infantry (serving with the 4th); 8th Infantry, Captain H. M'Kavett; Baltimore Battalion, Colonel Watson; 1st Ohio, Lieutenant Hett; 1st Tennessee, Captain Allen, Lieutenant Putnam; Captain Gillespie, Texan Rangers. Wounded: Major-general Butler, Major Mansfield; 1st Infantry, Major J. S. Abercrombie, Captain

J. H. Lamotte; 3d Infantry, Major W. W. Lear, Captain H. Bainbridge; 4th Infantry, Lieut. R. H. Graham; 5th Infantry N. B. Rossell; 7th Infantry, Capt. R. C. Gatlin, Lieutenant J. Potter; 8th Infantry, Lieutenant G. Wainwright; 1st Ohio, Colonel Mitchell, Captain George, Lieutenants Armstrong, Niles, Morter, McCarty; 1st Tennessee, Major Alexander, Lieutenants Allen, Scudder, and Nixon; 1st Mississippi, Lieutenant Colonel M'Clung, Captain Downing, Lieutenants Cook and Arthur.

It is astonishing that the city could be taken at all by so few. The citadel is a regular bastion work with revetments of solid masonry, with thirty-four embrasures. Inside are the remnants of an unfinished cathedral, which is itself a work of defence. Two magazines were discovered, with ammunition enough to have fired at us for a month. In nearly every street were works of defence. Barricades overlapped each other, and ditches were dug in front, and every house seemed to be a fortification. On the eastern part of the city there were barricades defending each other, and it is surprising that Worth's division who operated there, were not all cut to pieces. The Bishop's Palace has two or three heavy guns mounted, in Barbette, pointing towards the city. There were many fortifications around the-city, Making it a perfect Gibraltar.

Sept. 26th, the enemy were seen in great numbers mounted on every thing that looked like a horse, from the mustang to the donkey, preparing to follow the army. Ampudia left on the 25th with two divisions. The troops of the enemy had left the city before the close of the first week in October. General Worth and his division occupied the city, and Capt. Miles was his executive officer. The Governor of the city was allowed to go on as usual, excepting that he was required to furnish supplies for our army, for

which we were to pay cash.   Several deserters were observed in the ranks of the enemy, among which was Riley,
who was appointed a captain in the artillery of the enemy.
Immediately after the battle, the Texas troops were discharged.

When Ampudia reached Saltillo, he issued a proclamation, declaring that he had repulsed us with a loss of fifteen
hundred men, on the 21st, that, being scarce of amunition
and provisions, a conference was held on the 24th and terms
were agreed to, which saved their honor and they marched
out with their arms.   That Santa Anna was coming and
then they would see who would be the conquerors.

On the 16th of August, General Santa Anna arrived at
Vera Cruz, and was allowed to land, as our governmen
thought that he would use his best exertions to bring
about a peace ; but the duplicity of the Mexican character
must be learned by sad experience.   His proclamation, on
the day of his arrival, told his warlike intentions.   He was
immediately invested with the command of the army,
while General Salas acted as President of the republic.   He
went to San Luis Potosi to raise an army.

Oct. 12th, Lieutenant R. H. Graham, 4th Infantry, died
of his wcunds received Sept. 21st.

It was said that a woman named Dos Amades, commanded a company of Mexican lancers, who fought desperately and killed many of our men.

Oct. 25th, Capt. Ridgely's horse fell with him in Monterey and so injured him that he died on the 27th, and was
buried with military honors the next day.   He was a fine
officer and a graduate of West Point.

The troops on the Rio Grande were under General Patterson, whose head quarters were at Camargo.   The fol-

lowing were the different regiments, and the mode of their distribution:

At Camargo, 2d Brigade, General Pillow commanding, composed of 2d Tennessee, Colonel Haskell; Alabama, Colonel Coffee; Ohio and Kentucky Brigade, General Marshall commanding, composed of the 2d Kentucky, Colonel McKee, 2d Ohio, Col. Morgan; Illinois, Brigade, General Shields commanding, composed of 3d Illinois, Colonel Forman, 4th Illinois, Colonel Baker, 2d Infantry, Colonel Riley.

At Reynosa, Company H. 2d Artillery and two companies of the 1st Indiana, Captain Swartwout commanding.

Matamoras, 3d Ohio, Colonel Curtis, Captains Louds, Vanness, and Norman's companies of Artillery, Colonel Clarke commanding.

Camp Belknap, Indiana Brigade, General Lane commanding; 2d Indiana, Colonel Bowles, 3d Indiana, Colonel Lane.

Mouth of the Rio Grande, 1st Indiana, Colonel Drake.

Brasos Island, Captain Porter's company of Artillery.

Point Isabel, one company of Artillery, Major Gardner commanding

Nov. 2d, 1846, orders were received from Washington, directing General Taylor to announce to the Mexican authorities that the armstice was broken up and that we were to commence hostilities with greater energy than ever Major Graham, with a small escort was dispatched to give the information to the Mexican forces. General Patterson was ordered to Tampico with a part of our forces at Monterey. General Worth was ordered with his division excepting the 7th Infantry, a company of artillery and McKall's

Battery and Colonel Smith, to march to Saltillo on the 12th (Nov.)

Santa Anna took away the commissions and placed in confinement all the principal officers of Ampudia's army, excepting Mejia and Racina. Parades had gone to Havana. On the 8th news arrived in camp that Gen. Wool had arrived at Monclova and would not advance upon Chihuahua until further orders.

On the 10th Major Graham returned, not having gone farther than Saltillo. He learned that Santa Anna was at San Luis Potosi, with sixteen thousand men, and expected six thousand more; but he was nearly destitute of funds and the army had a scarcity of provisions and clothing.

On the 12th Mr. McLane arrived from Washington ordering our army to take all the towns between Monterey and Tampico.

On the 13th, Generals Taylor and Worth moved towards Satillo, and took possession of the city on the 16th. It is seventy-five miles from Monterey. Capt. Harden with his Dragoons, was left in the city.

On the 24th Capt. Taylor arrived from Camargo, with two eighteen-pounders and two eight inch howitzers. Gen. Shields and Col. Harny, arrived from General Wool's command on the 24th. The former is to go to Tampico and take the command. Brevet Major Buchanan, 4th Infantry, was appointed to command the Baltimore Batallion of Volunteers. Col. Benton sailed for Tampico, from Brasos, with six companies of artillery, about the same time. Santa Anna destroyed the water tanks between Monterey and Tampico. Seven Texans had been taken prisoners at China, before our army reached Monterey. General Taylor demanded their release. Santa Anna complied. They reported that Santa Anna had about 27,000 men at San

Luis Potosi. The Mexicans caused some of our men, mostly English and Germans, to desert, by giving them $60 each, citizens clothes, a horse, guide to the army, and 50 cents to drink the health of Santa Anna. Dec. 5th General Wool was ordered to Parras, east of Satillo. On the 2nd of Dec. Brigadier General Thomas L. Hamer, of Ohio, died of dysentery, and was burried on the 4th with military honors. He was very much esteemed.

———

NAVAL BATTLES.

During this time, the navy was engaged in blockading Mexican ports. The brig Truxton, commanded by Commander Carpenter, was run aground on the 15th of August, on the bar off Tuspan, and deserted. Lieut. Hunter, with a boat's crew, reached a vessel of the squadron, and the other officers and men surrendered to the enemy. They were afterwards exchanged for General La Vega and other Mexican officers. It was impossible to save the vessel and she was burned. An attempt had been made to capture Alvarado, and failed as the vessels could not cross the bar. Oct. 15th, another attempt was made by the steamers Vixen and Mc'Lane, three gun-boats, Schooners Nonata and Forward, and steamer Mississippi, Commander, Perry. The whole commanded by Commodore Connor. There was a battery at the mouth of the river, mounting seven guns. The first division consisting of the Reefer and Bonita, towed by the Vixen, crossed the bar and engaged with the battery. The second division consisted of the Nonata Forward and Petrel. towed by the Mc'Lane. The steamer run agronnd, and the others could not be towed over. Commodore Connor thought it would be useless to go forward with one division and retired. Oct. 16th. Commodore Perry sailed to attack Tobasco with the Vixen, Capt. Sands, schooners Bonita, Berham, Reefer, Sterret, Nonata, and Hazard, schooner Forward, Capt. Nones, and steamer Mc'Lane, Capt. Howard. Capt. Forest had a command of about 200 marines and sailors. He crossed the bar Oct. 23rd, and took, withuot resistance, Frontera, capturing two steamers, and all the vessels in port. Tobasco is seventy-four miles up the river from Frontera. Our forces reached Fort Aceachappa, commanding a difficult pass•in the river, Oct. 25th, and spiked the cannon, the enemy having left the fort. The vessels were all before Tobasco on the same day, about noon The town was summoned to surrender, but it refused. The boats soon captured five merchant vessels. The vessels fired upon the town, and Capt. Forest, with his command was ordered to advance into the city. There was a sharp engagement, and the command were ordered back at night. At the desire of the foreign merchants the town was spared. On the 26th they left with their prizes. One, under Lieut. Parker, grounded and was fired upon, but Parker defended it and got the vessel off, with one man killed and two wounded. Lieutenant Morris was wounded in carrying a message to Lieut. Parker, and died November 1st.

This expedition captured two steamers and seven vessels. Nov. 12th, Commodore Connor sailed for Tampico, with a considerable part of the squadron, and on the 14th the city surrendered unconditionally, without opposition. Nov. 20th Lieutenant Parker with Midshipman Rodgers, and Hynson at night with a small boat, and crew of six men, rowed in under the guns of San Juan d'Ullao, and burned the bark Creole, anchored there. This was very daring and brave. Midshipman Rodgers, Doct. J. W. Wright, and J. G. Fox, went ashore to reconnoitre one of the enemies magazines, in order to destroy it. After they had gone a little distance from the boat they were surrounded by seven Mexicans. Dr. Wright escaped, but the other two were taken prisoners.

The last of August 1846, by order of the President, Brigadier General J. E. Wool concentrated an army (called the " Central Division Army of Mexico") in Texas, for the purpose of moving against Chihuahua, the capital of the state of the same name. The command was composed of the 1st Illinois, Colonel Hardin, 2nd Illinois, Col. Bissell; six companies of Arkansas mounnted men, Col. Yell, a company of Kentucky volnnteers under Capt. Williams; two companies of 1st dragoons, Capt. Steen ; two companies 2d dragoons, Major Beall; three companies of 6th Infantry, Major Bonneville, and Capt. Washington's company of horse artillery, in all 2,829. The first column moved from San Antonio Sept. 26th, commanded by Colonel Harney, and the second column marched Oct. 14th, under Col. Churchill.

Oct. 29th, the command arrived at Monclora, and took possession without resistance. Here General Wool decided to go no farther towards Chihuahua.

The command from Monterey moved on towards San Luis Potosi. It was reported that Santa Anna was advancing upon Saltillo and a part of our forces returned, Dec. 18th, to Monterey and found that the alarm was false.

At this time Salas was president of the Mexican Congress

and had, in his message, recommended a vigorous prosecution of the war.

Dec. 31st, the rear guard of Colonel May, in passing from Labadores to Linares, was attacked by the enemy and cut off together with the baggage train.

General Quitman took possession of Victoria on the 30th, without resistance.

Just beyond San Pedro, on the way to San Luis Potosi, when our men were passing through a defile with high mountains each side, a mine was sprung and showers of stones thrown down among us while we were fired upon from the other side. The *arrieros* deserted their mules and the rear guard, consisting of eleven men, fled. Colonel May dismounted twenty men and went through the pass. Only an occasional shot was fired at them. Eleven men, twelve horses and all the baggage were lost. At Tula, one hundred and fifty miles from Victoria, towards San Luis Potosi, Generals Valencia and Urea, had concentrated, as was reported, Jan. 6th, a large force.

The order was issued January 12th, 1847, to proceed to Tampico. We set out on the 13th. As General Taylor was about starting, he received orders from General Scott to send his whole command, excepting two batteries of light artillery, and squadron of dragoons, to Tampico, where Scott would meet them about the first of February. General Taylor was ordered to return to Monterey and remain on the defensive. He left immediately, taking, in addition to the above named forces, the 1st Mississippi regiment. Thus Taylor was deprived of almost all of his regulars, which blasted all of his hopes in reference to advancing upon San Luis Potosi.

Upon parting with his old veteran soldiers, General Taylor said:

"It is with deep sensibility that the commanding general finds himself separated from the troops he so long commanded. To those corps, regular and volunteer, who have shared with him the active services of the field, he feels the attachment due such associations; while to those making their first campaign, he must express his regret that he can not participate with them in its eventful scenes. To all, both officers and men, he extends his heartfelt wishes for their continued success and happiness, confident that their achievements on another theatre will redound to the credit of their country and its arms."

General Scott reached the Brasos, Dec. 28th, 1846 and took the command of the army. Gen. Worth was ordered to move, with all the regulars, excepting Washington's, Webster's, Sherman's and Bragg's batteries, to Point Isabel.

The force that set out for Tampico, Jan. 13, arrived on the 23rd. General Taylor and his command, arrived at Monterey on his return from Victoria, the last of Jan. 1847. General Wool had established a camp at the rancho. Taylor kept possession of Saltillo and the strong passes in advance of it, and stationed his forces, at these points.

Jan. 22, a scouting party, under Major Borland and Gaines, the former of the Arkansas and the latter of the Kentucky cavalry, were surrounded by General Minon with three thousand men, and captured, sixty miles from Saltillo. Our men numbered sixty-four privates and six officers and they were immediately marched off to Mexico. This capture exhibited great carelessness in the officers. Capt Henrie, a Texan Volunteer, escaped and reached Sal tillo in safety.

Jan. 27th Capt Heady with seventeen Kentucky volun teers was captured by the enemy, while on a scouting party, without any resistance.

BATTLE OF BUENA VISTA.

On the 5th of February, General Taylor, having heard reports of the advancement of Santa Anna with a large force, moved his head quarters eighteen miles south of Saltillo, to Agua Nueva. By the 8th all of his army excepting Major Warren's command, which was left at Saltillo, concentrated at that point. The forces consisted of two companies of the 1st Dragoons, under Captain Steen; two companies 2d Dragoons, under Brevet Lieutenant-colonel May; Bragg's and Sherman's batteries, 3d Artillery; Washington's battery, 4th Artillery; one regiment Arkansas cavalry, under Colonel Yell; one regiment of Kentucky cavalry, under Colonel Marshall; 2d Kentucky foot under Colonel M'Kee; 1st Regiment Mississippi Rifles, under Colonel Davis; 3d Indiana, under Colonel Lane; 1st Illinois, under Colonel Hardin; 2d Illinois, under Colonel Bissell; and two companies of Texas volunteers, one commanded by Captain Conner, the other a spy company, commanded by the celebrated Captain (now Major) M'Cullough, in all amounting to three hundred and thirty-four officers, and four thousand four hundred and twenty-five men.

It was evident that there must be a terrible conflict and General Taylor selected a pass two miles in advance of Buena Vista, as his position. There was a valley about three miles broad, with irregular surface, containing occasionally hills and ravines, and was surrounded by high mountains The road passed by the side of a deep arroyo, which was impassable. On the right side of the road, there were great gullies which it was impossible to cross, extending to the mountains. On the left of the road were steep ascents to the tops of the spurs of the mountain and there was formed a plain, suitable for a battle field. The choice of this place showed much skill and good judgment in the General. By the 21st of Feb. our forces were stationed at this position. Col. Yell was left, with some cavalry to cover the removal of the stores and were driven in by the enemy. Our men secured most of the stores and burned the remainder. General Taylor went to Saltillo immediately, to make arrangements for its defence, leaving Gen. Wool to command the army. Our forces prepared for the advance of the enemy. Capt. Washington's battery was so placed as to command the road. The 1st and 2d Illinois regiments containing sixteen hundred strong, and the 2nd Kentucky regiment, occupied crests of ridges in the rear and to the left. Near the base of the mountain at the extreme left, stood the Arkansas and Kentucky cavalry The Indiana Brigade under General Lane, the Mississippi Riflemen, the two squadrons of dragoons, and Sherman's and Bragg's batteries were held in reserve.

On the morning of the 22nd the enemy approached, and General Taylor returned immediately to camp. Tremendous clouds of dust announced the advance of the enemy, who arrived in position, with immense masses, between 10 and 11 A. M. All was silence, waiting for the attack, when a white flag was brought into our camp, by Surgeon-general Lindenberger, with the following message from Santa Anna:

"You are surrounded by twenty thousand men, and cannot in any human probability avoid suffering a route, and being cut to pieces with your troops; but as you deserve consideration and particular esteem, I wish to save you from a catastrophe, and for that purpose give you this notice in order that you may surrender at discretion, under the assurance that you will be treated with the consideration belonging to the Mexican character, to which end you will be granted an hour's time to make up your mind, to commence from the moment when my flag of truce arrives in your camp.

" With this view, I assure you of my particular consideration.

" God and Liberty. Camp at Encantada, February 22d, 1847.

" ANTONIO LOPEZ DE SANTA ANNA.
"To Gen. Z. Taylor, comm'g the forces of the United States."

Old Rough and Ready answered thus:

" Headquarters, Army of Occupation,)
Near Buena Vista, Feb. 22, 1847. }

" *Sir,*—In reply to your note of this date, summoning me to surrender my force at discretion, I beg leave to say that I decline acceding to your request. With high respect, I am , sir,

" Your obedient servant,   Z. TAYLOR,
" Maj. Gen. U. S. Army, commanding.

" Senor Gen. D. Antonio Lopez de Santa Anna,)
Commander-in-chief, La Encantada." }

Several hours passed before any attack was made. The columns of the enmy's rear could be seen moving up. There was a slight demonstration of our right and a section of Bragg,s battery, supported by the 2d Kentucky foot, were detached to that point. They bivoucked for the night. Near evening, the light troops of the enemy commenced upon our left, consisting of detachments of Arkansas and Kentucky cavalry dismounted, and a battalion of Indiana

Riflemen, under Major Gorman and all commanded by Colonel Marshall. Some shells were thrown into this part of our line, by the enemy without effect, This skirmishing was continued until after dark, with slight loss on our side. Three pieces of Washington's battery under Capt. O'Brien, took position to the left. Here the troops rested during the night on their arms.

Genral Taylor proceeded to Saltillo with the Mississippi regiment and squadron of 2nd dragoons, and while there about fifteen hundred Mexicans under General Minon had advanced into the valley, by a pass through the mountains, and were seen in the rear of the city. They were designed to harass us and cut off our retreat. There were in the city, four companies of Illinois volunteers under Major Warren of the first regiment. There was a field-work commanding the approaches and was garrisoned by Capt. Webster's company with two twenty-four pound howitzers. Two companies of Mississippi riflemen, under Capt. Rodgers with one field-piece under Capt. Shower, defended the train.

Jan. 22nd, during the night, the enemy stationed a large force of light troops upon the side of the mountain, to outflank our left.

On the morning of the 23rd, the action was renewed at this point. Col. Marshall with his riflemen, re-enforced by three companies of Illinois volunteers, under Major Trail, stood firm and did considerable execution with their sure rifles. At 8 o'clock a large column of the enemy moved up the road and threatened our centre, but Washington's energetic battery kept them back., The enemy could do nothng on account of the nature of the ground, where they stood ; but our left being on an extensive plain, Santa Anna thought that he could outflank us. Large bodies of the enemy passed up the ravines under cover of the ridges, and concentrated near our left. The 2d Indiana and 2 Illinois regiments formed the extreme left of our line and the former supported O'Brien's three pieces of artillery. The commander on the left was Brigadier-general Lane. O'Brien was ordered to advance towards the enemy with his guns. The fight was now very severe upon the enemy; but they poured upon our men volleys of grape and cannister. The action was so warm that the Indiana regiment broke, not being able to stand against such a fire and left the artillery unprotected. Thus Capt. O'Brien was obliged to retire leaving one of his pieces, at which every man and horse was either killed or wounded. The cowardly Indiana regiment could not be rallied, though Major Dix, Paymaster U. S. Army, induced a few to return and join, together with their Colonel Bowles, the Mississippi regiment. They were very useful during the remainder of the day. Our left giving way, encouraged the enemy, and large masses of them pressed forward and forced our light troops on the side of the mountain, to retire, and many of them could not be rallied until they reached the depot at Buena Vista. The 2nd Illinois regiment, to which a section of Sherman's battery was attached, were driven before the enemy.

The Mexican Infantry and cavalry poured in so rapidly that our rear was in danger. Thus far evidently, every move went against us. But General Taylor now arrived and took a commanding position on the elevated plateau. His presence was enough to animate our troops. The Missssippi regiment, under Davis, was ordered to the left, and came in contact, immediately with large portions of the enemy, who had turned our flank.

The struggle was severe, but in favor of our troops. The 2nd Kentucky, under Col. M'Kee, with a section of artilery under Bragg, had been ordered to support our left. These with a part of the 1st Illinois under Col. Hardin were now fiercely engaged with the enemy, and recovered to some extent, the lost ground.

The batteries of Bragg and Sherman were very effective in the columns of the enemy, and especially those who were in our rear. The Mississippi regiment exhibited grea bravery, sustaining the attacks of the enemy without flinching. The 3rd Indiana, under Colonel Lane, and a piece of artillery under Colonel Kilburn, finally moved to their aid. The Mexican infantry and cavalry repeatedly advanced with the most determined impetuosity, intending to force our line, but they were received so firmly and warmly that they were glad to fall back. Our artillery made awful havoc. Brevet Lieutenant Colonel May commanded the regu lar cavalry, and Captain Pike's of the Arkansas cav- alry. May, with the Kentucky and Arkansas cavalry, un- der Colonels Marshall and Yell, were directed to keep in check the masses that had gained our rear. The enemy still were determined at all hazards, to break our left. Our forces were pouring upon the enemy a terrific fire from dif- ferent sections and pieces, under O'Brien, Bragg, Sherman Thomas. Kilburn, Reynolds, French and Bryan, forming a long line. The thick columns of the enemy were made to stagger, fearful inroads were made in their ranks, and they were finally, after many desperate struggles, obliged to give way. Their success was short, and their shouts of tri- umph were soon at an end. Just as they began to give way a little Lieutenant Rucker, with his squadron of 1st dragoons, was ordered to dash in among them, which was done with great effect.

It was feared that the portion of the enemy in our rear might attack the train at Buena Vista, and Col. May, with his command, and two pieces of artillery under Lieutenant Reynolds, was ordered to that place. But, before they arri- ved, the Arkansas and Keutucky cavalry had met the enemy and repulsed them. They broke in two columns, one escaped by the ranch, and received a destructive fire from the fugitive forces of a part of Major Trail's and Gorman's command, whom Major Munroe had reorganized. The other column of the enemy gained the mountain, but received a terrible fire from the pieces under, Lieutenant Reynolds.

Colonel Yell was killed, in the charge, at Buena Vista, at the head of his regiment. Adjutant Vaughn, also, of the Kentucky cavalry fell in that engagement.

A part of the Arkansas and Indiana troops, and Col. May, with his command, kept in check the enemy's right. They were crowded in vast numbers in ravines, and our guns made horrid work with them. Those who had gained our rear were now in the greatest danger. Santa Anna perceived it and in his deceptive and cowardly manner, sent a white flag into our camp, and asked General Taylor " what he wanted." Taylor immediately ordered the firing to cease, and sent General Wool, with a white flag, to answer the message. No consultation could be had, as the Mexicans kept on firing. Santa Anna had gained time for his forces to reach their lines and he cared no more for the truce. This was barbarous enough in the Mexican General. While the enemy were retreating, they were severely handled by our artillery.

The cavalry under General Minon, were in the road between the battle ground and Saltillo, and it was feared that they would fall upon the city. Capt. Webster fired upon them from the redoubt, and they moved towards Buena Vista. Capt. Shover, with some volunteers and a piece of artillery, accompanied by a piece of Webster's battery, under Lieut. Donaldson, aided by Capt. Wheeler, with his Illinois volunteers, drove the enemy into the ravines, leading to the lower valley. The enemy endeavored to charge once or twice, out were driven back every time in confusion. Firing had now nearly ceased; but one struggle more was to come. Santa Anna, being reinforced by cavalry. under cover of artillery, charged our line in a most desperate manner, by horse and foot. Great masses came rushing on, and poured among us a deadly fire. The 2nd Kentucky, 1st Illinois, and O'Brien, with two pieces, received the severest part of the attack. The infantry supporting O'Brien's piece was routed and their piece left in the hands of the enemy.

Our batteries, however, finally turned the tide. Their fire was so firm, precise and awful, that the enemy could not resist, and fell back in disorder. Harden and McKee, charged the enemy with great bravery and impetuosity. They fled, but seeing the few pursuing, turned suddenly and came up in vast numbers. There was dreadful carnage on both sides. We had but a mere handful compared with the enemy, and our men were again routed, and it seemed that we must be beaten. Brent and Whiting of Washington's battery covered their retreat.

General Taylor looked on calmly and unmoved, while the balls were flying all around him.

Bragg's battery had now reached the place of attack. Bragg told his Captain to unlimber the piece and wait till the enemy had arrived nearly to the muzzle, They rushed on certain that they should conquer us; but the battery opened and poured into their masses a plenty of grape. They staggered at the first fire, and the second opened streets through them and the third volley entirely dispersed them and they fled in dismay. Our loss was heavy in this last struggle.

In this desperate conflict, Colonels Hardin and McKee, and Lieutenant-Colonel Clay, fell at the head of their regiments. Our artillery turned the tide of battle three times

during the day. It was now ten hours that the battle had
been raging. The enemy did not make another attempt to
force our lines, and our troops, weary, dropped upon the
battle ground to seek rest to prepare them for the morrow.
among the dead and dying, without any fires to warm their
benumbed limbs. The wounded were removed to Saltillo and
our men prepared for an attack in the morning; but the
enemy retired very early to Agua Nueva, leaving many
of their dead and dying. Brigadier-general Marshall made a
forced march for Rinconada to reinforce our troops there;
but he was too late to participate in the action.

In the battle of Buena Vista, we had two hundred and
sixty-seven killed, four hundred and fifty-six wounded, and
twenty-three missing. The enemy must have lost two
thousand. There were five hundred of their dead left upon
the field. We had twenty-eight officers killed and forty-one
wounded.

What an awful responsibility rests upon somebody for
ushering so many innocent persons into the presence of their
Judge!

The names of the officers killed and wounded are the
following:

General Staff: killed, Captain George Lincoln, Assistant Adjutant General; wounded, H. W. Benham, 1st
Lieutenant Engineers; F. S. Bryan, brevet 2d Lieutenant Topographical engineers. 1st Regiment of dragoons:
wounded, Captain E. Steen. 2d regiment of dragoons:
wounded, Brevet Lieutenant-colonel C. A. May. 3d Regiment Artillery: wounded, Lieutenant S. G. French. 4th
Artillery: wounded, 1st Lieutenant J. P. O'Brien. Mississippi Rifles: killed, 1st Lieutenant R. L. Moore, 2d Lieut.
F. M'Nulty; wounded, Colonel Davis, Captains Sharp
and Stockaw, 1st Lieutenants Corwin and Posey. 1st

Regiment Illinois: killed, Colonel Hardin, Captain Zabris-
xie, and 1st Lieutenant Houghton. 2d Regiment Illinois;
killed, Captain Woodward, Lieutenants Rountree, Fletcher
Ferguson, Robbins, Steel, Kelly, Bartleson, Atherton, and
Price; wounded, Captains Coffee and Baker, Lieutenants
Picket, Engleman, West, and Whiteside. Texas volunteers;
killed, 1st Lieutetenant Campbell, 2d Lieutenant Leonhard;
wounded Captain Connor. Indiana volunteers: Brigade
Staff; Brigadier-aeneral Lane. 2d Indiana: killed, Cap-
tains Kinder and Walker, and Lieutenant Parr; wounded,
Captains Sanderson and Osborn, Lieutenants Cayce, Davis,
Pennington, Lewis, Moore, and Epperson. 3d Indiana ·
killed, Captain Taggart; wounded, Major Gorman, Cap-
tains Sleep and Connover. 2d Kentucky foot; killed,
Colonel M'Kee, Lieutenant-Colonel Clay, and Captain
Willis; wounded, Lieutenants Barber and Napier. Arkan-
sas Cavalry: killed, Colonel Yell, Captain Porter: wounded,
Lieutenant Reader.

A large portion of officers fell showing their unconquera-
ble bravery. It was a battle of artillery. General Taylor
said,—

"The services of the light artillery, always conspicuous,
were more than usually distinguished. Moving rapidly over
the roughest ground, it was always in action at the right
place and at the right time, and its well-directed fire dealt
destruction in the masses of the enemy."

The General was necessarily much exposed. Two balls
passed through his clothes. Our forces consisted of five
thousand, and but four hundred and fifty-three of them were
regulars. We were not able to follow up our success for
the want of more men.

On the 26th General Taylor issued the following order:

"Headquarters, Army of Occupation, ⎱
Buena Vista, Feb. 26, 1847.　　　⎰

Order No. 12.

1. The commanding general has the grateful task of congratulating the troops upon the brilliant success which attended their arms in the conflict of the 22nd and 23rd. Confident in the immense superiority of numbers, and stimulated by the presence of a distinguished leader, the Mexican troops were yet repulsed in every effort to force our lines, and finally withdrew with immense loss from the field.

11. The general would express his obligations to the men and officers engaged for the cordial support which they rendered throughout the action. It will be his highest pride to bring to the notice of the government the conspicuos gallantry of particular officers and corps, whose unwavering steadiness more than once saved the fortunes of the day. He would also express his high satisfaction with the small command left at Saltillo. Though not so seriously engaged as their comrades, their services were very important, and efficiently rendered. While bestowing this just tribute to the good conduct of the troops, the general deeply regrets to say that there were not a few exceptions. He trusts that those who fled ingloriously to Buena Vista, and even to Saltillo, will seek an opportunity to retrieve their reputation, and to emulate the bravery of their comrades who bore the brunt of the battle, and sustained, against fearful odds, the honor of the flag.

III. The exhultation of success is checked by the heavy sacrifice of life which it has cost, embracing many officers of high rank and rare merit. While the sympathy of a grateful country will be given to the bereaved families and friends of those who nobly fell, their illustrious example will remain for the benefit and admiration of the army.

By order,   Major-general TAYLOR.

Signed,   W. W .S. BLISS.

      Assistant Adjutant-general.

This order will be read at the head of every company.

      By order:

Signed,   W. W. S. BLISS.

It was found that the enemy were retiring towards San Luis Potosi.

Our forces returned to Agua Nueva on the 27th. The road was strewed with dead and wounded Mexicans, and their army seemed to be in a perfect state of disorganization.

Had it not been for the astonishing bravery of our men, in this battle, (5000 against 21,000,) we must have been overwhelmed.

General Urea, with about 8000 cavalry, had cut off all communication between Camargo and Monterey, previous to the battle of Buena Vista. A train of waggons, escorted by thirty men, was attacked and captured Feb. 24th, at Ramos. The wagons were burned and the teamsters dreadfully mutilated and their bodies cast into the flames.

March 7th, Major Giddings, in charge of a train of one hundred and fifty waggons, was attacked near Ceralvo. After a severe struggle, the enemy was repulsed, but we lost fifteen teamsters, two privates of Ohio volunteers, and fifty wagons.

General Taylor returned to Monterey early in March and pursued Urea, for a while and drove him over the mountaints. In April six thousand volunteers were called out by government to re-enforce the army. General

Taylor was to receive enough of them, to make, with what he had, about ten thousand men.

After this, nothing of much interest occurred in northern Mexico. The theatre of war was changed to another part of the country. The strong forts had been taken and the enemy conquered in every battle.

General Scott had been ordered to Mexico by the government, Nov. 23rd, 1846, in the following language:

WAR DEPARTMENT, WASHINGTON, *November*, 23, 1847

Sir,—The President, several days since communicated, in person to you his orders to repair to Mexico, to take command of the forces there assembled, and particularly to organize and set on foot an expedition to operate on the Gulf coast, if, on arriving at the theatre of action, you shall deem it to be practicable. It is not proposed to control your operations by definite and positive instructions, but you are left to prosecute them as your judgment, under a full view of all the circumstances, shall dictate. The work is before you, and the means provided, or to be provided, for accomplishing it, are committed to you, in the full confidence that you will use them to the best advantage.

The objects which it is desirable to obtain have been indicated, and it is hoped that you will have the requisite force to accomplish them.

Of this you must be the best judge, when preparations are made and the time for action arrived.

Very respectfully,

your obedient servant,

W. L. MARCY,

Secretary of War

Gen WINFIELD SCOTT.

Vera Cruz is situated in 19 degrees 11 minutes 52 seconds north latitude. One portion of its walls is washed by the Atlantic, and the shore on the opposite side is a dry and sandy plain.

General Scott sailed from New York, Nov. 30th and reached the Rio Grande Jan 1st 1847.

AMERICAN FLEET SALUTING THE CASTLE AT VERA CRUZ

BATTLE OF VERA CRUZ.

THE new army was designated to attack the city of Vera Cruz and the Castle of San Juan de Ulloa. The naval squadron, under Commodore Conner, was to assist the :and forces. The squadron landed at Anton Lizardo, March 7th. The troops, sent from General Taylor, arrived in February, and increased his army to 12,000 men.

DESCRIPTION OF THE CITY OF VERA CRUZ AND CASTLE OF SAN JUAN DE ULLOA.

"Vera Cruz is situated in 19° 11' 52" north latitude. One portion of its walls is washed by the Atlantic, and the shore on the opposite side is a dry and sandy plain.

" The city is small, but from the regularity which marks its laying out, it is beautiful. The streets are wide, straight, and well paved. The houses, of which there are one thousand and sixty-three, are mostly two stories high, and built of the Muscara stone, taken from the sea-beach.

" The fortifications of the city consist of nine towers connected together by means of a stone and mortar wall, which, however, is not very thick. The two towers named Santiago and Conception are the most important. They are situated at that portion of the walls looking toward the castle of San Juan, and are distant from each other one thousand two hundred and seventy varas. The other towers, including the one called San Fernando, are almost equal in shape, size, and strength. All of them can mount one hundred pieces of artillery of various sizes; and save those of the middle ones, their fires all cross in front of the guard-houses, the external walls of which form part of the walls which surround the city.

" Although the port of Vera Cruz is the principal one in the Gulf of Mexico, it is very dangerous during the seasons of the northers—that which is called the bay, being, in reality, nothing more than a bad roadstead. Baron Humboldt but too faithfully described the harbor of Vera Cruz when he said, that the only shelter it affords shipping is a dangerous anchorage among shoals.

" The *castle of San Juan de Ulloa* is unquestionably the most celebrated of all American fortresses. Its construction was commenced in the year 1582, upon a bar or bank, in front of the town of Vera Cruz, at the distance of one thousand and sixty-two Castilian varas or yards, and it is entirely surrounded by water. The centre of the area occupied by this fortress is a small island, upon which Juan de Grijalva landed a year previous to the arrival of Cortes upon the Continent, and, at that period, it accidentally received the name which it retains to this present day. It seems that there was a shrine or temple erected upon it, in which human victims were sacrificed to the Indian gods ; and as the Spaniards were informed that these offerings were made in accordance with the commands of the kings of Acolhua (one of the provinces of the empire), they confounded or abbreviated this name into the word Ulloa, which they affixed to the island.

" According to a report made on the 17th of January, 1775, it was the opinion of a council of war, composed of distinguished officers, that this fortress, after all its defences were completed, would require a garrison for effective service, composed of seventeen hundred infantry soldiers, three hundred artillery, two hundred and twenty-eight sailors, and a hundred supernumeraries.

" The exterior polygon, which faces Vera Cruz, extends three hundred yards in length, whilst that which defends the north channel is, at least, two hundred yards long. Besides this, there is a low battery situated in the bastion of Santiago, which doubles the fire on that channel. The southern channel is commanded also by the battery of San Miguel.

" The whole fortress is constructed of *Madrepora Astrea*, a species of soft coral, which abounds in the neighboring islands. Its walls are from four to five yards in thickness, their exterior being faced with a harder stone. It is well supplied with water, having seven cisterns within the castle, which altogether contain ninety-three thousand seven hundred and sixty-seven cubic feet of water. Its full equipment of artillery pieces is three hundred and seventy; but it contained only a hundred and seventy-seven when attacked by the French in 1838."

A regiment of Louisiana volunteers, under Colonel Russey, were wrecked in February near the island of Lobos. They were met by a large force under General Cos and ordered to surrender. They were without arms, but Colonel Russey delayed his answer until night, presenting at the same time a bold front. He lighted up camp fires, left his baggage, and, by forced marches, reached the American quarters at Tampico.

The two commanding officers, immediately after landing at Lizardo, reconnoitred the city in the steamer Petrita, and thought best to land on the beach due west of the island of Sacrificios. At daybreak on the 9th, about 2,800 troops were transferred, in each frigate, and proportionate numbers in smaller vessels, to Sacrificios. A little after 11 A. M. the squadron moved off majestically The day was fine, with a gentle breeze from the south east, and a smooth sea. The passage occupied between two and

.hree hours, and the vessels were anchored without confusion . Gen. Scott ordered the landing to be commenced immediately, ordering the steamers Spitfire and Vixen, and five gun-boats, to form a line parallel with and near the beach, in order to cover the landing of our men in the surf-boats. As the boats, 65 in number, received the troops, they assembled in a line, abreast, between the fleet and the gun-boats and pulled for the shore, all at once, landing without resistance. General Worth commanded this first line of the army and formed his men, 4,500 strong, on the beach and neighboring heights just before sunset, and by 10 P. M. an army of 10,000 men were on shore, without any accident occurring. All but a few companies had landed. The next day the artillery, horses, provisions, and other materials were landed, and the remaining troops, making more than eleven thousand men. General Scott landed early in the morning, and preparations were immediately made to surround the city. As our men advanced, some shot and shells were fired from the town and castle, but without effect. At 2 o'clock, March 10th, a brisk fire from the enemy commenced. One of our men had his thigh broken, and two others were wounded. A small detachment was sent out under Captain Gordon to reconnoitre. He found himself, after going two or three hundred yards, near a body of men and hailed them. They answered in English, and soon answered again by a volley of bullets, which was returned by the detachment, and the Mexicans were obliged to retire into the town. At sunrise, the steamer Spitfire, Capt. Tatnall, took position in front of the city and castle, and commenced firing. She continued for an hour, and the city and castle returned the compliment. Soon after the Spitfire opened her fire, the 1st and 2d divisions moved up the beach towards the city about a mile and commenced to invest the place. Four or five regiments of Mexican infantry and cavalry appeared in front of the city, half a mile from our men, and commenced firing upon us. One of our mountain howitzers and some rockets were placed on the hills. A few shots were fired and rockets sent; but without effect. Captain Taylor was ordered to try the six-pounder, which caused the Mexicans to retire behind the hill. One Mexican was killed.

General Worth was successful in taking his position on the right of the investment by 11 o'clock. The line, circumvallating the city, was to run along a chain of sand-hills about 3 miles from the city, ranging from 300 to 1500 feet high, entirely commanding the town and fortifications. The heavy guns from the castle could reach the right wing.

After Worth had taken his position, General Patterson's division took up its line of march, with General Pillow's brigade in advance, in order to form on the left of Worth's division. After proceeding a mile, they met the enemy in a thick chaparral. There was a smart fire for about twenty minutes. The Mexicans retreated. Gen. Pillow had great difficulty in advancing through the chaparral. He proceeded about half a mile farther by 4 P. M., and met the enemy again, in ambuscade. Their fire was heavy upon our men, and General Patterson sent the New York regiment of Shields' brigade to aid General Pillow; but only one New York company arrived, before General Pillow had routed the enemy by a charge. Only two of our men were slightly wounded. A body of the enemy were seen at a little distance, at a house known as a magazine, on the left flank of Pillow's command. A 6-pounder was directed towards them, and a few shots were enough to disperse them. Towards sun-down, Gen. Pillow reached, by great effort, one of the highest points in the rear of the city, and erected the star spangled banner. The batteries from the town and castle, kept up a continued firing till dark. One shell exploded in front of General Worth and staff.

At 7 A. M., (March 11th) General Quitman's brigade was ordered to relieve General Pillow from the place which he occupied during the night. The Mexicans, thinking that our men were deserting the heights, approached and were met by General Quitman, who advanced to the top of the hill. A smart fire was kept up for an hour.

Capt. Davis, of the Georgia regiment, with twenty riflemen, were sent as skirmishers, to move round under the hill and engage the enemy in close quarters. About 200 of the enemy advanced on him, and he held them in check until Colonel Jackson, with the balance of three companies, and Col. Dickerson and his regiment, came to his aid. The enemy were obliged to retire, with the loss of several dead and wounded. We had seven slightly wounded.

At 9 A. M., General Twiggs, with his mounted rifles in advance, moved up to take position on the left of the line. It was very difficult as the cannon had to be lifted over sand-ridges by the men, in many cases. The force all reached their destination by the sea-shore, above the town, about sun-down. Thus the city was surrounded by us, our line reaching about eight miles. General Worth occupied the right, General Twiggs the left, and General Patterson the centre.

Our men now commenced placing their heavy batteries in position to open upon the town.

By the 22d, seven ten-inch mortars were in battery,

and the others nearly ready. At two, P. M., General Scott addressed a summons to the Governor of Vera Cruz, and received an answer in two hours. The Governor supposed that Scott ordered him to surrender the town and castle (though that was not the case, as Scott was not prepared to make such a demand).

Scott now determined to open his seven mortars upon the town. The small vessels of Commodore Perry's squadron, two steamers and five schooners, came within a mile and an eighth of the city and opened a brisk fire, which continued till 9, A. M. (March 23), when the Com modore called the vessels away from so dangerous a posi-tion. By noon we had ten mortars battering the walls of the city. The ten inch mortars planted about eight hun-dred yards from the city, were very effective. Our men, thus far, from the time of their landing had only four or five men wounded, and one officer and one private killed. The officer was Capt. J. R. Vinton, of the U. S. 3d ar-tillery. He was killed in the trenches, March 24th, at ten, A. M. The naval battery, No. 5, consisting of three thirty-two pounders and three eight inch Paixhans, open-ed a terrific fire, under Capt. Aulick. The battery was active till two, P. M. We lost four sailors killed, and Lieut. Baldwin was slightly wounded.

March 25th, battery No. 4, consisting of four twenty-four pounders, and two eight inch Paixhans, opened.

Now, batteries 1, 2, 3, 4 and 5, were shaking the whole foundation of the city, by their tremendous fire.

On the evening of the 24th, the foreign consuls signed a memorial, requesting General Scott to grant a truce, so that the neutrals and women and children might retire from the city. Our heavy guns made dreadful havoc, destroying many women and children. General Scott replied:

First, That a truce could only be granted on the application of Governor Morales, with a view to surrender; second, That in sending safeguards to the different consuls, beginning as far back as the 13th instant, he distinctly admonished them, particularly the French and Spanish consuls—and, of course, through the two, the other consuls—of the dangers that have followed; third. That although, at that date, he had already refused to allow any person whatsoever to pass the line of investment either way, yet the blockade had been left open to the consuls and other neutrals to pass out to their respective ships of war up to the 22d instant; and, fourth, he enclosed to the memorialists a copy of his summons to the governor, to show that he had fully considered the impending hardships and distresses of the place, including those of women and children, before one gun had been fired in that direction.

On the 26th, General Scott received overtures from General Landero, on whom General Morales had devolved the command, and on account of a heavy norther, he was unable to communicate with the ships until the 27th.

The American Commissioners were, Generals Worth and Pillow, Colonel Totten, and Capt. Aulick.

It was finally agreed that the city and castle should surrender to us.

The following are the terms of capitulation:

" 1. The whole garrison, or garrisons, to be surrendered to the arms of the United States, as prisoners of war, the 29th instant, at 10 o'clock, A. M.; the garrisons to be permitted to march out with all the honors of war, and to lay down their arms to such officers as may be appointed by the general-in-chief of the United States' armies, and at a point to be agreed upon by the commissioners.

" 2. Mexican officers shall preserve their arms and private effects, including horses and horse-furniture, and to be allowed, regular and irregular officers, as also the rank and file, five days to retire to their respective homes, on parole, as hereinafter prescribed.

" 3. Coincident with the surrender, as stipulated in article 1, the Mexican flags of the various forts and stations shall be struck, saluted by their own batteries; and, immediately thereafter, Forts Santiago and Concet...on, and the castle of San Juan de Ulloa, occupied by the forces of the United States.

" 4. The rank and file of the regular portion of the prisoners to be disposed of after surrender and parole, as their general-in-chief may desire, and the irregular to be permitted to return to their homes. The officers, in respect to all arms and descriptions of force, giving the usual parole, that the said rank and file, as well as themselves, shall not serve again until duly exchanged.

" 5. All the *materiel* of war, and all public property of every description found in the city, the castle of San Juan de Ulloa and their dependencies, to belong to the United States ; but the armament of the same (not injured or destroyed in the further prosecution of the actual war), may be considered as liable to be restored to Mexico by a definite treaty of peace.

" 6. The sick and wounded Mexicans to be allowed to remain in the city, with such medical officers and attendants, and officers of the army, as may be necessary to their care and treatment.

" 7. Absolute protection is solemnly guaranteed to per-

sons in the city, and property, and it is clearly understood that no private building or property is to be taken
or used by the forces of the United States, without previous arrangement with the owners, and for a fair equivalent.

" 8. Absolute freedom of religious worship and cere
monies is solemnly guaranteed."

At the surrender on the 27th, our army were drawn up
in two lines, facing each other, and stretching more than a
mile. The enemy left the city at ten o'clock, passed between our lines, laid down their arms and colors and
marched for the interior. General Worth superintended
the evacuation and then entered the city. Our flag was
erected over the Plaza and saluted by the guns of the city
and squadron. General Worth was appointed Military
Governor.

BATTLE OF SIERRA GORDA.

GENERAL TWIGGS' division of our army arrived, within
three miles of the position of the enemy, April 11th, and
General Patterson's on the 12th. On the 16th, we had
six thousand men ready for action, while the enemy numbered from eight to twelve thousand. They occupied
a chain of works along the road, the nearest of which was
about a mile and a quarter from General Scott's head-
quarters. The road over which we had to pass, was barricaded and cut up in every way to impede our progress.
Beyond the first fortification there are several others completely commanding the gorge, through which the road to

Jalapa runs. There were twenty-four pieces of field artillery besides about fourteen heavy cannon in position. The high and rocky ravine of the river protected their right flank and a series of abrupt and apparently impassable mountains and ridges covered their left. A front attack, which the enemy expected on account of our bravery, must have been fatal to us. General Scott outwitted the *One Leg* and had a road cut to the right, so as to escape the front fire, and turn his position on the left flank. A deserter from our camp made this known to the enemy, and they sent General La Vega with a large force to aid the left flank.

General Scott, on the 17th of April, to cover his flank movements, sent General Twiggs against the fort on the steep ascent in front, and a little to the left of the Sierra. This expedition was commanded by Colonel Harney, who carried the position under a heavy fire of grape and musketry. This was an important post gained, situated in front and near the enemy's strongest fortification. By great labor, one of our large guns was placed upon the top of the fort, and blazed away at a strong fort in the rear ; but with little effect.

April 18th, early in the morning, our army moved to the attack in columns. General Twiggs's division attacked the enemy's left and carried the breast works after a slight resistance, at the point of the bayonet, and completely routed the enemy at that point. Pillow's brigade, accompanied by General Shields's, passed along the Jalapa road with rapidity, and took a position to stop the retreat of the enemy. General Worth moved forward toward the left to aid Twiggs. Twiggs had steep and ough ground to pass over, was constantly exposed to the fire of the enemy in front and to the cross-fire of the forts and batteries.

The fight was tremendous for a short time, and finally the enemy gave way on all sides. Three thousand men with field and other officers surrendered. A large amount of small arms, ordnance and batteries were taken. Six thousand of the enemy gained the rear of our army on the Jalapa road and were pursued. We lost two hundred and fifty killed and wounded, and among the latter was General Shields. The Mexican loss was about one hundred more than ours, besides those taken prisoners. We captured thirty pieces of cannon, much ammunition, and the private baggage and money chest of Santa Anna, containing twenty thousand dollars. On the 19th, Jalapa, and on the 22d, Perote, were taken without opposition.

Nothing prevented our men from being utterly destroyed but the steepness of the ascent under which they could shelter. But they sought no shelter, and onward rushed against a hailstorm of balls and musket-shot, led by the gallant Harney, whose noble bearing elicited the applause of the whole army. His conspicuous and stalwart frame at the head of his brigade, his long arm waving his men on to the charge, his sturdy voice ringing above the clash of arms and din of conflict, attracted the attention and admiration alike of the enemy and of our own men. On, on, he led the columns, whose front lines melted before the enemy's fire like snow-flakes in a torrent, and staid not their course until leaping over the rocky barriers, and bayonetting their gunners, they drove the enemy pell mell from the fort, delivering a deadly fire into their ranks, from their own guns, as they hastily retired.

General Scott, between whom and Colonel Harney there had existed some coolness, rode up to the colonel after this achievement, and remarked to him—"Colonel Harney, I cannot now adequately express my admiration of your gallant achievement, but at the proper time I shall take great pleasure in thanking you in proper terms."

It was here the enemy received their heaviest loss, and their General Vasquez was killed. A little after, General Worth, having, by great exertions, passed the steep and craggy heights on the enemy's left, summoned a strong fort in the rear of the Sierra to surrender. This fort was manned by a large force under General Pinzon, a mulatto officer of considerable ability and courage, who, seeing the Sierra carried, thought prudent to surrender, which he did with all his force. General Shields was not so fortunate in the battery which he attacked, and which was commanded by General la Vega. A heavy fire was opened on him, under which the fort was carried with some loss by the gallant Illinoisians, under Baker and Bennett, supported by the New Yorkers, under Burnett. Among those who fell under this fire was the gallant general, who received a grape-shot through his lungs, by which he was completely paralyzed, and at the last account was in a lingering state. On the enemy's right, General Pillow commenced the attack against the strong forts near the river. The Tennesseeans, under Haskell, led the column, and the other volunteer regiments followed. This column unexpectedly encountered a heavy fire from a masked battery, by which Haskell's regiment was nearly cut to pieces, and the other volunteer regiments were severely handled. General Pillow withdrew his men, and was preparing for another attack, when the operations at the other points having proved successful, the enemy concluded to surrender. Thus the victory was complete, and four generals, and about six thousand men, were taken prisoners by our army. One of their principal generals and a large number of other officers killed. The Mexican force on this occasion certainly exceeded our own."

In addition to the loss of the enemy in killed and taken they lost about thirty pieces of brass cannon, mostly of large calibre, manufactured at the royal foundry of Seville. A large quantity of fixed ammunition, of a very superior quality, together with the private baggage and money-chest of Santa Anna, containing twenty thousand dollars, was also captured.

On the same day that the battle of Sierra Gordo was fought, a portion of the American Gulf Squadron, under Commodore Perry, captured the town of Tuspan, on the Gulf.

On the 19th, the city of Jalapa was captured by a detachment under General Twiggs; and on the 22d, General Worth entered the town of Perote. Both these cities were taken without opposition; and in the latter were found immense stores of small arms, ammunition, and the large guns of the city and castle.

BATTLE OF CHURUBUSCO.

GENERAL SCOTT remained inactive for awhile before entering the capital, hoping to be re-enforced, his head-quarters being at Puebla, while the Mexicans, notwithstanding their repulses and severe losses, were busy in collecting another army and fortifying every entrance to the city. (For representation of this Battle, see cover.)

Aug. 8th, our army, having received a few re-enforcements, marched towards the capital, and reached Ayotla on the 12th, where there was a strong fortification called St. Pinon. It was reconnoitred and found to be very strong by nature and art. It was thought, that it would be hazardous to attack it, as was anticipated by the Mexicans. Scott here again outwitted Santa Anna, for he found a road south of Lake Charles, opening into that from Vera Cruz, below Ayotla, which would enable our army to pass around the fort; but the march was a very difficult one, for heavy rains had filled the low places so that the soldiers were often obliged to wade. The steep and rugged heights were to be crossed : and the paths and gorges were filled with immense stones, which had been rolled in by the enemy. The men became weary during the day, and the nights were dark and wet, which added to their discouragements.

On the 17th, our advance arrived at San Augustin, a small town about twelve miles south of the capital; General Worth led on his men to take possession of a hacienda near the fortification of San Antonio, for the purpose of attacking that place. They captured the village; but Capt. Thornton was killed in taking a reconnoissance, from a heavy discharge of artillery by the enemy. One or two of our men were wounded. A squadron of artillery and a battalion of infantry were near the redoubt, hoping to make an attack in the afternoon, but a rain set in, and General Scott thought best to withdraw them. Had the batteries of the enemy opened with energy upon this detachment, it would probably have been obliged to retire or been cut to pieces; but fortunately the guns were silent all night.

During the night, the divisions of Pillow and Twiggs marched towards the strong works of Contreras, to be prepared for an assault in the morning. This was a very fatiguing march. The darkness of the night, the torrents of rain pouring down upon them, the wild roaring of the winds, the ridges from rocks of lava to pass over, the denseness of the brushwood, the swollen streams to cross, presented difficulties rarely surpassed.

At eight the next morning, the batteries of the enemy opened upon the hacienda of San Antonio, where General Worth was posted. This cannonading was heavy. The air was shaken by the heavy explosions, while houses and even strong fortifications were shattered to pieces and fell in thundering ruins, beneath the showers of shot and shells. Almost all of the streets were swept by bullets and large bombs which burst in the air, and hurled slugs, shot and fragments among our ranks, making sad havoc. But the Yankees were not frightened yet. They placed themselves behind walls and buildings, and calmly, amid this scene of confusion, prepared for action. Soon the divisions of Pillow and Twiggs moved on towards Contreras, arriving about one P. M. General P. F. Smith was ordered to march up in front of the enemy's works, and Colonel Riley, to move with rapidity towards the right, gain the main road, and prevent any re-enforcements of the enemy. Smith dashed forward under a tremendous fire and secured a good position for his artillery. Every battery and gun on both sides roared away with horrible sublimity and actually shook the ground for miles around, and their reverberations rolled with grandeur along the lofty ridges of the mountains. The few guns of our advanced battery were soon silenced, and General Pierce proceeded to the relief of General Smith.

At this time, large re-enforcements of the enemy approached Contreras, and General Cadwallader hastened to re-enforce Riley. The contest was now terrific. Neither army would yield an inch of ground.

At four o'clock, General Scott passed along the lines, and was welcomed by an enthusiastic shout. Perceiving the immense strength of the enemy, he ordered General Shields to re-enforce Riley and Cadwallader, and strengthen our army in front of the enemy. Now the battle raged nigher still, and hundreds fell to rise no more. This dreadful carnage was kept up for six hours, when the darkness of night closed the scene, and the cannons ceased their roar. Our men were disappointed, as they expected by that time to have been in the "Halls of the Montezumas." They were obliged to lie upon the cold, wet ground, without blankets, to rest for the night.

At eight o'clock in the evening, General Scott retired to San Augustin, and Twiggs and Pillow went at eleven.

Scott and Worth set out for Contreras early the next morning. Firing was heard, and soon a messenger came, saying that General Worth had carried the whole line of fortifications at Contreras. He planned and executed the undertaking in a skilful manner and with little loss. He took fifteen hundred of the enemy prisoners, including Generals Salas, Blanco, Garcia and Mendoza. He also captured an immense amount of ammunition and camp equipage, and fifteen pieces of artillery, among them the two taken from Capt. O'Brien at Buena Vista; seven hundred of the enemy were killed and many more wounded.

General Scott now sent General Worth to attack San Antonio, while he with a force would go in its rear. The soldiers passed over the battle-field of the previous day, and the scene which was presented was enough to make the hardy soldier shudder and feel sick in view of the horrors of war. Hundreds lay covered with blood, stiff and cold in death, while others were uttering piteous groans and begged for water. The streams actually run with human blood. What a shocking scene! How surprising that nations will thus imbue their hands in each other's blood!

When the force reached San Pablo, another action commenced, and at the same time Worth's cannon were heard roaring away at Churubusco. The flower of both armies were now engaged in terrible combat. The rattling of the musketry, the clash of arms, and the deafening roar of the cannon and the groans of the dying, made the scene truly awful!

Scott was in the midst of danger encouraging his men, while Worth and Twiggs were cheering their soldiers on. Thus, one of the severest conflicts ever witnessed on this continent, raged with increasing power for two hours. Finally our forces gained full possession of all the works, and the enemy fled in dismay to the city. Worth followed them almost to the gates.

The next morning, a detachment of our men entered Chapultepec without opposition.

Soon after this, Santa Anna sent flags, proposing a suspension of hostilities. Negotiations took place, and the following armistice was adopted, August 20th:

THE ARMISTICE.

The undersigned, appointed respectively, the first three by Major-general Winfield Scott, commander-in-chief of the armies of the United States, and the last two by his Excellency D. Antonio Lopez de Santa Anna, President of the Mexican Republic, and commander-in-chief of its armies, met with full powers, which were fully verified in the village of Tucubaya, on the 23d day of August, 1847, to enter into an armistice for the purpose of giving the Mexican government an opportunity of receiving propositions of peace from the commissioners appointed by the President of the United States, and now with the American army ; when the following articles were agreed upon :

ART. 1. Hostilities shall instantly and absolutely cease between the armies of the United States of America and the United Mexican States, within thirty leagues of the capital of the latter States, to allow time to the commissioners appointed by the United States and the commissioners to be appointed by the Mexican Republic to negotiate.

2. The armistice shall continue as long as the commissioners of the two governments may be engaged on negotiations, or until the commander of either of the said armies shall give formal notice to the other of the cessation of the armistice for forty-eight hours after such notice.

3. In the mean time, neither army shall, within thirty leagues of the city of Mexico, commence any new fortification or military work of offence or defence, or do any thing to enlarge or strengthen any existing work or fortification of that character within the said limits.

4. Neither army shall be reinforced within the same. Any reinforcements in troops or munitions of war, other than subsistence now approaching either army, shall be stopped at the distance of twenty-eight leagues from the city of Mexico.

5. Neither army, nor any detachment from it, shall advance beyond the line it at present occupies.

6. Neither army, nor any detachment or individual of either, shall pass the neutral limits established by the last article, except under a flag of truce bearing the correspondence between the two armies, or on the business authorized by the next article; and individuals of either army, who may chance to straggle within the neutral limits, shall, by the opposite party, be kindly warned off, or sent back to their own armies under flags of truce.

7. The American army shall not, by violence, obstruct the passage from the open country into the city of Mexico, of the ordinary supplies of food necessary to the consumption of its inhabitants, or the Mexican army within the city; nor shall the Mexican authorities, civil or military, do any act to obstruct the passage of supplies from the city or country, needed by the American army.

8. All American prisoners of war remaining in the hands of the Mexican army, and not heretofore exchanged, shall immediately, or as soon as practicable, be restored to the American army, against a like number, having regard to rank, of Mexican prisoners captured by the American army.

9. All American citizens who were established in the city of Mexico prior to the existing war, and who have since been expelled from that city, shall be allowed to return to their respective business or families therein, without delay or molestation.

10. The better to enable the belligerent armies to execute these articles, and to favor the great object of peace, it is further agreed between the parties, that any courier with despatches that either army shall desire to send along the line from the city of Mexico or its vicinity, to and from Vera Cruz, shall receive a safe conduct from the commander of the opposing army.

11. The administration of justice between Mexicans, according to the general and state constitutions and laws, by the local authorities of the towns and places occupied by the American forces, shall not be obstructed in any manner.

12. Persons and property shall be respected in the towns and places occupied by the American forces. No person shall be molested in the exercise of his profession; nor shall the services of any one be required without his consent. In all cases where services are voluntarily rendered, a just price shall be paid, and trade remain unmolested.

13. Those wounded prisoners who may desire to remove to some more convenient place, for the purpose of being cured of their wounds, shall be allowed to do so without molestation, they still remaining prisoners.

14. The Mexican medical officers who may wish to attend the wounded shall have the privilege of doing so, if their services be required.

15. For the more perfect execution of this agreement, two commissioners shall be appointed, one by each party, who, in case of disagreement, shall appoint a third.

16. This convention shall have no force or effect, unless approved by their excellencies, the commanders respectively of the two armies, within twenty-four hours, reckoning from the sixth hour of the 23d day of August, 1847.

> A. Quitman, *Maj. Gen. U. S. A.*
> Persifor F. Smith, *Brig. Gen.*
> Franklin Pierce, *Brig. Gen. U. S. A.*
> Ignacio de Mara y Villamil.
> Benito Quijano.

It is believed that the whole force of the Mexicans, in these brilliant engagements, was about thirty-two thousand men. They lost between five and six thousand, including thirteen generals and forty-five pieces of cannon. Our army consisted of seven thousand, eleven hundred of whom were killed or wounded. What a terrible slaughter!

After the armistice was agreed upon, various meetings took place between Mr. Trist, the American minister, and Mexican Commissioners, and endeavors were made to effect a treaty of peace, until September 2d, when Trist handed in his ultimatum in reference to the boundary line, and the Commissioners were to meet again on the 16th.

Some infractions of the truce were made by the enemy, in reference to our supplies from the city; but the Mexicans apologized.

It appears that as soon as the propositions of Trist were considered in a grand council of ministers and others, Santa Anna, on the 4th and 5th, without giving any notice to General Scott, commenced again fortifying the city, directly in opposition to the armistice. Scott immediately sent him a note, which was answered in a false and impudent manner.

Our arrangements were delayed more than two weeks by the armistice. It is probable that Santa Anna only entered into it for the purpose of gaining time.

BATTLE OF MEXICO.

SEPT. 7th, General Scott began to reconnoitre the different approaches to the city within his reach. In the afternoon, a large body of the enemy were seen around the *Molinos del Rey* (Mills), about a mile and a third from Tucubaya, the head-quarters of our army. These mills were repositories of ammunition, and there was a foundry there for casting cannon. There was a formidable castle in the hands of the enemy on the heights of Chapultepec, between the mills and the gates of the capital. There were eight city gates strongly fortified. It was impossible to stop communication between the mills and the capital, without first taking the castle. Preparatory to storming it, it was thought best to capture the mills. Accordingly, on the 8th, General Worth's division, re-enforced by Cadwallader's brigade, Pillow's division, three squadrons of dragoons under Major Sumner, and some heavy guns of the siege train under Capt. Huger of the ordnance, and Capt. Drum of the 7th artillery, undertook the enterprise. They moved towards the enemy and soon met them. There was much energy manifested on both sides. The enemy several times were re-enforced, and the action becoming much more general than was expected, General Scott called to our aid from the distance of three miles, Gen. Pillow, with his remaining brigade (Pierce's), and then Riley's brigade of Twiggs' division. These forces approached with great rapidity; but the victory was won just as General Pierce reached the ground and placed his command between Worth's division and the retreating enemy. Thus again were our forces victorious.   Various daring reconnoisances **now** **took** place, of the castle and approaches to the city.   The latter stands on a slight swell of ground, near the **centre** **of** an irregular basin, and is girdled with a ditch in **its** greater extent—a navigable canal of great breadth **and** depth—very difficult to bridge, in the presence of an ene- **my,** having eight entrenches or gates, over arches—**each** **of** which was defended by a system of strong works **that** seemed to require nothing but some men and guns to **be** impregnable.

Outside and within the cross-fire of those gates, to **the** south, are other obstacles but little less formidable.   **All** approaches near the city were over elevated **causeways,** cut in many places (to oppose us) and flanked on **both** sides, by ditches also of unusual dimensions.   The nume- rous cross-roads were flanked, in like manner, **having** bridges at the intersections, recently broken.   The mead- ows thus checked, were, moreover, in many spots, **under** water or marshy.

After close observation, it was decided, on the 11th, **to** move round to the south-west and west part of the **capital,** believing that the approaches would present less formida- ble obstacles.   Accordingly, Scott ordered Quitman's di- vision from Coyoacan, to join Pillow *by daylight,* before the southern gates, and that they should *by night,* proceed (two miles) to join Scott at Tucubaya, where he was quar- tered with Worth's division.   Twiggs, with Riley's brigade and Captains Taylor's and Steptoe's field batteries—the latter 12-pounders—was left in front of those gates—to manœuvre, to threaten, or to make false attacks, in order to occupy and deceive the enemy.   Twiggs' other brigade (Smith's) was left at supporting distance, in the rear, **at**

San Angel, till the morning of the 13th, and also to support our general depôt at Miscoaque. The stratagem against the south was admirably executed throughout the 12th, and down to the afternoon of the 13th, when it was too late for the enemy to recover from the effects of his delusion.

The first step in the new movement was to carry the Castle of Chapultepec. Besides a numerous garrison, here was the military college of the Republic with a large number of sub-lieutenants and other students. Those works were within direct gun-shot of the village of Tucubaya, and until carried, we could not approach the city on the west without making a circuit too wide and too hazardous.

During the same night (that of the 11th) heavy batteries were established. No. 1, on the right, under the command of Capt. Drum, 4th artillery (relieved late next day, for some hours, by Lieut. Andrews of the 3d), and No. 2, commanded by Lieut. Huger, ordnance—both supported by Quitman's division. Nos. 3 and 4, on the opposite side, supported by Pillow's division, were commanded, the former by Capt. Brooks and Lieut. S. S. Anderson, 2d artillery, alternately, and the latter by Lieut. Stone, ordnance.

The bombardment and cannonade, under the direction of Capt. Huger, were commenced early in the morning of the 12th, and before night a good impression had been made on the castle and its outworks.

Pillow and Quitman had been in position since early in the night of the 11th. In the morning, Worth was ordered to hold his division in reserve, near the foundry, to support Pillow; and Brigadier General Smith, of Twiggs' division, had just arrived with his brigade, from Piedad,

[2 miles] to support Quitman. Twiggs' guns, before the southern gates, again reminded us, as the day before, that he, with Riley's brigade, and Taylor's and Steptoe's batteries, was in activity, threatening the southern gates, and there holding a great part of the Mexican army on the defensive.

Worth's division furnished Pillow's attack with an assaulting party of some 250 volunteer officers and men, under Capt. McKenzie, of the 2d artillery, and Twiggs' division supplied a similar one, commanded by Captain Casey, 2d infantry, to Quitman. Each of those little columns was furnished with scaling ladders.

The signal for the attack was to be the momentary cessation of fire on the part of our heavy batteries. About 8 o'clock A. M., of the 13th, Scott sent to Pillow and Quitman, with notice that the concerted signal was about to be given.

Both columns now advanced. The batteries threw shots and shells upon the enemy over the heads of our men, with good effect.

Major General Pillow's approach, on the west side, lay through an open grove, filled with sharp shooters, who were speedily dislodged ; when, being up hill with the front of the attack, and emerging into open space, at the foot of a rocky acclivity, that gallant leader was struck down by an agonizing wound.

The immediate command devolved on General Cadwallader. On a previous call of Pillow, Worth had just sent him a reinforcement, Col. Clark's brigade.

The broken declivity was still to be ascended and a strong redoubt midway to be carried, before reaching the castle on the heights. The advance of our men, though necessarily slow, was unwavering, over rocks, chasms and mines, and under the hottest fire of cannon and musketry.

The enemy were steadily driven from shelter to shelter. —The retreat allowed not time to fire a single mine, without the certainty of blowing up friend and foe. Those, who, at a distance, attempted to apply matches to the long trains were shot down by our men.

There was death below as well as above ground. At length the ditch and wall of the main work were reached; the scaling ladders were brought up and planted by the storming parties; some of the daring spirits first in the assault were cast down—killed or wounded; but a lodgment was soon made; streams of heroes followed; all opposition was overcome, and several of our regimental colors flung out from the upper walls, amidst long-continued shouts and cheers, which sent dismay into the capital. No scene could have been more animating.

General Quitman, supported by Generals Shields and Smith, [P. F.] his other officers and men, was up with the part assigned him. Simultaneously with the movement on the west, he approached the southeast of the same works over a causeway with cuts and batteries, and defended by an army strongly posted outside, to the east of the works. Those formidable obstacles Quitman had to face, with but little shelter for his troops or space for manœuvring. Deep ditches, flanking the causeway, made it difficult to cross on either side into the adjoining meadows, and these again were intersected by other ditches. Smith and his brigade made a sweep to the right, in order to present a front against the enemy's line (outside), and to turn into intervening batteries, near the foot of Chapultepec. This movement was also intended to support

Quitman's storming parties, both on the causeway. The first of these, furnished by Twiggs' division, was commanded in succession by Capt. Casey, 2d infantry, and Capt. Paul, 7th infantry, after Casey had been severely wounded; and the second, under Major Twiggs, marine corps, killed, and then Capt. Miller, 2d Pennsylvania volunteers. The storming party, now commanded by Capt. Paul, seconded by Captain Roberts of the rifles, Lieut. Stewart, and others of the same regiment, Smith's brigade, carried the two batteries in the road, took some guns, with many prisoners, and drove the enemy posted behind in support. The New York and South Carolina volunteers (Shields' brigade) and the 2d Pennsylvania volunteers, all on the left of Quitman's line, together with portions of his storming parties, crossed the meadows in front, under a heavy fire, and entered the outer enclosure of Chapultepec, just in time to join in the final assault from the west.

Generals Pillow, Quitman, Shields, Smith, and Cadwallader, distinguished themselves in these brilliant operations. Also Colonel Andrews, Lieut. Col. Johnstone, Major Caldwell. Captains Barnard and Biddle.

These operations all occurred on the west, southeast, and heights of Chapultepec. To the north, and at the base of the mound, inaccessible on that side, the 11th infantry, under Lieut. Col. Hebert, the 14th, under Col. Trousdale, and Capt. Magruder's field battery, 1st artillery —one section advanced under Lieut. Jackson all of Pillow's division—had, at the same time, some spirited affairs against superior numbers, driving the enemy from a battery in the road, and capturing a gun. Col. Trousdale, the commander, though twice wounded, continued on duty until the heights were carried.

Early in the morning of the 13th, Scott ordered Worth to support the movement of Pillow from our left. The latter soon called for that entire division, standing momentarily in reserve, and Worth sent him Col. Clark's brigade. The enemy in the road in front of Quitman's right, was receiving reinforcements from the city—less than a mile and a half to the east—and Worth, on our opposite flank, was ordered to return to Chapultepec with his *division*, and to proceed cautiously by the road at its northern base, in order, if not met by very superior numbers, to threaten or to attack, in rear, that body of the enemy.

Worth promptly advanced with his remaining brigade —Col. Garland's—Lieut. Col. C. F. Smith's light battalion, Lieut. Col. Duncan's squadrons of dragoons, under Major Sumner.

Having turned the forest on the west, and arriving opposite to the north centre of Chapultepec, Worth came up with the troops in the road, under Col. Trousdale, and aided by a flank movement of a part of Garland's brigade in taking the one-gun breastwork, then under the fire of Lieut. Jackson's section of Captain Magruder's field battery. Continuing to advance, this division passed Chapultepec, attacking the right of the enemy's line, resting on that road, about the moment of the general retreat consequent upon the capture of the formidable castle and its outworks.

There are two routes from Chapultepec to the capital— the one on the right entering the same gate, Belen, with the road from the south, *via* Piedad; and the other obliquing to intersect the great western, or San Cosme road, in a suburb outside of the gate of San Cosme.

Each of these routes (an elevated causeway) presents

a double roadway on the sides of an aqueduct of strong
masonry, and great height, resting on open arches and
massive pillars, which, together, afford fine points both
for attack and defence. The sideways of both aqueducts
are, moreover, defended by many strong breastworks at
the gates, and before reaching them.

Worth and Quitman were prompt in pursuing the retreating enemy—the former by the San Cosme aqueduct,
and the latter along that of Belen. Each had now advanced some hundred yards. The enemy fled in dismay.

Scott now despatched from Chapultepec—first Clarke's
brigade, and then Cadwallader's, to the support of Worth,
and gave orders that the necessary heavy guns should
follow. Pierce's brigade was, at the same time, sent to
Quitman, and, in the course of the afternoon, some additional siege pieces were added to his train. Scott
joined the advance of Worth, within the suburb, and
beyond the turn at the junction of the aqueduct with the
great highway from the west, to the gate of San Cosme.

At this junction of roads, we first passed one of those
formidable systems of city defences spoken of above, and
it had not a gun !

Within those disgarnished works our troops were engaged in a street fight against the enemy posted in gardens,
at windows, and on house-tops—all flat, with parapets.
Worth ordered forward the mountain howitzers of Cadwallader's brigade, preceded by skirmishers and pioneers,
with pickaxes and crowbars, to force windows and doors,
and burrow through walls. The assailants were soon in
an equality of position fatal to the enemy. By 8 o'clock
in the evening Worth had carried two batteries in this
suburb. He here posted guards and sentinels, and placed

his troops under shelter for the night. There was but one more obstacle—the San Cosme gate (custom house)—between him and the great square in front of the cathedral and palace—the heart of the city; and that barrier, it was known, could not, by daylight, resist our siege guns thirty minutes.

Scott had gone back to the foot of Chapultepec, the point from which the two aqueducts begin to diverge, some hours earlier, in order to be near that new depôt, and in easy communication with Quitman and Twiggs, as well as with Worth.

General Scott ordered all detachments and stragglers to their respective corps, then in advance; sent to Quitman additional siege guns, ammunition, entrenching tools; directed Twiggs' remaining brigade (Riley's) from Piedad, to support Worth, and Captain Steptoe's field battery, also at Piedad, to rejoin Quitman's division.

Quitman, supported by Shields and Smith—Shields badly wounded at Chapultepec and refusing to retire—as well as by all the officers and men of the column—continued to press forward under flank and direct fires; carried an intermediate battery of two guns, and then the Belen or South-Western gate, before two o'clock in the afternoon, but not without severe loss, increased by his steady maintenance of that position.

Here, of the heavy battery—Capt. Drum and Lieut. Benjamin were mortally wounded, and Lieut Porter, its third in rank, slightly. Lieuts. J. B. Moragne and Wm. Canty, of the South Carolina volunteers, also of high merit, fell on the same occasion—besides many of our bravest non-commissioned officers and men.

Quitman, within the city—adding several new defences

to the position he had won, and sheltering his corps as well as practicable—now awaited the return of daylight, under the guns of the formidable citadel yet to be subdued.

At about four o'clock next morning (Sept. 14), a deputation of the *ayuntamiento* (city council) waited on General Scott to report that the federal government and the army of Mexico had fled from the capital some three hours before, and to demand terms of capitulation in favor of the church, the citizens, and the municipal authorities. Scott promptly replied that he would sign no capitulation; that the city had been virtually in our possession from the time of the lodgments effected by Worth and Quitman the day before; that he regretted the silent escape of the Mexican army; that he should levy upon the city a moderate contribution, for special purposes; and that the American army should come under no terms, not *self*-imposed—such only as its own honor, the dignity of the United States, and the spirit of the age should, in his opinion, imperiously demand and impose.

At the termination of the interview with the city deputation, Worth and Quitman were ordered to advance slowly and cautiously (to guard against treachery) towards the heart of the city, and to occupy its stronger and more commanding points. Quitman proceeded to the great *plaza* or square, planted guards, and hoisted the colors of the United States on the national palace, containing the halls of Congress and executive apartments of federal Mexico.

Soon after we entered, and were in the act of occupying the city, a fire was opened upon us from the flat roofs of the houses, from windows and corners of streets, by some 2,000 convicts, liberated the night before by the flying government—joined by, perhaps, as many more soldiers, who had disbanded themselves and thrown off their uniforms. This unlawful war lasted for more than twenty-four hours, in spite of the exertions of the municipal authorities, and was not put down till we had lost many men, including several officers, killed or wounded, and had punished the miscreants.

BATTLE OF HUAMANTLA

After tne brilliant achievements of the American forces in and around the city of Mexico, there was little to do excepting to clear the great thoroughfares of the multitudes of guerillas that infested them. Some sharp engagements occurred between Mexico and Vera Cruz before these bodies of robbers could be dispersed. One of these battles took place at the town of *Huamantla*.

Gen. Lane having arrived at Perote, early in October, was there joined by Capt. Walker and his command; both advanced together on the Puebla road till they reached the town of Dreyes, at which place Capt. Walker, by order of the commanding General, took up his line of march to Huamantla, by way of the town of San Francisco and Guapastla. On his arrival at Huamantla, a sanguinary engagement took place in the streets, between the force of Capt. Walker, consisting of 250 men, and that of the Mexicans numbering 1,600.

The result of this contest was the total expulsion of the enemy from the town, and its occupation by our valiant little army, which lost in the battle only six men. But the gallant Walker, after performing prodigies of valor, and feats of the most daring character, fell in single combat, pierced by the spear of an enraged father who was goaded to actual frenzy by the death of his son, whose fall by the arm of Captain Walker he had just witnessed. The father rushed forward, heedless of all danger, to revenge his child's death, and attacking the Captain with almost irresistible violence, plunged his spear into his body and slew him almost instantly. In this engagement the Mexicans lost 200 men and three pieces of artillery. The latter were thrown into a gully adjoining the town, by the victors. At the battle of Huamantla an interesting struggle occurred between the Indiana Volunteers and a detachment of the 1st Pennsylvania Regiment, as to who should first reach town and plant the AMERICAN FLAG on the walls. Lieutenant Beany and Private Stebbes, of Pennsylvania, were successful.

After the achievement of their object, which was the dispersion of the enemy, for which they were despatched to Huamantla, the Americans evacuated the place and directed their course to Pinal, on the Puebla road, which they reached without any opposition. There meeting with Gen. Lane, the combined American force continued its march upon Puebla.

They found this city in a state of insurrection, and accordingly entered it in platoons—delivering at every step a constant and well-directed fire of musketry, which ceased not till the enemy retired, and order had been restored in every quarter.

Gen. Rea, of whom we heard so much, lately, fled with 400 guerillas towards Atlixco.

General Santa Anna was at Tehuacan de las Grenadas, having been deserted by all his followers, with the exception of 200.

BATTLE OF ATLIXCO.

Gen. Lane, with a considerable detachment, after a forced

march from Perote ten leagues distant, reached the vicinity of Atlixco on the evening of October 19th; and after
fighting his way through the forces of Gen, Rea, to a summit overlooking the town, he there posted his artillery, and
for three quarters of an hour threw shot and shells into the
"most thickly populated parts," the bright light of the moon
enabling the practised gunners to fire with terrific effect.
The crash of the walls and roofs of the houses, when struck
by our shot and shells, was mingled with the roar of artillery.   Two hundred and nineteen Mexicans were killed,
and three hundred wounded, while our own loss was only
one killed and one wounded.   It was thought necessary to
strike these people with terror, because their city had been
the refuge and headquarters of guerillas, whence many an
expedition had issued against our troops.

EXPEDITION TO TEHUACAN,

NARROW ESCAPE OF SANTA ANNA.

The detachment, consisting of, 350 men and officers, un-
derthe c ommand of Gen. Lane, left Mexico on the 18th of
January.   Maj. Polk, Col. Hays and Capt. Crittenden, accompanied it.   Passing Chalco and Rio Frio, the band,
took a circuitous route to Puebla, where it arrived on the
21st.
    Leaving Puebla at dark the same day, the company took
the road to Vera Cruz as far as Amazoque, where General
Lane took a road entirely unknown to any one but himself
and the guide. It was little better than a mule path over rocky
hills, and after a forty mile march, the troops arrived next
morning at the hacienda of Santa Clara.   They were then
informed that their object was to take Santa Anna, who
was then at Tehuacan, distant forty miles, with 150 men.
In order that the Mexican chieftain might not obtain information of the presence of our troops in this section of the
country, the General ordered every Mexican in the *hacienda*,

and every one found on the road during the day, to be arrested and kept close until they left in the evening.

After leaving the hacienda at dark, they came upon a party of mounted Mexicans, with a carriage whose occupant bore a passport from General Smith to travel to Orizaba. He was permitted to pass, with his attendants.

At dawn our army were within half a mile of Tehuacan. The report of a solitary gun of the enemy, gave hope that the bird was about to be caged. Our dragoons and riflemen dashed to the right and left, closing every outlet; while the rangers, with cocked revolvers, galoped toward the Plaza to secure their prey: but their amazement and mortification may be imagined, when they learned that, two hours before, the object of their search had fled to Oajaca, with seventy-five men. With chagrin, they also learned, that the Mexican, whose coach was stopped the evening before, had despatched a messenger across the mountain, to inform Santa Anna, that the American troops were on the road, with the probable intention of making him prisoner. Had it not been for this treachery, the surprise would have been complete.

OCCUPATION OF ORIZABA.

Leaving Tehuacan, on the 23d, the troops, after a rough march of several miles, came down, Feb. 26, 1848, into the valley of Orizaba. On arriving at the gates of the city, the authorities delivered up the keys; and on entering, they discovered a white flag, at the window of every house, and found the entire population assembled to witness their entry, with apparent satisfaction.

The inhabitants of the neighboring city of Cordova, sent a deputation requesting its occupation by the American Army.

Nothing of importance occurred afterwards, until Feb. 2d, 1848, when the Treaty of Peace was signed by the American and Mexican governmens.

NAMES OF THE KILLED, WOUNDED, AND MISSING,

On the part of the American Army, in the storming of Monterey, on the 21st, and subsequent engagements on the 22d and 23d of September, 1846.

GEN. TWIGGS' DIVISION

KILLED.

Lt Col Wm H Watson
Capt L N Morris
Capt G P Field
Bvt Major P N Barbour
1st Lt and Adj C Hoskins
1st Lieut J C Terrett
1st Lt and Adj D S Irwin
2d Lt R'Haslett
Bvt 1st Lieut J S Woods
Bvt 2d Lieut R Dilworth
1st Sergt George Waitman
John Eagle
Lovel Gregory
Henry Snower
Sergt T J Rabb
W Patrick
J Newman
C Torskay
J Young

Sergt Wm Brown
Wm Mickle
J Harper
C K Brown
J Stubert
Edgar Lavalette
Edward Rielly
Corpl Benjamin Bradt
Thomas Salsbury
Henry Conline
Edward Carey
Allen J Vanceal
Michael McGouth
John Weeks
James S Doble
Peter Andrews
Peter Judge
James C Pennington
Martin Enwul

Thomas W Gibson
Thomas Perkins
Lawson Stuart
Joseph Wolf
George Beck
Richard Bunchan
H K Brown
J Carroll
Marcus French
John Savage
Micah Hatch
William Raymond
Corpl Francis Sheridan
1st Sergt John Truscott
Sergt G A Herring
Alexander Ramsey
Joseph Worry
Patrick O'Brien

WOUNDED

Maj W W Lear
Capt H Bainbridge
Bvt Maj J J Abercrombie
Bvt Maj J F H Mansfield
Capt W G Williams
Capt J H Lemott
1st Lieut R H Graham
Sergt Philip Swartout
John Edwards
William P Holschea
John Lee
Michael McCarthy
Theodore Fricken
Bendt Nelson
Bartholomew Stokes
Corpl George Wolf
S D Coal
Thomas Henson
William Gilmore
John McCarthy
M Rielly
Corpl W R Goed
Austin Clark
P E Holcomb
Thomas Wajan, musician
Sergt G Brownley
Emit Hadduck
D Maloney
J Hogan
P White
C Iohle
N Farley
C Leslie

D Preslie
J D Ritters
W H McDonne
Ischa B Tucker
M Tyler
Joseph Morris
W Mullen
W Rooke
J Treel
D Boyle
T Clair
Wm H Bowden
J Mansfield
C Adams
Edward Astin
James Calhonn
J Kerns
M Regan
L Sours
David Pottsdaner
G E Radwell
Thomas O'Bryen
Sergt George W Anderson
   "   Robert Sanders
   "   Thomas Mannigan
   "   James Ryan
Corpl Thomas Hyam
   "   James Wyley
   "   Daniel McDonnell
   "   William Albison
   "   Matthew McCormick
William Taylor
E Henderson

William Holborn
William Petty
William Johnson
John Hill
E Barnum
Robert Halden
William A Jones
James Myers
Aaron Wriggle
Andrew Smith
William C Jones
John Maguire
John McDuffy
1st Sergt John Banks
   "   Patrick Myles
   "   E Bessie
   "   T H Haller
   "   John Tigart
   "   E Garver
Corpl Denton Connor
   "   Robert Aikens
   "   Augustus Lapple
C Smith, musician
William McCarty
Patrick Neele
John Saunders
William Norlin
Robert E Wooley
Jrmes Crawley
H Duchart
Francis Faulkner
A Ryan
John Wilson

Jacob Smidt
Charles Ratcliffe
James Delany
H Schrieder
John Gallagher
Levi Smith
Peter M Cabe
1st Sergt W P Foulson

Robert Caples
James Piles
Albert Hart
William Lee
Jacob Hemming
George Aunuld
Charles Peck
Andrew J Norris

George Allen
James Henry
Harry Elting
William Kelly
H Gifford
Melvin J Stone
E W Stevenson
William P Alexander

MISSING

R Gromley

Geo O'Brien

GEN. BUTLER'S DIVISION.—OHIO REGIMENT.

KILLED.

1st Lieut Matthew Hett
1st Sergt W G Davis
D F Smith
O B Coxe
Elijah Reese

Thomas McMurray
Corpl W H Harris
Richard Weish
James McCockey
George Phale

William Weber
John Havolett
T D Egan
Stephen Freeman
Oscar Behnee

WOUNDED.

Major Gen W O Butler
Col A M Mitchell
Lt and Adj A W Armstrong
1st Lieut Lewis Morter
"   N H Niles
2d Lieut H McCarty
Capt James George
Samuel Myers
Josiah A Kellam
Edward Wade
1st Sergt Wm Maloney
John Farrell
John Clarken
William Work

Thomas Vande Venter
John Flannigan
Jeremiah Ryan
Michael Gilligan
Tobias Went
Charles Segar
Griffin Lowerd
Alfred Dunaghue
Joseph Lombeck
Silas Burrill
Sergt William Miller
Corpl G W Fitzhugh
Robert Doney

Adam F Shane
John Fletcher
A B McKee
Corpl George Myer
E J Spoole
Henry Weber
Henry Myer
Sergt George Webster
"   George Longfellow
Corpl John F Longley
John Pearson
R H Alcott
Henry Humphries

TENNESSEE REGIMENT.

KILLED.

Capt W B Allen
2d Lieut S M Putnam
John B Porter
William H Robinson
Sergt John A Hill
B F Coffee
E W Thomas
Booker H Dolton
Isaac Gurman Elliot

Peter H Martin
Edward Pryor
Benjamin Soaper
Henry Collins
James H Allison
James H Johnston
James B Turner
R D Willis
Joseph B Burkitt

James M L Campbell
A J Eaton
A J Gibson
Finlay Glover
A J Pratt
William Rhodes
John W Sanders
G W Wilson

WOUNDED

Maj R B Alexander
1st Lt J L Sbudder
"   G H Nixon
2d Lt J C Allen
Corpl F F Winston
JL Bryant

Alexander Bigam
D C Fleming
Mackey Roney
Samuel Davis
James Thompson
David Collins

A S Duval
T B Powell
William B Davis
Joseph Law
James York
William Young

Richard Gifford
A V Stanfield
Asa Lamb
Corpl. J J Argo
James Todd
Thomas Vickens
W D Cabler
1st Sergt. James M Vance
Sergt. George W Gilbert
Charles M Talley
Michael Crantze
R C Locke
J F Raphile
Thomas Kelly
Albert Tomlinson
Corpl. Julius C Elliott
R A Cole
James H Jenkins
A G Stewart
Sergt. Gulinger Holt
Corpl. James Patterson

Charles Arnold
J J Blackwell
Joseph Crutchfield
J Freeman
J D Gilmer
P O Hale
Daniel C King
C B Maguire
S S Reaves
A W Reaves
Augustin Stevens
Thomas N Smith
C B Ward
1st Sergt. Charles Davis
Corpl. Robert W Green
Eli Brown
W F Bowen
Peter Engles
Robert Flannigan
William Lowery

S N Macey
E G Zachary
Corpl. W M Alfred
     "   John H Kay
A S Alexander
M C Abinathy
Jesse Brashars
J M Bailey
Campbell G Boyd
B L Commons
J W Curtis
H H Dadson
John Gavin
Aaron Parks
F Richardson
A O Richardson
Thomas C Ramsay
John Vining
M D Watson
Thomas Thompson

MISSING.

Felix Wordzinoki

R R Morehead

MISSISSIPPI REGIMENT.

KILLED

L M Troeur
Silas Mitcham
Samuel Potts

Joseph H Tenelle
Corpl. William H Grisam
Joseph Heaton

Joseph Downing
Daniel D Dubois
John M Tyree

WOUNDED.

Lieut. Col. Alexander R Mc-
    Clung
Capt. R N Downing
1st Lieut. Henry T Cook
2d Lieut. Rufus K Arthur
    "   L T Howard
Henry H Miller
J H Jackson
A Lainhart
J L Anderson
G H Jones
Corpl. John D Markham
H B Thompson
Sergt. E W Hollingsworth
Dr. G W Ramsay
Alphius Cobb
George Wills
W Huffman

O W Jones
William Orr
D Love
Sergt. Joseph H Langford
A P Barnham
H W Pierce
William Shadt
W H Fleming
Jacob Frederick
John Coleman
William P Spencer
M M Smith
James Kilvey
J Williamson
A W Taig
Warren White
Robert Bowen
Frederick Mathews

Benjamin F Roberts
Avery Noland
Sergt Francis A Wolf
C F Cotton
George Williams
Nathaniel Massie
Sergt. William H Bell
E B Lewis
D B Lewis
Charles Martin
James L Thompson
John Stewart
John McNorris
R W Chance
P W Johnson
Robert Grigg
Platt Snedicor

KENTUCKY REGIMENT.

WOUNDED.

Valentine Deutche
Lewis Young

Joseph Bartlett
Philip Smith

Thomas Alexder

GEN. WORTH'S DIVISION.

KILLED.

Capt. H McKavet
W Rihl
Charles Hamm

J F Wagner
Irwing
Miller

P Fickicson
S G Alleng
John Francis

WOUNDED

1st Lieut. N L Rossel.
Sergt. Maj. Brand
McManus
Grubb
Schriveigman
Bell
Ingalls
Grelan
McGuirk
Hendricks
Capt. Capt. R C Gatlin
2d Lieut. J H Potter
Sergt. R S Cross
Corpl. S P Oakley
M Fleming
C Gersbenberger

James Myers
A Renebeck
N White
Corpl. Morron
James Harvey
Louis Kirk
J W, Miller
W Burton
M Morton
Basse
Michael Noonan
Joseph Grey
Stephen Edwards
Theopolis Bowis
James Lynch

Mark Collins
Dennis Kelly
Amos Collins
John Reinecke
Isaac Dyer
Boyd
Artificer Ragan
Paul Bunzey
2d Lieut George Wainwright
Sergt Rock
    "   Willis
    "   Marshall
R Riley
Lance Tacey
James McKnight

COL. HAY'S REGIMENT.

KILLED.

Herman S Thomas
Daniel McCarty

J W D Austin
Capt R A Gillespie

Corpl John M Fullerton

WOUNDED.

Armstrong
Fielding Alston
John P Waters
C D De Witt
Oliver Jenkins
J F Minter

Thomas Law
John Rabb
Lieut William E Reese
Jesse Perkins
N P Browning
Sergt Roundtree

Corpl J B Walker
William Carley
Gilbert Brush
Sergt J B Barry
F F Keys

J Buchanan, H P Lyon, and C W Tufts were left behind on special duty, and are supposed to be killed.

COL. WOOD'S REGIMENT OF TEXAS RANGERS.

Operating in the eastern part of the city on the 23d

KILLED.

George Short | Thomas Gregory

WOUNDED.

Baker Barton
Charles G Davenport

Ira Grisby

Calvin Reese

RECAPITULATION.

Names of the commissioned officers killed ana wounded during the operations before Monterey, Mexico, from September 21 to September 23, 1846, inclusive.

KILLED.—*Sept.* 21.—J S Woods, bvt, 1st Lieut, 2d Infantry; L N Morris. Capt, 3d Infantry; George P Field. Capt, 3d Infantry; P N Barbour, Capt and bvt Major, 3d Infantry; D S Irwin, 1st Lieut and adj, 3d Infantry; R Hazlitt, 2d Lieut, 3d Infantry; C Hoskins, 1st Lieut and Adj. 4th Infantry; H McKavett, Capt, 8th Infantry; W E Watson, Lieut Col. Balt and Wash volunteers; M Hett, 1st Lieut, 1st Ohio regiment; W B Allen, Capt, 1st Tenn regiment; S N Putnam. 2d Lieut 1st Tenn regiment.

WOUNDED.—*Sept.* 21.—W G Williams, Capt, Top Engineers, mortally; J H F Mansfield. bvt Major, Engineers, severely; J L Abercrombie, bvt Major, 1st Infantry, slightly J H Lamotte, Capt, 1st Infantry severely; J C Terrett, 1st Lieut, 1st Infantry, mortally, R Dilworth, 2d Lieut, 1st Infantry, mortally; W W Lear, Major, 3d Infantry, dangerously; H Bainbridge, Capt, 3d infantry, slightly; R H Graham, 1st Lieut, 4th Infantry, dangerously; N B Rossell, 1st Lieut. 5th Infantry, slightly.

Sept. 22.—J H Potter, 2d Lieut, 7th Infantry, severely; George Wainwright, 2d Lieut, 8th Infantry, severely.

Sept. 23.—R C Gatlin, Capt, 7th Infantry, severely.

Sept 21.—W O Butler, Major Gen, volunteer service, severely; A M Mitchell, Col, 1st Ohio regiment, severely; A W Armstrong, Adj, 1st Ohio regiment, severely; James George, Capt, 1st Ohio regiment, slightly; Lewis Matter, 1st Lieut, 1st Ohio regiment, slightly; A McCarty, 2d Lieut, 1st Ohio regiment, slightly; N H Niles, 2d Lieut, 1st Ohio regiment, slightly; R B Alexander, Major, 1st Tenn regiment, severely; J L Scudder, 1st Lieut, 1st Ten regiment. severely; G H Nixon, 1st Lieut, 1st Tenn regiment, slightly; J C Allen, 2d Lieut, 1st Tenn regiment, severely: A K McClung, Lieut Col, Miss regiment, severely; R N Downing, Capt, Miss Regiment, slightly; H F Cook, 1st Lieut, Miss regiment, slightly; R H Arthur, 2d Lieut, Miss regiment. slightly.

Sept. 22.—R A Gillespie, Capt, 1st Texas regiment, mortally; W E Reese, 1st Lieut. 1st Texas regiment.

Sept. 23.—L S Howard, 2d Lieut, Miss regiment, severely.

The returns of the killed, wounded, and missing, show the following results

Commissioned officers.. 43
Non-commissioned officers, musicians, and privates........................ 447
Missing... 2
    Making a total of.. ———— 492

MUNITIONS CAPTURED AT MONTEREY.

PARK OF ARTILLERY.—DIVISION OF THE NORTH.

Invoice of Artillery, Arms, Ammunition, and other Munitions of War, given in virtue of the articles of capitulation, signed September 24, 1846.

Pieces of Artillery with Equipments and Sets of Arms.

2 4-pounders, culverine, mounted.
5 4-pounders
4 7-inch howitzers.
1 12-pounder, dismounted.
1 6-pounder, mounted.
1 8-pounder, mounted.
1 4-pounder, dismounted, conical.
1 3-pounder, dismounted,
1 iron howitzer, unserviceable
1 bronze howitzer, unserviceable
7 rampart guns. (bronzed.)

Arms for Infantry and Cavalry.

149 English muskets.
102 carbines
122 bayonets.

305 gun barrels, (loose)
100 carbine barrels, (loose.)
43 lances.

Munitions for Infantry and Artillery.

882 18-pound balls, (in pile.)
329 12-pound balls, do.
18 boxes blank 12-pound cartridges—12 in each.
19 boxes 8-pound canister shot, do.
49 rounds 8-pound canister shot, (loose.)
3 boxes 7-pound blank cartriges.
17 boxes 6-pound ball cartridges—fixed; 15 and 18 in each box.
59 boxes 4-pound ball cartridges—fixed; 18 and 24 in each box
2 boxes 4-pound blank cartridges—100 in both together
123 rounds 3-pound ball cartridges.
1½ boxes 7-inch howitzer blank cartridges.
½ box 5½-inch do do
15 boxes 6-pound canister cartridges—10 and 12 each
14 boxes 4-pound do 12 and 16 each
40 8-pound balls.
17 boxes 12-pound canister cartridges
79 rounds do do
12 rounds 8-pound do
28 rounds do do (loose.,
15 boxes 7-inch howitzer canister cartridges.
70 rounds 7-inch do (loose.)
253 pound cartridges.
27 boxes loaded grenades, 7-inch howitzer—3 in each box.
20 boxes loaded grenades, 5¾-inch howitzer—4 in each.
350 loose grenades, (part loaded.)
248 boxes musket-ball cartridges—1200 in each.
13 boxes do do (double ball) 1200 in each.
93 boxes cannon powder, (good) 12,450 lbs. net.
35 boxes do (damaged)—5,250 lbs. net— not examined, probably good
8 boxes musket powder, (damaged)—1200 lbs. net.
2 boxes rifle powder, (fine)—300 lbs net.
680 pounds slow match.
70 quintals lead, in balls. [The reader can calculate this.]
101 quintals lead, in bars.
10 dozen signal rockets.
[Here follows a long list of tools, &c.]

PARK OF ARTILLERY.—POST OF THE CITADEL.

Statement of Ordnance and Ordnance Stores which are at this Post on the 24th of September, 1846

60,000 musket cartridges, with ball.
594 12-pound blank cartridges.
334 8-pound do
723 8-pound cartridges, with ball.
394 6-pound do
201 7-inch howitzer blank cartridges
71 6-pound cartridges, with grape.
171 12-pound canister shot.
390 8-pound do
50 6-pound do
102 7-inch howitzer canister shot.
112 7-inch do loaded shells.
218 12-pound balls, (loose.)
710 12-pound priming tubes, (paper.)
1,200 8-pound do do
160 6-pound do do
300 4-pound do do
15 port-fires. 6 arobas slow-match, (150 lbs.)
4 8-pounders. 2 6-pounders. 2 7-inch howitzers

LIST OF KILLED AND WOUNDED.

FIRST DIVISION.—MAJ. GEN. WORTH.

Names of the Killed, Wounded, and Missing, in the action of Molino del Rey, September 8, 1847.

KILLED.

Hugh Donahue
Jacobus
Ullembrook
Brown
Lane
Taasen
Lansing
John Gracie
Samuel Grove
Timothy Sullivan
A L Grenier
John Connor
Wm Hanson
Jacob Frank
David Campbell
Jacob Dyas
1st Lieut Wm Armstrong
Sergt A B Howe
Wm J Barnhard
John C Elloes
Herman Levy
Bvt Capt G W Ayres
J F Farry
John Walsh
Simon Margarum
Benj M Harris
Sergt B Henry
Corpl John Cameron
Stillman Coburn
Patrick Ronnan
John McLoskey
Frederick Workman
2d Lieut W S Burwell
Bvt Lieut Col Martin Scott
Capt M E Merrill
2d Lieut E B Strong
Sergt John Gottenger
Sergt Augustus Quitman

Sergt Stanislaus Minot
Corpl Saml Carr
Timothy Howby
Thos Wiedman
Frederick Hobber
Hy Mamark
Francis McKay
Thos S Pole
John P Ronner
Charles Steward
Samuel Calhoun
Robt Crawford
Griffith Owens
David Sharp
Thomas Gooding
Peter Pentz
Owen Marry
John B Honer
John Koarstsupfads
Peter G Moore
Wm McCloskey
Sergt James McGlynn
Bernard Althor
Martin Munneman
Michael Sheehan
Matthew Murphy
Victor Durand
John H Bond
Nicholas Ramsey
Wm Agol
Wm Fahee
John H Plant
Christian Schuman
Wm Looey
Michael Murphy
John Brodrick
Peter Koite
Isham Canalizo

Sergt Edw Bertram
Sergt Nicholas Ford
Corpl James Crogan
" John Hughes
" Wm Sandys
" John Clark
Sergt Reuben Brown
Patrick McGrash, mus
Thos Lanson
Geo McGraff
Gabriel Wilson
Patrick Green
Alex Prentice
Peter Caffery
Bernard McFarlin
Jacob Neish
Charles Schwarykoryt
Wm Irvin
John A Jackson
Geo M Lightfell
Barthol Mahon
Henry Fassor
Lewis Hemne
Thomas Flea
Saml Clark
Robt Simson
Sidney W Gunroyer
Corpl Henry W Erwin
Lt Col Wm M Graham
1st Lt R H L Johnson
Sergt Geo Johnson
Corpl Chas Fenner
Corpl John McMahon
John Segler
John Buchanan
John Manning
James Simpson
Daniel Kippy

WOUNDED

Capt. J L Mason, Eng'rs.
2d Lieut. J B Foster
John Dougherty
Capt. C Kerr
2d Lieut. Smith
" Tree
" Walker
Sergt. McGuire
Corpl. Slade
Sergt. Young
Corpl. Buxton
" Buckley
Sergt's. Murphy
" Brooks
Usher
Boling
Klaws

Zink
Sweeney
Russell
Kerr
Walters
Thomas Murphy
Porthouse
Zalikiwick
White
Fielding
Freeman
Kohle
Mundel
Westerdelof
Drawn
Wyatt
Gardener

Flitshe
Hamilton
Paul
Cottrell
Carter
Harris
Sergt. Jacob Price
Richards
Boone
J M Quick
1st Lieut. H. J Hunt
" W Hayes
2d Lieut. H F. Clark
Corpl. Hugh McCoy
Richard Gilmore
James Whitter
George Wagner

Abram Hart
2d Lieut. and Aid-de-camp H Thorn
1st Lieut. M L Shackleford
" C B Daniels
Sergt. George Gordon
" James McCormick
Corpl. Henry Belleman, dead
" Hugh McDonald
Mus. Thomas Clark
William Shoppe, dead
Christie Bower dead
James Rochford
Charles Hoover
Hy Derlin
Martin Sharbuck
William Moore
Patrick Kean
John Conway
John Garrey
John Hill
Frederick Blunt
Thomas Furian
Francis Webb
William Crook
Samuel S Dickman
Arch'd. McFayden, dead
Robert Alexander
James Montgomery
Thomas O'Brien
Thomas Starr
Robert Michan
John Wiley
J D Reynolds, dead
William Sharp
Edward Ellsworth
James Bonahan
James Heany
John McNeil
John R Smith
William Cook
Capt. R Anderson
Oswold Drury
William Ehrenbaum
James Keenan
Christian Smallbark
David Coleman
John P Smith
Henry Stenoham
John Clancey
John Montgomery
Martin Rush
William Allen
John Gallagher
Lewis Merans
Joseph L Moody
Philip Hady, dead
Richard Abercrombie
Samuel Collier
Robert Kuntz
Michael Bonet
Edward McKeon
Peter W Syms
William C Goddard
Daniel F McKee
Meredith Qualls

Levi Leitz
John Coyle
John Hill
Justin O'Brien
William Lawrence
Maron Meyers
E McCready
Gilbert Goodrich, dead
Lile Barton
Alexander Miller
John T DeHart
Jules Gasse, dead
John Housmen
Lawrence Kenny
Adam Beecker
Theo Cranz
William Wiernest
John S Beach
William A Place, dead
Abner Dixon
John Clark
William Wheeler
Henry Wilkie
Moses Papiner
Thomas McDermott
Edward Annison
John Cogli
Josiah Ettinger
William Cain
Bernard Riley
James Shepherd
Patrick McAlroy
William O Mocht
Thomas Hogg
Josiah Cartwright, dead
Edward H Brown
John Eisdar
Patrick McCue
Patrick Scanlan
Peter Yorrick
Leonard Johnson
Charles Butterling
James Burns
Charles Evans
John Hunter
John Wrick
John Helm
Matthew Switzer
William H Morris
William Shaffer
Michael Coll
J M Montgomery
Charles Sanders
Edward B Conner
Peter Bragine
George McElrie
Joseph W Brush
Joseph Wolf
Thomas Foster, dead
John Harvey, dead
William Chapman
William Curtis
John Gorlan
John McCameron
Cornelius O'Neill
Samuel Tucker

Chester R Tully
Thomas H Wood
Jacob Watson
Benjamin Slater
Thomas Gloveen
Augustus De Lonza
Owen Melvin
Capt. A Cady
" W H T Walker
2d Lieut. R F Ernst
Sergt. P F Jackson
" George Williams
" John McIntyre
" James E Dresser
" John Cummings
" John Webb, dead
Corpl. John Ferguson
" Sylvester Jones
" Chas. Rafferty, dead
William Sheppard
L B Hanley
Abraham Fitzpatrick
P R Maloed
J A Burlyman
Solomon Viedenburg
Melon Miller
Lyman H Royce
Joseph Schwager
Henry Stevens
Henry Jordon, dead
E Hamar
Anthony Brooks
Robert Hawkins
James Wilson
L Kinney
John Graves
James Edmonds
Charles Evanson
William Angel
W T Bishop
George Coffee
Charles Hess
Michael McEwen
Michael Picket
William Smith
Thomas A Wilson
Lawrence Fagan
William Gibbard
James Hannigan
James B Hill
James B Kelly, dead
Charles Brown
William Smith
Lawrence Dunivan
John Forgy
Samuel Stanley
David Wheeler
John Murphy
Richard Harper
Joshua H Corwin
James Devine
Christopher Yeager
Capa E K Smith, since dead
2d Lieut. F S Dent
Sergt. Joseph Updigraff
" Thomas Johnson

Corpl. Samuel Meeker
   "   Gilbert G Francher
   "   Jacob Nichols
Edward Green
Darius Ballard
Thomas Low
Patrick Reily
James Alexander, mus.
George Barr
William Cordes
Herman Knickerbocker
Anthony Rounder
Thomas Sullivan
Andrew Casey
Alphonso Schaffer, dead
Daniel Rodgers
Charles Linder
James H Brooke
George Kraffenbaner
Augus Beaver
William Bell
Joseph McGarlin
Patrick O'Rourke
Thomas L Sleck
George W E Sherman
Edward Kinneford
Elijah J Cain
Levi Miles
John Kanavagh
Timothy Collins
Ezra Higgins
Michael Leonard
Thomas Pardon
Thomas Joyce
Nicholas Seminoff
William Wright
John Fleming
2d Lieut. G P Andrews
Sergt. Anton Achenback, dead
Corpl. John Matthews, dead
   "   John Hynes
James Walsh
George Wilcox
William F Taylor
Philip Rouse
Julius Martial
John Coogan, dead
Thomas Juit
Charles Beistrenger
Thomas Brady
William Bloom
Samuel Brown
John Conner
Peter Derit
Robert McGee
Dedrick Deer
William Parker, dead
Watchman, dead
Joseph Finch
John Tornis
Marshall Kimball, dead
Philip Bacher
William W Walker
Michael Ley
John Sullivan
Assist. Surgeon J Seniors

Adj. H Prince
2d Lieut. A B Lincoln
1st Lieut. S Smith
Sergt. George W Anderson
   "   William Quinn
Joseph Holybee, dead
John B Weeder
Charles Metz
Corpl. William Castigan
Ephraim Cain
James Carroll
Michael McGuire
James Steel, dead
John P Wirrick
Charles Skolinski
Edward Kirevin
Philip Felby, dead
Martin Loughest
Bvt. Col. J S McIntosh, dead
Asst. Surgt. William Roberts
2d Lieut C S Hamilton
Sergt. Alfred Landrage
   "   Elisha Buel
   "   Henry Farmer
   "   James O'Brien
   "   Alex McClellan
   "   David Thompson
   "   James Eversteine, dead
Corpl. William Godfrey
   "   H J Haskell
   "   Francis Smith
   "   John Doyle
   "   George Eimerick
   "   George Molely
   "   Nich Reid
   "   John Clarit
William Babb, mus.
Corpl. Dediah Meir
Morris Sayers, dead
William Witherspoon
William Goodwin
Hugh Frazer
Jeremiah Delong
S. Tiffans
J Weight
George Kingsman, dead
Isaac Baker, dead
Isaac Christman
John Lyons
Adam Eichstein
John Irwing
James Lollen
Corpl. Michael Eannes
Francis Kline, dead
Samuel Morgan
Bennet Keere.
John Finnerghty
Jacob Kennard
Richard Wilkinson
James Bradley
J B Johnson
William Spears
Calvin Wells
Henry Cropp
John Martin

John King
D Loundensborough
Michael McAuley, dead
E W Dexter
Loreny Flood
John McGuire
James Victory
William P Moore
Jefferson Wells
Abraham Riber
Henry Bertoled
George Smith
Joseph Roland, dead
David Brudy
Daniel Emerson
Daniel Boughanan
Richard Cherry
Brian Curry
Thomas Down
William C Howe
Deobald Snyder
Alfred Carlisle
John A Reading
Jeremiah Ryan
Ebenezer Gill
Gregory Kepler
S P Aretz
John Meon
Matthew Kols
William Jones, dead
Major C A Waite
Brevet-Maj. A Montgomery
Captain L Smith
1st Lieut. J Burbank, dead
   "   J Beardsley
   "   C Morris, dead
   "   J D Clark
2d Lieut. G Wainwright
Lieut. J G S Snelling
Sergt. John Fink
   "   Thomas Moir
   "   David Pink
   "   Thomas Sewell
   "   John Robinson
   "   James H Kearney
   "   John Smith
   "   Frederick Backhans
   "   George Simmons
Corpl. A T Osbourne
   "   A C Edson
   "   William Fairchilds
   "   David Lawyer
   "   Joseph Scanson
   "   Caleb Smith
David Springham, dead
William McDonald
DeWitt McDaniel
John McCarthy
Bernard Malone
James Mooney
John Paul
John M Rentor
Henry Rumears, dead
Oscar F Sweet
S Poler. dead
P McMillan

John H McGuire	J Silverhorn	J Brown
John Bermingham, dead	J Malony	D Wymp
S T Templeman	W Allison	A Wamsall
John Weith	D Deraughn	J Porter
S A Weller	J Rowenski	G W Seaton
W Wilson, dead	J Spencer	R Simpson
John T Blair	T C Parish	J Thompson
William Sourley	J Doney	J Metcalf
James Raby, dead	J J Nickerson	A Adamson
Charles Daniels	M Benton	T Davis
Mark Chapple	G W Burgeant	J Howell
Michael Conrey	John Sloan	J Pugh
William C Morris	J L Hisse	J Bunger
H Horinar	T Evans	A Funlay
William Thomas	H Kidwell	T Firish
James A Terril	A W Millbright	T Pugh
Henry Bohan, dead	J McCaslin	H White
Major George W Tatres	J Cromley	W Baldhurst
2d Lieut. G L Kitsing	D Davis	Major John H Savage
" R Swate	J V Franklin	Capt. Thomas Glenn
" William J Martin	S Field	Lieut. Hays
Patrick Castin	T Higginson	Thomas Shields
David Doace	A Idler	Samuel B Davis
Chester C Kennedy	G Kriner	Corpl. L Warren
Peter King	H Keenan	" Munroe Fliming
Patrick McCarty	R Lemon	Thomas Pierson
Henry L Snellers	W S Wendenhall	James M Cox
Nat Ross	J Massey	Robert Brenton
Joseph Arnold	P Morrell	Fielding Young
Patrick Keany	B McCape	Jackson W Lowry
Benjamin Burritt	J V Perry	A Sawyer
James Gamble	J Picken	Kaylams Lynch
Oliver W H Kellogg	J Pierce	William Farrell
Patrick Green, dead	B J Ross	Louis H, Mallerhy
Augustus Bliss, dead	W Jackson	David Hall
H Buckland	O Morton	James Gillespie
William Collan	G Spencer	Hardy Johnson
John Chari	J Kock	James R Attstin
John K Knock	C Eckhart	Thomas H Hayter
Theobald Shinard	G Backenschitz	Henry Dannigan
Jacob Missil, dead	F Kerse	Capt William H Irwin
Luther Schouts	J Rutter	" P M Guthrie
S W Pumroyer, dead	T Grooves	Adj. D S Lee
William Shad	J Sigmac	Sergt. John P Weldon
William Looney	J F Dentlenger	" Freeze
Michael Walsh, dead	J A Yates	" Lenox Lea
John Young	G W Jones	" J G Handy
Th Brennan	W H Fitzhue	Corpl. Charles Barturksy
Thomas Burke	2d Lieut. Wash Terrill	" Michael Freeney
John Cosgrove	Sergt. W B Vertrees	" Robert Raasch
Ph Cook	" C D Weymouth	Isaac Mahon
H Euhank	" F W Jennings	Uriah Kitchen
John Gordon	" J C Malbon	John Hayes
Nicholas Hoyt	" W J Herbert	James Rager
J L Knott	" R Harding	McCluny Radcliff
S A Evans	" C R Edwards	Robert D Brown
M Conway	" S Elliott	Foster R Carson
V Collins	" J G Gardiner	James Dilks
Holandorf	Corpl. W S McCorrett	William S Sashall
T Clark	" E D Denson	James Hight
R Sylvester	" B Ogle	Schmidt
H Wells	" J H Walker	William R Call
H Kilgrove	Sergt R H Turner	Jesse Flowers
W A Ward	D Grayheer	William Dolman
J Bean	A R Shasklett	Isaac Pierce
M G Good	J Hall	James Nesbitt

Herman Bickerstine | Simon Pickett | Oscar Wood
Fred Babe | John Romering | John Wilson, dead
Benjamin Dickie | Albert McGill | Christian Papst

MISSING

Privates Robert McKee, Joseph Scott, since discovered to have been blown up at Casa del Mata ; Francis Beed, Artificer Israel Barton, killed; Private John Jacob Divine ; Sergt. John Coble; Privates John Gillespie, Thomas Hardy, William Reynolds, James Smith, Conrad Young, Henry Muller. Jackson Adams, James Leary, H A Wood, S Vandergriff, J L Hass David Ayrs, Joseph G Smith.

Names of the killed, wounded, and missing, of the First Division, in tne actions of the 13th and 14th September.

KILLED.

Richard Gilmore | Corpl. James Hagan | 2d Lieut. J P Smith
Sergt. John Scar | Conrad Graf | V E Reed
Joseph Cook. mus. | Isaac I Jonson | James McLoy
Charles Carroll | Alexander McCoy | Patrick Hines
John Kennedy | Karl Sigmond | William Mooney
William O'Neil | Michael Kelley | David Trush
Lieut. A J Rogers | William Billington | Andrew Leet
Sergt. William Donegan | Joel Barrom | Henry Jones
" George Blast | |

WOUNDED.

A A Gen. W W Markall | Sergt. David Toobwiller | William O'Shaughnessy
A D C George W Kendall | Corpl. Theodore Gregg | John A Schuber
1st Lieut. J J Stevens | Daniel Bennett, dead | Wiliam Montgomery
Sergt. D Hastings | Joseph F Cooper | John Dillon
" P Maguire | Hamilton Sparks | James Harny
Davis | John Whitnell | Thomas Oats
Artificer Edmund Ring | William Grant | George Gill
Thomas Murphy | Patrick Toole | 1st Lieut. L A Armistead
Joseph Bateman | Lonesee | Sergt. Maj. Edw Thompson
William Smith | William Burton | George Ernst
John Wolfe | James Lawless | Alexander Maddox
Francis Desmond | Stephen Mann | William Dowley
Sergt. James McCormick | Adolphus Schuyer | Sergt. Francis Fox
Corpl. Henry Reigle | Jacob Shores | Bernard Lynch
Anthony Baker, mus. | J M Mallinder | Andrew Piper
John Sweeny | William Wilson | 2d Lieut. James Longhurst
Herman Von Steen | Mark Spaulding | 1st " Joseph Seldon
Carl Chapparean | V B West | Sergt. John A Noon
George Chiveton | George Henry | " J L Fisk
Frederick Brugh | William Lawrence | Corpl. Robert Shaw
Jeremiah Cavaugh | Duwilda Myers | " Thomas Smith
W Garlick | Thomas Collis | William Shaw
David Rikin | William Cross | John Hisner
Patrick Born | Joseph Peck | John Flummery
John Young | John C Christie | M Monaghyn
Michael Halloran | Mortonier Crofort | James C McIntyre
John Klinz | William Thompson | Stephen MConnell
Nathan Randall | Henry Byrnes | John McAulay
John Zear | James Fisher | William Palmoter
Godfrey Piermont | James Parker | John Kibler
Marcus Bain | Grapincamp | William Fox
John Haggerty | Aganus Dowis | Alexander Reinhart
Lieut. Col. John Garland | Capt D H McPhail | Nathaniel Clegg
1st Lieut. S Smith, dead | Sergt. Henry Farmer | Charles McClosky
2d Lieut. Maurice Maloney | Corpl. Darius Ballard | Hanson Palmer
Sergt. William Blaisdell | Joseph McGartin | William Verrel

MISSING.

Charles Quick
Valentine Imporf
James Farramier

Edward Blackman
Victor Whipple
James Leise

John Briolon
Charles Whitty

SECOND DIVISION—BRIG. GEN. TWIGGS.

List of the killed, wounded, and missing, of the Second D: vision, in the action at Chapultepec and the Garita de Belen, on the 13th, and in the city of Mexico on the 14th and 15th of September, 1847.

FIRST BRIGADE.

KILLED.

Corpl Dennis Byrne
" C C Arms
Thomas D Wheeler
George Town
William Donovan
Elijah O Pointer
James L Reed
Jesse James

Myron Bell
Hiram Dengh
William Hagan
William Finney
James Harrigan
Thomas McGlone
Sergt. John Bald
Corpl. James Huntley

William Fortition
John J O'Donnell
James Welsh
John Alexander
Walter Scott
Henry Boyle
Michael O'Loughlin
Florence McCarty

WOUNDED.

1st Lieut. Earl Van Dorn
Maj. W W Doring
Capt. J S Simonson
" J B Backenstos
" S S Tucker
2d Lieut. T S K Russell
Bvt. 2d Lieut. J A Palmer
Capt. George Nauman
1st Lieut. and Adj. J M Brannan
" Lieut. J H Haskin
Sergt. Maj. Alonzo Stanton
" Samuel Harp
" Z M P Hand
1st Sergt. James Manly
Sergt. William P Sanders
" Hiram Dwyer
" D M Frame
Corpl. William M Winter
" L L Worcester
" George Taylor
" J M L Addison
" Rufus Peck
" Jeremiah O'Connell
" J Freeman
" J Millard
Lance Corpl. Thomas Davis
" William P Cook
James Farrell
Edward Allen
Christopher Lidden
Frederick Pilgrim
J M Cannon
A Stickler
George W Raymond
Stans Moroski
Joseph Newhouse

John Barber
John Richardson
Joseph Hoban
W F Herrington
J C Morrison
George B Moshers
J W Robinson
Joseph Watson
Levi Grunsby
Benj Tabler
John Dillon
John G Myers
Lindsey Hooker
Daniel Williams
Lewis Copsey
Thomas B Brasheno
John Fickle
Lawrence J Filsome
Bartholomew W Wilson
Joshua P Santmyne
Clinton Frazer
William W Wilson
William Spear
M Hamilton
M Batsner
Francis Whitebread
J Hak
J Murray
S Young
J C Roberts
J C Christman
Joseph Patterson
C A B Phelps
Robert Williams
Josh Garrison
Josh Debeuque
Allen Overly

Daniel Wills
1st Sergt. Thomas Williams
Corpl. Henry D Sitner
" William Ferry
" Daniel B Baker
Art. John Weins
Richard J Shephard
Thomas S Perkins
Amos Kingsley
Bradly Laud
John McFarne
John Thompson
Robert Kugan
Henry Wutts
Harvey Gamperd
John Miller
Lewis Russell
Francis Fletcher
Frederick Wissail
Sergt. Stewart Dougherty
" Dixon Ashworth
" Orlando B Miles
Corpl. Nel Chamberlain
" John Storm
" William Adams
James McNulty
Henry Varner
Moses Gleason
Banva Upton
Edgar Watson
Francis J Slathan
Francis Oestrich
Henry Haldman
John O'Brien
Harry Aberlee
Amos Bardhart
William Campbell

John Childers
Cornelius Crowley
John Hamilton
William Myers
Philip Ryan
Timothy Sullivan
William Kenny
Charles F E Hyer
Edward Zimmerman

Edward Quin
Isaac Tracy

Patrick Morron
Henry McCampbill
Thomas Brisbard
Leonard Elias
David Jermon
Eli Gable
Charles McKinne
Jacob Varnes
Jos Butterfield

MISSING

John Witty
John Venator

George Frank
Thom McFarland
Tarr s
Charles J Truman
Frederick A Collins
Elliott Ellmer
Daniel Smith
Daniel Wise

John Montgomery
Theodore Woodbury

SECOND BRIGADE.

KILLED

1st. Lient. Levi Cautt
Sergt. William A Morrison
Corpl. James Tierney
Michael Elwood, mus.

John M Nash
Patrick Sheridan
Lewis Rinhart
William Steinson

Joseph N Garnett
Keyran Temple
Richard Shore
Neill Donnelly

WOUNDED.

Capt. Silas Casey
1st Lieut. N Lyon
Corpl. Robert Bailey
  " William Bond
  " William Evans
F McNally
John Keely
George Martin
John Wallace
Corpl. Ellis
Stevenson
William Feather
Titus S Gillow
William Hughes
Ervin Levin
Patrick Gallagher
John Daly
Hiram Shippey
Richard G Martin

William T Ray
Thomas Graham
Lewis Hastings
John Kavanagh
Patrick Kelly
John Semple
Daniel Lanahan
John Lynch
James Sullivan
John Steevier
Samuel Noble
Nicholas C James
Patrick McKenna
Jacob Miller
Abraham Sammons
Capt. Thomas Handey
Charles Clark
Benjamin Little
Sergt. Asabel H Wells

Thomas Rose, mus
John Brown
Daniel Carr
Peter Kerr
Alexander Beebe
Augustus Walker
Corpl. William Anderson
Francis H Fox
John McLaughlin
Thomas Navy
James Lilly
Joseph Gilhully
Patrick Murphy
Charles Howard
John Barnes
George F Flegg
John Hughes
Patrick Murphy

MISSING.

Stephen L Rouse
John Pierce

Michael Gilmore
David Mayer

TOTAL - Killed 36; Wounded 194; Missing 10.

THIRD DIVISION—MAJ. GEN PILLOW.

Return of the killed, wounded, and missing, of the Third Division, commanded by Major General Pillow, during the attack on Chapultepec and the city of Mexico on the 13th and 14th September, 1847.

WOUNDED

Major Gen. Gideon J Pillow | | Lieut. G T Beauregard

FIRST ARTILLERY, CO. I—FIELD BATTERY.

WOUNDED.

Capt. J B Magrauder
Paul Dalym

Edmond Lanergan
J Donelly

Anthony Kreiss
William Merriak

NINTH REGIMENT INFANTRY.

KILLED.

Col. T B Ransom
Sergt. George C Spencer
Corpl. John Balleneau

Corpl. George E Barnes
Foster
Edson

John Dorset
George Ball

WOUNDED.

George W King, mus.
E T Pike
Charles B Horsewell
Clark H Green
William March
James Mohan
Patrick Connars
William Welsh

Robert M Brown
N W King
Benjamin Osgood
N G Shett
William H White
H B Stone
Charles Twist

John Welston
John S Lock
Isaac Ware
A Noyce
W A Brown
J Moody
J Bridges

FOURTEENTH REGIMENT INFANTRY

KILLED.

Benjamin Hall
Robert Arnold

H R Manning
James M Moneypenny

WOUNDED.

Col. William Trousdale
Capt. J M Scantland
" Robert G Beale
2d Lieut. Richard Steel
Robert W Bedford
Sergt. Wm M Bledsoe
Corpl. H Montgomery

Wm D Pharris
S Sutzenhizer
W F Beatty
James Kennedy
Stewart White
John Philand
Bolivar Vincent

Calvin C Forola
A D Aujon
A Chadwick
John Wilkinson
F Faoball
J Donelly

MISSING.

John Crawford
Wm Doaring

James McDermott
John Blair

W R Wacaon

FIFTEENTH REGIMENT INFANTRY

KILLED.

Joseph Grant
John Haviland

John Herrick
Henry W Stoy

James D Kensil

WOUNDED

Capt. E A King
Sergt. Jonathan Jones
Corpl. Wm Kech
" Jos McGill
" Harvey Lyon
Enos McClaren

Jacob Ebeham
Seth Millington
Jonas Augtemyer
Geo Momeny
Caleb B Sly
Marvin Ward

Lewis Anderson
Christian Hammell
Duncumb McKinsey
Frank L Hartinaw
Henry Hess

MISSING—Harkin.

VOLTIGEUR REGIMENT

KILLED.

H Frick
E Miller

S Richardson
N Salisbury

WOUNDED

Lieut. Col. Jos E Johnson
Capt. Moses J Barnard
1st Lieut James Tilton
1st Lieut Gangenecker
2d Lieut. J L Meno
" W J Martin
Sergt. W Peat

J C Marbou
T S Gardner
H C Long
Corpl. H E Reed
" M Finder
" M Conway
" J Muldoon

Corpl. R Cooper
" J McGown
A Fair, mus
M Bancrof
E Brass
S McCall
W H Fitshugh

W Wood
2 Cox
Dwyer
T Evans
W K Fletcher
J Amey
J Smith
C Redding

M Rain
G Spencer
C Miller
J Young
P Henry
D Doughney
J Deitz

T Wallace
O Russell
E T Gooden
J H Malbon
J M Floyd
T H Gill
T Trumble

MISSING.

James Hall
J Medcalf

J A Maples
G Weygand

TOTAL—Killed 21; wounded 111; missing 10—142.   Horses—killed 9; wounded 3—12.

FOURTH DIVISION—MAJ. GEN. QUITMAN.

List of the killed, wounded, and missing, in the several actions near the city on the 14th and 15th September, 1847.

KILLED.

John Herbert
Mathew Banks
Thomas Kelly
1st Sergt Wm Blocker
   "   B F Mattison
T McHenry
Corpl L Goode
W B Devlin
J Morwood
C Meyer
D H Tresevant
H Calahan
T Cooper
T Lyles

M Martin
John Patrick
J C Tunison
T Golden
Andrew Jelard
John Wright
John Seaman
Thed Zimmerman
John Homer
Corpl James Williams
Jos A Dennis
John Shaw
John L Young

WOUNDED.

Jno Snyder
Corpl. A Patterson
   "   E A Downey
   "   F C McDermot
   "   B F Davis
   "   G W Neff
Se.gt. David Mecklin
   "   R McClelland
   "   George Decker
   "   Hugh Fiskill
   "   Chaney F Sergeant
Lieut. A S Towrison
Corpl. William H Sogour
Thomas Humphreys
John Vauson
James T Sample
John Bechter
John Copehart
William Rice
Samuel E Major
Capt. E S Williams
   "   Chris Sieb
J Palmer
M Flaxter
P Ward
Corpl. Jacob Meyer

R Rodgers
J Cosgrove
E Moyer
Sergt. A Cummins
McDonald, mus.
Millourn, mus.
Maj. A H Gladden
Act. Adj. M Clarke
Sergt. Maj. O T Gibbs
Thomas Gathey
Sergt. R Payen
   "   J Dunnogant
   "   W Triplett
M M Adams
J Thomas
M Ward
Y Muller
Y Evans
J Only
Corpl. J Hood
Y Cahill
N R Evans
J Ferguson
Y Robins
C Ingram
H Laherty

Bennett
Sergt L B Weaver
Y Anderson
C H Kenny
A Delany
2d Lieut. F Sellock
R Watson
Corpl. W L Rodgers
J H Saxton
H J Caughman
H Polock
J D Stanford
Manning Brown
J Fitzsinmons
B Hutchinson
J Kelly
1st Lieut A B O'Bannon
2d Lieut C J Kirkland
J G Atkinson
J K Parker
Capt. J H Williams
Sergt. J Caldbeeth
Corpl. J J Feagle
T Chapman
J Graham
J C Higgins
D Brown
H Suber
A Little
R B Lyles
A Feagle
Lieut. Col. Charles Baxter,
    dead
McGennis
Rowalt
Corpl. McGowen
Fife
Duncan
Waggoner
2d Lieut. Mayne
    "   Reede
John Eber
John Hunt
Jas Kelly
Corpl. John Hall
John Keeber
Charles Newman
Capt. J Barclay
Capt. S W Peel
J White
John Russell
Corpl. James Saxon
C Reymansmyder
B Van Deif
Henry Rist
Sam Morgan
Wm Mendenhall
Arch Graham
I N Hoods
Fred Myers
Capt. James Miller
W Clemens

J Horn
James Bustard
John Solomon
Emor M Davis
William Snyder
William Smyth
M Hastson
H Thomas
Edward Blain
Lieut John Keefe
Corpl. A J Jones
Wm Smyth
Jos Lutz
Thomas Davis
Chris Malone
James Stewart
Wm Bishop
Wm Crabb
Capt James Caldwell
Josh Hamilton
John Keever
David Shine
Charles Epler
Benjamin Shine
Lewis Bonnetts
Saxfere Heabbly
1st Lt and Adj D D Baker
    "   "   AQM J S Devlin
2d Lt Chas A Henderson
Sergt Maj Jas Montgomery
Comy Sergt James Orr
Sergt John Roach
    "   John Curran
    "   W J Wilson
    "   Graddisen L Tansill
Seebeck
Martin Fogg
Hugh Roney
John McGuignan
Philip Phoenix
Saml Williamson
Biggs
Connor
Francis Quinn
Thos B Smith
Elhanan Stevens
Edward Cooper
J Lions
Corpl John Whaley
P Anderson
John Cassedy
Jas Smith
Jas Kenneda
D Standerwick
L Strobill
Capt C H Pearson
Wm Connell
Y Donovan
S Calvert
J Davis
R Jenkin
D L McCowen

2d Lieut Bell
Sergt J N Easterby
Corpl Bold
R Hitchfelt
J Martin
P S Graham
C Rankin
C Anderson
W L Beadou
2d Lieut J W Steen
N Scott
D Nolan
James Walsh
2d Lieut J B Davis
Sergt J W Shett
S Camak
E Duke
W S Tidwell
R J Barker
W Claxton
James M Craig
C J Gladney
J W Brittendenham
J E Odom
A Tunison
J B Glass
R S Morrison
J T Olneys
J Burke
G Barry
M Cohlin
H Hardenbrook
W Tompkins
Capt D Hungerford
1st Lieut Chas H Janes
Sergt D Montgomery
Corpl Chas Thompson
Owen Elwood
Thos Healey
John McKinne
John Snyder
V Van Slyke
James Hart
Sergt John Duffy
Pat Roney
O Hanzel
Michael Butler, dead
Capt M Fairchild
Lieut J W Green
1st Sergt Barker
Thos L Decker
Jas Franklin
Geo Pemberton
John L Gardner
A Hendrick
Wm Daly
D Robertson
Geo Thistleton
Sergt John M Lane
Corpl Clipole Everett
Alex Cook
J Woodward

The Beautiful Rio Grande Classics

Author / Title	Price
Amsden, Charles A. — NAVAHO WEAVING, ITS TECHNIC AND HISTORY	12.00
Audubon, John W. — WESTERN JOURNALS	7.50
Bandelier, Adolph F. A. — GILDED MAN	7.00
Bandelier, Fanny — JOURNEY OF CABEZA DE VACA	7.50
Bourke, John G. — ON THE BORDER WITH CROOK	7.50
Bourke, John G. — SNAKE DANCE OF THE MOQUIS OF ARIZONA	8.00
Browne, J. Ross — ADVENTURES IN THE APACHE COUNTRY	8.00
Browne, J. Ross — NOTES ON THE SILVER MINING REGIONS OF NEVADA	7.50
Cooke, Philip St. G. — CONQUEST OF NEW MEXICO AND CALIFORNIA 1846-1848	8.00
Coues, Elliott — JOURNAL OF JACOB FOWLER	7.50
Davis, William W. H. — EL GRINGO; OR, NEW MEXICO AND HER PEOPLE	7.50
Dellenbaugh, Frederick S. — ROMANCE OF THE COLORADO RIVER	7.50
Falconer, Thomas — TEXAN-SANTA FE EXPEDITION	7.00
Fewkes, Jesse W. — HOPI KATCINAS DRAWN BY NATIVE ARTISTS	15.00
Forrest, Earle R. — MISSIONS AND PUEBLOS OF THE OLD SOUTHWEST	7.00
Grant, Blanche C. — WHEN OLD TRAILS WERE NEW	7.50
Henderson, Alice Corbin — BROTHERS OF LIGHT, THE PENITENTES	7.00
Hodge, Hiram C. — ARIZONA AS IT WAS 1877	6.00
Hughes, John T. — DONIPHANS EXPEDITION 1846-1848	8.00
James, Thomas — THREE YEARS AMONG INDIANS AND MEXICANS	7.50
Kubler, George — RELIGIOUS ARCHITECTURE OF NEW MEXICO	12.00
Lummis, Charles F. — SPANISH PIONEERS	7.00
McKenna, James A. — BLACK RANGE TALES	7.00
Otero-Warren, Nina — OLD SPAIN IN OUR SOUTHWEST	6.00
Sedgwick, Mrs. W. T. — ACOMA, THE SKY CITY	7.50
Shea, John Gilmary — PENALOSA EXPEDITION OF 1662	6.00
Sitgreaves, Lorenzo — EXPEDITION DOWN THE ZUNI AND COLORADO RIVERS	8.00
Twitchell, Ralph E. — MILITARY OCCUPATION OF NEW MEXICO	8.50
Twitchell, Ralph E. — OLD SANTA FE	12.00
Tyler, Sgt. Daniel — THE MORMON BATTALION 1846-1848	8.00
Villagra, Gasper de (Translated: Gilberto Espinosa) — A HISTORY OF NEW MEXICO 1610	7.50
Winship, George Parker — CORONADO EXPEDITION 1540-1542	15.00

7808·